Accele

Trey Nash

Apress®

Accelerated C# 2008

Copyright © 2007 by Weldon W. Nash, III

ISBN-13 (pbk): 978-1-59059-873-3

ISBN-10 (pbk): 1-59059-873-3

Printed and bound in the United States of America 9 8 7 6 5 4 3 2 1

Trademarked names may appear in this book. Rather than use a trademark symbol with every occurrence of a trademarked name, we use the names only in an editorial fashion and to the benefit of the trademark owner, with no intention of infringement of the trademark.

Lead Editor: Dominic Shakeshaft
Technical Reviewer: Shawn Wildermuth
Editorial Board: Steve Anglin, Ewan Buckingham, Tony Campbell, Gary Cornell, Jonathan Gennick, Jason Gilmore, Kevin Goff, Jonathan Hassell, Matthew Moodie, Joseph Ottinger, Jeffrey Pepper, Ben Renow-Clarke, Dominic Shakeshaft, Matt Wade, Tom Welsh
Project Manager: Sofia Marchant
Copy Editor: Jim Compton
Assistant Production Director: Kari Brooks-Copony
Production Editor: Laura Cheu
Compositor: Jimmie Young
Proofreader: April Eddy
Indexer: Beth Palmer
Artist: April Milne
Cover Designer: Kurt Krames
Manufacturing Director: Tom Debolski

Distributed to the book trade worldwide by Springer-Verlag New York, Inc., 233 Spring Street, 6th Floor, New York, NY 10013. Phone 1-800-SPRINGER, fax 201-348-4505, e-mail orders-ny@springer-sbm.com, or visit http://www.springeronline.com.

For information on translations, please contact Apress directly at 2855 Telegraph Avenue, Suite 600, Berkeley, CA 94705. Phone 510-549-5930, fax 510-549-5939, e-mail info@apress.com, or visit http://www.apress.com.

The information in this book is distributed on an "as is" basis, without warranty. Although every precaution has been taken in the preparation of this work, neither the author(s) nor Apress shall have any liability to any person or entity with respect to any loss or damage caused or alleged to be caused directly or indirectly by the information contained in this work.

The source code for this book is available to readers at http://www.apress.com.

This book is dedicated to the memory of my grandfather

Weldon W. Nash, Sr.
December 19, 1912 – April 29, 2007

To Svetlana
for believing in me

Contents at a Glance

Contents

Foreword

Programming is exhilarating. It is a breathtaking venture through problems of the mind accented by beautiful vistas as solutions are discovered. Throughout the process, a programmer's view of the problems he solves and the solutions to these problems is formed through the lens of the language that he uses and thinks in. So, it is important for a programmer to become intimately familiar with that language.

The problems that developers work on are as varied as the developers themselves. They range from medical applications to insurance software, from multimedia applications to data mining tools. The evolution of C# really is about the evolution of the problems that developers face. As the problems become ever more complex, the language becomes simpler and more powerful to deal with the complexity.

C# began its life as a way to describe reusable components that run in a variety of execution environments. During this phase, it solidified its role as a great language for describing the architecture of components and systems while embracing and extending its roots as a C-like language. One of the major contributions it added was a fully object-oriented type system that unifies the concepts of primitive and complex types and garbage collection.

While the first version of C# was a major accomplishment, the second release became the defining moment for the language. The type system became much richer with the inclusion of generics. The language also began to provide features like iterators and anonymous methods that encourage simpler and more elegant designs. These features enabled more flexible and powerful frameworks to be developed.

The third version of C# really breaks new ground. It blurs the line between code and data. It introduces declarative query syntax. It empowers programmers through functional features. All of these additions enable programmers to deal with the difficulties of data whether in-memory, in a database, or from a web server. Programmers will find that these features put the fun back in programming.

In this book, Trey Nash provides a refreshingly clear explanation of the C# language. He not only understands C#, but he is also able to guide the reader through the process of learning to excel in the language. He makes the journey to understanding enjoyable through thought-provoking examples while taking the time to motivate each feature and demonstrate common and best practices. I am confident that the reader will write better code by reading this book.

Wes Dyer
C# Compiler and Language Design Teams
Microsoft Corporation

About the Author

TREY NASH currently develops software at a market-leading security software company. Prior to that, he called Macromedia Inc. home for five years. At Macromedia, he worked on a cross-product engineering team for several years, designing solutions for a wide range of products throughout the company, including Flash and Fireworks. He specialized in COM/DCOM using C/C++/ATL until the .NET revolution. He's been glued to computers ever since he scored his first, a TI-99/4A, when he was a mere 13 years old. He astounded his parents by turning a childhood obsession into a decent paying career, much to their dismay. Trey received his bachelor of science and his master of engineering degrees in electrical engineering from Texas A&M University. When he's not sitting in front of a computer, you can find him working in his garage, honing his skills in card magic (strange but true), playing his piano, brushing up on a foreign language (Russian and Icelandic are the current favorites), or playing ice hockey.

About the Technical Reviewer

SHAWN WILDERMUTH is a Microsoft MVP (C#), MCSD.NET, MCT and is the founder of Wildermuth Consulting Services, LLC, a company that is dedicated to delivering architecture, mentoring, and software solutions in the Atlanta, Georgia area. He is also a speaker on the INETA Speaker's Bureau and has spoken at several national conferences on a variety of subjects. He is currently teaching Silverlight across the country during his Silverlight Tour (http://www.silverlight-tour.com).

Shawn is also the author of several books, including *Pragmatic ADO.NET* for Addison-Wesley, and is also the co-author of four Microsoft Certification Training Kits for Microsoft Press, as well as the upcoming book, *Prescriptive Data Architectures*.

He has been writing articles for a number of years for a variety of magazines and web sites, including *MSDN, MSDN Online, DevSource, InformIT, Windows IT Pro, The ServerSide, ONDotNet* and Intel's *Rich Client* series. Shawn has enjoyed building data-driven software for more than 20 years. He can be reached at his web site at http://www.wildermuthconsulting.com.

Acknowledgments

Writing a book is a long and arduous process, during which I have received tons of great support, which I greatly appreciate, from friends and family. The process would have been much more difficult, and arguably much less fruitful, without their support.

I would like to specifically call out the following individuals for their contribution to the first edition of this work. I would like to thank (in no particular order) David Weller, Stephen Toub, Rex Jaeschke, Vladimir Levin, Jerry Maresca, Chris Pels, Christopher T. McNabb, Brad Wilson, Peter Partch, Paul Stubbs, Rufus Littlefield, Tomas Restrepo, John Lambert, Joan Murray, Sheri Cain, Jessica D'Amico, Karen Gettman, Jim Huddleston, Richard Dal Porto, Gary Cornell, Brad Abrams, Ellie Fountain, Nicole Abramowitz and the entire Apress crew, and finally, Shelley Nash.

During the development of the second edition, I would like to call out the following individuals for their help and support (again in no particular order): Shawn Wildermuth, Sofia Marchant, Jim Compton, Dominic Shakeshaft, Wes Dyer, Kelly Winquist, and Laura Cheu.

If I have left anyone out, it is purely my mistake and not one I intended. I could not have done it without all of your support. Thank you all!

Introduction

Visual C# .NET (C#) is relatively easy to learn for anyone familiar with another object-oriented language. Even someone familiar with Visual Basic 6.0, who is looking for an object-oriented language, will find C# easy to pick up. However, although C#, coupled with the .NET Framework, provides a quick path for creating simple applications, you still need a wealth of information and must understand how to use it correctly in order to produce sophisticated, robust, fault-tolerant C# applications. In *Accelerated C# 2008* I teach you what you need to know and explain how best to use your knowledge so that you can quickly develop true C# expertise.

Idioms and design patterns are invaluable for developing and applying expertise, and I show you how to use many of them to create applications that are efficient, robust, fault tolerant, and exception safe. Although many of these patterns are familiar to C++ and Java programmers, some are unique to .NET and its Common Language Runtime (CLR). The following chapters show you how to apply these indispensable idioms and design techniques to seamlessly integrate your C# applications with the .NET runtime, focusing on the new capabilities of C# 3.0.

Design patterns document best practices in application design that many different programmers have discovered and rediscovered over time. In fact, the .NET Framework itself implements many well-known design patterns. Similarly, over the past three versions of the .NET Framework and the past two versions of C#, many new idioms and best practices have come to light. You will see these practices detailed throughout this book. Also, it is important to note that the invaluable tool chest of techniques is evolving constantly.

With the arrival of C# 3.0, you can easily incorporate functional programming techniques using lambda expressions, extension methods, and Language Integrated Query (LINQ). Lambda expressions make it easy to declare and instantiate function delegates at one point. Additionally, with lambda expressions, it's trivial to create functionals, which are functions that accept functions as arguments and typically return another function. Even though you could implement functional programming techniques in C# (albeit with some difficulty), the new language features in C# 3.0 foster an environment where functional programming can flourish interweaved with the typical imperative programming style of C#. LINQ allows you to express data query operations (which are typically functional in nature) using a syntax that is native to the language. Once you see how LINQ works, you will realize you can do much more than simple data query; you can use it to implement complex functional programs.

.NET and the CLR provide a unique and stable cross-platform execution environment. C# is only one of the languages that target this powerful runtime. You will find that many of the techniques explored in this book are also applicable to any language that targets the .NET runtime. For those of you who have significant C++ experience and are familiar with such concepts as C++ canonical forms, exception safety, Resource Acquisition Is Initialization (RAII), and const correctness, this book explains how to apply these concepts in C#. If you're a Java or Visual Basic programmer who has spent years developing your toolbox of techniques and you want to know how to apply them effectively in C#, you'll find out how to do that here.

As you'll see, it doesn't take years of trial-and-error experience to become a C# expert. You simply need to learn the right things and the right ways to use them. That's why I wrote this book for you.

About This Book

I assume that you already have a working knowledge of some object-oriented programming language, such as C++, Java, or Visual Basic .NET. Since C# derives its syntax from both C++ and Java, I don't spend much time covering C# syntax, except where it differs starkly from C++ or Java. If you already know some C#, you may find yourself skimming or even skipping Chapters 1 through 3.

Chapter 1, "C# Preview," gives a quick glimpse of what a simple C# application looks like, and it describes some basic differences between the C# programming environment and the native C++ environment.

Chapter 2, "C# and the CLR," expands on Chapter 1 and quickly explores the managed environment within which C# applications run. I introduce you to assemblies, the basic building blocks of applications into which C# code files are compiled. Additionally, you'll see how metadata makes assemblies self-describing.

Chapter 3, "C# Syntax Overview," surveys the C# language syntax. I introduce you to the two fundamental kinds of types within the CLR: value types and reference types. I also describe namespaces and how you can use them to logically partition types and functionality within your applications.

Chapters 4 through 13 provide in-depth descriptions of how to employ useful idioms, design patterns, and best practices in your C# programs and designs. I've tried hard to put these chapters in logical order, but inevitably one chapter may reference a technique or topic covered in a later chapter.

Chapter 4, "Classes, Structs, and Objects," provides details about defining types in C#. You'll learn more about value types and reference types in the CLR. I also touch upon the native support for interfaces within the CLR and C#. You'll see how type inheritance works in C#, as well as how every object derives from the System.Object type. This chapter also contains a wealth of information about the managed environment and what you must know in order to define types that are useful in it. I introduce many of these topics in this chapter and discuss them in much more detail in later chapters.

Chapter 5, "Interfaces and Contracts," details interfaces and the role they play in the C# language. Interfaces provide a functionality contract that types may choose to implement. You'll learn the various ways that a type may implement an interface, as well as how the runtime chooses which methods to call when an interface method is called.

Chapter 6, "Overloading Operators," details how you may provide custom functionality for the built-in operators of the C# language when applied to your own defined types. You'll see how to overload operators responsibly, since not all managed languages that compile code for the CLR are able to use overloaded operators.

Chapter 7, "Exception Handling and Exception Safety," shows you the exception-handling capabilities of the C# language and the CLR. Although the syntax is similar to that of C++, creating exception-safe and exception-neutral code is tricky—even more so than creating exception-safe code in native C++. You'll see that creating fault-tolerant, exception-safe code doesn't require the use of try, catch, or finally constructs at all. I also describe some of the new capabilities added to the .NET 2.0 runtime that allow you to create more fault-tolerant code than was possible in .NET 1.1.

Chapter 8, "Working with Strings," describes how strings are a first-class type in the CLR and how to use them effectively in C#. A large portion of the chapter covers the string-formatting capabilities of various types in the .NET Framework and how to make your defined types behave similarly by implementing `IFormattable`. Additionally, I introduce you to the globalization capabilities of the framework and how to create custom `CultureInfo` for cultures and regions that the .NET Framework doesn't already know about.

Chapter 9, "Arrays, Collection Types, and Iterators," covers the various array and collection types available in C#. You can create two types of multidimensional arrays, as well as your own collection types while utilizing collection-utility classes. You'll see how to define forward, reverse, and bidirectional iterators using the new iterator syntax introduced in C# 2.0, so that your collection types will work well with `foreach` statements.

Chapter 10, "Delegates, Anonymous Functions, and Events," shows you the mechanisms used within C# to provide callbacks. Historically, all viable frameworks have always provided a mechanism to implement callbacks. C# goes one step further and encapsulates callbacks into callable objects called *delegates*. Additionally, C# 2.0 allows you to create delegates with an abbreviated syntax called *anonymous functions*. Anonymous functions are similar to lambda functions in functional programming. Also, you'll see how the framework builds upon delegates to provide a publish/subscribe event notification mechanism, allowing your design to decouple the source of the event from the consumer of the event.

Chapter 11, "Generics," introduces you to probably the most exciting feature added to C# 2.0 and the CLR. Those familiar with C++ templates will find generics somewhat familiar, though many fundamental differences exist. Using generics, you can provide a shell of functionality within which to define more specific types at run time. Generics are most useful with collection types and provide great efficiency compared to the collections used in previous .NET versions.

Chapter 12, "Threading in C#," covers the tasks required in creating multithreaded applications in the C# managed virtual execution environment. If you're familiar with threading in the native Win32 environment, you'll notice the significant differences. Moreover, the managed environment provides much more infrastructure for making the job easier. You'll see how delegates, through use of the I Owe You (IOU) pattern, provide an excellent gateway into the process thread pool. Arguably, synchronization is the most important concept when getting multiple threads to run concurrently. This chapter covers the various synchronization facilities available to your applications.

Chapter 13, "In Search of C# Canonical Forms," is a dissertation on the best design practices for defining new types and how to make them so you can use them naturally and so consumers won't abuse them inadvertently. I touch upon some of these topics in other chapters, but I discuss them in detail in this chapter. This chapter concludes with a checklist of items to consider when defining new types using C#.

Chapter 14, "Extension Methods," covers a feature new to C# 3.0. Since you can invoke extension methods, like instance methods, on a type they extend, they can appear to augment the contract of types. But they are much more than that. In this chapter, I show you how extension methods can begin to open up the world of functional programming in C#.

Chapter 15, "Lambda Expressions," covers another new feature C# 3.0. You can declare and instantiate delegates using lambda expressions using a syntax that is brief and visually descriptive. Although anonymous functions can serve the same purpose just mentioned, they are much more verbose and less syntactically elegant. However, in C# 3.0, you can convert lambda expressions into expression trees. That is, the language has a built-in capability to convert code into data structures. By itself, this capability is useful, but not nearly as useful as when coupled with Language Integrated Query (LINQ). Lambda expressions, coupled with extension methods, really bring functional programming full circle in C#.

Chapter 16, "LINQ: Language Integrated Query," is the culmination of all of the new features of C# 3.0. Using LINQ expressions via the new C# 3.0 LINQ-oriented keywords, you can seamlessly integrate data queries into your code. LINQ forms a bridge between the typically imperative programming world of C# programming and the functional programming world of data query. LINQ expressions can be used to manipulate normal objects as well as data originating from SQL databases, Datasets, and XML, just to name a few.

CHAPTER 1

■■■

C# Preview

Since this is a book for experienced object-oriented developers, I assume that you already have some familiarity with the .NET runtime. *Essential .NET Volume 1: The Common Language Runtime* by Don Box (Boston, MA: Addison-Wesley, 2002) is an excellent book specifically covering the .NET runtime. Additionally, it's important to look at some of the similarities and differences between C# and C++, and then go through an elementary "Hello World!" example for good measure. If you already have experience building .NET applications, you may want to skip this chapter. However, you may want to read the section "Overview of What's New in C# 3.0."

Differences Between C# and C++

C# is a strongly typed object-oriented language whose code visually resembles C++ (and Java). This decision by the C# language designers allows C++ developers to easily leverage their knowledge to quickly become productive in C#. C# syntax differs from C++ in some ways, but most of the differences between these languages are semantic and behavioral, stemming from differences in the runtime environments in which they execute.

C#

C# source code compiles into *managed code*. Managed code, as you may already know, is an intermediate language (IL) because it is halfway between the high-level language (C#) and the lowest-level language (assembly/machine code). At run time, the Common Language Runtime (CLR) compiles the code on the fly by using Just In Time (JIT) compiling. As with just about anything in engineering, this technique comes with its pros and cons. It may seem that an obvious con is the inefficiency of compiling the code at run time. This process is different from interpreting, which is typically used by scripting languages such as Perl and JScript. The JIT compiler doesn't compile a function or method each and every time it's called; it does so only the first time, and when it does, it produces machine code native to the platform on which it's running. An obvious pro of JIT compiling is that the working set of the application is reduced, because the memory footprint of intermediate code is smaller. During the execution of the application, only the needed code is JIT-compiled. If your application contains printing code, for example, that code is not needed if the user never prints a document, and therefore the JIT compiler never compiles it. Moreover, the CLR can optimize the program's execution on the fly at run time. For example, the CLR may determine a way to reduce page faults in the memory manager by rearranging compiled code in memory, and it could do all this at run time. Once you weigh all the pros together, you find that they outweigh the cons for most applications.

■**Note** Actually, you can choose to code your programs in raw IL while building them with the IL Assembler (ILASM). However, it will likely be an inefficient use of your time. High-level languages can nearly always provide any capability that you can achieve with raw IL code.

C++

Unlike C#, C++ code traditionally compiles into *native code*. Native code is the machine code that's native to the processor for which the program was compiled. For the sake of discussion, assume that we're talking about natively compiled C++ code rather than managed C++ which can be achieved by using C++/CLI. If you want your native C++ application to run on different platforms, such as on both a 32-bit platform and a 64-bit platform, you must compile it separately for each. The native binary output is generally not compatible across platforms.

IL, on the other hand, is compatible across platforms, because it, along with the Common Language Infrastructure (CLI) upon which the CLR is built, is a defined international standard.[1] This standard is rapidly gaining traction and being implemented beyond the Microsoft Windows platform.

■**Note** I recommend you check out the work the Mono team has accomplished toward creating alternate, open source Virtual Execution Systems (VESs) on other platforms.[2]

Included in the CLI standard is the Portable Executable (PE) file format for managed modules. Therefore, you can actually compile a C# program on a Windows platform and execute the output on both Windows and Linux without having to recompile, because even the file format is standardized.[3] This degree of portability is extremely convenient and was in the hearts and minds of the COM/DCOM designers back in the day, but for various reasons, it failed to succeed across disparate platforms at this level.[4] One of the major reasons for that failure is that COM lacked a sufficiently expressive and extensible mechanism for describing types and their dependencies. The CLI specification solves this nicely by introducing metadata, which I'll describe in Chapter 2.

CLR Garbage Collection

One of the key facilities in the CLR is the *garbage collector* (GC). The GC frees you from the burden of handling memory allocation and deallocation, which is where many software errors can occur. However, the GC doesn't remove all resource-handling burdens from your plate, as you'll see in

---

1. You can find the CLI standard document Ecma-335 at www.ecma-international.org. Additionally, Ecma-334 is the standard document for the C# language.

2. You can find the Mono project on the Internet at www.mono-project.com.

3. Of course, the target platform must also have all of the dependent libraries installed. This is quickly becoming a reality, given the breadth of the .NET Standard Library. For example, check out www.go-mono.com/docs/ to see how much coverage the Mono project libraries have.

4. For all the gory details, I recommend reading Don Box and Chris Sells' *Essential .NET, Volume I: The Common Language Runtime* (Boston, MA: Addison-Wesley Professional, 2002). (The title leads one to believe that Volume II is due out any time now, so let's hope it's not titled in the same vein as Mel Brooks' *History of the World: Part I*.)

Chapter 4. For example, a file handle is a resource that must be freed when the consumer is finished with it, just as memory must be freed in the same way. The GC handles only memory resources directly. To handle resources other than memory, such as database connections and file handles, you can use a finalizer (as I'll show you in Chapter 13) to free your resources when the GC notifies you that your object is being destroyed. However, an even better way is to use the Disposable pattern for this task, which I'll demonstrate in Chapters 4 and 13.

■**Note** The CLR references all objects of *reference type* indirectly, similar to the way you use pointers and references in C++, except without the pointer syntax. When you declare a variable of a reference type in C#, you actually reserve a storage location that has a type associated with it, either on the heap or on the stack, which stores the reference to the object. So when you copy an object reference in one variable into another variable, you end up with two variables referencing the same object. All reference type instances live on the managed heap. The CLR manages the location of these objects, and if it needs to move them around, it updates all the outstanding references to the moved objects to point to the new location. Also, *value types* exist in the CLR, and instances of them live on the stack or as a field of an object on the managed heap. Their usage comes with many restrictions and nuances. You normally use them when you need a lightweight structure to manage some related data. Value types are also useful when modeling an immutable chunk of data. I cover this topic in much more detail in Chapter 4.

C# allows you to develop applications rapidly while dealing with fewer mundane details than in a C++ environment. At the same time, C# provides a language that feels familiar to either C++ or Java developers.

Example of a C# Program

Let's take a close look at a C# program. Consider the venerable "Hello World!" program that everyone knows and loves. A console version of it looks like this in C#:

```
class EntryPoint {
    static void Main() {
        System.Console.WriteLine( "Hello World!" );
    }
}
```

Note the structure of this C# program. It declares a type (a class named EntryPoint) and a member of that type (a method named Main). This differs from C++, where you declare a type in a header and define it in a separate compilation unit, usually a .cpp file. Also, metadata (which describes all of the types in a module and is generated transparently by the C# compiler) removes the need for the forward declarations and inclusions as required in C++. In fact, forward declarations don't even exist in C#.

C++ programmers will find the static Main method familiar, except for the fact that its name begins with a capital letter. Every program requires an entry point, and in the case of C#, it is the static Main method. There are some further differences. For example, the Main method is declared within a class (in this case, named EntryPoint). In C#, you must declare all methods within a type definition. There is no such thing as a static, free function as there is in C++. The return type for the Main method may be either of type int or void, depending on your needs. In my example, Main has no parameters, but if you need access to the command-line parameters, your Main method can declare a parameter (an array of strings) to access them.

■**Note** If your application contains multiple types with a static `Main` method, you can select which one to use via the `/main` compiler switch.

You may notice that the call to `WriteLine` seems verbose. I had to qualify the method name with the class name `Console`, and I also had to specify the namespace that the `Console` class lives in (in this case, `System`). .NET (and therefore C#) supports namespaces to avoid name collisions in the vast global namespace. However, instead of having to type the fully qualified name, including the namespace, every time, C# provides the `using` directive, which is analogous to Java's `import` and C++'s `using namespace`. So you could rewrite the previous program slightly, as Listing 1-1 shows.

Listing 1-1. *hello_world.cs*

```
using System;

class EntryPoint {
    static void Main() {
        Console.WriteLine( "Hello World!" );
    }
}
```

With the `using System;` directive, you can omit the `System` namespace when calling `Console.WriteLine`.

To compile this example, execute the following command from a Windows command prompt:

```
csc.exe /r:mscorlib.dll /target:exe hello_world.cs
```

Let's take a look at exactly what this command line does:

- `csc.exe` is the Microsoft C# compiler.

- The `/r` option specifies the assembly dependencies this program has. Assemblies are similar in concept to DLLs in the native world. `mscorlib.dll` is where the `System.Console` object is defined. In reality, you don't need to reference the `mscorlib` assembly because the compiler will reference it automatically, unless you use the `/nostdlib` option.

- The `/target:exe` option tells the compiler that you're building a console application, which is the default if not specified. Your other options here are `/target:winexe` for building a Windows GUI application, `/target:library` for building a DLL assembly with the `.dll` extension, and `/target:module` for generating a DLL with the `.netmodule` extension. `/target:module` generated modules don't contain an assembly manifest, so you must include it later into an assembly using the assembly linker `al.exe`. This provides a way to create multiple-file assemblies.

- `hello_world.cs` is the C# program you're compiling. If multiple C# files exist in the project, you could just list them all at the end of the command line.

Once you execute this command line, it produces `hello_world.exe`, and you can execute it from the command line and see the expected results. If you want, you can rebuild the code with the `/debug` option. Then you may step through the execution inside of a debugger. To give an example of C# platform independence, if you happen to have a Linux OS running and you have the Mono VES installed on it, you can copy this `hello_world.exe` directly over in its binary form and it will run as expected, assuming everything is set up correctly on the Linux box.

Overview of Features Added in C# 2.0

Since its initial release in late 2000, the C# language has evolved considerably. This evolution has likely been accelerated thanks to the wide adoption of C#. With the release of Visual Studio 2005 and the .NET Framework 2.0, the C# compiler supported the C# 2.0 enhancements to the language. This was great news, since C# 2.0 included some handy features that provided a more natural programming experience as well as greater efficiency. This section provides an overview of what those features are and what chapters of the book contain more detailed information.

Arguably, the meatiest addition to C# 2.0 was support for generics. The syntax is similar to C++ templates, but the main difference is that constructed types created from .NET generics are dynamic in nature—that is, they are bound and constructed at run time. This differs from C++ concrete types created from templates, which are static in the sense that they are bound and created at compile time.[5] Generics are most useful when used with container types such as vectors, lists, and hash tables, where they provide the greatest efficiency gains. Generics can treat the types that they contain specifically by their type, rather than by using the base type of all objects, System.Object. I cover generics in Chapter 11, and I cover collections in Chapter 9.

C# 2.0 added support for anonymous methods. An anonymous method is sometimes referred to as a *lambda function*, which comes from functional programming disciplines. C# anonymous methods are extremely useful with delegates and events. Delegates and events are constructs used to register callback methods that are called when triggered. Normally, you wire them up to a defined method somewhere. But with anonymous methods, you can define the delegate's or event's code inline, at the point where the delegate or event is set up. This is handy if your delegate merely needs to perform some small amount of work for which an entire method definition would be overkill. What's even better is that the anonymous method body has access to all variables that are in scope at the point it is defined.[6] I cover anonymous methods in Chapter 10. Lambda expressions, which are new to C# 3.0, supersede anonymous methods and make for more readable code.

C# 2.0 added support for iterators. Anyone familiar with the C++ Standard Template Library (STL) knows about iterators and their usefulness. In C#, you typically use the foreach statement to iterate over an object that behaves as a collection. That collection object must implement the IEnumerable interface, which includes the GetEnumerator method. Implementing the GetEnumerator method on container types is typically very tedious. However, when using C# iterators, implementing the GetEnumerator method is a snap. You can find more information regarding iterators in Chapter 9.

Finally, C# 2.0 added support for partial types. Prior to C# 2.0, you had to define each C# class entirely in one file (also called a *compilation unit*). This requirement was relaxed with the support for partial types. This was great news for those who rely upon code generators to provide skeleton code. For example, you can use the Visual Studio wizards to generate such useful things as System.Data.DataSet derived types for accessing data in a database. Prior to C# 2.0, it was problematic if you needed to make modifications to the generated code. You either had to derive from or contain the generated type in a new type while specializing its implementation, or you had to edit the generated code. Editing the generated code was risky because you normally lost those changes when the wizard was forced to regenerate the type for some reason. Partial types solve this problem, because now you can augment the generated code in a separate file so that your changes aren't lost when the wizard regenerates the code. For a great example of how partial types are used, look at the code automatically generated when you create a Windows Forms application using Visual Studio. You can find more information regarding partial types in Chapter 4.

---

5. Using C++/CLI, standardized in Ecma-372 and first made available with Visual Studio 2005, you can use generics and templates together.

6. This is referred to as either a *closure* or a *variable capture*.

Overview of What's New in C# 3.0

C# 3.0 includes some great new features. Most of the new features are stepping stones designed to support Language Integrated Query (LINQ). Nevertheless, all of them are extremely useful when used individually outside of the context of LINQ. Many of them allow programmers to employ functional programming techniques more easily.

C# now supports implicitly typed local variables by making use of a new keyword var. It's important to note that these variables are not typeless; rather, their type is inferred at compile time. You can read more about them in Chapter 3.

Have you ever wanted to create a simple type to hold some related data but been annoyed at having to create an entire new class? In many cases, the new support for anonymous types helps relieve you of this burden. Using anonymous types, you can define and instantiate a type all in one compound statement. I cover anonymous types in Chapter 4.

Auto-implemented properties are another helpful new feature to save us some typing and reduce the potential to introduce bugs. How many times have you simply declared a class to hold a few pieces of data and been annoyed with the amount of typing required to create property accessors for that data? After all, doing so follows good encapsulation practices. Thankfully, auto-implemented properties greatly reduce the amount of typing necessary to define properties on types. You can read more about them in Chapter 4.

While we're on the subject of conveniences, C# 3.0 also introduces two new features that help when instantiating and initializing object instances. Using object and collection initializers, you can instantiate and initialize either an object or a collection in one compound statement. I cover object initializers in Chapter 4 and collection initializers in Chapter 9.

C# 2.0 introduced partial class definitions to facilitate using code generators. C# 3.0 adds to that by introducing partial methods. Using partial methods, a code generator can declare a method signature, and the consumer of that generated code, the one that creates the rest of the partial class definition, can choose to implement it or not. You can read more about partial methods in Chapter 4.

Extension methods are one of the most exciting new features. Taken from the surface view, they are merely static methods that can be called as if they were instance methods. They do not get any special access into the instance they are operating on, so in that respect, they are just like static methods. However, the syntax they foster allows us to program in a more functional manner, usually resulting in clearer and more readable code. I devote the entire Chapter 14 to extension methods and what you can do with them.

Probably more compelling than extension methods is support for lambda expressions. Lambda expressions supersede support for anonymous methods. That is, if lambda expressions had existed in C# 2.0, there would have been no need for anonymous methods at all. However, lambda expressions offer much more than anonymous methods as they can be converted into both delegates and expression trees. Lambda expressions are covered in Chapter 15.

The granddaddy of all new C# 3.0 features has to be LINQ, which builds upon all of the new features, especially extension methods, lambda expressions, and anonymous types. It also adds some new language keywords to allow us to code intuitive query statements, thus seamlessly bridging the gap between the object-oriented world and the data world. You can use LINQ to access data from multiple sources. Visual Studio provides the capability to use LINQ on native object collections, SQL data stores, and XML. Support for many other data sources is coming soon from both Microsoft and third parties. For example, you'll be able to use LINQ to connect to Windows Management Instrumentation (WMI), the Document Object Model (DOM), and the Web. Additionally, there are implementations in the works to use LINQ against popular web sites such as Google and Flickr. Chapter 16 is devoted to LINQ.

Summary

In this chapter, I've touched upon the high-level characteristics of programs written in C#. That is, all code is compiled into IL rather than the native instructions for a specific platform. Additionally, the CLR implements a GC to manage raw memory allocation and deallocation, freeing you from having to worry about one of the most common errors in software development: improper memory management. However, as with most engineering trade-offs, there are other aspects (read: complications) of memory and resource management that the GC can introduce in certain situations.

Using the venerable "Hello World!" example, I was able to quickly show the usefulness of namespaces as well as the fact that C# is devoid of any kind of inclusion syntax as available in C++. Instead, all other external types are brought into the compilation unit via metadata, which is a rich description format of the types contained within an assembly. Therefore, the metadata and the compiled types are always contained in one neat package.

Generics open up such a huge area of development that you'll probably still be learning handy tricks of applying them over the next several years. Some of those tricks can be borrowed from the C++ template world, but not all of them, since the two concepts are fundamentally different. Iterators and anonymous methods offer a concise way of expressing common idioms such as enumeration and callback methods, while support for partial type declarations within C# makes it easier to work with tool-generated code.

C# 3.0 offers many new and exciting features that allow one to employ functional programming techniques very easily with little overhead. Some of the new features add convenience to programming in C#. LINQ provides a seamless mechanism to bridge to the data storage world from the object-oriented world.

In the next chapter, I'll briefly cover more details regarding the JIT compilation process. Additionally, I'll dig into assemblies and their contained metadata a bit more. Assemblies are the basic building blocks of C# applications, analogous to DLLs in the native Windows world.

CHAPTER 2

■ ■ ■

C# and the CLR

As mentioned in the previous chapter, managed applications and native applications have many differences, mainly because managed applications run inside the Microsoft CLR. The CLR is a Virtual Execution System (VES) that implements the CLI. The CLR provides many useful facilities to managed applications, including a highly tuned GC for memory management, a code access security layer, and a rich self-describing type system, among others. In this chapter, I'll show you how the CLR compiles, packages, and executes C# programs.

■**Note** In-depth coverage of the CLR is outside the scope of this book, because I focus closely on C# concepts and usage. However, I recommend that you become familiar with the CLR. It's always best to know and understand your target platform, and in the case of managed applications such as C#, the platform is the .NET CLR. For further, in-depth coverage of the CLR and everything covered in this chapter, see Don Box and Chris Sells' *Essential .NET, Volume I: The Common Language Runtime* (Boston, MA: Addison-Wesley Professional, 2002) and Andrew Troelsen's *Pro C# 2005 and the .NET 2.0 Platform, Third Edition* (Berkeley, CA: Apress, 2005). After that, you may find many of the other, more specific books on the CLR more informative. For complete coverage of the CLR layer that provides complete interoperability with native environments such as COM objects and the underlying platform, I recommend Adam Nathan's *.NET and COM: The Complete Interoperability Guide* (Indianapolis, IN: Sams, 2002). For topics dealing with .NET code access security, I recommend *.NET Framework Security* by Brian A. LaMacchia, et al. (Upper Saddle River, NJ: Pearson Education, 2002). Because no developer should ever ignore platform security when designing new systems, I recommend Keith Brown's *The .NET Developer's Guide to Windows Security* (Boston, MA: Addison-Wesley Professional, 2004).

This chapter provides a high-level and cursory description of the mechanisms involved with compiling C# and loading code for execution. Once the code is loaded, it must be compiled into native machine code for the platform it's running on. Therefore, you need to understand the concept of JIT compilation.

The JIT Compiler in the CLR

C# is compiled into IL, and IL is what the CLR processes. The IL specification is contained in the CLI standard. You can see what IL looks like by loading the "Hello World!" application (from the previous chapter) into the Intermediate Language Disassembler (ILDASM) provided with the .NET SDK.[1] ILDASM shows you a tree view of the type data from the assembly, and you can open up individual methods and see the IL code that the C# compiler generated for them. As shown in Listing 2-1, IL looks similar to assembly language; in essence, it's the assembly language of the CLR. It's called IL because it acts as an intermediate step between a specific language and a specific platform.

Listing 2-1. *HelloWorld.exe Main Method IL*

```
.method private hidebysig static void Main() cil managed
{
  .entrypoint
  // Code size       13 (0xd)
  .maxstack  8
  IL_0000:  nop
  IL_0001:  ldstr       "Hello World!"
  IL_0006:  call        void [mscorlib]System.Console::WriteLine(string)
  IL_000b:  nop
  IL_000c:  ret
} // end of method EntryPoint::Main
```

The CLR is not an interpreter. It doesn't retranslate the IL code each time it executes it. Although interpreters provide many flexible solutions (as in the JScript interpreter for the Windows Scripting Host, for example), they're generally not efficient runtime platforms. The CLR actually compiles IL code into machine code before it executes it—called JIT compiling. This process takes some time, but for each part of a program, it generally means only a one-time performance hit per process. Once the code is compiled, the CLR holds on to it and simply executes the compiled version the next time it's needed, just as quickly as traditionally compiled code (and sometimes even more quickly).

Although the JIT compilation phase adds some complexity and has an initial runtime performance penalty associated with it, the benefits of a JIT compiler coupled with the CLR can outweigh the time penalty of JIT compiling because

- *Managed applications can consume far less memory*: In general, IL code has a smaller footprint than native code. In other words, the *working set* of managed applications—that is, the number of memory pages the application consumes—is normally smaller than native applications. With a fair amount of work, you can reduce the working set of native applications to be comparable to managed applications, but with the CLR, you get this for free.

- *Only IL code that is executed ever gets JIT-compiled*: IL code is generally more compact than machine code, so keeping the compiled code to a minimum reduces the memory footprint of the application.

- *The CLR can keep track of the frequency of calls*: If it sees that a JIT-compiled code section has not been called in a long time, it can free the space occupied by it. The code will be recompiled if it's called again.

---

1. You can find ILDASM.exe in the bin directory of the .NET SDK, or if you have Visual Studio 2008 installed, you can normally find it in the following directory: C:\Program Files\Microsoft SDKs\Windows\v6.0A\ bin\ildasm.exe. You can launch it easily by invoking it after opening an instance of the Visual Studio 2008 command prompt.

The CLR also may perform optimizations at run time. In native applications, you define the optimizations at compile time. But, since compilation occurs at run time in the CLR, it can apply optimizations at any time. It may be the case that a CLR implementation can compile code faster with fewer optimizations, and it may default to doing it that way. However, for code that it sees getting called frequently, it could recompile such code with more optimizations turned on so that it executes faster. For example, the CLR efficiency model can be vastly different depending on how many CPUs are on the target platform or even what architecture family the CPUs belong to. For native applications, you have to do more manual work—either at run time or compile time—to accommodate such a situation. But the CLR provides facilities so you can create multi-CPU performance enhancements more readily. Additionally, if the CLR determines that different parts of code scattered all over the application are called rather frequently, it has the liberty to move them in memory so that they are all within the same group of memory pages, thus minimizing the number of page faults and increasing the cache hits as the application runs.

These are only a few of the reasons why the CLR is a flexible platform to target, and why its benefits quickly outweigh the initial perceived performance hit of JIT compiling.

Assemblies and the Assembly Loader

An *assembly* is a discrete unit of reusable code within the CLR, similar in nature to a DLL in the unmanaged world, but that's where the similarities end. An assembly can consist of multiple modules all linked together by a *manifest*, which describes the contents of the assembly. With respect to the operating system, a module is identical to a DLL. Assemblies can have a version attached to them so that multiple assemblies with the same name but different versions are identifiable separately. Assemblies also contain metadata describing the contained types. When you distribute a native DLL, you typically include a header file and/or documentation describing the exported functions. Metadata fulfills this requirement, completely describing the types contained within the assembly. In short, assemblies are versioned, self-describing units of reuse within the CLR environment.

As discussed in the previous chapter, when you compile the "Hello World!" program, the result is an .exe file that is, in fact, an assembly. You can create managed assemblies using any managed language. Moreover, in most cases, any other managed language can consume managed assemblies. Therefore, you can easily create complex systems developed with multiple managed languages. For example, when creating some low-level types, C++ /CLI may be the most natural languages to get the job done, but it may make more sense to code the top-level user interface using either C# or Visual Basic. To provide interoperability between the various languages, the CLI defines a subset of the type system known as the Common Language Specification (CLS). If you use only CLS-compliant types in your assemblies, you are guaranteed that any managed language can consume them.

Minimizing the Working Set of the Application

In the "Hello World!" example, the resulting assembly consists of only one file. However, assemblies can consist of multiple files. These files can include compiled modules, resources, and any other components listed in the *assembly manifest*. The assembly manifest is typically included in the main assembly module and contains essential identification information, including which pieces belong to the assembly. By using this information, the assembly loader can determine, among other things, if an assembly is incomplete or has been tampered with. Assemblies are either strongly named or not strongly named. A strongly named assembly has a hash code built into its manifest that the loader can use to test the integrity of the assembly. Assemblies can also be digitally signed in order to identify their producer.

When a C# executable launches, the CLR loads the assembly and starts executing the entry-point method. Of course, before it can do that, it must JIT-compile the entry-point method. At that stage, the CLR may have to resolve some external references to be able to JIT-compile the code. For example, if your `Main` method creates an instance of a class named `Employee`, the CLR must find and load the assembly that contains the `Employee` type before the JIT compiler can continue. However, the great thing is that the CLR loads assemblies on demand. So, if you have a type that provides a method to print a document, and it lives in a separate assembly from the one containing the main application, but the application never exercises the dependency, then the separate assembly never gets loaded. This keeps the working set of the application from growing unnecessarily large. Therefore, when designing applications, it makes sense to segregate less commonly used features into separate assemblies so that the CLR loads them only when needed. Any time you can trim the working set of the application, you speed up start-up time as well as shrink the memory footprint of the running application. The key is to partition your code into cohesive units, or assemblies. There's no point in creating multiassembly applications if code executed in common code paths is scattered across various assemblies, since you'll lose the benefit of multiple assemblies.

Naming Assemblies

You can name assemblies in two main ways:

- *Strongly (fully) named*: This assembly has a name that consists of four parts: the short assembly name, a version number, a culture identifier in ISO format, and a hash token. If an assembly is named with all four parts, it is considered to be strongly named.

- *Partially named*: This assembly has a name that's missing some of the detail in strongly named assemblies.

To get a good idea of what assembly names look like, open up Windows Explorer and navigate to your Global Assembly Cache (GAC), which is in the `%systemroot%\assembly` directory. In reality, the directory structure is very complex, but the GAC Explorer plug-in presents what you see in your browser. If you navigate to the same directory by using a command prompt, you see the encoded directory names that the GAC uses to store the assemblies. Do not tamper with this directory structure, or you may cause serious damage to your GAC. Focusing on the view in Explorer, you can see the assemblies' four-part names. If the Culture entry is blank for an assembly, it means that it is culture-neutral, which is common for assemblies that contain only code. I recommend that you isolate all of your resources in a separate assembly, so you can tag them as culture-specific and swap them out easily with a different culture without affecting your code. Similar guidelines have existed in native Win32 programming for years and greatly facilitate easy localization of your application to other languages.

The benefit of strongly named assemblies is that they can be registered in the GAC and become available for use by all applications on the system. Registering an assembly in the GAC is analogous to registering a COM server in the registry. If the assembly is not strongly named, the application may only use it locally. In other words, the assembly must reside somewhere in the directory of the application using it or in a subdirectory thereof. Such assemblies are commonly referred to as *private* assemblies.

Loading Assemblies

The assembly loader goes through a detailed process to load an assembly. Part of this process determines which version of the assembly to load. By using application configuration files, you can give the loader some hints during version resolution. The CLR can load assemblies on an as-needed basis, or you can load assemblies explicitly via `AppDomain.Load()`. The loader looks for partially named assemblies in the same directory as the running application or in a subdirectory. (Such assemblies are called *local* assemblies.) The loader can also reference the GAC when searching for the assembly—for example, when loading an assembly with its fully qualified name, the loader searches the GAC before probing the local directories.

Versioning plays a key role at assembly load time, and all assemblies are versioned. Versioning was built into the CLR loader from the beginning and removes the affliction known as *DLL Hell*, where replacing a shared DLL with a newer version breaks applications that use the older version. You veterans out there who have developed software on Windows throughout the past 15 years or so definitely have felt this pain. In the CLR, multiple versions of the same assembly can exist simultaneously on the same machine without conflicting with each other. Moreover, applications can choose to default to using the most recent version of an assembly on the machine, or they can specify the exact version they prefer by applying a version policy in their configuration files.

■Note Assembly loading and versioning is a fairly complex topic that is outside the scope of this book. Before loading an assembly, the loader uses various heuristics to determine which version to load. Once it knows the version, it passes the information down to the low-level assembly loading method. For more detailed information regarding assembly loading, reference Don Box and Chris Sells' *Essential .NET, Volume I: The Common Language Runtime* (Boston, MA: Addison-Wesley Professional, 2002).

Metadata

Let's look closely at the "Hello World!" example back in Listing 1-1 and compare it to what you may be used to if you come from the native C++ world. First, notice that it doesn't include any headers. That's because C# does not need to include headers. Instead, it uses something much more reliable and descriptively rich: metadata. By using metadata, managed modules are self-describing. In the C++ world, to consume a library in your application, you would need two things: a static library or a DLL, and, normally, a header file. Since they exist as two separate entities that you must treat as a whole, it's entirely possible that the header file and the library could get out of sync if you're not careful. That could spell disaster. Managed modules, on the other hand, contain all necessary information inside the metadata that is contained in the module itself. The unit of reuse in the managed world is an assembly. So it is the assembly that is, in fact, self-describing.

Metadata is also extensible, allowing you to define new types and attributes that can be contained in the metadata. To top it all off, you can access metadata at run time. For example, at run time, you can iterate over all the fields of an arbitrary class type without having to know its declaration ahead of time or at compile time. Astute readers may recognize that this power opens up the possibility of entire programs and types being generated at run time, which is also something that is impossible with native C++ unless you integrate a full C++ compiler into your application.

Metadata is an extensible description format for describing the contents of assemblies. Also, if it's not expressive enough for your needs, you can define new custom "attributes" that are easily included in the metadata for a type. In the managed world, just about every entity in a program with a type can have metadata attached to it, including classes, methods, parameters, return values, assemblies, and so on. You can define custom attributes by deriving from the System.Attribute class, and then you can easily associate an instance of your custom attribute to just about any entity in your assembly.

With metadata, you can access and examine type definitions and the attributes attached to them. Metadata can tell you if a particular object's class supports a given method before attempting to call it, or if a given class is derived from another. The process of inspecting metadata is called *reflection*. Typically, you start with a System.Type object when you reflect upon types in the assembly. You can get hold of one of these type instances by using the typeof keyword in C#, by calling System.Assembly.GetType(), and a few other ways. Generally, the typeof keyword is more efficient because it is computed at compile time, whereas GetType(), although more flexible since you can pass it an arbitrary string, is executed at run time. Once you have a type object, you can find out if it is a class, an interface, a struct, or so on, what methods it has, and the number and types of fields it contains.

■Note If you're wondering, "Why metadata?", COM/DCOM employ some other techniques. If you've ever created COM components, you may be familiar with the Interface Description Language (IDL), which is a platform-independent description language for interfaces and components. Typically, you provide your consumer with the COM component packaged in either a DLL or an executable along with the IDL. Again, it serves the same purpose as the header file for C++ libraries or the documentation for DLL exports. You typically take the IDL and pass it through an IDL compiler to produce native code that you can then interface with. A Type Library (TLB) serves much the same purpose as IDL, but it is a binary format that high-level languages, such as Visual Basic, typically consume. Unfortunately, IDL and TLBs don't overlap entirely. Some things can be described in IDL but not in TLBs, and vice versa.

Because assemblies are self-describing, the only thing the C# compiler needs in order to resolve type usages is a list of referenced assemblies as it compiles and builds the program. Once it has a list of the referenced assemblies, it can access the metadata contained inside them to resolve the dependencies. It's a beautiful system, and it removes some typically error-prone mundane details from the C# coding process.

In the managed world, you no longer have to carry around any extra baggage in the form of header files or IDL files. I won't go so far as to say you don't have to provide any documentation, because documentation is always useful. But with an assembly, you have a nicely packaged entity that contains both the code and the descriptions needed to use its contents. If your assembly consists of a single file, as most do, that one file contains everything needed to consume the code in the assembly.

Cross-Language Compatibility

Because assemblies are self-describing and contain portable IL code, they are easily shared across multiple languages. Finally, you have a viable solution to put together complex systems, where some components are coded using one language and others are coded using different languages. For example, in a complex system used for engineering analysis, you may have a group of C# developers coding the system infrastructure and a group of engineers developing the mathematical components. Many engineers still program in languages such as Fortran. That's OK, because Fortran compilers are available that emit IL and create managed assemblies. Thus, each development group can work in a language that is more natural to it and to its problem domains.

Metadata is essential to such sharing. Jim Miller and Susann Ragsdale describe the metadata format completely in *The Common Language Infrastructure Annotated Standard* (Boston, MA: Addison-Wesley Professional, 2003). I recommend that you read this book or the CLI Ecma standards documents[2] to get the best understanding of the CLR and how metadata is generated and consumed.

Summary

This chapter briefly covered the essentials of how C# is compiled, packaged, and executed.

I discussed how JIT compiling can actually compete with traditionally compiled applications in performance. One of the requirements for optimizing JIT compilation is an expressive and extensible type mechanism that the compiler can understand. By packaging IL into assemblies that are self-documenting, both the CLR and the JIT compiler have all the information they need to manage code execution. Additionally, you can explicitly load an assembly on demand by providing either its strong name or a partial name. Assemblies make it possible to run distinct versions of code without experiencing DLL Hell, and they also provide the basis for developing and sharing components across languages.

In the next chapter, I'll lead you on a whirlwind 20,000-foot view of the C# language syntax. Since I don't have the space to cover every minute syntactic detail, I recommend that you also reference the C# language specification as well.

---

2. The Ecma-334 document covers the Ecma CLI standard, and the Ecma-334 document found at www.ecma-international.org covers the C# language. ISO/IEC 23271 also covers the CLI, and ISO/IEC 23270 at www.iso.org also covers the C# language. However, the Ecma standards are generally more current, and you can download them freely.

CHAPTER 3

■■■

C# Syntax Overview

This chapter introduces you to the syntax of the C# language. It's assumed that you have a reasonable amount of experience with C++ or Java, since C# shares a similar syntax. This is no accident. The designers of C# clearly meant to leverage the knowledge of those who have already developed with C++ and Java, which are arguably the dominant languages in object-oriented (OO) software development.

I've noted nuances and differences that are specific to the C# language. But if you're familiar with either C++ or Java, you'll feel right at home with C# syntax.

C# Is a Strongly Typed Language

Like C++ and Java, C# is a strongly typed language, which means that every variable and object instance in the system is of a well-defined type. This enables the compiler to check that the operations you try to perform on variables and object instances are valid. For example, suppose you have a method that computes the average of two integers and returns the result. You could declare the C# method as follows:

```
double ComputeAvg( int param1, int param2 )
{
    return (param1 + param2) / 2.0;
}
```

This tells the compiler that this method accepts two integers and returns a double. Therefore, if the compiler attempts to compile code where you inadvertently pass an instance of type Apple, it will complain and stop. Suppose you wrote the method slightly differently:

```
object ComputeAvg( object param1, object param2 )
{
    return ((int) param1 + (int) param2) / 2.0;
}
```

The second version of ComputeAvg is still valid, but you have forcefully stripped away the type information. Every object and value in C# implicitly derives from System.Object. The object keyword in C# is an alias for the class System.Object. So it is perfectly valid to declare these parameters as type object. However, object is not a numeric type. In order to perform the calculation, you must first *cast* the objects into integers. After you're done, you return the result as an instance of type object. Although this version of the method can seem more flexible, it's a disaster waiting to happen. What if some code in the application attempts to pass an instance of type Apple into ComputeAvg? The compiler won't complain, because Apple derives from System.Object, as every other class does. However, you'll get a nasty surprise at run time when your application throws an exception declaring that it cannot convert an instance of Apple to an integer. The method will fail, and unless you have an exception handler in place, it could terminate your application. That's not something you want to happen in your code that is running on a production server somewhere.

It is *always* best to find bugs at compile time rather than run time. That is the moral of this story. If you were to use the first version of ComputeAvg, the compiler would have told you how ridiculous it was that you were passing an instance of Apple. This is much better than hearing it from an angry customer whose ecommerce server just took a dirt nap. The compiler is your friend, so let it be a good one and provide it with as much type information as possible to strictly enforce your intentions.

Expressions

Expressions in C# are practically identical to expressions in C++ and Java. The important thing to keep in mind when building expressions is operator precedence. C# expressions are built using operands, usually variables or types within your application, and operators. Many of the operators can be overloaded as well. Operator overloading is covered in Chapter 6. Table 3-1 lists the precedence of the operator groups. Entries at the top of the table have higher precedence, and operators within the same category have equal precedence.

Table 3-1. *C# Operator Precedence*

Operator Group	Operators Included	Description
Primary	x.m	Member access
	X(...)	Method invocation
	X[...]	Array access
	X++, x--	Postincrement and postdecrement
	new T(...), new T[...]	Object and array creation
	typeof(T)	Gets System.Type object for T
	checked(x), unchecked(x)	Evaluates expression in checked and unchecked environments
Unary	+x, -x	Identity and negation
	!x	Logical negation
	~x	Bitwise negation
	++x, --x	Preincrement and predecrement
	(T) x	Casting operation
Multiplicative	x*y, x/y, x%y	Multiplication, division, and remainder
Additive	x+y, x-y	Addition and subtraction
Shift	x<<y, x>>y	Left and right shift
Relational and type testing	x<y, x>y, x<=y, x>=y	Less than, greater than, less than or equal to, greater than or equal to
	x is T	True if x is convertible to T; false otherwise
	x as T	Returns x converted to T, or null if conversion is not possible
Equality	x == y, x != y	Equal and not equal

Operator Group	Operators Included	Description
Logical AND	x & y	Integer bitwise AND, Boolean logical AND
Logical XOR	x ^ y	Integer bitwise XOR, Boolean logical XOR
Logical OR	x | y	Integer bitwise OR, Boolean logical OR
Conditional AND	x && y	Evaluates y only if x is true
Conditional OR	x || y	Evaluates y only if x is false
Null coalescing	x ?? y	If x is non-null, evaluates to x; otherwise, y
Conditional	x ? y : z	Evaluates y if x is true; otherwise, evaluates z
Assignment	x = y	Simple assignment
	x op= y	Compound assignment; could be any of *=, /=, %=, +=, -=, <<=, >>=, &=, ^=, or |=

Note These operators can have different meanings in different contexts. Regardless, their precedence never changes. For example, the + operator can mean string concatenation if you're using it with string operands. By using operator overloading when defining your own types, you can make some of these operators perform whatever semantic meaning makes sense for the type. But again, you may never alter the precedence of these operators except by using parentheses to change the grouping of operations.

Statements and Expressions

Statements in C# are identical in form to those of C++ and Java. A semicolon terminates one-line expressions. However, code blocks, such as those in braces in an if or a while statement, do not need to be terminated with a semicolon. Adding the semicolon is optional at the end of a block.

Most of the statements that are available in C++ and Java are available in C#, including variable declaration statements, conditional statements, control flow statements, try/catch statements, and so on. However, C# (like Java) has some statements that are not available in C++. For example, C# provides a try/finally statement, which I discuss in detail in Chapter 7. In Chapter 12, I'll show you the lock statement, which synchronizes access to code blocks by using the sync block of an object. C# also overloads the using keyword, so you can use it either as a directive or a statement. You can use a using statement in concert with the Disposable pattern I describe in Chapters 4 and 13. The foreach statement, which makes iterating through collections easier, also deserves mention. You'll see more of this statement in Chapter 9, when I discuss arrays.

Types and Variables

Every entity in a C# program is an object that lives on either the stack or the managed heap. Every method is defined in a class or struct declaration. There are no such things as free functions, defined outside the scope of class or struct declarations, as there are in C++. Even the built-in value types, such as int, long, double, and so on, have methods associated with them implicitly. So, in C#, it's perfectly valid to write a statement such as the following:

```
System.Console.WriteLine( 42.ToString() );
```

A statement like this, where a method is invoked on the immediate value 42, will feel unfamiliar if you're used to C++ or Java. But, it emphasizes how everything in C# is an object, even down to the most basic types. In fact, the built-in type keywords in C# are actually mapped directly into types in the System namespace that represent them. You can even elect not to use the C# built-in types and explicitly use the types in the System namespace that they map to (but this practice is discouraged as a matter of style). Table 3-2 describes the built-in types, showing their size and what type they map to in the System namespace.

Table 3-2. *C# Built-In Types*

C# Type	Size in Bits	System Type	CLS-Compliant
sbyte	8	System.SByte	No
short	16	System.Int16	Yes
int	32	System.Int32	Yes
long	64	System.Int64	Yes
byte	8	System.Byte	Yes
ushort	16	System.Uint16	No
uint	32	System.Uint32	No
ulong	64	System.UInt64	No
char	16	System.Char	Yes
bool	8	System.Boolean	Yes
float	32	System.Single	Yes
double	64	System.Double	Yes
decimal	128	System.Decimal	Yes
string	N/A	System.String	Yes
object	N/A	System.Object	Yes

For each entry in the table, the last column indicates whether the type is compliant with the Common Language Specification (CLS). The CLS is defined as part of the CLI standard to facilitate multilanguage interoperability. The CLS is a subset of the Common Type System (CTS). Even though the CLR supports a rich set of built-in types, not all languages that compile into managed code support all of them. However, all managed languages are required to support the types in the CLS. For example, Visual Basic hasn't supported unsigned types traditionally. So the designers of the CLI defined the CLS to standardize types in order to facilitate interoperability between the languages. If your application will be entirely C#-based and won't create any components consumed from another language, then you don't have to worry about adhering to the strict guidelines of the CLS. But if you work on a project that builds components using various languages, then conforming to the CLS will be much more important to you.

In the managed world of the CLR, there are two kinds of types:

Value types: Defined in C# using the `struct` keyword. Instances of value types are the only kind of instances that can live on the stack. They live on the heap if they're members of reference types or if they're boxed, which I discuss later. They are similar to structures in C++ in the sense that they are copied by value by default when passed as parameters to methods or assigned to other variables. Although C#'s built-in value types represent the same kinds of values as Java's primitive types, there are no Java counterparts.

Reference types: Defined in C# using the `class` keyword. They are called reference types because the variables you use to manipulate them are actually references to objects on the managed heap. In fact, in the CLR reference-type variables are like value types that reference an object on the heap. In this way, C# and Java are identical. C++ programmers can think of them as pointers that you don't have to dereference to access objects. Some C++ programmers like to think of these as smart pointers.

Value Types

Value types can live on either the stack or the managed heap. You use them commonly when you need to represent some immutable data that is generally small in its memory footprint. You can define user-defined value types in C# by using the `struct` keyword.

■**Note** Even though C++ has a `struct` keyword, the meaning in C# is different in that it's the only way to create value types in C#.

User-defined value types behave in the same way that the built-in value types do. When you create a value during the flow of execution, the value is created on the stack, as shown in this code snippet:

```
int theAnswer = 42;
System.Console.WriteLine( theAnswer.ToString() );
```

Not only is the `theAnswer` instance created on the stack, but if it gets passed to a method, the method will receive a copy of it. Value types are typically used in managed applications to represent lightweight pieces or collections of data, similar to the way built-in types and structs are sometimes used in C++, and primitive types are used in Java.

Values can also live on the managed heap, but not by themselves. The only way this can happen is if a reference type has a field that is a value type. Even though a value type inside an object lives on the managed heap, it still behaves the same as a value type on the stack when it comes to passing it into a method; that is, the method will receive a copy by default. Any changes made to the value instance are only local changes to the copy unless the value was passed by reference. The following code illustrates these concepts:

```
public struct Coordinate  //this is a value type
{
    public int x;
    public int y;
}

public class EntryPoint //this is a reference type
```

```
{
    public static void AttemptToModifyCoord( Coordinate coord ) {
        coord.x = 1;
        coord.y = 3;
    }

    public static void ModifyCoord( ref Coordinate coord ) {
        coord.x = 10;
        coord.y = 10;
    }

    static void Main() {
        Coordinate location;
        location.x = 50;
        location.y = 50;

        AttemptToModifyCoord( location );
        System.Console.WriteLine( "( {0}, {1} )", location.x, location.y );

        ModifyCoord( ref location );
        System.Console.WriteLine( "( {0}, {1} )", location.x, location.y );
    }
}
```

In the Main method, the call to AttemptToModifyCoord actually does nothing to the location value. This is because AttemptToModifyCoord modifies a local copy of the value that was made when the method was called. The location value is passed by reference into the ModifyCoord method. Thus, any changes made in the ModifyCoord method are actually made on the location value in the calling scope. It's similar to passing a value by a pointer in C++. The output from the example is as follows:

```
( 50, 50 )
( 10, 10 )
```

Enumerations

Enumerations (enums) in C# are similar to enumerations in C++, and the defining syntax is almost identical. At the point of use, however, you must fully qualify the values within an enumeration using the enumeration type name. All enumerations are based upon an underlying integral type, which if not specified, defaults to int.

Note The underlying type of the enum must be an integral type that is one of the following: byte, sbyte, short, ushort, int, uint, long, or ulong.

Each constant that is defined in the enumeration must be defined with a value within the range of the underlying type. If you don't specify a value for an enumeration constant, the value takes the default value of 0 (if it is the first constant in the enumeration) or 1 plus the value of the previous constant. This example is an enumeration based upon a long:

```
public enum Color : long
{
```

```
    Red,
    Green = 50,
    Blue
}
```

In this example, if I had left off the colon and the long keyword after the Color type identifier, the enumeration would have been of int type. Notice that the value for Red is 0, the value for Green is 50, and the value for Blue is 51.

To use this enumeration, write code such as the following:

```
static void Main() {
    Color color = Color.Red;
    System.Console.WriteLine( "Color is {0}", color.ToString() );
}
```

If you compile and run this code, you'll see that the output actually uses the name of the enumeration rather than the ordinal value 0. The System.Enum type's implementation of the ToString method performs this magic.

Many times, you may use enumeration constants to represent bit flags. You can attach an attribute in the System namespace called System.FlagsAttribute to the enumeration to make this explicit. The attribute is stored in the metadata, and you can reference it at design time to determine whether members of an enumeration are intended to be used as bit flags. Also, you can reference this attribute in some places at run time—for example, when an enumeration value is converted to a string. Note that System.FlagsAttribute doesn't modify the behavior of the values defined by the enumeration. At run time, however, certain components can use the metadata generated by the attribute to process the value differently. This is a great example of how you can use metadata effectively in an aspect-oriented programming (AOP) manner.

■**Note** AOP, also called aspect-oriented software development (AOSD), is a concept originally developed by Gregor Kiczales and his team at Xerox PARC. Object-oriented methodologies generally do a great job of partitioning the functionality, or concerns, of a design into cohesive units. However, some concerns, called *crosscutting concerns*, cannot be modeled easily with standard OO designs. For example, suppose you need to log entry into and exit from various methods. It would be a horrible pain to modify the code for each and every method that you need to log. It would be much easier if you could simply attach a property—or in this case, an attribute—to the method itself so that the runtime would log the method's call when it happens. This keeps you from having to modify the method, and the requirement is applied out-of-band from the method's implementation. Microsoft Transaction Server (MTS) was one of the first widely known examples of AOP.

Using metadata, and the fact that you can attach arbitrary, custom attributes to types, methods, properties, and so on, you can use AOP in your own designs.

Here is an example of a bit flag enumeration:

```
[Flags]
public enum AccessFlags

{
    NoAccess = 0x0,
    ReadAccess = 0x1,
    WriteAccess = 0x2,
    ExecuteAccess = 0x4
}
```

Here is an example of using the AccessFlags enumeration:

```
static void Main() {
   AccessFlags access = AccessFlags.ReadAccess |
      AccessFlags.WriteAccess;

   System.Console.WriteLine( "Access is {0}", access );
}
```

If you compile and execute this example, you'll see that the Enum.ToString method implicitly invoked by WriteLine does, in fact, output a comma-separated list of all the bits that are set in this value.

Reference Types

The garbage collector (GC) inside the CLR manages everything regarding the placement of objects. It can move objects at any time. When it moves them, the CLR makes sure that the variables that reference them are updated. Normally, you're not concerned with the exact location of the object within the heap, and you don't have to care if it gets moved around or not. There are rare cases, such as when interfacing with native DLLs, when you may need to obtain a direct memory pointer to an object on the heap. It is possible to do that using *unsafe* (or *unmanaged*) code techniques, but that is outside the scope of this book.

■**Note** Conventionally, the term *object* refers to an instance of a reference type, whereas the term *value* refers to an instance of a value type, but all instances of any type are also derived from type object.

Variables of a reference type are either initialized by using the new operator to create an object on the managed heap, or they are initialized by assignment from another variable of a compatible type. The following code snippet points two variables at the same object:

```
string idTag = "423-XYZ";
string theTag = idTag;
```

Like the Java runtime, the CLR manages all references to objects on the heap. In C++, you must explicitly delete heap-based objects at some carefully chosen point. But in the managed environment of the CLR, the GC takes care of this for you. This frees you from having to worry about deleting objects from memory and minimizes memory leaks. The GC can determine, at any point in time, how many references exist to a particular object on the heap. If it determines there are none, it is free to start the process of destroying the object on the heap. (Chapter 13 discusses at length the intricacies of this process and the factors that influence it.) The previous code snippet includes two references to the same object. You initialize the first one, idTag, by creating a string object. You initialize the second one, theTag, from idTag. The GC won't collect the string object on the heap until both of these references are outside any usable scope. Had the method containing this code returned a copy of the reference to whatever called it, then the GC would still have a reference to track even when the method was no longer in scope.

■**Note** For those coming from a C++ background, the fundamental way in which objects are treated in the C++ world is reversed in the C# world. In C++, objects are allocated on the stack unless you create them explicitly with the new operator, which then returns a pointer to the object on the native heap. In C#, you cannot create objects of a reference type on the stack. They can only live on the heap. So, it's almost as if you were writing C++ code, where you create every object on the heap without having to worry about deleting the objects explicitly to clean up.

Default Variable Initialization

By default, the C# compiler produces what is called *safe code*. One of the safety concerns is making sure the program doesn't use uninitialized memory. The compiler wants every variable to be set to a value before you use it, so it is useful to know how different types of variables are initialized.

The default value for references to objects is null. At the point of declaration, you can optionally assign references from the result of a call to the new operator; otherwise, they will be set to null. When you create an object, the runtime initializes its internal fields. Fields that are references to objects are initialized to null, of course. Fields that are value types are initialized by setting all bits of the value type to zero. Basically, you can imagine that all the runtime is doing is setting the bits of the underlying storage to 0. For references to objects, that equates to a null reference, and for value types, that equates to a value of zero.

For value types that you declare on the stack, the compiler does not zero-initialize the memory automatically. However, it does make sure that you initialize the memory before the value is used.

■**Note** Since enumerations are actually value types, you should always declare an enumeration member that equates to zero, even if the name of the member is InvalidValue or None and is otherwise meaningless. If an enumeration is declared as a field of a class, instances of that class will have the field set to zero upon default initialization. Declaring a member that equates to zero allows users of your enumeration to deal with this case easily.

Implicitly Typed Local Variables

Because C# is a strongly typed language, every variable declared in the code must have an explicit type associated with it. When the CLR stores the contents of the variable in a memory location, it also associates a type with that location. But sometimes, when writing code for strongly typed languages, the amount of typing needed to declare such variables can be tedious, especially if the type is a generic one. For complex types, such as query variables created using Language Integrated Query (LINQ), discussed in Chapter 16, the type names can be downright unwieldy. Enter implicitly typed variables.

By declaring a local variable using the new var keyword, you effectively ask the compiler to reserve a local memory slot and attach an inferred type to that slot. At compilation time, there is enough information available at the point the variable is initialized for the compiler to deduce the actual type of that variable without your having to tell it the type explicitly. Let's have a look at what these look like.

Here you see an example of what an implicitly typed variable declaration looks like:

```
using System;
using System.Collections.Generic;

public class EntryPoint
{
    static void Main() {
        var myList = new List<int>();

        myList.Add( 1 );
        myList.Add( 2 );
        myList.Add( 3 );

        foreach( var i in myList ) {
            Console.WriteLine( i );
        }
    }
}
```

The first things you should notice are the keywords in bold that show the usage of the new var keyword. In the first usage, I have declared a variable named myList, asking the compiler to set the type of the variable based upon the type from which it is assigned. It's important to note that an implicitly typed variable declaration must include an initializer. If you tried to state the following in code, you would be greeted with the compiler warning CS0818, stating that "Implicitly typed locals must be initialized":

```
var newValue;    // emits error CS0818
```

Similarly, if you try to declare a class field member as an implicitly typed variable, even if it has an initializer, you will get the compiler error CS0825, stating that "The contextual keyword 'var' may only appear within a local variable declaration."

Finally, you may be used to declaring multiple variables in one line by separating each identifier with a comma, as in the following two examples:

```
int a = 2, b = 1;
int x, y = 4;
```

However, you cannot do this with implicitly typed variables. The compiler gives you the error CS0819, stating "Implicitly typed locals cannot have multiple declarators."

■ Note Early copies of the C# 3.0 draft standard floating around the Internet indicate that implicitly typed variables can be initialized using multiple declarators as long as each initializer results in the same type. However, the pre-release version of the compiler that I am using while writing this book does not support it.

THE COMPLEXITY OF ADDING NEW KEYWORDS TO THE LANGUAGE

Adding new features like implicitly typed variables to the compiler is not as trivial as it may appear at first. That's because any time you introduce a new keyword to the language, you have to be concerned about breaking existing code and not allowing backward compatibility. For example, imagine what would happen if you had a huge code base written with C# 1.0 or C# 2.0 that had a type, say a class, named var. Now, you are in the process of making the switch to C# 3.0 and you compile your application using the new compiler. Clearly, you will most likely have some variable declarations that create instances of your var class. What should the compiler do? This is a very difficult question to answer.

In my tests with the pre-release version of the compiler I am using as I write this, the compiler does nothing. But should it do nothing? It could choose to emit a compiler warning stating something like "declared type has same name as built-in 'var' keyword." But in reality, that's not necessary, as I'll show soon. In fact, it's probably best that the compiler does not emit a warning. Good development teams use the /WARNASERRORS+ compiler option to halt compilation if there is a warning in the code. So if the compiler emitted a warning, your application would fail to compile as you migrated to C# 3.0 and Microsoft would take the blame for being so flagrant as to ignore backward compatibility.

The bottom line is that if you have a type defined using the name var, you simply cannot use implicitly typed variables in any C# code where that type's namespace is imported into the local scope. If you do, you'll typically get the CS0029 compiler error, which says in essence that the type you are trying to assign to an implicitly typed variable cannot be implicitly converted to your custom var type. Whew! What a mouthful. For example, the following code exhibits this behavior:

```
using System;
using System.Collections.Generic;
```

```
public class var
{
}

public class EntryPoint
{
    static void Main() {
        var myList = new List<int>();    // Won't compile!  Error CS0029
    }
}
```

Compiler developers typically take this problem extremely seriously and sometimes won't even introduce a new keyword if it could possibly break existing code. However, the C# compiler developers have a trump card. If you follow the recommended conventions for naming .NET types with an initial capital letter, you'll never find yourself in this situation. Additionally, if you use Visual Studio code analysis or FxCop (the stand-alone version of code analysis) during the development of your application, you will never encounter this problem. These rules and guidelines are also covered in detail in *Framework Design Guidelines: Conventions, Idioms, and Patterns for Reusable .NET Libraries* by Krzysztof Cwalina and Brad Abrams (Boston, MA: Addison-Wesley Professional, 2005). I highly recommend you read their book if you have not already.

Type Conversion

Many times, it's necessary to convert instances of one type to another. In some cases, the compiler does this conversion implicitly whenever a value of one type is assigned from another type that, when converted to the assigned type, will not lose any precision or magnitude. In cases where precision could be lost, an explicit conversion is required. For reference types, the conversion rules are analogous to the pointer conversion rules in C++.

The semantics of type conversion are similar to both C++ and Java. Explicit conversion is represented using the familiar casting syntax that all of them inherited from C—that is, the type to convert to is placed in parentheses before whatever needs to be converted:

```
int defaultValue = 12345678;
long value = defaultValue;
int  smallerValue = (int) value;
```

In this code, the (int) cast is required to be explicit since the underlying size of an int is smaller than a long. Thus, it's possible that the value in the long may not fit into the space available to the int. The assignment from the defaultValue variable to the value variable requires no cast, since a long has more storage space than an int. If the conversion will lose magnitude, it's possible that the conversion may throw an exception at run time. The general rule is that implicit conversions are guaranteed never to throw an exception, whereas explicit conversions may throw exceptions.

The C# language provides the facilities to define custom implicit and explicit conversion operators to various types for your user-defined types. Chapter 6 covers these in more detail. The exception requirements for built-in conversion operators apply to user-defined conversion operators. Namely, implicit conversion operators are guaranteed never to throw.

Conversion to and from reference types models that of Java and of conversions between pointers in C++. For example, a reference to type DerivedType can be implicitly converted to a reference to type BaseType if DerivedType is derived from BaseType. However, you must explicitly cast a conversion in the opposite direction. Also, an explicit cast may throw a System.InvalidCastException if the CLR cannot perform the conversion at run time.

One kind of implicit cast is available in C# that is not easily available in C++, mainly because of the default value semantics of C++. It is possible to implicitly convert from an array of one reference type to an array of another reference type, as long as the target reference type is one that can be implicitly converted from the source reference type and the arrays are of the same dimension. For example, the following conversion is valid:

```
public class EntryPoint
{
    static void Main() {
        string[] names = new string[4];
        object[] objects = names;  //implicit conversion statement

        string[] originalNames =
            (string[]) objects;  // explicit conversion statement
    }
}
```

Because System.String derives from System.Object and, therefore, is implicitly convertible to System.Object, this implicit conversion of the string array names into the object array objects variable is valid. However, to go in the other direction, as shown, requires an explicit cast that may throw an exception at run time if the conversion fails.

Keep in mind that implicit conversions of arguments may occur during method invocation if arguments must be converted to match the types of parameters. If you cannot make the conversions implicitly, you must cast the arguments explicitly.

Finally, another type of common conversion is a *boxing conversion*. Boxing conversions are required when you must pass a value type as a reference type parameter to a method or assign it to a variable that is a reference type. What happens is that an object is allocated dynamically on the heap that contains a field of the value's type. The value is then copied into this field. I cover boxing in C# extensively in Chapter 4. The following code demonstrates boxing:

```
public class EntryPoint
{
    static void Main() {
        int employeeID = 303;
        object boxedID = employeeID;

        employeeID = 404;
        int unboxedID = (int) boxedID;

        System.Console.WriteLine( employeeID.ToString() );
        System.Console.WriteLine( unboxedID.ToString() );
    }
}
```

At the point where the object variable boxedID is assigned from the int variable employeeID, boxing occurs. A heap-based object is created and the value of employeeID is copied into it. This bridges the gap between the value type and the reference type worlds within the CLR. The boxedID object actually contains a copy of the employeeID value. I demonstrate this point by changing the original employeeID value after the boxing operation. Before printing out the values, I unbox the value and copy the value contained in the object on the heap back into another int on the stack. Unboxing requires an explicit cast in C#, because it can fail with a bad cast exception.

as and is Operators

Because explicit conversion can fail by throwing exceptions, times arise when you may want to test the type of a variable without performing a cast and seeing if it fails or not. Testing this way is tedious and inefficient, and exceptions are generally expensive at run time. For this reason, C# has two operators that come to the rescue, and they are guaranteed not to throw an exception:

- is

- as

The is operator results in a Boolean that determines whether you can convert a given expression to the given type as either a reference conversion or a boxing or unboxing operation. For example, consider the following code:

```
using System;

public class EntryPoint
{
    static void Main() {
        String derivedObj = "Dummy";
        Object baseObj1 = new Object();
        Object baseObj2 = derivedObj;

        Console.WriteLine( "baseObj2 {0} String",
                           baseObj2 is String ? "is" : "isnot" );
        Console.WriteLine( "baseObj1 {0} String",
                           baseObj1 is String ? "is" : "isnot" );
        Console.WriteLine( "derivedObj {0} Object",
                           derivedObj is Object ? "is" : "isnot" );

        int j = 123;
        object boxed = j;
        object obj = new Object();

        Console.WriteLine( "boxed {0} int",
                           boxed is int ? "is" : "isnot" );
        Console.WriteLine( "obj {0} int",
                           obj is int ? "is" : "isnot" );
        Console.WriteLine( "boxed {0} System.ValueType",
                           boxed is ValueType ? "is" : "isnot" );

    }
}
```

The output from this code is as follows:

```
baseObj2 is String
baseObj1 isnot String
derivedObj is Object
boxed is int
obj isnot int
boxed is System.ValueType
```

As mentioned previously, the is operator considers only reference conversions. This means that it won't consider any user-defined conversions that are defined on the types.

The as operator is similar to the is operator, except that it returns a reference to the target type. Because it is guaranteed never to throw an exception, it simply returns a null reference if the conversion cannot be made. Similar to the is operator, the as operator only considers reference conversions or boxing conversions. For example, look at the following code:

```
using System;

public class BaseType {}

public class DerivedType : BaseType {}

public class EntryPoint {
    static void Main() {
        DerivedType derivedObj = new DerivedType();
        BaseType baseObj1 = new BaseType();
        BaseType baseObj2 = derivedObj;

        DerivedType derivedObj2 = baseObj2 as DerivedType;
        if( derivedObj2 != null ) {
            Console.WriteLine( "Conversion Succeeded" );
        } else {
            Console.WriteLine( "Conversion Failed" );
        }

        derivedObj2 = baseObj1 as DerivedType;
        if( derivedObj2 != null ) {
            Console.WriteLine( "Conversion Succeeded" );
        } else {
            Console.WriteLine( "Conversion Failed" );
        }

        BaseType baseObj3 = derivedObj as BaseType;
        if( baseObj3 != null ) {
            Console.WriteLine( "Conversion Succeeded" );
        } else {
            Console.WriteLine( "Conversion Failed" );
        }
    }
}
```

The output from this code is as follows:

```
Conversion Succeeded
Conversion Failed
Conversion Succeeded
```

Sometimes you need to test whether a variable is of a certain type and, if it is, then do some sort of operation on the desired type. You could test the variable for the desired type using the is operator and then, if true, cast the variable to the desired type. However, doing it that way is inefficient. The better approach is to follow the idiom of applying the as operator to obtain a reference of the variable with the desired type, and then test whether the resulting reference is null, which would mean that the conversion succeeded. That way, you perform only one type lookup operation instead of two.

Generics

Support for generics is one of the most exciting new additions to the C# language. Using the generic syntax, you can define a type that depends upon another type that is not specified at the point of definition, but rather at the point of usage of the generic type. For example, imagine a collection type. Collection types typically embody things such as lists, queues, and stacks. The collection types that have been around since the .NET 1.0 days are adequate for containing any type in the CLR, since they contain Object instances and everything derives from Object. However, all of the type information for the contained type is thrown away, and the compiler's power to catch type errors is rendered useless. You must cast every type reference that you obtain from these collections into the type you think it should be, and that could fail at run time. Also, the original collection types can contain a heterogeneous blend of types rather than force the user to insert only instances of a certain type. You could go about fixing this problem by writing types such as ListOfIntegers and ListOfStrings for each type you want to contain in a list. However, you will quickly find out that most of the management code of these lists is similar, or generic, across all of the custom list types. The key word is *generic*. Using generic types, you can declare an open (or generic) type and only have to write the common code once. The users of your type can then specify which type the collection will contain at the point they decide to use it.

Additionally, using generics involves efficiency gains. The concept of generics is so large that I've devoted Chapter 11 entirely to their declaration and usage. However, I believe it's important to give you a taste of how to use a generic type now, since I mention them several times prior to Chapter 11.

■**Note** The generic syntax will look familiar to those who use C++ templates. However, it's important to note that there are significant behavioral differences, which I'll explain in Chapter 11.

The most common use of generics is during the declaration of collection types. For example, take a look at the following code:

```
using System;
using System.Collections.Generic;
using System.Collections.ObjectModel;

class EntryPoint
{
    static void Main() {
        Collection<int> numbers =
            new Collection<int>();
        numbers.Add( 42 );
        numbers.Add( 409 );

        Collection<string> strings =
            new Collection<string>();
        strings.Add( "Joe" );
        strings.Add( "Bob" );

        Collection< Collection<int> > colNumbers
            = new Collection<Collection<int>>();
        colNumbers.Add( numbers );
```

```
        IList<int> theNumbers = numbers;
        foreach( int i in theNumbers ) {
            Console.WriteLine( i );
        }
    }
}
```

This example shows usage of the generic Collection type. The telltale sign of generic type usage is the angle brackets surrounding a type name. In this case, I have declared a collection of integers, a collection of strings, and, to show an even more complex generic usage, a collection of collections of integers. Also, notice that I've shown the declaration for a generic interface, namely, IList<>.

When you specify the type arguments for a generic type by listing them within the angle brackets, as in Collection<int>, you are declaring a closed type. In this case, Collection<int> only takes one type parameter, but had it taken more, then a comma would have separated the type arguments. When the CLR first encounters this type declaration, it will generate the closed type based on the generic type and the provided type arguments. Using closed types formed from generics is no different than using any other type, except that the type declaration uses the special angle bracket syntax to form the closed type.

Now that you've seen a glimpse of what generics look like, you should be prepared for the casual generic references mentioned prior to Chapter 11.

Namespaces

C#, like C++ and analogous to Java packages, supports namespaces for grouping components logically. Namespaces help you avoid naming collisions between your identifiers.

Using namespaces, you can define all of your types such that their identifiers are qualified by the namespace that they belong to. You have already seen namespaces in action in many of the examples so far. For instance, in the "Hello World!" example from Chapter 1, you saw the use of the Console class, which lives in the .NET Framework Class Library's System namespace and whose fully qualified name is System.Console. You can create your own namespaces to organize components. The general recommendation is that you use some sort of identifier, such as your organization's name, as the top-level namespace, and then more specific library identifiers as nested namespaces.

Namespaces provide an excellent mechanism with which you can make your types more discoverable, especially if you're designing libraries meant for consumption by others. For example, you can create a general namespace such as MyCompany.Widgets, where you put the most commonly used types of widgets. Then you can create a MyCompany.Widgets.Advanced namespace where you place all of the less commonly used, advanced types. Sure, you could place them all in one namespace. However, users could become confused when browsing the types and seeing all of the types they least commonly use mixed in with the ones they use the most.

■Note When picking a name for your namespace, the general guideline suggests that you name it using the formula <CompanyName>.<Technology>.*, such that the first two dot-separated portions of the namespace name start with your company name followed by your company's technology. Then you can further subclassify the namespace. You can see examples of this in the .NET Framework—for example, the Microsoft.Win32 namespace.

Defining Namespaces

The syntax for declaring a namespace is simple. The following code shows how to declare a namespace named Acme:

```
namespace Acme
{
    class Utility {}
}
```

Namespaces don't have to live in only one compilation unit (i.e., the C# source code file). In other words, the same namespace declaration can exist in multiple C# files. When everything is compiled, the set of identifiers included in the namespace is a union of all of the identifiers in each of the namespace declarations. In fact, this union spans across assemblies. If multiple assemblies contain types defined in the same namespace, the total namespace consists of all of the identifiers across all the assemblies that define the types.

It's possible to nest namespace declarations. You can do this in one of two ways. The first way is obvious:

```
namespace Acme
{
    namespace Utilities
    {
        class SomeUtility {}
    }
}
```

Given this example, to access the SomeUtility class using its fully qualified name, you must identify it as Acme.Utilities.SomeUtility. The following example demonstrates an alternate way of defining nested namespaces:

```
namespace Acme
{
}

namespace Acme.Utilities
{
class SomeUtility {}
}
```

The effect of this code is exactly the same as the previous code. In fact, you may omit the first empty namespace declaration for the Acme namespace. I left it there only for demonstration purposes to point out that the Utilities namespace declaration is not physically nested within the Acme namespace declaration.

Any types that you declare outside a namespace become part of the global namespace.

■**Note** You should always avoid defining types in the global namespace. Such practice is known as "polluting the global namespace" and is widely considered poor programming practice. This should be obvious since there would be no way to protect types defined by multiple entities from potential naming collisions.

Using Namespaces

In the "Hello World!" example in Chapter 1, I quickly touched on the options available for using namespaces. Let's examine some code that uses the SomeUtility class I defined in the previous section:

```
public class EntryPoint
{
    static void Main() {
        Acme.Utilities.SomeUtility util =
            new Acme.Utilities.SomeUtility();
    }
}
```

This practice of always qualifying names fully is rather verbose and might eventually lead to a bad case of carpal tunnel syndrome. The using namespace directive avoids this. It tells the compiler that you're using an entire namespace in a compilation unit or another namespace. What the using keyword does is effectively import all of the names in the given namespace into the enclosing namespace, which could be the global namespace of the compilation unit. The following example demonstrates this:

```
using Acme.Utilities;

public class EntryPoint
{
    static void Main() {
        SomeUtility util = new SomeUtility();
    }
}
```

The code is now much easier to deal with and somewhat easier to read. The using directive, because it is at the global namespace level, imports the type names from Acme.Utilities into the global namespace. Sometimes when you import the names from multiple namespaces, you may still have naming conflicts if both imported namespaces contain types with the same name. In this case, you can import individual types from a namespace, creating a naming alias. This technique is available via namespace aliasing in C#. Let's modify the usage of the SomeUtility class so that you alias only the SomeUtility class rather than everything inside the Acme.Utilities namespace:

```
namespace Acme.Utilities
{
    class AnotherUtility() {}
}

using SomeUtility = Acme.Utilities.SomeUtility;

public class EntryPoint
{
    static void Main() {
        SomeUtility util = new SomeUtility();
        Acme.Utilities.AnotherUtility =
            new Acme.Utilities.AnotherUtility();
    }
}
```

In this code, the identifier SomeUtility is aliased as Acme.Utilities.SomeUtility. To prove the point, I augmented the Acme.Utilities namespace and added a new class named AnotherUtility. This class must be fully qualified in order for you to reference it, since no alias is declared for it. Incidentally, it's perfectly valid to give the previous alias a different name than SomeUtility. Although giving the alias a different name may be useful when trying to resolve a naming conflict, it's generally better to alias it using the same name as the original class name in order to avoid maintenance confusion in the future.

Note If you follow good partitioning principles when defining your namespaces, you shouldn't have to deal with this problem. It is bad design practice to create namespaces that contain a grab bag of various types covering different groups of functionality. Instead, you should create your namespaces with intuitively cohesive types contained within them. In fact, many times in the .NET Framework, you'll see a namespace with some general types for the namespace included in it, with more advanced types contained in a nested namespace named Advanced. In many respects, for creating libraries, these guidelines mirror the principle of discoverability applied when creating intuitive user interfaces. In other words, name and group your types intuitively and make them easily discoverable.

Control Flow

Like C, C++, and Java, the C# language contains all the usual suspects when it comes to control flow structure. C# even implements the dastardly goto statement.

if-else, while, do-while, and for

The if-else construct within C# is identical to those in C++ and Java. As a stylistic recommendation, I'm a proponent of always using blocks in if statements, or any other control flow statement as described in the following sections, even when they contain only one statement, as in the following example:

```
if( <test condition> ) {
    Console.WriteLine( "You are here." );
}
```

The while, do, and for statements are identical to those in C++ and Java.

switch

The syntax of the C# switch statement is very similar to the C++ and Java switch syntax. The main difference is that the C# switch doesn't allow falling through to the next section. It requires a break (or other transfer of control) statement to end each section. I believe this is a great thing. Countless hard-to-spot bugs exist in C++ and Java applications because developers forgot a break statement or rearranged the order of sections within a switch when one of them falls through to another. In C#, the compiler will immediately complain with an error if it finds a section that falls through to the next. The one exception to this rule is that you can have multiple switch labels (using the case keyword) per switch section, as shown in the following code snippet. You can also simulate falling through sections with the goto statement:

```
switch( k ) {
    case 0:
        Console.WriteLine( "case 0" );
        goto case 1;
    case 1:
    case 2:
        Console.WriteLine( "case 1 or 2" );
        break;
}
```

Notice that each one of the cases has a form of *jump* statement that terminates it. Even the last case must have one. Many C++ and Java developers would omit the break statement in the final section because it would just fall through to the end of the switch anyway. Again, the beauty of the "no fall-through" constraint is that even if a developer maintaining the code at a later date whimsically decides to switch the ordering of the labels, no bugs can be introduced, unlike in C++ and Java. Typically, you use a break statement to terminate switch sections, and you can use any statement that exits the section. These include throw and return, as well as continue if the switch is embedded within a loop where the continue statement makes sense.

foreach

The foreach statement allows you to iterate over a collection of objects in a syntactically natural way. Note that you can implement the same functionality using a while loop. However, this can be ugly, and iterating over the elements of a collection is such a common task that foreach syntax is a welcome addition to the language. If you had an array (or any other type of collection) of strings, for example, you could iterate over each string using the following code:

```
static void Main() {
    string[] strings = new string[5];
    strings[0] = "Bob";
    strings[1] = "Joe";
    foreach( string item in strings ) {
        Console.WriteLine( "{0}", item );
    }
}
```

Within the parentheses of the foreach loop, you declare the type of your iterator variable. In this example, it is a string. Following the declaration of the iterator type is the identifier for the collection to iterate over. You may use any object that implements the Collection pattern. Chapter 9 covers collections in greater detail, including what sorts of things a type must implement in order to be considered a collection. Naturally, the elements within the collection used in a foreach statement must be convertible, using an explicit conversion, to the iterator type. If they're not, the foreach statement will throw an InvalidCastException at run time. If you'd like to experience this inconvenience yourself, try running this modification to the previous example:

```
static void Main() {
    object[] strings = new object[5];
    strings[0] = 1;
    strings[1] = 2;
    foreach( string item in strings ) {
        Console.WriteLine( "{0}", item );
    }
}
```

Note, however, that it's invalid for the code embedded in a foreach statement to modify the iterator variable at all. It should be treated as read-only. That means you cannot pass the iterator variable as an out or a ref parameter to a method, either. If you try to do any of these things, the compiler will quickly alert you to the error of your ways.

break, continue, goto, return, and throw

C# includes a set of familiar statements that unconditionally transfer control to another location. These include break, continue, goto, return, and throw. Their syntax should be familiar to any C++ or Java developer (though Java has no goto). Their usage is essentially identical in all three languages.

Summary

This chapter introduced the C# syntax, emphasizing that C#, like similar object-oriented languages, is a strongly typed language. For these languages, you want to utilize the type-checking engine of the compiler to find as many errors as possible at compile time rather than find them later at run time. In the CLR, types are classified as either value types or reference types, and each category comes with its own stipulations, which I'll continue to dig into throughout this book. I also introduced namespaces and showed how they help keep the global namespace from getting polluted with too many types whose names could conflict. And finally, I showed how control statements work in C#, which is similar to how they work in C++ and Java.

In the next chapter, I'll dig deeper into the structure of classes and structs, while highlighting the behavioral differences of instances thereof.

■■■

## CHAPTER 4

Classes, Structs, and Objects

Everything is an object! At least, that is the view from inside the CLR and the C# programming language. This is no surprise, because C# is, after all, an object-oriented language. The objects that you create through class definitions in C# have all the same capabilities as the other predefined objects in the system. In fact, keywords in the C# language such as int and bool are merely aliases to predefined value types within the System namespace, in this case System.Int32 and System.Boolean, respectively.

Note This chapter is rather long, but don't allow it to be intimidating. In order to cater to a wider audience, this chapter covers as much C# base material as reasonably possible. If you're proficient with either C++ or Java, you may find yourself skimming this chapter and referencing it as you read subsequent chapters. Some of the topics touched upon in this chapter are covered in more detail in later chapters.

The first section of this chapter covers class definitions, which is followed by a section discussing value type definitions. These are the two most fundamental classifications of types in the .NET runtime. Then you'll learn about System.Object (the base type of all types), the nuances of creating and destroying instances of objects, expressions for initializing objects, and the topic of boxing and unboxing. Anonymous types are new to C# 3.0 and I have devoted a section to them. Finally, I cover inheritance and polymorphism, and the differences between inheritance and containment with regard to code reuse.

The ability to invent your own types is tantamount to object-oriented systems. The cool thing is that, since even the built-in types of the language are plain-old CLR objects, the objects you create are on a level playing field with the built-in types. In other words, the built-in types don't have special powers that you cannot muster in user-defined types. The cornerstone for creating these types is the *class definition*. Class definitions, using the C# class keyword, define the internal state and the behaviors associated with the objects of that class's type. The internal state of an object is represented by the fields that you declare within the class, which can consist of references to other objects, or values. Sometimes, but rarely, you will hear people describe this as the "shape" of the object, since the instance field definitions within the class define the memory footprint of the object on the heap.

The objects created from a class encapsulate the data fields that represent the internal state of the objects, and the objects can tightly control access to those fields. The behavior of the objects is defined by implementing methods, which you declare and define within the class definition. By calling one of the methods on an object instance, you initiate a unit of work on the object. That work can possibly modify the internal state of the object, inspect the state of the object, or anything else for that matter.

You can define constructors, which the system executes whenever a new object is created. You can also define a method called a finalizer, which works when the object is garbage-collected. As you'll see in Chapter 13, you should avoid finalizers if at all possible. This chapter covers construction and destruction in detail, including the detailed sequence of events that occur during the creation of an object.

Objects support the concept of *inheritance*, whereby a *derived class* inherits the fields and methods of a *base class*. Inheritance also allows you to treat objects of a derived type as objects of its base type. For example, a design in which an object of type Dog derives from type Animal is said to model an *is-a* relationship (i.e., Dog is-a(n) Animal). Therefore, you can implicitly convert references of type Dog to references of type Animal. Here, *implicit* means that the conversion takes the form of a simple assignment expression. Conversely, you can *explicitly* convert references of type Animal, through a cast operation, to references of type Dog if the particular object referenced through the Animal type is, in fact, an object created from the Dog class. This concept, called *polymorphism*, whereby you can manipulate objects of related types as though they were of a common type, should be familiar to you. Computer wonks always try to come up with fancy five-dollar words for things such as this, and *polymorphism* is no exception, when all it means is that an object can take on multiple type identities. This chapter discusses inheritance, as well as its traps and pitfalls.

The CLR tracks object references. This means each variable of *reference type* actually contains a reference to an object on the heap (or is null, if it doesn't currently refer to an object). When you copy the value of a reference-type variable into another reference-type variable, another reference to the same object is created—in other words, the reference is copied. Thus, you end up with two variables that reference the same object. In the CLR, you have to do extra work to create copies of objects—e.g., you must implement the ICloneable interface or a similar pattern.

All objects created from C# class definitions reside on the system heap, which the CLR garbage collector manages. The GC relieves you from the task of cleaning up your objects' memory. You can allocate them all day long without worrying about who will free the memory associated with them. The GC is smart enough to track all of an object's references, and when it notices that an object is no longer referenced, it marks the object for deletion. Then, the next time the GC compacts the heap, it destroys the object and reclaims the memory.

■**Note** In reality, the process is much more complex than this. There are many hidden nuances to how the GC reclaims the memory of unused objects. I talk about this in the section titled "Destroying Objects" later this chapter. Consider this: The GC removes some complexity in one area, but introduces a whole new set of complexities elsewhere.

Along with classes, the C# language supports the definition of new *value types* through the struct keyword. Value types are lightweight objects that typically don't live on the heap, but instead live on the stack. To be completely accurate, a value type can live on the heap, but only if it is a field inside an object on the heap. Value types cannot be defined to inherit from another class or value type, nor can another value type or class inherit from them.

Value types can have constructors, but they cannot have a finalizer. By default, when you pass value types into methods as parameters, the method receives a copy of the value. I cover the many details of value types, along with their differences from reference types, in this chapter and in Chapter 13.

That said, let's dive in and get to the details. Don't be afraid if the details seem a little overwhelming at first. The fact is, you can start to put together reasonable applications with C# without knowing every single detailed behavior of the language. That's a good thing, because C#, along with the Visual Studio IDE, is meant to facilitate rapid application development. However, the more details you know about the language and the CLR, the more effective you'll be at developing and designing robust C# applications.

Class Definitions

Class definitions in C# look similar to class definitions in C++ and Java. Let's look at a simple class now, so you can get a feel for things. In the following code, I've shown the basic pieces for creating a class definition:

```
//NOTE: This code is not meant to be compiled as-is
[Serializable]
public class Derived : Base, ICloneable
{
    private Derived( Derived other ) {
        this.x = other.x;
    }

    public object Clone() {  //implement the IClonable.Clone interface
        return new Derived( this );
    }

    private int x;
}
```

This class declaration defines a class `Derived`, which derives from the class `Base` and also implements the `ICloneable` interface.

▓**Note** If this is the first time you've encountered the interface concept, don't worry. Chapter 5 is devoted entirely to interfaces and contract-based programming.

The *access modifier* in front of the `class` keyword controls the visibility of the type from outside the assembly (I describe assemblies in Chapter 2). The class `Derived` is publicly accessible, which means that consumers of the assembly that contains this class can create instances of it. This type contains a private constructor that is used by the public method `Clone`, which implements the `ICloneable` interface. When a class implements an interface, you are required to implement all of the methods of the interface.

You can apply *attributes* to just about any nameable entity within the CLR type system. In this case, I've attached the `Serializable` attribute to the class to show an example of attribute usage syntax. These attributes become part of the metadata that describes the type to consumers. In addition, you can create custom attributes to attach to various entities, such as classes, parameters, return values, and fields, which easily exercise the capabilities of AOP.

Fields

Fields are the bread and butter that make up the state of objects. Typically, you declare a new class only if you need to model some new type of object with its own custom internal state, represented by its instance fields.

You declare fields with a type, just like all other variables in C. The possible field modifiers are as follows:

```
new
public
protected
internal
private
static
readonly
volatile
```

Many of these are mutually exclusive. Those that are mutually exclusive control the accessibility of the field and consist of the modifiers `public`, `protected`, `internal`, and `private`. I discuss these in more detail in the "Accessibility" section. However, for now, I'll detail the remaining modifiers.

The `static` modifier controls whether a field is a member of the type or a member of objects instantiated from the type. In the absence of the `static` modifier, a field is an *instance* field, and thus each object created from the class has its own copy of the field. This is the default. When decorated with the `static` modifier, the field is shared among all objects of a class on a per-application-domain basis.

Note that static fields are not included in the memory footprint of the object instances. In other words, objects don't encapsulate the static fields; rather, types encapsulate the static fields. It would be inefficient for all instances of the object to contain a copy of the same static variable in their memory footprint. And worse than that, the compiler would have to generate some sort of code under the hood to make sure that when the *static* field is changed for one instance, it would change the field in all instances. For this reason, the static fields actually belong to the class and not to the object instances. In fact, when a static field is publicly accessible outside the class, you use the class name and not the object instance variable to access the field.

■**Note** Static fields have another important quality: They are global to the application domain within which their containing types are loaded. Application domains are an abstraction that is similar to the process abstraction within an operating system, but it's a more lightweight mechanism. You can have multiple application domains in one operating system process. If your CLR process contains multiple application domains, each will have a copy of the class's static fields. A static field's value in one application domain can be different from the same static field in another application domain. Unless you create extra application domains yourself, your application will have only one application domain: the default application domain. However, it's important to note this distinction when working in environments such as ASP.NET, where the concept of the application domain is used as the isolation mechanism between two ASP.NET applications. In fact, you can easily jump to the conclusion that ASP.NET was the driving motivation behind the application domain notion.

You can initialize fields during object creation in various ways. One straightforward way of initializing fields is through *initializers*. You use these initializers at the point where the field is defined, and they can be used for either static or instance fields—for example:

```
private int x = 789;
private int y;
private int z = A.InitZ();
```

The field x is initialized using an initializer. The notation is rather convenient. Note that this initialization occurs at run time and not at compile time. Therefore, this initialization statement could have used something other than a constant. For example, the variable z is initialized by calling a method, `A.InitZ`. At first, this field initialization notation may seem like a great shortcut, saving you from having to initialize all of the fields inside the body of the constructor. However, I suggest that you initialize instance fields within the instance constructor body. I cover static and instance initialization in all of its gory detail in the "Creating Objects" section later in this chapter, and you'll see why initializing fields in the constructor can facilitate code that's easier to maintain and debug.

Another field modifier that comes in handy from time to time is the readonly modifier. As you can guess, it defines the field so that you can only read from it. You can write to it only during object creation. You can emulate the same behavior with greater flexibility using a read-only *property*, which I discuss in the section titled "Properties." Static readonly fields are initialized in a static constructor, while instance readonly fields are initialized in an instance constructor. Alternatively, you can initialize readonly fields using initializers at the point of their declaration in the class definition, just as you can do with other fields. Within the constructor, you can assign to the readonly field as many times as necessary. Only within the constructor can you pass the readonly field as a ref or out parameter to another function. Consider the following example:

```
public class A
{
    public A()
    {
        this.y = 456;

        // We can even set y again.
        this.y = 654;

        // We can use y as a ref param.
        SetField( ref this.y );
    }

    private void SetField( ref int val )
    {
        val = 888;
    }

    private readonly int x = 123;
    private readonly int y;
    public const     int z = 555;

    static void Main()
    {
        A obj = new A();

        System.Console.WriteLine( "x = {0}, y = {1}, z = {2}",
                                  obj.x, obj.y, A.z );
    }
}
```

You should note one important nuance here: The z field is declared using the const keyword. At first, it may seem that it has the same effect as a readonly field, but it does not. First, a const field such as this is known and used at compile time. This means that the code generated by the compiler in the Main routine can be optimized to replace all uses of this variable with its immediate const value. The compiler is free to use this performance trick, simply because the value of the field is known at compile time. Also, note that you access the const field using the class name rather than the instance name. This is because const values are implicitly static and don't affect the memory footprint, or shape, of the object instances. Again, this makes sense because the compiler would optimize away access to that memory slot in the object instance anyway, since it would be the same for all instances of this object.

But one more detail is lurking here with regard to the difference between readonly and const fields. readonly fields are guaranteed to be computed at run time. Therefore, suppose you have one class with both a readonly field and a const field that lives in assembly A, and code in assembly B creates and uses an instance of that class in assembly A. Now, suppose you rebuild assembly A at a later date, and you modify the field initializers for the readonly field and the const field. The consumer in assembly B would see the change in the const field only after you recompile the code in assembly B. This behavior is expected, because when assembly B was built referencing the initial incarnation of assembly A, the compiler optimized the use of the const values by inserting the literal value into the generated IL code. Because of this, you need to be careful when deciding whether to use a readonly field or a const value and, if you choose to use a readonly field, you need to choose carefully between using a readonly field or a read-only property, which I introduce in a later section titled "Properties." Properties provide greater design-time and maintenance-time flexibility over readonly fields.

Lastly, the volatile modifier indicates, as its name implies, that the field is sensitive to read and write timing. Technically, the modifier indicates to the compiler that the field may be accessed or modified by the operating system or hardware running on that system, or more likely, by another thread at any time. The latter case is the most typical. Normally, access to a field by multiple threads only becomes a problem when you don't use any synchronization techniques, such as when not using the C# lock statement or OS synchronization objects. When a field is marked as volatile, it tells the implementation—and by that, I mean the CLR JIT compiler—that it must not apply optimizations to that field's access. Because it is questionable and error-prone to access fields with multiple threads without using synchronization techniques, I won't spend any more time describing the use of the volatile modifier. The fact is, you'll rarely ever need it or come into contact with it unless you're doing some fancy type of interoperation with a device or something of that nature.

I've already covered some of the ways that field initialization can occur within an object instance during class initialization. I cover many more nuances of field initialization in the "Field Initialization" section. However, note that C# has rules about default field initialization that are applied before any field initialization code that occurs in the constructor method's code block. C#, by default, creates verifiably type-safe code, which is guaranteed not to use uninitialized variables and fields. The compiler goes to great lengths to ensure that this requirement is satisfied. For example, it initializes all fields, whether they're instance or static fields, to a default value before any of your variable initializers execute. The default value for just about anything can easily be represented by either the value 0 or null. For example, you can initialize an integer or any other similar value type by setting all of the bits in its storage space to 0. For reference types, you set the initial default value to null. Again, this is usually the result of the implementation setting all of the bits of the reference to 0. These default initializations occur before any code executes on the instance or class. Therefore, it's impossible to inspect the uninitialized values of an object or a class during initial construction.

Constructors

Constructors are called when a class is first loaded by the CLR or an object is created. There are two types of constructors: *static constructors* and *instance constructors*. A class can have only one static constructor, and it can have no parameters. The name of the static constructor must match the name of the class it belongs to. As with any other class member, you can attach metadata attributes to the static constructor.

Instance constructors, on the other hand, are called when an instance of a class is created. They typically set up the state of the object by initializing the fields to a desired predefined state. You can also do any other type of initialization work, such as connecting to a database and opening a file. A class can have multiple instance constructors that can be *overloaded* (i.e., have different parameter types). As with the static constructor, instance constructor names must match the name of the defining class. One notable capability of an instance constructor is that of the optional constructor initializer clause. Using the initializer, which follows a colon after the parameter list, you can call a base class constructor or another constructor in the same class through the keywords base and this, respectively. I have more to say about the base keyword in the section titled "base Keyword." Consider the following sample code and the two comments:

```
class Base
{
    public int x = InitX();

    public Base( int x )
    {
        this.x = x;     // disambiguates the parameter and the instance variable
    }
}

class Derived : Base
{
    public Derived( int a )
        :base( a )     // calls the base class constructor
    {
    }
}
```

Methods

A method defines a procedure that you can perform on an object or a class. If the method is an *instance* method, you can call it on an object. If the method is a *static* method, you can call it only on the class. The difference is that instance methods have access to the instance fields of the object instance, whereas static methods don't have access to instance fields or methods. Static methods can only access static class members.

Methods can have metadata attributes attached to them, and they can also have optional modifiers attached. I discuss them throughout this chapter. These modifiers control the accessibility of the methods, as well as facets of the methods that are germane to inheritance. Every method either does or does not have a return type. If a method doesn't have a return type, the declaration must declare the return type as void. Methods may or may not have parameters.

Static Methods

You call static methods on the class rather than on instances of the class. Static methods only have access to the static members of the class. You declare a method as static by using the static modifier, as in the following example:

```
public class A
{
    public static void SomeFunction()
    {
        System.Console.WriteLine( "SomeFunction() called" );
    }

    static void Main()
    {
        A.SomeFunction();
        SomeFunction();
    }
}
```

Notice that both methods in this example are static. In the Main method, I first access the SomeFunction method using the class name. I then call the static method without qualifying it. This is because the Main and SomeFunction methods are both defined in the same class and are both static methods. Had SomeFunction been in another class, say class B, I would have had no choice but to reference the method as B.SomeFunction.

Instance Methods

Instance methods operate on objects. In order to call an instance method, you need a reference to an instance of the class that defines the method. The following example shows the use of an instance method:

```
public class A
{
    private void SomeOperation()
    {
        x = 1;
        this.y = 2;
        z = 3;

        // assigning this in objects is an error.
        // A newinstance = new A();
        // this = newinstance;
    }

    private int x;
    private int y;
    private static int z;

    static void Main()
    {
        A obj = new A();

        obj.SomeOperation();

        System.Console.WriteLine( "x = {0}, y = {1}, z= {2}",
                                  obj.x, obj.y, A.z );
    }
}
```

In the Main method, you can see that I create a new instance of the A class and then call the SomeOperation method through the instance of that class. Within the method body of SomeOperation, I have access to the instance and static fields of the class, and I can assign to them simply by using their identifiers. Even though the SomeOperation method can assign the static field z without qualifying it, as I mentioned before, I believe it makes for more readable code if the assignment of static fields is qualified by the class name even in the methods of the same class. Doing so is helpful for whoever comes after you and has to maintain your code—someone who could even be you!

Notice that when I assign to y, I do so through the this identifier. You should note a few important things about this when used within an instance method body. It is treated as a read-only reference whose type is that of the class. Using this, you can access the fields of the instance, as I did when assigning the value of y in the previous code example. Because the this value is read-only, you may not assign it, which would make it reference a different instance. If you try to do so, you'll hear about it when the compiler complains to you and fails to compile your code.

Properties

Properties are one of the nicest mechanisms within C# and the CLR that enable you to enforce encapsulation better. In short, you use properties for strict control of access to the internal state of an object.

A property, from the point of view of the object's client, looks, smells, and behaves just like a public field. The notation to access a property is the same as that used to access a public field on the instance. However, a property doesn't have any associated storage space within the object, as a field does. Rather, a property is a shorthand notation for defining *accessors* used to read and write fields. The typical pattern is to provide access to a private field in a class through a public property. C# 3.0 makes this even easier with its support for auto-implemented properties.

Properties significantly enhance your flexibility as a class designer. For example, if a property represents the number of table rows in a database table object, the table object can defer the computation of the value until the point where it is queried through a property. It knows when to compute the value, because the client will call an accessor when it accesses the property.

Declaring Properties

The syntax for declaring properties is straightforward. As with most class members, you can attach metadata attributes to a property. Various modifiers that are valid for properties are similar to ones for methods. Other modifiers include the ability to declare a property as virtual, sealed, override, abstract, and so on. I also cover these in detail in the section titled "Inheritance and Virtual Methods" later in this chapter.

The following code defines a property, Temperature, in class A:

```
public class A
{
    private int temperature;

    public int Temperature
    {
        get
        {
            System.Console.WriteLine( "Getting value for temperature" );
            return temperature;
        }

        set
        {
            System.Console.WriteLine( "Setting value for temperature" );
            temperature = value;
        }
    }
}

public class MainClass
{
    static void Main()
    {
        A obj = new A();

        obj.Temperature = 1;
        System.Console.WriteLine( "obj.Temperature = {0}",
                                  obj.Temperature );
    }
}
```

First I defined a property named Temperature, which has a type of int. Each property declaration must define the type that the property represents. That type should be visible to the compiler at the point where it is declared in the class, and it should have at least the same accessibility as the property being defined. By that, I mean that if a property is public, the type of the value that the property represents must at least be declared public in the assembly within which it is defined. In the example, the int type is an alias for Int32. That class is defined in the System namespace, and it is public. So, you can use int as a property type in this public class A.

You can also give this property the name Temperature. This is the name with which the clients will refer to the property as if it were a field. In the example, I merely return the private field temperature from the internal state of the object instance. This is the universal convention. You name the private field with a leading lowercase character, while naming the property with a leading uppercase character. Of course, you're not obligated to follow this convention, but there is no good reason not to and C# programmers expect it.

Accessors

In the previous example, you can see that there are two blocks of code within the property block. These are the accessors for the property, and within the blocks of the accessors, you put the code that reads and writes the property. As you can see, one is named get and the other is named set. It should be obvious from their names which does what.

The get block is called when the client of the object reads the property. As you would expect, this accessor must return a value or an object reference that matches the type of the property declaration. It can also return an object that is implicitly convertible to the type of the property declaration. For example, if the property type is a long and the getter returns an int, the int will be implicitly converted to a long without losing precision. Otherwise, the code in this block is just like a parameterless method that returns a value or reference of the same type as the property.

The set accessor is called when the client attempts to write to the property. Note that there is no return value. Note also that a special variable named value is available to the code within this block, and it's the same type as that of the property declaration. When you write to the property, the value variable will have been set to the value or object reference that the client has attempted to assign to the property. If you attempt to declare a local variable named value in the set accessor, you'll receive a compiler error. The set accessor is like a method that takes one parameter of the same type as the property and returns void.

Read-Only and Write-Only Properties

If you define a property with only a get accessor, that property will be read-only. Likewise, if you define a property with only a set accessor, you'll end up with a write-only property. And lastly, a property with both accessors is a read-write property.

You may be wondering why a read-only property is any better or worse than a readonly public field. At first thought, it may seem that a read-only property is less efficient than a readonly public field. However, given the fact that the CLR can inline the code to access the property, in the case where the property simply returns a private field, this argument of inefficiency does not hold. Now, of course, writing the code is not as efficient. However, because programmers aren't lazy and C# 3.0 auto-implemented properties make it so simple, that's really no argument either.

The fact is, in 99% of all cases, a read-only property is more flexible than a readonly public field. One reason is that you can defer a read-only property's computation until the point where you need it (a technique known as *lazy evaluation*, or *deferred execution*). So, in reality, it could provide for more efficient code, when the property is meant to represent something that takes significant time to compute. If you're using a readonly public field for this purpose, the computation would have to happen in the block of the constructor. All the necessary data to make the computation may not even be available at that point. Or, you may waste time in the constructor computing the value, when the user of the object may not ever access the value.

Also, read-only properties help enforce encapsulation. If you originally had a choice between a read-only property and a `readonly` public field, and you chose the read-only property, you would have had greater flexibility in future versions of the class to do extra work at the point where the property is accessed without affecting the client. For example, imagine if you wanted to do some sort of logging in debug builds each time the property is accessed. The client would effectively be calling a method implicitly, albeit one of the special property methods, to access the data. The flexibility of things that you can do in that method is almost limitless. Had you accessed the value as a public `readonly` field, you wouldn't call a method or be able to do anything without switching it over to a property and forcing the client code to recompile. This discussion leads directly into the discussion regarding encapsulation in the later section titled "Encapsulation."

Auto-Implemented Properties

Many times, you need a type, say a class, that contains a few fields that are treated as a cohesive unit. For example, imagine an `Employee` type that contains a full name and an identification number but, for the sake of example, manages this data using strings as shown below:

```
public class Employee
{
    string fullName;
    string id;
}
```

As written, this class is essentially useless. The two fields are private and must be made accessible. For the sake of encapsulation, we don't want to just make the fields public. However, for such a simple little type, it sure is painful to code up basic property accessors as shown below:

```
public class Employee
{
    public string FullName {
        get { return fullName; }
        set { fullName = value; }
    }

    public string Id {
        get { return id; }
        set { id = value; }
    }

    string fullName;
    string id;
}
```

What a lot of code just to get a type with a couple of read/write properties!

Note I'd be willing to bet that there are many developers out there who have simply avoided properties and used public fields in these kinds of helper types simply because of the typing overhead alone. The problem with that short-sighted approach is that you cannot do any sort of validation upon setting the field or perform any lazy evaluation during property access.

Thankfully, C# 3.0 has a new feature called auto-implemented properties that reduce this burden significantly. Look how the previous Employee type changes after using auto-implemented properties:

```
public class Employee
{
    public string FullName { get; set; }
    public string Id { get; set; }
}
```

That's it! Basically, what you're telling the compiler is, "I want a string property named FullName and I want it to support get and set." Behind the scenes the compiler generates a private field in the class for the storage and implements the accessors for you. The beauty of this is that it's just a little more typing than declaring public fields but at the same time, since they are properties, you can change the underlying implementation without having to modify the public interface of the type. That is, if you later decided you wanted to customize the accessors for Id, you could do so without forcing the clients of Employee to recompile.

■**Note** If you're curious about the private field that the compiler declares in your type for auto-implemented properties, you can always look at the field using ILDASM. Using my current implementation, the private field providing storage for FullName in the Employee class is named <>k__AutomaticallyGeneratedPropertyField0 and is of type string. Notice that the field name is "unspeakable," meaning that you cannot type it into code and compile without getting syntax errors. The C# compiler implementers do this on purpose so we don't use the type name directly. After all, the name of the field is a compiler implementation detail that is subject to change in the future.

You can also create a read-only auto-implemented property by inserting the private keyword as shown below:

```
public class Employee
{
    public string FullName { get; private set; }
    public string Id { get; set; }
}
```

At this point, you may be wondering how the FullName field ever gets set. After all, it's read-only and the private field representing the underlying storage has a compiler-generated name that we cannot use in a constructor to assign to it. The solution is to use another new C# 3.0 feature called *object initializers*, as shown in the following example:

```
using System;

public class Employee
{
    public string FullName { get; private set; }
    public string Id { get; set; }
}

public class AutoProps
{
```

```
static void Main() {
    Employee emp = new Employee {
        FullName = "John Doe",
        Id = "111-11-1111"
    };
}
}
```

Object initializers complement auto-implemented properties. Not only do they allow you a means to set read-only auto-implemented properties, but they also give the instantiator of the instance syntax similar to that normally provided by constructors whereby one passes values to the constructor during instantiation to initialize the type appropriately. You can find out more about object initializers in the "Object Initializers" section later in this chapter.

Encapsulation

Arguably, one of the most important concepts in object-oriented programming is that of encapsulation. Encapsulation is the discipline of tightly controlling access to internal object data and procedures. It would be impossible to consider any language that does not support encapsulation as belonging to the set of object-oriented languages.

You always want to follow this basic concept: Never define the data fields of your objects as publicly accessible. It's as simple as that. However, you would be surprised how many programmers still declare their data fields as public. Typically, this happens when a small utility object is defined and the creators are either lazy or think they are in too much of a hurry. There are some things, though, you should just not do; and cutting corners like this is one of them.

You want the clients of your object to speak to it only through controlled means. This normally means controlling communication to your object via methods on the object (or properties which, under the covers, are method calls). In this way, you treat the internals of the object as if they are inside a black box. No internals are visible to the outside world, and all communications that could modify those internals are done through controlled channels. Through encapsulation, you can engineer a design whereby the integrity of the object's state is never compromised.

A simple example of what I'm talking about is in order. In this example, I create a dummy helper object to represent a rectangle. The example itself is a tad contrived, but it's a good one for the sake of argument because of its minimal complexity:

```
class MyRectangle
{
    public uint width;
    public uint height;
}
```

You can see a crude example of a custom rectangle class. Currently, I'm only interested in the width and the height of the rectangle. Of course, a useful rectangle class for a graphics engine would contain an origin as well, but for the sake of this example, I'll only be interested in the width and height. So, I declare the two fields for width and height as public. Maybe I did that because I was in a hurry as I was designing this basic little class. But as you'll soon see, just a little bit more work up front will provide much greater flexibility.

Now, let's say that time has passed, and I have merrily used my little rectangle class for many uses. Never mind the fact that my little rectangle class is not very useful in and of itself, but let's say I have come up with a desire to make it a little more useful. Suppose I have some client code that uses my rectangle class and needs to compute the area of the rectangle. Good object-oriented principles guide me to consider that the best way to do this is to let the instances of MyRectangle tell the client what their area values are. Back in the days of ANSI C and other purely procedural imperative programming languages, you would have created a function named something like ComputeArea, which would take, as a parameter, a pointer to an instance of MyRectangle. Thankfully, those days are behind us if we're using an object-oriented approach. So, let's do it:

```
class MyRectangle
{
    public uint width;
    public uint height;

    public uint GetArea()
    {
        return width * height;
    }
}
```

As you can see, I've added a new member: the GetArea method. When called on an instance, the trusty MyRectangle will compute the area of the rectangle and return the result. Now, I've still just got a basic little rectangle class that has one helper function defined on it to make clients' lives a little bit easier if they need to know the area of the rectangle. But let's suppose I have some reason to precompute the value of the area, so that each time the GetArea method is called, I don't have to recompute it every time. Maybe I want to do this because I know, for some reason, that GetArea will be called many times on the same instance during its lifetime. Ignoring the fact that early optimization is foolish, let's say that I decide to do it. Now, my new MyRectangle class could look something like this:

```
class MyRectangle
{
    public uint width;
    public uint height;

    public uint area;

    public uint GetArea()
    {
        return area;
    }
}
```

If you look closely, you can start to see my errors. Notice that all of the fields are public. This allows the consumer of my MyRectangle instances to access the internals of my rectangle directly. What would be the point of providing the GetArea method if the consumer can simply access the area field directly? Well, you say, maybe I should make the area field private. That way, clients are forced to call GetArea to get the area of the rectangle. This is definitely a step in the right direction. Let's do it:

```
class MyRectangle
{
    public uint width;
    public uint height;

    private uint area;

    public uint GetArea()
    {
```

```
        if( area == 0 ) {
            area = width * height;
        }

        return area;
    }
}
```

I've made the area field private, forcing the consumer to call GetArea in order to obtain the area. However, in the process, I realized that I have to compute the area of the rectangle at some point. So, since I'm lazy to begin with, I decide to check the value of the area field before returning it, and if it's 0, I assume that I need to compute the area before I return it. This is a crude attempt at an optimization. But now, I only compute the area if it is needed. Suppose a consumer of my rectangle instance never needed to know the area of the rectangle. Then, given the previous code, that consumer wouldn't have to lose the time it takes to compute the area. Of course, in my contrived example, this optimization will most likely be extremely negligible. But if you think for just a little bit, I'm sure you can come up with an example where it may be beneficial to use this lazy evaluation technique. Think about database access across a slow network where only certain fields in a table may be needed at run time. Or, for the same database access object, it may be expensive to compute the number of rows in the table. You should only use this technique when necessary.

A glaring problem still exists with my rectangle class. Since the width and height fields are public, what happens if consumers change one of the values after they've called GetArea on the instance? Well, then I'll have a really bad case of inconsistent internals. The integrity of the state of my object would be compromised. This is definitely not a good situation to be in. So, now you see the error of my ways yet again. I must make the width and height fields of my rectangle private as well:

```
class MyRectangle
{
    private uint width;
    private uint height;
    private uint area;

    public uint Width
    {
        get
        {
            return width;
        }

        set
        {
            width = value;
            ComputeArea();
        }
    }

    public uint Height
    {
        get
        {
            return height;
        }
```

```
      set
      {
         height = value;
         ComputeArea();
      }
   }

   public uint Area
   {
      get
      {
         return area;
      }
   }

   private void ComputeArea()
   {
      area = width * height;
   }
}
```

Now, in my latest incarnation of MyRectangle, I have become really wise. After making the width and height fields private, I realized that the consumer of the objects needs some way to get and set the values of the width and the height. That's where I use C# properties. Internally, I now handle the changes to the internal state through a method body, and the methods called belong to the set of specially named methods on the class. I have more to say about special—sometimes called *reserved*—member names in the section titled "Reserved Member Names." Now, I have tight control over access to the internals. And along with that control comes the most essential value of encapsulation. I can effectively manage the state of the internals so that they never become inconsistent. It's impossible to guarantee the integrity of the object's state when foreign entities have access to the state through back-door means.

In this example, my object knows exactly when the width and height fields change. Therefore, it can take the necessary action to compute the new area. If the object had used the approach of lazy evaluation, such that it contained a cached value of the area computed during the first call of the Area property getter, then I would know to invalidate that cache value as soon as either of the setters on the Width or Height properties is called.

So, the moral of the story is, a little bit of extra work up front to foster encapsulation goes a long way as time goes on. One of the greatest properties of encapsulation that you need to burn into your head and take to the bank is that, when used properly, the object's internals can change to support a slightly different algorithm without affecting the consumers. In other words, the interface visible to the consumer does not change. Interface-based design patterns help in this regard, too. For example, in the final incarnation of the MyRectangle class, the area is computed up front as soon as either of the Width or Height properties is set. Maybe once my software is nearing completion, I'll run a profiler and determine that computing the area early is really sapping the life out of the processor as my program runs. No problem. I can change the model to use a cached area value that is only computed when first needed, and because I followed the tenets of encapsulation, the consumers of my objects don't even need to know about it. They don't even know a change internal to the object occurred. That's the power of encapsulation. When the internal implementation of an object can change, and the clients that use it don't have to change, then you know encapsulation is working as it should.

■Note Encapsulation helps you achieve the age-old guideline of strong cohesion of objects with weak coupling between objects.

Accessibility

I've mentioned access modifiers several times up to this point. Their use may seem intuitive to you if you have any experience with any other object-oriented language, such as C++ or Java. However, certain nuances of C# and CLI member access modifiers bear mentioning. Before I discuss the various types of modifiers, let's talk a little bit about where you can apply them.

Essentially, you can use access modifiers on just about any defined entity in a C# program, including classes and any member within the class. Access modifiers applied to a class affect its visibility from outside the containing assembly. Access modifiers applied to class members, including methods, fields, properties, events, and indexers, affect the visibility of the member from outside of the class. Table 4-1 describes the various access modifiers available in C#.

Table 4-1. *Access Modifiers in C#*

Access Modifier	Meaning
public	Member is completely visible outside both the defining scope and the internal scope. In other words, access to a public member is not restricted at all.
protected	Member is visible only to the defining class and any class that derives from the defining class.
internal	Member is visible anywhere inside the containing assembly. This includes the defining class and any scope within the assembly that is outside the defining class.
protected internal	Member is visible within the defining class and anywhere else inside the assembly. This modifier combines protected and internal using a Boolean OR operation. The member is also visible to any class that derives from the defining class, whether it's in the same assembly or not.
private	Member is visible only within the defining class, with no exceptions. This is the strictest form of access and is the default access for class members.

Note that the CLR supports one more form of accessibility that the C# language designers felt strongly was unnecessary to implement. Within the CLR, it is known as *family-and-assembly* accessibility. In C# parlance, that equates to protected AND internal. If, for some reason, you absolutely must use this accessibility modifier, then you need to use a different language, such as C++/CLI or raw IL.

Now, let's examine the allowed usage of these modifiers on various defined entities within C#. Class members can use all five variants of the C# access modifiers. The default access of the class members, in the absence of any modifiers at all, is private. Classes defined either within or outside a namespace can only have one of two access modifiers; they can either be public or internal. By default, they are internal.

You can apply only public, private, and internal to struct member definitions. I cover struct definitions in greater detail later in the chapter in the section titled "Value Type Definitions." Notice the absence of protected and protected internal. They aren't needed, because structs are implicitly sealed, meaning they cannot be base classes. I cover the sealed modifier in more detail in the section titled "sealed Classes."

■Note One more important note is in order for those used to coding in C++: struct members are private by default, just like in class definitions, whereas they are public by default in C++.

Lastly, members of interfaces, which I describe fully in Chapter 5, and enums, which I covered in Chapter 3, are implicitly public by their very nature. Interfaces are meant to define a set of operations, or a contract, that a class can implement. It makes no sense for an interface to have any restricted access members, since restricted access members are normally associated with a class implementation, and interfaces, by their definition, contain no implementation. Enumerations, on the other hand, are normally used as a named collection of constants. Enumerations have no internal implementation either, so it makes no sense for enumeration members to have any restricted access. In fact, you get an error if you specify an access modifier, even public, on an interface member or an enumeration member.

As you can see, access for just about anything defaults to the strictest form of access that makes sense for that entity. In other words, you have to do work to allow others access to classes or class members. The only exception is the access for a namespace, which is implicitly public and cannot have any access modifiers applied to it.

Interfaces

Even though I devote much of Chapter 5 to the topic of interfaces, it is worth introducing interfaces at this point for the purpose of discussion in the rest of this chapter. Generally speaking, an *interface* is a definition of a contract. Classes can choose to implement various interfaces, and by doing so, they guarantee to adhere to the rules of the contract. When a class inherits from an interface, it is required to implement the members of that interface. A class can implement as many interfaces as it wants by listing them in the base class list of the class definition.

In general terms, an interface's syntax closely resembles that of a class. However, each member is implicitly public. In fact, you'll get a compile-time error if you declare any interface member with any modifiers. Interfaces can only contain instance methods; therefore, you can't include any static methods in the definition. Interfaces don't include an implementation; therefore, they are semantically abstract in nature. If you're familiar with C++, you know that you can create a similar sort of construct by creating a class that contains all public, pure virtual methods that have no default implementations.

The members of an interface can only consist of members that ultimately boil down to methods in the CLR. This includes methods, properties, events, and indexers. I cover indexers in the "Indexers" section, and I cover events in Chapter 10.

■Note If you're a stickler for terminology, the C# specification actually calls properties, events, indexers, operators, constructors, and destructors *function members*. It's actually a misnomer to call them *methods*. Methods contain executable code, so they're also considered function members.

The following code shows an example of an interface and a class that implements the interface:

```
public interface IMusician
//Note:A standard practice is that you preface interface names with a capital "I"
{
    void PlayMusic();
}
```

```csharp
public class TalentedPerson : IMusician
{
    public void PlayMusic() {}
    public void DoALittleDance() {}
}

public class EntryPoint
{
    static void Main()
    {
        TalentedPerson dude = new TalentedPerson();
        IMusician musician = dude;

        musician.PlayMusic();
        dude.PlayMusic();
        dude.DoALittleDance();
    }
}
```

In this example, I've defined an interface named IMusician. A class, TalentedPerson, indicates that it wants to support the IMusician interface. The class declaration is basically saying, "I would like to enter into a contract to support the IMusician interface, and I guarantee to support all the methods of that interface." The requirement of that interface is merely to support the PlayMusic method, which the TalentedPerson class does so faithfully. As a final note, it is customary to name an interface type with a leading uppercase I. When reading code, this stands as a marker to indicate that the type in question is, in fact, an interface.

Now, clients can access the PlayMusic method in one of two ways. They can either call it through the object instance directly, or they can obtain an interface reference onto the object instance and call the method through it. Because the TalentedPerson class supports the IMusician interface, references to objects of that class are implicitly convertible to references of IMusician. The code inside the Main method in the previous example shows how to call the method both ways.

The topic of interfaces is broad enough to justify devoting an entire chapter to them, which I do in Chapter 5. However, the information regarding interfaces that I've covered in this section is enough to facilitate the discussions in the rest of this chapter.

Inheritance

If you ask around, many developers will tell you that inheritance is the backbone of object-oriented programming. Although inheritance is a really slick concept to those who first encounter it, I beg to differ that inheritance is the backbone. I'm a firm believer that encapsulation is the strongest feature of object-oriented programming. Inheritance is an important concept and a useful tool. However, like many powerful tools, it can be dangerous when misused. My goal in this section is to introduce you to inheritance in a way that makes you respect its power and that helps you to avoid abusing it.

Earlier, I covered the syntax for defining a class. You specify the base class after a colon that follows the class name. In C#, a class can have only one base class. (Some other languages, such as C++, support multiple inheritance.)

Accessibility of Members

Accessibility of members plays an important aspect in inheritance, specifically with respect to accessing members of the base class from the derived class. Any public members of the base class become public members of the derived class.

Any members marked as protected are only accessible internally to the declaring class and to the classes that inherit from it. Protected members are never accessible publicly from outside the defining class or any class deriving from the defining class. Private members are never accessible to anything except the defining class. So even though a derived class inherits all the members of the base class, including the private ones, the code in the derived class cannot access the private members inherited from the base class. In addition, protected internal members are visible to all types that are defined within the containing assembly and to classes that derive from the class defining the member. The reality is that the derived class inherits every member of a base class, except instance constructors, static constructors, and destructors.

As you've seen, you can control the accessibility of the entire class itself when you define it. The only possibilities for the class type's accessibility are internal and public. When using inheritance, the rule is that the base class type must be at least as accessible as the deriving class. Consider the following code:

```
class A
{
    protected int x;
}

public class B : A
{
}
```

This code doesn't compile, because the A class is internal and is not at least as accessible as the deriving class B. Remember that in the absence of an access modifier, class definitions default to internal access—hence, the reason class A is internal. In order for the code to compile, you must either promote class A to public access or demote class B to internal access. Also note that it is legal for class A to be public and class B to be internal.

Implicit Conversion and a Taste of Polymorphism

You can view inheritance and what it does for you in several ways. First and most obvious, inheritance allows you to borrow an implementation. In other words, you can inherit class D from class A and reuse the implementation of class A in class D. It potentially saves you from having to do some work when defining class D. Another use of inheritance is *specialization*, where class D becomes a specialized form of class A. For example, consider the class hierarchy, as shown in Figure 4-1.

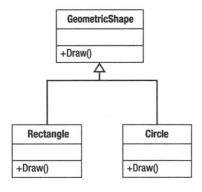

Figure 4-1. *Inheritance specialization*

As you can see, classes Rectangle and Circle derive from class GeometricShape. In other words, they are specializing the GeometricShape class. Specialization is meaningless without polymorphism and virtual methods. I cover the topic of polymorphism in more detail in the "Inheritance and Virtual Methods" section of this chapter. For the moment, I'll define basically what it means for the purpose of this conversation.

Polymorphism describes a situation in which a type referenced with a particular variable can behave like, and actually be, a different (more specialized) type instance. Chapter 5 examines the differences and similarities between interfaces and contracts. Figure 4-1 shows a method in GeometricShape named Draw. This same method appears in both Rectangle and Circle. You can implement the model with the following code:

```
public class GeometricShape
{
    public virtual void Draw()
    {
        // Do some default drawing stuff.
    }
}

public class Rectangle : GeometricShape
{
    public override void Draw()
    {
        // Draw a rectangle
    }
}

public class Circle : GeometricShape
{
    public override void Draw()
    {
        // Draw a circle
    }
}

public class EntryPoint
{
    private static void DrawShape( GeometricShape shape )
    {
        shape.Draw();
    }

    static void Main()
    {
        Circle circle = new Circle();
        GeometricShape shape = circle;

        DrawShape( shape );
        DrawShape( circle );
    }
}
```

You create a new instance of Circle in the Main method. Right after that, you obtain a GeometricShape reference on the same object. This is an important step to note. The compiler has implicitly converted the reference into a GeometricShape type reference by allowing you to use a simple assignment expression. Underneath the covers, however, it's really still referencing the same Circle object. This is the gist of type specialization and the automatic conversion that goes along with it.

Now let's consider the rest of the code in the Main method. After you get a GeometricShape reference on the Circle instance, you can pass it to the DrawShape method, which does nothing but call the Draw method on the shape. However, the shape object reference really points to a Circle, the Draw method is defined as virtual, and the Circle class overrides the virtual method, so calling Draw on the GeometricShape reference actually calls Circle.Draw. That is polymorphism in action. The DrawShape method doesn't need to care at all about what specific type of shape the object is. All it cares about is whether it is, in fact, a GeometricShape. And Circle is a GeometricShape. This is why inheritance is often referred to as an is-a relationship. In the given example, Rectangle is-a GeometricShape, and Circle is-a GeometricShape. The key to determining whether inheritance makes sense or not is to apply the is-a relationship, along with some good old common sense, to your design. If a class D inherits from a class B, and class D semantically is-not-a class B, then inheritance is not the correct tool for that relationship.

One last important note about inheritance and convertibility is in order. I've said that the compiler implicitly converts the Circle instance reference into a GeometricShape instance reference. Implicit, in this case, means that the code doesn't have to do anything special to do the conversion, and by something special, I typically mean a cast operation. Because the compiler has the ability to do this based upon its knowledge of the inheritance hierarchy, it would seem to make sense that you don't have to get a GeometricShape reference before you can call DrawShape with the Circle object instance. In fact, this is exactly true. The last line of the Main method demonstrates this. You can simply pass the Circle instance reference directly into the DrawShape method, and because the compiler can implicitly convert the type to a GeometricShape reference based upon the inheritance, it does all of the work for you. Again, you can see the power of this mechanism.

Now, you can pass any object instance that derives from GeometricShape. After the software is shrink-wrapped and labeled *version 1*, someone can come along later in version 2 and define new shapes that derive from GeometricShape, and the code for DrawShape does not need to change. It doesn't even need to know what the new specializations are. They could be Trapezoid, Square (a specialization of Rectangle), or Ellipse. It does not matter, as long as they derive from GeometricShape.

Member Hiding

From the previous section's discussion, you can see how the concept of inheritance, although a powerful one, can be overused. When programmers are first introduced to inheritance, they have a tendency to use it too much, creating designs and hierarchical structures that are hard to maintain. It's important to note that there are alternatives to using inheritance that in many cases make more sense. Among the various types of associations between classes in a software system design, inheritance is the strongest bond of them all. I uncover many more issues with regards to inheritance near the end of the chapter. However, let's go ahead and cover some basic effects of inheritance here.

Note that inheritance extends functionality but cannot remove functionality. For example, the public methods available on a base class are available through instances of the derived class and classes derived from that class. You cannot remove these capabilities from the derived class. Consider the following code:

```
public class A
{
    public void DoSomething()
    {
        System.Console.WriteLine( "A.DoSomething" );
    }
}
```

```
public class B : A
{
    public void DoSomethingElse()
    {
        System.Console.WriteLine( "B.DoSomethingElse" );
    }
}

public class EntryPoint
{
    static void Main()
    {
        B b = new B();

        b.DoSomething();
        b.DoSomethingElse();
    }
}
```

In Main, you create a new instance of class B, which derives from class A. Since class B inherits from class A, class B gets a union of the members of both class A and class B. That is why you can call both DoSomething and DoSomethingElse on the instance of class B. This is pretty obvious, since inheritance extends functionality.

But what if you want to inherit from class A but hide the DoSomething method? In other words, what if you just want to extend part of A's functionality? This is impossible with inheritance. However, you have the option of member *hiding*, as shown in the following code, which is a modified form of the previous example:

```
public class A
{
    public void DoSomething()
    {
        System.Console.WriteLine( "A.DoSomething" );
    }
}

public class B : A
{
    public void DoSomethingElse()
    {
        System.Console.WriteLine( "B.DoSomethingElse" );
    }

    public new void DoSomething()
    {
        System.Console.WriteLine( "B.DoSomething" );
    }
}

public class EntryPoint
{
    static void Main()
    {
        B b = new B();

        b.DoSomething();
```

```
            b.DoSomethingElse();

            A a = b;
            a.DoSomething();
        }
}
```

You can see that in this version I've introduced a new method on class B named DoSomething. Also notice the addition of the new keyword to the declaration of B.DoSomething. If you don't add this keyword, the compiler will complain with a warning. This is the compiler's way of telling you that you need to be more explicit about the fact that you're hiding a method in the base class. Arguably, the compiler does this because hiding members this way is generally considered bad design. Let's see why. The output from the previous code is as follows:

```
B.DoSomething
B.DoSomethingElse
A.DoSomething
```

First notice that which DoSomething method gets called depends on the type of reference it is being called through. This is rather nonintuitive, since B is-an A, and you know that inheritance models an is-a relationship. If that's the case, shouldn't the entire public interface for A be available to consumers of the instance of class B? The short answer is yes. If you really want the method to behave differently in subclasses, then at the point class A is defined, you would declare the DoSomething method as virtual. That way, you could utilize polymorphism to do the right thing. Then, the most derived DoSomething would get called no matter which type of reference it is called through.

I have more to say about virtual methods later on, but think about this for a moment. In order to declare DoSomething as virtual, you need to think about the future at the point you define it. That is, you have to anticipate the possibility that someone could inherit from your class and possibly may want to override this functionality. This is just one reason why inheritance can be more complicated during the design process than it initially seems. As soon as you employ inheritance, you have to start thinking about a lot more things like this. And we all know that nobody can predict the future.

Even though class B now hides class A's implementation of DoSomething, remember, it does not remove it. It hides it when calling the method through a B reference on the object. However, in the Main method, you can see that you can easily get around this by using implicit conversion to convert the B instance reference into an A instance reference and then calling the A.DoSomething implementation through that. So, it's not gone—it's just hidden. You have to do a little more work to get to it.

Suppose you passed the B instance reference to a method that accepted an A instance reference, similar to the DrawShape example. The B instance reference would be implicitly converted to an A instance reference, and if that method called DoSomething on that A instance reference passed to it, it would get to A.DoSomething rather than B.DoSomething. That's probably not what the caller of the method would expect.

This is a classic demonstration that just because the language allows you to do something like this doesn't mean that doing so fosters good design. Just about any language available out there, including C++, has features in the backwaters of its spec that, when used (or used improperly), really just add unnecessary complexity.

The base Keyword

When you derive from a class, often you need to call a method or access a field, a property, or an indexer on the base class from within a method on the derived class. The base keyword exists for this purpose. You can use the base keyword just like any other instance variable, but you can use it only within the block of an instance constructor, instance method, or instance property accessor. You cannot use it in static methods. This makes complete sense, because base allows access to base class implementations of an instance, much like this allows access to the instance owning the method. Let's look at the following code block:

```
public class A
{
    public A( int var )
    {
        this.x = var;
    }

    public virtual void DoSomething()
    {
        System.Console.WriteLine( "A.DoSomething" );
    }

    private int x;
}

public class B : A
{
    public B()
        : base( 123 )
    {
    }

    public override void DoSomething()
    {
        System.Console.WriteLine( "B.DoSomething" );
        base.DoSomething();
    }

}

public class EntryPoint
{
    static void Main()
    {
        B b = new B();

        b.DoSomething();
    }
}
```

In this example, you can see two uses of the base keyword. The first is in the constructor for class B. Remember that the base class doesn't inherit instance constructors. However, when initializing the object, it is sometimes necessary to call one of the base class constructors explicitly during initialization of the derived class. This explains the notation in the class B instance constructor. The base class initialization occurs after the declaration of the derived class constructor's parameter list, but before the constructor code block. I discuss the ordering of constructor calls and object initialization in greater detail later, in the section titled "Creating Objects."

The second use of the base keyword is in the B.DoSomething implementation. I have decided that, in my implementation of class B, I want to borrow the DoSomething implementation in class A while implementing B.DoSomething. I can call the A.DoSomething implementation directly from within the B.DoSomething implementation by going through the base keyword.

If you're familiar with virtual methods, you may have raised an eyebrow at this point. If the DoSomething method is virtual, and the base keyword acts like an instance variable on the base class, wouldn't the call to base.DoSomething actually end up calling B.DoSomething? After all, that's how polymorphism works, and base.DoSomething is equivalent to doing ((B)this).DoSomething, which is just casting the this reference into a class B reference on this and then calling B.DoSomething, isn't it? Well, if that were the case, then the code in B.DoSomething would introduce an infinite loop.

The answer to the question is that no infinite loop has been introduced. The base keyword is treated specially when used inside an instance member to call a virtual method. Normally, calling a virtual method on an instance calls the most derived implementation of the virtual method, which in this case is B.DoSomething. However, when it's called through the base keyword, the most derived method with respect to the base class is called. Thus, this is how you can implement an override method while borrowing the implementation of the base class. If you're curious about the details, the fact is that the generated IL code calls through the base reference using the call instruction rather than callvirt.

sealed Classes

I hinted previously that inheritance is such a powerful tool that it's easily abused. In fact, this is so true that I devote an entire discussion to the pitfalls of inheritance in the section titled "Inheritance, Containment, and Delegation" later in this chapter. When you create a new class, sometimes you create it with the express intent for it to serve as a base class or to allow for specialization. Often, though, classes are designed with no knowledge or foresight about whether they will be used as base classes or not. In fact, it's likely that a class you design today will be used as a base class tomorrow, even though you never intended for it to be used as a base class.

C# offers the sealed keyword for the occasions when you never want a client to derive from a class. When applied to the entire class, the sealed keyword indicates that this class is a *leaf* class. By that, I mean that nothing can inherit from this class. If you visualize your inheritance diagrams in your design as trees, then it makes sense to call sealed classes *leaf classes*. At first, you might think that you should rarely use the sealed keyword. However, I believe that the contrary is true. You should use the sealed keyword as often as possible when designing new classes. In fact, use it by default.

Inheritance is such a tricky beast that, in order for a class to serve as a good base class, you must design it with that goal in mind. If not, you should mark it as sealed. It's as simple as that. Now, you may be thinking, "Shouldn't I leave it unsealed so that someone can possibly derive from it in the future, thus retaining maximum flexibility?" The answer is no, in a good design. Again, a class that is meant to serve as a base class must be designed with that in mind from the start. If it is not, then it's likely that you'll hit pitfalls while trying to derive from the class effectively.

Note In many cases, classes that are meant to serve as extendable base classes are contained in consumable libraries. Creating libraries is a detail-oriented business that you must focus lots of time on for your library to be maximally useful. Additionally, once you publish a library, you may be stuck with supporting it for a long time; therefore, you want to get it right the first time. I suggest you reference Krzysztof Cwalina and Brad Abrams' *Framework Design Guidelines: Conventions, Idioms, and Patterns for Reusable .NET Libraries* (Boston, MA: Addison-Wesley Professional, 2005) if you're planning to create libraries; the book originated from the internal design guidelines that the .NET Base Class Library team used while developing the framework.

abstract Classes

At the opposite end of the spectrum from sealed classes are abstract classes. Sometimes, you need to design a class whose only purpose is to serve as a base class. You should mark classes such as these with the abstract keyword.

The abstract keyword tells the compiler that this class is meant to be used only as a base class, and therefore it does not allow code to create instances of that class. Let's revisit the GeometricShape example from earlier in the chapter:

```
public abstract class GeometricShape
{
   public abstract void Draw();
}

public class Circle : GeometricShape
{
   public override void Draw()
   {
      // Do some drawing.
   }
}

public class EntryPoint
{
   static void Main()
   {
      Circle shape = new Circle();

      // This won't work!
      // GeometricShape shape2 = new GeometricShape();

      shape.Draw();
   }
}
```

It makes no sense to create a GeometricShape object all by itself, so I've marked the GeometricShape class as abstract. Therefore, if the code in Main attempts to create an instance of GeometricShape, a compiler error will be emitted. You may have also noted the use of the abstract keyword on the GeometricShape.Draw method. I cover this usage of the keyword in more detail in the "Virtual and Abstract Methods" section. In short, using the abstract keyword is a way of saying to the compiler that the deriving classes must override the method. Since the method must be overridden by the derived classes, it makes no sense for GeometricShape.Draw to have an implementation when you can't ever create an instance of GeometricShape anyway. Therefore, abstract methods don't need to have an implementation. If you come from the C++ world, you may be exclaiming that C++ allows an abstract method to have an implementation. This is true, but the designers of C# considered the idea unnecessary. In my experience, I've rarely found the need to use a default implementation of an abstract method except in debug builds.

As you can see, there can be times in a design when you use a base class to define a sort of template of behavior by providing an implementation to inherit. The leaf classes can inherit from this base template of an implementation and flesh out the details.

Nested Classes

You define nested classes within the scope of another class definition. Classes that are defined within the scope of a namespace, or outside the scope of a namespace but not inside the scope of another class, are called *non-nested classes*. Nested classes have some special capabilities and lend themselves well to situations where you need a helper class that works on behalf of the containing class.

For example, a container class might maintain a collection of objects. Imagine that you need some facility to iterate over those contained objects and also allow external users who are doing the iteration to maintain a marker, or an iterator of sorts, representing their place during the iteration. This is a common design technique. Preventing the users from holding on to direct references to the contained objects gives you much greater flexibility to change the internal behavior of the container class without breaking code that uses the container class. Nested classes provide a great solution to this problem for several reasons.

First, nested classes have access to all of the members that are visible to the containing class, even if they're private. Consider the following code, which represents a container class that contains instances of GeometricShape:

```
using System.Collections;

public abstract class GeometricShape
{
   public abstract void Draw();
}

public class Rectangle : GeometricShape
{
   public override void Draw()
   {
      System.Console.WriteLine( "Rectangle.Draw" );
   }
}

public class Circle : GeometricShape
{
   public override void Draw()
   {
      System.Console.WriteLine( "Circle.Draw" );
   }
}

public class Drawing : IEnumerable
{
   private ArrayList shapes;

   private class Iterator : IEnumerator
   {
      public Iterator( Drawing drawing )
      {
         this.drawing = drawing;
         this.current = -1;
      }

      public void Reset()
      {
         current = -1;
      }

      public bool MoveNext()
      {
```

```csharp
            ++current;
            if( current < drawing.shapes.Count ) {
                return true;
            } else {
                return false;
            }
        }

        public object Current
        {
            get
            {
                return drawing.shapes[ current ];
            }
        }

        private Drawing    drawing;
        private int        current;
    }

    public Drawing()
    {
        shapes = new ArrayList();
    }

    public IEnumerator GetEnumerator()
    {
        return new Iterator( this );
    }

    public void Add( GeometricShape shape )
    {
        shapes.Add( shape );
    }
}

public class EntryPoint
{
    static void Main()
    {
        Rectangle rectangle = new Rectangle();
        Circle circle = new Circle();
        Drawing drawing = new Drawing();

        drawing.Add( rectangle );
        drawing.Add( circle );

        foreach( GeometricShape shape in drawing ) {
            shape.Draw();
        }
    }
}
```

This example introduces a few new concepts, such as the IEnumerable and IEnumerator interfaces, which I detail in Chapter 9. For now, let's focus primarily on the nested class usage. As you can see, the Drawing class supports a method called GetEnumerator, which is part of the IEnumerable implementation. It creates an instance of the nested Iterator class and returns it.

Here's where it gets interesting. The Iterator class takes a reference to an instance of the containing class, Drawing, as a parameter to its constructor. It then stores away this instance for later use so that it can get at the shapes collection within the drawing object. However, notice that the shapes collection in the Drawing class is private. It doesn't matter, since nested classes have access to the containing class's private members.

Also, notice that the Iterator class itself is declared private. Non-nested classes can only be declared as either public or internal, and they default to internal. You can apply the same access modifiers to nested classes as you can to any other member of the class. In this case, you declare the Iterator class as private so that external code, such as in the Main routine, cannot create instances of the Iterator directly. Only the Drawing class itself can create instances of Iterator. It doesn't make sense for anyone other than Drawing.GetEnumerator to be able to create an Iterator instance.

Nested classes that are declared public can be instantiated by code external to the containing class. The notation for addressing the nested class is similar to that of namespace qualification. In the following example, you can see how to create an instance of a nested class:

```
public class A
{
   public class B
   {
   }
}

public class EntryPoint
{
   static void Main()
   {
      A.B b = new A.B();
   }
}
```

Sometimes, when you introduce a nested class, its name may hide a member name within a base class using the new keyword, similar to the way method hiding works. This is extremely rare, and can, for the most part, be avoided. Let's take a look at an example:

```
public class A
{
   public void Foo()
   {
   }
}

public class B : A
{
   public new class Foo
   {
   }
}
```

In this case, you define a nested class Foo inside the class B definition. Since the name is the same as the Foo method in class A, you must use the new keyword, or else the compiler will let you know about the collision in names. Again, if you get into a situation like this, it's probably time to rethink your design or simply rename the nested class unless you really meant to hide the base member. Hiding base members like this is questionable design and not something you should generally do just because the language allows it.

Indexers

Indexers allow you to treat an object instance as if it were an array. This allows for a more natural usage of objects that are meant to behave as a collection, such as instances of the Drawing class from the previous section.

Generally, indexers look a little bit like a method whose name is this. As with just about every entity in the C# type system, you can apply metadata attributes to indexers. You can also apply the same modifiers to them that just about every other class member can have, except one: Indexers may not be static. Indexers are, therefore, always instance-based and work on a specific instance of an object of the defining class. Following the modifiers in the declaration is the type of the indexer. The indexer will return this type of the object to the caller. Then you put the this keyword, followed by the parameter list in square brackets, which I show in the next example.

Essentially, an indexer behaves a lot like a hybrid between a property and a method. After all, under the covers, it is one of the special methods defined by the compiler when you define an indexer. Conceptually, an indexer is similar to a method, in that it can take a set of parameters when used. However, it also behaves like a property, as you define the accessors with a similar syntax. You can apply many of the same modifiers to indexers as you can to a method. For example, indexers can be virtual, they can be an override of a base class indexer, or they can be overloaded based on the parameter list, just as methods can. Following the parameter list is the code block for the indexer, which is just like a property code block in its syntax. The main difference is that the accessors for the indexer can access the parameter list variables, whereas the accessors of a property don't have user-defined parameters. Let's add an indexer to the Drawing object and see how you can use it:

```csharp
using System.Collections;

public abstract class GeometricShape
{
    public abstract void Draw();
}

public class Rectangle : GeometricShape
{
    public override void Draw()
    {
        System.Console.WriteLine( "Rectangle.Draw" );
    }
}

public class Circle : GeometricShape
{
    public override void Draw()
    {
        System.Console.WriteLine( "Circle.Draw" );
    }
}

public class Drawing
{
    private ArrayList shapes;

    public Drawing()
    {
        shapes = new ArrayList();
    }
```

```
   public int Count
   {
      get
      {
         return shapes.Count;
      }
   }

   public GeometricShape this[ int index ]
   {
      get
      {
         return (GeometricShape) shapes[index];
      }
   }

   public void Add( GeometricShape shape )
   {
      shapes.Add( shape );
   }
}

public class EntryPoint
{
   static void Main()
   {
      Rectangle rectangle = new Rectangle();
      Circle circle = new Circle();
      Drawing drawing = new Drawing();

      drawing.Add( rectangle );
      drawing.Add( circle );

      for( int i = 0; i < drawing.Count; ++i ) {
         GeometricShape shape = drawing[i];
         shape.Draw();
      }
   }
}
```

As you can see, you can access the elements of the Drawing object in the Main method as if they were inside a normal array. Most collection types support some type of indexer such as this. Also, since this indexer only has a get accessor, it is read-only. However, keep in mind that if the collection maintains references to objects, the client code can still change the state of the contained object through that reference. But since the indexer is read-only, the client code cannot swap out the object reference at a specific index with a reference to a completely different object.

One difference is worth noting between a real array and an object that provides an indexer. You cannot pass the results of calling an indexer on an object as an out or ref parameter to a method as you can do with a real array. This is similar to the same restriction placed on properties.

partial Classes

Classes defined as partial were a new addition to C# 2.0. So far, I've shown you how to define classes in one single file. This was a requirement in C# 1.0. It was impossible to split the definition of a class across multiple files.

At first, such a convenience may not seem worthwhile. After all, if a class has become so large that the file is hard to manage, that may be an indication of poor design. But arguably, the main reason partial classes were introduced is to support code-generation tools.

Normally, when you work within the confines of the IDE, the IDE tries to help you out by generating some code for you. For example, a wizard generates helpful `DataSet`-derived classes when using ADO.NET facilities. The classic problem has always been editing the resulting code generated by the tool. It was always a dangerous proposition to edit the output from the tool, because any time the parameters to the tool change, the tool regenerates the code, thus overwriting any changes made. This is definitely not desired. Previously, the only way to work around this was to use some form of reuse, such as inheritance or containment, thus inheriting a class from the class produced by the code-generation tool. Many times these were not natural solutions to the problem. And many times, the code generated by these tools was not designed to take inheritance into consideration.

Now, you can slip the `partial` keyword into the class definition right before the `class` keyword, and voilà—you can split the class definition across multiple files. One requirement is that each file that contains part of the partial class must use the `partial` keyword, and all of the partial pieces must be defined within the same namespace, if you declare them in a namespace at all. Now, with the addition of the `partial` keyword, the code generated from the code-generation tool can live in a separate file from the additions to that generated class, and when the tool regenerates the code, you don't lose your changes.

You should know some things about the process the compiler goes through to assemble partial classes into a whole class. You must compile all the partial pieces of a class together at once so the compiler can find all of the pieces. For the most part, all of the members and aspects of the class are merged together using a union operation. Therefore, they must coexist together as if you had declared and defined them all in the same file. Base interface lists are unioned together. However, since a class can have one base class at most, if the partial pieces list a base class, they must all list the same base class. Other than those obvious restrictions, I think you'll agree that partial classes are a welcome addition to the C# language.

partial Methods

C# 3.0 introduced the `partial` keyword for methods to complement partial classes. A partial method is simply a method whose signature is declared without a body in one piece of the partial class and defined in another piece of the partial class. Just like partial classes, partial methods come in really handy when you are consuming code created by wizards and code generators. But the beauty of partial methods is that if a generator creates a declaration for a partial method in one part of the class declaration and you don't implement it in your part, then the method is not included as part of the final assembled class. Moreover, any code in the generated piece that calls the partial method will not break. It will simply not call the partial method at all. There are several restrictions on partial methods necessary to provide this behavior.

- Partial methods must have a return type of `void`.

- Partial methods may not accept `out` parameters but may accept `ref` parameters.

- Partial methods may not be `extern` as well.

- Partial methods cannot be marked `virtual` and may not be decorated with access modifiers because they are implicitly private.

- Partial methods can be marked either `static` or `unsafe`.

- Partial methods can be generic and may be decorated with constraints, although repeating the constraints in the declaration of the implementation is optional.

- Delegates may not be wired up to call partial methods since they are not guaranteed to exist in the final compiled product.

With all of that in mind, let's look at a short example of partial methods. Imagine one partial class that is, for the sake of this example, a result of some code generator and is shown below:

```
public partial class DataSource
{
    // Some useful methods
    // ...

    partial void ResetSource();
}
```

Let's pretend that this DataSource class that the generator created represents some sort of back-end data store that, in order to satisfy some design requirement, needs to be able to be reset from time to time. Moreover, let's assume that the steps required to reset the data source are only known by the one who completes and consumes this partial class and implements the partial method. With that in mind, a possible completion of this partial class by the consumer could look like the following:

```
using System;

public partial class DataSource
{
    partial void ResetSource() {
        Console.WriteLine( "Source was reset" );
    }

    public void Reset() {
        ResetSource();
    }
}

public class PartialMethods
{
    static void Main() {
        DataSource ds = new DataSource();

        ds.Reset();
    }
}
```

You can see that I had to add a public method named Reset in order for Main to be able to reset instances of DataSource. That's because the ResetSource method is implicitly private. If you inspect the resultant executable with ILDASM, you will see the private method DataSource.ResetSource and if you inspect the IL generated for DataSource.Reset, you will see it calling through to ResetSource. If you were to comment out, or remove, the partial implementation of ResetSource and recompile, ILDASM would show that the DataSource.ResetSource method does not exist and the call to ResetSource within the Reset method is simply removed.

Static Classes

C# 2.0 introduced a new class modifier that allows you to designate that a class is nothing more than a collection of static members and cannot have objects instantiated from it. The way you do this is by decorating the class declaration with the static modifier. Once you do that, several restrictions are placed upon the class, as follows:

- The class may not derive from anything other than System.Object, and if you don't specify any base type, derivation from System.Object is implied.

- The class may not be used as a base class of another class.

- The class can only contain static members, which can be public or private. However, they cannot be marked protected or protected internal, since the class cannot be used as a base class.

- The class may not have any operators, since defining them would make no sense if you cannot create instances of the class.

Even though the entire class is marked static, you still must mark each individual member as static as well. Although it would be nice for the compiler to just assume that any member within a static class is static itself, it would add unnecessary complexity to an already complex compiler. However, constants and nested types declared within a static class are static with respect to the declaring class by default. But if you put the static modifier on a nested class, it too will be a static class just as the containing class is, but you'll be able to instantiate nested classes not decorated with static.

■Note In essence, declaring a class static is just the same as declaring it sealed and abstract at the same time, but the compiler won't let you do such a thing. However, if you look at the IL code generated for a static class, you'll see that this is exactly what the compiler is doing—that is, the class is decorated with the abstract and sealed modifiers in the IL.

The following code shows an example of a static class:

```
using System;

public static class StaticClass
{
    public static void DoWork() {
        ++callCount;
        Console.WriteLine( "StaticClass.DoWork()" );
    }

    public class NestedClass {
        public NestedClass() {
            Console.WriteLine( "NestedClass.NestedClass()" );
        }
    }

    private static long callCount = 0;
    public static long CallCount {
        get {
            return callCount;
        }
    }
}

public static class EntryPoint
{
    static void Main() {
        StaticClass.DoWork();

        // OOPS! Cannot do this!
        // StaticClass obj = new StaticClass();
```

```
        StaticClass.NestedClass nested =
            new StaticClass.NestedClass();

        Console.WriteLine( "CallCount = {0}",
                            StaticClass.CallCount );
    }
}
```

The `StaticClass` type contains one method, a field, a property, and a nested class. Notice that since the `NestedClass` is not declared `static`, you can instantiate it just like any other class. Also, since the `EntryPoint` class merely contains the static `Main` method, it too is marked as `static` to prevent anyone from instantiating it inadvertently.

Static classes are useful when you need a logical mechanism to partition a collection of methods. An example of a static class within the Base Class Library is the venerable `System.Console` class. It contains static methods, properties, and events, which are all static since only one console can be attached to the process at a single time.

THE SINGLETON PATTERN

Probably the most popular design pattern is the Singleton pattern, which typically models a situation in which you can create only one instance of a class at one time. Historically, you implement the Singleton pattern with private constructors and with a static method named something like `GetInstance` to obtain a reference to the one possible running instance. Although you can use this technique in C#, the static class provides an excellent tool for implementing the Singleton pattern in certain situations, as you see with `System.Console`.

If your Singleton is not required to be an instance of a class, then the static class is an excellent tool for implementing it. For example, if you don't ever need to destroy and re-create your class, and if you won't use your Singleton with .NET Remoting, then each application domain has its own *instance* of the Singleton, since static fields are application-domain-specific. In fact, such a Singleton will not live on the heap, and all of the bookkeeping involved with managing the single instance is unnecessary. What's even better is that since it's not an actual object instance, you can use the static class effectively within an object's finalizer body safely. In Chapter 13, I describe why using objects in finalizers is so dangerous and how you cannot guarantee in what order finalizers for multiple objects will be called.

Reserved Member Names

Several of the capabilities provided by the C# language are really just syntactic sugar that boils down to methods and method calls in the IL code that you never see, unless you open the generated assembly with a tool such as ILDASM. It's important to be aware of this, just in case you attempt to declare a method whose name conflicts with one of these underlying reserved method names. These syntactic shortcuts include properties, events, and indexers. If you try to declare a method with one of these special internal names and you also have a property, an event, or an indexer already defined that declares the same method names internally, the compiler will complain about duplicate symbols.

■**Note** If you follow the conventions in *Framework Design Guidelines: Conventions, Idioms, and Patterns for Reusable .NET Libraries* by Krzysztof Cwalina and Brad Abrams (Boston, MA: Addison-Wesley Professional, 2005) or you use FxCop to regularly analyze your code, you should never encounter a name conflict between one of your class members and a reserved member name.

Reserved Names for Properties

For a property named Prop of type T, the following signatures are reserved for the implementation of the property:

```
T get_Prop();
void set_Prop( T value );
```

Reserved Names for Indexers

If the class contains an indexer that is of type T and takes a parameter list represented by Params, it will contain the following reserved method names:

```
T get_Item( Params );
void set_Item( Params, T value );
```

Reserved Names for Destructors

If the class is defined with a finalizer (using the destructor syntax), it will contain a definition of the following method:

```
void Finalize();
```

I have a lot more to say about destructors and the Finalize method later in this chapter and in Chapter 13.

Reserved Names for Events

If the class contains an event definition of type T that is named Event, the following methods are reserved on the class:

```
void add_Event( T callback );
void remove_Event( T callback );
```

I discuss events in Chapter 10, when I cover delegates and anonymous methods.

Value Type Definitions

A value type is a lightweight type that you typically don't create on the heap. The only exception to this rule is a value type that is a field in an object that lives on the heap. A value type is a type that behaves with value semantics. That is, when you assign a value-type variable to another value-type variable, the contents of the source are copied into the destination and a full copy of the instance is made. This is in contrast to reference types, or object instances, where the result of copying one reference-type variable to another is that there is now a new reference to the same object. Also, when you pass a value type as a parameter to a method, the method body receives a local copy of the value, unless the parameter was declared as a ref or an out parameter. All of the C# built-in types except string, arrays, and delegates are value types. In C#, you declare a value type using the struct keyword rather than the class keyword.

On the whole, the syntax of defining a struct is the same as for a class—with some notable exceptions, as you'll soon see. A struct cannot declare a base class. Also, a struct is implicitly sealed. That means that nothing else can derive from a struct. Internally, a struct derives from System. ValueType, which in turn extends System.Object. This is so that ValueType can provide implementations of Object.Equals and Object.GetHashCode, among others, which are meaningful for value types. In the section titled "System.Object," I cover the nuances involved with implementing the methods inherited from System.Object for a value type. Like classes, structs can be declared in partial pieces, and the same rules for partial pieces apply to structs as they do to classes.

Constructors

Types defined as structs can have static constructors just like classes. Structs can also have instance constructors, with one notable exception. They cannot have a user-defined default, parameterless constructor, nor can they have instance field initializers in the struct definition. Static field initializers are permitted, though. Parameterless constructors are not necessary for value types, since the system provides one, which simply sets the fields of the value to their default values. In all cases, that amounts to setting the bits of the field's storage to 0. So, if a struct contains an int, the default value will be 0. If a struct contains a reference type field, the default value will be null. Each struct gets this implicit, parameterless constructor, which takes care of this initialization. It's all part of the language's endeavor to create verifiably type-safe code. However, it's completely possible for a user to declare a struct without calling a constructor on it at all. If that happens, the coder is responsible for setting up the struct appropriately before any methods on it can be called. Consider the following code:

```
using System;

public struct Square
{
    // Not a good idea to have public fields, but I use them
    // here only for the sake of example.  Prefer to expose
    // these with properties instead.
    public int width;
    public int height;
}

public class EntryPoint
{
    static void Main()
    {
        Square sq;
        sq.width = 1;

        // Can't do this yet.
        // Console.WriteLine( "{0} x {1}", sq.width, sq.height );

        sq.height = 2;

        Console.WriteLine( "{0} x {1}", sq.width, sq.height );
    }
}
```

In Main, I've allocated space on the stack for a Square object. However, immediately after, I only assign to the width field. I've commented out a call to Console.WriteLine immediately after that because it won't compile. The reason is that you can't call methods on a struct before it is fully initialized. Properties are really method calls under the covers. After I initialize the height field, I can successfully use the Square instance to send the width and height to the console. Can you spot the problem in the following code?

```
using System;

public struct Square
{
    public int Width
    {
        get
        {
            return width;
        }

        set
        {
            width = value;
        }
    }

    public int Height
    {
        get
        {
            return height;
        }

        set
        {
            height = value;
        }
    }

    private int width;
    private int height;
}

public class EntryPoint
{
    static void Main()
    {
        Square sq;
        sq.Width = 1;
        sq.Height = 1;
    }
}
```

The problem is in the Main method. If you try to compile this code, the compiler will fail with an error. You cannot initialize the fields since they're now private. Also, you cannot initialize them with the properties, because properties are really methods, and it's illegal to call methods on a value that is not fully initialized. The only way to get out of this pickle is to use the new keyword when you declare the new Square instance. You can either call one of the constructors on the struct or the default constructor. In this case, I'll call the default constructor so the Main method will change to the following:

```
public class EntryPoint
{
    static void Main()
    {
        Square sq = new Square();
        sq.Width = 1;
        sq.Height = 1;
    }
}
```

Since a struct cannot derive from another struct or class, it is not permitted to call any base constructor through the base keyword while inside the constructor block. Even though you know that a struct derives from System.ValueType internally, you may not invoke the constructor of the base type explicitly.

The Meaning of this

Previously, I said that the this keyword within class methods behaves as a constant, read-only value that contains a reference to the current object instance. In other words, it's a read-only object reference in class methods. However, with value types, this behaves like a regular ref parameter. In instance constructors that don't have an initialization list, the this value behaves as an out parameter. That means that you can actually assign a value to this, as in the following example:

```
public struct ComplexNumber
{
    public ComplexNumber( double real, double imaginary )
    {
        this.real = real;
        this.imaginary = imaginary;
    }

    public ComplexNumber( ComplexNumber other )
    {
        this = other;
    }

    private double real;
    private double imaginary;
}

public class EntryPoint
{
    static void Main()
    {
        ComplexNumber valA = new ComplexNumber( 1, 2 );
        ComplexNumber copyA = new ComplexNumber( valA );
    }
}
```

Notice that the second constructor takes, as a parameter, another ComplexNumber value. This constructor behaves similarly to a copy constructor in C++. But instead of having to assign each field individually, you can simply assign to this, thus making a copy of the parameter's state in one line of code. Again, the this keyword acts like an out parameter in this case.

Remember that out parameters behave similarly to ref parameters, with one special difference. When a parameter is marked as an out parameter, the compiler knows that the value is uninitialized at the point the method body starts executing. Therefore, the compiler must make sure that every field of the value is initialized before the constructor exits. For example, consider the following code, which doesn't compile:

```
public struct ComplexNumber
{
    public ComplexNumber( double real, double imaginary )
    {
        this.real = real;
        this.imaginary = imaginary;
    }

    public ComplexNumber( double real )
    {
        this.real = real;
    }

    private double real;
    private double imaginary;
}
```

The problem with this code lies in the second constructor. Since value types typically are created on the stack, the allocation of such values merely requires adjustment of the stack pointer. Of course, an allocation of this sort says nothing about the state of the memory. The odds are that the memory reserved on the stack for the value contains random garbage. The CLR could elect to zero-initialize these blocks of memory, but that would defeat half the purpose of value types. Value types are meant to be lightweight and fast. If the CLR has to zero-initialize the stack memory for a value type each time the memory is reserved, that's hardly a fast operation. Of course, the default parameterless constructor generated by the system does exactly this. But you must call it explicitly by creating the instance with the new keyword. Since the this keyword is treated as an out parameter in the instance constructors, the instance constructor must initialize each field of the value before it exits. And it is the duty of the C# compiler, which is supposed to generate verifiably type-safe code, to make sure you do so. That's why the previous code example produces a compiler error.

Even though instance constructors in value types cannot use the base keyword to call base class constructors, they can have an initializer. It is valid for the initializer to use the this keyword to call other constructors on the same struct during initialization. So you can make one minor modification to the preceding code example to make it compile:

```
public struct ComplexNumber
{
    public ComplexNumber( double real, double imaginary )
    {
        this.real = real;
        this.imaginary = imaginary;
    }

    public ComplexNumber( double real )
        :this( real, 0 )
    {
        this.real = real;
    }

    private double real;
    private double imaginary;
}
```

```
public class EntryPoint
{
   static void Main()
   {
      ComplexNumber valA = new ComplexNumber( 1, 2 );
   }
}
```

Notice the difference in the second constructor. I've now introduced an initializer that calls the first constructor from the second one. Even though the single line of code in the second constructor's body is redundant, I left it there to prove a point. Notice that it only assigns the real value as in the previous example, but the compiler doesn't complain. That's because, when an instance constructor contains an initializer, the this keyword behaves as a ref parameter in that constructor's body rather than an out parameter. And, since it is a ref parameter, the compiler can assume that the value has been initialized properly before entry into the method's code block. In essence, the initialization burden is deferred to the first constructor, whose duty it is to make sure it initializes all fields of the value.

One last note to consider is that even though the system generates a default, parameterless initializer under the covers, you can't call it using the this keyword. For example, the following code doesn't compile:

```
public struct ComplexNumber
{
   public ComplexNumber( double real, double imaginary )
   {
      this.real = real;
      this.imaginary = imaginary;
   }

   public ComplexNumber( double real )
      :this()
   {
      this.real = real;
   }

   private double real;
   private double imaginary;
}
```

If you had a struct that had quite a few fields in it and you wanted to initialize all but one of them to 0 or null, it would save you a little bit of typing to be able to do this. But, alas, the compiler doesn't allow it.

Finalizers

Value types are not allowed to have a finalizer. The concept of finalization, or nondeterministic destruction, is reserved for instances of classes, or objects. If structs had finalizers, the runtime would have to manage the calling of the finalizer each time the value goes out of scope.

Keep in mind that you want to be careful about initializing resources within constructors of value types. Just don't do it. Consider a value type that has a field, which is a handle to some sort of low-level system resource. Suppose this low-level resource is allocated, or acquired, in a special constructor that accepts parameters. You now have a couple of problems to deal with. Since you cannot create a default, parameterless constructor, how can you possibly acquire the resource when the user creates an instance of the value without using one of the custom constructors? The answer is, you cannot. The second problem is that you have no automatic trigger to clean up and release the resource, since you have no destructor. You would have to force the user of the value to call some special method to clean up before the value goes out of scope. Requiring the user to remember to do something like that is poor design.

Interfaces

Although it's illegal for a struct to derive from another class, it can still implement interfaces. Supported interfaces are listed in the same way as they are for classes, in a base interface list after the struct identifier. Generally, supporting interfaces for structs is the same as supporting interfaces for classes. I cover interfaces in much more detail in Chapter 5. There are performance implications of implementing interfaces on structs, in that doing so incurs a boxing operation to call methods through an interface reference on the struct value instances.

Anonymous Types

How many times have you needed a lightweight class to hold a handful of related values for use within a particular method and you lamented having to type a whole type definition complete with private fields and public property accessors? Enter anonymous types! C# 3.0 allows you to introduce these types using an extended syntax of the new operator. Let's see what this looks like:

```
using System;

public class EntryPoint
{
    static void Main() {
        var employeeInfo = new { Name = "Joe", Id = 42 };
        var customerInfo = new { Name = "Jane", Id = "AB123" };

        Console.WriteLine( "Name: {0}, Id: {1}",
                           employeeInfo.Name,
                           employeeInfo.Id );

        Console.WriteLine( "employeeInfo Type is actually: {0}",
                           employeeInfo.GetType() );
        Console.WriteLine( "customerInfo Type is actually: {0}",
                           customerInfo.GetType() );
    }
}

using System;

public class EntryPoint
{
    static void Main() {
        var employeeInfo = new { Name = "Joe", Id = 42 };
        var customerInfo = new { Name = "Jane", Id = "AB123" };

        Console.WriteLine( "Name: {0}, Id: {1}",
                           employeeInfo.Name,
                           employeeInfo.Id );
```

```
        Console.WriteLine( "employeeInfo Type is actually: {0}",
                            employeeInfo.GetType() );
        Console.WriteLine( "customerInfo Type is actually: {0}",
                            customerInfo.GetType() );
    }
}
```

Notice the interesting and new syntax within the braces after the new keyword while declaring employeeInfo. The name/value pairs declare a property name within the anonymous type and initialize it to the given value. In this case, two anonymous types are created with two properties. In the first anonymous type, the first property is a System.String called Name, and the second is a System.Int32 called Id. It's important to note that the underlying type of the instance created is a strong type, it's just compiler generated and you don't know the name of it. But as you can see from the following output from the code above, you can figure out the name of the type:

```
Name: Joe, Id: 42
employeeInfo Type is actually: <>f__AnonymousType0`2[System.String,System.Int32]
customerInfo Type is actually: <>f__AnonymousType0`2[System.String,System.String]
```

■Note The compiler-generated type names are implementation specific, so you should never rely on them. Additionally, you'll notice that they are "unspeakable" to the compiler; if you were to attempt to declare an instance using that type name, the compiler would complain with a syntax error.

Since you do not know the compiler-generated name of the type, you are forced to declare the variable instance as an implicitly typed local variable using the var keyword, as I did in the code.

Also, notice that the compiler-generated type is a generic type that takes two type parameters. It would be inefficient for the compiler to generate a new type for every anonymous type that contains two types with the same field names. The output above indicates that the actual type of employeeInfo looks similar to the type name below:

```
<>f__AnonymousType0<System.String, System.Int32>
```

And since the anonymous type for customerInfo contains the same number of fields with the same names, the generated generic type is reused and the type of customerInfo looks similar to the type below:

```
<>f__AnonymousType0<System.String, System.String>
```

Had the anonymous type for customerInfo contained different field names than those for employeeInfo, then another generic anonymous type would have been declared.

Now that you know the basics about anonymous types, I want to show you an abbreviated syntax for declaring them. Pay attention to the bold statements in the following example:

```
using System;

public class ConventionalEmployeeInfo
{
    public ConventionalEmployeeInfo( string Name, int Id ) {
        this.name = Name;
        this.id = Id;
    }
```

```
    public string Name {
        get {
            return name;
        }

        set {
            name = value;
        }
    }

    public int Id {
        get {
            return id;
        }

        set {
            id = value;
        }
    }

    private string name;
    private int id;
}

public class EntryPoint
{
    static void Main() {
        ConventionalEmployeeInfo oldEmployee =
            new ConventionalEmployeeInfo( "Joe", 42 );

        var employeeInfo = new { oldEmployee.Name,
                                 oldEmployee.Id };

        string Name = "Jane";
        int Id = 1234;

        var customerInfo = new { Name, Id };

        Console.WriteLine( "employeeInfo Name: {0}, Id: {1}",
                           employeeInfo.Name,
                           employeeInfo.Id );
        Console.WriteLine( "customerInfo Name: {0}, Id: {1}",
                           customerInfo.Name,
                           customerInfo.Id );

        Console.WriteLine( "Anonymous Type is actually: {0}",
                           employeeInfo.GetType() );
    }
}
```

For illustration purposes, I have declared a type named ConventionalEmployeeInfo that is not an anonymous type. Notice that at the point where I instantiate the anonymous type for employeeInfo, I do not provide the names of the fields as before. In this case, the compiler uses the names of the properties of the ConventionalEmployeeInfo type, which is the source of the data. This same technique works using local variables, as you can see when I declare the customerInfo instance. In this case, customerInfo is an anonymous type that implements two read/write properties named Name and Id. Member declarators for anonymous types that use this abbreviated style are called projection initializers.[1]

If you inspect the compiled assembly in ILDASM, you'll notice that the generated types for anonymous types are of class type. The class is also marked private and sealed. However, the class is extremely basic and does not implement anything like a finalizer or IDisposable.

■**Note** Anonymous types, even though they are classes, do not implement the IDisposable interface. As I mention in Chapter 13, the general guideline for types that contain disposable types is that they, too, should be disposable. But since anonymous types are not disposable, you should avoid placing instances of disposable types within them.

Be careful not to strip the type off of anonymous types. For example, if you put instances of anonymous types in a System.List, how are you supposed to cast those instances back into the anonymous type when you reference them later? Remember, System.List stores references to System.Object. And even though the anonymous types derive from System.Object, how are you going to cast them back into their concrete types to access their properties? You could attempt to use reflection to overcome this. But then you introduce so much work that you lose any benefit from using anonymous types in the first place. Similarly, if you want to pass instances of anonymous types out of functions via out parameters or via a return statement, you must pass them out as references to System.Object, thus stripping the variables of their useful type information. If you need to pass instances out of a method, then you really should be using an explicitly defined type such as ConventionalEmployeeInfo instead of anonymous types.

After all of these restrictions placed on anonymous types, you may be wondering how they are useful except in rare circumstances within the local scope. It turns out that they are extremely useful when used with projection operators in LINQ (Language Integrated Query), which I will show you in Chapter 16.

Object Initializers

C# 3.0 introduces a shorthand you can use while instantiating new instances of objects. How many times have you written code similar to this?

```
Employee developer = new Employee();
developer.Name = "Fred Blaze";
developer.OfficeLocation = "B1";
```

Right after creating an instance of Employee, you immediately start initializing the accessible properties of the instance. Wouldn't it be nice if you could do this all in one statement? Of course, you could always create a specialized overload of the constructor that accepts the parameters to use while initializing the new instance. However, there may be times where it is more convenient not to do so.

---

1. Projection initializers are very handy when used together with LINQ, which I cover in Chapter 16.

■Note If your type contains one or more read-only auto-implemented properties, you must use an object initializer to initialize the properties at instantiation.

The new object initializer syntax is shown below:

```
using System;

public class Employee
{
    public string Name {
        get; set;
    }

    public string OfficeLocation {
        get; set;
    }
}

public class InitExample
{
    static void Main() {
        Employee developer = new Employee {
            Name = "Fred Blaze",
            OfficeLocation = "B1"
        };
    }
}
```

Notice how the `developer` instance is initialized in the `Main` method. Under the hood, the compiler generates the same code it would have if you had initialized the properties manually after creating the `Employee` instance. Therefore, this technique only works if the properties, in this case `Name` and `OfficeLocation`, are accessible at the point of initialization.

You can even nest object initializers as shown in the example below:

```
using System;

public class Employee
{
    public string Name { get; set; }
    public string OfficeLocation { get; set; }
}

public class FeatureDevPair
{
    public Employee Developer { get; set; }
    public Employee QaEngineer { get; set; }
}
```

```
public class InitExample
{
    static void Main() {
        FeatureDevPair spellCheckerTeam = new FeatureDevPair {
            Developer = new Employee {
                Name = "Fred Blaze",
                OfficeLocation = "B1"
            },
            QaEngineer = new Employee {
                Name = "Marisa Bozza",
                OfficeLocation = "L42"
            }
        };
    }
}
```

Notice how the two properties of spellCheckerTeam are initialized using the new syntax. Each of the Employee instances assigned to those properties is itself initialized using an object initializer, too. Finally, let me show you an even more abbreviated way to initialize the object above that saves a bit more typing at the expense of hidden complexity:

```
using System;

public class Employee
{
    public string Name { get; set; }
    public string OfficeLocation { get; set; }
}

public class FeatureDevPair
{
    private Employee developer = new Employee();
    private Employee qaEngineer = new Employee();

    public Employee Developer {
        get { return developer; }
        set { developer = value; }
    }

    public Employee QaEngineer {
        get { return qaEngineer; }
        set { qaEngineer = value; }
    }
}

public class InitExample
{
    static void Main() {
        FeatureDevPair spellCheckerTeam = new FeatureDevPair {
            Developer = {
                Name = "Fred Blaze",
                OfficeLocation = "B1"
            },
```

```
            QaEngineer = {
                Name = "Marisa Bozza",
                OfficeLocation = "L42"
            }
        };
    }
}
```

Notice that I was able to leave out the new expressions when initializing the Developer and QaEngineer properties of spellCheckerTeam. However, this abbreviated syntax requires that the fields of spellCheckerTeam exist before the properties are set, that is, the fields cannot be null. Therefore, you see that I had to change the definition of FeatureDevPair to create the contained instances of the Employee type at the point of initialization.

▓Note If you do not initialize fields exposed by properties during object initialization, and then later write code that initializes instances of those objects using the abbreviated syntax shown above, you will get a nasty surprise at run time. You might have guessed that your code will generate a NullReferenceException in those cases. Unfortunately, the compiler cannot detect this potential disaster at compile time. So be very careful when using the abbreviated syntax shown above. For example, if you are using this syntax to intialize instances of objects that you did not write, then you should be even more careful because unless you look at the implementation of that third-party class using ILDASM, you have no way of knowing if the fields are initialized at object initialization time or not.

Boxing and Unboxing

Allow me to introduce boxing and unboxing. All types within the CLR fall into one of two categories: reference types (objects) or value types (values). You define objects using classes, and you define values using structs. A clear divide exists between these two. Objects live on the memory heap and are managed by the garbage collector. Values normally live in temporary storage spaces, such as on the stack. The one notable exception already mentioned is that a value type can live on the heap as long as it is contained as a field within an object. However, it is not autonomous, and the GC doesn't control its lifetime directly. Consider the following code:

```
public class EntryPoint
{
    static void Print( object obj )
    {
        System.Console.WriteLine( "{0}", obj.ToString() );
    }
    static void Main()
    {
        int x = 42;
        Print( x );
    }
}
```

It looks simple enough. In Main, there is an int, which is a C# alias for System.Int32, and it is a value type. You could have just as well declared x as type System.Int32. The space allocated for x is on the local stack. You then pass it as a parameter to the Print method. The Print method takes an object reference and simply sends the results of calling ToString on that object to the console. Let's analyze this. Print accepts an object reference, which is a reference to a heap-based object. Yet, you're passing a value type to the method. What's going on here? How is this possible?

The key is a concept called *boxing*. At the point where a value type is defined, the CLR creates a runtime-created wrapper class to contain the value type. Instances of the wrapper live on the heap and are commonly called boxing objects. This is the CLR's way of bridging the gap between value types and reference types. In fact, if you use ILDASM to look at the IL code generated for the Main method, you'll see the following:

```
.method private hidebysig static void  Main() cil managed
{
  .entrypoint
  // Code size       15 (0xf)
  .maxstack  1
  .locals init (int32 V_0)
  IL_0000:  ldc.i4.s    42
  IL_0002:  stloc.0
  IL_0003:  ldloc.0
  IL_0004:  box         [mscorlib]System.Int32
  IL_0009:  call        void EntryPoint::Print(object)
  IL_000e:  ret
} // end of method EntryPoint::Main
```

Notice the IL instruction, box, which takes care of the boxing operation before the Print method is called. This creates an object, which Figure 4-2 depicts.

Figure 4-2 depicts the action of copying the value type into the boxing object that lives on the heap. The boxing object behaves just like any other reference type in the CLR. Also, note that the boxing type implements the interfaces of the contained value type. The boxing type is a class type that is generated internally by the virtual execution system of the CLR at the point where the contained value type is defined. The CLR then uses this internal class type when it performs boxing operations as needed.

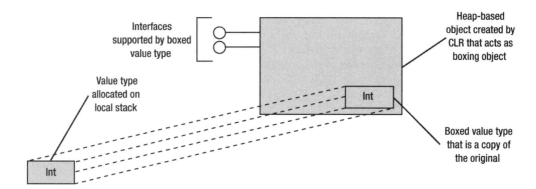

Figure 4-2. *Result of boxing operation*

The most important thing to keep in mind with boxing is that the boxed value is a copy of the original. Therefore, any changes made to the value inside the box are not propagated back to the original value. For example, consider this slight modification to the previous code:

```
public class EntryPoint
{
  static void PrintAndModify( object obj )
```

```
  {
    System.Console.WriteLine( "{0}", obj.ToString() );
    int x = (int) obj;
    x = 21;
  }
  static void Main()
  {
    int x = 42;
    PrintAndModify( x );
    PrintAndModify( x );
  }
}
```

The output from this code might surprise you:

42
42

The fact is, the original value, x, declared and initialized in Main, is never changed. As you pass it to the PrintAndModify method, it is boxed, since the PrintAndModify method takes an object as its parameter. Even though PrintAndModify takes a reference to an object that you can modify, the object it receives is a boxing object that contains a copy of the original value. The code also introduces another operation called *unboxing* in the PrintAndModify method. Since the value is boxed inside an instance of an object on the heap, you can't change the value because the only methods supported by that object are methods that System.Object implements. Technically, it also supports the same interfaces that System.Int32 supports. Therefore, you need a way to get the value out of the box. In C#, you can accomplish this syntactically with casting. Notice that you cast the object instance back into an int, and the compiler is smart enough to know that what you're really doing is unboxing the value type and using the unbox IL instruction, as the following IL for the PrintAndModify method shows:

```
.method private hidebysig static void  PrintAndModify(object obj) cil managed
{
  // Code size       28 (0x1c)
  .maxstack  2
  .locals init (int32 V_0)
  IL_0000:  ldstr      "{0}"
  IL_0005:  ldarg.0
  IL_0006:  callvirt   instance string [mscorlib]System.Object::ToString()
  IL_000b:  call       void [mscorlib]System.Console::WriteLine(string,
                                                                object)
  IL_0010:  ldarg.0
  IL_0011:  unbox      [mscorlib]System.Int32
  IL_0016:  ldind.i4
  IL_0017:  stloc.0
  IL_0018:  ldc.i4.s   21
  IL_001a:  stloc.0
  IL_001b:  ret
} // end of method EntryPoint::PrintAndModify
```

Let me be very clear about what happens during unboxing in C#. The operation of unboxing a value is the exact opposite of boxing. The value in the box is copied into an instance of the value on the local stack. Again, any changes made to this unboxed copy are not propagated back to the value contained in the box. Now, you can see how boxing and unboxing can really become confusing. As shown, the code's behavior is not obvious to the casual observer who is not familiar with the fact that boxing and unboxing are going on internally. What's worse is that two copies of the int are created between the time the call to PrintAndModify is initiated and the time that the int is manipulated in the method. The first copy is the one put into the box. The second copy is the one created when the boxed value is copied out of the box.

Technically, it's possible to modify the value that is contained within the box. However, you must do this through an interface. The runtime-generated box that contains the value also implements the interfaces that the value type implements and forwards the calls to the contained value. So, you could do the following:

```
public interface IModifyMyValue
{
    int X
    {
        get;
        set;
    }
}

public struct MyValue : IModifyMyValue
{
    public int x;

    public int X
    {
        get
        {
            return x;
        }

        set
        {
            x = value;
        }
    }

    public override string ToString()
    {
        System.Text.StringBuilder output =
            new System.Text.StringBuilder();
        output.AppendFormat( "{0}", x );
        return output.ToString();
    }
}

public class EntryPoint
{
    static void Main()
    {
        // Create value
        MyValue myval = new MyValue();
        myval.x = 123;
```

```
      // box it
      object obj = myval;
      System.Console.WriteLine( "{0}", obj.ToString() );

      // modify the contents in the box.
      IModifyMyValue iface = (IModifyMyValue) obj;
      iface.X = 456;
      System.Console.WriteLine( "{0}", obj.ToString() );

      // unbox it and see what it is.
      MyValue newval = (MyValue) obj;
      System.Console.WriteLine( "{0}", newval.ToString() );
   }
}
```

You can see that the output from the code is as follows:

```
123
456
456
```

As expected, you're able to modify the value inside the box using the interface named
IModifyMyValue. However, it's not the most straightforward process. And keep in mind that before
you can obtain an interface reference to a value type, it must be boxed. This makes sense if you
think about the fact that references to interfaces are object reference types.

When Boxing Occurs

Since C# handles boxing implicitly for you, it's important to know the instances when C# boxes a
value. Basically, a value gets boxed when one of the following conversions occurs:

- Conversion from a value type to an object reference

- Conversion from a value type to a System.ValueType reference

- Conversion from a value type to a reference to an interface implemented by the value type

- Conversion from an enum type to a System.Enum reference

In each case, the conversion normally takes the form of an assignment expression. The first
two cases are fairly obvious, since the CLR is bridging the gap by turning a value type instance into a
reference type. The third one can be a little surprising. Any time you implicitly cast your value into
an interface that it supports, you incur the penalty of boxing. Consider the following code:

```
public interface IPrint
{
   void Print();
}

public struct MyValue : IPrint
{
   public int x;
```

```
      public void Print()
      {
         System.Console.WriteLine( "{0}", x );
      }
   }

   public class EntryPoint
   {
      static void Main()
      {
         MyValue myval = new MyValue();
         myval.x = 123;

         // no boxing
         myval.Print();

         // must box the value
         IPrint printer = myval;
         printer.Print();
      }
   }
```

The first call to Print is done through the value reference, which doesn't incur boxing. However, the second call to Print is done through an interface. The boxing takes place at the point where you obtain the interface. At first, it looks like you can easily sidestep the boxing operation by not acquiring an explicit reference typed on the interface type. This is true in this case, since Print is also part of the public contract of MyValue. However, had you implemented the Print method as an explicit interface, which I cover in Chapter 5, then the only way to call the method would be through the interface reference type. So, it's important to note that any time you implement an interface on a value type explicitly, you force the clients of your value type to box it before calling through that interface. The following example demonstrates this:

```
public interface IPrint
{
   void Print();
}

public struct MyValue : IPrint
{
   public int x;

   void IPrint.Print()
   {
      System.Console.WriteLine( "{0}", x );
   }
}

public class EntryPoint
{
   static void Main()
   {
      MyValue myval = new MyValue();
      myval.x = 123;
```

```
    // must box the value
    IPrint printer = myval;
    printer.Print();
  }
}
```

As another example, consider that the System.Int32 type supports the IConvertible interface. However, most of the IConvertible interface methods are implemented explicitly. Therefore, even if you want to call an IConvertible method, such as IConvertible.ToBoolean on a simple int, you must box it first.

■**Note** Typically, you want to rely upon the external class System.Convert to do a conversion like the one mentioned previously. I only mention calling directly through IConvertible as an example.

Efficiency and Confusion

As you might expect, boxing and unboxing are not the most efficient operations in the world. What's worse is that the C# compiler silently does the boxing for you. You really must take care to know when boxing is occurring. Unboxing is usually more explicit, since you typically must do a cast operation to extract the value from the box, but there is an implicit case I'll cover soon. Either way, you must pay attention to the efficiency aspect of things. For example, consider a container type, such as a System.Collections.ArrayList. It contains all of its values as references to type object. If you were to insert a bunch of value types into it, they would all be boxed! Thankfully, generics, which were introduced in C# 2.0 and .NET 2.0 and are covered in Chapter 10, can solve this inefficiency for you. However, note that boxing is inefficient and should be avoided as much as possible. Unfortunately, since boxing is an implicit operation in C#, it takes a keen eye to find all of the cases of boxing. The best tool to use if you're in doubt whether boxing is occurring or not is ILDASM. Using ILDASM, you can examine the IL code generated for your methods, and the box operations are clearly identifiable. You can find ILDASM.exe in the .NET SDK \bin folder.

As mentioned previously, unboxing is normally an explicit operation introduced by a cast from the boxing object reference to a value of the boxed type. However, unboxing is implicit in one notable case. Remember how I talked about the differences in how the this reference behaves within methods of classes vs. methods of structs? The main difference is that, for value types, the this reference acts as either a ref or an out parameter, depending on the situation. So when you call a method on a value type, the hidden this parameter within the method must be a managed pointer rather than a reference. The compiler handles this easily when you call directly through a value-type instance. However, when calling a virtual method or an interface method through a boxed instance—thus, through an object—the CLR must unbox the value instance so that it can obtain the managed pointer to the value type contained within the box. After passing the managed pointer to the contained value type's method as the this pointer, the method can modify the fields through the this pointer, and it will apply the changes to the value contained within the box. Be aware of hidden unboxing operations if you're calling methods on a value through a box object.

■**Note** Unboxing operations in the CLR are not inefficient in and of themselves. The inefficiency stems from the fact that C# typically combines that unboxing operation with a copy of the value.

System.Object

Every object in the CLR derives from System.Object. Object is the base type of every type. In C#, the object keyword is an alias for System.Object. It can be convenient that every type in the CLR and in C# derives from Object. For example, you can treat a collection of instances of multiple types homogenously simply by casting them to Object references.

Even System.ValueType derives from Object. However, some special rules govern obtaining an Object reference. On reference types, you can turn a reference of class A into a reference of class Object with a simple implicit conversion. Going the other direction requires a runtime type check and an explicit cast using the familiar cast syntax of preceding the instance to convert with the new type in parentheses. Obtaining an Object reference directly on a value type is, technically, impossible. Semantically, this makes sense, because value types can live on the stack. It can be dangerous for you to obtain a reference to a transient value instance and store it away for later use if, potentially, the value instance is gone by the time you finally use the stored reference. For this reason, obtaining an Object reference on a value type instance involves a boxing operation, as described in the previous section.

The definition of the System.Object class is as follows:

```
public class Object
{
    public Object();

    public virtual void Finalize();

    public virtual bool Equals( object obj );
    public static bool Equals( object obj1,
                               object obj2 );

    public virtual int GetHashCode();
    public Type GetType();
    protected object MemberwiseClone();
    public static bool ReferenceEquals( object obj1,
                                        object obj2 );
    public virtual string ToString();
}
```

Object provides several methods, which the designers of the CLI/CLR deemed to be important and germane for each object. The methods dealing with equality deserve an entire discussion devoted to them; I cover them in detail in the next section. Object provides a GetType method to obtain the runtime type of any object running in the CLR. Such a capability is extremely handy when coupled with reflection—the capability to examine types in the system at run time. GetType returns an object of type Type, which represents the real, or concrete, type of the object. Using this object, you can determine everything about the type of the object on which GetType is called. Also, given two references of type Object, you can compare the result of calling GetType on both of them to find out if they're actually instances of the same concrete type.

System.Object contains a method named MemberwiseClone, which returns a shallow copy of the object. I have more to say about this method in Chapter 13. When MemberwiseClone creates the copy, all value type fields are copied on a bit-by-bit basis, whereas all fields that are references are simply copied such that the new copy and the original both contain references to the same object. When you want to make a copy of an object, you may or may not desire this behavior. Therefore, if objects support copying, you should consider supporting ICloneable and do the correct thing in the implementation of that interface. Also, note that this method is declared as protected. The main reason for this is so that only the class for the object being copied can call it, since MemberwiseClone can create an object without calling its instance constructor. Such behavior could potentially be destabilizing if it were made public.

> **Note** Be sure to read more about `ICloneable` in Chapter 13 before deciding whether to implement this interface.

Four of the methods on `Object` are virtual, and if the default implementations of the methods inside `Object` are not appropriate, you should override them. `ToString` is useful when generating textual, or human-readable, output and a string representing the object is required. For example, during development, you may need the ability to trace an object out to a debug output at run time. In such cases, it makes sense to override `ToString` so that it provides detailed information about the object and its internal state. The default version of `ToString` simply calls the `ToString` implementation on the `Type` object returned from a call to `GetType`, thus providing the name of the object's type. It's more useful than nothing, but it's probably not useful enough for you if you need to call `ToString` on an object in the first place.[2] Try to avoid adding side effects to the `ToString` implementation, since the Visual Studio debugger can call it to display information at debug time. In fact, `ToString` is most useful for debugging purposes and rarely useful otherwise.

The `Finalize` method deserves special mention. C# doesn't allow you to explicitly override this method. Also, it doesn't allow you to call this method on an object. If you need to override this method for a class, you can use the destructor syntax in C#. I have much more to say about destructors and finalizers in Chapter 13.

Equality and What It Means

Equality between reference types that derive from `System.Object` is a tricky issue. By default, the equality semantics provided by `Object.Equals` represent identity equivalence. What that means is that the test returns `true` if two references point to the same instance of an object. However, you can change the semantic meaning of `Object.Equals` to value equivalence. That means that two references to two entirely different instances of an object may equate to `true` as long as the internal states of the two instances match. Overriding `Object.Equals` is such a sticky issue that I've devoted several sections within Chapter 13 to the subject.

The IComparable Interface

The `System.IComparable` interface is a system-defined interface that objects can choose to implement if they support ordering. If it makes sense for your object to support ordering in collection classes that provide sorting capabilities, then you should implement this interface. For example, it may seem obvious, but `System.Int32`, aliased by `int` in C#, implements `IComparable`. In Chapter 13, I show how you can effectively implement this interface and its generic cousin, `IComparable<T>`.

Creating Objects

Object creation is a topic that looks simple on the surface, but in reality is relatively complex under the hood. You need to be intimately familiar with what operations take place during creation of a new object instance or value instance in order to write constructor code effectively and use field initializers effectively. Also, in the CLR, not only do object instances have constructors, but so do the types they're based on. By that, I mean that even the struct and the class types have a constructor,

---

2. Be sure to read Chapter 8, where I give reasons why `Object.ToString` is not what you want when creating software for localization to various locales and cultures.

which is represented by a static constructor definition. Constructors allow you to get work done at the point the type is loaded and initialized into the application domain.

The new Keyword

The new keyword lets you create new instances of objects or values. However, it behaves slightly differently when used with value types than with object types. For example, new doesn't always allocate space on the heap in C#. Let's discuss what it does with value types first.

Using new with Value Types

The new keyword is only required for value types when you need to invoke one of the constructors for the type. Otherwise, value types simply have space reserved on the stack for them, and the client code must initialize them fully before you can use them. I covered this in the "Value Type Definitions" section on constructors in value types.

Using new with Class Types

You need the new operator to create objects of class type. In this case, the new operator allocates space on the heap for the object being created. If it fails to find space, it will throw an exception of type System.OutOfMemoryException, thus aborting the rest of the object-creation process.

After it allocates the space, all of the fields of the object are initialized to their default values. This is similar to what the compiler-generated default constructor does for value types. For reference-type fields, they are set to null. For value-type fields, their underlying memory slots are filled with all zeros. Thus, the net effect is that all fields in the new object are initialized to either null or 0. Once this is done, the CLR calls the appropriate constructor for the object instance. The constructor selected is based upon the parameters given and is matched using the overloaded method parameter matching algorithm in C#. The new operator also sets up the hidden this parameter for the constructor, which is a read-only reference that references the new object created on the heap, and that reference's type is the same as the class type. Consider the following example:

```
public class MyClass
{
    public MyClass( int x, int y )
    {
        this.x = x;
        this.y = y;
    }

    public int x;
    public int y;
}

public class EntryPoint
{
    static void Main()
    {
        // We can't do this!
        // MyClass objA = new MyClass();

        MyClass objA = new MyClass( 1, 2 );
        System.Console.WriteLine( "objA.x = {0}, objA.y = {1}",
                                  objA.x, objA.y );
    }
}
```

In the Main method, notice that you cannot create a new instance of MyClass by calling the default constructor. The C# compiler doesn't create a default constructor for a class unless no other constructors are defined. The rest of the code is fairly straightforward. I create a new instance of MyClass and then output its values to the console. Shortly, in the section titled "Instance Constructor and Creation Ordering," I cover the minute details of object instance creation and constructors.

Field Initialization

When defining a class, it is sometimes convenient to assign the fields a value at the point where the field is declared. The fact is, you can assign a field from any immediate value or any callable method as long as the method is not called on the instance of the object being created. For example, you can initialize fields based upon the return value from a static method on the same class. Let's look at an example:

```
using System;

public class A
{
    private static int InitX()
    {
        Console.WriteLine( "A.InitX()" );
        return 1;
    }
    private static int InitY()
    {
        Console.WriteLine( "A.InitY()" );
        return 2;
    }
    private static int InitA()
    {
        Console.WriteLine( "A.InitA()" );
        return 3;
    }
    private static int InitB()
    {
        Console.WriteLine( "A.InitB()" );
        return 4;
    }

    private int y = InitY();
    private int x = InitX();

    private static int a = InitA();
    private static int b = InitB();
}

public class EntryPoint
{
    static void Main()
    {
        A a = new A();
    }
}
```

Notice that you're assigning all of the fields using field initializers and setting the fields to the return value from the methods called. All of those methods called during field initialization are

static, which helps reinforce a couple of important points regarding field initialization. The output
from the preceding code is as follows:

```
A.InitA()
A.InitB()
A.InitY()
A.InitX()
```

Notice that two of the fields, a and b, are static fields, whereas the fields x and y are instance
fields. The runtime initializes the static fields before the class type is used for the first time in this
application domain. In the next section, "Static (Class) Constructors," I show how you can relax the
CLR's timing of initializing the static fields.

During construction of the instance, the instance field initializers are invoked. As expected,
proof of that appears in the console output after the static field initializers have run. Note one
important point: Notice the ordering of the output regarding the instance initializers and compare
that with the ordering of the fields declared in the class itself. You'll see that field initialization,
whether it's static or instance initialization, occurs in the order in which the fields are listed in the
class definition. Sometimes this ordering can be important if your static fields are based on expressions or methods that expect other fields in the same class to be initialized first. You should avoid
writing such code at all costs. In fact, any code that requires you to think about the ordering of the
declaration of your fields in your class is bad code. If initialization ordering matters, you should
consider initializing all of your fields in the body of the static constructor. That way, people maintaining your code at a later date won't be unpleasantly surprised when they reorder the fields in
your class for some reason.

Static (Class) Constructors

I already touched upon static constructors in the "Fields" section, but let's look at them in a little
more detail. A class can have at most one static constructor, and that static constructor cannot
accept any parameters. Static constructors can never be invoked directly. Instead, the CLR invokes
them when it needs to initialize the type for a given application domain. The static constructor is
called before an instance of the given class is first created or before some other static fields on the
class are referenced. Let's modify the previous field initialization example to include a static constructor and examine the output:

```
using System;

public class A
{
    static A()
    {
        Console.WriteLine( "static A::A()" );
    }

    private static int InitX()
    {
        Console.WriteLine( "A.InitX()" );
        return 1;
    }
    private static int InitY()
    {
        Console.WriteLine( "A.InitY()" );
        return 2;
    }
```

```csharp
    private static int InitA()
    {
        Console.WriteLine( "A.InitA()" );
        return 3;
    }
    private static int InitB()
    {
        Console.WriteLine( "A.InitB()" );
        return 4;
    }

    private int y = InitY();
    private int x = InitX();

    private static int a = InitA();
    private static int b = InitB();
}

public class EntryPoint
{
    static void Main()
    {
        A a = new A();
    }
}
```

I've added the static constructor and want to see that it has been called in the output. The output from the previous code is as follows:

```
A.InitA()
A.InitB()
static A::A()
A.InitY()
A.InitX()
```

Of course, the static constructor was called before an instance of the class was created. However, notice the important ordering that occurs. The static field initializers are executed before the body of the static constructor executes. This ensures that the instance fields are initialized properly before possibly being referenced within the static constructor body.

It is the default behavior of the CLR to call the type initializer before any member of the type is accessed. By that, I mean that the type initializer will execute before any code accesses a field or a method on the class or before an object is created from the class. However, you can apply a metadata attribute defined in the CLR, beforefieldinit, to the class to relax the rules a little bit. In the absence of the beforefieldinit attribute, the CLR is required to call the type initializer before any member on the class is touched. With the beforefieldinit attribute, the CLR is free to defer the type initialization to the point right before the first static field access and not any time sooner. This means that if beforefieldinit is set on the class, you can call instance constructors and methods all day long without requiring the type initializer to execute first. But as soon as anything tries to access a static field on the class, the CLR invokes the type initializer first. Keep in mind that the beforefieldinit attribute gives the CLR this leeway to defer the type initialization to a later time, but the CLR could still initialize the type long before the first static field is accessed.

The C# compiler sets the beforefieldinit attribute on all classes that don't specifically define a static constructor. To see this in action, you can use ILDASM to examine the IL generated for the previous two examples. For the example in the previous section, where I didn't specifically define a static constructor, the class A metadata looks like the following:

```
.class public auto ansi beforefieldinit A
       extends [mscorlib]System.Object
{
} // end of class A
```

For the class A metadata in the example in this section, the metadata looks like the following:

```
.class public auto ansi A
       extends [mscorlib]System.Object
{
} // end of class A
```

This behavior of the C# compiler makes good sense. When you explicitly define a type initializer, you usually want to guarantee that it will execute before anything in the class is utilized or before any instance of the class is created. However, if you don't provide an explicit type initializer and you do have static field initializers, the C# compiler will create a type initializer of sorts that merely initializes all of the static fields. Since you didn't provide user code for the type initializer, the C# compiler can let the class defer the static field initializers until one of the static fields is accessed.

After all of this discussion regarding beforefieldinit, you should make note of one important point. Suppose you have a class similar to the ones in the examples, where a static field is initialized based upon the result of a method call. If your class doesn't provide an explicit type initializer, it would be erroneous to assume that the code called during the static field initialization will be called prior to an object creation based on this class. For example, consider the following code:

```
using System;

public class A
{
    public A()
    {
        Console.WriteLine( "A.A()" );
    }

    static int InitX()
    {
        Console.WriteLine( "A.InitX()" );
        return 1;
    }

    public int x = InitX();
}

public class EntryPoint
{
    static void Main()
    {
        // No guarantee A.InitX() is called before this!
        A a = new A();
    }
}
```

If your implementation of InitX contains some side effects that are required to run before an object instance can be created from this class, then you would be better off putting that code in a static constructor so that the compiler will not apply the beforefieldinit metadata attribute to the class. Otherwise, there's no guarantee that your code with the side effect in it will run prior to a class instance being created.

Instance Constructor and Creation Ordering

Instance constructors follow a lot of the same rules as static constructors, except they're more flexible and powerful, so they have some added rules of their own. Let's examine those rules.

Instance constructors can have what's called an *initializer expression*. An initializer expression allows instance constructors to defer some of their work to other instance constructors within the class, or more importantly, to base class constructors during object initialization. This is important if you rely on the base class instance constructors to initialize the inherited members. Remember, constructors are never inherited, so you must go through explicit means such as this in order to call the base class constructors during initialization if you need to.

If your class doesn't implement an instance constructor at all, the compiler will generate a default parameterless instance constructor for you, which really only does one thing—it merely calls the base class default constructor through the base keyword. If the base class doesn't have an accessible default constructor, a compiler error is generated. For example, the following code doesn't compile:

```
public class A
{
   public A(int x) {
      this.x = x;
   }

   private int x;
}

public class B : A
{
}

public class EntryPoint
{
   static void Main()
   {
      B b = new B();
   }
}
```

Can you see why it won't compile? The problem is that a class with no explicit constructors is given a default parameterless constructor by the compiler; this constructor merely calls the base class parameterless constructor, which is exactly what the compiler tries to do for class B. However, the problem is that, since class A does have an explicit instance constructor defined, the compiler doesn't produce a default constructor for class A. So, there is no accessible default constructor available on class A for class B's compiler-provided default constructor to call. Therein lies another caveat to inheritance. In order for the previous example to compile, either you must explicitly provide a default constructor for class A, or class B needs an explicit constructor. Now, let's look at an example that demonstrates the ordering of events during instance initialization:

```
using System;

class Base
{
   public Base( int x )
   {
```

```
        Console.WriteLine( "Base.Base(int)" );
        this.x = x;
    }

    private static int InitX()
    {
        Console.WriteLine( "Base.InitX()" );
        return 1;
    }

    public int x = InitX();
}

class Derived : Base
{
    public Derived( int a )
        :base( a )
    {
        Console.WriteLine( "Derived.Derived(int)" );
        this.a = a;
    }

    public Derived( int a, int b )
        :this( a )
    {
        Console.WriteLine( "Derived.Derived(int, int)" );
        this.a = a;
        this.b = b;
    }

    private static int InitA()
    {
        Console.WriteLine( "Derived.InitA()" );
        return 3;
    }

    private static int InitB()
    {
        Console.WriteLine( "Derived.InitB()" );
        return 4;
    }

    public int a = InitA();
    public int b = InitB();
}

public class EntryPoint
{
    static void Main()
    {
        Derived b = new Derived( 1, 2 );
    }
}
```

Before I start detailing the ordering of events here, look at the output from this code:

```
Derived.InitA()
Derived.InitB()
Base.InitX()
Base.Base(int)
Derived.Derived(int)
Derived.Derived(int, int)
```

Are you able to determine why the ordering is the way it is? It can be quite confusing upon first glance, so let's take a moment to examine what's going on here. The first line of the Main method creates a new instance of class Derived. As you see in the output, the constructor is called. But, it's called in the last line of the output! Clearly, a lot of things are happening before the constructor body for class Derived executes.

At the bottom, you see the call to the Derived constructor that takes two int parameters. Notice that this constructor has an initializer using the this keyword. This delegates construction work to the Derived constructor that takes one int parameter.

The Derived constructor that takes one int parameter also has an initialization list, except it uses the base keyword, thus calling the constructor for the class Base, which takes one int parameter. However, if a constructor has an initializer that uses the base keyword, the constructor will invoke the field initializers defined in the class before it passes control to the base class constructor. And remember, the ordering of the initializers is the same as the ordering of the fields in the class definition. This behavior explains the first two entries in the output. The output shows that the initializers for the fields in Derived are invoked first, before the initializers in Base.

After the initializers for Derived execute, control is then passed to the Base constructor that takes one int parameter. Notice that class Base has an instance field with an initializer, too. The same behavior happens in Base as it does in Derived, so before the constructor body for the Base constructor is executed, the constructor implicitly calls the initializers for the class. I have more to say about why this behavior is defined in this way later in this section, and it involves virtual methods. This is why the third entry in the output trace is that of Base.InitX.

After the Base initializers are done, you find yourself in the block of the Base constructor. Once that constructor body runs to completion, control returns to the Derived constructor that takes one int parameter, and execution finally ends up in that constructor's code block. Once it's done there, it finally gets to execute the body of the constructor that was called when the code created the instance of Derived in the Main method. Clearly, a lot of initialization work is going on under the covers when an object instance is created.

As promised, I'll explain why the field initializers of a derived class are invoked before the constructor for the base class is called through an initializer on the derived constructor, and the reason is subtle. Virtual methods, which I cover in more detail in the section titled "Inheritance and Virtual Methods," work inside constructors in the CLR and in C#.

■Note If you're coming from a C++ programming environment, you should recognize that this behavior of calling virtual methods in constructors is completely different. In C++, you're never supposed to rely on virtual method calls in constructors, since the vtable is not set up while the constructor body is running.

Let's look at an example:

```
using System;

public class A
{
```

```
    public virtual void DoSomething()
    {
        Console.WriteLine( "A.DoSomething()" );
    }

    public A()
    {
        DoSomething();
    }
}

public class B : A
{
    public override void DoSomething()
    {
        Console.WriteLine( "B.DoSomething()" );
        Console.WriteLine( "x = {0}", x );
    }

    public B()
        :base()
    {
    }

    private int x = 123;
}

public class EntryPoint
{
    static void Main()
    {
        B b = new B();
    }
}
```

The output from this code is as follows:

```
B.DoSomething()
x = 123
```

As you can see, the virtual invocation works just fine from the constructor of A. Notice that
B.DoSomething uses the x field. Now, if the field initializers were not run before the base invocation,
imagine the calamity that would ensue when the virtual method is invoked from the class A constructor. That, in a nutshell, is why the field initializers are run before the base constructor is called
if the constructor has an initializer. The field initializers are also run before the constructor's body is
entered, if there is no initializer defined for the constructor.

Destroying Objects

If you thought object creation was complicated, hold onto your hats. As you know, the CLR environment contains a garbage collector, which manages memory on your behalf. You can create new
objects as much as you want, but you never have to worry about freeing their memory explicitly. A
huge majority of bugs in native applications come from memory allocation/deallocation mis-

matches, otherwise known as memory leaks. Garbage collection is a technique meant to avoid that type of bug, since the execution environment now handles the tracking of object references and destroys the object instances when they're no longer in use.

The CLR tracks every single managed object reference in the system that is just a plain-old object reference that you're already used to. Once the CLR realizes that an object is no longer reachable via a reference, it flags the object for deletion. The next time the garbage collector compacts the heap, these flagged objects either have their memory reclaimed or are moved over into a queue for deletion if they have a finalizer. It is the responsibility of another thread, the finalizer thread, to iterate over this queue of objects and call their finalizers before freeing their memory. Once the finalizers have completed, the memory for the object is freed on the next collection pass, and the object is completely dead, never to return.

Finalizers

There are many reasons why you should rarely write a finalizer. When used unnecessarily, finalizers can degrade the performance of the CLR, because finalizable objects live longer than their nonfinalizable counterparts. Even allocating finalizable objects is more costly. Additionally, finalizers are difficult to write, because you cannot make any assumptions about the state that other objects in the system are in.

When the finalization thread iterates through the objects in the finalization queue, it calls the Finalize method on each object. The Finalize method is an override of a virtual method on System.Object; however, it's illegal in C# to explicitly override this method. Instead, you write a destructor that looks like a method that has no return type, cannot have access modifiers applied to it, accepts no parameters, and whose identifier is the class name immediately prefixed with a tilde. Destructors cannot be called explicitly in C#, and they are not inherited, just as constructors are not inherited. A class can have only one destructor.

When an object's finalizer is called, each finalizer in an inheritance chain is called, from the most derived class to the least derived class. Consider the following example:

```
using System;

public class Base
{
    ~Base()
    {
        Console.WriteLine( "Base.~Base()" );
    }
}

public class Derived : Base
{
    ~Derived()
    {
        Console.WriteLine( "Derived.~Derived()" );
    }
}

public class EntryPoint
{
    static void Main()
    {
        Derived derived = new Derived();
    }
}
```

As expected, the result of executing this code is as follows:

```
Derived.~Derived()
Base.~Base()
```

Although the garbage collector now handles the task of cleaning up memory so that you don't have to worry about it, you have a whole new host of concerns to deal with when it comes to the destruction of objects. I've mentioned that finalizers run on a separate thread in the CLR. Therefore, whatever objects you use inside your destructor must be thread-safe, but the odds are you should not even be using other objects in your finalizer, since they may have already been finalized or destroyed. This includes objects that are fields of the class that contains the finalizer. You have no guaranteed way of knowing exactly when your finalizer will be called or in what order the finalizer will be called between two independent or dependent objects. This is one more reason why you shouldn't introduce interdependencies on objects in the destructor code block. After all this dust has settled, it starts to become clear that you shouldn't do much inside a finalizer except basic housecleaning, if anything.

Essentially, you only need to write a finalizer when your object manages some sort of unmanaged resource. However, if the resource is managed through a standard Win32 handle, I highly recommend that you use the SafeHandle type to manage it. Writing a wrapper such as SafeHandle is tricky business, mainly because of the finalizer and all of the things you must do to guarantee that it will get called in all situations, even the diabolical ones such as an out-of-memory condition or in the face of unexpected exceptions. Finally, any object that has a finalizer must implement the Disposable pattern, which I cover in the forthcoming section titled "Disposable Objects."

Deterministic Destruction

So far, everything that you've seen regarding destruction of objects in the garbage-collected environment of the CLR is known as nondeterministic destruction. That means that you cannot predict the timing of the execution of the destructor code for an object. If you come from a native C++ world, you'll recognize that this is completely different.

In C++, heap object destructors are called when the user explicitly deletes the object. With the CLR, the garbage collector handles that for you, so you don't have to worry about forgetting to do it. However, for a C++-based stack object, the destructor is called as soon as the execution scope in which that object is created is exited. This is known as deterministic destruction and is extremely useful for managing resources.

Let's examine the case of an object that holds a system file handle. You can use such a stack-based object in C++ to manage the lifetime of the file handle. When the object is created, the constructor of the object acquires the file handle, and as soon as the object goes out of scope, the destructor is called and its code closes the file handle. This frees the client code of the object from having to manage the resource explicitly. It also prevents resource leaks, because if an exception is thrown from that code block where the object is used, C++ guarantees that the destructors for all stack-based objects will be called no matter how the block is exited.

This idiom is called Resource Acquisition Is Initialization (RAII), and it's extremely useful for managing resources. C# has almost completely lost this capability of automatic cleanup in a timely manner. Of course, if you had an object that held a file open and closed it in the destructor, you wouldn't have to worry about *whether* the file gets closed or not, but you will definitely have to consider *when* it gets closed. The fact is, you don't know exactly when it will get closed if the code to close it is in the finalizer, which is fallout from nondeterministic finalization. For this very reason, it would be bad design to put resource management code, such as closing file handles, in the finalizer. What if the object is already marked for finalization but has not had its finalizer called yet, and you try to create a new instance of the object whose constructor tries to open the resource? Well, with an exclusive-access resource, the code will fail in the constructor for the new instance. I'm sure you'll agree that this is not desired, and most definitely would not be expected by the client of your object.

Let's revisit the finalization ordering problem mentioned a little while ago. If an object contains another object, and the outer object is put on the finalization queue, the internal objects possibly are, too. However, the finalizer thread just goes through the queue finalizing the objects individually. It doesn't care who was an internal object of whom. So clearly, it's possible that if destructor code accesses an object reference in a field, that object could already have been finalized. Accessing such a field produces the dreaded *undefined behavior exception*.

This is a perfect example of how the garbage collector removes one bit of complexity but replaces it with another. In reality, you should avoid finalizers if possible. Not only do they add complexity, but they hamper memory management, since they cause objects to live longer than objects with no finalizer. This is because they're put on the finalization list, and it is the responsibility of an entirely different thread to clean up the finalization list. In the "Disposable Objects" section and in Chapter 13, I describe an interface, IDisposable, that was included in the Framework Class Library in order to facilitate a form of deterministic destruction.

Exception Handling

It's important to note the behavior of exceptions when inside the scope of a finalizer. If you come from a native C++ world, you know that it is bad behavior to allow exceptions to propagate out from a destructor, because in certain situations, that may cause your application to abort. In C#, an exception thrown in a finalizer that leaves the block uncaught will be treated as an unhandled exception, and by default, the process will be terminated after notifying you of the exception.

■Note This behavior starting with .NET 2.0 is a breaking change from .NET 1.1. Before .NET 2.0, unhandled exceptions in the finalization thread were swallowed after notifying the user, and the process was allowed to continue. The danger with this behavior is that the system could be running in a half-baked or inconsistent state. Therefore, it's best to kill the process rather than run the risk of it causing more damage. In Chapter 7, I show you how you can force the CLR to revert to the pre-2.0 behavior if you absolutely must.

Disposable Objects

In the previous section on finalizers, I discussed the differences between deterministic and nondeterministic finalization, and you also saw that you lose a lot of convenience along with deterministic finalization. For that reason, the IDisposable interface exists, and in fact, it was only added during beta testing of the first release of the .NET Framework when developers were shouting about not having any form of deterministic finalization built into the framework. It's not a perfect replacement for deterministic finalization, but it does get the job done at the expense of adding complexity to the client of your objects.

The IDisposable Interface

The IDisposable definition is as follows:

```
public interface IDisposable
{
    void Dispose();
}
```

Notice that it has only one method, Dispose, and it is within this method's implementation that the dirty work is done. Thus, you should completely clean up your object and release all resources inside Dispose. Even though the client code rather than the system calls Dispose automatically, it's the client code's way of saying, "I'm done with this object and don't intend to use it ever again."

Even though the IDisposable pattern provides a form of deterministic destruction, it is not a perfect solution. Using IDisposable, the onus is thrown on the client to ensure that the Dispose method is called. There is no way for the client to rely upon the system, or the compiler, to call it for them automatically. C# makes this a little easier to manage in the face of exceptions by overloading the using keyword, which I discuss in the next section.

When you implement Dispose, you normally implement the class in such a way that the finalizer code reuses Dispose. This way, if the client code never calls Dispose, the finalizer code will take care of it at finalization time. Another factor makes implementing IDisposable painful for objects, and that is that you must chain calls of IDisposable if your object contains references to other objects that support IDisposable. This makes designing classes a little more difficult, since you must know whether a class that you use for a field type implements IDisposable, and if it does, you must implement IDisposable and you must make sure to call its Dispose method inside yours.

Given all of this discussion regarding IDisposable, you can definitely start to see how the garbage collector adds complexity to design, even though it reduces the chance for memory bugs. I'm not trying to say the garbage collector is worthless; in fact, it's very valuable when used appropriately. However, as with any design, engineering decisions typically have pros and cons in both directions.

Let's look at an example implementation of IDisposable:

```csharp
using System;

public class A : IDisposable
{
    private bool disposed = false;
    public void Dispose( bool disposing )
    {
        if( !disposed ) {
            if( disposing ) {
                // It is safe to access other objects here.
            }

            Console.WriteLine( "Cleaning up object" );
            disposed = true;
        }
    }
    public void Dispose()
    {
        Dispose( true );
        GC.SuppressFinalize( this );
    }

    public void DoSomething()
    {
        Console.WriteLine( "A.SoSomething()" );
    }

    ~A()
    {
        Console.WriteLine( "Finalizing" );
```

```
        Dispose( false );
    }
}

public class EntryPoint
{
    static void Main()
    {
        A a = new A();
        try {
            a.DoSomething();
        }
        finally {
            a.Dispose();
        }
    }
}
```

Let's go over this code in detail to see what's really going on. The first thing to notice in the class is an internal Boolean field that registers whether or not the object has been disposed. It's there because it's perfectly legal for client code to call Dispose multiple times. Therefore, you need some way to know that you've done the work already.

You'll also see that I've implemented the finalizer in terms of the Dispose implementation. Notice that I have two overloads of Dispose. I've done this so that I know inside the Dispose(bool) method whether I got here through IDisposable.Dispose or through the destructor. It tells me whether I can safely access contained objects inside the method.

One last point: The Dispose method makes a call to GC.SuppressFinalize. This method on the garbage collector allows you to keep the garbage collector from finalizing an object. If the client code calls Dispose, and if the Dispose method completely cleans up all resources, including all the work a finalizer would have done, then there is no need for this object to ever be finalized. You can call SuppressFinalize to keep this object from being finalized. This handy optimization helps the garbage collector get rid of your object in a timely manner when all references to it cease to exist.

Now, let's take a look at how to use this disposable object. Notice the try/finally block within the Main method. I cover exceptions in Chapter 7. For now, understand that this try/finally construct is a way of guaranteeing that certain code will be executed no matter how a code block exits. In this case, no matter how the execution flow leaves the try block—whether normally, through a return statement, or even by exception—the code in the finally block will execute. View the finally block as a sort of safety net. It is within this finally block that you call Dispose on the object. No matter what, Dispose will get called.

This is a perfect example of how nondeterministic finalization throws the onus on the client code, or the user, to clean up the object, whereas deterministic finalization doesn't require the user to bother typing these ugly try/finally blocks or to call Dispose. This definitely makes life harder on the user, as it makes it much more tedious to create exception-safe and/or exception-neutral code. The designers of C# have tried to lessen this load by overloading the using keyword. Although it lessens the load, it doesn't remove the burden put on the client code altogether.

■**Note** C++/CLI allows you to use RAII in a way familiar to C++ developers without requiring you to call Dispose explicitly or use a using block. It would be nice if C# could do the same, but it would cause too much of a calamity to introduce such a breaking change in the language at this point.

The using Keyword

The using keyword was overloaded to support the IDisposable pattern, and the general idea is that the using statement acquires the resources within the parentheses following the using keyword, while the scope of these local variables is confined to the declaration scope of the following curly braces.

Let's look at a modified form of the previous example:

```
using System;

public class A : IDisposable
{
   private bool disposed = false;
   public void Dispose( bool disposing )
   {
      if( !disposed ) {
         if( disposing ) {
            // It is safe to access other objects here.
         }

         Console.WriteLine( "Cleaning up object" );
         disposed = true;
      }
   }
   public void Dispose()
   {
      Dispose( true );
      GC.SuppressFinalize( this );
   }

   public void DoSomething()
   {
      Console.WriteLine( "A.SoSomething()" );
   }

   ~A()
   {
      Console.WriteLine( "Finalizing" );
      Dispose( false );
   }
}

public class EntryPoint
{
   static void Main()
   {
      using( A a = new A() ) {
         a.DoSomething();
      }

      using( A a = new A(), b = new A() ) {
         a.DoSomething();
         b.DoSomething();
      }
   }
}
```

The meat of the changes is in the Main method. Notice that I've replaced the ugly try/finally construct with the cleaner using statement. Under the covers, the using statement expands to the try/finally construct I already had. Now, granted, this code is much easier to read and understand. However, it still doesn't remove the burden from the client code of having to remember to use the using statement in the first place.

The using statement requires that all resources acquired in the acquisition process be implicitly convertible to IDisposable. That is, they must implement IDisposable. If they don't, you'll see a compiler warning.

Method Parameter Types

Method parameters follow the same general rules as those of C/C++. That is, by default, parameters declare a variable identifier that is valid for the duration and scope of the method itself. There are no const parameters as in C++, and method parameters may be reassigned at will. Unless the parameter is declared a certain way as a ref or an out parameter, such reassignment will remain local to the method.

I have found that one of the biggest stumbling blocks for C++ developers in C# is dealing with the semantics of variables passed to methods. Since the dominant type of type instance within the CLR is a reference, variables to such objects merely point to their instances on the heap—i.e., arguments are passed to the method using reference semantics. C++ developers are used to copies of variables being made as they're passed into methods by default, unless they're passed by reference or as pointers. In other words, arguments are passed using value semantics.

In C#, arguments are actually passed by value. However, for references, the value that is copied is the reference itself and not the object that it references. Changes in state that are made to the reference object within the method are visible to the caller of the method.

Since there is no notion of a const parameter within C#, you should create immutable objects to pass where you would have wanted to pass a const parameter. I have more to say about immutable objects in Chapter 13.

■**Note** Those C++ developers who are used to using handle/body idioms to implement copy-on-write semantics must take these facts into consideration. It doesn't mean that you cannot employ those idioms in C#; rather, it just means that you must implement them differently.

Value Arguments

In reality, all parameters passed to methods are value arguments, assuming they're normal, plain, undecorated parameters that get passed to a method. By undecorated, I mean they don't have special keywords such as out, ref, and params attached to them. They can, however, have attributes attached to them just as almost everything else in the CLR type system can. As with all parameters, the identifier is in scope within the method block following the parameter list (i.e., within the curly braces), and the method receives a copy of the passed variable at invocation time. Be careful about what this means, though. If the passed variable is a struct, or value type, then the method receives a copy of the value. Any changes made locally to the value are not seen by the caller. If the passed variable is a reference to an object on the heap, as any variable for a class instance is, then the method receives a copy of the *reference*. Thus, any changes made to the object through the reference are seen by the caller of the method.

ref Arguments

Passing parameters by reference is indicated by placing the ref modifier ahead of the parameter type in the parameter list for the method. When a variable is passed by reference, a new copy of the variable is not made, and the caller's variable is directly affected by any actions within the method. As is usually the case in the CLR, this means two slightly different things, depending on whether the variable is an instance of a value type (struct) or an object (class).

When a value instance is passed by reference, a copy of the caller's value is not made. It's as if the parameter were passed as a C++ pointer, even though you access the methods and fields of the variable in the same way as value arguments. When an object (reference) instance is passed by reference, again, no copy of the variable is made, which means that a new reference to the object on the heap is not created. In fact, the variable behaves as if it were a C++ pointer to the reference variable, which could be viewed as a C++ pointer to a pointer. Additionally, the verifier ensures that the variable referenced by the ref parameter has been definitely assigned before the method call. Let's take a look at some examples to put the entire notion of ref parameters into perspective:

```
using System;

public struct MyStruct
{
    public int val;
}

public class EntryPoint
{
    static void Main() {
        MyStruct myValue = new MyStruct();
        myValue.val = 10;

        PassByValue( myValue );
        Console.WriteLine( "Result of PassByValue: myValue.val = {0}",
                           myValue.val );

        PassByRef( ref myValue );
        Console.WriteLine( "Result of PassByRef: myValue.val = {0}",
                           myValue.val );
    }

    static void PassByValue( MyStruct myValue ) {
        myValue.val = 50;
    }

    static void PassByRef( ref MyStruct myValue ) {
        myValue.val = 42;
    }
}
```

This example contains two methods: PassByValue and PassByRef. Both methods modify a field of the value type instance passed in. However, as the following output shows, the PassByValue method modifies a local copy, whereas the PassByRef method modifies the caller's instance as you would expect:

```
Result of PassByValue: myValue.val = 10
Result of PassByRef: myValue.val = 42
```

Also, pay attention to the fact that the ref keyword is required at the point of call into the PassByRef method. This is necessary because the method could be overloaded based upon the ref keyword. In other words, another PassByRef method could just as well have taken a MyStruct by value rather than by ref. Plus, the fact that you have to put the ref keyword on at the point of call makes the code easier to read in my opinion. When programmers read the code at the point of call, they can get a pretty clear idea that the method could make some changes to the object being passed by ref.

Now, let's consider an example that uses an object rather than a value type:

```
using System;

public class EntryPoint
{
    static void Main() {
        object myObject = new Object();

        Console.WriteLine( "myObject.GetHashCode() == {0}",
                           myObject.GetHashCode() );
        PassByRef( ref myObject );
        Console.WriteLine( "myObject.GetHashCode() == {0}",
                           myObject.GetHashCode() );
    }

    static void PassByRef( ref object myObject ) {
        // Assign a new instance to the variable.
        myObject = new Object();
    }
}
```

In this case, the variable passed by reference is an object. But, as I said, instead of the method receiving a copy of the reference, thus creating a new reference to the same object, the original reference is referenced instead. Yes, this can be confusing. In the previous PassByRef method, the reference passed in is reassigned to a new object instance. The original object is left with no references to it, so it is now available for collection. To illustrate that the myObject variable references two different instances between the point before it is called and the point after it is called, I sent the results of myObject.GetHashCode to the console to prove it.

out Parameters

Out parameters are almost identical to ref parameters, with two notable differences. First, instead of using the ref keyword, you use the out keyword, and you still have to provide the out keyword at the point of call as you do with the ref keyword. However, the variable referenced by the out variable is not required to have been definitely assigned before the method is called as it is with ref parameters. That's because the method is not allowed to use the variable for anything useful until it has assigned the variable. For example, the following is valid code:

```
public class EntryPoint
{
    static void Main() {
        object obj;
        PassAsOutParam( out obj );
    }

    static void PassAsOutParam( out object obj ) {
        obj = new object();
    }
}
```

Notice that the `obj` variable in the `Main` method is not directly assigned before the call to `PassAsOutParam`. That's perfectly fine, since it is marked an out parameter. The `PassAsOutParam` method won't be referencing the variable unless it has already assigned it. If you were to replace the two occurrences of `out` with `ref` in the previous code, you would see a compiler error similar to the following:

```
error CS0165: Use of unassigned local variable 'obj'
```

param Arrays

C# makes it a snap to pass a variable list of parameters. Simply declare the last parameter in your parameter list as an array type and precede the array type with the `params` keyword. Now, if the method is invoked with a variable number of parameters, those parameters are passed to the method in the form of an array that you can easily iterate through, and the array type that you use can be based on any valid type. Here's a short example:

```
using System;

public class EntryPoint
{
    static void Main() {
        VarArgs( 42 );
        VarArgs( 42, 43, 44 );
        VarArgs( 44, 56, 23, 234, 45, 123 );
    }

    static void VarArgs( int val1, params int[] vals ) {
        Console.WriteLine( "val1: {0}", val1 );
        foreach( int i in vals ) {
            Console.WriteLine( "vals[]: {0}",
                               i );
        }
        Console.WriteLine();
    }
}
```

In each case, `VarArgs` is called successfully, but in each case, the array referenced by the `vals` parameter is different. As you can see, referencing a variable number of parameters is pretty easy in C#. You can code an efficient `Add` method to a container type using parameter arrays where only one call is necessary to add a variable number of items.

Method Overloading

C# overloading is a compile-time technique in which, at a call point, the compiler chooses a method from a set of methods with the same name. The compiler uses the argument list of the method to choose the method that fits best. The argument types and the `ref`, `out`, and `param` parameter modifiers play a part in method overloading, since they form part of the method signature. Methods without variable-length parameter arrays get preference over those that have them. Similar to C++, the method return type is not part of the signature (except in one rare case of conversion operators, which I cover in Chapter 6). So you cannot have methods within an overloaded class where the only difference is the return type. Finally, if the compiler gets to a point where multiple methods are ambiguous with respect to overloading, it stops with an error.

Overall, there's really nothing different about method overloading in C# compared to C++. It can't possibly cause any runtime exceptions, because the entire algorithm is applied at compile time. When the compiler fails to find an exact match based on the parameters given, it then starts hunting for a best match based on implicit convertibility of the instances in the parameter list. Thus, if a single parameter method accepts an object of type A, and you have passed an object of type B that is derived from type A, in the absence of a method that accepts type B, the compiler will implicitly convert your instance into a type A reference to satisfy the method call. Depending on the situation and the size of the overloaded method set, the selection process can still be a tricky one. I've found that it's best to minimize too many confusing overloads where implicit conversion is necessary to satisfy the resolution. Too many implicit conversions can make code difficult to follow, requiring you to actually execute it in a debugger to see what happens. That makes it hard on maintenance engineers who need to come in behind you and figure out what you were doing. It's not to say that implicit conversion is bad during overload resolution, but just use it judiciously and sparingly to minimize future surprises.

Inheritance and Virtual Methods

C# implements the notion of virtual methods just as the C++ and Java languages do. That's no surprise at all, since C# is an object-oriented language, and virtual methods are the primary mechanism for implementing dynamic polymorphism. That said, some notable differences from those languages deserve special mention.

Virtual and Abstract Methods

You declare a virtual method using either the `virtual` or `abstract` modifiers on the method at the point of declaration. They both introduce the method into the declaration space as one that a deriving class can override. The difference between the two is that abstract methods are required to be overridden, whereas virtual methods are not. Abstract methods are similar to C++ pure virtual methods, except that C++ pure virtual methods may have an implementation associated with them, whereas C# abstract methods may not. Virtual methods, in contrast to abstract methods, are required to have an implementation associated with them. Virtual methods, along with interfaces, are the only means of implementing polymorphism within C#.

■Note Under the covers, the CLR implements virtual methods differently from C++. Whereas C++ can create multiple vtables (dynamic method tables pointing to virtual methods) for an individual object of a class depending on its static hierarchical structure, CLR objects have only one method table that contains both virtual and nonvirtual methods. Additionally, the table in the CLR is built early on in the lifetime of the object. Not only does the creation order of objects affect the ordering of static initializers and constructor calls in a hierarchy, but it also gives C# a capability that C++ lacks. In C#, virtual method calls work when called inside constructor bodies, whereas they don't in C++. For more information on how the CLR manages method tables for object instances, read Don Box and Chris Sells' *Essential .NET, Volume 1: The Common Language Runtime* (Boston, MA: Addison-Wesley Professional, 2002).

---

override and new Methods

To override a method in a derived class, you must tag the method with the `override` modifier. If you don't, you'll get a compiler warning telling you that you need to provide either the new modifier or the override modifier in the derived method declaration. The compiler defaults to using the new modifier, which probably does the exact opposite of what you intended. This behavior is different than C++, since in C++, once a method is marked as virtual, any derived method of the same name and signature is automatically an override of the virtual method, and the virtual modifier on those derived methods is completely optional. Personally, I prefer the fact that C# requires you to tag the overriding method simply for the purpose of code readability. I cannot tell you how many poorly designed C++ code bases I've worked on with deep hierarchies where developers were too lazy to keep tagging the virtual override methods with the virtual keyword. I had no way of knowing if a method overrides a virtual in a base class without looking at the base class declaration. These terribly designed code bases had such deep hierarchies that they forced me to rifle through a whole plethora of files just to find the answer. C# drives a stake through the heart of this problem. Check out the following code:

```
using System;

public class A
{
    public virtual void SomeMethod() {
        Console.WriteLine( "A.SomeMethod" );
    }
}

public class B : A
{
    public void SomeMethod() {
        Console.WriteLine( "B.SomeMethod" );
    }
}

public class EntryPoint
{
    static void Main() {
        B b = new B();
        A a = b;

        a.SomeMethod();
    }
}
```

This code compiles, but not without the following warning:

```
test.cs(12,17): warning CS0114: 'B.SomeMethod()' hides inherited member 'A.SomeMethod()'.
To make the current member override that implementation, add the override keyword.
Otherwise add the new keyword.
```

When the code is executed, A.SomeMethod gets called. So what does the new keyword do? It breaks the virtual chain at that point in the hierarchy. When a virtual method is called through an object reference, the method called is determined from the method tables at run time. If a method is virtual, the runtime searches down through the hierarchy looking for the most derived version of the method, and then it calls that one. However, during the search, if it encounters a method marked with the new modifier, it backs up to the method of the previous class in the hierarchy and uses that one instead. That is why A.SomeMethod is the method that gets called. Had B.SomeMethod been marked as override, then the code would have called B.SomeMethod instead. Since C# defaults to using the new modifier when none of them are present, it throws off the warning possibly to get the attention of those of us who are used to the C++ syntax. Finally, the new modifier is orthogonal to the virtual modifier in meaning, in the sense that the method marked new could either also be virtual or not. In the previous example, I did not also attach the virtual modifier to B.SomeMethod, so there cannot be a class C derived from B that overrides B.SomeMethod, since it's not virtual. Thus, the new keyword not only breaks the virtual chain, but it redefines whether the class and the derived classes from class B will get a virtual SomeMethod.

Another issue to consider with regard to overriding methods is whether to call the base class version of the method and when. In C#, you call the base class version using the base identifier as shown:

```csharp
using System;

public class A
{
    public virtual void SomeMethod() {
        Console.WriteLine( "A.SomeMethod" );
    }
}

public class B : A
{
    public override void SomeMethod() {
        Console.WriteLine( "B.SomeMethod" );
        base.SomeMethod();
    }
}


public class EntryPoint
{
    static void Main() {
        B b = new B();
        A a = b;

        a.SomeMethod();
    }
}
```

As expected, the output of the previous code prints A.SomeMethod on the line after it prints B.SomeMethod. Is this the correct ordering of events? Should it not be the other way around? Shouldn't B.SomeMethod call the base class version before it does its work? The point is that you don't have enough information to answer this question. Therein lies a problem with inheritance and virtual method overrides. How do you know when and if to call the base class method? The answer is that the method should be well documented so that you know how to do the right thing. Thus, inheritance with virtual methods increases your documentation load, because now you must provide the consumers of your class with information above and beyond just the public interface. For example, if you follow the Non-Virtual Interface (NVI) pattern that I describe in Chapter 13, the virtual method in question is protected, so now you must document both public methods and some protected methods, and the virtual methods must clearly state whether the base class should call them and when. Ouch!

sealed Methods

For the reasons stated previously, I believe you should seal your classes by default and only make classes inheritable in well-thought-out circumstances. Many times I see hierarchies where the developer was thinking, "I'll just mark all of my methods as virtual to give my deriving classes the most flexibility." All this does is create a rat's nest of bugs later down the line. This thought pattern is typical of less-experienced designers who are grappling with the complexities of inheritance and virtual methods. The fact is that inheritance coupled with virtual methods is so surprisingly complex that it's best to explicitly turn off the capability rather than leave it wide open for abuse. Therefore, when designing classes, you should prefer to create sealed, noninheritable classes, and you should document the public interface well. Consumers who need to extend the functionality can still do so, but through containment rather than inheritance. Extension through containment coupled with crafty interface definitions is far more powerful than class inheritance.

In rare instances, you're deriving from a class with virtual methods and you want to force the virtual chain for a specific method to end at your override. In other words, you don't want further derived classes to be able to override the virtual method. To do so, you also mark the method with the sealed modifier. As is obvious from the name, it means that no further derived classes can override the method. They can, however, provide a method with the same signature, as long as the method is marked with the new modifier, as discussed in the previous section. In fact, you could mark the new method as virtual, thus starting a new virtual chain in the hierarchy. This is not the same as sealing the entire class, which doesn't even allow a class to derive from this one in the first place. Therefore, if the deriving class is marked as sealed, then marking override methods within that class with sealed is redundant.

A Final Few Words on C# Virtual Methods

Clearly, C# provides a lot of flexible keywords to make some interesting things happen when it comes to inheritance and virtual methods. However, just because the language provides them does not mean that it's wise to use them. Over the past decade, many experts have published countless books describing how to design C++- and Java-based applications safely and effectively. Many times, those works indicate things that you should not do rather than things that you should do. That's because C++, along with C#, provides you with the power to do things that don't necessarily fall within the boundaries of what's considered good design. In the end, you want to strive for classes and constructs that are intuitive to use and carry few hidden surprises.

The savvy reader probably noticed that the new modifier is the quickest way to introduce some serious surprises into a class hierarchy. If you ever find yourself using that modifier on a method, you're most likely using a class in a way it was not intended to be used. You could be deriving from a class that should have been marked sealed in the first place. And you may be cursing the developer of that class for not marking a particular method virtual so you can easily override it. Therefore, you resort to using the new modifier. Just because it exists, don't assume it's wise to use it. The designer of the class you're deriving from probably never intended you to derive from it and just forgot to mark it sealed. And if the designer intentionally left it unsealed, he probably did not intend for you to replace the method you're trying to override. Therefore, always strive to follow time-tested design techniques and avoid the whiz-bang features of the language that go against that grain of good design.

Inheritance, Containment, and Delegation

When many people started programming in object-oriented languages some years ago, they thought inheritance was the greatest thing since sliced bread. In fact, many people consider it an integral, important part of object-oriented programming. Some argue that a language that doesn't support inheritance is not an object-oriented language at all. This arguing point for many people over the years has almost taken on the form of a religious war at times. As time went on, though, some astute designers started to notice the pitfalls of inheritance.

Choosing Between Interface and Class Inheritance

When you first discover inheritance, you have a tendency to overuse it and abuse it. This is easy to do. Misuse can make software designs hard to understand and maintain, especially in languages such as C++ that support multiple inheritance. It can also make it hard for those designs to adapt to future needs, thus forcing them to be thrown out and replaced with a completely new design. In languages that only support single inheritance, such as C# and Java, you're forced to apply more diligence to your use of inheritance.

For example, when modeling a human-resources system at company XYZ, one naïve designer could be inclined to introduce classes such as Payee, BenefitsRecipient, and Developer. Then, using multiple inheritance, he could build or compose a full-time developer, represented by the class FulltimeDeveloper, by inheriting from all three, as in Figure 4-3.

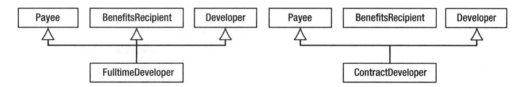

Figure 4-3. *Example of bad inheritance*

As you can see, this forces our designer to create a new class for contract developers, where the concrete class doesn't inherit from BenefitsRecipient. After the system grows by leaps and bounds, you can quickly see the flaw in the design when the inheritance lattice becomes complex and deep. Now he has two classes for types of developers, thus making the design hard to manage. Now, let's look at a bad attempt of the same problem with a language that supports only single inheritance. Figure 4-4 shows you that this solution is hardly a good one.

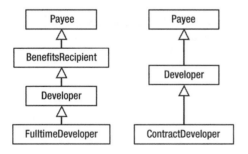

Figure 4-4. *Example of bad single-inheritance hierarchy*

If you look closely, you can see the ambiguity that is present. It's impossible that the Developer class can be derived from both Payee and BenefitsRecipient in an environment where only single inheritance is allowed. Because of that, these two hierarchies cannot live within the same design. You could create two different variants of the Developer class—one for FulltimeDeveloper to derive from, and one for `ContractDeveloper` to derive from. However, that would be a waste of time. More importantly, code reuse—the main benefit of inheritance—is gone if you have to create two versions of essentially the same class.

A better approach is to have a `Developer` class that contains various properties that represent these qualities of developers within the company. For example, the support of a specific interface could represent the support of a certain property. An inheritance hierarchy that is multiple levels deep is a telltale sign that the design needs some rethinking.

To see what's really going on here, let's take a moment to analyze what inheritance does for you. In reality, it allows you to get a little bit of work for free by inheriting an implementation. There is an important distinction between inheritance and interface implementation. Although the object-oriented languages, including C#, typically use a similar syntax for the two, it's important to note that classes that implement an interface don't get any implementation at all. When using inheritance, not only do you inherit the public contract of the class, but you also inherit the layout, or the guts.

A good rule of thumb is that when your purpose is primarily to inherit a contract, choose interface implementation over inheritance. This will guarantee that your design has the greatest flexibility. To understand more why that's the case, let's investigate more pitfalls of inheritance.

Delegation and Composition vs. Inheritance

Another very important aspect of inheritance that is unfavorable: *Inheritance can break encapsulation and always increases coupling*. I'm sure we all agree, or at least we should all agree, that encapsulation is the most fundamental and important object-oriented concept. If that's the case, then why would you want to break it? Yet any time you use encapsulation where the base type contains protected fields, you're cracking the shell of encapsulation and exposing the internals of the base class. This cannot be good. Let me explain why it's not and what sorts of alternatives you have at your disposal that can create better designs.

Many describe inheritance as white-box reuse. A better form of reuse is black-box reuse, meaning that the internals of the object are not exposed to you. You can achieve this by using containment. Yes, that's correct. Instead of inheriting your new class from another, you can contain an instance of the other class in your new class, thus reusing the class of the contained type without cracking the encapsulation. The downside to this technique is that in most languages, including C#, it requires a little more coding work, but not too much. In the end, it can provide a much more adaptable design.

For a simple example of what I'm talking about, consider a problem domain where a class handles some sort of custom network communications. Let's call this class `NetworkCommunicator`, and let's say it looks like this:

```
public class NetworkCommunicator
{
    public void SendData( DataObject obj )
    {
        // Send the data over the wire.
    }

    public DataObject ReceiveData()
    {
        // Receive data over the wire.
    }
}
```

Now, let's say that you come along later and decide it would be nice to have an
EncryptedNetworkCommunicator object, where the data transmission is encrypted before it is sent. A
common approach would be to derive EncryptedNetworkCommunicator from NetworkCommunicator.
Then, the implementation would look like this:

```
public class EncryptedNetworkCommunicator : NetworkCommunicator
{
    public override void SendData( DataObject obj )
    {
        // Encrypt the data.
        base.SendData( obj );
    }

    public override DataObject ReceiveData()
    {
        DataObject obj = base.ReceiveData();

        // Decrypt data.

        return obj;
    }
}
```

There is a major drawback here. First of all, good design dictates that if you're going to modify
the functionality of the base class methods, you should override them. To override them properly,
you need to declare them as virtual in the first place. This requires you to be able to tell the future
when you design the NetworkCommunicator class and mark the methods as virtual. Yes, you can hide
them in C# using the new keyword when you define the method on the derived class. But if you do
that, you're breaking the tenet that the inheritance relationship models an is-a relationship. Now,
let's look at the containment solution:

```
public class EncryptedNetworkCommunicator
{
    public EncryptedNetworkCommunicator()
    {
        contained = new NetworkCommunicator();
    }

    public void SendData( DataObject obj )
    {
        // Encrypt the data.
        contained.SendData( obj );
    }

    public DataObject ReceiveData()
    {
        DataObject obj = contained.ReceiveData();

        // Decrypt data

        return obj;
    }

    private NetworkCommunicator contained;
}
```

As you can see, it's only slightly more work. But the good thing is, you're able to reuse the NetworkCommunicator as if it were a black box. The designer of NetworkCommunicator could have created the thing sealed, and you would still be able to reuse it. Had it been sealed, you definitely could not have inherited from it.

Another downfall of using inheritance is that it is not dynamic. It is static by the very fact that it is determined at compile time. This can be very limiting, to say the least. You can remove this limitation by using containment. However, in order to do that, you have to also employ your good friend, polymorphism. By doing so, the contained type can be, say, an interface type. Then, the contained object merely has to support the contract of that interface in order to be reused by the container. Moreover, you can change this object at run time. Think about this for a moment and let it sink in. Consider an object that represents a container of sortable objects. Let's say that this container type comes with a default sort algorithm. If you implement this default algorithm as a contained type that you can swap at run time, then if the problem domain required it, you could replace it with a custom sort algorithm as long as the new sort algorithm object implements the required interface that the container type expects. This technique is known as the Strategy design pattern. You've just seen an excellent use of a design pattern.

In conclusion, you can see that designs are much more flexible if you favor dynamic rather than static constructs. This includes favoring containment over inheritance in many reuse cases. This type of reuse is also known as delegation, since the work is delegated to the contained type. Containment also preserves encapsulation, whereas inheritance breaks encapsulation. One word of caution is in order, though. As with just about anything, you can overdo containment. For smaller utility classes, it may not make sense to go to too much effort to favor containment. And in some cases, you need to use inheritance to implement specialization. But, in the grand scheme of things, designs that favor containment over inheritance as a reuse mechanism are magnitudes more flexible and stand the test of time much better. Always respect the power of inheritance, including the damage it can cause through its misuse.

Summary

In this very long chapter, I've covered the important points regarding the C# type system, which allows you to create new types that have all of the capabilities of implicit types defined by the runtime. I started out by covering class definitions used to define new reference types, then I followed that with struct definitions used to create instances of new value types within the CLR, and I described the major differences between the two. Related to the topic of value types is that of boxing and unboxing, which I showed can introduce unintended inefficiencies when you don't understand all of the places boxing can be introduced by the compiler. (In Chapter 11, which covers generics, you'll see how you can eliminate boxing and unboxing entirely in some cases.)

I then turned to the complex topics of object creation and initialization, as well as object destruction. Destruction is a rather tricky topic in the CLR, since your reference types can support either deterministic or nondeterministic destruction. (I cover destruction in more detail with more examples in Chapter 13.) Then, I quickly discussed method overloading in C# and the various modifiers you can place on methods to control whether they're modified as virtual, override, or sealed. Finally, I spent some time discussing inheritance, polymorphism, and containment, and I provided some pointers for choosing when to use them.

The last sections in this chapter lead right into the next chapter, where I'll cover the all-important topic of interface-based, or contract-based, programming and how to use it in the CLR.

CHAPTER 5

■■■

Interfaces and Contracts

During your years as a software developer, you've likely come across the notion of *interface-based programming*. If you're familiar with the seminal book, *Design Patterns: Elements of Reusable Object-Oriented Software* by Erich Gamma, Richard Helm, Ralph Johnson, and John Vlissides (known as the "Gang of Four"),[1] then you know that many design patterns employ interface-style "contracts." If you're not familiar with that book and its concepts, I urge you to read it. In this chapter, it is my goal to show you how you can model well-defined, versioned contracts using interfaces. In this context, a contract is an agreement by a type to support a set of functionality.

If you've done any COM or CORBA development over the years, then you've most definitely been doing interface-based development. In fact, the interface is the only form of communication between components in COM. Therefore, much of the design complexity rests in developing solid interfaces before you write any line of implementation code. Failure to follow this paradigm has been the source of many problems. For example, Visual Studio 2003 offered an easy environment from which you could create web services. By simply annotating methods of a class a certain way, you could expose those methods as methods of the web service. However, the IDE fostered an approach whereby the interface was the result of annotating methods on a class rather than the other way around. Thus, the cart was put before the horse. Instead, you should clearly define the web service interface before doing any coding, and then code the implementation to implement the interface. To name just one benefit of this approach, you can code both the client and the server concurrently rather than one after the other. Another part of the problem is that once an interface is published to the world, you cannot change it. Doing so would break all implementations based upon it. Unfortunately, the Visual Studio environment encourages you to break this rule by making it easy for you to add a new method to a class and annotate it as a web service method.

In a well-designed, interface-based system, such as in service-oriented architecture (SOA) systems, you should always design the interface first, as it's the contract between components. The contract drives the implementation rather than the implementation driving, or defining, the contract. Unfortunately, too many tools in the past and even up to the present have promoted this backward development. But just because they promote it does not mean you need to follow their erroneous lead. After all, a contract, when applied to a type, imposes a set of requirements on that type. It makes no sense for the requirements to be driven by the types themselves. In the .NET environment, interfaces are types.

---

1. *Design Patterns: Elements of Reusable Object-Oriented Software* by Erich Gamma, Richard Helm, Ralph Johnson, and John Vlissides (Boston, MA: Addison-Wesley Professional, 1995) is cited in the references at the end of this book.

Interfaces Define Types

An interface declaration defines a reference type. Within variables of this type, you can store a reference to an object that implements the contract of the interface type. Each variable in the CLR is stored in a storage location, whether it be on the heap or on the stack. Each storage location has a type associated with it. Therefore, an interface type can describe the type associated with a specific storage location. When a variable—say, a reference to an object—is stored in that location, it must be the same type as the location, or it must be convertible to the type attached to the location. If it can be converted automatically to the type of the location, then it is implicitly convertible to the storage location type. If it requires a specific cast syntax to perform the conversion, then it is explicitly convertible to the storage location type.

Many examples use a fictitious GUI framework as their basis for demonstration purposes, so I'll do the same here. Take a look at the following code snippet:

```
public interface IUIControl
{
   void Paint();
}

public class Button : IUIControl
{
   public void Paint() {
      // Paint the Button
   }
}

public class ListBox : IUIControl
{
   public void Paint() {
      // Paint the Listbox
   }
}
```

This example declares an interface named IUIControl that simply exposes one method, Paint. This interface defines a contract, which states that any type that implements this interface must implement the Paint method. Of course, some documentation describing the semantic meaning of what Paint is supposed to do would be nice. For example, you can imagine that an interface named IArtist could have a method named Paint, but the meaning would probably not be reflexive as it is in the previous example—i.e., IUIControl.Paint likely asks a control to paint itself, while IArtist.Paint likely means that the artist should paint something.

■**Note** I've found it useful to name methods according to both the action they perform and where the action is directed. For example, suppose the IUIControl.Paint method takes a Graphics object as a parameter telling it where to paint itself. In my opinion, it makes the code more readable if the method is named IUIControl. PaintSelfTo. This way, the method call sort of reads like a spoken language in the sense that a method call that looks like control.PaintSelfTo(myGraphicsObject) is saying, "control, please paint yourself to myGraphicsObject."

Once the classes ListBox and Button in the previous example implement the interface, they can both be treated as type IUIControl. It's handy to consider how the CLR manages the situation. If you were to attempt to store any instance of either Button or ListBox into a variable declared as IUIControl, the operation would succeed. The reference to those concrete types is implicitly convertible to the IUIControl interface type because they both implement the interface. However, to cast an IUIControl reference back into a ListBox or Button reference requires an explicit cast, and that explicit cast could fail at run time if, in fact, the IUIControl reference does not point to an instance of the desired concrete type.

Defining Interfaces

In the previous section, you got a taste of what a C# interface declaration looks like. It looks similar to a class declaration where the keyword class is simply replaced with the word interface and the methods have no body. Note some important things, though. If you follow the recommended convention, your interface names will start with the letter I. Thus, you can spot interface types in code easily. Interfaces can have an access modifier attached to them. This determines whether the interface type declaration is visible outside the assembly. Since most interfaces represent contracts of communication between consumers and providers, interface declarations are typically declared as public.

Interface members cannot have any access modifiers attached to them. However, they can be decorated with the new modifier, which I discuss later on. Interface members are implicitly public. What would be the point of having a nonpublic interface member when the purpose of the interface is to allow two objects to talk to each other?

INTERFACES DEFINE CONTRACTS

To stress the fact that an interface only specifies a contract, I like to draw an analogy between interface declarations and IDL and Web Services Description Language (WSDL). Both COM and CORBA use IDL to define interfaces. The syntax is similar to C++. It is typically passed through a translator, such as midl.exe for COM, to generate wrappers—and possibly proxies and stubs—for whatever language you desire. WSDL is another example, although it is much more expressive than IDL. An XML schema defines the format of WSDL, and a WSDL document is used to describe a contract, or interface, into a network service. The usage pattern is similar to IDL. Once you have a WSDL document, you pass it through a translator for whatever language you're using to implement or consume the service. The translator helps you out by generating a shell of an implementation, or interfaces that are native to the language you're using. Declaring and consuming interfaces in the .NET environment should follow the same pattern.

In practice, it usually make sense to house your interface declarations in a separate assembly that contains only interface definitions and constants, so that the consumer and the provider can base their implementations on exactly the same version of the interfaces.

What Can Be in an Interface?

Interface declarations may declare zero or more methods, properties, events, and indexers. All are implicitly public and cannot be static. Interfaces may inherit from one or more other interfaces. The syntax is the same as that of class inheritance. When it comes to interfaces, I prefer to think of interface B deriving from interface A as meaning that if you implement interface B, you must also implement interface A. Class inheritance implies an is-a relationship, where the base implementation is also inherited. Even though interface inheritance borrows the same syntax as class inheritance, which is an is-a relationship, it's not completely accurate to consider them one and the same, since interface inheritance merely declares a generalization and no implementation is inherited. Therefore, whenever you say *interface inheritance*, try to think of it more in terms of an *implements* relationship. This becomes clearer when I discuss how a derived class can reimplement interfaces and how the compiler does interface implementation mapping in the concrete types that implement the interface.

Here's an example of what you can declare in an interface:

```
public delegate void DBEvent( IMyDatabase sender );²

public interface IMyDatabase : ISerializable, IDisposable
{
   void Insert( object element );
   int  Count { get; }
   object this[ int index ] { get; set; }
   event DBEvent dbChanged;
}
```

In this example, IMyDatabase also implements ISerializable and IDisposable. Therefore, any concrete type that implements IMyDatabase must also implement ISerializable and IDisposable; otherwise, the concrete type will not compile. If you were to compile this code snippet into an assembly and look at it with ILDASM, you would see that the IMyDatabase type contains nothing more than instance method declarations. Of course, some of those will have special names based on the fact that they're accessors for the property, indexer, or event.

Interface Inheritance and Member Hiding

As mentioned previously, interfaces support multiple inheritance from other interfaces in the syntactic sense. As with multiple inheritance in C++, you may also have diamond-lattice hierarchies, such as in the following code:

```
public interface IUIControl
{
    void Paint();
}

public interface IEditBox : IUIControl
{
}

public interface IDropList : IUIControl
{
}

public class ComboBox : IEditBox, IDropList
{
    public void Paint() {
        // paint implementation for ComboBox
    }
}
```

---

2. If you're unfamiliar with the delegate keyword and how delegates are used to declare events, don't worry. You'll find a thorough discussion of delegates and events in Chapter 10.

In this example, both the IEditBox and IDropList interfaces implement the IUIControl interface. And since ComboBox implements both of those interfaces, it must implement the union of all the methods declared in the interfaces it directly implements, plus the interfaces those interfaces implement recursively. In this case, that only includes the IUIControl.Paint method.

Quite simply, all of the methods from all of the interfaces are merged together into one big union to form the set of methods that the concrete class or structure must implement. Therefore, the ComboBox class gets only one implementation of the Paint method. If you were to cast a ComboBox instance into both an IEditBox reference and an IDropList reference, then calling Paint through both of those would call into exactly the same implementation.

■**Note** If you come from a native C++ background, you might know all of the intricacies of multiple inheritance and diamond-lattice inheritance diagrams and how they relate to virtual inheritance in C++ and the multiple compiler-generated vtables involved. To understand how C# differs, imagine that C# flattens all of those vtables into one table at compile time.

Sometimes—although rarely—you need to declare a method in an interface that hides a method in an inherited interface. You must use the new keyword if you want to keep the compiler from complaining about it with a warning.

■**Note** Traditionally, Object-Oriented Analysis and Design (OOA-D) considers it bad design to hide a nonvirtual inherited member. The implementation that actually gets called depends on the type of reference held, even if the two references point to the same instance. For example, if A.DoWork isn't virtual, and B derives from A and introduces a new B.DoWork that hides the base method, then calling DoWork on a reference to B will call B.DoWork, and calling DoWork on a reference to A obtained by casting a B reference to an A reference will call A.DoWork. This behavior is nonintuitive in object-oriented systems. Just because the language allows you to do something does not mean that it's the correct thing to do. Now you see why the compiler warning exists in the first place.

In the following example, IEditBox, for one reason or another, needs to declare a Paint method whose signature is exactly that of the one in IUIControl. Therefore, it must use the new keyword:

```
using System;

public interface IUIControl
{
    void Paint();
}

public interface IEditBox : IUIControl
{
    new void Paint();
}

public interface IDropList : IUIControl
{
}

public class ComboBox : IEditBox, IDropList
{
    public void Paint() {
        Console.WriteLine( "ComboBox.IEditBox.Paint()" );
    }
}
```

```
public class EntryPoint
{
    static void Main() {
        ComboBox cb = new ComboBox();
        cb.Paint();
        ((IEditBox)cb).Paint();
        ((IDropList)cb).Paint();
        ((IUIControl)cb).Paint();
    }
}
```

In all calls to the Paint method in the Main method, it always boils down to a call on
ComboBox.Paint. That's because the set of required methods that ComboBox must implement are
merged together into one set. Both signatures from Paint—the one from IEditBox and the one from
IUIControl—are merged into one slot in the requirements list. In the end, they both map to
ComboBox.Paint. You can change this behavior by using explicit interface implementation (which I
discuss in the section "Explicit Interface Implementation"), where ComboBox can elect to implement
two different versions of Paint—one for IEditBox and one for IUIControl.

When the IEditBox interface declares the Paint method using the new keyword, it is said to hide
the Paint method declared in IUIControl. When you call ComboBox.Paint, it will invoke the
IEditBox.Paint method as if it chose the IEditBox path in the inheritance hierarchy over the
IDropList path. In essence, any time any path hides a method, it hides the method for all paths.
This will become clearer when I discuss how the compiler matches up a concrete method with an
interface method when you call an interface method. That process is called *interface mapping*, and
I cover it in the section titled "Interface Member Matching Rules" later in this chapter.

Implementing Interfaces

When implementing interfaces in C#, you have the choice of implementing them one of two ways.
By default, interface implementations are said to be implicit implementations. The method implementations are part of the public contract of the class but also implement the interface implicitly.
Alternatively, you can implement the interface explicitly, whereby the method implementations are
private to the implementing class and don't become part of the public interface. Explicit implementation provides some flexibility, especially when implementing two interfaces that have methods
with the same name in them.

Implicit Interface Implementation

When a concrete type implements the methods in inherited interfaces, and those methods are
marked public, it's known as *implicit interface implementation*. What good is it to say that a concrete type implements the contract of a specific interface if a consumer of the objects of that type
cannot call the methods in that contract? For example, the following is not valid:

```
public interface IUIControl
{
    void Paint();
}

public class StaticText : IUIControl
{
    void Paint();   // !!! WON'T COMPILE !!!
}
```

If you try to compile this, the compiler will immediately complain that the StaticText class doesn't implement all of the methods of the derived interfaces—in this case, IUIControl. In order for this to work, you could rewrite it as in the following:

```
public interface IUIControl
{
    void Paint();
}

public class StaticText : IUIControl
{
    public void Paint();   //Notice that we've added 'public' to the method declaration
}
```

Now, not only will the code compile, but when you call Paint through a reference to StaticText or through a reference to IUIControl, the StaticText.Paint method will be called. Thus, consumers can treat instances of StaticText polymorphically as instances of type IUIControl.

Explicit Interface Implementation

When a concrete type implements an interface implicitly, the interface methods also become part of the public contract of the concrete type itself. However, you might not always want the interface method implementations to become part of the public interface of the class that implements the interface. For example, the System.IO.FileStream class implements IDisposable, but you cannot call Dispose through an instance of FileStream. Instead, you must first cast the reference to the FileStream object to an IDisposable interface, and then you may call Dispose. When you need this behavior in your own types, you must implement the interfaces using explicit interface implementation.

■Note To achieve the same result as Dispose using a reference to a FileStream object, you must call FileStream.Close. In the implementation of FileStream.Close calls straight through to the internal implementation of the Dispose method. Why did the designers of FileStream do this? Most likely because it makes more linguistic sense to "close" a file rather than "dispose of" it.

You can also use explicit implementation to provide separate implementations for overlapping methods in inherited interfaces. Let's look again at the ComboBox example from the previous section. If you want to provide a separate implementation for IEditBox.Paint and IUIControl.Paint inside ComboBox, you can do that using explicit interface implementation, as shown here:

```
using System;

public interface IUIControl
{
    void Paint();
}

public interface IEditBox : IUIControl
{
    new void Paint();
}
```

```
public interface IDropList : IUIControl
{
}

public class ComboBox : IEditBox, IDropList
{
    void IEditBox.Paint() {
        Console.WriteLine( "ComboBox.IEditBox.Paint()" );
    }

    void IUIControl.Paint() {
        Console.WriteLine( "ComboBox.IUIControl.Paint()" );
    }

    public void Paint() {
        ((IUIControl)this).Paint();
    }
}

public class EntryPoint
{
    static void Main() {
        ComboBox cb = new ComboBox();
        cb.Paint();
        ((IEditBox)cb).Paint();
        ((IDropList)cb).Paint();
        ((IUIControl)cb).Paint();
    }
}
```

Pay attention to the change in syntax. Now, ComboBox has three implementations for Paint. One is specific for the IEditBox interface, the other is specific to the IUIControl interface, and the last one is simply there for convenience to provide a Paint method for the public interface of the ComboBox class. When you implement interface methods explicitly, not only do you add the interface name followed by a dot before the method name, but you also remove the access modifier. This keeps it from being in the public contract for ComboBox. However, the explicit interface implementations aren't exactly private in the sense that you can call them after you cast the instance of the ComboBox to the required interface type. In my implementation of ComboBox.Paint—the one that contributes to the ComboBox public contract—I get to choose which version of Paint to call. In this case, I chose to call IUIControl.Paint. I could just as easily have chosen to implement IEditBox.Paint explicitly and IUIControl.Paint implicitly, and then I wouldn't have needed the third implementation of Paint. But in this case, I believe it adds more flexibility and makes more sense for ComboBox to implement its own Paint method so that it can reuse the other and add value to it at the same time. If you compile and run the previous example, you'll see output similar to the following:

```
ComboBox.IUIControl.Paint()
ComboBox.IEditBox.Paint()
ComboBox.IUIControl.Paint()
ComboBox.IUIControl.Paint()
```

Granted, this example is rather contrived, but it's meant to exhibit the intricacies of explicit interface implementation and member hiding during multiple interface inheritance.

Overriding Interface Implementations in Derived Classes

Suppose you have a handy implementation of ComboBox, as in the previous section, and the implementer decided not to seal the class so that you can inherit from it.

Note I suggest that you declare all classes sealed unless the designer explicitly intends them to be inherited from. In Chapter 4 I explain in detail why this is desired.

Now, suppose you create a new class, FancyComboBox, and you want it to paint itself better, maybe with some new psychedelic theme. You could try something like this:

```
using System;

public interface IUIControl
{
    void Paint();
    void Show();
}

public interface IEditBox : IUIControl
{
    void SelectText();
}

public interface IDropList : IUIControl
{
    void ShowList();
}

public class ComboBox : IEditBox, IDropList
{
    public void Paint() { }
    public void Show() { }

    public void SelectText() { }

    public void ShowList() { }
}

public class FancyComboBox : ComboBox
{
    public void Paint() { }
}

public class EntryPoint
{
    static void Main() {
        FancyComboBox cb = new FancyComboBox();
    }
}
```

However, the compiler will promptly warn you that FancyComboBox.Paint hides ComboBox.Paint and that you probably meant to use the new keyword. This will surprise you if you were assuming that methods that implement interface methods are automatically virtual. They are not in C#.

■Note Under the covers, interface method implementations are called as if they are virtual methods. Any interface method implementations not marked virtual in the C# code are marked as virtual and final (sealed) in the generated IL. If the method is marked virtual in the C# code, then the method is marked with virtual and newslot (new) in the generated IL. This can be the source of some confusion.

When faced with a problem such as this, you have a couple of options. One option is to have FancyComboBox reimplement the IUIControl interface:

```
using System;

public interface IUIControl
{
    void Paint();
    void Show();
}

public interface IEditBox : IUIControl
{
    void SelectText();
}

public interface IDropList : IUIControl
{
    void ShowList();
}

public class ComboBox : IEditBox, IDropList
{
    public void Paint() {
        Console.WriteLine( "ComboBox.Paint()" );
    }
    public void Show() { }

    public void SelectText() { }

    public void ShowList() { }
}

public class FancyComboBox : ComboBox, IUIControl
{
    public new void Paint() {
        Console.WriteLine( "FancyComboBox.Paint()" );
    }
}

public class EntryPoint
{
    static void Main() {
        FancyComboBox cb = new FancyComboBox();
        cb.Paint();
```

```
        ((IUIControl)cb).Paint();
        ((IEditBox)cb).Paint();
    }
}
```

In this example, note a couple of things. First, FancyComboBox lists IUIControl in its inheritance list. That's how you indicate that FancyComboBox is planning to reimplement the IUIControl interface. Had IUIControl inherited from another interface, FancyComboBox would have had to reimplement the methods from those inherited interfaces as well. I also had to use the new keyword for FancyComboBox.Paint, since it hides ComboBox.Paint. This wouldn't have been a problem had ComboBox implemented the IUIControl.Paint method explicitly, since it wouldn't have been part of the ComboBox public contract. When the compiler matches class methods to interface methods, it also considers public methods of base classes. In reality, FancyComboBox could have indicated that it reimplements IUIControl but without redeclaring any methods, as the compiler would have just wired up the interface to the base class methods. Of course, doing so would be pointless, since the reason you reimplement an interface in a derived class is to modify behavior.

▓**Note** The ability to reimplement an interface is a powerful one. It highlights the vast differences between the way C# and the CLR handle interfaces and the C++ treatment of interfaces as abstract class definitions. Gone are the intricacies of C++ vtables, as well as the question of when you should use C++ virtual inheritance. As I've said before, and don't mind saying again, C#/CLR interfaces are nothing more than contracts that say, "You, Mr. Concrete Class, agree to implement all of these methods in said contract, a.k.a. interface."

When you implement methods in an interface contract implicitly, they must be publicly accessible. As long as they meet those requirements, they can also have other attributes, including the virtual keyword. In fact, implementing the IUIControl interface in ComboBox using virtual methods as opposed to nonvirtual methods would make the previous problem a lot easier to solve, as demonstrated here:

```
using System;

public interface IUIControl
{
    void Paint();
    void Show();
}

public interface IEditBox : IUIControl
{
    void SelectText();
}

public interface IDropList : IUIControl
{
    void ShowList();
}

public class ComboBox : IEditBox, IDropList
{
    public virtual void Paint() {
        Console.WriteLine( "ComboBox.Paint()" );
    }
    public void Show() { }
```

```
    public void SelectText() { }

    public void ShowList() { }
}

public class FancyComboBox : ComboBox
{
    public override void Paint() {
        Console.WriteLine( "FancyComboBox.Paint()" );
    }
}

public class EntryPoint
{
    static void Main() {
        FancyComboBox cb = new FancyComboBox();
        cb.Paint();
        ((IUIControl)cb).Paint();
        ((IEditBox)cb).Paint();
    }
}
```

In this case, FancyComboBox doesn't have to reimplement IUIControl. It merely has to override the virtual ComboBox.Paint method. It's much cleaner for ComboBox to declare Paint virtual in the first place. Any time you have to use the new keyword to keep the compiler from warning you about hiding a method, consider whether the method of the base class should be virtual.

Caution Hiding methods causes confusion and makes code hard to follow and debug. Again, just because the language allows you to do something does not mean that you should.

Of course, the implementer of ComboBox would have had to think ahead and realize that someone might derive from ComboBox, and anticipated these issues. In my opinion, it's best to seal the class and avoid any surprises by people who attempt to derive from your class when you never meant for it to be derived from. Imagine who they will scream at when they encounter a problem. Have you ever used Microsoft Foundation Classes (MFC) in the past and come to a point where you're pulling your hair out because you're trying to derive from an MFC class and wishing a particular method were virtual? In that case, it's easy to blame the designers of MFC for being so flagrantly thoughtless and not making the method virtual when, in reality, it's more accurate to consider the fact that they probably never meant for you to derive from the class in the first place. Chapter 13 describes how containment rather than inheritance is the key in situations like these.

Beware of Side Effects of Value Types Implementing Interfaces

All the examples so far have shown how classes may implement interface methods. In fact, value types can implement interfaces as well. However, there's one major side effect to doing so. If you cast a value type to an interface type, you'll incur a boxing penalty. Even worse, if you modify the value via the interface reference, you're modifying the boxed copy and not the original. Given the intricacies of boxing that I cover in Chapters 4 and 13, you may consider that to be a bad thing.

As an example, consider System.Int32. I'm sure you'll agree that it is one of the most basic types in the CLR. However, you may or may not have noticed that it also implements several interfaces: IComparable, IFormattable, and IConvertible. Consider System.Int32's implementation of IConvertible, for example. All of the methods are implemented explicitly. IConvertible has quite a few methods declared within it. However, none of those are in the public contract of System.Int32. If you want to call one of those methods, you must first cast your Int32 value type into an IConvertible interface reference. Only then may you call one of the IConvertible methods. And of course, since interface-typed variables are references, the Int32 value must be boxed.

PREFER THE CONVERT CLASS OVER ICONVERTIBLE

Even though I use the IConvertible interface implemented by a value type as an example to prove a point, the documentation urges you not to call the methods of IConvertible on Int32; rather, it recommends using the Convert class instead. The Convert class provides a collection of methods with many overloads of common types for converting a value to just about anything else, including custom types (by using Convert.ChangeType), and it makes your code easier to change later. For example, if you have the following

```
int i = 0;
double d = Int32.ToDouble(i);
```

and you want to change the type of i to long, you have to also change the Int32 type to Int64. On the other hand, if you write

```
int i = 0;
double d = Convert.ToDouble(i);
```

then all you have to do is change the type of i.

Interface Member Matching Rules

Each language that supports interface definitions has rules about how it matches up method implementations with interface methods. The interface member matching rules for C# are pretty straightforward and boil down to some simple rules. However, to find out which method actually gets called at run time, you need to consider the rules of the CLR as well. These rules are only relevant at compile time. Suppose you have a hierarchy of classes and interfaces. To find the implementation for SomeMethod on ISomeInterface, start at the bottom of the hierarchy and search for the first type that implements the interface in question. In this case, that interface is ISomeInterface. This is the level at which the search for a matching method begins. Once you find the type, recursively move up through the type hierarchy and search for a method with the matching signature, while first giving preference to explicit interface member implementations. If you don't find any, look for public instance methods that match the same signature.

The C# compiler uses this algorithm when matching up method implementations with interface implementations. The method that it picks must be a public instance method or an explicitly implemented instance method, and it may or may not be tagged in C# as virtual. However, when the IL code is generated, all interface method calls are made through the IL callvirt instruction.

So, even though the method is not necessarily marked as virtual in the C# sense, the CLR treats interface calls as virtual. Be sure that you don't confuse these two concepts. If the method is marked as virtual in C# and has methods that override it in the types below it, the C# compiler will generate vastly different code at the point of call. Be careful, as this can be quite confusing, as shown by the following contrived example:

```
using System;

public interface I
{
    void Go();
}

public class A : I
{
    public void Go() {
        Console.WriteLine( "A.Go()" );
    }
}

public class B : A
{
}

public class C : B, I
{
    public new void Go() {
        Console.WriteLine( "C.Go()" );
    }
}

public class EntryPoint
{
    static void Main() {
        B b1 = new B();

        C c1 = new C();
        B b2 = c1;

        b1.Go();
        c1.Go();
        b2.Go();
        ((I)b2).Go();
    }
}
```

The output from this example is as follows:

```
A.Go()
C.Go()
A.Go()
C.Go()
```

The first call, on b1, is obvious, as is the second call on c1. However, the third call, on b2, is not obvious at all. Since the A.Go method is not marked as virtual, the compiler generates code that calls A.Go. The fourth and final call is almost equally confusing, but not if you consider the fact that the CLR handles virtual calls on class type references and calls on interface references significantly differently. The generated IL for the fourth call makes a call to I.Go, which, in this case, boils down to a call to C.Go, since b2 is actually a C, and C reimplements I.

You have to be careful when searching for the actual method that gets called, since you must consider whether the type of your reference is a class type or an interface type. The C# compiler generates IL virtual method calls in order to call through to interfaces methods, and the CLR uses interface tables internally to achieve this.

■Note C++ programmers must realize that interface tables are different from C++ vtables. Each CLR type only has one method table, whereas a C++ instance of a type may have multiple vtables.

The contents of these interface tables are defined by the compiler using its method-matching rules. For more detailed information regarding these interface tables, see Don Box and Chris Sells' *Essential .NET, Volume I: The Common Language Runtime* (Boston, MA: Addison-Wesley Professional, 2002), as well as the CLI standard document itself.

The C# method-matching rules explain the situation I discussed previously in the section "Interface Inheritance and Member Hiding." Hiding a method in one hierarchical path of a diamond-shaped hierarchy hides the method in all inheritance paths. The rules state that when you walk up the hierarchy, you short-circuit the search once you find a method at a particular level. These simple rules also explain how interface reimplementation can greatly affect the method-matching process, thus short-circuiting the compiler's search during its progression up the hierarchy. Let's consider an example of this in action:

```
using System;

public interface ISomeInterface
{
    void SomeMethod();
}

public interface IAnotherInterface : ISomeInterface
{
    void AnotherMethod();
}

public class SomeClass : IAnotherInterface
{
    public void SomeMethod() {
        Console.WriteLine( "SomeClass.SomeMethod()" );
    }

    public virtual void AnotherMethod() {
        Console.WriteLine( "SomeClass.AnotherMethod()" );
    }
}
```

```
public class SomeDerivedClass : SomeClass
{
    public new void SomeMethod() {
        Console.WriteLine( "SomeDerivedClass.SomeMethod()" );
    }

    public override void AnotherMethod() {
        Console.WriteLine( "SomeDerivedClass.AnotherMethod()" );
    }
}

public class EntryPoint
{
    static void Main() {
        SomeDerivedClass  obj = new SomeDerivedClass();
        ISomeInterface    isi = obj;
        IAnotherInterface iai = obj;

        isi.SomeMethod();
        iai.SomeMethod();
        iai.AnotherMethod();
    }
}
```

Let's apply the search rules to each method call in Main in the previous example. In all cases, I've implicitly converted an instance of SomeDerivedClass to references of the two interfaces, ISomeInterface and IAnotherInterface. I place the first call to SomeMethod through ISomeInterface. First, walk up the class hierarchy, starting at the concrete type of the reference, looking for the first class that implements this interface or an interface derived from it. Doing so leaves us at the SomeClass implementation, because, even though it does not implement ISomeInterface directly, it implements IAnotherInterface, which derives from ISomeInterface. Thus, we end up calling SomeClass.SomeMethod. You may be surprised that SomeDerivedClass.SomeMethod was not called. But if you follow the rules, you'll notice that you skipped right over SomeDerivedClass, looking for the bottom-most class in the hierarchy that implements the interface. In order for SomeDerivedClass.SomeMethod to be called instead, SomeDerivedClass would need to reimplement ISomeInterface. The second call to SomeMethod through the IAnotherInterface reference follows exactly the same path when finding the matching method.

Things get interesting in the third call in Main, where you call AnotherMethod through a reference to IAnotherInterface. As before, the search begins at the bottom-most class in the hierarchy that implements this interface, inside SomeClass. Since SomeClass has a matching method signature, your search is complete. However, the twist is that the matching method signature is declared virtual. So when the call is made, the virtual method mechanism places execution within SomeDerivedClass.AnotherMethod. It's important to note that AnotherMethod doesn't change the rules for interface method matching, even though it is implemented virtually. It's not until after the interface method has been matched that the virtual nature of the method has an impact on exactly which implementation gets called at run time.

■**Note** Interface method matching is applied statically at compile time. Virtual method dispatching happens dynamically at run time. You should note the difference between the two when trying to determine which method implementation gets invoked.

The output from the previous example code is as follows:

```
SomeClass.SomeMethod()
SomeClass.SomeMethod()
SomeDerivedClass.AnotherMethod()
```

Explicit Interface Implementation with Value Types

Many times, you'll encounter general-use interfaces that take parameters in the form of a reference to System.Object. These interfaces are typically general usage, nongeneric interfaces. For example, consider the IComparable interface, which looks like the following:

```
public interface IComparable
{
    int CompareTo( object obj );
}
```

■ Note NET 2.0 added support for IComparable<T>, which you should always consider using along with IComparable in order to offer greater type safety.

It makes sense that the CompareTo method accepts such a general type, because it would be nice to be able to pass it just about anything to see how the object in question compares to the one that implements it. When dealing strictly with reference types, there's really no loss of efficiency here, since conversion to and from System.Object on reference types is free for all practical purposes. But things get a little sticky when you consider value types. Let's look at some code to see the gory details:

```
using System;

public struct SomeValue : IComparable
{
    public SomeValue( int n ) {
        this.n = n;
    }

    public int CompareTo( object obj ) {
        if( obj is SomeValue ) {
            SomeValue other = (SomeValue) obj;

            return n - other.n;
        } else {
            throw new ArgumentException( "Wrong Type!" );
        }
    }

    private int n;
}
```

```
public class EntryPoint
{
    static void Main() {
        SomeValue val1 = new SomeValue( 1 );
        SomeValue val2 = new SomeValue( 2 );

        Console.WriteLine( val1.CompareTo(val2) );
    }
}
```

In the innocuous call to WriteLine in Main, you see val1 being compared to val2. But look closely at how many boxing operations are required. First, since CompareTo takes an object reference, val2 must be boxed at the point of the method call. Had you implemented the CompareTo method explicitly, you would have needed to cast the val1 value into an IComparable interface, which would incur a boxing penalty. But once you're inside the CompareTo method, the boxing nightmare is still not over. Ouch. Thankfully, you can employ an optimization when SomeValue is compared to certain types. Take, for example, the case where an instance of SomeValue is compared to another SomeValue instance. You can provide a type-safe version of the CompareTo method to get the job done, as shown here:

```
using System;

public struct SomeValue : IComparable
{
    public SomeValue( int n ) {
        this.n = n;
    }

    int IComparable.CompareTo( object obj ) {
        if( obj is SomeValue ) {
            SomeValue other = (SomeValue) obj;

            return n - other.n;
        } else {
            throw new ArgumentException( "Wrong Type!" );
        }
    }

    public int CompareTo( SomeValue other ) {
        return n - other.n;
    }

    private int n;
}

public class EntryPoint
{
    static void Main() {
        SomeValue val1 = new SomeValue( 1 );
        SomeValue val2 = new SomeValue( 2 );

        Console.WriteLine( val1.CompareTo(val2) );
    }
}
```

In this example, there is absolutely no boxing in the call to CompareTo. That's because the compiler picks the one with the best match for the type. In this case, since you implement IComparable. CompareTo explicitly, there is only one overload of CompareTo in the public contract of SomeValue. But even if IComparable.CompareTo had not been implemented explicitly, the compiler would have still chosen the type-safe version. The typical pattern involves hiding the typeless versions from casual use so that the user must do a boxing operation explicitly. This operation converts the value to an interface reference in order to get to the typeless version.

The bottom line is that you'll definitely want to follow this idiom any time you implement an interface on a value type where you determine that you can define overloads with better type safety than the ones listed in the interface declaration. Avoiding unnecessary boxing is always a good thing, and your users will appreciate your detail and commitment to efficiency.

Versioning Considerations

The concept of versioning is essentially married to the concept of interfaces. When you create, define, and publish an interface, you're defining a contract—or viewed in more rigid terms—a standard. Any time you have a standard form of communication, you must adhere to it so as not to break any clients of that contract. For example, consider the 802.11 standard upon which many WiFi devices are based. It's important that access points from one vendor work with devices from as many vendors as possible. This works as long as all of the vendors agree and follow the standard. Can you imagine the chaos that would erupt if a single vendor's WiFi card were the only one that worked at your favorite Pacific Northwest-based coffee shops? It would be pandemonium. Therefore, we have standards.

Now, nothing states that the standard cannot be augmented. Certain manufacturers do just that. In some cases, if you use Manufacturer A's access point with the same manufacturer's wireless card, you can achieve speeds greater than those supported by the standard. However, note that those augmentations only augment, and don't alter, the standard. Similarly, nothing states that a standard cannot be revised. Standards normally have version numbers attached to them, and when they are revised, the version number is incremented. Most of the time, devices that implement the new version also support the previous version. Although not required, it's a good move for those manufacturers who want to achieve maximum market saturation. In the 802.11 example, 802.11a, 802.11b, and 802.11g represent the various revisions of the standard.

The point of this example is that you should apply these same rules to your interfaces once you publish them. You don't normally create interfaces unless you're doing so to allow entities to interact with each other using a common contract. So, once you're done with creating that contract, do the right thing and slap a version number on it. You can create your version number in many ways. For new revisions of your interface, you could simply give it a new name—the key point being that you never change the original interface. You've probably already seen exactly the same idiom in use in the COM world. Typically, if someone, probably Microsoft, decides they have a good reason to augment the behavior of an interface, you'll find a new interface definition ending with either an *Ex* suffix or a numeric suffix. At any rate, it's a completely different interface than the previous one, even though the contract of the new interface could inherit the original interface, and the implementations may be shared.

■**Note** Current design guidelines in wide use suggest that if you need to create an augmented interface based upon another, you shouldn't use the suffix Ex as COM does. Instead, you should follow the interface name with an ordinal. So, if the original interface is ISomeContract, then you should name the augmented interface ISomeContract2.

In reality, if your interface definitions live within a versioned assembly, you may define a newer version of the same interface, even with the same name, in an assembly with the same name but with a new version number. The assembly loader will resolve and load the proper assembly at run time. However, this practice can become confusing to the developers using your interface, since they now have to be more explicit about which assembly to reference at build time.

Contracts

Many times, you need to represent the notion of a contract when designing an application or a system. A programming contract is no different than any other contract. You usually define a contract to facilitate communication between two types in your design. For example, suppose you have a virtual zoo, and in your zoo, you have animals. Now, an instance of your ZooKeeper needs a way to communicate to the collection of these ZooDweller objects that they should fly to a specific location. Ignoring the fact that they had all better be fairly obedient, they had also better be able to fly. However, not all animals can fly, so clearly not all of the types in the zoo can support this flying contract.

Contracts Implemented with Classes

Let's consider one way to manage the complexity of getting these creatures to fly from one location to the next. First, consider the assumptions that you can make here. Let's say that this Zoo can have only one ZooKeeper. Second, let's assume that you can model the locations within this Zoo by using a simple two-dimensional Point structure. It starts to look as though you can model this system by the following code:

```
using System;
using System.Collections.ObjectModel;

namespace CityOfShanoo.MyZoo
{

public struct Point
{
    public double X;
    public double Y;
}

public abstract class ZooDweller
{
    public void EatSomeFood() {
        DoEatTheFood();
    }

    protected abstract void DoEatTheFood();
}

public sealed class ZooKeeper
{
    public void SendFlyCommand( Point to ) {
        // Implementation removed for clarity.
    }
}
```

```
public sealed class Zoo
{
    private static Zoo theInstance = new Zoo();
    public static Zoo GetInstance() {
        return theInstance;
    }

    private Zoo() {
        creatures = new Collection<ZooDweller>();³
        zooKeeper = new ZooKeeper();
    }

    public ZooKeeper ZooKeeper {
        get {
            return zooKeeper;
        }
    }

    private ZooKeeper zooKeeper;
    private Collection<ZooDweller> creatures;
}

}
```

Since there can only be one zoo in the CityOfShanoo, the Zoo is modeled as a singleton object, and the only way to obtain the instance of the one and only Zoo is to call Zoo.GetInstance. Also, you can get a reference to the ZooKeeper via the Zoo.ZooKeeper property. It is common practice in the .NET Framework to name the property after the custom type that it represents.

Note The Singleton design pattern is one of the most widely used and well-known design patterns. Essentially, the pattern allows only one instance of its type to exist at one time. Many people still argue about the best way to implement it. Implementation difficulty varies depending on the language you're using. But in general, some static private instance within the type declaration is lazily initialized at the point of first access. The previous implementation of the Zoo class does that, since the static initializer is not called until the type is first accessed through the GetInstance method.

This initial design defines the ZooDweller as an abstract class that implements a method EatSomeFood. The ZooDweller uses the Non-Virtual Interface (NVI) pattern described in Chapter 13, where the virtual method that the concrete type overrides is declared protected rather than public.

It's important to note that the ZooDweller type does, in fact, define a contract even though it is not an interface. The contract, as written, states that any type that derives from ZooDweller must implement EatSomeFood. Any code that uses a ZooDweller instance can be guaranteed that this method is supported.

Note Notice that an interface is not required in order to define a contract.

---

3. If the syntax of Collection<ZooDweller> looks foreign to you, don't worry. It is a declaration of a collection based on a generic collection type. I will cover generics in detail in Chapter 11.

So far, this design is missing a key operation, and that is the one commanding the creatures to fly to a destination within the zoo. Clearly, you cannot put a Fly method on the ZooDweller type, because not all animals in the zoo can fly. You must express this contract in a different way.

Interface Contracts

Since not all creatures in the zoo can fly, an interface provides an excellent mechanism for defining the flying contract. Consider the following modifications to the example from the previous section:

```
public interface IFly
{
    void FlyTo( Point destination );
}

public class Bird : ZooDweller, IFly
{
    public void FlyTo( Point destination ) {
        Console.WriteLine( "Flying to ({0}. {1}).",
                           destination );
    }

    protected override void DoEatTheFood() {
        Console.WriteLine( "Eating some food." );
    }
}
```

Now, using the interface IFly, Bird is defined such that it derives from ZooDweller and implements IFly.

Note If you intend to have various bird types derive from Bird, and those various birds have different implementations of ToFly, consider using the NVI pattern. You could introduce a protected virtual method named DoFlyTo that the base types override, while having Bird.FlyTo call through to DoFlyTo. Read the section titled "Use the Non-Virtual Interface (NVI) Pattern" in Chapter 13 for more information on why this is a good idea.

Choosing Between Interfaces and Classes

The previous section on contracts shows that you can implement a contract in multiple ways. In the C# and .NET environments, the two main methods are interfaces and classes, where the classes may even be abstract. In the zoo example, it's pretty clear as to when you should use an interface rather than an abstract class to define an interface. However, the choice is not always so clear, so let's consider the ramifications of both methods.

Since C# supports abstract classes, you can easily model a contract using abstract classes. But which method is more powerful? And which is more appropriate? These are not easy questions to answer, although the guideline tends to be that you should prefer a class if possible. Let's explore this.

■**Note** Since COM became so popular, some developers have a false notion that the only way to define a contract is by defining an interface. It's easy to jump to that conclusion when moving from the COM environment to the C# environment, simply because the basic building block of COM is the interface, and C# and .NET support interfaces natively. However, jumping to that conclusion would be perilous to your designs.

If you're familiar with COM and you've created any serious COM projects in the past, you most certainly implemented the COM objects using C++. You probably even used the Active Template Library (ATL) to shield yourself from the intricacies of the mundane COM development tasks. But at the core of it all, how does C++ model COM interfaces? The answer is with abstract classes.

When you implement a contract by defining an interface, you're defining a versioned contract. That means that the interface, once released, must never change, as if it were cast into stone. Sure, you could change it later, but you would not be very popular when all of your clients' code fails to compile with the modified interface. Consider the following example:

```
public interface IMyOperations
{
    void Operation1();
    void Operation2();
}

// Client class
public class ClientClass : IMyOperations
{
    public void Operation1() { }
    public void Operation2() { }
}
```

Now, you've released this wonderful IMyOperations interface to the world, and thousands of clients have implemented it. Then, you start getting requests from your clients asking for Operation3 support in your library. It seems like it would be easy enough to simply add Operation3 to the IMyOperations interface, but that would be a terrible mistake. If you add another operation to IMyOperations, then all of a sudden your clients' code won't compile until they implement the new operation. Also, code in another assembly that knows about the newer IMyOperations could attempt to cast a ClientClass instance into an IMyOperations reference and then call Operation3, thus creating a runtime failure. Clearly, you shouldn't modify an already published interface.

■**Caution** Never modify an already publicly published interface declaration.

You could also address this problem by defining a completely new interface, say IMyOperations2. However, ClientClass would need to implement both interfaces in order to get the new behavior, as shown here:

```
public interface IMyOperations
{
    void Operation1();
    void Operation2();
}
```

```
public interface IMyOperations2
{
    void Operation1();
    void Operation2();
    void Operation3();
}

// Client class
public class ClientClass : IMyOperations,
                           IMyOperations2
{
    public void Operation1() { }
    public void Operation2() { }
    public void Operation3() { }
}

public class AnotherClass
{
    public void DoWork( IMyOperations ops ) {
    }
}
```

Modifying ClientClass to support the new operation from IMyOperations2 isn't terribly diffi-cult, but what about the code that already exists, such as what is shown in AnotherClass? The problem is that the DoWork method accepts a type of IMyOperations. In order to make it to where the new Operation3 method can be called, the prototype of DoWork must change, or the code within it must do a cast to IOperations2, which could fail at run time. Since you want the compiler to be able to catch as many type bugs as possible, it would be better if you change the prototype of DoWork to accept a type of IMyOperations2.

Note If you define your original IMyOperations interface within a fully versioned, strongly named assembly, then you can get away with creating a new interface with the same name in a new assembly, as long as the ver-sion of the new assembly is different. Although the .NET Framework supports this explicitly, it doesn't mean you should do it without careful consideration, since introducing two IMyOperations interfaces that differ only by ver-sion number of the containing assembly could be confusing to your clients.

That was a lot of work just to make a new operation available to clients. Let's examine the same situation, except using an abstract class:

```
public abstract class MyOperations
{
    public virtual void Operation1() {
    }

    public virtual void Operation2() {
    }
}

// Client class
public class ClientClass : MyOperations
{
```

```
    public override void Operation1() { }
    public override void Operation2() { }
}

public class AnotherClass
{
    public void DoWork( MyOperations ops ) {
    }
}
```

MyOperations is a base class of ClientClass. One advantage is that MyOperations can contain default implementations if it wants to. Otherwise, the virtual methods in MyOperations could have been declared abstract. The example also declares MyOperations abstract, since it makes no sense for clients to be able to create instances of MyOperations. Now, let's suppose you want to add a new Operation3 method to MyOperations, and you don't want to break existing clients. You can do this as long as the added operation is not abstract, such that it forces changes on derived types, as shown here:

```
public abstract class MyOperations
{
    public virtual void Operation1() {
    }

    public virtual void Operation2() {
    }

    public virtual void Operation3() {
        // New default implementation
    }
}

// Client class
public class ClientClass : MyOperations
{
    public override void Operation1() { }
    public override void Operation2() { }
}

public class AnotherClass
{
    public void DoWork( MyOperations ops ) {
        ops.Operation3();
    }
}
```

Notice that the addition of MyOperations.Operation3 doesn't force any changes upon ClientClass, and AnotherClass.DoWork can make use of Operation3 without making any changes to the method declaration. This technique doesn't come without its drawbacks, though. You're restricted by the fact that the managed runtime only allows a class to have one base class. Since ClientClass has to derive from MyOperations to get the functionality, it uses up its only inheritance ticket. This may put complicated restrictions upon your client code. For example, what if one of your clients needs to create an object for use with .NET Remoting? In order to do so, the class must derive from MarshalByRefObject.

Sometimes, it's tricky to find a happy medium when deciding between interfaces and classes. I use the following rules of thumb:

- *If modeling an is-a relationship, use a class*: If it makes sense to name your contract with a noun, then you should probably model it with a class.

- *If modeling an IMPLEMENTS relationship, use an interface*: If it makes sense to name your contract with an adjective, as if it is a quality, then you should probably model it as an interface.

- *Consider wrapping up your interface and abstract class declarations in a separate assembly*: Implementations in other assemblies can then reference this separate assembly.

- *If possible, prefer classes over interfaces*: This can be helpful for the sake of extensibility.

You can see examples of these techniques throughout the .NET Framework Base Class Library (BCL). Consider using them in your own code as well.

Summary

This chapter introduced you to interfaces and how you can model a well-defined, versioned contract using an interface. Along with showing you the various ways that classes can implement interfaces, I also described the process that the C# compiler follows when matching up interface methods to implementations in the implementing class. I described interfaces from the perspective of reference types and value types—specifically, how expensive boxing operations can cause you pain when using interfaces on value types. Finally, I spent some time comparing and contrasting the use of interfaces and classes when modeling contracts between types in your design.

In the next chapter, I'll explain the intricacies of operator overloading in the C# language and why you may want to avoid it when creating code used by other .NET languages.

## CHAPTER 6

Overloading Operators

C# adopted the capability of operator overloading from C++. Just as you can overload methods, you can overload operators such as +, -, *, and so on. In addition to overloading arithmetic operators, you can also create custom conversion operators to convert from one type to another. You can overload other operators to allow objects to be used in Boolean test expressions.

Just Because You Can Doesn't Mean You Should

Overloading operators can make certain classes and structs more natural to use. However, overloading operators in a slipshod way can make code much more difficult to read and understand. You must be careful to consider the semantics of a type's operators. Be careful not to introduce something that is hard to decipher. Always aim for the most readable code, not only for the next fortunate soul who claps eyes on your code, but also for yourself. Have you ever looked at code and wondered, "Who in their right mind wrote this stuff?!?" only to find out it was you? I know I have.

Another reason not to overload operators is that not all .NET languages support overloaded operators, because overloading operators is not part of the CLS. Languages that target the CLI aren't required to support operator overloading. For example, Visual Basic 2005 was the first .NET version of the language to support operator overloading. Therefore, it's important that your overloaded operators be syntactic shortcuts to functionality provided by other methods that perform the same operation and can be called by CLS-compliant languages. In fact, I recommend that you design types as if overloaded operators don't exist. Then, later on, you can add overloaded operators in such a way that they simply call the methods you defined that carry the same semantic meaning.

Types and Formats of Overloaded Operators

You define all overloaded operators as public static methods on the classes they're meant to augment. Depending on the type of operator being overloaded, the method may accept either one or two parameters, and it always returns a value. For all operators except conversion operators, one of the parameter types must be of the same type as the enclosing type for the method. For example, it makes no sense to overload the + operator on class `Complex` if it adds two `double` values together, and, as you'll see shortly, it's impossible.

A typical + operator for a class `Complex` could look like the following:

```
public static Complex operator+( Complex lhs, Complex rhs )
```

Even though this method adds two instances of `Complex` together to produce a third instance of `Complex`, nothing says that one of the parameters cannot be that of type `double`, thus adding a `double` to a `Complex` instance. Now, how you add a `double` value to a `Complex` instance and produce another `Complex` instance is for you to decipher. In general, operator overloading syntax follows the previous pattern, with the + replaced with the operator du jour, and of course, some operators accept only one parameter.

■**Note** When comparing C# operators with C++ operators, note that C# operator declarations are more similar to the friend function technique of declaring C++ operators since C# operators are not instance methods.

There are essentially three different groups of overloadable operators. Unary operators accept only one parameter. Familiar unary operators include the ++ and -- operators. Binary operators, as the name implies, accept two parameters and include familiar mathematical operators such as +, -, /, and *, as well as the familiar comparison operators. Finally, conversion operators define a user-defined conversion. They must have either the operand or the return value type declared the same as the containing class or struct type.

Even though operators are static and public, and thus are inherited by derived classes, operator methods must have at least one parameter in their declaration that matches the *enclosing* type, making it impossible for the derived type's operator method to match the signature of the base class operator method exactly. For example, the following is not valid:

```
public class Apple
{
    public static Apple operator+( Apple rhs, Apple lhs ) {
        // Method does nothing and exists only for example.
        return rhs;
    }
}

public class GreenApple : Apple
{
    // INVALID!! – Won't compile.
    public static Apple operator+( Apple rhs, Apple lhs ) {
        // Method does nothing and exists only for example.
        return rhs;
    }
}
```

If you attempt to compile the previous code, you'll get the following compiler error:

```
error CS0563: One of the parameters of a binary operator must be the containing type
```

Operators Shouldn't Mutate Their Operands

You already know that operator methods are static. Therefore, it is highly recommended (read: required) that you do *not* mutate the operands passed into the operator methods. Instead, you should create a new instance of the return value type and return the result of the operation. Structs and classes that are immutable, such as System.String, are perfect candidates for implementing custom operators. This behavior is natural for operators such as boolean operators, which usually return a type different from the types passed into the operator.

■**Note** "Now wait just a minute!" some of you from the C++ community may be saying. "How in the world can you implement the postfix and prefix operators ++ and -- without mutating the operand?" The answer lies in the fact that the postfix and prefix operators as implemented in C# are somewhat different than those of C++. All C# operators are static, and that includes the postfix and prefix operators, whereas in C++ they are instance methods that modify the object instance through the `this` pointer. The beauty of the C# approach is that you don't have to worry about implementing two different versions of the ++ operator in order to support both postfix and prefix incrementing, as you do in C++. The compiler handles the task of making temporary copies of the object to handle the difference in behavior between postfix and prefix. This is yet another reason why your operators must return new instances while never modifying the state of the operands themselves. If you don't follow this practice, you're setting yourself up for some major debugging heartbreak.

Does Parameter Order Matter?

Suppose you create a struct to represent simple complex numbers—say, struct `Complex`—and you need to add instances of `Complex` together. It would also be convenient to be able to add a plain old `double` to the `Complex` instance. Adding this functionality is no problem, since you can overload the `operator+` method such that one parameter is a `Complex` and the other is a `double`. That declaration could look like the following:

```
static public Complex operator+( Complex lhs, double rhs )
```

With this operator declared and defined on the `Complex` struct, you can now write code such as the following:

```
Complex cpx1 = new Complex( 1.0, 2.0 );
Complex cpx2 = cpx1 + 20.0;
```

This saves you the time of having to create an extra `Complex` instance with just the real part set to `20.0` in order to add it to `cpx1`. However, suppose you want to be able to reverse the operands on the operator and do something like the following instead:

```
Complex cpx2 = 20.0 + cpx1;
```

If you want to support different orderings of operands of different types, you must provide different overloads of the operator. If you overload a binary operator that uses different parameter types, you can create a *mirror* overload—that is, another operator method that reverses the parameters.

Overloading the Addition Operator

Let's take a look at a cursory example of a `Complex` struct, which is by no means a complete implementation, but merely a demonstration of how to overload operators. Throughout this chapter, I'll build upon this example and add more operators to it:

```
using System;

public struct Complex
{
    public Complex( double real, double imaginary ) {
        this.real = real;
        this.imaginary = imaginary;
    }
```

```csharp
        static public Complex Add( Complex lhs,
                                   Complex rhs ) {
            return new Complex( lhs.real + rhs.real,
                                lhs.imaginary  + rhs.imaginary );
        }

        static public Complex Add( Complex lhs,
                                   double rhs ) {

            return new Complex( rhs + lhs.real,
                                lhs.imaginary );
        }

        public override string ToString() {
            return String.Format( "({0}, {1})",
                                  real,
                                  imaginary );
        }

        static public Complex operator+( Complex lhs,
                                         Complex rhs ) {
            return Add( lhs, rhs );
        }

        static public Complex operator+( double lhs,
                                         Complex rhs ) {
            return Add( rhs, lhs );
        }

        static public Complex operator+( Complex lhs,
                                         double rhs ) {
            return Add( lhs, rhs );
        }

        private double real;
        private double imaginary;
}

public class EntryPoint
{
    static void Main() {
        Complex cpx1 = new Complex( 1.0, 3.0 );
        Complex cpx2 = new Complex( 1.0, 2.0 );

        Complex cpx3 = cpx1 + cpx2;
        Complex cpx4 = 20.0 + cpx1;
        Complex cpx5 = cpx1 + 25.0;

        Console.WriteLine( "cpx1 == {0}", cpx1 );
        Console.WriteLine( "cpx2 == {0}", cpx2 );
        Console.WriteLine( "cpx3 == {0}", cpx3 );
        Console.WriteLine( "cpx4 == {0}", cpx4 );
        Console.WriteLine( "cpx5 == {0}", cpx5 );
    }
}
```

Notice that, as recommended, the overloaded operator methods call methods that perform the same operation. In fact, doing so makes supporting both orderings of operator+ that add a double to a Complex a snap.

■**Tip** If you're absolutely sure that your type will only be used in a C# environment or in a language that supports overloaded operators, then you can forgo this exercise and simply stick with the overloaded operators.

Operators That Can Be Overloaded

Let's take a quick look at which operators you can overload. Unary operators, binary operators, and conversion operators are the three general types of operators. It's impossible to list all of the conversion operators here, since the set is limitless. Additionally, you can use the one ternary operator—the familiar ?: operator—for conditional statements, but you cannot overload it directly. Later, in the "Boolean Operators" section, I describe what you can do to play nicely with the ternary operator. Table 6-1 lists all of the operators except the conversion operators.

Table 6-1. *Unary and Binary Operators*

Unary Operators	Binary Operators
+	+
-	-
!	*
~	/
++	%
--	&
true and false	|
	^
	<<
	>>
	== and !=
	> and <
	>= and <=

Comparison Operators

The binary comparison operators == and !=, < and >, and >= and <= are all required to be implemented as pairs. Of course, this makes perfect sense, because I doubt there would ever be a case where you would like to allow users to use operator== and not operator!=. Moreover, if your type allows ordering via implementation of the IComparable interface or its generic counterpart IComparable<T>, then it makes the most sense to implement all comparison operators. Implementing these operators is trivial if you follow the canonical guidelines given in Chapters 4 and 13 by overriding Equals and GetHashCode and implementing IComparable (and optionally IComparable<T> and IEquatable<T>) appropriately. Given that, overloading the operators merely requires you to call those implementations. Let's look at a modified form of the Complex number that follows this pattern to implement all of the comparison operators:

```
using System;

public struct Complex : IComparable,
                        IEquatable<Complex>,
                        IComparable<Complex>
{
    public Complex( double real, double img ) {
        this.real = real;
        this.img = img;
    }

    // System.Object override
    public override bool Equals( object other ) {
        bool result = false;
        if( other is Complex ) {
            result = Equals( (Complex) other );
        }
        return result;
    }

    // Typesafe version
    public bool Equals( Complex that ) {
        return (this.real == that.real &&
                this.img == that.img);
    }

    // Must override this if overriding Object.Equals()
    public override int GetHashCode() {
        return (int) this.Magnitude;
    }

    // Typesafe version
    public int CompareTo( Complex that ) {
        int result;
        if( Equals( that ) ) {
            result = 0;
        } else if( this.Magnitude > that.Magnitude ) {
            result = 1;
        } else {
            result = -1;
        }

        return result;
    }

    // IComparable implementation
    int IComparable.CompareTo( object other ) {
        if( !(other is Complex) ) {
            throw new ArgumentException( "Bad Comparison" );
        }

        return CompareTo( (Complex) other );
    }
```

```csharp
        // System.Object override
        public override string ToString() {
            return String.Format( "({0}, {1})",
                                  real,
                                  img );
        }

        public double Magnitude {
            get {
                return Math.Sqrt( Math.Pow(this.real, 2) +
                                  Math.Pow(this.img, 2) );
            }
        }

        // Overloaded operators
        public static bool operator==( Complex lhs, Complex rhs ) {
            return lhs.Equals( rhs );
        }

        public static bool operator!=( Complex lhs, Complex rhs ) {
            return !lhs.Equals( rhs );
        }

        public static bool operator<( Complex lhs, Complex rhs ) {
            return lhs.CompareTo( rhs ) < 0;
        }

        public static bool operator>( Complex lhs, Complex rhs ) {
            return lhs.CompareTo( rhs ) > 0;
        }

        public static bool operator<=( Complex lhs, Complex rhs ) {
            return lhs.CompareTo( rhs ) <= 0;
        }

        public static bool operator>=( Complex lhs, Complex rhs ) {
            return lhs.CompareTo( rhs ) >= 0;
        }

        // Other methods omitted for clarity.

        private double real;
        private double img;
    }

public class EntryPoint
{
    static void Main() {
        Complex cpx1 = new Complex( 1.0, 3.0 );
        Complex cpx2 = new Complex( 1.0, 2.0 );

        Console.WriteLine( "cpx1 = {0}, cpx1.Magnitude = {1}",
                           cpx1, cpx1.Magnitude );
        Console.WriteLine( "cpx2 = {0}, cpx2.Magnitude = {1}\n",
                           cpx2, cpx2.Magnitude );
        Console.WriteLine( "cpx1 == cpx2 ? {0}", cpx1 == cpx2 );
        Console.WriteLine( "cpx1 != cpx2 ? {0}", cpx1 != cpx2 );
```

```
        Console.WriteLine( "cpx1 <  cpx2 ? {0}", cpx1 < cpx2 );
        Console.WriteLine( "cpx1 >  cpx2 ? {0}", cpx1 > cpx2 );
        Console.WriteLine( "cpx1 <= cpx2 ? {0}", cpx1 <= cpx2 );
        Console.WriteLine( "cpx1 >= cpx2 ? {0}", cpx1 >= cpx2 );
    }
}
```

Notice that the operator methods merely call the methods that implement Equals and Com-pareTo. Also, I've followed the guideline of providing type-safe versions of the two methods by implementing IComparable<Complex> and IEquatable<Complex>, since the Complex type is a value type and I want to avoid boxing if possible.[1] Additionally, I implemented the IComparable.CompareTo method explicitly to give the compiler a bigger type-safety hammer to wield by making it harder for users to call the wrong one inadvertently. Anytime you can utilize the compiler's type system to sniff out errors at compile time rather than run time, you should do so. Had I not implemented IComparable.CompareTo explicitly, then the compiler would have happily compiled a statement where I attempt to compare an Apple instance to a Complex instance. Of course, you would expect an InvalidCastException at run time if you were to attempt something so silly, but again, always prefer compile-time errors over run time errors.

Conversion Operators

Conversion operators are, as the name implies, operators that convert objects of one type into objects of another. Conversion operators can allow implicit conversion as well as explicit conver-sion. Implicit conversion is done with a simple assignment, whereas explicit conversion requires the familiar casting syntax with the target type of the conversion provided in parentheses immedi-ately preceding the instance being assigned from.

There is an important restriction on implicit operators. The C# standard requires that implicit operators do not throw exceptions and that they're always guaranteed to succeed with no loss of information. If you cannot meet that requirement, then your conversion must be an explicit one. For example, when converting from one type to another, there's always the possibility for loss of information if the target type is not as expressive as the original type. Consider the conversion from long to short. Clearly, it's possible that information could be lost if the value in the long is greater than the highest value a short can represent. Even though an exception is not thrown by default in this case if truncation occurs, in some cases it may make sense to throw an exception at run time. Such a conversion must be an explicit one and require the user to use the casting syntax. Now, sup-pose you were going the other way and converting a short into a long. Such a conversion will always succeed, so therefore it can be implicit.

■**Note** Performing explicit conversions from a type with larger storage to a type with smaller storage may result in a truncation error if the original value is too large to be represented by the smaller type. For example, if you explicitly cast a long into a short, you may trigger an overflow situation. By default, your compiled code will silently perform the truncation. If you compile your code with the /checked+ compiler option, it actually would throw a System.OverflowException if your explicit conversion from a long to a short caused an overflow. I recommend that you lean toward building with /checked+ turned on.

Let's see what kind of conversion operators you should provide for Complex. I can think of at least one definite case, and that's the conversion from double to Complex. Definitely, such a

---

1. I describe this guideline in more detail in Chapter 5 in the section titled "Explicit Interface Implementation with Value Types."

conversion should be an implicit one. Another consideration is from Complex to double. Clearly, this conversion requires an explicit conversion. (Since casting a Complex to double makes no sense anyway and is only shown here for the sake of example, you can choose to return the magnitude rather than just the real portion of the complex number when casting to a double.) Let's look at an example of implementing conversion operators:

```
using System;

public struct Complex
{
    public Complex( double real, double imaginary ) {
        this.real = real;
        this.imaginary = imaginary;
    }

    // System.Object override
    public override string ToString() {
        return String.Format( "({0}, {1})", real, imaginary );
    }

    public double Magnitude {
        get {
            return Math.Sqrt( Math.Pow(this.real, 2) +
                              Math.Pow(this.imaginary, 2) );
        }
    }

    public static implicit operator Complex( double d ) {
        return new Complex( d, 0 );
    }

    public static explicit operator double( Complex c ) {
        return c.Magnitude;
    }

    // Other methods omitted for clarity.

    private double real;
    private double imaginary;
}

public class EntryPoint
{
    static void Main() {
        Complex cpx1 = new Complex( 1.0, 3.0 );
        Complex cpx2 = 2.0;           // Use implicit operator.

        double d = (double) cpx1;    // Use explicit operator.

        Console.WriteLine( "cpx1 = {0}", cpx1 );
        Console.WriteLine( "cpx2 = {0}", cpx2 );
        Console.WriteLine( "d = {0}", d );
    }
}
```

The syntax in the Main method uses conversion operators. However, be careful when implementing conversion operators to make sure that you don't open up users to any surprises or confusion with your implicit conversions. It's difficult to introduce confusion with explicit operators when the users of your type must use the casting syntax to get it to work. After all, how can users be surprised when they must provide the type to convert to within parentheses? On the other hand, inadvertent use or misguided use of implicit conversion can be the source of much confusion. If you write a bunch of implicit conversion operators that make no semantic sense, I guarantee your users will find themselves in a confusing spot one day when the compiler decides to do a conversion for them when they least expect it. For example, the compiler could do an implicit conversion when trying to coerce an argument on a method call. Even if the conversion operators do make semantic sense, they can still provide plenty of surprises, because the compiler will have the liberty of silently converting instances of one type to another when it feels it's necessary.

C# requires that you explicitly write an implicit operator on the types that you define.[2] Thus, you can't accidentally create an implicit conversion operator without realizing you're doing so (as you can in C++). However, in order to provide these conversions, you must bend the rules of method overloading ever so slightly for this one case. Consider the case where Complex provides another explicit conversion operator to convert to an instance of Fraction as well as to an instance of double. This would give Complex two methods with the following signatures:

```
public static explicit operator double( Complex d )
public static explicit operator Fraction( Complex f )
```

These two methods take the same type, Complex, and return another type. However, the overload rules clearly state that the return type doesn't participate in the method signature. Going by those rules, these two methods should be ambiguous and result in a compiler error. In fact, they are not ambiguous, because a special rule exists to allow the return type of conversion operators to be considered in the signature. Incidentally, the implicit and explicit keywords don't participate in the signature of conversion operator methods. Therefore, it's impossible to have both implicit and explicit conversion operators with the same signature. Naturally, at least one of the types in the signature of a conversion operator must be the enclosing type. It is invalid for a type Complex to implement a conversion operator from type Apples to type Oranges.

Boolean Operators

It makes sense for some types to participate in Boolean tests, such as within the parentheses of an if block or with the ternary operator ?:. In order for this to work, you have two alternatives. The first is that you can implement two conversion operators, known as operator true and operator false. You must implement these two operators in pairs to allow the Complex number to participate in Boolean test expressions. Consider the following modification to the Complex type, where you now want to use it in expressions where a value of (0, 0) means false and anything else means true:

```
using System;

public struct Complex
{
```

---

2. Yes, I realize the implications of my explicit, and possible confusing, use of the words *implicit* and *explicit*. I explicitly hope that I have not implicitly confused you.

```
        public Complex( double real, double imaginary ) {
            this.real = real;
            this.imaginary = imaginary;
        }

        // System.Object override
        public override string ToString() {
            return String.Format( "({0}, {1})",
                                  real,
                                  imaginary );
        }

        public double Magnitude {
            get {
                return Math.Sqrt( Math.Pow(this.real, 2) +
                                  Math.Pow(this.imaginary, 2) );
            }
        }

        public static bool operator true( Complex c ) {
            return (c.real != 0) || (c.imaginary != 0);
        }

        public static bool operator false( Complex c ) {
            return (c.real == 0) && (c.imaginary == 0);
        }

        // Other methods omitted for clarity.

        private double real;
        private double imaginary;
    }

    public class EntryPoint
    {
        static void Main() {
            Complex cpx1 = new Complex( 1.0, 3.0 );
            if( cpx1 ) {
                Console.WriteLine( "cpx1 is true" );
            } else {
                Console.WriteLine( "cpx1 is false" );
            }

            Complex cpx2 = new Complex( 0, 0 );
            Console.WriteLine( "cpx2 is {0}", cpx2 ? "true" : "false" );
        }
    }
```

You can see the two operators for applying the true and false tests to the Complex type. Notice that the declaration syntax is a bit quirky. The syntax looks almost the same as the conversion operators, except that it includes the return type of bool. I'm not quite sure why this is necessary, since you can't provide a type other than bool as the return type. If you do, the compiler will quickly tell you that the only valid return type from operator true or operator false is a bool. Nevertheless, you must supply the return type for these two operators. Also, notice that you cannot mark these operators explicit or implicit, because they're not conversion operators. Once you define these two operators on the type, you can use instances of Complex in Boolean test expressions, as shown in the Main method.

Alternatively, you can choose to implement a conversion to type `bool` to achieve the same result. Typically, you'll want to implement this operator implicitly for ease of use. Consider the modified form of the previous example using the implicit `bool` conversion operator rather than `operator true` and `operator false`:

```
using System;

public struct Complex
{
    public Complex( double real, double imaginary ) {
        this.real = real;
        this.imaginary = imaginary;
    }

    // System.Object override
    public override string ToString() {
        return String.Format( "({0}, {1})",
                              real,
                              imaginary );
    }

    public double Magnitude {
        get {
            return Math.Sqrt( Math.Pow(this.real, 2) +
                              Math.Pow(this.imaginary, 2) );
        }
    }

    public static implicit operator bool( Complex c ) {
        return (c.real != 0) || (c.imaginary != 0);
    }

    // Other methods omitted for clarity.

    private double real;
    private double imaginary;
}

public class EntryPoint
{
    static void Main() {
        Complex cpx1 = new Complex( 1.0, 3.0 );
        if( cpx1 ) {
            Console.WriteLine( "cpx1 is true" );
        } else {
            Console.WriteLine( "cpx1 is false" );
        }

        Complex cpx2 = new Complex( 0, 0 );
        Console.WriteLine( "cpx2 is {0}", cpx2 ? "true" : "false" );
    }
}
```

The end result is the same with this example. Now, you may be wondering why you would ever want to implement operator true and operator false rather than just an implicit bool conversion operator. The answer lies in whether it is valid for your type to be converted to a bool type or not. With the latter form, where you implement the implicit conversion operator, the following statement would be valid:

```
bool f = cpx1;
```

This assignment would work because the compiler would find the implicit conversion operator at compile time and apply it. However, if you were extremely tired the night you coded this line and really meant to assign f from a completely different variable, it might be a long time before you find the bug. This is one example of how gratuitous use of implicit conversion operators can get you in trouble.

The rule of thumb is this: Provide only enough of what is necessary to get the job done and no more. If all you want is for your type—in this case, Complex—to participate in Boolean test expressions, only implement operator true and operator false. Do not implement the implicit bool conversion operator unless you have a real need for it. If you do happen to have a need for it, and thus implement the implicit bool conversion operator, you don't have to implement operator true and operator false, because they would be redundant. If you do provide all three, the compiler will go with the implicit conversion operator rather than operator true and operator false, because invoking one is not more efficient than the other, assuming you code them the same.

Summary

In this chapter, I covered some useful guidelines for overloading operators, including unary, binary, and conversion operators. Operator overloading is one of the features that makes C# such a powerful and expressive .NET language. However, just because you can do something doesn't mean that you should. Misuse of implicit conversion operators and improperly defined semantics in other operator overloads has proven time and time again to be the source of great user confusion (and that user could be the author of the type) as well as unintended behavior. When it comes to overloading operators, provide only enough of what is necessary, and don't go counter to the general semantics of the various operators. Since the CLS doesn't require overloaded operator support, not all .NET languages support overloaded operators. Therefore, it's important to always provide explicitly named methods that provide the same functionality. Sometimes, those methods are already defined in system interfaces, such as IComparable or IComparable<T>. Never isolate functionality strictly within overloaded operators unless you're 100% sure that your code will be consumed by .NET languages that do support operator overloading.

In the next chapter, I'll cover the intricacies and tricks involved in creating exception-safe and exception-neutral code in the .NET Framework.

## CHAPTER 7

Exception Handling and Exception Safety

The CLR contains strong support for exceptions. Exceptions can be created and thrown at a point where code execution cannot continue because of some exceptional condition (usually a method failure or an invalid state). Writing exception-safe code is a difficult art to master. It would be a mistake to assume that the only tasks required when writing exception-safe code are simply throwing exceptions when an error occurs and catching them at some point. Such a view of exception-safe code is shortsighted and will lead you down a path of despair. Instead, exception-safe coding means guaranteeing the integrity of the system in the face of exceptions. When an exception is thrown, the runtime will iteratively unwind the stack while cleaning up. Your job as an exception-safe programmer is to structure your code in such a way that the integrity of the state of your objects is not compromised as the stack unwinds. That is the true essence of exception-safe coding techniques.

In this chapter, I will show you how the CLR handles exceptions and the mechanics involved with handling exceptions. However, there is more to exception handling than just that. For example, I'll describe which areas of code should handle exceptions as well as pitfalls to avoid when implementing exception handling. Most importantly, I will show you how writing exception-safe code may not even involve handling exceptions at all. Such code is typically called *exception-neutral* code. It may sound surprising, but read on for all of the details.

How the CLR Treats Exceptions

Once an exception is thrown, the CLR begins the process of unwinding the execution stack iteratively, frame by frame.[1] As it does so, it cleans up any objects that are local to each stack frame. At some point, a frame on the stack could have an exception handler registered for the type of exception thrown. Once the CLR reaches that frame, it invokes the exception handler to remedy the situation. If the stack unwinds completely and a handler is not found for the exception thrown, then the unhandled-exception event for the current application domain may be fired and the application could be aborted.

---

1. If you're not familiar with the term *stack frame*, you may want to reference http://en.wikipedia.org/wiki/ Stack_frame. In short, as each method is called throughout the execution of a program, a frame is built on the stack that contains the passed parameters and any local parameters to the method. The frame is deleted upon return from the method. However, as the method calls other methods, and so on, new frames are stacked on top of the current frame, thus implementing a nested call-frame structure.

Mechanics of Handling Exceptions in C#

If you've ever used exceptions in other C-style languages such as C++, Java, or even C/C++ using the Microsoft structured exception-handling extensions (__try/__catch/__finally), then you're already familiar with the basic syntax of exceptions in C#. In that case, you may find yourself skimming the next few sections or treating the material as a refresher. I've tried to point out any areas that are significantly different from the other C-style languages in the process.

Throwing Exceptions

The act of throwing an exception is actually quite easy. You simply execute a throw statement whose parameter is the exception you would like to throw. For example, suppose you have written a custom collection class that allows users to access items by index, and you would like to notify users when an invalid index is passed as a parameter. You could throw an ArgumentOutOfRange exception, as in the following code:

```
public class MyCollection
{
    public object GetItem( int index ) {
        if( index < 0 || index >= count ) {
            throw new ArgumentOutOfRangeException();
        }

        // Do other useful stuff here
    }

    private int count;
}
```

The runtime can also throw exceptions as a side effect to code execution. An example of a system-generated exception is NullReferenceException, which occurs if you attempt to access a field or call a method on an object when, in fact, the reference to the object doesn't exist.

Changes with Unhandled Exceptions Starting with .NET 2.0

When an exception is thrown, the runtime begins to search up the stack for a matching catch block for the exception. As it walks up the execution stack, it unwinds the stack at the same time, cleaning up each frame along the way.

If the search ends in the last frame for the thread, and it still finds no handler for the exception, the exception is considered unhandled at that point. What happens next depends on what version of the .NET Framework your code uses.

■**Note** You can install an unhandled-exception filter by registering a delegate with AppDomain. UnhandledException. When an unhandled exception comes up through the stack, this delegate will be called and will receive an instance of UnhandledExceptionEventArgs.

■**Note** The CLR translates unhandled exceptions passing through static constructors. I'll cover that in more detail in the section titled "Exceptions Thrown in Static Constructors."

In .NET 1.1, the CLR designers decided to swallow certain unhandled exceptions in the pursuit of greater stability. For example, if a finalizer throws an exception in .NET 1.1 instead of aborting the finalizer thread and the process, the exception is swallowed and not allowed to kill the finalizer thread or terminate the process. Similarly, if an unhandled exception percolates up in a thread other than the main thread, that thread is terminated without affecting the rest of the process. In a thread-pool thread, the exception is swallowed and the thread is returned to the pool, which is behavior that is similar to exception handling in the finalizer thread. If an unhandled exception propagates up from the main thread, then it behaves as expected, and either the process is terminated or the JIT debugging dialog is displayed, asking the user what to do.

This behavior sounds good in concept, but in reality, it gives the opposite of the desired result. Instead of providing greater stability, systems become unstable because code runs in a nondeterministic state. For example, consider a finalizer that does some crucial work. Suppose that halfway through that work, an exception is thrown. The second half of the work in the finalizer never runs. Now, the system is in a potentially unstable, half-baked state. Everything continues to run normally, although the state of the system could be far from normal. In practice, this causes great instability because the sources of the errors are hard to find since the exceptions are swallowed.

.NET 2.0 solves this problem by requiring that any unhandled exception, except AppDomainUnloadException and ThreadAbortException, causes the thread to terminate. It sounds rude, but in reality, this is the behavior you should want from an unhandled exception. After all, it's an *unhandled* exception. Now that the thread terminates as expected, a big red flag is raised at the point of the exception that allows you to find the problem immediately and fix it. This is always a good thing. You always want errors to present themselves as soon as possible; never swallow exceptions and just let the system keep running as if everything were normal.

■Note If you really want the unhandled-exception behavior to emulate the .NET 1.1 behavior, you can request that by adding the following option to the application's configuration file:

```
<system>
    <runtime>
        <legacyUnhandledExceptionPolicy enabled="1"/>
    </runtime>
</system>
```

Syntax Overview of the try Statement

The code within a try block is guarded against exceptions such that, if an exception is thrown, the runtime searches for a suitable catch block to handle the exception. Whether a suitable catch block exists or not, if a finally block is provided, the finally block is always executed no matter how execution flow leaves the try block. Let's look at an example of a C# try statement:

```
using System;
using System.Collections;
using System.Runtime.CompilerServices;

// Disable compiler warning: CS1058
[assembly: RuntimeCompatibility(WrapNonExceptionThrows = false)]

public class Entrypoint
{
```

```
static void Main() {
    try {
        ArrayList list = new ArrayList();
        list.Add( 1 );

        Console.WriteLine( "Item 10 = {0}", list[10] );
    }
    catch( ArgumentOutOfRangeException x ) {
        Console.WriteLine( "=== ArgumentOutOfRangeException"+
                           " Handler ===" );
        Console.WriteLine( x );
        Console.WriteLine( "=== ArgumentOutOfRangeException"+
                           " Handler ===\n\n" );
    }
    catch( Exception x ) {
        Console.WriteLine( "=== Exception Handler ===" );
        Console.WriteLine( x );
        Console.WriteLine( "=== Exception Handler ===\n\n" );
    }
    catch {
        Console.WriteLine( "=== Unexpected Exception" +
                           " Handler ===" );
        Console.WriteLine( "An exception I was not" +
                           " expecting..." );
        Console.WriteLine( "=== Unexpected Exception" +
                           " Handler ===" );
    }
    finally {
        Console.WriteLine( "Cleaning up..." );
    }
}
```

Once you see the code in the try block, you know it is destined to throw an ArgumentOutOfRange exception. Once the exception is thrown, the runtime begins searching for a suitable catch clause that is part of this try statement and matches the type of the exception as best as possible. Clearly, the first catch clause is the one that fits best. Therefore, the runtime will immediately begin executing the statements in the first catch block. Had I not been interested in the actual exception contents, I could have left off the declaration of the exception variable x in the catch clause and only declared the type. But in this case, I wanted to demonstrate that exception objects in C# produce a nice stack trace that can be useful during debugging. While generating the output for this chapter, I compiled the samples without debugging symbols turned on. However, if you turn on debugging symbols, you'll notice that the stack trace also includes file and line numbers of the various levels in the stack.

The second catch clause will catch exceptions of the general Exception type. Should the code in the try block throw an exception derived from System.Exception other than ArgumentOutOfRangeException, then this catch block would handle it. In C#, multiple catch clauses associated with a single try block must be ordered such that more specific exception types are listed first. The C# compiler will simply not compile code in which more general catch clauses are listed before more specific catch clauses. You can verify this by swapping the order of the first two catch clauses in the previous example.

In C#, every exception that you can possibly throw must derive from System.Exception. Since I declared a catch clause that traps exceptions of type System.Exception specifically, what's the story with the third and last catch clause? Even though it is impossible to throw an exception of any type not derived from System.Exception in the C# language, it is not impossible in the CLR. (For example, you can throw an exception of any type in C++.) Therefore, if you wrote `ArrayList` in a language that allows this, it's possible that the code could throw a not-very-useful type, such as `System.Int32`. It sounds strange, but it is possible. In this case, you can catch such an exception in C# by using a `catch` clause with neither an explicit exception type nor a variable. Unfortunately, there's no easy way to know what type the thrown exception is. Also, a `try` statement can have, at most, one such general `catch` clause.

■**Note** Starting with .NET 2.0, the situation regarding general catch clauses is a little different than in .NET 1.1. It features a new attribute, `RuntimeCompatibilityAttribute`, that you can attach to your assembly. The C# and Visual Basic compilers that target .NET 2.0 apply this property by default. It tells the runtime to wrap exceptions that are not derived from `System.Exception` inside an exception of type `RuntimeWrappedException`, which is derived from `System.Exception`. This is handy, because it allows your C# code to access the thrown exception. Previously, you could not access the thrown exception, since it was caught by a general, parameterless `catch` clause. You can access the actual thrown exception type via the `RuntimeWrappedException.WrappedException` property. If your code contains a parameterless `catch` clause, the compiler emits a warning of type `CS1058` by default, unless you disable the attribute as I did in the previous example.

Last of all, there is the `finally` block. No matter how the `try` block is exited, whether by reaching the end point of the block or via an exception or a `return` statement, the `finally` block will always execute. If there is a suitable `catch` block in the same frame as the `finally` block, it will execute before the `finally` block. You can see this by looking at the output of the previous code example, which looks like the following:

```
=== ArgumentOutOfRangeException Handler ===
System.ArgumentOutOfRangeException: Index was out of range.  Must be ?
non-negative and less than the size of the collection.
Parameter name: index
   at System.Collections.ArrayList.get_Item(Int32 index)
   at Entrypoint.Main()
=== ArgumentOutOfRangeException Handler ===


Cleaning up...
```

Rethrowing Exceptions and Translating Exceptions

Within a particular stack frame, you may find it necessary to catch all exceptions, or a specific subset of exceptions, long enough to do some cleanup and then rethrow the exception in order to let it continue to propagate up the stack. To do this, you use the `throw` statement with no parameter:

```
using System;
using System.Collections;

public class Entrypoint
{
    static void Main() {
        try {
            try {
                ArrayList list = new ArrayList();
```

```
                list.Add( 1 );

                Console.WriteLine( "Item 10 = {0}", list[10] );
            }
            catch( ArgumentOutOfRangeException ) {
                Console.WriteLine( "Do some useful work and" +
                                   " then rethrow" );

                // Rethrow caught exception.
                throw;
            }
            finally {
                Console.WriteLine( "Cleaning up..." );
            }
        }
        catch {
            Console.WriteLine( "Done" );
        }
    }
}
```

Note that any finally blocks associated with the exception frame that the catch block is associated with will execute before any higher-level exception handlers are executed. You can see this in the output from the code:

```
Do some useful work and then rethrow
Cleaning up...
Done
```

In the "Achieving Exception Neutrality" section, I introduce some techniques that can help you avoid having to catch an exception, do cleanup, and then rethrow the exception. That sort of work flow is cumbersome, since you must be careful to rethrow the exception appropriately. If you accidentally forget to rethrow, things could get ugly, since you would not likely be remedying the exceptional situation. The techniques that I show you help you achieve a goal where the only place to introduce a catch block is at the point where correctional action can occur.

Sometimes, you may find it necessary to "translate" an exception within an exception handler. In this case, you catch an exception of one type, but you throw an exception of a different, possibly more precise, type in the catch block for the next level of exception handlers to deal with. Consider the following example:

```
using System;
using System.Collections;

public class MyException : Exception
{
    public MyException( String reason, Exception inner )
        :base( reason, inner ) {
    }
}

public class Entrypoint
{
    static void Main() {
        try {
            try {
                ArrayList list = new ArrayList();
```

```
                list.Add( 1 );

                Console.WriteLine( "Item 10 = {0}", list[10] );
            }
            catch( ArgumentOutOfRangeException x ) {
                Console.WriteLine( "Do some useful work" +
                                   " and then rethrow" );
                throw new MyException( "I'd rather throw this",
                                       x ) ;
            }
            finally {
                Console.WriteLine( "Cleaning up..." );
            }
        }
        catch( Exception x ) {
            Console.WriteLine( x );
            Console.WriteLine( "Done" );
        }
    }
}
```

One special quality of the System.Exception type is its ability to contain an inner exception reference via the Exception.InnerException property. This way, when the new exception is thrown, you can preserve the chain of exceptions for the handlers that process them. I recommend you use this useful feature of the standard exception type of C# when you translate exceptions. The output from the previous code is as follows:

```
Do some useful work and then rethrow
Cleaning up...
MyException: I'd rather throw this --> System.ArgumentOutOfRangeException: ➥
Index was out of range. ➥
Must be non-negative and less than the size of the collection.
Parameter name: index
    at System.Collections.ArrayList.get_Item(Int32 index)
    at Entrypoint.Main()
    -- End of inner exception stack trace --
    at Entrypoint.Main()
Done
```

Keep in mind that you should avoid translating exceptions if possible. The more you catch and then rethrow within a stack, the more you insulate the code that handles the exception from the code that throws the exception. That is, it's harder to correlate the point of catch to the original point of throw. Yes, the Exception.InnerException property helps mitigate some of this disconnect, but it still can be tricky to find the root cause of a problem if there are exception translations along the way.

Exceptions Thrown in finally Blocks

It is possible, but highly inadvisable, to throw exceptions within a finally block. The following code shows an example:

```
using System;
using System.Collections;

public class Entrypoint
```

```
{
    static void Main() {
        try {
            try {
                ArrayList list = new ArrayList();
                list.Add( 1 );

                Console.WriteLine( "Item 10 = {0}", list[10] );
            }
            finally {
                Console.WriteLine( "Cleaning up..." );
                throw new Exception( "I like to throw" );
            }
        }
        catch( ArgumentOutOfRangeException ) {
            Console.WriteLine( "Oops!  Argument out of range!" );
        }
        catch {
            Console.WriteLine( "Done" );
        }
    }
}
```

The first exception is simply lost, and the new exception is propagated up the stack. Clearly, this is not desirable. You never want to lose track of exceptions, because it becomes virtually impossible to determine what caused an exception in the first place.

Exceptions Thrown in Finalizers

C# destructors are not really deterministic destructors, but rather CLR finalizers. Finalizers are run in the context of the finalizer thread, which is effectively an arbitrary thread context. If the finalizer were to throw an exception, the CLR might not know how to handle the situation and might simply shut down the thread (and the process). Consider the following code:

```
using System;

public class Person
{
    ~Person() {
        Console.WriteLine( "Cleaning up Person..." );
        Console.WriteLine( "Done Cleaning up Person..." );
    }
}

public class Employee : Person
{
    ~Employee() {
        Console.WriteLine( "Cleaning up Employee..." );
        object obj = null;

        // The following will throw an exception.
        Console.WriteLine( obj.ToString() );
        Console.WriteLine( "Done cleaning up Employee..." );
    }
}
```

```
public class Entrypoint
{
    static void Main() {
        Employee emp = new Employee();
        emp = null;
    }
}
```

The output from executing this code is as follows:

```
Cleaning up Employee...

Unhandled Exception: System.NullReferenceException: Object reference not set ➥
to an instance of an object.
   at Employee.Finalize()
Cleaning up Person...
Done Cleaning up Person...
```

You will notice slightly different behavior with this example between the .NET 1.1 and .NET 2.0 runtimes. In .NET 1.1, the exception is swallowed while it is logged in the console, and execution then continues. In .NET 2.0, your development environment presents you with the familiar JIT debugger dialog, asking if you would like to debug the application. The problem is, you have a limited amount of time within which to respond before the .NET 2.0 runtime aborts your application. If you haven't already, be sure to read about how .NET 1.1 and .NET 2.0 treat unhandled exceptions differently in this chapter's previous section, "Changes with Unhandled Exceptions in .NET 2.0."

You should avoid knowingly throwing exceptions in finalizers at all costs, because you could abort the process. As a final note, be sure to read about all of the pros and cons of creating a finalizer in the first place in Chapter 13.

Exceptions Thrown in Static Constructors

If an exception is thrown and there is no handler in the stack, so that the search for the handler ends up in the static constructor, the runtime handles this case specially. It translates the exception into a System.TypeInitializationException and throws that instead. Before throwing the new exception, it sets the InnerException property of the new exception to the original exception. That way, any handler for type initialization exceptions can easily find out exactly why things failed.

Translating such an exception makes sense because constructors cannot, by their very nature, have a return value to indicate success or failure. Exceptions are the only mechanism you have to indicate that a constructor has failed. More importantly, since the system calls static constructors at system-defined times,[2] it makes sense for them to use the TypeInitializationException type in order to be more specific about when something went wrong. For example, suppose you have a static constructor that can potentially throw an ArgumentOutOfRangeException. Now, imagine the frustration users would have if your exception propagated out to the enclosing thread at some seemingly random time, because the exact moment of a static constructor call is system-defined. It could appear that the ArgumentOutOfRange exception materialized out of thin air. Wrapping your exception inside a TypeInitializationException takes a little of the mystery out of it and tips off users, or hopefully the developer, that the problem happened during type initialization.

---

2. The system could call static constructors at type load time or just prior to a static member access, depending on how the CLR is configured for the current process.

The following code shows an example of what a `TypeInitializationException` with an inner exception looks like:

```
using System;
using System.IO;

class EventLogger
{
    static EventLogger() {
        eventLog = File.CreateText( "logfile.txt" );

        // Statement below will throw an exception.
        strLogName = (string) strLogName.Clone();
    }

    static public void WriteLog( string someText ) {
        eventLog.Write( someText );
    }

    static private StreamWriter eventLog;
    static private string       strLogName;
}

public class EntryPoint
{
    static void Main() {
        EventLogger.WriteLog( "Log this!" );
    }
}
```

When you run this example, the output looks like the following:

```
Unhandled Exception: System.TypeInitializationException:
The type initializer for 'EventLogger' threw
an exception. --> System.NullReferenceException: Object reference not set ➥
to an instance of an object.
   at EventLogger..cctor()
   -- End of inner exception stack trace --
   at EntryPoint.Main()
```

Notice that along with describing that the outermost exception is of type `TypeInitializationException`, the output also shows that the inner exception, which started it all, is a `NullReferenceException`.

Who Should Handle Exceptions?

Where should you handle exceptions? You can find the answer by applying a variant of the Expert pattern, which states that work should be done by the entity that is the expert with respect to that work. That is a circuitous way of saying that you should catch the exception at the point where you can actually handle it with some degree of knowledge available to remedy the exceptional situation. Sometimes, the catching entity could be close to the point of the exception generation within the stack frame. The code could catch the exception, then take some corrective action, and then allow the program to continue to execute normally. In other cases, the only reasonable place to catch an exception is at the entry-point `Main` method, at which point you could either abort the process after providing some useful data, or reset the process as if the application were just restarted. The bottom line is that you should figure out the best way to recover from exceptions, if that is possible, and the best place to do so based upon where it makes the most sense to do it.

Avoid Using Exceptions to Control Flow

It can be tempting to use exceptions to manage the flow of execution in complex methods. This is never a good idea, for a couple of reasons. First, exceptions are generally expensive to generate and handle. Therefore, if you were to use them to control execution flow within a method that is at the heart of your application, your performance would likely degrade. Second, it trivializes the exceptional nature of exceptions in the first place. The whole point of exceptions is to indicate an exceptional condition in a way that can be handled or reported cleanly.

Historically, programmers have been rather lazy when it comes to handling error conditions. How many times have you seen code where the programmer never even bothered to check the return value of an API function or a method call? Such lackadaisical approaches to error handling can lead to headaches in a hurry. Exceptions provide a syntactically succinct way to indicate and handle error conditions without littering your code with a plethora of `if` blocks and other traditional (nonexception-based) error-handling constructs. At the same time, the runtime supports exceptions, and it does a lot of work on your behalf when exceptions are thrown. Unwinding the stack is no trivial task in itself. Lastly, the point where an exception is thrown and the point where it's handled can be disjointed and have no connection to each other. Thus, it can be difficult when reading code to determine where an exception will be caught and handled. These reasons alone are enough for you to stick to traditional techniques when managing normal execution flow.

■**Note** You can find an article, "The Cost of Exceptions," on Rico Mariani's blog at `http://blogs.msdn.com/ ricom/archive/2003/12/19/44697.aspx`. Rico is an expert on performance-related issues in the CLR.

Achieving Exception Neutrality

When exceptions were first added to C++, many developers were excited to be able to throw them, catch them, and handle them. In fact, a common misconception at the time was that exception handling simply consisted of strategically placing `try` statements throughout the code and tossing in an occasional `throw` when necessary. Over time, the developer community realized that dropping `try` statements all over the place made their code difficult to read when, most of the time, the only thing they wanted to do was clean up gracefully when an exception was thrown and allow the exception to keep propagating up the stack. Even worse, it made the code hard to write and difficult to maintain. Code that doesn't handle exceptions but is expected to behave properly in the face of exceptions is generally called *exception-neutral* code.

Clearly, there had to be a better way to write exception-neutral code without having to rely on writing `try` statements all over the place. In fact, the only place you need a `try` statement is the point at which you perform any sort of system recovery or logging in response to an exception. Over time, everyone started to realize that writing `try` statements was, in fact, the least significant part of writing exception-safe and exception-neutral code. Generally, the only code that should catch an exception is code that knows specifically how to remedy the situation. That code could even be in the main entry point and could merely reset the system to a known start state, effectively restarting the application.

By exception-neutral code, I mean code that doesn't really have the capability to specifically handle the exception but that must be able to handle exceptions gracefully. Usually, this code sits somewhere on the stack in between the code that throws the exception and the code that catches the exception, and it must not be adversely affected by the exception passing through on its way up the stack. At this point, some of you are probably starting to think about the throw statement with no parameters that allows you to catch an exception, do some work, and then rethrow the exception. However, I want to introduce you to an arguably cleaner technique that allows you to write exception-neutral code without using a single try statement and that also produces code that is easier to read and more robust.

Basic Structure of Exception-Neutral Code

The general idea behind writing exception-neutral code is similar to the idea behind creating commit/rollback code. You write such code with the guarantee that if it doesn't finish to completion, the entire operation is reverted with no change in state to the system. The changes in state are committed only if the code reaches the end of its execution path. You should code your methods like this in order for them to be exception-neutral. If an exception is thrown before the end of the method, the state of the system should remain unchanged. The following shows how you should structure your methods in order to achieve these goals:

```
void ExceptionNeutralMethod()
{
    //————————
    // All code that could possibly throw exceptions is in this
    // first section. In this section, no changes in state are
    // applied to any objects in the system including this.
    //————————


    //————————
    // All changes are committed at this point using operations
    // strictly guaranteed not to throw exceptions.
    //————————
}
```

As you can see, this technique doesn't work unless you have a set of operations that are guaranteed never to throw exceptions. Otherwise, it would be impossible to implement the commit/rollback behavior as illustrated. Thankfully, the .NET runtime does provide quite a few operations that the specification guarantees will never throw exceptions.

Let's start by building an example to describe what I mean. Suppose you have a system or an application where you're managing employees. For the sake of argument, say that once an employee is created and represented by an Employee object, it must exist within one and only one collection in the system. Currently, the only two collections in the system are one to represent active employees and one to represent terminated employees. Additionally, the collections exist within an EmployeeDatabase object, as shown in the following example:

```
using System.Collections;

class EmployeeDatabase
{
    private ArrayList activeEmployees;
    private ArrayList terminatedEmployees;
}
```

The example uses collections of the ArrayList type, which is contained in the System. Collections namespace. A real-world system would probably use something more useful, such as a database.

Now, let's see what happens when an employee quits. Naturally, you need to move that employee from the activeEmployees to the terminatedEmployees collection. A naïve attempt at such a task could look like the following:

```
using System.Collections;

class Employee
{
}

class EmployeeDatabase
{
    public void TerminateEmployee( int index ) {
        object employee = activeEmployees[index];
        activeEmployees.RemoveAt( index );
        terminatedEmployees.Add( employee );
    }

    private ArrayList activeEmployees;
    private ArrayList terminatedEmployees;
}
```

This code looks reasonable enough. The method that does the move assumes that the calling code somehow figured out the index for the current employee in the activeEmployees list prior to calling TerminateEmployee. It copies a reference to the designated employee, removes that reference from activeEmployees, and adds it to the terminatedEmployees collection. So what's so bad about this method?

Look at the method closely, and see where exceptions could be generated. The fact is, an exception could be thrown upon execution of any of the method calls in this method. If the index is out of range, you would expect to see ArgumentOutOfRange exceptions thrown from the first two lines. Of course, if the range exception is thrown from the first line, execution would never see the second line, but you get the idea. And, if memory is scarce, it's possible that the call to Add could fail with an exception. The danger comes from the possibility of the exception being thrown after the state of the system is modified. Suppose the index passed in is valid. The first two lines will likely succeed. However, if an exception is thrown while trying to add the employee to terminatedEmployees, then the employee will get lost in the system. So, what can you do to fix the glitch?

An initial attempt could use try statements to avoid damage to the system state. Consider the following example.

```
using System.Collections;

class Employee
{
}

class EmployeeDatabase
{
    public void TerminateEmployee( int index ) {
        object employee = null;
        try {
            employee = activeEmployees[index];
        }
```

```
        catch {
            // oops!  We must be out of range here.
        }

        if( employee != null ) {
            activeEmployees.RemoveAt( index );

            try {
                terminatedEmployees.Add( employee );
            }
            catch {
                // oops! Allocation may have failed.
                activeEmployees.Add( employee );
            }
        }
    }

    private ArrayList activeEmployees;
    private ArrayList terminatedEmployees;
}
```

Look how quickly the code becomes hard to read and understand, thanks to the `try` statements. You have to pull the `employee` reference out of the `try` statement and initialize it to `null`. Once you attempt to get the reference to the employee, you have to check the reference for `null` to make sure you actually got a reference to it. Once that succeeds, you can proceed to add the `employee` to the `terminatedEmployees` list. However, if that fails for some reason, you need to put the `employee` back into the `activeEmployees` list.

You may have already spotted a multitude of problems with this approach. First of all, what happens if you have a failure to add the `employee` back into the `activeEmployees` collection? Do you just fail at that point? That's unacceptable, since the state of the system has changed already. Second, you probably need to return an error code from this method to indicate why it may have failed. That's something I didn't do in the previous code. The method can't just return happily as if everything went smoothly when, in fact, the action failed to complete. Third, the code is just plain ugly and hard to read. Lastly, a variety of problems still exist with this code that I won't waste time going into.

So what's the solution? Well, think of what you attempted to do with the `try` statements. You want to do the actions that possibly throw exceptions, and if they fail, revert to the previous state. You can actually perform a variation on this theme without `try` statements that goes like this: Attempt all of the actions in the method that could throw exceptions up front, and once you get past that point, commit those actions using operations that can't throw exceptions.

■**Note** The C++ community has accepted these techniques, thanks, in part, to the excellent works published by Herb Sutter in his *Exceptional C++* series (Boston, MA: Addison-Wesley Professional). There is no good reason you cannot apply the same techniques wholesale in the C# world.

Let's see what this method would look like:

```
using System.Collections;

class Employee
{
}
```

```
class EmployeeDatabase
{
    public void TerminateEmployee( int index ) {
        // Clone sensitive objects.
        ArrayList tempActiveEmployees =
            (ArrayList) activeEmployees.Clone();
        ArrayList tempTerminatedEmployees =
            (ArrayList) terminatedEmployees.Clone();

        // Perform actions on temp objects.
        object employee = tempActiveEmployees[index];
        tempActiveEmployees.RemoveAt( index );
        tempTerminatedEmployees.Add( employee );

        // Now commit the changes.
        ArrayList tempSpace = null;
        ListSwap( ref activeEmployees,
                  ref tempActiveEmployees,
                  ref tempSpace );
        ListSwap( ref terminatedEmployees,
                  ref tempTerminatedEmployees,
                  ref tempSpace );
    }

    void ListSwap( ref ArrayList first,
                   ref ArrayList second,
                   ref ArrayList temp ) {
        temp = first;
        first = second;
        second = temp;
        temp = null;
    }

    private ArrayList activeEmployees;
    private ArrayList terminatedEmployees;
}
```

First, notice the absence of any try statements. The nice thing about their absence is that the method doesn't need to return a result code. The caller can expect the method to either work as advertised or throw an exception otherwise. The only two lines in the method that affect the state of the system are the last two calls to ListSwap. ListSwap was introduced to allow you to swap the references of the ArrayList objects in the EmployeeDatabase with the references to the temporary modified copies that you made.

How is this technique so much better when it appears to be so much less efficient? There are two tricks here. The obvious one is that, no matter where in this method an exception is thrown, the state of the EmployeeDatabase will remain unaffected. But what if an exception is thrown inside ListSwap? Ah! Here you have the second trick: ListSwap will never throw an exception. One of the most important features required in order to create exception-neutral code is that you have a small set of operations that are guaranteed not to fail under normal circumstances. No, I'm not including the case of some bozo pulling the plug on the computer in the middle of a ListSwap call, nor am I considering the case of a catastrophic earthquake or tornado at that point either. Let's see why ListSwap won't throw any exceptions.

In order to create exception-neutral code, it's imperative that you have a handful of operations, such as an assignment operation, that are guaranteed not to throw. Thankfully, the CLR provides such operations. The assignment of references, when no conversion is required, is one example of a nonthrowing operation. Every reference to an object is stored in a location, and that location has a type associated with it. However, once the locations exist, copying a reference from one to the other is a simple memory copy to already allocated locations, just like a regular pointer copy in C++, and that cannot fail. That's great for when you're copying references of one type to references of the same type.

But what happens when a conversion is necessary? Can that throw an exception? The C# standard specifies that conforming implicit conversion operators will never throw an exception. If your assignment invokes an implicit conversion, you're covered, assuming that any custom implicit conversion operators don't throw.[3] If you find a custom implicit conversion that throws an exception, I suggest you throw the C# specification at the author immediately. However, explicit conversions, in the form of casts, can throw. The bottom line is, a simple assignment from one reference to another, whether it requires implicit conversion or not, will not throw.

Simple assignment from one reference location to another is all that ListSwap is doing. After you set up the temporary ArrayList objects with the desired state, and you've gotten to the point of even executing the ListSwap calls, you've arrived at a point where you know that no more exceptions in the TerminateEmployee method are possible. Now you can make the switch safely. The ArrayList objects in the EmployeeDatabase object are swapped with the temporary ones. Once the method completes, the original ArrayList objects are free to be collected by the GC.

One more thing that you may have noticed regarding ListSwap is that the temporary location to store an ArrayList instance during the swap is allocated outside the ListSwap method and passed in as a ref parameter. I did this in order to avoid a StackOverflowException inside ListSwap. It's remotely possible that, when calling ListSwap, the stack could be running on vapors, and the mere allocation of another stack slot could fail and generate an exception. So, I performed that step outside of the confines of the ListSwap method. Once execution is inside ListSwap, all the locations are allocated and ready for use.

This technique, when applied liberally in a system that requires rigid stability, will quickly point out methods that may be too complex and need to be broken up into smaller functional units. In essence, this idiom amplifies the complexity of a particular method it is applied to. Therefore, if you find that it becomes unwieldy and difficult to make the method bulletproof, you should analyze the method and make sure it's not trying to do too much work that you could break up into smaller units.

Incidentally, you may find it necessary to make swap operations, similar to ListSwap, atomic in a multithreaded environment. You could modify ListSwap to use some sort of exclusive lock object, such as a mutex or a System.Threading.Monitor object. However, you may find yourself inadvertently making ListSwap capable of throwing exceptions, and that violates the requirements on ListSwap. Thankfully, the System.Threading namespace offers the Interlocked class to perform these swap operations atomically, and best of all, the methods are guaranteed never to throw exceptions. The Interlocked class provides a generic overload of all of the useful methods, making them very efficient. The generic Interlocked methods come with a constraint that they only work with reference types.

The bottom line is, you should do everything that can possibly throw an exception before modifying the state of the object being operated on. Once you know you're past the point of possibly causing any exceptions, commit the changes using operations that are guaranteed not to throw exceptions.

If you're tasked to create a robust, real-world system where many people rely on the integrity of the system, I cannot stress how much this idiom is a must. Sure, it's not as efficient as the naïve approach, and it requires more system resources to succeed effectively, but your clients will prefer

---

3.   The C# reference explicitly states that custom implicit conversion operators must not throw exceptions.

the inefficiency over corrupt data any day. Your colleagues will thank you, too, since resource leaks and other related glitches caused as a side effect of a thrown exception are tricky to find due to their out-of-band nature.

Constrained Execution Regions

The example in the previous section demonstrates some of the level of paranoia you must endure in order to write bulletproof, exception-neutral code. I was so paranoid that a stack overflow would occur that I allocated the extra space needed by ListSwap before I called the method. You would think that would take care of all of the issues. Unfortunately, you'd be wrong. In the CLR environment, other asynchronous exceptions could occur, such as a ThreadAbortException (which I cover in Chapter 12) and OutOfMemoryException and StackOverflowException exceptions.

For example, what if, during the commit phase of the TerminateEmployee method, the application domain is shut down, forcing a ThreadAbortException? Or what if, during the first call to ListSwap, the JIT compiler fails to allocate enough memory to compile the method in the first place? Clearly, these bad situations are difficult to deal with. In fact, in the .NET 1.1 days, you couldn't do much to handle these diabolical situations. However, starting in .NET 2.0, you can use a *constrained execution region* (CER) or a *critical finalizer*.

A CER is a region of code that the CLR prepares prior to executing, so that when the code is needed, everything is in place and the failure possibilities are mitigated. Moreover, the CLR postpones the delivery of any asynchronous exceptions, such as ThreadAbortException exceptions, if the code in the CER is executing. You can perform the magic of CERs using the RuntimeHelpers class in the System.Runtime.CompilerServices namespace. To create a CER, simply call RuntimeHelpers.PerpareConstrainedRegions prior to a try statement in your code. The CLR then examines the catch and finally blocks and prepares them by walking through the call graph and making sure all methods in the execution path are JIT-compiled and sufficient stack space is available.[4] Even though you call PrepareConstrainedRegions prior to a try statement, the actual code within the try block is not prepared. Therefore, you can use the following idiom for preparing arbitrary sections of code by wrapping the code in a finally block within a CER:

```
RuntimeHelpers.PrepareConstrainedRegions();
try {} finally
{
    // critical code goes here
}
```

Let's look at how you can modify the previous example using a CER to make it even more reliable:

```
using System.Collections;
using System.Runtime.CompilerServices;
using System.Runtime.ConstrainedExecution;

class Employee
{
}
```

---

4. Incidentally, virtual methods and delegates pose a problem, because the call graph is not deducible at preparation time. However, if you know the target of the virtual method or delegate, you can prepare it explicitly by calling RuntimeHelpers.PrepareDelegate. I recommend reading Stephen Toub's article "Keep Your Code Running with the Reliability Features of the .NET Framework," available at http://msdn.microsoft.com/msdnmag/issues/05/10/Reliability/default.aspx.

```
class EmployeeDatabase
{
    public void TerminateEmployee( int index ) {
        // Clone sensitive objects.
        ArrayList tempActiveEmployees =
            (ArrayList) activeEmployees.Clone();
        ArrayList tempTerminatedEmployees =
            (ArrayList) terminatedEmployees.Clone();

        // Perform actions on temp objects.
        object employee = tempActiveEmployees[index];
        tempActiveEmployees.RemoveAt( index );
        tempTerminatedEmployees.Add( employee );

        RuntimeHelpers.PrepareConstrainedRegions();
        try {} finally {
            // Now commit the changes.
            ArrayList tempSpace = null;
            ListSwap( ref activeEmployees,
                      ref tempActiveEmployees,
                      ref tempSpace );
            ListSwap( ref terminatedEmployees,
                      ref tempTerminatedEmployees,
                      ref tempSpace );
        }
    }

    [ReliabilityContract( Consistency.WillNotCorruptState,
                          Cer.Success )]
    void ListSwap( ref ArrayList first,
                   ref ArrayList second,
                   ref ArrayList temp ) {
        temp = first;
        first = second;
        second = temp;
        temp = null;
    }

    private ArrayList activeEmployees;
    private ArrayList terminatedEmployees;
}
```

Notice that the commit section of the TerminateEmployee method is wrapped inside a CER. At run time, prior to executing that code, the CLR prepares the code by also preparing the ListSwap method and ensuring that the stack can handle the work. Of course, this preparation operation may fail, and that's OK, because you're not yet into the code that commits the changes. Notice the addition of the ReliabilityContractAttribute to the ListSwap method. This informs the runtime of what sorts of guarantees the ListSwap method adheres to so that the CER can be formed properly. You could also attach a ReliabilityContractAttribute to the TerminateEmployee method, but it really is only useful for code executed inside a CER. If you want to attach this attribute to the TerminateEmployee method so that you can use it in a CER created elsewhere, you could add the following attribute:

```
[ReliabilityContract(Consistency.WillNotCorruptState, Cer.MayFail)]
```

This `ReliabilityContractAttribute` expresses the goal that you set out to achieve with `TerminateEmployee` in the first place. That is, it may fail, but if it does, the state of the system won't be corrupted.

■**Note** Even though the CLR guarantees that asynchronous exceptions won't be injected into the thread while inside a CER, it doesn't provide any guarantee about suppressing all exceptions. It only suppresses the ones that are outside of your control. That means that if you create objects within a CER, you must be prepared to deal with `OutOfMemoryException` or any other such code-induced exception.

Critical Finalizers and SafeHandle

Critical finalizers are similar to CERs, in that the code within them is protected from asynchronous exceptions and other such dangers caused by running in a virtual execution system that are outside your control. To mark your object as having a critical finalizer, simply derive from `CriticalFinalizerObject`. By doing so, you guarantee your object to have a finalizer that runs within the context of a CER, and therefore, must abide by all of the rules imposed by a CER. Additionally, the CLR will execute critical finalizers after it finishes dealing with all other noncritical finalizable objects.

In reality, it's rare that you'll ever need to create a critical finalizable object. Instead, you can usually get the behavior you need by deriving from `SafeHandle`. `SafeHandle` is a critical tool when creating native interop code through P/Invoke or COM interop, since it allows you to guarantee that you won't leak any unmanaged resources from within the CLR. Prior to .NET 2.0, this was not possible. In the .NET 1.1 days, you would typically represent an opaque native handle type with a managed `IntPtr` type. This works just fine, except that you cannot guarantee that the underlying resource will be cleaned up in the event of an asynchronous exception such as a `ThreadAbortException`. As usual, by adding an extra level of indirection[5] in the form of a `SafeHandle`, you can mitigate these problems in .NET 2.0.

■**Caution** Before you jump to the conclusion that you need to create a `SafeHandle` derivative, be sure to check if one of the supplied `SafeHandle` derivatives in the .NET Framework will work for you. For example, if you're creating code to talk directly to a device driver by calling the Win32 `DeviceIoControl` function via P/Invoke, then the `SafeFileHandle` type is sufficient for holding the handle that you open directly on the driver.

When creating your own `SafeHandle` derived class, you must follow a short list of steps. As an example, let's create a `SafeHandle` derived class, `SafeBluetoothRadioFindHandle`, to enumerate through the Bluetooth radios on a system, assuming there are any. The pattern for enumerating Bluetooth radios in native code is quite simple and a common theme used throughout the Win32 API. You call the Win32 `BluetoothFindFirstRadio` function, and if it succeeds, it returns the first radio handle through an out parameter and an enumeration handle through the return value. You can find any additional radios by calling the Win32 function `BluetoothFindNextRadio`. When

---

5. Andrew Koenig of C++ fame likes to call this the Fundamental Theorem of Software Engineering—that is, that any software engineering problem can be solved by adding a level of indirection.

finished, you must be sure to call the Win32 function `BluetoothFindRadioClose` on the enumeration handle. Consider the following code:

```
using System;
using System.Runtime.InteropServices;
using System.Runtime.ConstrainedExecution;
using System.Security;
using System.Security.Permissions;
using System.Text;
using Microsoft.Win32.SafeHandles;


//
// Matches Win32 BLUETOOTH_FIND_RADIO_PARAMS
//
[StructLayout( LayoutKind.Sequential )]
class BluetoothFindRadioParams
{
    public BluetoothFindRadioParams() {
        dwSize = 4;
    }
    public UInt32 dwSize;
}

//
// Matches Win32 BLUETOOTH_RADIO_INFO
//
[StructLayout( LayoutKind.Sequential,
               CharSet = CharSet.Unicode )]
struct BluetoothRadioInfo
{
    public const int BLUETOOTH_MAX_NAME_SIZE = 248;

    public UInt32 dwSize;
    public UInt64 address;
    [MarshalAs( UnmanagedType.ByValTStr,
                SizeConst = BLUETOOTH_MAX_NAME_SIZE )]
    public string szName;
    public UInt32 ulClassOfDevice;
    public UInt16 lmpSubversion;
    public UInt16 manufacturer;
}

//
// Safe Bluetooth Enumeration Handle
//
[SecurityPermission( SecurityAction.Demand,
                     UnmanagedCode = true )]
sealed public class SafeBluetoothRadioFindHandle
    : SafeHandleZeroOrMinusOneIsInvalid
{
    private SafeBluetoothRadioFindHandle() : base( true ) { }

    override protected bool ReleaseHandle() {
        return BluetoothFindRadioClose( handle );
    }

    [DllImport( "Irprops.cpl" )]
```

```
        [ReliabilityContract( Consistency.WillNotCorruptState,
                              Cer.Success )]
        [SuppressUnmanagedCodeSecurity]
        private static extern bool BluetoothFindRadioClose(
                                            IntPtr hFind );
}

public class EntryPoint
{
    private const int ERROR_SUCCESS = 0;

    static void Main() {
        SafeFileHandle radioHandle;
        using( SafeBluetoothRadioFindHandle radioFindHandle
            = BluetoothFindFirstRadio(new BluetoothFindRadioParams(),
                                      out radioHandle) ) {
            if( !radioFindHandle.IsInvalid ) {
                BluetoothRadioInfo radioInfo = new BluetoothRadioInfo();
                radioInfo.dwSize = 520;
                UInt32 result = BluetoothGetRadioInfo( radioHandle,
                                                       ref radioInfo );

                if( result == ERROR_SUCCESS ) {
                    // Let's send the contents of the radio info to the
                    // console.
                    Console.WriteLine( "address = {0:X}",
                                       radioInfo.address );
                    Console.WriteLine( "szName = {0}",
                                       radioInfo.szName );
                    Console.WriteLine( "ulClassOfDevice = {0}",
                                       radioInfo.ulClassOfDevice );
                    Console.WriteLine( "lmpSubversion = {0}",
                                       radioInfo.lmpSubversion );
                    Console.WriteLine( "manufacturer = {0}",
                                       radioInfo.manufacturer );
                }

                radioHandle.Dispose();
            }
        }
    }

    [DllImport( "Irprops.cpl" )]
    private static extern SafeBluetoothRadioFindHandle
        BluetoothFindFirstRadio( [MarshalAs(UnmanagedType.LPStruct)]
                                 BluetoothFindRadioParams pbtfrp,
                                 out SafeFileHandle phRadio );

    [DllImport( "Irprops.cpl" )]
    private static extern UInt32
        BluetoothGetRadioInfo( SafeFileHandle hRadio,
                               ref BluetoothRadioInfo pRadioInfo );
}
```

The crux of this example is SafeBluetoothRadioFindHandle. You could have derived it directly from SafeHandle, but the runtime provides two helper classes, SafeHandleZeroOrMinusOneIsInvalid and SafeHandleMinusOneIsInvalid, to derive from in order to make things easier.

■Caution Be careful when dealing with Win32 functions via P/Invoke, and always read the documentation carefully to see what constitutes an invalid handle value. The Win32 API is notorious for making this confusing. For example, the Win32 CreateFile function returns -1 to represent a failure. The CreateEvent function returns a NULL handle in the event of an error. In both cases, the return type is HANDLE.

Take several things into consideration when providing your own SafeHandle derivative:

- *Apply a code access security demand on the class requiring the ability to call unmanaged code*: Of course, you don't need to do this unless you really do call unmanaged code, but the odds of your ever creating a SafeHandle derivative and not calling unmanaged code are very slim.

- *Provide a default constructor that initializes the* SafeHandle *derivative*: Notice that SafeBluetoothRadioFindHandle declares a private default constructor. Since the P/Invoke layer possesses special powers, it can create instances of the object even though the constructor is private. The private constructor keeps clients from creating instances without calling the Win32 functions that create the underlying resource.

- *Override the virtual* IsInvalid *property*: In this case, that was not necessary since the base class SafeHandleZeroOrMinusOneIsInvalid handles that for you.

- *Override the virtual* ReleaseHandle *method, which is used to clean up the resource*: Typically, this is where you'll make your call through P/Invoke to release the unmanaged resource. In the example, you make a call to BluetoothFindRadioClose. Note that when declaring the method for P/Invoke, you apply a reliability contract, since the ReleaseHandle method is called within the context of a CER. Additionally, it's wise to apply the SuppressUnmanagedCodeSecurityAttribute to the method.

Once you define your SafeHandle derivative, you're ready to use it in your P/Invoke declarations. In the preceding example, you declare the BluetoothFindFirstRadio method to be called through P/Invoke. If you look up this function in the Microsoft Developer Network (MSDN), you'll see that it returns a BLUETOOTH_RADIO_FIND type, which is a handle to an internal radio enumeration object. In the .NET 1.1 days, you would have declared the method as returning an IntPtr. Starting with .NET 2.0, you indicate that it returns a SafeBluetoothRadioFindHandle type, and the P/Invoke marshaling layer handles the rest. Now, the enumeration handle is safe from being leaked by the runtime in the event of some asynchronous exception introduced by the virtual execution system.

■Caution When marshaling between a COM method or Win32 function that returns a handle in a structure, the interop layer doesn't provide support for dealing with SafeHandle derivatives. In these rare cases, you'll need to call SetHandle on the SafeHandle derivative after getting the structure back from the function or COM method. However, if you have to do such a thing, you want to make sure that the operation that creates the handle and the subsequent SetHandle method call occurs within a CER so that nothing can interrupt the process of allocating the resource and assigning the handle to the SafeHandle object; otherwise, your application could leak resources.

Creating Custom Exception Classes

System.Exception has three public constructors and one protected constructor. The first is the default constructor, which doesn't really do much of anything. The second is a constructor that accepts a reference to a string object. This string is a general, programmer-defined message that you can consider a more user-friendly description of the exception. The third is a constructor that takes a message string, like the second constructor, but it also accepts a reference to another Exception. The reference to the other exception allows you to keep track of originating exceptions when one exception is translated into another exception within a try block. A good example of that is when an exception is not handled and percolates up to the stack frame of a static constructor. In that case, the runtime throws a TypeInitializationException, but only after it sets the inner exception to that of the original exception so that the one who catches the TypeInitializationException will at least know why this exception occurred in the first place. Finally, the protected constructor allows creation of an exception from a SerializationInfo object. You always want to create serializable exceptions so you can use them across context boundaries—for example, with .NET Remoting. That means you'll also want to mark your custom exception classes with the SerializableAttribute as well.

The System.Exception class is very useful with these three public constructors. However, it would constitute a bad design to simply throw objects of type System.Exception any time anything goes wrong. Instead, it would make much more sense to create a new, more specific, exception type that derives from System.Exception. That way, the type of the exception is much more expressive about the problem at hand. Even better than that is the fact that your derived exception class could contain data that is germane to the reason the exception was thrown in the first place. And remember, in C#, all exceptions must derive from System.Exception. Let's see what it takes to define custom exceptions effectively.

Consider the previous EmployeeDatabase example. Suppose that in order to add an employee to the database, the employee's data must be validated. If an employee's data does not validate, the Add method will throw an exception of type EmployeeVerificationException. Notice that I'm ending the new exception's type name with the word Exception. This is a good habit to get into, and a recommended convention, since it makes it easy to spot exception types within your type system. It's also considered good style within the C# programming community. Let's see what such an exception type could look like:

```
using System;
using System.Runtime.Serialization;

[Serializable()]
public class EmployeeVerificationException : Exception
{
    public enum Cause {
        InvalidSSN,
        InvalidBirthDate
    }

    public EmployeeVerificationException( Cause reason )
        :base() {
        this.reason = reason;
    }

    public EmployeeVerificationException( Cause reason,
                                          String msg )
        :base( msg ) {
        this.reason = reason;
    }
```

```
    public EmployeeVerificationException( Cause reason,
                                          String msg,
                                          Exception inner )

        :base( msg, inner ) {
        this.reason = reason;
    }

    protected EmployeeVerificationException(
                SerializationInfo info,
                StreamingContext  context )
             :base( info, context ) { }

    private Cause reason;
    public Cause Reason {
        get {
            return reason;
        }
    }
}
```

In the `EmployeeDatabase.Add` method, you can see the simple call to `Validate` on the `emp` object. This is a rather crude example, where you force the validation to fail by throwing an `EmployeeVerificationException`. But the main focus of the example is the creation of the new exception type. Many times, you'll find that just creating a new exception type is good enough to convey the extra information you need to convey. In this case, I wanted to illustrate an example where the exception type carries more information about the validation failure, so I created a `Reason` property whose backing field must be initialized in the constructor. Also, notice that `EmployeeVerificationException` derives from `System.Exception`. At one point, the school of thought was that all .NET Framework-defined exception types would derive from `System.Exception`, while all user-defined exceptions would derive from `ApplicationException`, thus making it easier to tell the two apart. This goal has been lost partly due to the fact that some .NET Framework-defined exception types derive from `ApplicationException`.[6]

You may be wondering why I defined four exception constructors for this simple exception type. The traditional idiom when defining new exception types is to define the same four public constructors that `System.Exception` exposes. Had I decided not to carry the extra reason data, then the `EmployeeVerificationException` constructors would have matched the `System.Exception` constructors exactly in their form. If you follow this idiom when defining your own exception types, users will be able to treat your new exception type in the same way as other system-defined exceptions. Plus, your derived exception will be able to leverage the message and inner exception already encapsulated by `System.Exception`.

Working with Allocated Resources and Exceptions

If you're a seasoned C++ pro, then one thing you have most definitely been grappling with in the C# world is the lack of deterministic destruction. C++ developers have become accustomed to using constructors and destructors of stack-based objects to manage precious resources. This idiom even

---

6. For more on this subject and many other useful guidelines, reference Krzysztof Cwalina and Brad Abrams' *Framework Design Guidelines: Conventions, Idioms, and Patterns for Reusable .NET Libraries* (Boston, MA: Addison-Wesley Professional, 2005).

has a name: *Resource Acquisition Is Initialization* (RAII). This means that you can create objects on the C++ stack where some precious resource is allocated in the constructor of those objects, and if you put the deallocation in the destructor, you can rely upon the destructor getting called at the proper time to clean up. For example, no matter how the stack-based object goes out of scope— whether it's through normal execution while reaching the end of the scope or via an exception—you can always be guaranteed that the destructor will execute, thus cleaning up the precious resource.

When C# and the CLR were first introduced to developers during the beta program, many developers immediately became very vocal about this omission in the runtime. Whether you view it as an omission or not, it clearly was not addressed to its fullest extent until after the beta developer community applied a gentle nudge. The problem stems, in part, from the garbage-collected nature of objects in the CLR, coupled with the fact that the friendly destructor in the C# syntax was reused to implement object finalizers. It's also important to remember that finalizers are very different from destructors. Using the destructor syntax for finalizers only added to the confusion of the matter. There were also other technical reasons, some dealing with efficiency, why deterministic destructors as we know them were not included in the runtime.

After knocking heads for some time, the solution put on the table was the Disposable pattern that you utilize by implementing the IDisposable interface. For more detailed discussions relating to the Disposable pattern and your objects, refer to Chapter 4 and Chapter 13. Essentially, if your object needs deterministic destruction, it obtains it by implementing the IDisposable interface. However, you have to call your Dispose method explicitly in order to clean up after the disposable object. If you forget to, and your object is coded properly, then the resource won't be lost—rather, it will just be cleaned up when the GC finally gets around to calling your finalizer. Within C++, you only have to remember to put your cleanup code in the destructor, and you never have to remember to clean up after your local objects, since cleanup happens automatically once they go out of scope.

Consider the following contrived example that illustrates the danger you can face:

```
using System;
using System.IO;
using System.Text;

public class EntryPoint
{
    public static void DoSomeStuff() {
        // Open a file.
        FileStream fs = File.Open( "log.txt",
                                   FileMode.Append,
                                   FileAccess.Write,
                                   FileShare.None );
        Byte[] msg = new UTF8Encoding(true).GetBytes("Doing Some"+
                                                     " Stuff");
        fs.Write( msg, 0, msg.Length );
    }

    public static void DoSomeMoreStuff() {
        // Open a file.
        FileStream fs = File.Open( "log.txt",
                                   FileMode.Append,
                                   FileAccess.Write,
                                   FileShare.None );
        Byte[] msg = new UTF8Encoding(true).GetBytes("Doing Some"+
                                                     " More Stuff");
        fs.Write( msg, 0, msg.Length );
    }
```

```
static void Main() {
    DoSomeStuff();

    DoSomeMoreStuff();
}
}
```

This code looks innocent enough. However, if you execute this code, you'll most likely encounter an IOException. The code in DoSomeStuff creates a FileStream object with an exclusive lock on the file. Once the FileStream object goes out of scope at the end of the function, it is marked for collection, but you're at the mercy of the GC and when it decides to do the cleanup. Therefore, when you find yourself opening the file again in DoSomeMoreStuff, you'll get the exception, since the precious resource is still locked by the unreachable FileStream object. Clearly, this is a horrible position to be in. And don't even think about making an explicit call to GC.Collect in Main before the call to DoSomeMoreStuff. Fiddling with the GC algorithm by forcing it to collect at specific times is a recipe for poor performance. You cannot possibly help the GC do its job better, since you have no specific idea how it is implemented.

So what is one to do? One way or another, you must ensure that the file gets closed. However, here's the rub: No matter how you do it, you must remember to do it. This is in contrast to C++, where you can put the cleanup in the destructor and then just rest assured that the resource will get cleaned up in a timely manner. One option would be to call the Close method on the FileStream in each of the methods that use it. That works fine, but it's much less automatic and something you must always remember to do. However, even if you do, what happens if an exception is thrown before the Close method is called? You find yourself back in the same boat as before, with a resource dangling out there that you can't get to in order to free it.

Those of you who are savvy with exception handling will notice that you can solve the problem using some try/finally blocks, as in the following example:

```
using System;
using System.IO;
using System.Text;

public class EntryPoint
{
    public static void DoSomeStuff() {
        // Open a file.
        FileStream fs = null;
        try {
            fs = File.Open( "log.txt",
                            FileMode.Append,
                            FileAccess.Write,
                            FileShare.None );
            Byte[] msg =
                new UTF8Encoding(true).GetBytes("Doing Some"+
                                                " Stuff\n");
            fs.Write( msg, 0, msg.Length );
        }
        finally {
            if( fs != null ) {
                fs.Close();
            }
        }
    }

    public static void DoSomeMoreStuff() {
        // Open a file.
```

```
        FileStream fs = null;
        try {
            fs = File.Open( "log.txt",
                            FileMode.Append,
                            FileAccess.Write,
                            FileShare.None );
            Byte[] msg =
                new UTF8Encoding(true).GetBytes("Doing Some"+
                                                " More Stuff\n");
            fs.Write( msg, 0, msg.Length );
        }
        finally {
            if( fs != null ) {
                fs.Close();
            }
        }
    }

    static void Main() {
        DoSomeStuff();

        DoSomeMoreStuff();
    }
}
```

The try/finally blocks solve the problem. But, yikes! Notice how ugly the code just got. Plus, let's face it, many of us are lazy typists, and that was a lot of extra typing. Moreover, more typing means more places for bugs to be introduced. Lastly, it makes the code difficult to read. As you'd expect, there is a better way. Many objects, such as FileStream, that have a Close method also implement the IDisposable pattern. Usually, calling Dispose on these objects is the same as calling Close. Of course, calling Close over Dispose or vice versa is arguing over apples and oranges, if you still have to explicitly call one or the other. Thankfully, there's a good reason why most classes that have a Close method implement Dispose—so you can use them effectively with the using state-ment, which is typically used as part of the Disposable pattern in C#. Therefore, you could change the code to the following:

```
using System;
using System.IO;
using System.Text;

public class EntryPoint
{
    public static void DoSomeStuff() {
        // Open a file.
        using( FileStream fs = File.Open( "log.txt",
                                          FileMode.Append,
                                          FileAccess.Write,
                                          FileShare.None ) ) {
            Byte[] msg =
                new UTF8Encoding(true).GetBytes("Doing Some" +
                                                " Stuff\n");
            fs.Write( msg, 0, msg.Length );
        }
    }

    public static void DoSomeMoreStuff() {
        // Open a file.
```

```
        using( FileStream fs = File.Open( "log.txt",
                                          FileMode.Append,
                                          FileAccess.Write,
                                          FileShare.None ) ) {
            Byte[] msg =
                new UTF8Encoding(true).GetBytes("Doing Some" +
                                                " More Stuff\n");
            fs.Write( msg, 0, msg.Length );
        }
    }

    static void Main() {
        DoSomeStuff();

        DoSomeMoreStuff();
    }
}
```

As you can see, the code is much easier to follow, and the using statement takes care of having to type all those explicit try/finally blocks. You probably won't be surprised to notice that if you look at the generated code in ILDASM, the compiler has generated the try/finally blocks in place of the using statement. You can also nest using statements within their compound blocks, just as you can nest try/finally blocks.

Even though the using statement solves the "ugly code" symptom and reduces the chances of typing in extra bugs, it still requires that you remember to use it in the first place. It's not as convenient as the deterministic destruction of local objects in C++, but it's better than littering your code with try/finally blocks all over the place, and it's definitely better than nothing. The end result is that C# does have a form of deterministic destruction via the using statement, but it's only deterministic if you remember to make it deterministic.

Providing Rollback Behavior

When producing exception-neutral methods, as covered in the "Achieving Exception Neutrality" section of this chapter, you'll often find it handy to employ a mechanism that can roll back any changes if an exception happens to be generated. You can solve this problem by using the classic technique of introducing one more level of indirection in the form of a helper class. For the sake of discussion, let's use an object that represents a database connection, and that has methods named Commit and Rollback.

In the C++ world, a popular solution to this problem involves the creation of a helper class that is created on the stack. The helper class also has a method named Commit. When called, it just passes through to the database object's method, but before doing so, it sets an internal flag. The trick is in the destructor. If the destructor executes before the flag is set, there are only a couple of ways that is possible. First, the user might have forgotten to call Commit. Since that's a bug in the code, let's not consider that option. The second way to get into the destructor without the flag set is if the object is being cleaned up because the stack is unwinding as it looks for a handler for a thrown exception. Depending on the state of the flag in the destructor code, you can instantly tell if you got here via normal execution or via an exception. If you got here via an exception, all you have to do is call Rollback on the database object, and you have the functionality you need.

Now, this is all great in the land of native C++, where you can use deterministic destruction. However, you can get the same end result using the C# form of deterministic destruction, which is the marriage between IDisposable and the using keyword. Remember, a destructor in native C++ maps into an implementation of the IDisposable interface in C#. All you have to do is take the code that you would have put into the destructor in C++ into the Dispose method of the C# helper class. Let's take a look at what this C# helper class could look like:

```csharp
using System;
using System.Diagnostics;

public class Database
{
    public void Commit() {
        Console.WriteLine( "Changes Committed" );
    }

    public void Rollback() {
        Console.WriteLine( "Changes Abandoned" );
    }
}

public class RollbackHelper : IDisposable
{
    public RollbackHelper( Database db ) {
        this.db = db;
    }

    ~RollbackHelper() {
        Dispose( false );
    }

    public void Dispose() {
        Dispose( true );
    }

    public void Commit() {
        db.Commit();
        committed = true;
    }

    private void Dispose( bool disposing ) {
        // Don't do anything if already disposed.  Remember, it is
        // valid to call Dispose() multiple times on a disposable
        // object.
        if( !disposed ) {
            // Remember, we don't want to do anything to the db if
            // we got here from the finalizer, because the database
            // field could already be finalized!  However, we do
            // want to free any unmanaged resources.  But, in this
            // case, there are none.
            if( disposing ) {
                if( !committed ) {
                    db.Rollback();
                }
            } else {
                Debug.Assert( false, "Failed to call Dispose()" +
                                     " on RollbackHelper" );
            }
        }
    }
}
```

```
        private Database db;
        private bool    disposed = false;
        private bool    committed = false;
    }

    public class EntryPoint
    {
        static private void DoSomeWork() {
            using( RollbackHelper guard = new RollbackHelper(db) ) {
                // Here we do some work that could throw an exception.

                // Comment out the following line to cause an
                // exception.  nullPtr.GetType();

                // If we get here, we commit.
                guard.Commit();
            }

        }

        static void Main() {
            db = new Database();
            DoSomeWork();
        }

        static private Database db;
        static private Object   nullPtr = null;
    }
```

Inside the DoSomeWork method is where you'll do some work that could fail with an exception. Should an exception occur, you'll want any changes that have gone into the Database object to be reverted. Inside the using block, you've created a new RollbackHelper object that contains a reference to the Database object. If control flow gets to the point of calling Commit on the guard reference, all is well, assuming the Commit method does not throw. Even if it does throw, you should code it in such a way that the Database remains in a valid state. However, if your code inside the guarded block throws an exception, the Dispose method in the RollbackHelper will diligently roll back your database.

No matter what happens, the Dispose method will be called on the RollbackHelper instance, thanks to the using block. If you forget the using block, the finalizer for the RollbackHelper will not be able to do anything for you, since finalization of objects goes in random order, and the Database referenced by the RollbackHelper could be finalized prior to the RollbackHelper instance. To help you find the places where you brain-froze, you can code an assertion into the helper object as I have done above. Since the whole use of this pattern hinges on the using block, for the sake of discussion, let's assume you didn't forget it.

Once execution is safely inside the Dispose method, and it got there via a call to Dispose rather than through the finalizer, it simply checks the committed flag, and if it's not set, it calls Rollback on the Database instance. That's all there is to it. It's almost as elegant as the C++ solution except that, as in previous discussions in this chapter, you must remember to use the using keyword to make it work. If you'd like to see what happens in a case where an exception is thrown, simply uncomment the attempt to access the null reference inside the DoSomeWork method.

You may have noticed that I haven't addressed what happens if Rollback throws an exception. Clearly, for robust code, it's optimal to require that whatever operations RollbackHelper performs in the process of a rollback should be guaranteed never to throw. This goes back to one of the most basic requirements for generating strong exception-safe and exception-neutral code: In order to create robust exception-safe code, you must have a well-defined set of operations that are guaranteed not to throw. In the C++ world, during the stack unwind caused by an exception, the rollback happens within a destructor. Seasoned C++ salts know that you should never throw an exception in a destructor, because if the stack is in the process of unwinding during an exception when that happens, your process is aborted very rudely. And there's nothing worse than an application disappearing out from under users without a trace. But what happens if such a thing happens in C#? Remember, a using block is expanded into a try/finally block under the covers. And you may recall that when an exception is thrown within a finally block that is executing as the result of a previous exception, that previous exception is simply lost and the new exception gets thrown. What's worse is that the finally block that was executing never gets to finish. That, coupled with the fact that losing exception information is always bad and makes it terribly difficult to find problems, means that it is strongly recommended that you never throw an exception inside a finally block. I know I've mentioned this before in this chapter, but it's so important it deserves a second mention. The CLR won't abort your application, but your application will likely be in an undefined state if an exception is thrown during execution of a finally block, and you'll be left wondering how it got into such an ugly state.

Summary

In this chapter, I covered the basics of exception handling along with how you should apply the Expert pattern to determine the best place to handle a particular exception. I touched upon the differences between .NET 1.1 and later versions of the CLR when handling unhandled exceptions and how .NET 2.0 and later respond in a more consistent manner. The meat of this chapter described techniques for creating bulletproof exception-safe code that guarantees system stability in the face of unexpected exceptional events. I also described constrained execution regions that you can use to postpone asynchronous exceptions during thread termination. Creating bulletproof exception-safe and exception-neutral code is no easy task. Unfortunately, the huge majority of software systems in existence today flat-out ignore the problem altogether. It's an extremely unfortunate situation, given the wealth of resources that have become available ever since exception handling was added to the C++ language years ago.

   Sadly, for many developers, exception safety is an afterthought. They erroneously assume they can solve any exception problems during testing by sprinkling try statements throughout their code. In reality, exception safety is a crucial issue that you should consider at software design time. Failure to do so will result in substandard systems that will do nothing but frustrate users and lose market share to those companies whose developers spent a little extra time getting exception safety right. Moreover, there's always the possibility, as computers integrate more and more into people's daily lives, that government regulations could force systems to undergo rigorous testing in order to prove they are worthy for society to rely upon. Don't think you may be the exception, either (no pun intended). I can envision an environment where a socialist government could force such rules on any commercially sold software (shudder). Have you ever heard stories about how, for example, the entire integrated air traffic control system in a country or continent went down because of a software glitch? Wouldn't you hate to be the developer who skimped on exception safety and caused such a situation? I rest my case.

   In the next chapter, I'll cover the main facets of dealing with strings in C# and the .NET Framework. Additionally, I'll cover the important topic of globalization.

CHAPTER 8

■ ■ ■

Working with Strings

Within the .NET Framework base class library, the System.String type is the model citizen. It offers an ideal example of how to create an immutable reference type that semantically acts like a value type.

String Overview

Instances of String are immutable in the sense that once you create them, you cannot change them. Although it may seem inefficient at first, this approach actually does make code more efficient. When you copy String instances liberally within the application, you create a new instance that points to the same raw string data as the source instance. Even if you call the ICloneable.Clone method on a string, you get an instance that points to the same string data as the source. This is entirely safe because the String public interface offers no way to modify the actual String data. Sure, you can subvert the system by employing unsafe code trickery, but I trust you wouldn't want to do such a thing. In fact, if you require a string that is a deep copy of the original string, you may call the Copy method to do so.

Note Those of you who are familiar with common design patterns and idioms may recognize this usage pattern as the handle/body or envelope/letter idiom. In C++, you typically implement this idiom when designing reference-based types that you can pass by value. Many C++ standard library implementations implement the standard string this way. However, in C#'s garbage-collected heap, you don't have to worry about maintaining reference counts on the underlying data.

In many environments, such as C++ and C, the string is not usually a built-in type at all, but rather a more primitive, raw construct, such as a pointer to the first character in an array of characters. Typically, string-manipulation routines are not part of the language but rather a part of a library used with the language. Although that is mostly true with C#, the lines are somewhat blurred by the .NET runtime. The designers of the CLI specification could have chosen to represent all strings as simple arrays of System.Char types, but they chose to annex System.String into the collection of built-in types instead. In fact, System.String is an oddball in the built-in type collection, since it is a reference type and most of the built-in types are value types. However, this difference is blurred by the fact that the String type behaves with value semantics.

You may already know that the System.String type represents a Unicode character string, and System.Char represents a 16-bit Unicode character. Of course, this makes portability and localization to other operating systems—especially systems with large character sets—easy. However, sometimes you might need to interface with external systems using encodings other than Unicode character strings. For times like these, you can employ the System.Text.Encoding class to convert to and from various encodings, including ASCII, UTF-7, UTF-8, and UTF-32. Incidentally, the Unicode format used internally by the runtime is UTF-16.[1]

String Literals

When you declare a string in your C# code, the compiler creates a System.String object for you that it then places into an internal table in the module called the *intern pool*. The idea is that each time you declare a new string literal within your code, the compiler first checks to see if you've declared the same string elsewhere, and if you have, then the code simply references the one already interned. Let's take a look at an example of a way to declare a string literal within C#:

```
using System;

public class EntryPoint
{
    static void Main( string[] args ) {
        string lit1 = "c:\\windows\\system32";
        string lit2 = @"c:\windows\system32";

        string lit3 = @"
Jack and Jill
Went up the hill...
";
        Console.WriteLine( lit3 );

        Console.WriteLine( "Object.RefEq(lit1, lit2): {0}",
                           Object.ReferenceEquals(lit1, lit2) );

        if( args.Length > 0 ) {
            Console.WriteLine( "Parameter given: {0}",
                               args[0] );

            string strNew = String.Intern( args[0] );

            Console.WriteLine( "Object.RefEq(lit1, strNew): {0}",
                               Object.ReferenceEquals(lit1, strNew) );
        }
    }
}
```

First, notice the two declarations of the two literal strings lit1 and lit2. The declared type is string, which is the C# alias for System.String. The first instance is initialized via a regular string literal that can contain the familiar escaped sequences that are used in C and C++, such as \t and \n. Therefore, you must escape the backslash itself as usual—hence, the double backslash in the path. You can find more information about the valid escape sequences in the MSDN documentation. However, C# offers a type of string literal declaration called *verbatim strings*, where anything within the string declaration is put in the string as is. Such declarations are preceded with the @

---

1. For more information regarding the Unicode standard, visit www.unicode.org.

character as shown. Specifically, pay attention to the fact that the strange declaration for lit3 is perfectly valid. The newlines within the code are taken verbatim into the string, which is shown in the output of this program. Verbatim strings can be useful if you're creating strings for form submission and you need to be able to lay them out specifically within the code. The only escape sequence that is valid within verbatim strings is "", and you use it to insert a quote character into the verbatim string.

Clearly, lit1 and lit2 contain strings of the same value, even though you declare them using different forms. Based upon what I said in the previous section, you would expect the two instances to reference the same string object. In fact, they do, and that is shown in the output from the program, where I test them using Object.ReferenceEquals.

Finally, this example demonstrates the use of the String.Intern static method. Sometimes, you may find it necessary to determine if a string you're declaring at run time is already in the intern pool. If it is, it may be more efficient to reference that string rather than create a new instance. The code accepts a string on the command line and then creates a new instance from it using the String.Intern method. This method always returns a valid string reference, but it will either be a string instance referencing a string in the intern pool, or a new string copy based upon the passed-in value. Given the string of "c:\windows\system32" on the command line, this code produces the following output:

```
Jack and Jill
Went up the hill...

Object.RefEq(lit1, lit2): True
Parameter given: c:\windows\system32
Object.RefEq(lit1, strNew): True
```

Format Specifiers and Globalization

You often need to format the data that an application displays to users in a specific way. For example, you may need to display a floating-point value representing some tangible metric in exponential form or in fixed-point form. In fixed-point form, you may need to use a culture-specific character as the decimal mark. Traditionally, dealing with these sorts of issues has always been painful. C programmers have the printf family of functions for handling formatting of values, but it lacks any locale-specific capabilities. C++ took further steps forward and offered a more robust and extensible formatting mechanism in the form of standard I/O streams while also offering locales. The .NET standard library offers its own powerful mechanisms for handling these two notions in a flexible and extensible manner. However, before I can get into the topic of format specifiers themselves, let's cover some preliminary topics.

■Note It's important to address any cultural concerns your software may have early in the development cycle. Many developers tend to treat globalization as an afterthought. But if you notice, the .NET Framework designers put a lot of work into creating a rich library for handling globalization. The richness and breadth of the globalization API is an indicator of how difficult it can be. Address globalization concerns at the beginning of your product's development cycle, or you'll suffer from heartache later.

Object.ToString, IFormattable, and CultureInfo

Every object derives a method from System.Object called ToString that you're probably familiar with already. It's extremely handy to get a string representation of your object for output, even if only for debugging purposes. For your custom classes, you'll see that the default implementation of ToString merely returns the type of the object itself. You need to implement your own override to do anything useful. As you'd expect, all of the built-in types do just that. Thus, if you call ToString on a System.Int32, you'll get a string representation of the value within. But what if you want the string representation in hexadecimal format? Object.ToString is of no help here, because there is no way to request the desired format. There must be another way to get a string representation of an object. In fact, there is a way, and it involves implementing the IFormattable interface, which looks like the following:

```
public interface IFormattable
{
    string ToString( string format, IFormatProvider formatProvider )
}
```

You'll notice that all built-in numeric types as well as date-time types implement this interface. Using this method, you can specify exactly how you want the value to be formatted by providing a format specifier string. Before I get into exactly what the format strings look like, let me explain a few more preliminary concepts, starting with the second parameter of the IFormattable.ToString method.

An object that implements the IFormatProvider interface is—surprise—a format provider. A format provider's common task within the .NET Framework is to provide culture-specific formatting information, such as what character to use for monetary amounts, for decimal separators, and so on. When you pass null for this parameter, the format provider that IFormattable.ToString uses is typically the CultureInfo instance returned by System.Globalization.CultureInfo.CurrentCulture. This instance of CultureInfo is the one that matches the culture that the current thread uses. However, you have the option of overriding it by passing a different CultureInfo instance, such as one obtained by creating a new instance of CultureInfo by passing into its constructor a string representing the desired locale formatted as described in the RFC 1766 standard. For more information on culture names, consult the MSDN documentation for the CultureInfo class. Finally, you can even provide a culture-neutral CultureInfo instance by passing the instance provided by CultureInfo.InvariantCulture.

Note Instances of CultureInfo are used as a convenient grouping mechanism for all formatting information relevant to a specific culture. For example, one CultureInfo instance could represent the cultural-specific qualities of English spoken in the United States, while another could contain properties specific to English spoken in the United Kingdom. Each CultureInfo instance contains specific instances of DateTimeFormatInfo, NumberFormatInfo, TextInfo, and CompareInfo that are germane to the language and region represented.

Once the IFormattable.ToString implementation has a valid format provider—whether it was passed in or whether it is the one attached to the current thread—then it may query that format provider for a specific formatter by calling the IFormatProvider.GetFormat method. The formatters implemented by the .NET Framework are the NumberFormatInfo and DateTimeFormatInfo types. When you ask for one of these objects via IFormatProvider.GetFormat, you ask for it by type. This mechanism is extremely extensible, since you can provide your own formatter types, and other types that you create that know how to consume them can ask a custom format provider for instances of them.

Suppose you want to convert a floating-point value into a string. The execution flow of the IFormattable.ToString implementation on System.Double follows these general steps:

1. The implementation gets a reference to an IFormatProvider type, which is either the one passed in or the one attached to the current thread if the one passed in is null.

2. It asks the format provider for an instance of the type NumberFormatInfo via a call to IFormatProvider.GetFormat. The format provider initializes the NumberFormatInfo instance's properties based on the culture it represents.

3. It uses the NumberFormatInfo instance to format the number appropriately while creating a string representation of this based upon the specification of the format string.

Creating and Registering Custom CultureInfo Types

The globalization capabilities of the .NET Framework have always been strong. However, there was room for improvement, and much of that improvement came with the .NET 2.0 Framework. Specifically, with .NET 1.1, it was always a painful process to introduce cultural information into the system if the framework didn't know the culture and region information. The .NET 2.0 Framework introduced a new class named CultureAndRegionInfoBuilder in the System.Globalization namespace.

Using CultureAndRegionInfoBuilder, you have the capability to define and introduce an entirely new culture and its region information into the system and register them for global usage as well. Similarly, you can modify preexisting culture and region information on the system. And if that's not enough flexibility for you, you can even serialize the information into a Locale Data Markup Language (LDML) file, which is a standard-based XML format. Once you register your new culture and region with the system, you can then create instances of CultureInfo and RegionInfo using the string-based name that you registered with the system.

When naming your new cultures, you should adhere to the standard format for naming cultures. The format is generally [prefix-]language[-region][-suffix[...]], where the language identifier is the only required part and the other pieces are optional. The prefix can be either of the following:

- i- for culture names registered with the Internet Assigned Numbers Authority (IANA)

- x- for all others

Additionally, the prefix portion can be in uppercase or lowercase. The language part is the lowercase two-letter code from the ISO 639-1 standard, while the region is a two-letter uppercase code from the ISO 3166 standard. For example, Russian spoken in Russia is ru-RU. The suffix component is used to further subidentify the culture based on some other data. For example, Serbian spoken in Serbia could be either sr-SP-Cyrl or sr-SP-Latn—one for the Cyrillic alphabet and the other for the Latin alphabet. If you define a culture specific to your division within your company, you could create it using the name x-en-US-MyCompany-WidgetDivision.

To see how easy it is to use the CultureAndRegionInfoBuilder object, let's create a fictitious culture based upon a preexisting culture. In the United States, the dominant measurement system is English units. Let's suppose that the United States decided to switch to the metric system at some point, and you now need to modify the culture information on some machines to match. Let's see what that code would look like:

```
using System;
using System.Globalization;

public class EntryPoint
{
```

```csharp
static void Main() {
    CultureAndRegionInfoBuilder cib = null;
    cib = new CultureAndRegionInfoBuilder(
                    "x-en-US-metric",
                    CultureAndRegionModifiers.None );

    cib.LoadDataFromCultureInfo( new CultureInfo("en-US") );
    cib.LoadDataFromRegionInfo( new RegionInfo("US") );

    // Make the change.
    cib.IsMetric = true;

    // Create an LDML file.
    cib.Save( "x-en-US-metric.ldml" );

    // Register with the system.
    cib.Register();
    }
}
```

Note In order to compile the previous example, you'll need to reference the `sysglobl.dll` assembly specifically. If you build it using the command line, you can use the following:

`csc /r:sysglobl.dll example.cs`

You can see that the process is simple, since the CultureAndRegionInfoBuilder has a well-designed interface. For illustration purposes, I've sent the LDML to a file so you can see what it looks like, although it's too verbose to list in this text. One thing to consider is that you must have proper permissions in order to call the Register method. This typically requires that you be an administrator, although you could get around that by adjusting the accessibility of the %WINDIR%\Globalization directory and the HKEY_LOCAL_MACHINE\SYSTEM\CurrentControlSet\Control\Nls\CustomLocale registry key. Once you register the culture with the system, you can reference it using the given name when specifying any culture information in the CLR. For example, to verify that the culture and information region is registered properly, you can build and execute the following code to test it:

```csharp
using System;
using System.Globalization;

public class EntryPoint
{
    static void Main() {
        RegionInfo ri = new RegionInfo("x-en-US-metric");
        Console.WriteLine( ri.IsMetric );
    }
}
```

Format Strings

You must consider what the format string looks like. The built-in numeric objects use the standard numeric format strings or the custom numeric format strings defined by the .NET Framework, which you can find in the MSDN documentation by searching for "standard numeric format strings." The standard format strings are typically of the form Axx, where A is the desired format requested and xx is an optional precision specifier. Examples of format specifiers for numbers are "C" for currency, "D" for decimal, "E" for scientific notation, "F" for fixed-point notation, and "X" for hexadecimal notation. Every type also supports "G" for general, which is the default format specifier and is also the format that you get when you call Object.ToString, where you cannot specify a format string. If these format strings don't suit your needs, you can even use one of the custom format strings that allow you to describe what you'd like in a more-or-less picture format.

The point of this whole mechanism is that each type interprets and defines the format string specifically in the context of its own needs. In other words, System.Double is free to treat the G format specifier differently than the System.Int32 type. Moreover, your own type—say, type Employee—is free to implement a format string in whatever way it likes. For example, a format string of "SSN" could create a string based on the Social Security number of the employee.

■**Note** What is of even more utility is to allow your own types to handle a format string of "DBG", thus creating a detailed string that represents the internal state to send to a debug output log.

Let's take a look at some example code that exercises these concepts:

```
using System;
using System.Globalization;
using System.Windows.Forms;

public class EntryPoint
{
    static void Main() {
        CultureInfo current  = CultureInfo.CurrentCulture;
        CultureInfo germany  = new CultureInfo( "de-DE" );
        CultureInfo russian  = new CultureInfo( "ru-RU" );

        double money = 123.45;

        string localMoney = money.ToString( "C", current );
        MessageBox.Show( localMoney, "Local Money" );

        localMoney = money.ToString( "C", germany );
        MessageBox.Show( localMoney, "German Money" );

        localMoney = money.ToString( "C", russian );
        MessageBox.Show( localMoney, "Russian Money" );
    }
}
```

In this example, I display the strings using the MessageBox type defined in Windows.Forms, since the console isn't good at displaying Unicode characters. The format specifier that I've chosen is "C" to display the number in a currency format. For the first display, I use the CultureInfo instance attached to the current thread. For the following two, I've created a CultureInfo for both Germany and Russia. Note that in forming the string, the System.Double type has used the CurrencyDecimalSeparator, CurrencyDecimalDigits, and CurrencySymbol properties of the NumberFormatInfo instance returned from the CultureInfo.GetFormat method. Had I displayed a DateTime instance, then the DateTime implementation of IFormattable.ToString would have utilized an instance of DateTimeFormatInfo returned from CultureInfo.GetFormat in a similar way.

Console.WriteLine and String.Format

Throughout this book, you've seen me using Console.WriteLine extensively in the examples. One of the forms of WriteLine that is useful and identical to some overloads of String.Format allows you to build a composite string by replacing format tags within a string with a variable number of parameters passed in. In practice, String.Format is similar to the printf family of functions in C and C++. However, it's much more flexible and safer, since it's based upon the .NET Framework string-formatting capabilities covered previously. Let's look at a quick example of string format usage:

```
using System;
using System.Globalization;
using System.Windows.Forms;

public class EntryPoint
{
    static void Main( string[] args ) {
        if( args.Length < 3 ) {
            Console.WriteLine( "Please provide 3 parameters" );
            return;
        }

        string composite =
            String.Format( "{0} + {1} = {2}",
                           args[0],
                           args[1],
                           args[2] );

        Console.WriteLine( composite );
    }
}
```

You can see that a placeholder is contained with curly braces and that the number within them is the index within the following parameters that goes there. The String.Format method, as well as the Console.WriteLine method, has an overload that accepts a variable number of parameters to use as the replacement values. In this example, the String.Format method replaces each placeholder using the general formatting of the type that you can get via a call to the parameterless version of ToString. If the instance being placed in this spot supports IFormattable, the IFormattable.ToString method is called with a null format specifier, which usually is the same as if you had supplied the "G", or general, format specifier. Incidentally, within the source string, if you need to insert actual curly braces that will show in the output, you must double them by putting in either {{ or }}.

The exact format of the replacement item is {index[,alignment][:formatString]}, where the items within brackets are optional. The index value is a zero-based value used to reference one of the trailing parameters provided to the method. The alignment represents how wide the entry should be within the composite string. For example, if you set it to eight characters in width and the string is narrower than that, then the extra space is padded with spaces. Lastly, the formatString portion of the replacement item allows you to denote precisely what formatting to use for the item.

The format string is the same style of string that you would have used if you were to call
IFormattable.ToString on the instance itself, which I covered in the previous section. Unfortunately, you can't specify a particular IFormatProvider instance for each one of the replacement
strings. If you need to create a composite string from items using multiple format providers or
cultures, you must resort to using IFormattable.ToString directly.

Examples of String Formatting in Custom Types

Let's take a look at another example using the venerable Complex type that I've used throughout this
book. This time, let's implement IFormattable on it to make it a little more useful when generating a
string version of the instance:

```
using System;
using System.Text;
using System.Globalization;

public struct Complex : IFormattable
{
    public Complex( double real, double imaginary ) {
        this.real = real;
        this.imaginary = imaginary;
    }

    // IFormattable implementation
    public string ToString( string format,
                    IFormatProvider formatProvider ) {
        StringBuilder sb = new StringBuilder();

        if( format == "DBG" ) {
            // Generate debugging output for this object.
            sb.Append( this.GetType().ToString() + "\n" );
            sb.AppendFormat( "\treal:\t{0}\n", real );
            sb.AppendFormat( "\timaginary:\t{0}\n", imaginary );
        } else {
            sb.Append( "( " );
            sb.Append( real.ToString(format, formatProvider) );
            sb.Append( " : " );
            sb.Append( imaginary.ToString(format, formatProvider) );
            sb.Append( " )" );
        }

        return sb.ToString();
    }

    private double real;
    private double imaginary;
}

public class EntryPoint
{
    static void Main() {
        CultureInfo local = CultureInfo.CurrentCulture;
        CultureInfo germany = new CultureInfo( "de-DE" );
```

```
        Complex cpx = new Complex( 12.3456, 1234.56 );

        string strCpx = cpx.ToString( "F", local );
        Console.WriteLine( strCpx );

        strCpx = cpx.ToString( "F", germany );
        Console.WriteLine( strCpx );

        Console.WriteLine( "\nDebugging output:\n{0:DBG}",
                            cpx );
    }
}
```

The real meat of this example lies within the implementation of IFormattable.ToString. I've implemented a "DBG" format string for this type that will create a string that shows the internal state of the object and may be useful for debug purposes. I'm sure you can think of a little more information to display to a debugger output log that is specific to the instance, but you get the idea. If the format string is not equal to "DBG", then you simply defer to the IFormattable implementation of System.Double. Notice my use of StringBuilder to create the string that I eventually return. Also, I chose to use the Console.WriteLine method and its format item syntax to send the debugging output to the console just to show a little variety in usage.

ICustomFormatter

ICustomFormatter is an interface that allows you to replace or extend a built-in or already existing IFormattable interface for an object. Whenever you call String.Format or StringBuilder.AppendFormat to convert an object instance to a string, before the method calls through to the object's implementation of IFormattable.ToString, it first checks to see if the passed-in IFormatProvider provides a custom formatter. It does this by calling IFormatProvider.GetFormat while passing a type of ICustomFormatter. If the formatter returns an implementation of ICustomFormatter, then the method will use the custom formatter. Otherwise, it will use the object's implementation of IFormattable.ToString or the object's implementation of Object.ToString in cases where it doesn't implement IFormattable.

Consider the following example where I've reworked the previous Complex example, but I've externalized the debugging output capabilities outside of the Complex struct. I've bolded the code that has changed:

```
using System;
using System.Text;
using System.Globalization;

public class ComplexDbgFormatter : ICustomFormatter, IFormatProvider
{
    // IFormatProvider implementation
    public object GetFormat( Type formatType ) {
        if( formatType == typeof(ICustomFormatter) ) {
            return this;
        } else {
            return CultureInfo.CurrentCulture.
                GetFormat( formatType );
        }
    }
```

```
        // ICustomFormatter implementation
        public string Format( string format,
                              object arg,
                              IFormatProvider formatProvider ) {
            if( arg.GetType() == typeof(Complex) &&
                format == "DBG" ) {
                Complex cpx = (Complex) arg;

                // Generate debugging output for this object.
                StringBuilder sb = new StringBuilder();
                sb.Append( arg.GetType().ToString() + "\n" );
                sb.AppendFormat( "\treal:\t{0}\n", cpx.Real );
                sb.AppendFormat( "\timaginary:\t{0}\n", cpx.Img );
                return sb.ToString();
            } else {
                IFormattable formattable = arg as IFormattable;
                if( formattable != null ) {
                    return formattable.ToString( format, formatProvider );
                } else {
                    return arg.ToString();
                }
            }
        }
    }

public struct Complex : IFormattable
{
    public Complex( double real, double imaginary ) {
        this.real = real;
        this.imaginary = imaginary;
    }

    public double Real {
        get { return real; }
    }

    public double Img {
        get { return imaginary; }
    }

    // IFormattable implementation
    public string ToString( string format,
                    IFormatProvider formatProvider ) {
        StringBuilder sb = new StringBuilder();
        sb.Append( "( " );
        sb.Append( real.ToString(format, formatProvider) );
        sb.Append( " : " );
        sb.Append( imaginary.ToString(format, formatProvider) );
        sb.Append( " )" );

        return sb.ToString();
    }

    private double real;
    private double imaginary;
}
```

```
public class EntryPoint
{
    static void Main() {
        CultureInfo local = CultureInfo.CurrentCulture;
        CultureInfo germany = new CultureInfo( "de-DE" );

        Complex cpx = new Complex( 12.3456, 1234.56 );

        string strCpx = cpx.ToString( "F", local );
        Console.WriteLine( strCpx );

        strCpx = cpx.ToString( "F", germany );
        Console.WriteLine( strCpx );

        ComplexDbgFormatter dbgFormatter =
            new ComplexDbgFormatter();
        strCpx = String.Format( dbgFormatter,
                                "{0:DBG}",
                                cpx );
        Console.WriteLine( "\nDebugging output:\n{0}",
                           strCpx );
    }
}
```

Of course, this example is a bit more complex (no pun intended). But if you were not the original author of the Complex type, then this may be your only way to provide custom formatting for that type. Using this technique, you can provide custom formatting to any of the other built-in types in the system.

Comparing Strings

When it comes to comparing strings, the .NET Framework provides quite a bit of flexibility. You can compare strings based on cultural information as well as without cultural consideration. You can also compare strings using case sensitivity or not, and the rules for how to do case-insensitive comparisons vary from culture to culture. There are several ways to compare strings offered within the Framework, some of which are exposed directly on the System.String type through the static String.Compare method. You can choose from a few overloads, and the most basic of them use the CultureInfo attached to the current thread to handle comparisons.

You often need to compare strings, and you don't need to worry about, or want to carry, the overhead of culture-specific comparisons. A perfect example is when you're comparing internal string data from, say, a configuration file, or when you're comparing file directories. In the .NET 1.1 days, the main tool of choice was to use the String.Compare method while passing the InvariantCulture property. This works fine in most cases, but it still applies culture information to the comparison even though the culture information it uses is neutral to all cultures, and that is usually an unnecessary overhead for such comparisons. The .NET 2.0 Framework introduced a new enumeration, StringComparison, that allows you to choose a true nonculture-based comparison. The StringComparison enumeration looks like the following:

```
public enum StringComparison
{
    CurrentCulture,
    CurrentCultureIgnoreCase,
    InvariantCulture,
```

```
    InvariantCultureIgnoreCase,
    Ordinal,
    OrdinalIgnoreCase
}
```

The last two items in the enumeration are the items of interest. An ordinal-based comparison is the most basic string comparison; it simply compares the character values of the two strings based on the numeric value of each character compared (i.e., it actually compares the raw binary values of each character). Doing comparisons this way removes all cultural bias from the comparisons and increases the efficiency tremendously. On my computer, I ran some crude timing loops to compare the two techniques when comparing strings of equal length. The speed increase was almost nine times faster. Of course, had the strings been more complex with more than just lowercase Latin characters in them, the gain would have been even higher.

The .NET 2.0 Framework introduced a new class called StringComparer that implements the IComparer interface. Things such as sorted collections can use StringComparer to manage the sort. The System.StringComparer type follows the same pattern as the IFormattable locale support. You can use the StringComparer.CurrentCulture property to get a StringComparer instance specific to the culture of the current thread. Additionally, you can get the StringComparer instance from StringComparer.CurrentCultureIgnoreCase to do case-insensitive comparison. Also, you can get culture-invariant instances using the InvariantCulture and InvariantCultureIgnoreCase properties. Lastly, you can use the Ordinal and OrdinalIgnoreCase properties to get instances that compare based on ordinal string comparison rules.

As you may expect, if the culture information attached to the current thread isn't what you need, you can create StringComparer instances based upon explicit locales simply by calling the StringComparer.Create method and passing the desired CultureInfo representing the locale you want as well as a flag denoting whether you want a case-sensitive or case-insensitive comparer. The string used to specify which locale to use is the same as that for CultureInfo and is described in detail in the MSDN documentation.

When choosing between the various comparison techniques, take care to choose the appropriate choice for the job. The general rule of thumb is to use the culture-specific or culture-invariant comparisons for any user-facing data—that is, data that will be presented to end users in some form or fashion—and ordinal comparisons otherwise. However, it's rare that you'd ever use InvariantCulture compared strings to display to users. Use the ordinal comparisons when dealing with data that is completely internal. In fact, ordinal-based comparisons render InvariantCulture comparisons almost useless.

■**Note** Prior to version 2.0 of the .NET Framework, it was a general guideline that if you were comparing strings to make a security decision, you should use InvariantCulture rather than base the comparison on CultureInfo.CurrentCulture. In such comparisons, you want a tightly controlled environment that you know will be the same in the field as it is in your test environment. If you base the comparison on CurrentCulture, this is impossible to achieve, because end users can change the culture on the machine and introduce a probably untested code path into the security decision, since it's almost impossible to test under all culture permutations.

Naturally, in .NET 2.0 and onward, it is recommended that you base these security comparisons on ordinal comparisons rather than InvariantCulture for added efficiency and safety.

Working with Strings from Outside Sources

Within the confines of the .NET Framework, all strings are represented using Unicode UTF-16 character arrays. However, you often might need to interface with the outside world using some other form of encoding, such as UTF-8. Sometimes, even when interfacing with other entities that use 16-bit Unicode strings, those entities may use big-endian Unicode strings, whereas the Intel platform typically uses little-endian Unicode strings. The .NET Framework makes this conversion work easy with the System.Text.Encoding class.

In this section, I won't go into all of the details of System.Text.Encoding, but I highly suggest that you reference the documentation for this class in the MSDN for all of the finer details. Let's take a look at a cursory example of how to convert to and from various encodings using the Encoding objects served up by the System.Text.Encoding class:

```
using System;
using System.Text;

public class EntryPoint
{
    static void Main() {
        string leUnicodeStr = "здорово!";        // "What's up!"

        Encoding leUnicode = Encoding.Unicode;
        Encoding beUnicode = Encoding.BigEndianUnicode;
        Encoding utf8 = Encoding.UTF8;

        byte[] leUnicodeBytes = leUnicode.GetBytes(leUnicodeStr);
        byte[] beUnicodeBytes = Encoding.Convert( leUnicode,
                                                  beUnicode,
                                                  leUnicodeBytes);
        byte[] utf8Bytes = Encoding.Convert( leUnicode,
                                             utf8,
                                             leUnicodeBytes );

        Console.WriteLine( "Orig. String: {0}\n", leUnicodeStr );
        Console.WriteLine( "Little Endian Unicode Bytes:" );
        StringBuilder sb = new StringBuilder();
        foreach( byte b in leUnicodeBytes ) {
            sb.Append( b ).Append(" : ");
        }
        Console.WriteLine( "{0}\n", sb.ToString() );

        Console.WriteLine( "Big Endian Unicode Bytes:" );
        sb = new StringBuilder();
        foreach( byte b in beUnicodeBytes ) {
            sb.Append( b ).Append(" : ");
        }
        Console.WriteLine( "{0}\n", sb.ToString() );

        Console.WriteLine( "UTF Bytes:" );
        sb = new StringBuilder();
        foreach( byte b in utf8Bytes ) {
            sb.Append( b ).Append(" : ");
        }
        Console.WriteLine( sb.ToString() );
    }
}
```

The example first starts by creating a System.String with some Russian text in it. As mentioned, the string contains a Unicode string, but is it a big-endian or little-endian Unicode string? The answer depends on what platform you're running on. On an Intel system, it is normally little-endian. However, since you're not supposed to access the underlying byte representation of the string because it is encapsulated from you, it doesn't matter. In order to get the bytes of the string, you should use one of the Encoding objects that you can get from System.Text.Encoding. In my example, I get local references to the Encoding objects for handling big-endian Unicode, little-endian Unicode, and UTF-8. Once I have those, I can use them to convert the string into any byte representation that I want. As you can see, I get three representations of the same string and send the byte sequence values to standard output. In this example, since the text is based on the Cyrillic alphabet, the UTF-8 byte array is longer than the Unicode byte array. Had the original string been based on the Latin character set, the UTF-8 byte array would be shorter than the Unicode byte array usually by half. The point is, you should never make any assumption about the storage requirements for any of the encodings. If you need to know how much space is required to store the encoded string, call the Encoding.GetByteCount method to get that value.

■Caution Never make assumptions about the internal string representation format of the CLR. Nothing says that the internal representation cannot vary from one platform to the next. It would be unfortunate if your code made assumptions based upon an Intel platform and then failed to run on a Sun platform running the Mono CLR. Microsoft could even choose to run Windows on another platform one day, just as Apple has chosen to start using Intel processors.

Usually, you need to go the opposite way with the conversion and convert an array of bytes from the outside world into a string that the system can then manipulate easily. For example, the Bluetooth protocol stack uses big-endian Unicode strings to transfer string data. To convert the bytes into a System.String, use the GetString method on the encoder that you're using. You must also use the encoder that matches the source encoding of your data.

This brings up an important note to keep in mind. When passing string data to and from other systems in raw byte format, you must always know the encoding scheme used by the protocol you're using. Most importantly, you must always use that encoding's matching Encoding object to convert the byte array into a System.String, even if you know that the encoding in the protocol is the same as that used internally to System.String on the platform where you're building the application. Why? Suppose you're developing your application on an Intel platform and the protocol encoding is little-endian, which you know is the same as the platform encoding. So you take a shortcut and don't use the System.Text.Encoding.Unicode object to convert the bytes to the string. Later on, you decide to run the application on a platform that happens to use big-endian strings internally. You'll be in for a big surprise when the application starts to crumble because you falsely assumed what encoding System.String uses internally. Efficiency is not a problem if you always use the encoder, because on platforms where the internal encoding is the same as the external encoding, the conversion will essentially boil down to nothing.

In the previous example, you saw use of the StringBuilder class in order to send the array of bytes to the console. Let's now take a look at what the StringBuilder type is all about.

StringBuilder

Since System.String objects are immutable, sometimes they create efficiency bottlenecks when you're trying to build strings on the fly. You can create composite strings using the + operator as follows:

```
string compound = "Vote" + " for " + "Pedro";
```

However, this method isn't efficient, since this code creates four strings to get the job done. Creating all those intermediate strings could increase memory pressure. Although this line of code is rather contrived, you can imagine that the efficiency of a complex system that does lots of string manipulation can quickly go downhill due to memory usage. Consider a case where you implement a custom base64 encoder that appends characters incrementally as it processes a binary file. The .NET library already offers this functionality in the System.Convert class, but let's ignore that for the sake of example. If you repeatedly used the + operator in a loop to create a large base64 string, your performance would quickly degrade as the source data increased in size. For these situations, you can use the System.Text.StringBuilder class, which implements a mutable string specifically for building composite strings efficiently.

I won't go over each of the methods of StringBuilder in detail, since you can get all the details of each method within the MSDN documentation. However, I'll cover more of the salient points of note. StringBuilder internally maintains an array of characters that it manages dynamically. The workhorse methods of StringBuilder are Append, Insert, and AppendFormat. If you look up the methods in the MSDN, you'll see that they are richly overloaded in order to support appending and inserting string forms of the many common types. When you create a StringBuilder instance, you have various constructors to choose from. The default constructor creates a new StringBuilder instance with the system-defined default capacity. However, that capacity doesn't constrain the size of the string that it can create. Rather, it represents the amount of string data the StringBuilder can hold before it needs to grow the internal buffer and increase the capacity. If you know a ballpark figure of how big your string will likely end up being, you can give the StringBuilder that number in one of the constructor overloads, and it will initialize the buffer accordingly. This could help the StringBuilder instance from having to reallocate the buffer too often while you fill it.

You can also define the maximum-capacity property in the constructor overloads. By default, the maximum capacity is System.Int32.MaxValue, which is currently 2,147,483,647, but that exact value is subject to change as the system evolves. If you need to protect your StringBuilder buffer from growing over a certain size, you may provide an alternate maximum capacity in one of the constructor overloads. If an append or insert operation forces the need for the buffer to grow greater than the maximum capacity, an ArgumentOutOfRangeException is thrown.

For convenience, all of the methods that append and insert data into a StringBuilder instance return a reference to this. Thus, you can chain operations on a single string builder as shown:

```
using System;
using System.Text;

public class EntryPoint
{
    static void Main() {
        StringBuilder sb = new StringBuilder();

        sb.Append("StringBuilder ").Append("is ")
            .Append("very... ");

        string built1 = sb.ToString();

        sb.Append("cool");

        string built2 = sb.ToString();

        Console.WriteLine( built1 );
        Console.WriteLine( built2 );
    }
}
```

In this example, you can see that I converted the StringBuilder instance sb into a new System.String instance named built1 by calling sb.ToString. For maximum efficiency, the StringBuilder simply hands off a reference to the character buffer to the string instance so that a copy is not necessary. If you think about it, part of the utility of StringBuilder would be compromised if it didn't do it this way. After all, if you create a huge string—say, some megabytes in size, such as a base64-encoded large image—you don't want that data to be copied in order to create a string from it. However, once you create the System.String, you now have the System.String and the StringBuilder holding references to the same array of characters. Since System.String is immutable, the StringBuilder's internal character array now becomes immutable as well. StringBuilder then switches to using a copy-on-write idiom with that buffer. Therefore, at the place where I append to the StringBuilder after having created the built1 string instance, the StringBuilder must make a new copy of the internal character array, thus handing off complete ownership of the old buffer to the built1 System.String instance. It's important for you to keep this behavior in mind if you're using StringBuilder to work with large string data.

Searching Strings with Regular Expressions

The System.String type itself offers some rudimentary searching methods, such as IndexOf, IndexOfAny, LastIndexOf, LastIndexOfAny, and StartsWith. Using these methods, you can determine if a string contains certain substrings and where. However, these methods quickly become cumbersome and are a bit too primitive to do any complex searching of strings effectively. Thankfully, the .NET Framework library contains classes that implement regular expressions (regex). If you're not already familiar with regular expressions, I strongly suggest that you learn the regular-expression syntax and how to use it effectively. The regular-expression syntax is a language in and of itself. Excellent sources of information on the syntax include Jeffrey E. F. Friedl's *Mastering Regular Expressions, Third Edition* (Sebastapol, CA: O'Reilly Media, 2006) and the material under "Regular Expression Language Elements" within the MSDN. The capabilities of the .NET regular-expression engine are on a par with those of Perl 5 and Python. Full coverage of the capabilities of regular expressions with regard to their syntax is beyond the scope of this book. However, I'll describe the ways to use regular expressions that are specific to the .NET Framework.

There are really three main types of operations for which you employ regular expressions. The first is when searching a string just to verify that it contains a specific pattern, and if so, where. The search pattern can be extremely complex. The second is similar to the first, except, in the process, you save off parts of the searched expression. For example, if you search a string for a date in a specific format, you may choose to break the three parts of the date into individual variables. And finally, regular expressions are often used for search-and-replace operations. This type of operation builds upon the capabilities of the previous two. Let's take a look at how to achieve these three goals using the .NET Framework's implementation of regular expressions.

Searching with Regular Expressions

As with the System.String class itself, most of the objects created from the regular expression classes are immutable. The workhorse class at the bottom of it all is the Regex class, which lives in the System.Text.RegularExpressions namespace. One of the general patterns of usage is to create a Regex instance to represent your regular expression by passing it a string of the pattern to search for. You then apply it to a string to find out if any matches exist. The results of the search will include whether a match was found, and if so, where. You can also find out where all subsequent instances of the match occur within the searched string. Let's go ahead and look at an example of what a basic Regex search looks like and then dig into more useful ways to use Regex:

```
using System;
using System.Text.RegularExpressions;

public class EntryPoint
{
    static void Main( string[] args ) {
        if( args.Length < 1 ) {
            Console.WriteLine( "You must provide a string." );
            return;
        }

        // Create regex to search for IP address pattern.
        string pattern = @"\d\d?\d?\.\d\d?\d?.\d\d?\d?.\d\d?\d?";
        Regex regex = new Regex( pattern );
        Match match = regex.Match( args[0] );
        while( match.Success ) {
            Console.WriteLine( "IP Address found at {0} with " +
                               "value of {1}",
                               match.Index,
                               match.Value );

            match = match.NextMatch();
        }

    }
}
```

This example searches a string provided on the command line for an IP address. The search is crude, but I'll refine it a bit as I continue. Regular expressions can consist of literal characters to search for, as well as escaped characters that carry a special meaning. The familiar backslash is the method used to escape characters in a regular expression. In this example, \d means a numeric digit. The ones that are suffixed with a ? mean that there can be one or zero occurrences of the previous character or escaped expression. Notice that the period is escaped, because the period by itself carries a special meaning: An unescaped period matches any character in that position of the match. Lastly, you'll see that it is much easier to use the verbatim string syntax when declaring regular expressions in order to avoid the gratuitous proliferation of backslashes. If you were to invoke the previous example passing the following quoted string on the command line

```
"This is an IP address:123.123.1.123"
```

the output would look like the following:

```
IP Address found at 22 with value of 123.123.1.123
```

The previous example creates a new Regex instance named regex and then, using the Match method, applies the pattern to the given string. The results of the match are stored in the match variable. That match variable represents the first match within the searched string. You can use the Match.Success property to determine if the regex found anything at all. Next, you see the code using the Index and Value properties to find out more about the match. Lastly, you can go to the next match in the searched string by calling the Match.NextMatch method, and you can iterate through this chain until you find no more matches in the searched string.

Alternatively, instead of calling Match.NextMatch in a loop, you can call the Regex.Matches method to retrieve a MatchCollection that gives you all of the matches at once rather than one at a time. Also, all of the examples using Regex in this chapter are calling instance methods on a Regex instance. Many of the methods on Regex, such as Match and Replace, also offer static versions where you don't have to create a Regex instance first and you can just pass the regular expression pattern in the method call.

Searching and Grouping

From looking at the previous match, really all that is happening is that the pattern is looking for a series of four groups of digits separated by periods, where each group can be from one to three digits in length. The reason I say this is a crude search is that it will match an invalid IP address such as 999.888.777.666. A better search for the IP address would look like the following:

```
using System;
using System.Text.RegularExpressions;

public class EntryPoint
{
    static void Main( string[] args ) {
        if( args.Length < 1 ) {
            Console.WriteLine( "You must provide a string." );
            return;
        }

        // Create regex to search for IP address pattern.
        string pattern = @"([01]?\d\d?|2[0-4]\d|25[0-5])\." +
                         @"([01]?\d\d?|2[0-4]\d|25[0-5])\." +
                         @"([01]?\d\d?|2[0-4]\d|25[0-5])\." +
                         @"([01]?\d\d?|2[0-4]\d|25[0-5])";
        Regex regex = new Regex( pattern );
        Match match = regex.Match( args[0] );
        while( match.Success ) {
            Console.WriteLine( "IP Address found at {0} with " +
                               "value of {1}",
                               match.Index,
                               match.Value );

            match = match.NextMatch();
        }

    }
}
```

Essentially, four groupings of the same search pattern [01]?\d\d?|2[0-4]\d|25[0-5] are separated by periods, which of course, are escaped in the preceding regular expression. Each one of these subexpressions matches a number between 0 and 255. This entire expression for searching for regular expressions is better, but still not perfect. However, you can see that it's getting closer, and with a little more fine-tuning, you can use it to validate the IP address given in a string. Thus, you can use regular expressions to effectively validate input from users to make sure that it matches a certain form. For example, you may have a web server that expects US telephone numbers to be entered in a pattern such as (xxx) xxx-xxxx. Regular expressions allow you to easily validate that the user has input the number correctly.

You may have noticed the addition of parentheses in the IP address search expression in the previous example. Parentheses are used to define groups that group subexpressions within regular expressions into discrete chunks. Groups can contain other groups as well. Therefore, the IP address regular-expression pattern in the previous example forms a group around each part of the IP address. In addition, you can access each individual group within the match. Consider the following modified version of the previous example:

```
using System;
using System.Text.RegularExpressions;

public class EntryPoint
{
    static void Main( string[] args ) {
        if( args.Length < 1 ) {
            Console.WriteLine( "You must provide a string." );
            return;
        }

        // Create regex to search for IP address pattern.
        string pattern = @"([01]?\d\d?|2[0-4]\d|25[0-5])\." +
                          @"([01]?\d\d?|2[0-4]\d|25[0-5])\." +
                          @"([01]?\d\d?|2[0-4]\d|25[0-5])\." +
                          @"([01]?\d\d?|2[0-4]\d|25[0-5])";
        Regex regex = new Regex( pattern );
        Match match = regex.Match( args[0] );
        while( match.Success ) {
            Console.WriteLine( "IP Address found at {0} with " +
                               "value of {1}",
                               match.Index,
                               match.Value );
            Console.WriteLine( "Groups are:" );
            foreach( Group g in match.Groups ) {
                Console.WriteLine( "\t{0} at {1}",
                                   g.Value,
                                   g.Index );
            }

            match = match.NextMatch();
        }

    }
}
```

Within each match, I've added a loop that iterates through the individual groups within the match. As you'd expect, there will be at least four groups in the collection, one for each portion of the IP address. In fact, there is also a fifth item in the group—the entire match. So, one of the groups within the groups collection returned from Match.Groups will always contain the entire match itself. Given the following input to the previous example

```
"This is an IP address:123.123.1.123"
```

the result would look like the following:

```
IP Address found at 22 with value of 123.123.1.123
Groups are:
        123.123.1.123 at 22
        123 at 22
        123 at 26
        1 at 30
        123 at 32
```

Groups provide an excellent means of picking portions out of a given input string. For example, at the same time that you validate that a user has input a phone number of the required format, you could also capture the area code into a group for use later. Collecting substrings of a match into groups is handy. But what's even handier is being able to give those groups a name. Check out the following modified example:

```
using System;
using System.Text.RegularExpressions;

public class EntryPoint
{
    static void Main( string[] args ) {
        if( args.Length < 1 ) {
            Console.WriteLine( "You must provide a string." );
            return;
        }

        // Create regex to search for IP address pattern.
        string pattern = @"(?<part1>[01]?\d\d?|2[0-4]\d|25[0-5])\." +
                         @"(?<part2>[01]?\d\d?|2[0-4]\d|25[0-5])\." +
                         @"(?<part3>[01]?\d\d?|2[0-4]\d|25[0-5])\." +
                         @"(?<part4>[01]?\d\d?|2[0-4]\d|25[0-5])";
        Regex regex = new Regex( pattern );
        Match match = regex.Match( args[0] );
        while( match.Success ) {
            Console.WriteLine( "IP Address found at {0} with " +
                               "value of {1}",
                               match.Index,
                               match.Value );
            Console.WriteLine( "Groups are:" );
            Console.WriteLine( "\tPart 1: {0}",
                               match.Groups["part1"] );
            Console.WriteLine( "\tPart 2: {0}",
                               match.Groups["part2"] );
            Console.WriteLine( "\tPart 3: {0}",
                               match.Groups["part3"] );
            Console.WriteLine( "\tPart 4: {0}",
                               match.Groups["part4"] );

            match = match.NextMatch();
        }

    }
}
```

In this variation, I've captured each part into a group with a name, and when I send the result to the console, I access the group by name through an indexer on the GroupCollection returned by Match.Groups that accepts a string argument.

With the ability to name groups comes the ability to back-reference groups within searches. For example, if you're looking for an exact repeat of a previous match, you can reference a previous group in what's called a back-reference by including \k<name>, where name is the name of the group to back-reference. For example, consider the following example that looks for IP addresses where all four parts are the same:

```
using System;
using System.Text.RegularExpressions;
```

```
public class EntryPoint
{
    static void Main( string[] args ) {
        if( args.Length < 1 ) {
            Console.WriteLine( "You must provide a string." );
            return;
        }

        // Create regex to search for IP address pattern.
        string pattern = @"(?<part1>[01]?\d\d?|2[0-4]\d|25[0-5])\." +
                         @"\k<part1>\." +
                         @"\k<part1>\." +
                         @"\k<part1>";
        Regex regex = new Regex( pattern );
        Match match = regex.Match( args[0] );
        while( match.Success ) {
            Console.WriteLine( "IP Address found at {0} with " +
                               "value of {1}",
                               match.Index,
                               match.Value );

            match = match.NextMatch();
        }
    }
}
```

The following output shows the results of running this code on the string "My IP address is 123.123.123.123":

```
IP Address found at 17 with value of 123.123.123.123
```

Replacing Text with Regex

If you've ever used Perl to do any text processing, you know that the regular-expression engine within it is indispensable. But one of the greatest powers within Perl is the regular-expression text-substitution capabilities. You can do the same thing using .NET regular expressions via the Regex. Replace method overloads. Suppose that you want to process a string looking for an IP address that a user input, and you want to display the string. However, for security reasons, you want to replace the IP address with xxx.xxx.xxx.xxx. You could achieve this goal, as in the following example:

```
using System;
using System.Text.RegularExpressions;

public class EntryPoint
{
    static void Main( string[] args ) {
        if( args.Length < 1 ) {
            Console.WriteLine( "You must provide a string." );
            return;
        }

        // Create regex to search for IP address pattern.
        string pattern = @"([01]?\d\d?|2[0-4]\d|25[0-5])\." +
                         @"([01]?\d\d?|2[0-4]\d|25[0-5])\." +
                         @"([01]?\d\d?|2[0-4]\d|25[0-5])\." +
```

```
                        @"([01]?\d\d?|2[0-4]\d|25[0-5])";
         Regex regex = new Regex( pattern );
         Console.WriteLine( "Input given -> {0}",
                            regex.Replace(args[0],
                                          "xxx.xxx.xxx.xxx") );
    }
}
```

Thus, given the following input

```
"This is an IP address:123.123.123.123"
```

the output would look like the following:

```
Input given -> This is an IP address:xxx.xxx.xxx.xxx
```

Of course, when you find a match within a string, you may want to replace it with something that depends on what the match is. The previous example simply replaces each match with a static string. In order to replace based on the match instance, you can create an instance of the MatchEvaluator delegate and pass it to the Regex.Replace method. Then, whenever it finds a match, it calls through to the MatchEvaluator delegate instance given while passing it the match. Thus, the delegate can create the replacement string based upon the actual match. The MatchEvaluator delegate has the following signature:

```
public delegate string MatchEvaluator( Match match );
```

Suppose you want to reverse the individual parts of an IP address. Then you could use a MatchEvaluator coupled with Regex.Replace to get the job done, as in the following example:

```
using System;
using System.Text;
using System.Text.RegularExpressions;

public class EntryPoint
{
    static void Main( string[] args ) {
        if( args.Length < 1 ) {
            Console.WriteLine( "You must provide a string." );
            return;
        }

        // Create regex to search for IP address pattern.
        string pattern = @"(?<part1>[01]?\d\d?|2[0-4]\d|25[0-5])\." +
                         @"(?<part2>[01]?\d\d?|2[0-4]\d|25[0-5])\." +
                         @"(?<part3>[01]?\d\d?|2[0-4]\d|25[0-5])\." +
                         @"(?<part4>[01]?\d\d?|2[0-4]\d|25[0-5])";
        Regex regex = new Regex( pattern );
        Match match = regex.Match( args[0] );

        MatchEvaluator eval = new MatchEvaluator(
                                  EntryPoint.IPReverse );
        Console.WriteLine( regex.Replace(args[0],
                                         eval) );
    }

    static string IPReverse( Match match ) {
        StringBuilder sb = new StringBuilder();
```

```
            sb.Append( match.Groups["part4"] + "." );
            sb.Append( match.Groups["part3"] + "." );
            sb.Append( match.Groups["part2"] + "." );
            sb.Append( match.Groups["part1"] );
            return sb.ToString();
        }
    }
```

Whenever a match is found, the delegate is called to determine what the replacement string
should be. However, since all you're doing is changing the order, the job is not too complex for what
are called *regular-expression substitutions*. If, in the example prior to this one, you had chosen to
use the overload of Replace that doesn't use a MatchEvaluator delegate, you could have achieved the
same result, since the regex lets you reference the group variables in the replacement string. To reference one of the named groups, you can use the syntax shown in the following example:

```
using System;
using System.Text;
using System.Text.RegularExpressions;

public class EntryPoint
{
    static void Main( string[] args ) {
        if( args.Length < 1 ) {
            Console.WriteLine( "You must provide a string." );
            return;
        }

        // Create regex to search for IP address pattern.
        string pattern = @"(?<part1>[01]?\d\d?|2[0-4]\d|25[0-5])\." +
                         @"(?<part2>[01]?\d\d?|2[0-4]\d|25[0-5])\." +
                         @"(?<part3>[01]?\d\d?|2[0-4]\d|25[0-5])\." +
                         @"(?<part4>[01]?\d\d?|2[0-4]\d|25[0-5])";
        Regex regex = new Regex( pattern );
        Match match = regex.Match( args[0] );

        string replace = @"${part4}.${part3}.${part2}.${part1}" +
                         @" (the reverse of $&)";
        Console.WriteLine( regex.Replace(args[0],
                                         replace) );
    }
}
```

To include one of the named groups, simply use the ${name} syntax, where name is the name of
the group. You can also see that I reference the full text of the match using $&. Other substitutions
strings are available, such as $`, which substitutes the part of the input string prior to and up to the
match, and $', which substitutes all text after the match. Others are documented in the MSDN doc-
umentation.

As you can imagine, you can craft complex string-replacement capabilities using the regular-
expression implementation within .NET Framework just as you can using Perl.

Regex Creation Options

One of the constructor overloads of a Regex allows you to pass various options of type RegexOptions during creation of a Regex instance. Likewise, the methods on Regex, such as Match and Replace, have a static overload allowing you to pass RegexOptions flags. I'll discuss some of the more commonly used options in this section, but for a description of all of the options and their behavior, consult the RegexOptions documentation within the MSDN.

By default, regular expressions are interpreted at run time. Complex regular expressions can chew up quite a bit of processor time while the regex engine is processing them. For times like these, consider using the Compiled option. This option causes the regular expression to be represented internally by IL code that is JIT-compiled. This increases the latency for the first use of the regular expression, but if it's used often, it will pay off in the end. Also, don't forget that JIT-compiled code increases the working set of the application.

Many times, you'll find it useful to do case-insensitive searches. You could accommodate that in the regular-expression pattern, but it makes your pattern much more difficult to read. It's much easier to pass the IgnoreCase flag when creating the Regex instance. When you use this flag, the Regex engine will also take into account any culture-specific case-sensitivity issues by referencing the CultureInfo attached to the current thread. If you want to do case-insensitive searches in a culture-invariant way, combine the IgnoreCase flag with the CultureInvariant flag.

The IgnorePatternWhitespace flag is also useful for complex regular expressions. This flag tells the regex engine to ignore any white space within the match expression and to ignore any comments on lines following the # character. This provides a nifty way to comment regular expressions that are really complex. For example, check out the IP address search from the previous example rewritten using IgnorePatternWhitespace:

```
using System;
using System.Text.RegularExpressions;

public class EntryPoint
{
    static void Main( string[] args ) {
        if( args.Length < 1 ) {
            Console.WriteLine( "You must provide a string." );
            return;
        }

        // Create regex to search for IP address pattern.
        string pattern = @"
# First part match
([01]?\d\d?        # At least one digit,
                   # possibly prepended by 0 or 1
                   # and possibly followed by another digit
# OR
|2[0-4]\d          # Starts with a 2, after a number from 0-4
                   # and then any digit
# OR
|25[0-5])          # 25 followed by a number from 0-5

\.                 # The whole group is followed by a period.

# REPEAT
([01]?\d\d?|2[0-4]\d|25[0-5])\.
```

```
# REPEAT
([01]?\d\d?|2[0-4]\d|25[0-5])\.

# REPEAT
([01]?\d\d?|2[0-4]\d|25[0-5])
";
        Regex regex = new Regex( pattern,
                        RegexOptions.IgnorePatternWhitespace );
        Match match = regex.Match( args[0] );
        while( match.Success ) {
            Console.WriteLine( "IP Address found at {0} with " +
                            "value of {1}",
                            match.Index,
                            match.Value );

            match = match.NextMatch();
        }

    }
}
```

Notice how expressive you can be in the comments of your regular expression. And given how complex regular expressions can become, this is never a bad thing indeed.

Summary

In this chapter, I've touched the tip of the iceberg on the string-handling capabilities of the .NET Framework and C#. Since the string type is such a widely used type, rather than merely include it in the base class library, the CLR designers chose to annex it into the set of built-in types. This is a good thing considering how common string usage is. Furthermore, the library provides a thorough implementation of cultural-specific patterns, via CultureInfo, that you typically need when creating global software that deals with strings heavily.

I showed how you can create your own cultures easily using the CultureAndRegionInfoBuilder class. Essentially, any software that interacts directly with the user and is meant to be used on a global basis needs to be prepared to service locale-specific needs. Finally, I gave a brief tour of the regular-expression capabilities of the .NET Framework, even though a full treatment of the regular-expression language is outside the scope of this book. I think you'll agree that the string and text-handling facilities built into the CLR, the .NET Framework, and the C# language are well-designed and easy to use.

In Chapter 9, I cover arrays and other, more versatile, collection types in the .NET Framework. Also, I spend a fair amount of time covering the new support for iterators in C#.

Arrays, Collection Types, and Iterators

Collection types have been around in various forms since the dawn of programming. I'm sure you remember the linked list exercises when you were learning to write programs. In this chapter, I'll give a brief overview of arrays but won't go into much detail, as arrays have not changed much between the various .NET releases.

However, I'll spend more time explaining the major generic collection interfaces and iterators along with what sorts of cool things you can do with them. Traditionally, creating enumerators for collection types has been tedious and annoying. Iterators make this task a breeze, while making your code a lot more readable in the process.

Introduction to Arrays

C# arrays, as well as arrays in the CLR, are highly evolved from C/C++ arrays. In C/C++, you typically access an array by offsetting a pointer that points to the beginning of a contiguous range of items in a memory block somewhere. C/C++ arrays have no built-in range checking, which is the root of more bugs than you can shake a stick at. C# and the CLR solve this problem elegantly by making the array type a built-in, implicit type to the runtime.

When you declare a type—whether it's a class or struct—the runtime reserves the right to silently generate an array type based upon that new type. The array type that it generates is a reference type—thus, all array instances are of class type. The reference type that it generates is derived from System.Array, and ultimately from System.Object. Therefore, you can treat all C# arrays polymorphically through a reference to System.Array. Of course, that means that each array, no matter what concrete type of array it is, implements all of the methods and properties of System.Array.

The way that you declare an array within C# is similar to C/C++, except the designers of the language took the liberty to make the syntax a tad more intuitive in their minds, in that the square brackets in the declaration follow the type and not the array variable name. The following example shows three ways to create an array of integers and print them to the console:

```
using System;

public class EntryPoint
{
    static void Main() {
        int[] array1 = new int[ 10 ];
        for( int i = 0; i < array1.Length; ++i ) {
            array1[i] = i*2;
        }
```

```
        int[] array2 = new int[] { 2, 4, 6, 8 };

        int[] array3 = { 1, 3, 5, 7 };
    }
}
```

The longhand way to create an array instance and fill it with initial values is shown where array1 is initialized. Items are indexed using an indexer that is typically greater than or equal to 0. You may know that arrays in the CLR can have a user-defined lower bound. However, in C#, the lower bound is always 0 in order to meet the CLS restriction that arrays have a 0 lower bound. The initialization techniques used for array2 and array3 show a shorter notation for doing the same thing. Notice that in all cases, you must first allocate the array instances on the heap using the new operator. The same thing happens with the array3 instance, but the compiler does it for you in order to facilitate the notational shorthand. It's interesting to note that an array of type object—thus, System.Object[]—is itself of type System.Object.

One of the conveniences of .NET arrays is that they are range-checked. Therefore, if you step off the end of one of them, thus going out of bounds, the runtime will throw an IndexOutOfRangeException instead of changing random memory, as in native C/C++. So you can say goodbye to those lurking, hard-to-find range bugs, because the CLR won't allow them to lurk too long, and they definitely won't go unnoticed for long periods of time anymore.

Lastly, notice that you can conveniently iterate through the items in the array using the C# foreach statement. This works because System.Array implements IEnumerable. I have more to say about IEnumerable and its cousin IEnumerator later on, in the section titled "IEnumerable<T>, IEnumerator<T>, IEnumerable, and IEnumerator."

Implicitly Typed Arrays

C# 3.0 introduces an abbreviated way of initializing arrays when the type of the array can be inferred at runtime. Let's have a look at the new syntax in the following code snippet:

```
using System;

public class EntryPoint
{
    static void Main() {
        // A conventional array
        int[] conventionalArray = new int[] { 1, 2, 3 };

        // An implicitly typed array
        var implicitlyTypedArray = new [] { 4, 5, 6 };
        Console.WriteLine( implicitlyTypedArray.GetType() );

        // An array of doubles
        var someNumbers = new [] { 3.1415, 1, 6 };
        Console.WriteLine( someNumbers.GetType() );

        // Won't compile!
        // var someStrings = new [] { "int",
        //                            someNumbers.GetType() };
    }
}
```

For comparison purposes, the first array variable, named conventionalArray, uses one of the conventional syntaxes for declaring and instantiating an array. However, the next variable, implicitlyTypedArray, uses the new and shorter syntax, and so it is devoid of any type information. Instead of providing the compiler with type information, I instead rely on the compiler to deduce that each item in the array is of type int. And to save even more keystrokes and make my life a bit easier, implicitlyTypedArray is declared as an implicitly typed local variable. If you execute this code, you will see that the WriteLine() method call right below it shows that the implicitly typed variable is of type System.Int32[]. In fact, you could have expressed the same line of code as follows:

```
int[] implicitlyTypedArray = new [] { 4, 5, 6 };
```

However, since you've already got the compiler figuring out the type of the array elements, you may as well go a little further and let it deduce the entire array type, especially if the variable remains local to the scope of this method. But what happens if you declare the array using multiple types in the initialization list?

When the compiler is presented with multiple types within the initialization list of an implicitly typed array, it determines a type that all the given types are implicitly convertible to. And, of course, for all practical purposes, any type instance is convertible to its own type. Therefore, in the declaration of the someNumbers instance in the example, the compiler determines that all of the types within the braces are convertible to System.Double[]. Not surprisingly, the following WriteLine() method call confirms this. But what if the types are not all implicitly convertible to a single type?

When the compiler cannot find a common type that all of the array variables are convertible to, it will present the compiler warning CS0826, stating

---

```
No best type found for implicitly typed array
```

If you uncomment the line where I have declared the someStrings variable, you will see this behavior, since System.Type instances are not implicitly convertible to System.String.

But what happens if you declare an array with two items and both types are convertible to each other? Getting into a situation like this is very rare and usually has to be induced by having two custom types that both contain implicit conversion operators to each other's type.[1] Just to see what happened, I did just that. When I attempted to declare an implicitly typed array with an item of each type, I was greeted with the CS0826 compiler error again, which I expected.

You may already be thinking about many useful applications for implicitly typed arrays. But in most cases, they merely save you some typing.[2] This is handy if your array contains closed generic types that require a lot of typing to specify their type. So, in that respect, implicitly typed arrays can make more readable code. But in other cases, they can actually make code harder to follow for a maintenance engineer if knowing the type of the array at the point of declaration is essential to easily reading and understanding what the code is doing. However, since implicitly typed variables are actually implicitly typed **local** variables, then unless the method you are reading is overly complex and huge, you should have no trouble deducing the type yourself. If you have trouble deducing the type from looking at the code, it may mean that the function is too complex and in need of some refactoring.

---

1. I cover how you can define your own custom implicit and explicit conversion operators in Chapter 6.

2. Implicitly typed arrays are also very useful when used with LINQ. In fact, that's true of most of the new features of C# 3.0. Taken individually, they provide minimal added convenience, but taken as a whole and used with LINQ, they provide the ability to create incredibly expressive expressions. I cover LINQ in Chapter 16.

All of that said, implicitly typed arrays are great for instantiating n-tuples of items. For example, the following code snippet shows a succinct way to declare a matrix of integers:

```
using System;

public class EntryPoint {
    static void Main() {
        var threeByThree = new [] {
            new [] { 1, 2, 3 },
            new [] { 4, 5, 6 },
            new [] { 7, 8, 9 }
        };

        foreach( var i in threeByThree ) {
            foreach( var j in i ) {
                Console.Write( "{0}, ", j );
            }
            Console.Write( "\n" );
        }
    }
}
```

Type Convertibility and Covariance

When you declare an array to contain instances of a certain type, the instances that you may place in that array can actually be instances of a more derived type. For example, if you create an array that contains instances of type Animal, then you can feasibly insert an instance of Dog or Cat if both of them derive from Animal.

Note In C/C++, storing instances of type Dog or Cat into arrays as type Animal is strongly discouraged because the objects, if held by value, would get sheared off, the Cat-ness and Dog-ness would get chopped off, and all you'd end up with is Animal-ness. Not so in C#, because the array merely references the objects on the heap. If you want to make an analogy to C/C++ arrays, C# arrays are similar to C/C++ arrays holding pointers to Cat and Dog through pointers to type Animal.

You can coerce array types in another, even more interesting way:

```
using System;

public class Animal { }
public class Dog : Animal { }
public class Cat : Animal { }

public class EntryPoint
{
    static void Main() {
        Dog[] dogs = new Dog[ 3 ];
        Cat[] cats = new Cat[ 2 ];

        Animal[] animals = dogs;
        Animal[] moreAnimals = cats;
    }
}
```

The assignment from dogs to animals and from cats to animals is something that you definitely can't do in native C/C++. Arrays are assignable as long as their rank matches and the contained type is convertible from one to the other. This capability of array assignment in the CLR is provided by the fact that arrays are covariant as opposed to invariant. Since both arrays in the previous example have a rank of 1, and Dog and Cat are type-convertible to Animal, the assignment works. The C# creators included covariant array support in the CLR primarily to support the Java language.

■**Note** The full type information of an array comprises its rank (how many dimensions it has) and the type that it contains.

Sortability and Searchability

If you take a look at the entire System.Array interface as documented in the MSDN documentation, you'll notice that several methods have to do with sorting the items within the array. These methods are usable when the contained type implements IComparable, the standard interface through which items of a particular type are compared.[3] Naturally, you cannot sort a multidimensional array, and if you try, you'll need to be ready to catch an exception of type RankException. Also, if you attempt to sort an array where one or more of the members do not support IComparable, you can expect to see an exception of type InvalidOperationException. So, always be cognizant of what types of things could go wrong when you're calling methods on arrays to do what could appear to be fail-proof operations.

Using the static methods Index() and LastIndexOf(), you can locate a specific value within an array. If the method fails to find the requested value, it returns –1. No particular search algorithm is involved with these methods other than the fact that the former starts searching from the beginning of the array and the latter starts at the end. If you'd like to perform a faster search, you can use the BinarySearch static method. However, before you can do so, you must sort your array, and of course, that requires that the items within the array implement IComparable.

Synchronization

Many times, you'll find it necessary to synchronize access to an array or a collection type that implements ICollection.[4] The System.Array type implements ICollection as well as IList. One of the properties of ICollection is IsSynchronized, which always returns false for regular arrays. That's because regular arrays aren't synchronized by default, since enforcing such a rule would cause those who don't need synchronization to pay a penalty. Therefore, you must manage synchronization yourself.

---

3. IComparable<T>, the generic form of IComparable, is also available.

4. Chapter 12 covers synchronization and concurrency in detail, along with the subject of threading in the .NET Framework.

    You can find out more about System.Monitor and other synchronization techniques in Chapter 12.

The easiest way to manage synchronization is via the System.Monitor class, which you normally use via the C# lock keyword. The class allows you to acquire the built-in synchronization lock on an object.[5] However, instead of acquiring a lock on the array object itself, you should acquire a lock on the ICollection.SyncRoot object instead.

▮Note You can acquire a lock on any object referenced in the CLR. Each object has a lazily created sync block, which contains the lock variable that the CLR manages internally when System.Monitor attempts to acquire the lock.

Many array and collection implementations are free to return a reference to the actual container via the ICollection.SyncRoot property, but they might not for various reasons. ICollection.SyncRoot provides a common way for synchronizing access to both arrays and collections. I have more to say about synchronization when I cover the ICollection interface in the "Collection Synchronization" section.

Vectors vs. Arrays

It's interesting to note that the CLR supports two special types to deal with arrays in C# code. If your array happens to be single-dimensional, and it happens to have a lower bound of 0, which is usually true for C# arrays,[6] then the CLR uses a special built-in type called a *vector*, which is actually a subtype of System.Array. The CLR supports special IL instructions defined to work directly with vectors. If your array is multidimensional, then a CLR vector type is not used and an array object is used instead. To demonstrate this, let's take a quick look at some IL code generated by the following short example:

```
public class EntryPoint
{
    static void Main() {
        int val = 123;
        int newVal;

        int[] vector = new int[1];
        int[,] array = new int[1,1];
        vector[0] = val;
        array[0,0] = val;

        newVal = vector[0];
        newVal = array[0,0];
    }
}
```

---

5. You can find out more about System.Monitor and other synchronization techniques in Chapter 12.

6. Arrays declared with the C# array syntax always have a zero lower bound. If you need an array with a nonzero lower bound, you must create the instance via the System.Array.CreateInstance() method.

Take a look at the generated IL for the Main method:

```
.method private hidebysig static void  Main() cil managed
{
  .entrypoint
  // Code size       46 (0x2e)
  .maxstack  4
  .locals init ([0] int32 val,
           [1] int32 newVal,
           [2] int32[] 'vector',
           [3] int32[0...,0...] 'array')
  IL_0000:  nop
  IL_0001:  ldc.i4.s   123
  IL_0003:  stloc.0
  IL_0004:  ldc.i4.1
  IL_0005:  newarr     [mscorlib]System.Int32
  IL_000a:  stloc.2
  IL_000b:  ldc.i4.1
  IL_000c:  ldc.i4.1
  IL_000d:  newobj     instance void int32[0...,0...]::.ctor(int32,
                                                             int32)
  IL_0012:  stloc.3
  IL_0013:  ldloc.2
  IL_0014:  ldc.i4.0
  IL_0015:  ldloc.0
  IL_0016:  stelem.i4
  IL_0017:  ldloc.3
  IL_0018:  ldc.i4.0
  IL_0019:  ldc.i4.0
  IL_001a:  ldloc.0
  IL_001b:  call       instance void int32[0...,0...]::Set(int32,
                                                           int32,
                                                           int32)
  IL_0020:  ldloc.2
  IL_0021:  ldc.i4.0
  IL_0022:  ldelem.i4
  IL_0023:  stloc.1
  IL_0024:  ldloc.3
  IL_0025:  ldc.i4.0
  IL_0026:  ldc.i4.0
  IL_0027:  call       instance int32 int32[0...,0...]::Get(int32,
                                                            int32)
  IL_002c:  stloc.1
  IL_002d:  ret
} // end of method EntryPoint::Main
```

Notice the difference between usages of the two C# arrays. On line IL_0005, the newarr IL instruction creates the instance represented by the vector variable. The multidimensional array held in the variable array is created on line IL_000d. In the first case, a native IL instruction handles the operation, whereas a regular constructor call handles the operation in the second case. Similarly, when accessing the elements, the IL instructions stelem and ldelem are used for the vector, whereas regular method calls handle the access to the elements of the multidimensional array.

Since vector support is handled by specific IL instructions tailored specifically for vectors, it's safe to assume that vector use tends to be more efficient than multidimensional array use, even though instances of both derive from System.Array.

Multidimensional Rectangular Arrays

C# and the CLR contain direct support for multidimensional arrays, also known as *rectangular arrays*, which is something that C and C++ don't support directly. You can easily declare an array with multiple rank within C#. Simply introduce a comma into the square brackets to separate the rank, as shown in the following example:

```
using System;

public class EntryPoint
{
    static void Main() {
        int[,] twoDim1 = new int[5,3];

        int[,] twoDim2 = { {1, 2, 3},
                           {4, 5, 6},
                           {7, 8, 9} };

        foreach( int i in twoDim2 ) {
            Console.WriteLine( i );
        }
    }
}
```

There are several things to note when using rectangular arrays. All usage of these arrays boils down to method calls on a CLR-generated reference type, and the built-in vector types don't come into play here. Notice the two declarations. In each case, you don't need the size of each dimension when declaring the type. Again, that's because arrays are typed based on their containing type and rank. However, once you create an instance of the array type, you must provide the size of the dimensions. I did this in two different ways in this example. In creating twoDim1, I explicitly said what the dimension sizes are, and in the creation of twoDim2, the compiler figured it out based upon the initialization expression.

In the example, I listed all of the items in the array using the foreach loop as shown. foreach iterates over all items in the array in a row-major fashion. I could have achieved the same goal using two nested for loops, and I definitely would have needed to do that if I needed to iterate over the array elements in any other order. When doing so, keep in mind that the Array.Length property returns the total amount of items in the array. In order to get the count of each dimension, you must call the Array.GetLength method supplying the dimension that you're interested in. For example, I could have iterated over the items in the array using the following syntax, and the results would have been the same:

```
using System;

public class EntryPoint
{
    static void Main() {
        int[,] twoDim = { {1, 2, 3},
                          {4, 5, 6},
                          {7, 8, 9} };

        for( int i = 0; i != twoDim.GetLength(0); ++i ) {
            for( int j = 0; j != twoDim.GetLength(1); ++j ) {
                Console.WriteLine( twoDim[i,j] );
            }
        }
    }
```

```
for( int i = twoDim.GetLowerBound(0);
     i <= twoDim.GetUpperBound(0);
     ++i ) {
    for( int j = twoDim.GetLowerBound(1);
         j <= twoDim.GetUpperBound(1);
         ++j ) {
        Console.WriteLine( twoDim[i,j] );
    }
  }
 }
}
```

For good measure, I've shown how to iterate over the dimensions of the array using two methods. The first method assumes that the lower bound of each dimension is 0, and the second does not. In all of the calls to GetLength(), GetUpperBound(), and GetLowerBound(), you must supply a zero-based dimension of the Array that you're interested in.

■Note All arrays created within C# using the standard C# array declaration syntax will have a lower bound of 0. However, if you're dealing with arrays used for mathematical purposes, as well as arrays that come from assemblies written in other languages, you may need to consider that the lower bound may not be 0.

When you access the items of a multidimensional array, the compiler generates calls to Get and Set methods, which are similar to GetValue() and SetValue(). These methods are overloaded to accept a variable list of integers to specify the ordinal of each dimension within the array.

When mapping multidimensional arrays to mathematical concepts, the rectangular array is the most natural and preferred way to go. However, creating methods where an argument may be an array of varying rank is tricky, because you must accept the argument as type System.Array and dynamically deal with the rank of the array. You can access the rank of an array using the Array.Rank property. Thus, creating rank-general code is tricky due to the syntactical burden of accessing all array items through method calls to System.Array, but it is entirely possible. Moreover, the most general array-manipulation code should also handle the case of nonzero lower bounds in the individual ranks.

Multidimensional Jagged Arrays

If you come from a C/C++ or Java background, you're probably already familiar with jagged arrays, because those languages don't support rectangular multidimensional arrays like C# does. The only way to implement multidimensional arrays is to create arrays of arrays, which is precisely what a jagged array is. However, since each element of the top-level array is an individual array instance, each array instance in the top-level array can be any size. Therefore, the array isn't necessarily rectangular—hence, the name *jagged arrays*.

The syntactical pattern for declaring a jagged array in C# is similar to its cousins C++ and Java. The following example shows how to allocate and use a jagged array:

```
using System;
using System.Text;

public class EntryPoint
{
    static void Main() {
```

```
int[][] jagged = new int[3][];

jagged[0] = new int[] { 1, 2};
jagged[1] = new int[] {1, 2, 3, 4, 5};
jagged[2] = new int[] {6, 5, 4};

foreach( int[] ar in jagged ) {
    StringBuilder sb = new StringBuilder();
    foreach( int n in ar ) {
        sb.AppendFormat( "{0} ", n );
    }
    Console.WriteLine( sb.ToString() );
}
Console.WriteLine();

for( int i = 0; i < jagged.Length; ++i ) {
    StringBuilder sb = new StringBuilder();
    for( int j = 0; j < jagged[i].Length; ++j ) {
        sb.AppendFormat( "{0} ", jagged[i][j] );
    }
    Console.WriteLine( sb.ToString() );
}
    }
}
```

As you can see, allocating and creating a jagged array is a bit more complex than rectangular arrays because you must handle all of the subarray allocations individually, whereas a rectangular array gets allocated all at once. Notice how the output provides a jagged-looking output, since each subarray has a different size:

```
1 2
1 2 3 4 5
6 5 4
```

In the example, I show two ways to iterate through the array just to show the syntax for accessing the individual items within a jagged array and how that syntax differs from accessing items within a rectangular array. The syntax is similar to that of C++ and Java. The foreach method of iterating through the array is more elegant, and as I'll cover later on, using foreach allows you to use the same code to iterate through collections that may not be arrays.

Note It's preferable to use foreach to iterate through arrays and collections. That way, you can change the type of the container later, and as long as it supports the IEnumerable interface, the foreach block won't have to change. If you use a for loop instead, you may have to change the method used to access each individual element. Additionally, foreach handles cases where the array has a nonzero lower bound.

It often makes sense to use jagged arrays rather than rectangular arrays. For example, you may be reading in information from a database, and each entry in the top-level array may represent a collection where each subcollection may have a widely varying amount of items in it. If most of the subcollections contain just a handful of items and then one of them contains 100 items, a rectangular array would waste a lot of space since it would allocate 100 entries for each subcollection no matter what. Jagged arrays are generally more space efficient, but the trade-off is that accessing items within a jagged array requires more care, since you cannot assume that each subarray has the same number of items in it.

Note Jagged arrays can potentially be more computationally efficient, since jagged arrays are typically arrays of single-dimension, zero-lower-bound arrays, which the CLR represents with vectors, as described previously in this chapter.

Collection Types

Ever since its inception, the .NET Framework has offered a host of collection types for managing everything from an expandable array via `ArrayList`, a `Queue`, a `Stack`, or even a dictionary via the `HashTable` class. Over the years, newer version of the .NET Framework expanded these types. Generally, a collection is any type that holds on to a set of objects and implements `IEnumerable` or `IEnumerable<T>`. The objects in the set are typically related to each other in some way defined by the problem domain.

I'm assuming that you're already familiar with the nongeneric collection types and collection interfaces available in .NET 1.1—specifically, those defined in the `System.Collections` and `System.Collections.Specialized` namespaces. You can find plenty of documentation on these in the MSDN. Throughout this discussion, I'll call the old collection types the nongeneric collection types in order to distinguish them from the new collection types and interfaces defined within the `System.Collections.Generic` and `System.Collections.ObjectModel` namespaces.

Comparing ICollection<T> with ICollection

The most obvious additions to the collection types starting within the .NET 2.0 Framework are the types defined within the `System.Collections.Generic` namespace. These types are strongly typed, thus giving the compiler a bigger type-safety hammer to wield when ferreting out type-mismatch bugs at compile time. In addition, when used to contain value types, they are much more efficient, since there is no gratuitous boxing. Arguably, the root type of all the generic collection types is `ICollection<T>`. I have included the declaration for it here:

```
public interface ICollection<T> : IEnumerable<T>, IEnumerable
{
    int Count { get; }
    bool IsReadOnly { get; }
    void Add( T item );
    void Clear();
    bool Contains( T item );
    void CopyTo( T[] array, int arrayIndex );
    bool Remove( T item );
}
```

For the sake of comparison, I've included the nongeneric `ICollection` interface definition as well:

```
public interface ICollection : IEnumerable
{
    int Count { get; }
    bool IsSynchronized { get; }
```

```
    object SyncRoot { get; }
    void CopyTo( Array array, int index );
}
```

Now, let's take a look at the differences and what that means for your code. One thing that has been missing with the nongeneric collections is a uniform interface for managing the contents of the collection. For example, the nongeneric Stack and Queue types both have a Clear method to erase their contents. As expected, they both implement ICollection. However, since ICollection doesn't contain any modifying methods, you generally can't treat instances of these two types poly-morphically within code. Thus, you would always have to cast an instance variable to type Stack in order to call Stack.Clear(), and cast to type Queue in order to call Queue.Clear().

ICollection<T> helps this problem by declaring some methods for modifying the collection. As with most general-use solutions, it does not necessarily apply to all situations. For example, ICollection<T> also declares an IsReadOnly property, because sometimes you need to introduce an immutable collection in your design. For those instances, you would expect calls to Add(), Clear(), and Remove() to throw an InvalidOperationException.

■Note For better performance, it's recommended that calling code determine if such operations are forbidden by first checking the IsReadOnly property, thus avoiding the exception altogether.

Since a main purpose of ICollection<T> is to provide stronger type safety, it only makes sense that ICollection<T> provides its own version of CopyTo() that is strongly typed. Whereas ICollection.CopyTo() knows that the first parameter is an array, ICollection<T>.CopyTo() is also given the array rank as well as the containing type. Clearly, you can only pass a single dimension array to ICollection<T>.CopyTo(). The fact is that the nongeneric ICollection.CopyTo() only accepts an array of single dimension as well, but since the compiler cannot determine the rank of a System.Array type at compile time, you get a runtime exception of the type ArgumentException if you pass an array with more than one dimension to a proper implementation of ICollection.CopyTo(). Notice that I said "a proper implementation." Not only is the caller of ICollection.CopyTo() supposed to know this rule, but so is the type implementing ICollection. The added type information in ICollection<T>.CopyTo() not only protects both the caller and the implementer from making this mistake, it also provides greater efficiency.

You'll notice that all of the generic collection types implement both ICollection<T> and ICollection. Both interfaces provide useful utility to the container type. Any methods in ICollection that overlap with ICollection<T> should be implemented explicitly.

■Note When defining your own collection types, you should derive from Collection<T> in the System. Collections.ObjectModel namespace unless there is a good reason not to do so. For instance, Collection<T> might have some functionality that you don't want, or you must be explicit about how the items are stored in the collection. When you don't derive from Collection<T>, your job is much more laborious, since you must reimplement most of what Collection<T> already implements.

Collection Synchronization

One capability present in ICollection that is missing from its generic counterpart is the provision for handling multithreaded synchronization generally across all collections. By default, most collection types are not synchronized. You can access the IsSynchronized property to determine whether the collection is synchronized. Most of the time, including with System.Array, the answer will be false. However, sometimes you'll require synchronization while accessing these collections from multiple threads.

There are a couple of ways to control synchronization to collections that return false from ICollection.IsSynchronized. The most basic way is to use the ICollection.SyncRoot property, which returns an object that you can subsequently use with the System.Monitor—usually via the C# lock statement—to guard access to the collection. Handling it this way gives you much greater flexibility when accessing the collection, because you control the granularity of exactly when the lock is acquired and released. However, the burden is on you to make sure that locking is handled appropriately, since the collection doesn't attempt to acquire the lock internally.

■**Note** Choosing how to implement synchronization is a classic engineering trade-off decision to make when designing new collections that implement ICollection. You can implement synchronization internally to the collection, but clients that don't need it pay a performance penalty. You also can externalize the synchronization by implementing ICollection.SyncRoot, but then you rely on the clients to manage the synchronization correctly. You should consider your application domain thoroughly when choosing between the two.

In some cases, collection types simply return this for ICollection.SyncRoot. Therefore, it's important that you never synchronize access to a collection by passing its reference to the System.Monitor. Instead, always use the object obtained through the SyncRoot property, even though it may actually return this.

As an alternative to managing the SyncLock manually, most of the nongeneric collection types in the standard library implement a Synchronized method, which returns an object that wraps the collection and manages the synchronization lock for you. You may want to consider applying this same pattern when creating collection types of your own. By using the wrapper returned by the Synchronized method, client code that uses the collection doesn't have to change in order to work in a multithreaded environment. When implementing your own collections, always allow clients to choose whether synchronization is used and never force it upon them.

Lists

One thing that is missing from ICollection<T>, and for good reason, is an index operator that allows you to access the items within the collection using the familiar array-access syntax. The fact is that not all concrete types that implement ICollection<T> need to have an index operator, and in some of those cases, it makes no sense for them to have an index operator. For example, an index operator for a list of integers would probably accept a parameter of type int, whereas a dictionary type would accept a parameter type that is the same as the key type in the dictionary.

If you're defining a collection where it makes sense to index the items, then you want that collection to implement IList<T>. Concrete generic list collection types typically implement the IList<T> and IList interfaces. IList<T> implements ICollection<T>, and IList implements ICollection, so any type that is a list is also a collection. The IList<T> interface looks like the following:

```
public interface IList<T> : ICollection<T>, IEnumerable<T>, IEnumerable
{
    T this[ int index ] { get; set; }
    int IndexOf( T item );
    void Insert( int index, T item );
    void RemoveAt( int index );
}
```

The IList interface is a bit larger:

```
public interface IList : ICollection, IEnumerable
{
    bool IsFixedSize { get; }
    bool IsReadOnly { get; }
    object this[ int index ] { get; }
    int Add( object value );
    void Clear();
    bool Contains( object value );
    int IndexOf( object value );
    void Insert( int index, object value );
    void Remove( object value );
    void RemoveAt( int index );
}
```

As you can see, there is some overlap between IList<T> and IList, but there are plenty of useful properties and methods in IList that a generic container such as List<T>, or any other generic list that you create, would want. As with ICollection<T> and ICollection, the typical pattern is to implement both interfaces. You should explicitly implement the methods of IList that overlap in functionality with those of IList<T>, so that the only way to get to them is to convert the instance reference to the IList type first.

Note Generally, when implementing your own list types, you should derive your implementation from Collection<T> in the System.Collections.ObjectModel namespace.

Dictionaries

The .NET 2.0 Framework introduced the IDictionary<TKey, TValue> type as a generic and thus strongly typed counterpart to IDictionary. As usual, concrete types that implement IDictionary<TKey, TValue> should implement IDictionary as well. There is a lot of overlap, and the generic interface declares more type-safe versions of some properties and methods declared in IDictionary. However, there is also a new method available on IDictionary<TKey, TValue> called TryGetValue, which you can use to attempt to get a value based on the given key. The method returns the value through an out parameter, and the actual return value from the method indicates whether the item was in the dictionary. Although you can do this same thing using the index operator and catching the KeyNotFoundException when the item is not in there, it is always more efficient to avoid exceptions if you know the item is probably not there. Using exceptions for the purpose of control flow is a practice to avoid for two reasons. First, using exceptions for control flow is inefficient, since exceptions are expensive. Second, it trivializes the fact that an exception is a truly exceptional event. When using exceptions for control flow, you're using exceptions to handle an expected event. You'll find more cases of this Try... method call pattern throughout the .NET Framework, since the .NET team made a concerted effort to avoid efficiency bottlenecks such as these.

■**Note** When implementing generic dictionaries, you have a couple of choices from which to derive implementations. First, you can use `SortedDictionary<TKey, TValue>`, which provides O(log n) retrieval and implements
`IDictionary<TKey, TValue>` as well as the collection interfaces. However, you can also choose to use
`KeyedCollection<TKey, TValue>` in the `System.Collections.ObjectModel` namespace. Although it doesn't
actually implement the dictionary interfaces, it does provide O(1) retrieval most of the time. For more details, see
the MSDN documentation.

Sets

The .NET 3.5 Framework introduces yet another useful collection class, known as `HashSet`, which is
defined in the `System.Collections.Generic` namespace. `HashSet` implements the typical set operations that you would expect. For example, you can call the `IntersectWith` method to modify the
current set so that it will contain an intersection of the current items and the items contained in the
`IEnumerable<T>` type given. Conversely, `UnionWith` modifies the current set to contain the union of
two sets. Other useful methods include `IsSubsetOf`, `IsSupersetOf`, `ExceptWith`,
`SymmetricExceptWith`, `Contains`, etc. These are just a few of the useful methods available for sets.

■**Note** Notice that the various set operation methods implemented by `HashSet` accept parameters of type
`IEnumerable<T>`. This is very handy since it allows you to use any collection type as the parameter to these
methods rather than only `HashSet` instances.

As is typical with set operations, you can only add unique values to instances of `HashSet`. For
example, if you have already added the values 1, 2, and 3 to a `HashSet<int>` instance, then you cannot add another integer corresponding to one of those values. This is the reason the `Add` method
returns a Boolean indicating whether the operation succeeded or not. It would be inefficient to
throw an exception in such cases, so the result is indicated via the return value from `Add`.

System.Collections.ObjectModel

For those of you who need to define your own collection types, you'll find the types defined in the
`System.Collection.ObjectModel` namespace most useful. In fact, you should derive your implementations from the objects in this namespace if at all possible. This namespace contains only three
types, and the fact that this namespace exists has been the source of some controversy. There were
two main reasons these types were broken out into their own namespace. First, the Visual Basic
environment already contains a `Collection` type that is implemented by a namespace it imports by
default, and the Visual Basic team was concerned that VB users could become confused by seeing
two types with similar names and drastically different behaviors popping up in IntelliSense. Second, the Base Class Libraries (BCL) team thought that users would rarely need the types in this
namespace. Whether that is true will be shown over time. My opinion is that these types are
extremely useful for writing libraries or for code consumed by others. One of Microsoft's guidelines
even suggests that you should consider creating a subclass of these types when exposing collections, even if only to provide a richer type name describing the collection and an easily accessible
extensibility point.

These types are extremely useful if you're defining collection types of your own. You can derive your type from Collection<T> easily in order to get default collection behavior, including implementation of ICollection<T>, IList<T>, and IEnumerable<T>. Collection<T> also implements the nongeneric interfaces ICollection, IList, and IEnumerable. However, you may have to cast the type to one of these interfaces explicitly to access the properties and methods of them, since many of them are implemented explicitly. Moreover, the Collection<T> type uses the NVI pattern[7] to provide the derived type with a set of protected virtual methods that you can override. I won't list the entire public interface to Collection<T> here, since you can find the details in the MSDN documentation. However, the protected virtual methods that you may override are shown here:

```
public class Collection<T> : ICollection<T>, IList<T>, IEnumerable<T>,
                             ICollection, IList, IEnumerable
{
   ...
   protected virtual void ClearItems();
   protected virtual void InsertItem( int index, T item );
   protected virtual void RemoveItem( int index );
   protected virtual void SetItem( int index, T item );
   ...
}
```

You cannot modify the storage location of the collection by overriding these methods. Collection<T> manages the storage of the items, and the items are held internally through a private field of type IList<T>. However, you can override these methods to manage extra information triggered by these operations. Just be sure to call through to the base class versions in your overrides.

Finally, the Collection<T> type offers two constructors: one creates an empty instance, and the other accepts an IList<T>. The constructor copies the passed-in contents of the IList<T> instance into the new collection in the order that they are provided by the enumerator returned from IList<T>.GetEnumerator(). This ordering is important to note, as you'll see a way to control it in the following section on enumerators and iterator blocks. The implementation of the source list's enumerator can do such things as reverse the order of the items as they're put into the collection, simply by providing a proper enumerator implementation. Personally, I believe there should be more constructors on Collection<T> that accept an interface of type IEnumerator<T> and IEnumerable<T> in order to provide more flexible ways to fill a collection. You can solve this problem by introducing the extra constructors into a type that derives from Collection<T>, as I've shown here:

```
using System;
using System.Collections.Generic;
using System.Collections.ObjectModel;

public class MyCollection<T> : Collection<T>
{
   public MyCollection() : base() {
   }

   public MyCollection( IList<T> list )
      : base(list) { }

   public MyCollection( IEnumerable<T> enumerable )
      : base() {
      foreach( T item in enumerable ) {
         this.Add( item );
      }
   }
}
```

7. I describe the NVI pattern in Chapter 13.

```
    public MyCollection( IEnumerator<T> enumerator )
        : base() {
        while( enumerator.MoveNext() ) {
            this.Add( enumerator.Current );
        }
    }
}

public class EntryPoint
{
    static void Main() {
        MyCollection<int> coll =
            new MyCollection<int>( GenerateNumbers() );

        foreach( int n in coll ) {
            Console.WriteLine( n );
        }
    }

    static IEnumerable<int> GenerateNumbers() {
        for( int i = 4; i >= 0; --i ) {
            yield return i;
        }
    }
}
```

In Main, you can see the instance of MyCollection<int> created by passing in an
IEnumerable<int> type returned from the GenerateNumbers method. If the yield keyword in the
GenerateNumbers method looks foreign to you, it may be because it's a feature added in C# 2.0. I'll
explain this keyword a little later on in this chapter. Essentially, it defines what's called an *iterator
block*, which creates a compiler-generated enumerator from the code. After creating a
MyCollection<T> constructed type, you can still hold on to it and use it solely through a
Collection<T> reference. After all, MyCollection<T> is-a Collection<T>. Incidentally, I didn't bother
creating constructors that accept the nongeneric IEnumerable and IEnumerator, simply because I
want to favor stronger type safety.

You may have noticed the existence of List<T> in the System.Collections.Generic namespace.
It would be tempting to use List<T> in your applications whenever you need to provide a generic
list type to consumers. However, instead of using List<T>, consider Collection<T>. List<T> doesn't
implement the protected virtual methods that Collection<T> implements. Therefore, if you derive
your list type from List<T>, your derived type has no way to respond when modifications are made
to the list. On the other hand, List<T> serves as a great tool to use when you need to embed a raw
list-like storage implementation within a type, since it is devoid of virtual method calls such as
Collection<T> and is more efficient as a result.

Another useful type within the System.Collections.ObjectModel namespace is the type, which is
a wrapper you can use to implement read-only collections. Since the C# language lacks any const keyword like in C++, it is essential to create immutable types when necessary and pass those to methods
in lieu of const parameters. The constructor for ReadOnlyCollection<T> accepts an IList<T> parameter type. Thus, you can use a ReadOnlyCollection<T> to wrap any type that implements IList<T>,
including Collection<T>. Naturally, if users access the ICollection<T>.IsReadOnly property, the
answer will be true. Any time users call a modifying method such as ICollection<T>.Clear(), an
exception of type NotSupportedException will be thrown. Moreover, in order to call modifying methods, the ReadOnlyCollection<T> reference must be cast to the interface containing the method, since
ReadOnlyCollection<T> implements all modifying methods explicitly. The biggest benefit of implementing these methods explicitly is to help you avoid their use at compile time.

Efficiency

When given a choice, you should always prefer the generic collection types over the nongeneric versions because of added type safety and higher efficiency. Let's consider the efficiency standpoint a little more closely. When containing value types, the generic types avoid any unnecessary boxing and unboxing. Boxing is definitely a much more expensive operation than unboxing, since boxing requires a heap allocation but an unboxing operation doesn't. Rico Mariani pinpoints many other efficiency bottlenecks in his blog, *Rico Mariani's Performance Tidbits*.[8] He indicates that the development teams spent a lot of time focusing specifically on performance issues and simplifying things to make them better. One excellent example that he provides illustrates how List<T> is remarkably faster than ArrayList when used in many foreach iterations. However, the speed is not because of the obvious boxing/unboxing reasons, but rather because ArrayList uses a gratuitous amount of virtual methods, especially during enumeration. ArrayList.GetEnumerator() is virtual, and the nested enumerator type ArrayListEnumeratorSimple also implements the MoveNext() method and the Current property virtually. That adds up to many costly virtual methods to call during enumeration. Unless you're enumerating an ArrayList like a crazed demon, you won't notice this performance penalty, but it just goes to show how much attention the BCL development team has been putting on efficiency lately.

This is a great example of why you want to analyze your class designs clearly to ensure that you're making your classes inheritable for a good reason. Don't make a method virtual unless you're positive someone will need to override it, and if you do, make sure you use the NVI pattern covered in Chapter 13. It is my firm belief that you should tend toward creating sealed classes, unless you're absolutely sure that there is a good reason why people would want to inherit from your class. If you can't think of a reason why they would want to, don't leave it unsealed just because you think someone may come up with a good reason in the future. If you don't come up with a good reason, then it's unlikely that you created your class with inheritance in mind, and it may not work as expected for whatever derives from your class. Inheritability should be a conscious decision and not a subconscious one.

■**Note** Even if your class derives from a class that uses virtual methods, it will be more efficient if you declare it sealed, because the compiler can then call those virtual methods nonvirtually when calling through a reference to the derived type.

There is one caveat to everything mentioned so far: Gratuitous use of generics, or any feature for that matter, without knowing the ramifications is never good. Whenever a fully constructed type is created, the runtime must generate that code within memory. Also, fully constructed types created from generic types with static fields will each get their own copy of the static fields. Moreover, they'll all get their own version of the static constructor. So, if the generic contains a field like this:

```
public class MyGeneric<T>
{
    public static int staticField;
}
```

then MyGeneric<int>.staticField and MyGeneric<long>.staticField will both reference different storage locations.

The moral of the story is that you must consider the engineering trade-off. Although generics help avoid boxing and generally create more efficient code, they can also increase the size of your application's working set. If in doubt, measure the results using performance-analysis tools to determine the proper route to take.

---

8. You can find Rico's blog at http://blogs.msdn.com/ricom/.

IEnumerable<T>, IEnumerator<T>, IEnumerable, and IEnumerator

You've seen how you can use the C# foreach statement to conveniently iterate over a collection of objects, including a System.Array, ArrayList, List<T>, and so on. How does this work? The answer is that each collection that expects to work with foreach must implement the IEnumerable<T> or IEnumerable interface that foreach uses to obtain an object that knows how to enumerate, or iterate over, the items in the collection. The iterator object obtained from IEnumerable<T> must implement the IEnumerator<T> or IEnumerator interface. Generic collection types typically implement IEnumerable<T>, and the enumerator object implements IEnumerator<T>. IEnumerable<T> derives from IEnumerable, and IEnumerator<T> derives from IEnumerator. This allows you to use generic collections in places where nongeneric collections are used. Strictly speaking, your collection types are not required to implement enumerators, and users can iterate through the collection using a for loop if you provide an index operator by implementing IList<T>, for example. However, you won't make many friends that way, and once I show you how easy it is to create enumerators using iterator blocks, you'll see that it's a piece of cake to implement IEnumerable<T> and IEnumerator<T>.

Many of you may already be familiar with the nongeneric enumerator interfaces and how to implement enumerators on your collection types. In the rest of this section, I'll quickly go over the salient points of creating enumerators from scratch, and I'll quickly transition to how to create enumerators the new and improved way using iterator blocks. If you'd like, you may skip to the next section on iterators. Or if you want a refresher on implementing enumerators, go ahead and read the rest of this section.

The IEnumerable<T> interface exists so that clients have a well-defined way to obtain an enumerator on the collection. The following code defines the IEnumerable<T> and IEnumerable interfaces:

```
public interface IEnumerable<T> : IEnumerable
{
    IEnumerator<T> GetEnumerator();
}

public interface IEnumerable
{
    IEnumerator GetEnumerator();
}
```

Since both interfaces implement GetEnumerator() with the same overload signature (remember, the return value doesn't take part in overload resolution), any collection that implements IEnumerable<T> needs to implement one of the GetEnumerator methods explicitly. It makes the most sense to implement the non-generic IEnumerable.GetEnumerator method explicitly. The IEnumerator<T> and IEnumerator interfaces are shown here:

```
public interface IEnumerator<T> : IEnumerator, IDisposable
{
    T Current { get; }
}

public interface IEnumerator
{
    object Current { get; }
    bool MoveNext();
    void Reset();
}
```

Again, the two interfaces implement a member that has the same signature, which, in this case, is the Current property. When implementing IEnumerator<T>, you should implement IEnumerator. Current explicitly. Also, notice that IEnumerator<T> implements the IDisposable interface. Later, I'll explain why this is a good thing.

Now I'm going to show you how to implement IEnumerable<T> and IEnumerator<T> for a home-grown collection type. Good teachers always show you how to do something the "hard way" before introducing you to the "easy way." I think this technique is useful because it forces you to understand what is happening under the covers. When you know what's happening underneath, you're more adept at dealing with the technicalities that may come from using the "easy way." Let's look at an example of implementing IEnumerable<T> and IEnumerator<T> the hard way by introducing a home-grown collection of integers. I'll show how to implement the generic versions, since that implies that you must also implement the nongeneric versions as well. In this example, I haven't implemented ICollection<T> so as not to clutter the example, since I'm focusing on the enumeration interfaces:

```
using System;
using System.Threading;
using System.Collections;
using System.Collections.Generic;

public class MyColl<T> : IEnumerable<T>
{
    public MyColl( T[] items ) {
        this.items = items;
    }

    public IEnumerator<T> GetEnumerator() {
        return new NestedEnumerator( this );
    }

    IEnumerator IEnumerable.GetEnumerator() {
        return GetEnumerator();
    }

    // The enumerator definition.
    class NestedEnumerator : IEnumerator<T>
    {
        public NestedEnumerator( MyColl<T> coll ) {
            Monitor.Enter( coll.items.SyncRoot );
            this.index = -1;
            this.coll = coll;
        }

        public T Current {
            get { return current; }
        }

        object IEnumerator.Current {
            get { return Current; }
        }

        public bool MoveNext() {
            if( ++index >= coll.items.Length ) {
                return false;
            } else {
                current = coll.items[index];
```

```
                    return true;
                }
            }

        public void Reset() {
            current = default(T);
            index = 0;
        }

        public void Dispose() {
            try {
                current = default(T);
                index = coll.items.Length;
            }
            finally {
                Monitor.Exit( coll.items.SyncRoot );
            }
        }

        private MyColl<T> coll;
        private T current;
        private int index;
    }

    private T[] items;
}

public class EntryPoint
{
    static void Main() {
        MyColl<int> integers =
            new MyColl<int>( new int[] {1, 2, 3, 4} );

        foreach( int n in integers ) {
            Console.WriteLine( n );
        }
    }
}
```

■**Note** In most real-world cases, you would derive your custom collection class from `Collection<T>` and get the `IEnumerable<T>` implementation for free.

This example initializes the internal array within `MyColl<T>` with a canned set of integers, so that the enumerator will have some data to play with. Of course, a real container should implement `ICollection<T>` to allow you to populate the items in the collection dynamically. The `foreach` statements expands into code that obtains an enumerator by calling the `GetEnumerator` method on the `IEnumerable<T>` interface. The compiler is smart enough to use `IEnumerator<T>.GetEnumerator()` rather than `IEnumerator.GetEnumerator()` in this case. Once it gets the enumerator, it starts a loop, where it first calls `MoveNext()` and then initializes the variable `n` with the value returned from `Current`. If the loop contains no other exit paths, the loop will continue until `MoveNext()` returns `false`. At that point, the enumerator finishes enumerating the collection, and you must call `Reset()` on the enumerator in order to use it again.

Even though you could create and use an enumerator explicitly, I recommend that you use the foreach construct instead. You have less code to write, which means fewer opportunities to introduce inadvertent bugs. Of course, you might have good reasons to manipulate the enumerators directly. For example, your enumerator could implement special methods specific to your concrete enumerator type that you need to call while enumerating collections. If you must manipulate an enumerator directly, be sure to always do it inside a using block, since IEnumerator<T> implements IDisposable.

Notice that there is no synchronization built into enumerators by default. Therefore, one thread could enumerate over a collection, while another thread modifies it. If the collection is modified while an enumerator is referencing it, the enumerator is semantically invalid, and subsequent use could produce undefined behavior. If you must preserve integrity within such situations, then you may want your enumerator to lock the collection via the object provided by the ICollection. SyncRoot property. The obvious place to obtain the lock would be in the constructor for the enumerator. However, you must also release the lock at some point. You already know that in order to provide such deterministic cleanup, you must implement the IDisposable interface. That's exactly one reason why IEnumerator<T> implements the IDisposable interface. Moreover, the code generated by a foreach statement creates a try/finally block under the covers that calls Dispose() on the enumerator within the finally block. You can see the technique in action in my previous example.

Types That Produce Collections

I've already touched upon the fact that a collection's contents can change while an enumerator is enumerating the collection. If the collection changes, it could invalidate the enumerator. In the following sections on iterators, I show how you can create an enumerator that locks access to the container while it is enumerating. Although that's possible, it may not be the best thing to do from an efficiency standpoint. For example, what if it takes a long time to iterate over all of the items in the collection? The foreach loop could do some lengthy processing on each item, during which time anyone else could be blocked from modifying the collection.

In cases like these, it may make sense for the foreach loop to iterate over a copy of the collection rather than the original collection itself. If you decide to do this, you need to make sure you understand what a copy of the collection means. If the collection contains value types, then the copy is a deep copy, as long as the value types within don't hold on to reference types internally. If the collection contains reference types, you need to decide if the copy of the collection must clone each of the contained items. Either way, it would be nice to have a design guideline to follow in order to know when to return a copy.

The current rule of thumb when returning collection types from within your types is to always return a copy of the collection from methods, and return a reference to the actual collection if accessed through a property on your type. Although this rule is not set in stone, and you're in no way obligated to follow it, it does make some semantic sense. Methods tend to indicate that you're performing some sort of operation on the type and you may expect results from that operation. On the other hand, property access tends to indicate that you need direct access to the state of the object itself. Therefore, this rule of thumb makes good semantic sense. In general, it makes sense to apply this same semantic separation to all properties and methods within your types.

Iterators

In the previous section, I showed you a cursory and lightweight example of creating an enumerator for a collection type. After you do this a few times, the task becomes mundane. And any time a task becomes mundane, we as humans are more likely to introduce silly mistakes. C# introduces a new construct called an iterator block to make this task much easier. Before I go into the gory details of iterators, let's quickly look at how to accomplish the same task as the example in the previous section. This is the "easy way" that I was talking about:

```
using System;
using System.Collections;
using System.Collections.Generic;

public class MyColl<T> : IEnumerable<T>
{
    public MyColl( T[] items ) {
        this.items = items;
    }

    public IEnumerator<T> GetEnumerator() {
        foreach( T item in items ) {
            yield return item;
        }
    }

    IEnumerator IEnumerable.GetEnumerator() {
        return GetEnumerator();
    }

    private T[] items;
}

public class EntryPoint
{
    static void Main() {
        MyColl<int> integers =
            new MyColl<int>( new int[] {1, 2, 3, 4} );

        foreach( int n in integers ) {
            Console.WriteLine( n );
        }
    }
}
```

It doesn't get much easier than that. Notice that the enumerator implementation from the example in the previous section has boiled down to three lines within the GetEnumerator method. The key to the whole thing is the yield keyword. The presence of the yield keyword defines this block of code as a yield block. When you see it for the first time, it can be a little confusing to figure out exactly what's going on. When GetEnumerator() is called, the code in the method that contains the yield statement is not actually executed at that point in time. Instead, the compiler generates an enumerator class, and that class contains the yield block code. It is an instance of that class that is returned. Thus, when the foreach statement in Main() calls through to the IEnumerator<T> methods, the code in the yield block is utilized.

One thing missing that was in the example from the previous section is synchronization. Let's explore how to add synchronization to the enumerator returned by the yield block. The following is a replacement for the previous GetEnumerator method:

```
    public IEnumerator<T> GetEnumerator() {
        lock( items.SyncRoot ) {
            for( int i = 0; i < items.Length; ++i ) {
                yield return items[i];
            }
        }
    }
```

How amazingly simple is that? For the sake of example, I've changed the way I iterate over the collection using a for loop rather than foreach. Now, let me explain what magic the compiler is doing here. As before, the yield block code isn't executed immediately. Rather, an enumerator object is returned. Internally, the enumerator can be in one of several states. The first time MoveNext() is called on the enumerator, the block of code is executed up until the first yield statement is reached. Each subsequent call to MoveNext() continues execution of the loop until either a yield break statement is reached or the loop falls through to the end of the method. Once that happens, the enumerator goes into its final state, and you cannot use it to enumerate the collection anymore. In fact, the Reset method isn't available for use on enumerators generated from yield blocks, and if you call it, a NotSupportedException is thrown. At the end of enumeration, any finally blocks within the yield block are executed as expected. In this case, that means releasing the lock, since the C# lock statement boils down to a try/finally construct under the covers. Also, if the enumerator is disposed of before it reaches the end of the loop, the compiler is smart enough to put the code within the finally block into the implementation of Dispose() on the enumerator so that the lock always gets released.

As you can see, the compiler is doing a lot of work for you under the covers when you use iterators. As a final example, I've shown yet another way to iterate through the items in this collection:

```
public IEnumerator<T> GetEnumerator( bool synchronized ) {
    if( synchronized ) {
        Monitor.Enter( items.SyncRoot );
    }
    try {
        int index = 0;
        while( true ) {
            if( index < items.Length ) {
                yield return items[index++];
            } else {
                yield break;
            }
        }
    }
    finally {
        if( synchronized ) {
            Monitor.Exit( items.SyncRoot );
        }
    }
}

public IEnumerator<T> GetEnumerator() {
    return GetEnumerator( false );
}
```

It is not a pretty way to iterate over the items, but I wanted to show you an example of using the yield break statement. Also, notice that I created a new GetEnumerator method that accepts a bool denoting whether the caller wants a synchronized or nonsynchronized enumerator. The important thing to note here is that the enumerator object created by the compiler now has a public field named synchronized. Any parameters passed to the method containing the yield block are added as public fields to the generated enumerator class.

■**Note** Since the enumerator generated from the yield block captures local variables and parameters, it is invalid to attempt to declare ref or out parameters on methods that implement a yield block.

You could argue that the added fields should be private rather than public, since you can really mess up the enumerator if you access the fields and modify those public fields during enumeration. In this case, if you modify the `synchronized` field during enumeration and change it to `false`, other entities will have a hard time gaining access to the collection since the lock will never be released. Even though you have to use reflection to access the public fields of an enumerator generated from a yield block, it's easy and dangerous to do so if used improperly. That's not to say that this technique cannot be useful, as I show in an example in the section "Forward, Reverse, and Bidirectional Iterators," when I demonstrate how to create a bidirectional iterator.

You can avoid this whole can of worms by introducing the proverbial extra level of indirection. Instead of making the parameter to `GetEnumerator()` a bool, make it a custom defined type that is immutable, such as `ImmutableBool`. The following example shows how you can do this to avoid outside entities mucking with public fields of the compiler-generated enumerators:

```
using System;
using System.Threading;
using System.Reflection;
using System.Collections;
using System.Collections.Generic;

public struct ImmutableBool
{
    public ImmutableBool( bool b ) {
        this.b = b;
    }

    public bool Value {
        get { return b; }
    }

    private bool b;
}

public class MyColl<T> : IEnumerable<T>
{
    public MyColl( T[] items ) {
        this.items = items;
    }

    public IEnumerator<T> GetEnumerator(
                       ImmutableBool synchronized ) {
        if( synchronized.Value ) {
            Monitor.Enter( items.SyncRoot );
        }
        try {
            foreach( T item in items ) {
                yield return item;
            }
        }
        finally {
            if( synchronized.Value ) {
                Monitor.Exit( items.SyncRoot );
            }
        }
    }
}
```

```
    public IEnumerator<T> GetEnumerator() {
        return GetEnumerator( new ImmutableBool(false) );
    }

    IEnumerator IEnumerable.GetEnumerator() {
        return GetEnumerator();
    }

    private T[] items;
}

public class EntryPoint
{
    static void Main() {
        MyColl<int> integers =
            new MyColl<int>( new int[] {1, 2, 3, 4} );

        IEnumerator<int> enumerator =
            integers.GetEnumerator( new ImmutableBool(true) );

        // Get reference to synchronized field.
        object field = enumerator.GetType().
            GetField("synchronized").GetValue( enumerator );

        while( enumerator.MoveNext() ) {
            Console.WriteLine( enumerator.Current );

            // Throws an exception.
            field.GetType().GetProperty("Value").
                SetValue( field, false, null );
        }
    }
}
```

In Main, you can see that I'm using the enumerator directly rather than via foreach. Even though this is not recommended, I'm doing it anyway because I'm playing the part of the diabolical developer who wants to change the enumerator's state during enumeration. You can see in the while loop that I attempt to change the value of the property on the ImmutableBool in the enumerator using reflection. This throws an exception, since the property has no setter defined on it.

■**Note** Those of you familiar with the intricacies of reflection will recognize that it is technically possible for the code to modify the private field within the ImmutableBool instance. That, however, requires that the code pass the ReflectionPermission code access security (CAS) demand. This demand fails unless the person running this code has granted it explicitly, and that's unlikely. CAS is beyond the scope of this book, but for all the nitty-gritty details on CAS, including how to extend it to meet your needs, I recommend reading *.NET Framework Security* by Brian A. LaMacchia, et al. (Upper Saddle River, NJ: Pearson Education, 2002).

Using an immutable type, you can rest easy knowing that nobody can muck with the state of the enumerator and cause really bad things to happen.

So far, you've seen how iterator blocks are handy for creating enumerators. However, you can also use them to generate the enumerable type as well. For example, suppose you want to iterate through the first few powers of 2. You could do the following:

```
using System;
using System.Collections.Generic;

public class EntryPoint
{
    static public IEnumerable<int> Powers( int from,
                                           int to ) {
        for( int i = from; i <= to; ++i ) {
            yield return (int) Math.Pow( 2, i );
        }
    }

    static void Main() {
        IEnumerable<int> powers = Powers( 0, 16 );
        foreach( int result in powers ) {
            Console.WriteLine( result );
        }
    }
}
```

In this example, the compiler generates a single type that implements the four interfaces IEnumerable<int>, IEnumerable, IEnumerator<int>, and IEnumerator. Therefore, this type serves as both the enumerable and the enumerator. The bottom line is that any method that contains a yield block must return a type of IEnumerable<T>, IEnumerable, IEnumerator<T>, or IEnumerator, where T is the yield type of the method. The compiler will handle the rest. I recommend that you strive to use the generic versions, since they will avoid unnecessary boxing for value types and give the type-safety engine more muscle. In the previous example, the from and to values are stored as public fields in the enumerable type, as shown earlier in this section. So, you may want to consider wrapping them up inside an immutable type if you want to prevent users from modifying them during enumeration.

Tip *Framework Design Guidelines: Conventions, Idioms, and Patterns for Reusable .NET Libraries* by Krzysztof Cwalina and Brad Abrams (Boston, MA: Addison-Wesley Professional, 2005) suggests that a type should never implement both IEnumerable<T> and IEnumerator<T>, since a single type should semantically be either a collection or an enumerator but not both. However, the objects generated by yield blocks violate this rule. For hand-coded collections, you should try to adhere to the rule, even though it's clear that C# does this to make yield blocks more useful.

Forward, Reverse, and Bidirectional Iterators

Many libraries that support iterators on their container types support three main flavors of iterators in the form of forward, reverse, and bidirectional iterators. Forward iterators are analogous to regular enumerators implementing IEnumerator<T>, which the GetEnumerator methods of the container types in the .NET library typically expose. However, what if you need a reverse iterator or a bidirectional iterator? C# iterators make creating such things nice and easy.

To get a reverse iterator for your container, all you need to do is create a yield block that loops through the items in the collection in reverse order. Even more convenient, you can typically declare your yield block external to your collection, as shown in the following example:

```
using System;
using System.Collections.Generic;

public class EntryPoint
{
    static void Main() {
        List<int> intList = new List<int>();
        intList.Add( 1 );
        intList.Add( 2 );
        intList.Add( 3 );
        intList.Add( 4 );

        foreach( int n in CreateReverseIterator(intList) ) {
            Console.WriteLine( n );
        }
    }

    static IEnumerable<T> CreateReverseIterator<T>( IList<T> list ) {
        int count = list.Count;
        for( int i = count-1; i >= 0; −i ) {
            yield return list[i];
        }
    }
}
```

The meat of the example is in the CreateReverseIterator<T> method. This method only works on collections of type IList<T>, but you could easily write another form of CreateReverseIterator<T> that takes some other collection type. When you create utility methods of this sort, it's always best to be as generic as possible in the types that you accept. For example, would it be possible to make CreateReverseIterator<T> more general-purpose by accepting a type of ICollection<T>? No, because ICollection<T> doesn't declare an index operator. IList<T> does declare an index operator, though.

Now let's turn our attention to a bidirectional iterator. In order to make a bidirectional iterator out of an enumerator, you need to be able to toggle its direction. As I showed previously, enumerators created from methods that accept parameters and contain a yield block have public fields that you can modify. Although you must use reflection to access these fields, you can still do it nevertheless. First, let's look at a possible usage scenario for a bidirectional iterator:

```
static void Main() {
    LinkedList<int> intList = new LinkedList<int>();
    for( int i = 1; i < 6; ++i ) {
        intList.AddLast( i );
    }

    BidirectionalIterator<int> iter =
        new BidirectionalIterator<int>(intList,
                                       intList.First,
                                       TIteratorDirection.Forward);

    foreach( int n in iter ) {
        Console.WriteLine( n );

        if( n == 5 ) {
```

```
            iter.Direction = TIteratorDirection.Backward;
        }
    }
}
```

You need a way to create an iterator object that supports IEnumerable<T> and then use it within a foreach statement to start the enumeration. At any time within the foreach block, you want the ability to reverse the direction of iteration. The following example shows a BidirectionalIterator class that facilitates the previous usage model:

```
public enum TIteratorDirection {
    Forward,
    Backward
};

public class BidirectionalIterator<T> : IEnumerable<T>
{
    public BidirectionalIterator( LinkedList<T> list,
                                  LinkedListNode<T> start,
                                  TIteratorDirection dir ) {
        enumerator = CreateEnumerator( list,
                                       start,
                                       dir ).GetEnumerator();
        enumType = enumerator.GetType();
    }

    public TIteratorDirection Direction {
        get {
            return (TIteratorDirection) enumType.GetField("dir")
                        .GetValue( enumerator );
        }
        set {
            enumType.GetField("dir").SetValue( enumerator,
                                               value );
        }
    }

    private IEnumerator<T> enumerator;
    private Type enumType;

    private IEnumerable<T> CreateEnumerator( LinkedList<T> list,
                                             LinkedListNode<T> start,
                                             TIteratorDirection dir ) {
        LinkedListNode<T> current = null;
        do {
            if( current == null ) {
                current = start;
            } else {
                if( dir == TIteratorDirection.Forward ) {
                    current = current.Next;
                } else {
                    current = current.Previous;
                }
            }
```

```
            if( current != null ) {
                yield return current.Value;
            }
        } while( current != null );
    }

    public IEnumerator<T> GetEnumerator() {
        return enumerator;
    }

    IEnumerator IEnumerable.GetEnumerator() {
        return GetEnumerator();
    }
}
```

Technically speaking, I didn't have to wrap the enumerator inside the BidirectionalIterator class. I could have accessed the direction variable via reflection from within the foreach block directly. However, in order to do that, the code within the foreach block would have needed the name of the parameter passed into the BidirectionalIterator.CreateEnumerator method with the yield block. In order to avoid such disjoint coupling, I tidied it up within the BidirectionalIterator wrapper class and provided a Direction property to access the public field on the enumerator.

Finally, the following example shows how you can use the same technique to implement a circular iterator. You could use this for things such as game loops, where you must iterate indefinitely through a collection of entities, updating their state with each pass until requested to quit:

```
using System;
using System.Collections;
using System.Collections.Generic;

public class EntryPoint
{
    static void Main() {
        LinkedList<int> intList = new LinkedList<int>();
        for( int i = 1; i < 6; ++i ) {
            intList.AddLast( i );
        }

        CircularIterator<int> iter =
            new CircularIterator<int>(intList,
                                      intList.First);

        int counter = 0;
        foreach( int n in iter ) {
            Console.WriteLine( n );

            if( counter++ == 100 ) {
                iter.Stop();
            }
        }
    }
}

public class CircularIterator<T> : IEnumerable<T>
{
    public CircularIterator( LinkedList<T> list,
                             LinkedListNode<T> start ) {
```

```
        enumerator = CreateEnumerator( list,
                                       start,
                                       false ).GetEnumerator();
        enumType = enumerator.GetType();
    }

    public void Stop() {
        enumType.GetField("stop").SetValue( enumerator, true );
    }

    private IEnumerator<T> enumerator;
    private Type enumType;

    private IEnumerable<T> CreateEnumerator( LinkedList<T> list,
                                             LinkedListNode<T> start,
                                             bool stop ) {
        LinkedListNode<T> current = null;
        do {
            if( current == null ) {
                current = start;
            } else {
                current = current.Next;
                if( current == null ) {
                    current = start;
                }
            }

            yield return current.Value;
        } while( !stop );
    }

    public IEnumerator<T> GetEnumerator() {
        return enumerator;
    }

    IEnumerator IEnumerable.GetEnumerator() {
        return GetEnumerator();
    }
}
```

I've included a Stop method on CircularIterator<T> so that you can easily tell it to stop iterating. Of course, as with the bidirectional iterator example, the Stop method uses reflection to set the public field stop on the compiler-generated enumerator. I'm sure that you'll agree that there are many more creative uses for yield blocks for creating complex iteration paths.

Collection Initializers

C# 3.0 introduces a new abbreviated syntax for initializing collections, similar to the object initializer syntax shown in the section titled "Object Initializers." If the instance of the collection type you are attempting to initialize implements ICollection<T> from the System.Collections.Generic namespace, you can utilize this new syntax, shown in the following code:

```
using System;
using System.Collections.Generic;
```

```
public class Employee
{
    public string Name { get; set; }
}

public class CollInitializerExample
{
    static void Main() {
        var developmentTeam = new List<Employee> {
            new Employee { Name = "Michael Bolton" },
            new Employee { Name = "Samir Nagheenanajar" },
            new Employee { Name = "Peter Gibbons" }
        };

        Console.WriteLine( "Development Team:" );
        foreach( var employee in developmentTeam ) {
            Console.WriteLine( "\t" + employee.Name );
        }
    }
}
```

Under the covers the compiler generates a fair amount of code to help you out here. For each item in the collection initialization list, the compiler generates a call to the collection's Add() method. Notice that I have also used the new object initializer syntax to initialize each of the instances in the initializer list.

As I've mentioned, the collection type must implement ICollection<T>. If it does not, you will receive compile-time errors. Additionally, the collection must implement only one specialization of ICollection<T>; that is, it can only implement ICollection<T> for one type T. And finally, each item in the collection initialization list must be implicitly convertible to the type T.

Summary

In this chapter, I gave a brief overview of how arrays work in the CLR and in C#, in preparation for the discussion of generic collection types. After reviewing the generic collection types defined in System.Collections.Generic, I covered efficiency and usage concerns and introduced you to the useful types defined in System.Collections.ObjectModel. I then turned the spotlight on enumerators and showed you how to create effective enumerators efficiently by employing iterator yield blocks added in the C# 2.0 language. Finally, I showed you the new syntax in C# 3.0 that streamlines initializing a collection at instantiation time. Although this chapter didn't delve into the minute details of each of the collection types, after reading the chapter, you should be effectively armed with the information you need to make informed choices about which generic collection types to use and when. I encourage you to reference the MSDN documentation often for all of the finer details regarding the APIs for the collection types.

In the next chapter, I cover delegates, events, and anonymous methods. Anonymous methods are a nice addition to the language. They're useful for creating callable code inline at the point where you register the callback with the caller.

CHAPTER 10

■ ■ ■

Delegates, Anonymous Functions, and Events

Delegates provide a built-in, language-supported mechanism for defining and executing callbacks. Their flexibility allows you to define the exact signature of the callback, and that information becomes part of the delegate type itself. Anonymous functions are forms of delegates that allow you to shortcut some of the delegate syntax that, in many cases, is overkill and tedious.[1] Building on top of delegates is the support for events in C# and the .NET platform. Events provide a uniform pattern for hooking up callback implementations—and possibly multiple instances thereof—to the code that triggers the callback.

Overview of Delegates

The CLR provides a runtime that explicitly supports a flexible callback mechanism. From the beginning of time, or at least from the beginning of Windows time, there has always been the need for a callback function that the system, or some other entity, calls at specific times to notify you of something interesting. After all, callbacks provide a convenient mechanism whereby users can extend functionality of a component. Even the most basic component of a Win32 GUI application—the window procedure—is a callback function that is registered with the system. The system calls the function any time it needs to notify you that a message for the window has arrived. This mechanism works just fine in a C-based programming environment.

Things became a little trickier with the widespread use of object-oriented languages such as C++. Developers immediately wanted the system to be able to call instance methods on objects rather than global functions or static methods. Many solutions to this problem exist. But no matter which solution you use, the bottom line is that somewhere, someone must store an instance pointer to the object and call the instance method through that instance pointer. Implementations typically consist of a *thunk*, which is nothing more than an intermediate block of data or code that calls the instance method through the instance pointer. This thunk is the actual function registered with the system. Many creative thunk solutions have been developed in C++ over the years. Your trusty author can recall many iterations of such designs with sentimental fondness.

Delegates are now the preferred method of implementing callbacks in the CLR. A delegate instance is essentially the exact same thing as a thunk, except it is a first-class citizen of the CLR. In fact, when you declare a delegate in your code, the C# compiler generates a class derived from

---

1. Even better than anonymous functions are lambda expressions, which deserve an entire chapter and are covered in Chapter 15.

MulticastDelegate, and the CLR implements all of the interesting methods of the delegate dynamically at run time. That's why you won't see any IL code behind those delegate methods if you examine the compiled module with ILDASM.

The delegate contains a couple of useful fields. The first one holds a reference to an object, and the second holds a method pointer. When you invoke the delegate, the instance method is called on the contained reference. However, if the object reference is null, the runtime understands this to mean that the method is a static method. One delegate type can handle callbacks to either an instance or a static method. Moreover, invoking a delegate syntactically is the exact same as calling a regular function. Therefore, delegates are perfect for implementing callbacks.

As you can see, delegates provide an excellent mechanism to decouple the method being called on an instance from the actual caller. In fact, the caller of the delegate has no idea, or necessity to know, if it is calling an instance method or a static method or on what exact instance it is calling. To the caller, it is calling arbitrary code. The caller can obtain the delegate instance through any appropriate means, and it can be decoupled completely from the entity it actually calls. Think for a moment about UI elements in a dialog, such as a Commit button, and how many external parties may be interested in knowing when that button is selected. If the class that represents the button must call directly to the interested parties, it needs to have intimate knowledge of the layout of those parties, or objects, and it must know which method to call on each one of them. Clearly, this requirement adds way too much coupling between the button class and the interested parties, and with coupling comes complexity. Delegates come to the rescue and break this link. Now, interested parties only need to register a delegate with the button that is preconfigured to call whatever method they want. This decoupling mechanism describes events as supported by the CLR. I have more to say about CLR events later in this chapter in the "Events" section. Let's go ahead and see how to create and use delegates in C#.

Delegate Creation and Use

Delegate declarations look almost exactly like abstract method declarations, except they have one added keyword: the delegate keyword. The following is a valid delegate declaration:

```
public delegate double ProcessResults( double x, double y );
```

When the C# compiler encounters this line, it defines a type derived from MulticastDelegate, which also implements a method named Invoke that has exactly the same signature as the method described in the delegate declaration. For all practical purposes, that class looks like the following:

```
public class ProcessResults : System.MulticastDelegate
{
    public double Invoke( double x, double y );

    // Other stuff omitted for clarity
}
```

Even though the compiler creates a type similar to that listed, the compiler also abstracts the use of delegates behind syntactical shortcuts. In fact, the compiler won't allow you to call the Invoke method on a delegate directly. Instead, you use a syntax that looks similar to a function call, which I'll show shortly.

When you instantiate an instance of a delegate, you must wire it up to a method to call when it is invoked. The method that you wire it up to could be either a static or an instance method that has a signature compatible with that of the delegate. Thus, the parameter types and the return type must either match the delegate declaration or be implicitly convertible to the types in the delegate declaration.

■**Note** In .NET 1.x, the signature of the methods wired up to delegates had to match the delegate declaration exactly. In .NET 2.0, this requirement was relaxed to allow methods with compatible types in the declaration.

Single Delegate

The following example shows the basic syntax of how to create a delegate:

```
using System;

public delegate double ProcessResults( double x,
                                       double y );

public class Processor
{
    public Processor( double factor ) {
        this.factor = factor;
    }

    public double Compute( double x, double y ) {
        double result = (x+y)*factor;
        Console.WriteLine( "InstanceResults: {0}", result );
        return result;
    }

    public static double StaticCompute( double x,
                                        double y ) {
        double result = (x+y)*0.5;
        Console.WriteLine( "StaticResult: {0}", result );
        return result;
    }

    private double factor;
}

public class EntryPoint
{
    static void Main() {
        Processor proc1 = new Processor( 0.75 );
        Processor proc2 = new Processor( 0.83 );

        ProcessResults delegate1 = new ProcessResults( proc1.Compute );
        ProcessResults delegate2 = new ProcessResults( proc2.Compute );
        ProcessResults delegate3 = new ProcessResults( Processor.StaticCompute );

        double combined = delegate1( 4, 5 ) +
                          delegate2( 6, 2 ) +
                          delegate3( 5, 2 );

        Console.WriteLine( "Output: {0}", combined );
    }
}
```

In this example, I've created three delegates. Two of them point to instance methods, and one points to a static method. Notice that the delegates are created by creating instances of the ProcessResults type, which is the type created by the delegate declaration. When you create the delegate instances, you pass the methods they must call in the constructor. Take note of the format of the parameters. In the first two cases, you pass an instance method on the proc1 and proc2 instances. However, in the third case, you pass a method pointer on the type rather than an instance. This is the way you create a delegate that points to a static method rather than an instance method. At the point where the delegates are called, the syntax is identical and independent of whether the delegate points to an instance method or a static method. Of course, this example is rather contrived, but it gives a clear indication of the basic usage of delegates within C#.

In all of the cases in the previous code, a single action takes place when the delegate is called. It is possible to chain delegates together so that multiple actions take place.

Delegate Chaining

Delegate chaining allows you to create a linked list of delegates such that when the delegate at the head of the list is called, all of the delegates in the chain are called. The System.Delegate class provides a few static methods to manage lists of delegates. To create delegate lists, you rely on the following methods declared inside of the System.Delegate type:

```
public class Delegate : ICloneable, ISerializable
{
    public static Delegate Combine( Delegate[] );
    public static Delegate Combine( Delegate first, Delegate second );
}
```

Notice that the Combine methods take the delegates to combine and return another Delegate. The Delegate returned is a new instance of a MulticastDelegate. That is because Delegate instances are treated as immutable. For example, the caller of Combine may wish to create a delegate list but leave the original delegate instances in the same state they were in. The only way to do that is to treat delegate instances as immutable when creating delegate chains.

Notice that the first version of Combine listed previously takes an array of delegates to form the constituents of the new delegate list, and the second form takes just a pair of delegates. However, in both cases, any one of the Delegate instances could itself already be a delegate chain. So, you can see that some fairly complex nesting can take place here.

To remove delegates from a list, you rely upon the following two static methods on System.Delegate:

```
public class Delegate : IClonable, ISerializable
{
    public static Delegate Remove( Delegate source, Delegate value );
    public static Delegate RemoveAll( Delegate source, Delegate value );
}
```

As with the Combine methods, the Remove and RemoveAll methods return a new Delegate instance created from the previous two. The Remove method removes the last occurrence of value in the source delegate list, whereas RemoveAll removes all occurrences of the value delegate list from the source delegate list. Notice that I said that the value parameter may represent a delegate list rather than just a single delegate. Again, these methods have the ability to meet any complex delegate list management needs.

Let's look at a modified form of the code example in the last section to see how you can combine the delegates:

```
using System;

public delegate double ProcessResults( double x,
                                       double y );

public class Processor
{
    public Processor( double factor ) {
        this.factor = factor;
    }

    public double Compute( double x, double y ) {
        double result = (x+y)*factor;
        Console.WriteLine( "InstanceResults: {0}", result );
        return result;
    }

    public static double StaticCompute( double x,
                                        double y ) {
        double result = (x+y)*0.5;
        Console.WriteLine( "StaticResult: {0}", result );
        return result;
    }

    private double factor;
}

public class EntryPoint
{
    static void Main() {
        Processor proc1 = new Processor( 0.75 );
        Processor proc2 = new Processor( 0.83 );

        ProcessResults[] delegates = new ProcessResults[] {
            new ProcessResults( proc1.Compute ),
            new ProcessResults( proc2.Compute ),
            new ProcessResults( Processor.StaticCompute )
        };

        ProcessResults chained = (ProcessResults) Delegate.Combine( delegates );

        double combined = chained( 4, 5 );

        Console.WriteLine( "Output: {0}", combined );
    }
}
```

Notice that instead of calling all of the delegates, this example chains them together and then calls them by calling through the head of the chain. This example features some major differences from the previous example, which I have listed below.

- The resultant `double` that comes out of the chained invocation is the result of the last delegate called, which, in this case, is the delegate pointing to the static method `StaticCompute`. The return values from the other delegates in the chain are simply lost.

- If any of the delegates throws an exception, processing of the delegate chain will terminate and the CLR will begin to search for the next exception-handling frame on the stack.

- Be aware that if you declare delegates that take parameters by reference, then each delegate that uses the reference parameter will see the changes made by the previous delegate in the chain. This could be a desired effect, or it could be a surprise, depending on what your intentions are.

- Finally, notice that before invoking the delegate chain, you must cast the delegate back into the explicit delegate type. This is necessary for the compiler to know how to invoke the delegate. The type returned from the `Combine` and `Remove` methods is of type `System.Delegate`, which doesn't have enough type information for the compiler to figure out how to invoke it.

Iterating Through Delegate Chains

Sometimes you need to call a chain of delegates, but you need to harvest the return values from each invocation, or you may need to specify the ordering of the calls in the chain. For these times, the `System.Delegate` type, from which all delegates derive, offers the `GetInvocationList` method to acquire an array of delegates where each element in the array corresponds to a delegate in the invocation list. Once you obtain this array, you can call the delegates in any order you please, and you can process the return value from each delegate appropriately. You could also put an exception frame around each entry in the list so that an exception in one delegate invocation will not abort the remaining invocations. This modified version of the previous example shows how to call each delegate in the chain explicitly:

```
using System;

public delegate double ProcessResults( double x,
                                       double y );

public class Processor
{
    public Processor( double factor ) {
        this.factor = factor;
    }

    public double Compute( double x, double y ) {
        double result = (x+y)*factor;
        Console.WriteLine( "InstanceResults: {0}", result );
        return result;
    }

    public static double StaticCompute( double x,
                                        double y ) {
        double result = (x+y)*0.5;
        Console.WriteLine( "StaticResult: {0}", result );
        return result;
    }
```

```
        private double factor;
}

public class EntryPoint
{
    static void Main() {
        Processor proc1 = new Processor( 0.75 );
        Processor proc2 = new Processor( 0.83 );

        ProcessResults[] delegates = new ProcessResults[] {
            new ProcessResults( proc1.Compute ),
            new ProcessResults( proc2.Compute ),
            new ProcessResults( Processor.StaticCompute )
        };

        ProcessResults chained = (ProcessResults) Delegate.Combine( delegates );
        Delegate[] chain = chained.GetInvocationList();
        double accumulator = 0;
        for( int i = 0; i < chain.Length; ++i ) {
            ProcessResults current = (ProcessResults) chain[i];
            accumulator += current( 4, 5 );
        }

        Console.WriteLine( "Output: {0}", accumulator );
    }
}
```

Unbound (Open Instance) Delegates

All of the delegate examples so far show how to wire up a delegate to a static method on a specific type or to an instance method on a specific instance. This abstraction provides excellent decoupling, but the delegate doesn't really imitate or represent a pointer to a method per se, since it is bound to a method on a specific instance. What if you want to have a delegate represent an instance method, and then you want to invoke that same instance method, via the delegate, on a collection of instances?

For this task, you need to use an *open instance delegate*. When you call a method on an instance, there is a hidden parameter at the beginning of the parameter list known as this, which represents the current instance.[2] When you wire up a closed instance delegate to an instance method on an object instance, the delegate passes the object instance as the this reference when it calls the instance method. With open instance delegates, the delegate defers this action to whatever invokes the delegate. Thus, you can provide the object instance to call on at delegate invocation time.

Let's look at an example of what this would look like. Imagine a collection of Employee types, and the company has decided to give everyone a 10% raise at the end of the year. All of the Employee objects are contained in a collection type, and now you need to iterate over each employee, applying the raise by calling the Employee.ApplyRaiseOf method:

```
using System;
using System.Reflection;
using System.Collections.Generic;

delegate void ApplyRaiseDelegate( Employee emp,
                                  Decimal percent );
```

---

2. Reference Chapter 4 for more details on this with regards to reference and value types.

```
public class Employee
{
    private Decimal salary;

    public Employee( Decimal salary ) {
        this.salary = salary;
    }

    public Decimal Salary {
        get {
            return salary;
        }
    }

    public void ApplyRaiseOf( Decimal percent ) {
        salary *= (1 + percent);
    }
}

public class EntryPoint
{
    static void Main() {
        List<Employee> employees = new List<Employee>();

        employees.Add( new Employee(40000) );
        employees.Add( new Employee(65000) );
        employees.Add( new Employee(95000) );

        // Create open instance delegate.
        MethodInfo mi =
            typeof(Employee).GetMethod( "ApplyRaiseOf",
                                        BindingFlags.Public |
                                        BindingFlags.Instance );
        ApplyRaiseDelegate applyRaise = (ApplyRaiseDelegate )
            Delegate.CreateDelegate( typeof(ApplyRaiseDelegate),
                                     mi );

        // Apply raise.
        foreach( Employee e in employees ) {
            applyRaise( e, (Decimal) 0.10 );

            // Send new salary to console.
            Console.WriteLine( e.Salary );
        }
    }
}
```

First, notice that the declaration of the delegate has an Employee type declared at the beginning of the parameter list. This is how you expose the hidden instance pointer so that you can bind it later. Had you used this delegate to represent a closed instance delegate, the Employee parameter would have been omitted. Unfortunately, the C# language doesn't have any special syntax for creating open instance delegates. Therefore, you must use one of the more generalized Delegate. CreateDelegate overloads to create the delegate instance as shown, and before you can do that, you must use reflection to obtain the MethodInfo instance representing the method to bind to.

The key point to notice here is that nowhere during the instantiation of the delegate do you provide a specific object instance. You won't provide that until the point of delegate invocation. The foreach loop shows how you invoke the delegate and provide the instance to call upon at the same time. Even though the ApplyRaiseOf method that the delegate is wired to takes only one parameter, the delegate invocation requires two parameters, so that you can provide the instance on which to make the call.

The previous example shows how to create and invoke an open instance delegate; however, the delegate could still be more general and more useful in a broad sense. In that example, you declared the delegate such that it knew it was going to be calling a method on a type of Employee. Thus, at invocation time, you could have placed the call only on an instance of Employee or a type derived from Employee. You can use a generic delegate to declare the delegate such that the type on which it is called is unspecified at declaration time.[3] Such a delegate is potentially much more useful. It allows you to state the following: "I want to represent a method that matches this signature supported by an as-of-yet unspecified type." Only at the point of instantiation of the delegate are you required to provide the concrete type that will be called. Examine the following modifications to the previous example:

```
delegate void ApplyRaiseDelegate<T>( T instance,
                                     Decimal percent );

public class EntryPoint
{
    static void Main() {
        List<Employee> employees = new List<Employee>();

        employees.Add( new Employee(40000) );
        employees.Add( new Employee(65000) );
        employees.Add( new Employee(95000) );

        // Create open instance delegate
        MethodInfo mi =
            typeof(Employee).GetMethod( "ApplyRaiseOf",
                                        BindingFlags.Public |
                                        BindingFlags.Instance );
        ApplyRaiseDelegate<Employee> applyRaise =
            (ApplyRaiseDelegate<Employee> )
            Delegate.CreateDelegate(
                        typeof(ApplyRaiseDelegate<Employee>),
                        mi );

        // Apply raise.
        foreach( Employee e in employees ) {
            applyRaise( e, (Decimal) 0.10 );

            // Send new salary to console.
            Console.WriteLine( e.Salary );
        }
    }
}
```

3. I cover generics in Chapter 11.

Now, the delegate is much more generic. You can imagine that this delegate could be useful in some circumstances. For example, consider an imaging program that supports applying filters to various objects on the canvas. Suppose you need a delegate to represent a generic filter type that, when applied, is provided a percentage value to indicate how much of an effect it should have on the object. Using generic, open instance delegates, you could represent such a general notion.

Events

In many cases, when you use delegates as a callback mechanism, you may just want to notify someone that some event happened, such as a button press in a UI. Suppose that you're designing a media player application. Somewhere in the UI is a Play button. In a well-designed system, the UI and the control logic are separated by a well-defined abstraction, commonly implemented using a form of the Bridge pattern. The abstraction facilitates slapping on an alternate UI later, or even better, since UI operations are normally platform-specific, it facilitates porting the application to another platform. For example, the Bridge pattern works well in situations where you want to decouple your control logic from the UI.

■**Note** The purpose of the Bridge pattern, as defined in *Design Patterns: Elements of Reusable Object-Oriented Software* by Erich Gamma, Richard Helm, Ralph Johnson, and John Vlissides (Boston, MA: Addison-Professional, 1995), is to decouple an abstraction from an implementation so that the two can vary independently.

By using the Bridge pattern, you can facilitate the scenario where changes that occur in the core system don't force changes in the UI, and most importantly, where changes in the UI don't force changes in the core system. One common way of implementing this pattern is by creating well-defined interfaces into the core system that the UI then uses to communicate with it, and vice versa. Delegates are an excellent mechanism to use to help define such an interface. With a delegate, you can begin to say things as abstract as, "When the user wants to play, I want you to call registered methods passing any information germane to the action." The beauty here is that the core system doesn't care how the user indicates to the UI that he wants the player to start playing media. It could be a button press, or there could be some sort of brain-wave detection device that recognizes what the user is thinking. To the core system, it doesn't matter, and you can change and interchange both independently without breaking the other. Both sides adhere to the same agreed-upon interface contract, which in this case is a specifically formed delegate and a means to register that delegate with the event-generating entity.[4]

This pattern of usage, also known as publish/subscribe, is so common, even outside the realm of UI development, that the .NET runtime designers were so generous as to define a formalized built-in event mechanism. When you declare an event within a class, internally the compiler implements some hidden methods that allow you to register and unregister delegates, which are called when a specific event is raised. In essence, an event is a shortcut that saves you the time of having to write the register and unregister methods that manage a delegate chain yourself. Let's take a look at a simple event sample based on the previous discussion:

```
using System;

// Arguments passed from UI when play event occurs.
public class PlayEventArgs : EventArgs
{
```

---

4. In Chapter 5, I cover the topic of contracts and interfaces in detail.

```csharp
    public PlayEventArgs( string filename ) {
        this.filename = filename;
    }

    private string filename;
    public string Filename {
        get { return filename; }
    }
}

public class PlayerUI
{
    // define event for play notifications.
    public event EventHandler<PlayEventArgs> PlayEvent;

    public void UserPressedPlay() {
        OnPlay();
    }

    protected virtual void OnPlay() {
        // fire the event.
        EventHandler<PlayEventArgs> localHandler
            = PlayEvent;
        if( localHandler != null ) {
            localHandler( this,
                    new PlayEventArgs("somefile.wav") );
        }
    }
}

public class CorePlayer
{
    public CorePlayer() {
        ui = new PlayerUI();

        // Register our event handler.
        ui.PlayEvent += this.PlaySomething;
    }

    private void PlaySomething( object source,
                               PlayEventArgs args ) {
        // Play the file.
    }

    private PlayerUI ui;
}

public class EntryPoint
{
    static void Main() {
        CorePlayer player = new CorePlayer();
    }
}
```

Even though the syntax of this simple event may look complicated, the overall idea is that you're creating a well-defined interface through which to notify interested parties that the user wants to play a file. That well-defined interface is encapsulated inside the PlayEventArgs class. Events put certain rules upon how you use delegates. The delegate must not return anything, and it must accept two arguments. The first argument is an object reference representing the party generating the event. The second argument must be a type derived from System.EventArgs. Your EventArgs derived class is where you define any event-specific arguments.

■**Note** In .NET 1.1, you had to explicitly define the delegate type behind the event. Starting in .NET 2.0, you can use the new generic EventHandler<T> class to shield you from this mundane chore.

Notice that I've declared the event using the generic EventHandler<T> class. When registering handlers using the += operator, as a shortcut you can provide only the reference to the method to call, and the compiler will create the EventHandler<T> instance for you. You could optionally follow the += operator with a new expression creating a new instance of EventHandler<T>, but if the compiler provides the shortcut shown, why type more syntax that makes the code harder to read?

Notice the way that the event is defined within the PlayerUI class using the event keyword. The event keyword is first followed by the defined event delegate, which is then followed by the name of the event—in this case, PlayEvent. The PlayEvent identifier means two entirely different things depending on what side of the decoupling fence you're on. From the perspective of the event generator—in this case, PlayerUI—the PlayEvent event is used just like a delegate. You can see this usage inside the OnPlay method. Typically, a method such as OnPlay is called in response to a UI button press. It notifies all of the registered listeners by calling through the PlayEvent event (delegate).

■**Note** The popular idiom when raising events is to raise the event within a protected virtual method named On<event>, where <event> is replaced with the name of the event—in this case, OnPlay. This way, derived classes can easily modify the actions taken when the event needs to be raised. In C#, you must test the event for null before calling it; otherwise, the result could be a NullReferenceException. The OnPlay method makes a local copy of the event before testing it for null. This avoids the race condition where the event is set to null from another thread after the null check passes and before the event is raised.

From the event consumer side of the fence, the PlayEvent identifier is used completely differently, as you can see in the CorePlayer constructor. The C# language has overloaded the += and -= operators for events to provide a compact notation for registering and unregistering event listeners. In the CorePlayer constructor, you could have also registered the event as follows:

```
ui.PlayEvent += this.PlaySomething;
```

That's the basic structure of events. As I alluded to earlier, .NET events are a shortcut to creating delegates and the interfaces with which to register those delegates. As proof of this, you can examine the IL generated from compiling the previous example. Under the covers, the compiler has generated two methods, add_OnPlay and remove_OnPlay, which are called when you use the overloaded += and -= operators. These methods manage the addition and removal of delegates from the event delegate chain. In fact, the C# compiler doesn't allow you to call these methods explicitly, so you must use the operators.

The event mechanism defines two hidden function members, or accessors, which is similar to the way properties define hidden accessors. You may be wondering if there is some way to control the body of those function members as you can with properties. The answer is yes, and the syntax is similar to that of properties. I've modified the PlayerUI class to show the way to handle event add and remove operations explicitly:

```
public class PlayerUI
{
    // define event for play notifications.
    private EventHandler<PlayEventArgs> playEvent;
    public event EventHandler<PlayEventArgs> PlayEvent {
        add {
            playEvent = (EventHandler<PlayEventArgs>)
                        Delegate.Combine( playEvent, value );
        }
        remove {
            playEvent = (EventHandler<PlayEventArgs>)
                        Delegate.Remove( playEvent, value );
        }
    }

    public void UserPressedPlay() {
        OnPlay();
    }

    protected virtual void OnPlay() {
        // fire the event.
        EventHandler<PlayEventArgs> localHandler
            = playEvent;
        if( localHandler != null ) {
            localHandler( this,
                    new PlayEventArgs("somefile.wav") );
        }
    }
}
```

Inside the add and remove sections of the event declaration, the delegate being added or removed is referenced through the value keyword, which is identical to the way property setters work. This example uses Delegate.Combine and Delegate.Remove to manage an internal delegate chain named playEvent. This example is a bit contrived because the default event mechanism does essentially the same thing, but I show it here for the sake of example.

■Note You would want to define custom event accessors explicitly if you needed to define some sort of custom event storage mechanism, or if you needed to perform any other sort of custom processing when events are registered or unregistered.

One final comment regarding design patterns is in order. As described, you can see that events are ideal for implementing a publish/subscribe design pattern, where many listeners are registering for notification (publication) of an event. Similarly, you can use .NET events to implement a form of the Observer pattern, where various entities register to receive notifications that some other entity has changed. These are only two design patterns that events facilitate.

Anonymous Methods

Many times, you may find yourself creating a delegate for a callback that does something very simple. Imagine that you're implementing a simple engine that processes an array of integers. Let's say that you design the system flexibly, so that when the processor works on the array of integers, it uses an algorithm that you supply at the point of invocation. This pattern of usage is called the Strategy pattern. In this pattern, you can choose to use a different computation strategy by providing a mechanism to specify the algorithm to use at run time. A delegate is the perfect tool for implementing such a system. Let's see what an example would look like:

```
using System;

public delegate int ProcStrategy( int x );

public class Processor
{
    private ProcStrategy strategy;
    public ProcStrategy Strategy {
        set {
            strategy = value;
        }
    }

    public int[] Process( int[] array ) {
        int[] result = new int[ array.Length ];
        for( int i = 0; i < array.Length; ++i ) {
            result[i] = strategy( array[i] );
        }
        return result;
    }
}

public class EntryPoint
{
    private static int MultiplyBy2( int x ) {
        return x*2;
    }

    private static int MultiplyBy4( int x ) {
        return x*4;
    }

    private static void PrintArray( int[] array ) {
        for( int i = 0; i < array.Length; ++i ) {
            Console.Write( "{0}", array[i] );
            if( i != array.Length-1 ) {
                Console.Write( ", " );
            }
        }
        Console.Write( "\n" );
    }

    static void Main() {
        // Create an array of integers.
        int[] integers = new int[] {
            1, 2, 3, 4
        };
```

```
        Processor proc = new Processor();
        proc.Strategy = new ProcStrategy( EntryPoint.MultiplyBy2 );
        PrintArray( proc.Process(integers) );

        proc.Strategy = new ProcStrategy( EntryPoint.MultiplyBy4 );
        PrintArray( proc.Process(integers) );
    }
}
```

Conceptually, the idea sounds really easy. However, in practice, you must do a few complicated things to make this work. First, you have to define a delegate type to represent the strategy method. In the previous example, that's the ProcStrategy delegate type. Then, you have to write the various strategy methods themselves. After that, the delegates are created and bound to those methods and registered with the processor. In essence, these actions feel disjointed in their flow. It would feel much more natural to be able to define the delegate method in a less verbose way. Many times, the infrastructure required with using delegates makes the code hard to follow, since the pieces of the mechanism are sprinkled around various different places in the code.

Anonymous methods provide an easier and more compact way to define simple delegates such as these. Anonymous methods were introduced in C# 2.0, and in short, they allow you to define the method body of the delegate at the point where you instantiate the delegate. Let's look at how you can modify the previous example to use anonymous methods. The following is the revised portion of the example:

```
public class EntryPoint
{
    private static void PrintArray( int[] array ) {
        for( int i = 0; i < array.Length; ++i ) {
            Console.Write( "{0}", array[i] );
            if( i != array.Length-1 ) {
                Console.Write( ", " );
            }
        }
        Console.Write( "\n" );
    }

    static void Main() {
        // Create an array of integers.
        int[] integers = new int[] {
            1, 2, 3, 4
        };

        Processor proc = new Processor();
        proc.Strategy = delegate(int x) {
            return x*2;
        };
        PrintArray( proc.Process(integers) );

        proc.Strategy = delegate(int x) {
            return x*4;
        };
        PrintArray( proc.Process(integers) );

        proc.Strategy = delegate {
            return 0;
        };
        PrintArray( proc.Process(integers) );
    }
}
```

Notice that the two methods, MultiplyBy2 and MultiplyBy4, are gone. Instead, a delegate is created using a special syntax for anonymous methods at the point where it is assigned to the Processor.Strategy property. You can see that the syntax is almost as if you took the delegate declaration and the method you wired the delegate to and mashed them together into one. Basically, anywhere that you can pass a delegate instance as a parameter, you can pass an anonymous method instead.

When you pass an anonymous method in a parameter list that accepts a delegate, or when you assign a delegate type from an anonymous method, you must be concerned with anonymous method type conversion. Behind the scenes, your anonymous method is turned into a regular delegate that is treated just like any other delegate instance.

When you assign an anonymous method to a delegate instance storage location, a number of rules must apply. First, the parameter types of the delegate must be compatible with those of the anonymous method. In the previous example's first two delegate usages, I showed you the long way to declare an anonymous method. Some of you may have noticed the different syntax in the third usage in the example. I left out the parameter list because the body of the method doesn't even use it. Yet, I was still able to set the Strategy property based upon this anonymous method, so clearly, some type conversion has occurred. Basically, if the anonymous method has no parameter list, then it is convertible to a delegate type that has a parameter list, as long as the list doesn't include any out or ref parameters. If there are out parameters, the anonymous method is forced to list them in its parameter list at the point of declaration.

Second, if the anonymous method does list any parameters in its declaration, it must list the same count of parameters as the delegate type, and each one of those types must be implicitly convertible to the types in the delegate declaration. Finally, the return type returned from the anonymous method must be implicitly convertible to the declared return type of the delegate type it is being assigned to. Since the anonymous method declaration syntax doesn't explicitly state what the return type is, the compiler must examine each return statement within the anonymous method and make sure it returns a type that matches the convertibility rules.

So far, anonymous methods have saved a small amount of typing and made the code more readable. But let's look at the scoping rules involved with anonymous methods. With C#, you already know that curly braces define units of nested scope. The braces delimiting anonymous methods are no different. Take a look at the following modifications to the previous example:

```
using System;

public delegate int ProcStrategy( int x );

public class Processor
{
    private ProcStrategy strategy;
    public ProcStrategy Strategy {
        set { strategy = value; }
    }

    public int[] Process( int[] array ) {
        int[] result = new int[ array.Length ];
        for( int i = 0; i < array.Length; ++i ) {
            result[i] = strategy( array[i] );
        }
        return result;
    }
}

public class Factor
{
```

```
    public Factor( int fact ) {
        this.fact = fact;
    }

    private int fact;

    public ProcStrategy Multiplier {
        get {
            // This is an anonymous method.
            return delegate(int x) {
                return x*fact;
            };
        }
    }

    public ProcStrategy Adder {
        get {
            // This is an anonymous method.
            return delegate(int x) {
                return x+fact;
            };
        }
    }
}

public class EntryPoint
{
    private static void PrintArray( int[] array ) {
        for( int i = 0; i < array.Length; ++i ) {
            Console.Write( "{0}", array[i] );
            if( i != array.Length-1 ) {
                Console.Write( ", " );
            }
        }
        Console.Write( "\n" );
    }

    static void Main() {
        // Create an array of integers.
        int[] integers = new int[] {
            1, 2, 3, 4
        };

        Factor factor = new Factor( 2 );
        Processor proc = new Processor();
        proc.Strategy = factor.Multiplier;
        PrintArray( proc.Process(integers) );

        proc.Strategy = factor.Adder;
        factor = null;
        PrintArray( proc.Process(integers) );
    }
}
```

In particular, pay close attention to the Factor class in this example. I have made the Processor more flexible so that I can apply the factor differently, using either multiplication or addition. Notice that the anonymous methods in the Factor class are using a variable that is accessible within the scope they are defined in—namely, the factor instance field. You can do this because the regular scoping rules apply even to the block of the anonymous method. There's something tricky going on here, though. See where I set the factor instance variable in Main to null? Notice that I did it before the delegate obtained from the Factor.Adder property is used. That's fine, because the Adder property returns a delegate instance, even though I decided to declare the delegate as an anonymous method rather than the original way. But what about that Factor.fact instance field? If I set the factor variable to null in Main, then the GC can collect the factor object even before the delegate, which uses the field, is done with it, right? Could this actually be a volatile race condition if the GC collects the Factor.fact instance before the delegate is finished with it? The answer is no, because the delegate has captured the variable.

Within anonymous method declarations, any variables defined outside the scope of the anonymous method but accessible to the anonymous method's scope, including the this reference, are considered outer variables. And whenever an anonymous method body references one of these variables, it is said that the anonymous method has "captured" the variable. Thus, the Factor.fact field in the previous example will continue to live as it is still referenced in active delegates.

The ability of anonymous method bodies to access variables within their containing definition scope is enormously useful. Imagine how much more difficult it would have been to achieve the same mechanism as in the example if you'd used regular delegates. You would have to create a mechanism, external to the delegate, to maintain the factor that you want the delegate to use. One solution when using standard delegates is to introduce another level of indirection in the form of a class, as is so often done when solving problems like these. However, I'm sure you'll agree that anonymous methods can save a fair amount of work, not to mention that they can make your code significantly briefer and more readable.

Beware the Captured Variable Surprise

When a variable is captured by an instance of an anonymous method, you have to be careful of the implications that can have. Keep in mind that a captured variable's representation lives on the heap somewhere, and the variable in a delegate instance is merely a reference to that data. Therefore, it's entirely possible that two delegate instances created from an anonymous method can hold references to the same variable. Let me show an example of what I'm talking about:

```
using System;

public delegate void PrintAndIncrement();

public class EntryPoint
{
    public static PrintAndIncrement[] CreateDelegates() {
        PrintAndIncrement[] delegates = new PrintAndIncrement[3];
        int someVariable = 0;
        int anotherVariable = 1;
        for( int i = 0; i < 3; ++i ) {
            delegates[i] = delegate {
                Console.WriteLine( someVariable++ );
            };
        }
        return delegates;
    }

    static void Main() {
```

```
        PrintAndIncrement[] delegates = CreateDelegates();
        for( int i = 0; i < 3; ++i ) {
            delegates[i]();
        }
    }
}
```

The anonymous method inside the CreateDelegates method captures someVariable, which is a local variable in the CreateDelegates method scope. However, since three instances of the anonymous method are put into the array, three anonymous method instances have now captured the same instance of the same variable. Therefore, when the previous code is run, the result looks like this:

```
0
1
2
```

As each delegate is called, it prints and increments the same variable. Now, consider what effect a small change in the CreateDelegates method can have. If you move the someVariable declaration into the loop that creates the delegate array, a fresh instance of the local variable is instantiated every time you go through the loop. Notice the following change to the CreateDelegates method:

```
public static PrintAndIncrement[] CreateDelegates() {
    PrintAndIncrement[] delegates = new PrintAndIncrement[3];
    for( int i = 0; i < 3; ++i ) {
        int someVariable = 0;
        delegates[i] = delegate {
            Console.WriteLine( someVariable++ );
        };
    }
    return delegates;
}
```

This time, the output is as follows:

```
0
0
0
```

This is why you need to be careful when you use variable capture in anonymous delegates. In the first case, the three delegates all captured the same variable. In the second case, they all captured separate instances of the variable, because each iteration of the for loop creates a new (separate) variable on the stack. Although you should keep this powerful feature handy in your bag of tricks, you must know what you're doing so you don't end up shooting yourself in the foot.

Savvy readers may be wondering how the code can possibly work without blowing up, since the captured variables are value types that live on the stack by default. Remember that value types are created on the stack unless they happen to be declared as a field in a reference type that is created on the heap, which includes the case when they are boxed. However, someVariable is a local variable, so under normal circumstances, it is created on the stack. But these are not normal circumstances. Clearly, it's not possible for an instance of an anonymous method to capture a local variable on the stack and expect it to be there later when it needs to reference it. It must live on the heap. Local value type variables that are captured must have different lifetime rules than such variables that are not captured. Therefore, the compiler does quite a bit of magic under the covers when it encounters local value type captured variables.

When the compiler encounters a captured value type variable, it silently creates a class behind the scenes. Where the code initializes the local variable, the compiler generates IL code that creates an instance of this transparent class and initializes the field, which, in this case, represents someVariable. You can verify this with the first example if you open the compiled code in ILDASM. I included the dummy variable anotherVariable so you could see the difference in how the IL treats them. Since anotherVariable is not captured, it is created on the stack, as you'd expect. The following code contains a portion of the IL for the CreateDelegates call after compiling the example with debugging symbols turned on:

```
// Code size       85 (0x55)
.maxstack  5
.locals init ([0] class PrintAndIncrement[] delegates,
         [1] int32 anotherVariable,
         [2] int32 i,
         [3] class PrintAndIncrement '<>9__CachedAnonymousMethodDelegate1',
         [4] class EntryPoint/'<>c__DisplayClass2' '<>8__locals3',
         [5] class PrintAndIncrement[] CS$1$0000,
         [6] bool CS$4$0001)
IL_0000:  ldnull
IL_0001:  stloc.3
IL_0002:  newobj     instance void EntryPoint/'<>c__DisplayClass2'::.ctor()
IL_0007:  stloc.s    '<>8__locals3'
IL_0009:  nop
IL_000a:  ldc.i4.3
IL_000b:  newarr     PrintAndIncrement
IL_0010:  stloc.0
IL_0011:  ldloc.s    '<>8__locals3'
IL_0013:  ldc.i4.0
IL_0014:  stfld      int32 EntryPoint/'<>c__DisplayClass2'::someVariable
IL_0019:  ldc.i4.1
IL_001a:  stloc.1
IL_001b:  ldloc.1
IL_001c:  call       void [mscorlib]System.Console::WriteLine(int32)
```

Note the two variables' usages. In line IL_0002, a new instance of the hidden class is created. In this case, the compiler named the class <>c__DisplayClass2. That class contains a public instance field named someVariable, which is assigned in IL_0014. The compiler has transparently inserted the proverbial extra level of indirection in the form of a class to solve this sticky wicket of local value types captured by anonymous methods. Also, note the fact that anotherVariable is treated just like a normal stack-based variable, as can be shown by the fact that it is declared in the local variables portion of the method.

Anonymous Methods as Delegate Parameter Binders

Anonymous methods, coupled with variable capture, can provide a convenient means of implementing *parameter binding* on delegates. Parameter binding is a technique where you want to call a delegate, typically with more than one parameter, in such a way that one or more parameters are fixed while the others can vary per delegate invocation. For example, if you have a delegate that takes two parameters, and you'd like to convert it into a delegate that takes one parameter where the other parameter is fixed, you could use parameter binding to accomplish this feat. Those of you C++ programmers who are familiar with the STL or the Boost Library may be familiar with parameter binders. Let me show an example of what I'm talking about:

```
using System;

public delegate int Operation( int x, int y );
```

```
public class Bind2nd
{
    public delegate int BoundDelegate( int x );

    public Bind2nd( Operation del, int arg2 ) {
        this.del = del;
        this.arg2 = arg2;
    }

    public BoundDelegate Binder {
        get {
            return delegate( int arg1 ) {
                return del( arg1, arg2 );
            };
        }
    }

    private Operation del;
    private int arg2;
}

public class EntryPoint
{
    static int Add( int x, int y ) {
        return x + y;
    }

    static void Main() {
        Bind2nd binder = new Bind2nd(
                new Operation(EntryPoint.Add),
                4 );

        Console.WriteLine( binder.Binder(2) );
    }
}
```

In this example, the delegate of type Operation with two parameters, which calls back into the static EntryPoint.Add method, is converted into a delegate that only takes one parameter. The second parameter is fixed using the Bind2nd class. Basically, the instance field Bind2nd.arg2 is set to the value that you want the second parameter fixed to. Then, the Bind2nd.Binder property returns a new delegate in the form of an anonymous method instance, which captures the instance field and applies it along with the first parameter that is applied at the point of invocation.

Readers familiar with the C++ STL are probably exclaiming that this example would be infinitely more useful if Bind2nd was generic so it could support a generic two-parameter delegate, much like the binder in STL does. This would be nice indeed; however, some language barriers make it a bit tricky. Let's start with an attempt to make the delegate type generic in the Bind2nd class. You could try the following:

```
// WILL NOT COMPILE !!!
public class Bind2nd< DelegateType >
{
    public delegate int BoundDelegate( int x );

    public Bind2nd( DelegateType del, int arg2 ) {
        this.del = del;
        this.arg2 = arg2;
    }
```

```
    public BoundDelegate Binder {
        get {
            return delegate( int arg1 ) {
                return del( arg1, arg2 );   // OUCH!
            };
        }
    }

    private DelegateType del;
    private int arg2;
}
```

This is a noble attempt, but unfortunately, it fails miserably because the compiler gets confused inside the anonymous method body and complains that an instance field is being used like a
method. The compiler's correct. That's exactly what you want to do, even though the compiler cannot make heads or tails of it. What is a programmer to do?

Another attempt involves generic constraints. Using constraints, you can say that even though
the type is generic, it must derive from a certain base class or implement a specific interface. Fair
enough! Let's just help the compiler out and tell it that DelegateType will derive from System.
Delegate, as follows:

```
// STILL WILL NOT COMPILE !!!
public class Bind2nd< DelegateType >
    where DelegateType : Delegate
{
    public delegate int BoundDelegate( int x );

    public Bind2nd( DelegateType del, int arg2 ) {
        this.del = del;
        this.arg2 = arg2;
    }

    public BoundDelegate Binder {
        get {
            return delegate( int arg1 ) {
                return del( arg1, arg2 );   // OUCH!
            };
        }
    }

    private DelegateType del;
    private int arg2;
}
```

Alas, we're stuck again! This time the compiler says that a constraint of type Delegate is not
allowed. It turns out that the solution lies with using generic delegates coupled with the Delegate.
CreateDelegate static method to get the job done. The following is a solution to the problem:

```
using System;
using System.Reflection;

public delegate int Operation( int x, int y );

public class Bind2nd<Arg1Type, Arg2Type, ReturnType>
{
    public delegate ReturnType UnboundDelegate<UBArg1Type, UBArg2Type>(
```

```
                    UBArg1Type arg1,
                    UBArg2Type arg2 );
    public delegate ReturnType BoundDelegate<BArg1Type>( BArg1Type x );

    public Bind2nd( Delegate del, Arg2Type arg2 ) {
        // Get the types from the delegate.
        object target = del.Target;
        MethodInfo targetMethod = del.Method;
        Type targetType = targetMethod.ReflectedType;

        if( target == null ) {
            // Static method
            this.del = (UnboundDelegate<Arg1Type, Arg2Type>)
            Delegate.CreateDelegate(
                        typeof(UnboundDelegate<Arg1Type, Arg2Type>),
                        targetType,
                        targetMethod.Name );

        } else {
            // Instance method
            this.del = (UnboundDelegate<Arg1Type, Arg2Type>)
            Delegate.CreateDelegate(
                        typeof(UnboundDelegate<Arg1Type, Arg2Type>),
                        target,
                        targetMethod.Name );
        }
        this.arg2 = arg2;
    }

    public BoundDelegate<Arg1Type> Binder {
        get {
            return delegate( Arg1Type arg1 ) {
                return del( arg1, arg2 );
            };
        }
    }

    private UnboundDelegate<Arg1Type, Arg2Type> del;
    private Arg2Type arg2;
}

public class EntryPoint
{
    static int Add( int x, int y ) {
        return x + y;
    }

    static void Main() {
        Bind2nd<int,int,int> binder = new Bind2nd<int,int,int>(
                new Operation(EntryPoint.Add),
                4 );

        Console.WriteLine( binder.Binder(2) );
    }
}
```

The trickery behind this solution lies in two places. First, in order for the anonymous method to be able to use the del field as a method, the compiler must know that it is a delegate. Also, it cannot simply be of type System.Delegate. In order to call through to a delegate using the method call syntax, it must be a concrete delegate type. That's where the generic delegate UnboundDelegate comes in. For good measure, I've also introduced the BoundDelegate type, which is a generic delegate that only takes one parameter—the unbound parameter. The second trick is in the constructor. Unfortunately, the C# language doesn't allow a shortcut to convert a delegate of one type to another type, even if both delegate types support exactly the same method signature. Therefore, you have to crack the target type and method information out of the original delegate in order to build an UnboundDelegate instance via the call to Delegate.CreateDelegate. Armed with these two tricks, you now have a working generic binder.

The Strategy Pattern

Delegates offer up a handy mechanism to implement the Strategy pattern. In a nutshell, the Strategy pattern allows you to swap computational algorithms dynamically, based on the runtime situation. For example, consider the common case of sorting a group of items. Let's suppose that you want the sort to occur as quickly as possible. Because of system circumstances, however, more temporary memory is required in order to achieve this speed. This works great for collections of reasonably manageable size, but if the collection grows to be huge, it's possible that the amount of memory needed to perform the quick sort could exceed the system resource capacity. For those cases, you can provide a sort algorithm that is much slower but taxes the system resources far less. The Strategy pattern allows you to swap out these algorithms at run time depending on the conditions. This example, although a tad contrived, illustrates the purpose of the Strategy pattern perfectly.

Typically, you implement the Strategy pattern using interfaces. You declare an interface that all implementations of the strategy implement. Then, the consumer of the algorithm doesn't have to care which concrete implementation of the strategy it is using. Figure 10-1 features a diagram that describes this typical usage.

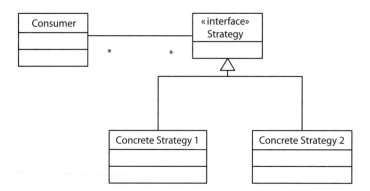

Figure 10-1. *Typical interface-based implementation of the Strategy pattern*

Delegates offer a more lightweight alternative to using interfaces to implement a simple strategy. Interfaces are merely a mechanism to implement a programming contract. Instead, imagine that your delegate declaration is used to implement the contract, and any method that matches the delegate signature is a potential concrete strategy. Now, instead of the consumer holding on to a reference to the abstract strategy interface, it simply retains a delegate instance. The following example illustrates this scenario:

```
using System;
using System.Collections;

public delegate Array SortStrategy( ICollection theCollection );

public class Consumer
{
    public Consumer( SortStrategy defaultStrategy ) {
        this.strategy = defaultStrategy;
    }

    private SortStrategy strategy;
    public SortStrategy Strategy {
        get { return strategy; }
        set { strategy = value; }
    }

    public void DoSomeWork() {
        // Employ the strategy.
        Array sorted = strategy( myCollection );

        // Do something with the results.
    }

    private ArrayList myCollection;
}

public class SortAlgorithms
{
    static Array SortFast( ICollection theCollection ) {
        // Do the fast sort.
    }

    static Array SortSlow( ICollection theCollection ) {
        // Do the slow sort.
    }
}
```

When the Consumer object is instantiated, it is passed a default sort strategy, which is nothing more than a method that implements the SortStrategy delegate signature. If the conditions are right at run time, the sort strategy is swapped out and the Consumer.DoSomeWork method automatically calls into the replacement strategy. You could argue that implementing a strategy pattern this way is even more flexible than using interfaces, since delegates can bind to both static methods and instance methods. Therefore, you could create a concrete implementation of the strategy that also contains some state data that is needed for the operation, as long as the delegate points to an instance method on a class that contains that state data. Similarly, the delegate could be an anonymous method returned by a property of that class.

Summary

Delegates offer a first-class system-defined and system-implemented mechanism for uniformly representing callbacks. In this chapter, you saw various ways to declare and create delegates of different types, including single delegates, chained delegates, open instance delegates, and anonymous methods, which are themselves delegates. Additionally, I showed how to use delegates as the building blocks of events. You can use delegates to implement a wide variety of design patterns, since delegates are a great means for defining a programming contract. And at the heart of just about all design patterns is a well-defined contract.

The next chapter covers the details of generics, which is arguably one of the most powerful features of the CLR and the C# language for creating type-safe code.

CHAPTER 11

■ ■ ■

Generics

Support for generics is one of the nicest features of C# and .NET. Generics allow you to create open-ended types that are converted into closed types at run time. Each unique closed type is itself a unique type. Only closed types may be instantiated. When you declare a generic type, you specify a list of type parameters in the declaration for which type arguments are given to create closed types, as in the following example:

```
public class MyCollection<T>
{
    public MyCollection() {
    }

    private T[] storage;
}
```

In this case, I've declared a generic type, MyCollection<T>, which treats the type within the collection as an unspecified type. In this example, the type parameter list consists of only one type, and it is described with syntax in which the generic types are listed, separated by commas, between angle brackets. The identifier T is really just a placeholder for any type. At some point, a consumer of MyCollection<T> will declare what's called a closed type, by specifying the concrete type that T is supposed to represent. For example, suppose some other assembly wants to create a MyCollection<T> constructed type that contains members of type int. Then it would do so as shown in the following code:

```
public void SomeMethod() {
    MyCollection<int> collectionOfNumbers = new MyCollection<int>();
}
```

MyCollection<int> in this example is the closed type. MyCollection<int> can be used just like any other declared type, and it also follows all of the same rules that other nongeneric types follow. The only difference is that it was born from a generic type. At the point of instantiation, the IL code behind the implementation of MyCollection<T> is JIT-compiled in a way that all of the usages of type T in the implementation of MyCollection<T> are replaced with type int.

Note that all unique constructed types created from the same generic type are, in fact, completely different types that share no implicit conversion capabilities. For example, MyCollection<long> is a completely different type than MyCollection<int>, and you cannot do something like the following:

```
// THIS WILL NOT WORK!!!
public void SomeMethod( MyCollection<int> intNumbers ) {
    MyCollection<long> longNumbers = intNumbers;        // ERROR!
}
```

If you're familiar with the array covariance rules that allow you to do the following, then you might be surprised that you cannot accomplish the same thing using constructed generic types:

```
public void ProcessStrings( string[] myStrings ) {
    object[] objs = myStrings;
    foreach( object o in objs ) {
        Console.WriteLine( o );
    }
}
```

The difference is that with array covariance, the source and the destination of the assignment are of the same type, System.Array. The array covariance rules simply allow you to assign one array from another, as long as the declared type of the elements in the array is implicitly convertible at compile time. However, in the case of two constructed generic types, they are completely separate types.

Difference Between Generics and C++ Templates

It's no accident that the syntax of generics is similar to that of C++ templates, when the syntax for every other element in C# is based on the corresponding C++ syntax. This approach allows you to leverage your existing knowledge. As is typical throughout C#, the designers have streamlined the syntax and removed some of the verbosity. However, the similarities end there, because C# generics behave very differently than C++ templates, and, if you come from the C++ world, you must make sure that you understand the differences. Otherwise, you may find yourself attempting to apply your C++ template knowledge in ways that simply won't work with generics.

The main difference between the two is that expansion of generics is dynamic, whereas expansion of C++ templates is static. In other words, C++ templates are always expanded at compile time. Therefore, the C++ compiler must have access to all template types—generally through header files—and any types used to create the closed types from the template types at compile time. For this reason alone, it is impossible to package C++ templates into libraries. I know that many developers become confused by this fact when learning C++ templates for the first time. I remember plenty of times when it would have been nice to be able to package a C++ template into a static library or a DLL. Unfortunately, that is not possible. That's why all of the code for C++ template types usually lives in headers. This makes it difficult to package proprietary library code within C++ templates, since you must essentially give your code away to anyone who needs to consume it. The STL is a perfect example: Notice how almost every bit of your favorite STL implementation exists in header files.

Generics, on the other hand, can be packaged in assemblies and consumed later. Instead of being formed at compile time, constructed types are formed at run time, or more specifically, at JIT-compile time. In many ways, this makes generics more flexible. However, as with just about anything in the engineering world, advantages come with disadvantages. You must treat generics significantly differently at design time than C++ templates, as you'll see at the end of this chapter.

■**Note** Each time the JIT compiler forms a closed type, a new type is initialized for the application domain that uses it. Naturally, this places a demand on the memory consumption of the application, also known as the working set. Once a type is initialized and loaded into an application domain, you cannot uninitialize and unload it without destroying the application domain as well. Under some rare circumstances, you may need to consider these ramifications when designing systems that use generics. In general, though, such concerns are typically minimal. If your generic type declares a lot of static fields, creating many closed types from it could place pressure on memory, since each closed type gets its own copy of those static fields. Additionally, if those closed types are used in multiple application domains, there will be a copy of that static data for each application domain the type is loaded into.

Efficiency and Type Safety of Generics

Arguably, the added efficiency when using value types in collections is one of the greatest gains from generics in C#. Whereas a regular array based on System.Array can contain a heterogeneous collection of instances created from many types as long as it holds references to a common base type such as System.Object, it does come with its drawbacks. Take a look at the following usage:

```
public void SomeMethod( ArrayList col ) {
    foreach( object o in col ) {
        ISomeInterface iface = (ISomeInterface) o;
        o.DoSomething();
    }
}
```

Since everything in the CLR is derived from System.Object, the ArrayList passed in via the col variable could possibly contain a hodgepodge of things. Some of those things may not actually implement ISomeInterface. As you'd expect, an InvalidCastException could erupt from this code. However, wouldn't it be nice to be able to utilize the C# compiler's type engine to help sniff out such things at compile time? That's exactly what generics allow you to do. Using generics, you can devise something like the following:

```
public void SomeMethod( IList<ISomeInterface> col ) {
    foreach( ISomeInterface iface in col ) {
        o.DoSomething();
    }
}
```

Here, the method accepts an interface of IList<T>. Since the type parameter to the constructed type is of type ISomeInterface, the only objects the list may hold are those of type ISomeInterface. Instantly, the compiler has a bigger stick to wield while enforcing type safety.

Note Added type safety at compile time is always a good thing, because it's much better to capture bugs based on type mismatches earlier at compile time rather than later at run time.

You could have solved the same problem without using generics, but it would have required writing a class by hand that would have served the same purpose as the List<ISomeInterface> constructed type. Thus, another beauty of generics is similar to that of C++ templates: They provide an easy-to-specialize shell for new types to be built from.

The compiler is your friend, and you should always provide it with as much type information as possible to help it do its job. Since everything in C# and the CLR derives from System.Object one way or another, you can easily cast away all type information from objects, thus crippling the compiler. If you come from a C++ environment, just imagine how ugly things could get if you preferred to pass around pointers to objects as void*. And that's not even mentioning the hard-to-find bugs that would come from such madness.

The example you've just seen shows how to use generics for better type safety. However, you haven't really gained much yet from an efficiency standpoint. The real efficiency gain comes into play when the type argument is a value type. Remember that a value type inserted into a collection in the System.Collections namespace, such as ArrayList, must first be boxed, since the ArrayList maintains a collection of System.Object types. An ArrayList meant to hold nothing but a bunch of integers suffers from severe efficiency problems, since the integers must be boxed and unboxed each time they are inserted and referenced or extracted from the ArrayList, respectively. Also, an unboxing operation in C# is normally formed with an IL unbox operation paired with a copy operation on the value type's data. Generics come to the rescue and stop this madness. As an example, compile the following code, and then load the assembly into ILDASM to compare the IL generated for each of the methods that accept a Stack instance:

```
using System;
using System.Collections;
using System.Collections.Generic;

public class EntryPoint
{
    static void Main() {
    }

    public void NonGeneric( Stack stack ) {
        foreach( object o in stack ) {
            int number = (int) o;
            Console.WriteLine( number );
        }
    }

    public void Generic( Stack<int> stack ) {
        foreach( int number in stack ) {
            Console.WriteLine( number );
        }
    }
}
```

You'll notice that the IL code generated by the NonGeneric method has at least 10 more instructions than the generic version. Most of this is attributed to the type coercing and unboxing that the NonGeneric method must do. Furthermore, the NonGeneric method could possibly throw an InvalidCastException if it encounters an object that cannot be explicitly cast and unboxed into an integer at run time.

Clearly, generics offer the compiler much greater latitude to help it do its job by not stripping away precious type information at compile time. However, you could argue that the efficiency gain is so high that the primary motivator for generics in the CLR was to avoid unnecessary boxing operations. Either way, both gains are extremely significant and worth utilizing to the fullest extent.

GENERIC TYPE PLACEHOLDER NAMING CONVENTIONS

Although there are no hard-and-fast rules for naming generic parameter placeholders, it is recommended that you at least provide a name that is somewhat descriptive of how the type is going to be used. Additionally, placeholder identifiers conventionally make the first letter a capital T to denote it as a type. Naming conventions like these, similar to the convention that interface names start with a capital I, provide for code that is generally easier to read. If the generic type definition has only one type parameter and it's simple to understand, it's conventional to name it T.

Generic Type Definitions and Constructed Types

As I touched upon previously, a generic type is a compiled type that is unusable until a closed type is created from it. A nongeneric type is also known as a closed type, whereas a generic type is known as an open type. However, it is possible to define a new open type via a generic, as shown in the following example:

```
public class MyClass<T>
{
    private T innerObject;
}

public class Consumer<T>
{
    private MyClass< Stack<T> > obj;
}
```

In this case, a generic type, Consumer<T>, is defined and also contains a field that is based on another generic type. When declaring the type of the Consumer<T>.obj field, MyClass< Stack<T> > remains open until someone declares a constructed type based on Consumer<T>, thus creating a closed type for the contained field.

Generic Classes and Structs

So far, all of the examples I've shown you have been generic classes, but all of the rules of generics map equally to structs. In fact, the most common types of generic declaration you will use are generic classes and structs. Also, I've been running pretty fast and loose with my terminology, so from now on, I'll be more explicit.

Overall, declarations of all generic struct and class types follow the same rules as those for regular struct and class types. Any time a class declaration contains a type parameter list, it is, from that point on, a generic type. Likewise, any nested class declaration—whether it's generic or not—that is declared within the scope of a generic type is a generic type itself. That's because the enclosing type's fully qualified name requires a type argument in order to completely specify the nested type.

Generic types are overloaded based upon the number of arguments in their type argument lists. The following example illustrates what I mean:

```
public class Container {}
public class Container<T> {}
public class Container<T, R> {}
```

Each of these declarations is valid within the same namespace. You can declare as many generic types based on the Container identifier as you want, as long as each one has a different count of type parameters. You cannot declare another type named Container<X, Y>, even though the identifiers used in the type parameters list are different. The name overloading rules for generic declarations are based on the count of type parameters rather than the names given to their placeholders.

When you declare a generic type, you're declaring what is called an open type. It's called that because its fully specified type is not yet known. When you declare another type based upon the generic type definition, you're declaring what's called a constructed type, as shown here:

```
public class MyClass<T>
{
    private Container<int> field1;
    private Container<T>   field2;
}
```

Both fields in the previous declaration of MyClass<T> are constructed types, since they declare a new type based upon the generic type Container<T>. However, not every constructed type is a closed type. Only field1 is a closed type, whereas field2 is an open type, since its final type must still be determined at run time based on the type arguments from MyClass<T>.

In C#, all identifiers are declared and are valid within a specific scope. Within the confines of a method, for example, any local variable identifiers declared within the curly braces of the method are only available within that scope. Similar rules exist for type parameter identifiers within generics. In the previous example, the identifier T is only valid within the scope of the class declaration itself. Consider the following nested class example:

```
public class MyClass<T>
{
    public class MyNestedClass<R>
    {
    }
}
```

The identifier R is only valid within the scope of the nested class, and you may not use it within the outer scope of the declaration for MyClass<T>. However, you may use T in the nested class, since the nested class is defined within the scope within which T is valid. It is generally considered to be bad form to hide outer argument identifiers within nested scopes, just as it is with variable name identifiers within nested execution scopes. For example, try to follow this confusing code:

```
public class MyClass<T>
{
    public class MyNestedClass<T>
    {
    }

    private Containter<T> field1;

    static void Main() {
        // What does this mean for MyNestedClass?
        MyClass<int> closedTypeInstance = null;
    }
}
```

When the closed type MyClass<int> is declared in Main, what does it mean for the nested type? The answer is, nothing. Even though the MyNestedClass<T> declaration uses the same type argument, it does not expand into the following:

```
// This is NOT what happens!
public class MyClass<int>
{
    public class MyNestedClass<int>
    {
    }

    private Containter<int> field1;
}
```

Just because the type parameter for the MyClass<T> type has been specified, it does not mean that the MyNestedClass<T> has been specified as well. In fact, it would be more accurate to describe the resultant MyClass<int> as follows:

```
public class MyClass<int>
{
    public class MyNestedClass<T>
    {
    }

    private Containter<int> field1;
}
```

MyNestedClass<T> still remains open, even though it used the same identifier in its parameter list as the containing type. What's actually happening is that within the curly braces of MyNestedClass<T>, the outer type argument to MyClass<T> is hidden from access by the identifier of the inner scope. It is better to declare it as follows:

```
public class MyClass<T>
{
    public class MyNestedClass<R>
    {
        private T innerfield1;
        private R innerfield2;
    }

    private Containter<T> field1;

    static void Main() {
        MyClass<int> closedTypeInstance = null;
    }
}
```

Now, the declaration scope of MyNestedClass<R> has access to both the T and R type parameters as illustrated.

Generic structs and classes, just like normal structs and classes, may contain static types. However, each closed type based on the generic type contains its own instance of the static type. When you consider that each closed type is a separate concrete type, this fact makes perfect sense. Therefore, if you need to share static data between different closed types based on the same generic type, you must devise some other means to do so. One technique involves a separate, nongeneric type that contains static data that is referenced by the generic types. Such a device is typically implemented with the Singleton pattern.

■**Note** Keep in mind that generic types with static initializers require that the initialization code be run each and every time the CLR creates a closed type based upon the generic type. Complex type initializers, or static constructors, can possibly increase the working set of the application if too many closed types are created based upon such a generic type. For example, if you create a sizable per-type data structure in a generic type initializer, you could create a hidden source of memory consumption if many types are formed from it.

Generic Interfaces

Along with classes and structs, you can also create generic interface declarations. This concept is a natural progression from struct and class generics. Naturally, a whole host of interfaces declared within the .NET 1.1 base class library make excellent candidates to have generic versions fashioned after them. A perfect example is IEnumerable<T>. Generic containers create much more efficient code than nongeneric containers when they contain value types, since they avoid any unnecessary boxing. It's only natural that any generic enumerable interface must have a means of enumerating the generic items within. Thus, IEnumerable<T> exists, and any enumerable containers you implement yourself should implement this interface. Alternatively, you could get it for free by deriving your custom containers from Collection<T>.

■**Note** When creating your own custom collection types, you should derive them from Collection<T> in the System.Collections.ObjectModel namespace. Other types, such as List<T>, are not meant to be derived from and are intended as a lower-level storage mechanism. Collection<T> implements protected virtual methods that you can override to customize its behavior, whereas List<T> does not.

Generic Methods

C# supports generic methods. Any method declaration that exists within a struct, a class, or an interface may be declared as a generic method. That includes static as well as virtual or abstract methods. Also, you can declare generic methods on non-generic types. To declare a generic method, simply append a type argument list to the end of the method name but before the parameter list for the method. You can declare any of the types in the method parameter list, including the method return type, using one of the generic parameters. As with nested classes, it is bad form to hide outer type identifiers by reusing the same identifier in the nested scope, which in this case, is the scope of the generic method. Let's consider an example of where a generic method may be useful. In the following code I've created a container to which I want to add the contents of another generic container:

```
using System;
using System.Collections.Generic;

public class MyContainer<T> : IEnumerable<T>
{
    public void Add( T item ) {
        impl.Add( item );
    }

    // Converter<TInput, TOutput> is a new delegate type introduced
    // in the .NET Framework 2.0 that can be wired up to a method that
    // knows how to convert the TInput type into a TOutput type.
    public void Add<R>( MyContainer<R> otherContainer,
                        Converter<R, T> converter ) {
        foreach( R item in otherContainer ) {
            impl.Add( converter(item) );
        }
    }

    public IEnumerator<T> GetEnumerator() {
        foreach( T item in impl ) {
            yield return item;
        }
    }

    System.Collections.IEnumerator System.Collections.IEnumerable.GetEnumerator() {
        return GetEnumerator();
    }

    private List<T> impl = new List<T>();
}

public class EntryPoint
{
    static void Main() {
```

```
        MyContainer<long> lContainer = new MyContainer<long>();
        MyContainer<int> iContainer = new MyContainer<int>();

        lContainer.Add( 1 );
        lContainer.Add( 2 );
        iContainer.Add( 3 );
        iContainer.Add( 4 );

        lContainer.Add( iContainer,
                        EntryPoint.IntToLongConverter );

        foreach( long l in lContainer ) {
            Console.WriteLine( l );
        }
    }

    static long IntToLongConverter( int i ) {
        return i;
    }
}
    static long IntToLongConverter( int i ) {
        return i;
    }
}
}
```

First of all, take note of the syntax of the generic Add<R> method, and also notice that there are two overloads of Add in MyContainer<T>. Clearly, you need to have a method to add instances of type T—thus, the need for Add(T). However, it would be really handy to be able to add an entire range of objects from another closed type formed from MyContainer<T>, as long as the enclosed type of the source container is convertible to the enclosed type of the target. If you look at Main, you can see the intent here. I want to place the objects contained within an instance of MyContainer<int> into an instance of MyContainer<long>. Therefore, I created a generic method, Add<R>, to allow me to accept another container that contains any arbitrary type.

This technique involves a twist, though. Logically, what I'm trying to do makes perfect type sense. I want to add a collection of ints to a collection of longs, and I know that an int is easily implicitly convertible to a long, so I should be able to do this. Although this is true, you have to take into consideration that generics are formed dynamically at run time. And at run time, there is no guarantee what closed type formed from MyContainer<T> the Add<R> method will see. It could be MyContainer<Apples>, and an Apple may not be implicitly convertible to a long, assuming it was passed to MyContainer<long>.Add<Apples>. Those of you who are used to C++ templates will recognize that doing such a thing won't work, since the compiler will let you know if you're trying to perform an invalid conversion at compile time. However, generics don't have this compile-time luxury, so more restrictions are in place during compile time to disallow such a thing. Therefore, you must seek out a different solution, and a good one is to provide a conversion delegate to get the job done.

The base class library provides the System.Converter<T, R> delegate specifically for this case. The syntax for this delegate may seem a bit foreign, but it's simply a generic delegate declaration, which I cover in detail in the section "Generic Delegates." When callers call Add<R>, they must also provide an instance of the generic Converter<T, R> delegate pointing to a method that knows how to convert from the source type to the target type. This explains the need for the IntToLongConverter method in the previous example. The Add<R> method then uses this delegate to do the actual conversion from one type to another. In this case, the conversion is an implicit one, but it still must be externalized this way since, at compile time, the compiler must accommodate the fact that the Add<R> method can have any type thrown at it.

To facilitate enumeration of the container, I have also declared MyContainer<T> such that it implements IEnumerable<T>. This allows you to use the syntactically intuitive foreach construct. You'll notice some syntax that may look foreign to you if you're not familiar with C# iterators.[1] However, notice how easy it is to create an enumerator for this class using the yield keyword. This was a welcome addition to the language, since declaring and constructing objects that enumerate containers is traditionally a laborious task.

Generic Delegates

Quite often, generics are used in the context of container types, where a closed type's field or internal array is based on the type argument given. Generic methods extend the capability of generic types by providing a finer granularity of generic scope. I have yet to discuss the power of generic delegates.

You're already familiar with the venerable delegate. If you were to declare a delegate that takes two parameters—the first being a long, and the second being an object—you would declare a delegate such as the following:

```
public delegate void MyDelegate( long l, object o );
```

In the previous section, you got a preview of a generic delegate when I showed the use of the generic converter delegate. The declaration for the generic converter delegate looks like this:

```
public delegate TOutput Converter<TInput, TOutput>(
    TInput input
);
```

It looks just like any other delegate, except it has the telltale form of a generic with a type parameter list immediately following the name of the delegate. Just as nongeneric delegates look similar to method declarations without a body, generic delegate declarations look almost identical to generic method declarations without a body. The type parameter list follows the name of the delegate, but it precedes the parameter list of the delegate.

The generic converter uses the placeholder identifiers TInput and TOutput within its type parameter list, and those types are used elsewhere in the declaration for the delegate. In generic delegate declarations, the types in the type parameter list are in scope for the entire declaration of the delegate, including the return type as shown in the previous declaration for the generic converter delegate.

Creating an instance of the Converter<TInput, TOutput> delegate is the same as creating an instance of any other delegate. When you create an instance of the generic delegate, you may use the new operator, and you may explicitly provide the type list at compile time. Or, you may simply use the abbreviated syntax that I used in the MyContainer<T> example in the previous section, in which case the compiler deduces the type parameters. For convenience, I have reprinted the Main method of that example:

```
static void Main() {
    MyContainer<long> lContainer = new MyContainer<long>();
    MyContainer<int> iContainer = new MyContainer<int>();

    lContainer.Add( 1 );
    lContainer.Add( 2 );
    iContainer.Add( 3 );
    iContainer.Add( 4 );
```

---

1. I covered iterators fully in Chapter 9.

```
lContainer.Add( iContainer,
                EntryPoint.IntToLongConverter );

foreach( long l in lContainer ) {
    Console.WriteLine( l );
}
}
```

Notice that the second parameter to the last Add method is simply a reference to the method rather than an explicit creation of the delegate itself. This works because of the method group conversion rules defined by the C# language. When the actual delegate is created from the method, the closed type of the generic is inferred using a complex pattern-matching algorithm from the parameter types of the IntToLongConverter method itself. In fact, the call to Add<T> is devoid of any explicit type parameter list at the point of invocation. The compiler is able to do the exact same type of pattern matching to infer the closed form of the Add<T> method called, which, in this case, is Add<int>. You could just as well have written the code as follows, where every type is provided explicitly:

```
static void Main() {
    MyContainer<long> lContainer = new MyContainer<long>();
    MyContainer<int> iContainer = new MyContainer<int>();

    lContainer.Add( 1 );
    lContainer.Add( 2 );
    iContainer.Add( 3 );
    iContainer.Add( 4 );

    lContainer.Add<int>( iContainer,
        new Converter<int, long>( EntryPoint.IntToLongConverter) );

    foreach( long l in lContainer ) {
        Console.WriteLine( l );
    }
}
```

In this example, all types are given explicitly, and the compiler is not left with the task of inferring them at compile time. Either way, the generated IL code is the same. Most of the time, you can rely on the type inference engine of the compiler. However, depending on the complexity of your code, you occasionally may find yourself needing to throw the compiler a bone by providing an explicit type list.

Along with providing a way to externalize type conversions from a container type, as in the previous examples, generic delegates help solve a special problem that I demonstrate in the following code:

```
// THIS WON'T WORK AS EXPECTED!!!
using System;
using System.Collections.Generic;

public delegate void MyDelegate( int i );

public class DelegateContainer<T>
{
    public void Add( T del ) {
        imp.Add( del );
    }
```

```
    public void CallDelegates( int k ) {
        foreach( T del in imp ) {
//          del( k );
        }
    }

    private List<T> imp = new List<T>();
}

public class EntryPoint
{
    static void Main() {
        DelegateContainer<MyDelegate> delegates =
            new DelegateContainer<MyDelegate>();

        delegates.Add( EntryPoint.PrintInt );
    }

    static void PrintInt( int i ) {
        Console.WriteLine( i );
    }
}
```

As written, the previous code will compile. However, notice the commented line within the
CallDelegates method. If you uncomment this line and attempt to recompile with the Microsoft
compiler, you'll get the following error:

```
error CS0118: 'del' is a 'variable' but is used like a 'method'
```

The problem is that the compiler has no way of knowing that the type represented by the
placeholder T is a delegate. Those of you who've been jumping ahead in this chapter may be wondering why there is no form of constraint (I cover constraints shortly) to give the compiler the hint
that it is a delegate. Well, even if there were, the compiler could not possibly know how to call the
delegate. The constraint would not carry the information about how many parameters the delegate
accepts. Remember, unlike C++ templates, generics are dynamic, and closed types are formed at
run time rather than at compile time. So, at run time, the delegate represented by del could take an
arbitrary number of parameters. I can only imagine the headache caused by trying to devise a way
to push a dynamic count of parameters onto the stack before calling the delegate. For all of these
reasons, it rarely makes sense to create a closed type from a generic where one of the type arguments is a delegate type, since, after all, you cannot call through to it normally.

What you can do to help in this situation is apply a generic delegate to give the compiler a bit
more information about what you want to do with this delegate. For example, using a generic delegate, you can effectively say, "I would like you to use delegates that only accept two parameters and
return an arbitrary type." That's enough information to get the compiler past the block and allow it
to generate code that makes sense for the generic. After all, if you give the compiler this amount of
information, at least it knows how many parameters to push onto the stack before making the call
through the delegate. The following code shows how you could remedy the previous situation:

```
using System;
using System.Collections.Generic;

public delegate void MyDelegate<T>( T i );

public class DelegateContainer<T>
{
```

```
    public void Add( MyDelegate<T> del ) {
        imp.Add( del );
    }

    public void CallDelegates( T k ) {
        foreach( MyDelegate<T> del in imp ) {
            del( k );
        }
    }

    private List<MyDelegate<T> > imp = new List<MyDelegate<T> >();
}

public class EntryPoint
{
    static void Main() {
        DelegateContainer<int> delegates =
            new DelegateContainer<int>();

        delegates.Add( EntryPoint.PrintInt );
        delegates.CallDelegates( 42 );
    }

    static void PrintInt( int i ) {
        Console.WriteLine( i );
    }
}
```

Generic Type Conversion

As I covered earlier in this chapter, there is no implicit type conversion for different constructed types formed from the same generic type. The same rules that apply when determining if an object of type X is implicitly convertible to an object of type Y apply equally when determining if an object of type List<int> is convertible to an object of type List<object>. When such conversion is desired, you must create a custom implicit conversion operator, just as in the case of converting objects of type X to objects of type Y when they share no inheritance relationship. Otherwise, you need to create a conversion method to go from one type to another. For example, the following code is invalid:

```
// INVALID CODE!!!
public void SomeMethod( List<int> theList ) {
    List<object> theSameList = theList; // Ooops!!!
}
```

If you've looked at the documentation of List<T>, you may have noticed a generic method named ConvertAll<TOutput>. Using this method, you can convert a generic list of type List<int> to List<object>. However, you must pass the method an instance of a generic conversion delegate as described in the previous section. That is the only way that the method can possibly know how to convert each contained instance from the source type to the destination type. Even though you may call a method to convert List<int> to List<object>, you must still provide the explicit means by which it converts an int into an object.

Those familiar with the Strategy pattern may find this a familiar notion. In essence, you can provide the ConvertAll<TOutput> method at run time with a means of doing the conversion on the contained instances that, depending on the complexity of the conversion, may be tuned for the platform that it is running on. In other words, if you were converting List<Apples> to

List<Oranges>, you could provide a few different conversion methods to select from, depending on the circumstances. For example, maybe one of them is highly tuned for an environment with lots of resources, so it runs faster in those environments. Another version may be optimized for minimal resource usage but is much slower. At run time, the proper conversion delegate is built to bind to the conversion method that is logical for the job at hand.

Default Value Expression

Sometimes when working with generic type definitions and generic method definitions, you need to initialize an object or a value instance of a parameterized type to its default value. Recall that the default value for a reference is the same as setting it to null, whereas the default value for a value type is equivalent to setting all of its underlying bits to 0. You need an expression for generics to account for these two semantic differences, and for that task, you can use the default value expression shown in the following code example:

```
using System;

public class MyContainer<T>
{
    public MyContainer() {
        // Create initial capacity.
        imp = new T[ 4 ];
        for( int i = 0; i < imp.Length; ++i ) {
            imp[i] = default(T);
        }
    }

    public bool IsNull( int i ) {
        if( i < 0 || i >= imp.Length ) {
            throw new ArgumentOutOfRangeException();
        }

        if( imp[i] == null ) {
            return true;
        } else {
            return false;
        }
    }

    private T[] imp;
}

public class EntryPoint
{
    static void Main() {
        MyContainer<int> intColl =
            new MyContainer<int>();

        MyContainer<object> objColl =
            new MyContainer<object>();

        Console.WriteLine( intColl.IsNull(0) );
        Console.WriteLine( objColl.IsNull(0) );
    }
}
```

Pay attention to the syntax within the MyContainer<T> constructor, where each item in the array is initialized explicitly to its default value. At run time, the type of T may be a value type or a reference type, so you cannot simply set the value to null and expect it to work for value types. In fact, if you attempt to assign imp[i] to null, the compiler will give you a friendly reminder with the following error:

```
default_value_1.cs(8,13): error CS0403: Cannot convert null to type parameter ➥
'T' because it could be a value type. Consider using 'default(T)' instead.
```

You should also use the default expression when testing a variable for null, since, after all, it could be a value type. However, in this case, the compiler cannot help you sniff out when you should do this, as you can see in the example. If you run the previous code, you get the output as follows:

```
False
True
```

This is probably not the intended result. If you modify the code so that the IsNull method looks like the following example, you'll get output that is more in line with the intended result:

```
public class MyContainer<T>
{
    public MyContainer() {
        // Create initial capacity.
        imp = new T[ 4 ];
        for( int i = 0; i < imp.Length; ++i ) {
            imp[i] = default(T);
        }
    }

    public bool IsNull( int i ) {
        if( i < 0 || i >= imp.Length ) {
            throw new ArgumentOutOfRangeException();
        }

        if( Object.Equals(imp[i], default(T)) ) {
            return true;
        } else {
            return false;
        }
    }

    private T[] imp;
}
```

Nullable Types

Related to the previous discussion is the concept of null values and what semantic meaning they carry. The null state for reference types is easily representable. If the value of the reference is set to null, it typically means that the variable has no value. This is much different, semantically, than saying that the value is 0. Semantically, a variable set to null has no value, not even the value of 0. With respect to value types, it has traditionally been much more cumbersome to represent the semantic meaning of null. If you set the value to 0, that could mean that the value is null. Then what do you do to represent the case when the value is actually 0, not null? Many techniques involve maintaining another Boolean value to indicate that the value type actually conveys meaning, such as a bool value named isNull.

To help you avoid having to manage such a mundane, error-prone mechanism, the .NET base class library provides you with the System.Nullable<T> type, as demonstrated in the following code:

```
using System;

public class Employee
{
    public Employee( string firstName,
                     string lastName ) {
        this.firstName = firstName;
        this.lastName = lastName;

        this.terminationDate = null;
        this.ssn = default(Nullable<long>);
    }

    public string firstName;
    public string lastName;

    public Nullable<DateTime> terminationDate;
    public long? ssn;    // Shorthand notation
}

public class EntryPoint
{
    static void Main() {
        Employee emp = new Employee( "Vasya",
                                     "Pupkin" );
        emp.ssn = 1234567890;

        Console.WriteLine( "{0} {1}",
                           emp.firstName,
                           emp.lastName );
        if( emp.terminationDate.HasValue ) {
            Console.WriteLine( "Start Date: {0}",
                               emp.terminationDate );
        }

        long tempSSN = emp.ssn ?? -1;
        Console.WriteLine( "SSN: {0}",
                           tempSSN );
    }
}
```

This code demonstrates two ways to declare a nullable type. The first nullable field within type Employee is the terminationDate field, which is declared using the System.Nullable<DateTime> type. One of the properties of Nullable<T> is HasValue, which returns true when the nullable value is non-null, and false otherwise. The second nullable value within Employee is the ssn field; however, this time I chose to use a C# shorthand notation for nullable types, where you simply follow the field's type declaration with a question mark. Internally, the compiler handles this in exactly the same way as with the declaration for the terminationDate field.

One last thing to consider when using nullable types is how you assign to and from them. In the constructor for Employee, you can see that I assign null to the nullable types at first. The compiler uses an implicit conversion for the null value to do the right thing. In fact, when I assign the ssn field in the constructor, I use the default expression syntax, which is the same thing the compiler does when I assign the terminationDate nullable value to null. Finally, you must consider what it means to assign a nullable type to a non-nullable type. For example, in the Main method, I want to assign tempSSN based upon the value of emp.ssn. However, since emp.ssn is nullable, what should tempSSN be assigned to if emp.ssn happens to have no value? This is when you must use the null coalescing operator ??. This operator allows you to designate what you want the non-nullable value to be set to in the event that the nullable value you're assigning from has no value. So, in the previous example, I'm saying, "Set the value of tempSSN to emp.ssn, and if emp.ssn has no value, set tempSSN to –1 instead." Armed with these tools, it's a snap to represent within a system values that may be semantically null, which is handy when you're using values to represent fields within a database field that is nullable.

Constructed Types Control Accessibility

When you build constructed types from generic types, you must consider the accessibility of both the generic type and the types provided as the type arguments, in order to determine the accessibility of the whole constructed type. For example, the following code is invalid and will not compile:

```
public class Outer
{
    private class Nested
    {
    }

    public class GenericNested<T>
    {
    }

    private GenericNested<Nested> field1;
    public GenericNested<Nested> field2; // Ooops!
}
```

The problem is with field2. The Nested type is private, so how can GenericNested<Nested> possibly be public? Of course, the answer is, it cannot. With constructed types, the accessibility is an intersection of the accessibility of the generic type and the types provided in the argument list.

Generics and Inheritance

C# generic types cannot directly derive from a type parameter. However, you can use the following type parameters to construct the base types they do derive from:

```
// This is invalid!!
public class MyClass<T> : T
{
}
```

```
// But this is valid.
public class MyClass<T> : Stack<T>
{
}
```

■Tip With C++ templates, deriving directly from a type parameter provides a special flexibility. If you've ever used the Active Template Library (ATL) to do COM development, you have no doubt come across this technique, since ATL employs it extensively to avoid the need for virtual method calls. The same technique is used with C++ templates to generate entire hierarchies at compile time. For more examples, I suggest you read Andrei Alexandrescu's *Modern C++ Design: Generic Programming and Design Patterns Applied* (Boston, MA: Addison-Wesley Professional, 2001). This is yet another example showing how C++ templates are static in nature, whereas C# generics are dynamic.

Let's examine techniques that you can use to emulate the same behavior to some degree. As is often the case, you can add one more level of indirection to achieve something similar. Many times, in C++, when a template type derives directly from one of the type arguments, it is assumed that the type specified for the type argument exhibits a certain desired behavior. For example, you can do the following using C++ templates:

```
// NOTE: This is C++ code used for the sake of example

class Employee
{
    public:
        long get_salary() {
            return salary;
        }
        void set_salary( long salary ) {
            this->salary = salary;
        }

    private:
        long salary;
};

template< class T >
class MyClass : public T
{
};

void main()
{
    MyClass<Employee> myInstance;
    myInstance.get_salary();
}
```

In the main function, pay attention to the call to get_salary. Even though it looks odd at first, it works just fine, because MyClass<T> inherits the implementation of whatever type is specified for T at compile time. In this case, that type, Employee, implements get_salary, and MyClass<Employee> inherits that implementation. Clearly, an assumption is being placed on the type that is provided for T in MyClass<T>, that the type will support a method named get_salary. If it does not, the C++ compiler will complain at compile time. This is a form of static polymorphism or policy-based programming. In traditional cases, polymorphism is explained within the context of virtual methods known as dynamic polymorphism. You cannot implement static polymorphism with C# generics. However, you can require that the type arguments given when forming a closed type support a specific contract by using a mechanism called *constraints*, which I cover in the following section.

Constraints

So far, the majority of generics examples that I've shown involve some sort of collection-style class that holds a bunch of objects or values of a specific type. But many times, you'll need to create generic types that not only contain instances of various types but also use those objects directly by calling methods or accessing properties on them. For example, suppose you have a generic type that holds instances of arbitrary geometric shapes that all implement a property named Area. Also, you need the generic type to implement a property—say, TotalArea—where all the areas of the contained shapes are accumulated. The guarantee here is that each geometric shape in the generic container will implement the Area property. You may be inclined to write code like the following:

```
using System;
using System.Collections.Generic;

public interface IShape
{
    double Area {
        get;
    }
}

public class Circle : IShape
{
    public Circle( double radius ) {
        this.radius = radius;
    }

    public double Area {
        get {
            return 3.1415*radius*radius;
        }
    }

    private double radius;
}

public class Rect : IShape
{
    public Rect( double width, double height ) {
        this.width = width;
        this.height = height;
    }

    public double Area {
        get {
            return width*height;
        }
    }
```

```
        private double width;
        private double height;
}

public class Shapes<T>
{
    public double TotalArea {
        get {
            double acc = 0;
            foreach( T shape in shapes ) {
                // THIS WON'T COMPILE!!!
                acc += shape.Area;
            }
            return acc;
        }
    }

    public void Add( T shape ) {
        shapes.Add( shape );
    }

    private List<T> shapes = new List<T>();
}

public class EntryPoint
{
    static void Main() {
        Shapes<IShape> shapes = new Shapes<IShape>();

        shapes.Add( new Circle(2) );
        shapes.Add( new Rect(3, 5) );

        Console.WriteLine( "Total Area: {0}",
                            shapes.TotalArea );
    }
}
```

There is one major problem, as the code won't compile. The offending line of code is inside the TotalArea property of Shapes<T>. The compiler complains with the following error:

```
error CS0117: 'T' does not contain a definition for 'Area'
```

All of this talk of requiring the contained type T to support the Area property sounds a lot like a contract, because it is! C# generics are dynamic as opposed to static in nature, so you cannot achieve the desired effect without some extra information. Whenever you hear the word *contract* within the C# world, you may start thinking about interfaces. Therefore, I've chosen to have both of my shapes implement the IShape interface. Thus, the IShape interface defines the contract, and the shapes implement that contract. However, that still is not enough for the C# compiler to be able to compile the previous code.

C# generics must have a way to enforce the rule that the type T supports a specific contract at run time, since constructed types are formed dynamically at run time. A naïve attempt to solve the problem could look like the following:

```
public class Shapes<T>
{
    public double TotalArea {
        get {
```

```
                double acc = 0;
                foreach( T shape in shapes ) {
                    // DON'T DO THIS!!!
                    IShape theShape = (IShape) shape;
                    acc += theShape.Area;
                }
                return acc;
            }
        }

        public void Add( T shape ) {
            shapes.Add( shape );
        }

        private List<T> shapes = new List<T>();
    }
```

This modification to Shapes<T> indeed does compile and work, most of the time. However, this generic has lost some of its innocence due to the type cast within the foreach loop. Just imagine if, during a late-night caffeine-induced trance, you attempted to create a constructed type Shapes<int>. The compiler would happily oblige. But what would happen if you tried to get the TotalArea property from a Shapes<int> instance? As expected, you would be treated to a runtime exception as the TotalArea property accessor attempted to cast an int into an IShape. One of the primary benefits of using generics is better type safety, but in this example, I've tossed type safety right out the window. So, what are you supposed to do? The answer lies in a concept called *generic constraints*. Check out the following correct implementation:

```
public class Shapes<T>
    where T: IShape
{
    public double TotalArea {
        get {
            double acc = 0;
            foreach( T shape in shapes ) {
                acc += shape.Area;
            }
            return acc;
        }
    }

    public void Add( T shape ) {
        shapes.Add( shape );
    }

    private List<T> shapes = new List<T>();
}
```

Notice the extra line under the first line of the class declaration using the where keyword. This says, "Define class Shapes<T> where T must implement IShape." Now the compiler has everything it needs to enforce type safety, and the JIT compiler has everything it needs to build working code at run time. The compiler has been given a hint to help it notify you, with a compile-time error, when you attempt to create constructed types where T does not implement IShape.

The syntax for constraints is pretty simple. There can be one where clause for each type parameter. Any number of interfaces may be listed following the type parameter in the where clause, but only one class at most. This restriction is intuitive, since a given type may only derive from one class but may implement an unlimited amount of interfaces. Additionally, you may use special keywords in the constraint clause for a particular type argument. Only one constraint can name a class type (since the CLR has no concept of multiple inheritance), so that constraint is known as the *primary constraint*. Additionally, instead of specifying a class name, the primary constraint may list the special words class or struct, which are used to indicate that the type parameter must be a class or a struct. The constraint clause can then include as many secondary constraints as possible, and they are usually a list of interfaces. Finally, you can list a constructor constraint that takes the form new( ). This constrains the parameterized type such that it is required to have a default, parameterless constructor. Class types must have an explicitly defined default constructor, whereas the new( ) constraint is automatic for value types since they have a system-generated default constructor.

It is customary to list each where clause on a separate line in any order under the class header. A comma separates each constraint following the colon in the where clause. That said, let's take a look at some constraint examples:

```
using System.Collections.Generic;

public class MyValueList<T>
    where T: struct
// But can't do the following
//   where T: struct, new()
{
    public void Add( T v ) {
        imp.Add( v );
    }

    private List<T> imp = new List<T>();
}

public class EntryPoint
{
    static void Main() {
        MyValueList<int> intList =
            new MyValueList<int>();

        intList.Add( 123 );

        // CAN'T DO THIS.
        // MyValueList<object> objList =
        //   new MyValueList<object>();
    }
}
```

In this code, you can see an example of the struct constraint. For one reason or another, you may find it necessary to create a container that can only contain value types. Alternatively, the constraint could have also claimed to allow only class types. Incidentally, in the Visual Studio version of the C# compiler, I'm unable to create a constraint that includes both class and struct. Of course, doing so is pointless, since the same effect comes from including neither struct nor class in the constraints list. Nevertheless, the compiler complains with an error if you try to do so, claiming the following:

```
error CS0449: The 'class' or 'struct' constraint must come before any ➥
other constraints
```

This looks like the compiler error could be better stated by saying that only one primary constraint is allowed in a constraint clause. You'll also see that I commented out an alternate constraint line, where I attempted to include the new() constraint to force the type given for T to support a default constructor. Clearly, for value types, this constraint is redundant and should be harmless to specify. Even so, the compiler won't allow you to provide the new() constraint together with the struct constraint. Now let's look at a slightly more complex example that shows two constraint clauses:

```
using System;
using System.Collections.Generic;

public interface IValue
{
    // IValue methods.
}

public class MyDictionary<TKey, TValue>
    where TKey: struct, IComparable<TKey>
    where TValue: IValue, new()
{
    public void Add( TKey key, TValue val ) {
        imp.Add( key, val );
    }

    private Dictionary<TKey, TValue> imp
        = new Dictionary<TKey, TValue>();
}
```

I've declared MyDictionary<TKey, TValue> in such a way that the key value is constrained to value types. I also want those key values to be comparable, so I've required the TKey type to implement IComparable<TKey>. This example shows two constraint clauses, one for each type parameter. In this case, I'm allowing the TValue type to be either a struct or a class, but I do require that it support the defined IValue interface as well as a default constructor.

Overall, the constraint mechanism built into C# generics is simple and straightforward. The complexity of constraints is easy to manage and decipher with few if any surprises. As the language and the CLR evolve, I suspect that this area will see some additions as more and more applications for generics are explored. For example, the ability to use the class and struct constraints within a constraint clause was a relatively late addition to the standard.

Finally, the format for constraints on generic interfaces is identical to that of generic classes and structs.

Constraints on Nonclass Types

So far, I've discussed constraints within the context of classes, structs, and interfaces. In reality, any entity that you can declare generically is capable of having an optional constraints clause. For generic method and delegate declarations, the constraints clauses follow the formal parameter list to the method or delegate. Using constraint clauses with method and delegate declarations does provide for some odd-looking syntax, as shown in the following example:

```
using System;

public delegate R Operation<T1, T2, R>( T1 val1,
                                        T2 val2 )
    where T1: struct
```

```
        where T2: struct
        where R:  struct;

public class EntryPoint
{
    public static double Add( int val1, float val2 ) {
        return val1 + val2;
    }

    static void Main() {
        Operation<int, float, double> op =
            new Operation<int, float, double>( EntryPoint.Add );

        Console.WriteLine( "{0} + {1} = {2}",
                           1, 3.2, op(1, 3.2f) );
    }
}
```

I've declared a generic delegate for an operator method that accepts two parameters and has a return value. My constraint is that the parameters and the return value all must be value types. For generic methods, the constraints clauses follow the method declaration but precede the method body. Notice that at the point of creation in the Main method, I had to tell the compiler the exact constructed type of the Operation<T1, T2, R> delegate I needed.

Generic System Collections

It seems that the most natural use of generics within C# and the CLR is for collection types. Maybe that's because you can gain a huge amount of efficiency when using generic containers to hold value types when compared to the collection types within the System.Collections namespace. Of course, you cannot overlook the added type safety that comes with using the generic collections. Any time you get added type safety, you're guaranteed to reduce runtime type conversion exceptions, since the compiler can catch many of those at compile time.

I encourage you to look at the .NET Framework documentation for the System. Collections.Generic namespace. There you will find all of the generic collection classes made available by the Framework. Included in the namespace are Dictionary<TKey, TValue>, LinkedList<T>, List<T>, Queue<T>, SortedDictionary<TKey, TValue>, SortedList<T>, HashSet<T>, and Stack<T>.

Based on their names, the uses of these types should feel familiar compared to the nongeneric classes under System.Collections. Although the containers within the System.Collections.Generic namespace may not seem complete for your needs, you have the possibility to create your own collections, especially given the extendable types in System.Collections.ObjectModel.

When creating your own collection types, you'll often find the need to be able to compare the contained objects. When coding in C#, it feels natural to use the built-in equality and inequality operators to perform the comparison. However, I suggest that you stay away from them, because the support of operators by classes and structs—although possible—is not part of the CLS. Some languages have been slow to pick up support for operators. Therefore, your container must be prepared for the case when it contains types that don't support operators for comparison. This is one of the reasons that interfaces such as IComparer and IComparable exist.

When you create an instance of the SortedList type within System.Collections, you have the opportunity to provide an instance of an object that supports IComparer. The SortedList then utilizes that object when it needs to compare two key instances that it contains. If you don't provide an object that supports IComparer, the SortedList looks for an IComparable interface on the contained key objects to do the comparison. Naturally, you'll need to provide an explicit comparer if the contained key objects don't support IComparable. The overloaded versions of the constructor that accept an IComparer type exist specifically for that case.

The generic version of the sorted list, SortedList<TKey, TValue>, follows the same sort of pattern. When you create a SortedList<TKey, TValue>, you have the option of providing an object that implements the IComparer<T> interface so it can compare two keys. If you don't provide one, the SortedList<TKey, TValue> defaults to using what's called the *generic comparer*. The generic comparer is simply an object that derives from the abstract Comparer<T> class and can be obtained through the static property Comparer<T>.Default. Based upon the nongeneric SortedList, you might think that if the creator of SortedList<TKey, TValue> did not provide a comparer, it would just look for IComparable<T> on the contained key type. This approach would cause problems, since the contained key type could either support IComparable<T> or the nongeneric IComparable. Therefore, the default comparer acts as an extra level of indirection. The default comparer checks to see if the type provided in the type parameter implements IComparable<T> and if it does not, looks to see if it supports IComparable, thus using the first one that it finds. Using this extra level of indirection provides greater flexibility with regard to the contained types. Let's look at an example to illustrate what I've just described:

```
using System;
using System.Collections.Generic;

public class EntryPoint
{
    static void Main() {
        SortedList<int, string> list1 =
            new SortedList<int, string>();

        SortedList<int, string> list2 =
            new SortedList<int, string>( Comparer<int>.Default );

        list1.Add( 1, "one" );
        list1.Add( 2, "two" );
        list2.Add( 3, "three" );
        list2.Add( 4, "four" );
    }
}
```

I've declared two instances of SortedList<TKey, TValue>. In the first instance, I've used the parameterless constructor, and in the second instance, I've explicitly provided a comparer for integers. In both cases, the result is the same because I provided the default generic comparer in the list2 constructor. I did this mainly so you could see the syntax used to pass in the default generic comparer. You could have just as easily provided any other type in the type parameter list for Comparer as long as it supports either IComparable or IComparable<T>.

Generic System Interfaces

Given the fact that the runtime library provides generic versions of container types, it should be no surprise that it also provides generic versions of commonly used interfaces. This is a great thing for those trying to achieve maximum type safety. For example, your classes and structs may implement IComparable<T> and/or IComparable as well as IEquatable<T>. Naturally, IComparable<T> is a more type-safe version of IComparable and should be preferred when possible.

■**Note** IEquatable<T> was added to .NET 2.0 and provides a type-safe interface through which you can perform equality comparisons on value types or reference types.

The System.Collections.Generic namespace also defines a whole host of interfaces that are generic versions of the ones in System.Collections. These include ICollection<T>, IDictionary<TKey, TValue>, and IList<T>. Two of these interfaces deserve special mention: IEnumerator<T> and IEnumerable<T>.[2] Late in the game, the development team at Microsoft decided it would be a good idea for IEnumerator<T> to derive from IEnumerator and for IEnumerable<T> to derive from IEnumerable. This decision has proven to be a controversial one. Anders Hejlsberg, one of the developers of the C# language, indicates that IEnumerable<T> inherits from IEnumerable because it can.

His argument goes something like this: You can imagine that it would be nice if the container that implements IList<T> also implemented IList. If IList<T> inherits from IList, it would be forced upon the author of the container to implement two versions of the Add method: Add<T> and Add. If the end user is able to call the nongeneric Add, then the whole benefit of added type safety through IList<T> would be lost, since the very existence of Add opens up the container implementation for runtime cast exceptions. So, deriving IList<T> from IList is a bad idea. IEnumerable<T> and IEnumerator<T>, on the other hand, differ from the other generic interfaces in that the type T is only used in return value positions. Therefore, no type safety is lost when implementing both.

That is the basis of the justification for saying that IEnumerable<T> can derive from IEnumerable and that IEnumerator<T> can derive from IEnumerator because they can. One of the developers at Microsoft working on the Framework library indicated that IEnumerable<T> and IEnumerator<T> are implemented this way in order to work around the lack of covariance with regard to generics. Yes, it's dizzying indeed.

Coding a type that implements IEnumerable<T> requires a bit of a trick in that you must implement the IEnumerable method using explicit interface implementation. Moreover, in order to keep the compiler from becoming confused, you may have to fully qualify IEnumerable with its namespace, as in the following example:

```
using System;
using System.Collections.Generic;

public class MyContainer<T> : IEnumerable<T>
{
    public void Add( T item ) {
        impl.Add( item );
    }

    public void Add<R>( MyContainer<R> otherContainer,
                        Converter<R, T> converter ) {
        foreach( R item in otherContainer ) {
            impl.Add( converter(item) );
        }
    }
}
```

---

2. Chapter 9 covers the facilities provided by IEnumerator<T> and IEnumerable<T> and how you can implement them easily using C# iterators.

```
    public IEnumerator<T> GetEnumerator() {
        foreach( T item in impl ) {
            yield return item;
        }
    }

    System.Collections.IEnumerator
        System.Collections.IEnumerable.GetEnumerator() {
        return GetEnumerator();
    }

    private List<T> impl = new List<T>();
}
```

Select Problems and Solutions

In this section, I want to illustrate some examples of creating generic types that show some useful techniques when creating generic code. I assure you that the pathway to learning how to use generics effectively will contain many surprises from time to time, since you must sometimes develop an unnatural or convoluted way of doing something that conceptually is very natural.

Note Many of you will undoubtedly get that unnatural feeling if you're transitioning from the notion of C++ templates to generics, as you discover the constraints that the dynamic nature of generics places upon you.

Conversion and Operators Within Generic Types

Converting from one type to another or applying operators to parameterized types within generics can prove to be tricky. To illustrate, let's develop a generic Complex struct that represents a complex number. Suppose that, for some reason, you want to be able to designate what value type is used internally to represent the real and imaginary portions of a complex number. This example is a tad contrived, since you would normally represent the components of an imaginary number using something such as System.Double. However, for the sake of example, let's imagine that you may want to be able to represent the components using System.Int64. Throughout this discussion, in order to reduce clutter and focus on the issues regarding generics, I'm going to ignore all of the canonical constructs that the generic Complex struct should implement.

You could start out by defining the Complex number as follows:

```
using System;

public struct Complex<T>
    where T: struct
{
    public Complex( T real, T imaginary ) {
        this.real = real;
        this.imaginary = imaginary;
    }

    public T Real {
        get { return real; }
        set { real = value; }
    }
```

```
    public T Img {
        get { return imaginary; }
        set { imaginary = value; }
    }

    private T real;
    private T imaginary;
}

public class EntryPoint
{
    static void Main() {
        Complex<Int64> c =
            new Complex<Int64>( 4, 5 );
    }
}
```

This is a good start, but now let's make this value type a little more useful. You could benefit from having a `Magnitude` property that returns the square root of the two components multiplied together. Let's attempt to create such a property:

```
using System;

public struct Complex<T>
    where T: struct
{
    public Complex( T real, T imaginary ) {
        this.real = real;
        this.imaginary = imaginary;
    }

    public T Real {
        get { return real; }
        set { real = value; }
    }

    public T Img {
        get { return imaginary; }
        set { imaginary = value; }
    }

    public T Magnitude {
        get {
            // WON'T COMPILE!!!
            return Math.Sqrt( real * real +
                             imaginary * imaginary );
        }
    }

    private T real;
    private T imaginary;
}

public class EntryPoint
{
    static void Main() {
        Complex<Int64> c =
            new Complex<Int64>( 3, 4 );
```

```
        Console.WriteLine( "Magnitude is {0}",
                            c.Magnitude );
    }
}
```

If you attempt to compile this code, you may be surprised to get the following compiler error:

```
error CS0019: Operator '*' cannot be applied to operands of type 'T' and 'T'
```

This is a perfect example of the problem with using operators in generic code. The compilation problem stems from the fact that you must compile generic code in a generic way to accommodate the fact that constructed types formed at run time can be formed from a value type that may not support the operator. In this case, it's impossible for the compiler to know if the type given for T in a constructed type at some point in the future even supports the multiplication operator. What are you to do? A common technique is to externalize the operation from the Complex<T> definition itself and then require the user of Complex<T> to provide the operation. A delegate is the perfect tool for doing this. Let's look at an example of Complex<T> that does that:

```
using System;

public struct Complex<T>
    where T: struct, IConvertible
{
    // Delegate for doing multiplication.
    public delegate T BinaryOp( T val1, T val2 );

    public Complex( T real, T imaginary,
                    BinaryOp mult,
                    BinaryOp add,
                    Converter<double, T> convToT ) {
        this.real = real;
        this.imaginary = imaginary;
        this.mult = mult;
        this.add = add;
        this.convToT = convToT;
    }

    public T Real {
        get { return real; }
        set { real = value; }
    }

    public T Img {
        get { return imaginary; }
        set { imaginary = value; }
    }

    public T Magnitude {
        get {
            double magnitude =
                Math.Sqrt( Convert.ToDouble(add(mult(real, real),
                                                mult(imaginary, imaginary))) );
            return convToT( magnitude );
        }
    }
```

```
        private T real;
        private T imaginary;
        private BinaryOp mult;
        private BinaryOp add;
        private Converter<double, T> convToT;
}

public class EntryPoint
{
    static void Main() {
        Complex<Int64> c =
            new Complex<Int64>(
                    3, 4,
                    EntryPoint.MultiplyInt64,
                    EntryPoint.AddInt64,
                    EntryPoint.DoubleToInt64 );

        Console.WriteLine( "Magnitude is {0}",
                        c.Magnitude );
    }

    static Int64 MultiplyInt64( Int64 val1, Int64 val2 ) {
        return val1 * val2;
    }

    static Int64 AddInt64( Int64 val1, Int64 val2 ) {
        return val1 + val2;
    }

    static Int64 DoubleToInt64( double d ) {
        return Convert.ToInt64( d );
    }
}
```

You're probably looking at this code and wondering what went wrong and why the complexity seems so much higher when all you're trying to do is find the magnitude of a complex number. As mentioned previously, you had to provide a delegate to handle the multiplication external to the generic type. Thus, I've defined the Complex<T>.Multiply delegate. At construction time, the Complex<T> constructor must be passed a third parameter that references a method for the multiplication delegate to refer to. In this case, EntryPoint.MultiplyInt64 handles multiplication. So, when the Magnitude property needs to multiply the components, it must use the delegate rather than the multiplication operator. Naturally, when the delegate is called, it boils down to a call to the multiplication operator. However, the application of the operator is now effectively external to the generic type Complex<T>.

No doubt you have noticed the extra complexities in the property accessor. First, Math.Sqrt accepts a type of System.Double. This explains the call to the Convert.ToDouble method. And to make sure things go smoothly, I added a constraint to T so that the type supplied supports IConvertible. But you're not done yet. Math.Sqrt returns a System.Double, and you have to convert that value type back into type T. In order to do so, you cannot rely on the System.Convert class, because you don't know what type you're converting to at compile time. Yet again, you have to externalize an operation, which in this case is a conversion. This is precisely one reason why the Framework defines the Converter<TInput, TOuput> delegate. In this case, Complex<T> needs a Converter<double, T> conversion delegate. At construction time, you must pass a method for this delegate to call through to, which in this case is EntryPoint.DoubleToInt64. Now, after all of this, the Complex<T>.Magnitude property works as expected, but not without an extra amount of work.

Note The complexity of using Complex<T>, as shown in the previous example, is greatly reduced by using lambda expressions, which are covered fully in Chapter 15. By using lambda expressions, you can completely bypass the need to define the operation methods such as MultiplyInt64, AddInt64, and DoubeToInt64 as shown in the example.

Let's say you want instances of Complex<T> to be able to be used as key values in a SortedList<TKey, TValue> generic type. In order for that to work, Complex<T> needs to implement IComparable<T>. Let's see what you need to do to make that a reality:

```
using System;

public struct Complex<T> : IComparable<Complex<T> >
    where T: struct, IConvertible, IComparable
{
    // Delegate for doing multiplication.
    public delegate T BinaryOp( T val1, T val2 );

    public Complex( T real, T imaginary,
                    BinaryOp mult,
                    BinaryOp add,
                    Converter<double, T> convToT ) {
        this.real = real;
        this.imaginary = imaginary;
        this.mult = mult;
        this.add = add;
        this.convToT = convToT;
    }

    public T Real {
        get { return real; }
        set { real = value; }
    }

    public T Img {
        get { return imaginary; }
        set { imaginary = value; }
    }

    public T Magnitude {
        get {
            double magnitude =
                Math.Sqrt( Convert.ToDouble(add(mult(real, real),
                                            mult(imaginary, imaginary))) );
            return convToT( magnitude );
        }
    }

    public int CompareTo( Complex<T> other ) {
        return Magnitude.CompareTo( other.Magnitude );
    }

    private T real;
    private T imaginary;
    private BinaryOp mult;
    private BinaryOp add;
```

```
        private Converter<double, T> convToT;
}

public class EntryPoint
{
    static void Main() {
        Complex<Int64> c =
            new Complex<Int64>(
                    3, 4,
                    EntryPoint.MultiplyInt64,
                    EntryPoint.AddInt64,
                    EntryPoint.DoubleToInt64 );

        Console.WriteLine( "Magnitude is {0}",
                        c.Magnitude );
    }

    static Int64 MultiplyInt64( Int64 val1, Int64 val2 ) {
        return val1 * val2;
    }

    static Int64 AddInt64( Int64 val1, Int64 val2 ) {
        return val1 + val2;
    }

    static Int64 DoubleToInt64( double d ) {
        return Convert.ToInt64( d );
    }
}
```

My implementation of the IComparable<Complex<T>> interface considers two Complex<T> types equivalent if they have the same magnitude. Therefore, most of the work required to do the comparison is done already. However, instead of being able to rely upon the inequality operator of the C# language, again you need to use a mechanism that doesn't rely upon operators. In this case, I've used the CompareTo method. Of course, this requires me to force another constraint on type T: It must support the nongeneric IComparable interface.

One thing worth noting is that the previous constraint on the nongeneric IComparable interface makes it a little bit difficult for Complex<T> to contain generic structs, because generic structs might implement IComparable<T> instead. In fact, given the current definition, it is impossible to define a type of Complex<Complex<int>>. It would be nice if Complex<T> could be constructed from types that may implement either IComparable<T> or IComparable or even both. Let's see how you can do this:

```
using System;
using System.Collections.Generic;

public struct Complex<T> : IComparable<Complex<T> >
    where T: struct
{
    // Delegate for doing multiplication.
    public delegate T BinaryOp( T val1, T val2 );

    public Complex( T real, T imaginary,
                    BinaryOp mult,
                    BinaryOp add,
                    Converter<double, T> convToT ) {
        this.real = real;
        this.imaginary = imaginary;
```

```
            this.mult = mult;
            this.add = add;
            this.convToT = convToT;
        }

    public T Real {
        get { return real; }
        set { real = value; }
    }

    public T Img {
        get { return imaginary; }
        set { imaginary = value; }
    }

    public T Magnitude {
        get {
            double magnitude =
                Math.Sqrt( Convert.ToDouble(add(mult(real, real),
                                        mult(imaginary, imaginary))) );
            return convToT( magnitude );
        }
    }

    public int CompareTo( Complex<T> other ) {
        return Comparer<T>.Default.Compare( this.Magnitude, other.Magnitude );
    }

    private T real;
    private T imaginary;
    private BinaryOp mult;
    private BinaryOp add;
    private Converter<double, T> convToT;
}

public class EntryPoint
{
    static void Main() {
        Complex<Int64> c =
            new Complex<Int64>(
                    3, 4,
                    EntryPoint.MultiplyInt64,
                    EntryPoint.AddInt64,
                    EntryPoint.DoubleToInt64 );

        Console.WriteLine( "Magnitude is {0}",
                        c.Magnitude );
    }

    static void DummyMethod( Complex<Complex<int> > c ) {
    }

    static Int64 AddInt64( Int64 val1, Int64 val2 ) {
        return val1 + val2;
    }
```

```
    static Int64 MultiplyInt64( Int64 val1, Int64 val2 ) {
        return val1 * val2;
    }

    static Int64 DoubleToInt64( double d ) {
        return Convert.ToInt64( d );
    }
}
```

In this example, I had to remove the constraint on T requiring implementation of the IComparable interface. Instead, the CompareTo method relies upon the default generic comparer defined in the System.Collections.Generic namespace.

■**Note** The generic comparer class Comparer<T> introduces one more level of indirection in the form of a class with regard to comparing two instances. In effect, it externalizes the comparability of the instances. If you need a custom implementation of IComparer, you should derive from Comparer<T>.

Additionally, I had to remove the IConvertible constraint on T to get DummyMethod to compile. That's because Complex<T> doesn't implement IConvertible, and when T is replaced with Complex<T> (thus forming Complex<Complex<T>>), the result is that T doesn't implement IConvertible.

■**Note** When creating generic types, try not to be too restrictive by forcing too many constraints on the contained types. For example, don't force all the contained types to implement IConvertible. Many times, you can externalize such constraints by using a helper object coupled with a delegate.

Think about the removal of this constraint for a moment. In the Magnitude property, you rely on the Convert.ToDouble method. However, since you removed the constraint, the possibility of getting a runtime exception exists—for example, when the type represented by T doesn't implement IConvertible. Since generics are meant to provide better type safety and help you avoid runtime exceptions, there must be a better way. In fact, there is, and you can do better by giving Complex<T> yet another converter in the form of a Convert<T, double> delegate in the constructor, as follows:

```
using System;
using System.Collections.Generic;

public struct Complex<T> : IComparable<Complex<T> >
    where T: struct
{
    // Delegate for doing multiplication.
    public delegate T BinaryOp( T val1, T val2 );

    public Complex( T real, T imaginary,
                    BinaryOp mult,
                    BinaryOp add,
                    Converter<T, double> convToDouble,
                    Converter<double, T> convToT ) {
        this.real = real;
        this.imaginary = imaginary;
        this.mult = mult;
        this.add = add;
```

```
                this.convToDouble = convToDouble;
                this.convToT = convToT;
            }

            public T Real {
                get { return real; }
                set { real = value; }
            }

            public T Img {
                get { return imaginary; }
                set { imaginary = value; }
            }

            public T Magnitude {
                get {
                    double magnitude =
                        Math.Sqrt( convToDouble(add(mult(real, real),
                                                    mult(imaginary, imaginary))) );
                    return convToT( magnitude );
                }
            }

            public int CompareTo( Complex<T> other ) {
                return Comparer<T>.Default.Compare( this.Magnitude, other.Magnitude );
            }

            private T real;
            private T imaginary;
            private BinaryOp mult;
            private BinaryOp add;
            private Converter<T, double> convToDouble;
            private Converter<double, T> convToT;
        }

        public class EntryPoint
        {
            static void Main() {
                Complex<Int64> c =
                    new Complex<Int64>(
                            3, 4,
                            EntryPoint.MultiplyInt64,
                            EntryPoint.AddInt64,
                            EntryPoint.Int64ToDouble,
                            EntryPoint.DoubleToInt64 );

                Console.WriteLine( "Magnitude is {0}",
                                    c.Magnitude );
            }

            static void DummyMethod( Complex<Complex<int> > c ) {
            }

            static Int64 MultiplyInt64( Int64 val1, Int64 val2 ) {
                return val1 * val2;
            }
```

```
static Int64 AddInt64( Int64 val1, Int64 val2 ) {
    return val1 + val2;
}

static Int64 DoubleToInt64( double d ) {
    return Convert.ToInt64( d );
}

static double Int64ToDouble( Int64 i ) {
    return Convert.ToDouble( i );
}
}
```

Now, the Complex<T> type can contain any kind of struct, whether it's generic or not. However, you must provide it with the necessary means to be able to convert to and from double as well as to multiply and add constituent types. This Complex<T> struct is by no means meant to be a reference for complex number representation at all. Rather, it is a somewhat contrived example meant to illustrate many of the concerns you must deal with in order to create effective generic types.

You'll see some of these techniques in practice as you deal with the generic containers that exist in the Base Class Library.

Creating Constructed Types Dynamically

Given the dynamic nature of the CLR and the fact that you can actually generate classes and code at run time, it is only natural to consider the possibility of constructing closed types from generics at run time. Up until now, all of the examples in this book have dealt with creating closed types at compile time.

This functionality stems from a natural extension of the metadata specification to accommodate generics. The type System.Type is the cornerstone of functionality whenever you need to work with types dynamically within the CLR, and naturally, it has been extended to deal with generics as well. Some of the new methods on System.Type are self-explanatory by name and include GetGenericArguments, GetGenericParameterConstraints, and GetGenericTypeDefinition. These methods are helpful when you already have a System.Type instance representing a closed type. However, the method that makes things interesting is MakeGenericType, which allows you to pass an array of System.Type objects that represent the types that are to be used in the argument parameter list for the resultant constructed type.

Those coming from a C++ template background have probably become frustrated from time to time with generics, since they lack the static compile-time capabilities of templates. However, I think you'll agree that the dynamic capabilities of generics make up for that in the end. Imagine how handy it is to be able to create closed types from generics at run time. For example, creating a parsing engine for some sort of XML-based language that defines new types from generics is a snap. Let's take a look at an example of how you use the MakeGenericType method:

```
using System;
using System.Collections.Generic;

public class EntryPoint
{
    static void Main() {
        IList<int> intList =
            (IList<int>) CreateClosedType<int>( typeof(List<>) );
```

```
        IList<double> doubleList =
            (IList<double>)
                CreateClosedType<double>( typeof(List<>) );

        Console.WriteLine( intList );
        Console.WriteLine( doubleList );
    }

    static object CreateClosedType<T>( Type genericType ) {
        Type[] typeArguments = {
            typeof( T )
        };

        Type closedType =
            genericType.MakeGenericType( typeArguments );

        return Activator.CreateInstance( closedType );
    }
}
```

The meat of this code is inside the generic method CreateClosedType<T>. All of the work is done in general terms via references to Type created from the available metadata. First, you need to get a reference to the generic, open type List<>, which is passed in as a parameter. After that, you simply create an array of Type instances to pass to MakeGenericType to obtain a reference to the closed type. Once that stage is complete, the only thing left to do is to call CreateInstance on the System.Activator class. System.Activator is the facility that you must use to create instances of types that are known only at run time. In this case, I'm calling the default constructor for the closed type. However, Activator has overloads of CreateInstance that allow you to call constructors that require parameters.

■**Note** I used the C# typeof operator rather than the Type.GetType method to obtain the Type instance for the types. If the type is known at compile time, the typeof operator performs the metadata lookup then rather than at run time—therefore, it is more efficient.

When you run the previous example, you'll see that the closed types are streamed to the console showing their fully qualified type names, thus proving that the closed types were created properly after all.

The ability to create closed types at run time is yet another powerful tool in your toolbox for creating highly dynamic systems. Not only can you declare generic types within your code so that you can write flexible code, but you can also create closed types from those generic definitions at run time. Take a moment to consider the extent of problems you could solve with these techniques, and it's easy to see that generics are an extremely potent addition to C# and the CLR.

Summary

In this chapter, I've shown how to declare and use generics using C#, including generic classes, structs, interfaces, methods, and delegates. I also discussed generic constraints, which are necessary for the compiler to create code where certain functional assumptions are placed upon the type arguments provided for the generic type arguments at run time. Collection types gain a real and measurable gain in efficiency and safety with generics.

Support for generics in .NET and C# is a welcome addition. Not only do generics allow you to generate more efficient code when using value types with containers, they also give the compiler much more power when enforcing type safety. As a rule, you should always prefer compile-time type safety over runtime type safety. You can fix a compile-time failure before software is deployed, but a runtime failure usually results in an `InvalidCastException` thrown in a production environment. Such a runtime failure could cost the end user huge sums of money, depending on the situation, and it could cause large amounts of embarrassment for you as the developer. Therefore, always provide the compiler with as much power as possible to enforce type safety, so it can do what it's meant to do best—and that's to be your friend.

The next chapter tackles the topic of threading in C# and the .NET runtime. Along with threading comes the ever-so-important topic of synchronization.

## CHAPTER 12

Threading in C#

The mere mention of multithreading can strike fear in the hearts of some programmers. For others, it fires them up for a good challenge. No matter how you react to the subject, multithreading is an area riddled with mine fields. Unless you show due diligence, a threading bug can jump up and bite you—and bite you in a place where you cannot seem to find it easily. Threading bugs can be among the hardest to find, because they are asynchronous. Threading bugs are hard enough to find on a single-processor machine, but add another processor, and the bugs can become even harder to find. In fact, some threading bugs don't even rear their ugly head until you run your application on a multiprocessor machine, since that's the only way to get true concurrent multithreading. For this reason, I always advise anyone developing a multithreaded application to test, and test often, on a multiprocessor machine. Otherwise, you run the risk of sending your product out the door with lurking threading bugs.

I remember it as if it were a meal ago: At a former employer of mine, we were soon to ship our gold master to the manufacturer and have hundreds of thousands of disks made, and then someone finally happened to test the application on a multiprocessor machine in the lab. Needless to say, a great lesson was learned across the entire team, and a nasty bug was snipped before it got out the door.

Threading in C# and .NET

Even though threading environments have presented many challenges and hurdles over the years, and will continue to do so, the CLR and the .NET base class library mitigate many of these risks and provide a clean model to build upon. It's still true that the greatest challenge of creating high-quality threaded code is that of synchronization. The .NET Framework makes it easier than ever to create new threads or utilize a system-managed pool of threads, and it provides intuitive objects that help you synchronize those threads with each other. However, it's still your duty to make sure you use those objects properly.

Managed threads are virtual threads in the sense that they don't map one-to-one to OS threads. Managed threads do actually run concurrently, but it would be erroneous to assume that the OS thread currently running a particular managed thread's code will only run managed code for that thread only. In fact, an OS thread could run managed code for multiple managed threads in multiple application domains in the current implementation of the CLR. The bottom line is, don't make any assumptions about the correlation between OS threads and managed threads. If you burrow down to the OS thread using the P/Invoke layer to make direct Win32 calls, be sure that you only use that information for debugging purposes and base no program logic on it at all. Otherwise, you'll end up with something that may break as soon as you run it on another CLR implementation.

It would be erroneous to conclude that multithreaded programming is just about creating extra threads to do something that can take a long time to do. Sure, that's part of the puzzle. And when you create a desktop application, you definitely want to use a threading technique to ensure that the UI stays responsive during a long computational operation, because we all know what impatient users tend to do when desktop applications become unresponsive: They kill them! But it's important to realize that there is much more to the threading puzzle than creating an extra thread to run some random code. That task is actually quite easy in the C# environment, so let's take a look and see how easy it really is.

Starting Threads

As I said, creating a thread is very simple. Take a look at the following example to see what I mean:

```
using System;
using System.Threading;

public class EntryPoint
{
    private static void ThreadFunc() {
        Console.WriteLine( "Hello from new thread {0}!",
                            Thread.CurrentThread.GetHashCode() );
    }

    static void Main() {
        // Create the new thread.
        Thread newThread =
            new Thread( new ThreadStart(EntryPoint.ThreadFunc) );

        Console.WriteLine( "Main Thread is {0}",
                            Thread.CurrentThread.GetHashCode() );
        Console.WriteLine( "Starting new thread..." );

        // Start the new thread.
        newThread.Start();

        // Wait for new thread to finish.
        newThread.Join();

        Console.WriteLine( "New thread has finished" );
    }
}
```

All you have to do is create a new System.Thread object and pass an instance of the ThreadStart delegate as the parameter to the constructor. The ThreadStart delegate references a method that takes no parameters and returns no parameters. In the previous example, I chose to use the static ThreadFunc method as the start of execution for the new thread. I could have just as easily chosen to use any other method visible to the code creating the thread, as long as it neither accepted nor returned parameters. Notice that the code also outputs the hash code from the thread to demonstrate how you identify threads in the managed world. In the unmanaged C++ world, you would use the thread ID obtained via the Win32 API. In the managed world, you instead use the value returned by GetHashCode. As long as this thread is alive, it is guaranteed never to collide with any other thread in any application domain of this process. The thread hash code is not globally unique on the entire system. Also, you can see how you can get a reference to the current thread by accessing the static property Thread.CurrentThread. Finally, notice the call to the Join method on the newThread object. In native Win32 code, you normally wait for a thread to finish by waiting on its handle. When the thread finishes running, the operating system signals its handle and the wait completes. The

Thread.Join method encapsulates this functionality. In this case, the code waits forever for the thread to finish. Thread.Join also provides a few overloads that allow you to specify a timeout period on the wait.

In the managed environment, the System.Thread class nicely encapsulates all of the operations that you may perform on a thread. If you have some sort of state data that you must transmit to the new thread so that it has that data available when it starts execution, you can simply create a helper object and initialize the ThreadStart delegate to point to an instance method on that object. Yet again, you solve another problem by introducing another level of indirection in the form of a class. Suppose you have a system where you fill multiple queues with tasks, and then at some point you want to create a new thread to process the items in a specific queue that you pass into it. The following code demonstrates one way you can achieve such a goal:

```
using System;
using System.Threading;
using System.Collections;

public class QueueProcessor
{
    public QueueProcessor( Queue theQueue ) {
        this.theQueue = theQueue;
        theThread = new Thread( new ThreadStart(this.ThreadFunc) );
    }

    private Queue theQueue;

    private Thread theThread;
    public Thread TheThread {
        get {
            return theThread;
        }
    }

    public void BeginProcessData() {
        theThread.Start();
    }

    public void EndProcessData() {
        theThread.Join();
    }

    private void ThreadFunc() {
        // ... drain theQueue here.
    }
}

public class EntryPoint
{
    static void Main() {
        Queue queue1 = new Queue();
        Queue queue2 = new Queue();

        // ... operations to fill the queues with data.

        // Process each queue in a separate thread.
        QueueProcessor proc1 = new QueueProcessor( queue1 );
```

```
        proc1.BeginProcessData();

        QueueProcessor proc2 = new QueueProcessor( queue2 );
        proc2.BeginProcessData();

        // ... do some other work in the meantime.

        // Wait for the work to finish.
        proc1.EndProcessData();
        proc2.EndProcessData();
    }
}
```

There are some potential synchronization problems here if anyone were to access the queues after the new threads begin their work. But I'll save synchronization issues until later in the chapter. This solution is a clean one and also loosely follows the typical pattern of asynchronous processing in the .NET Framework. The class adding the extra level of indirection is the QueueProcessor class. It cleanly encapsulates the worker thread and exposes a lightweight interface to get the work done. In this example, the main thread waits for the work to finish by calling EndProcessData. That method merely calls Join on the encapsulated thread. However, had you required some sort of status regarding the completion of the work, the EndProcessData method could have returned it to you.

When you create a separate thread, it is subject to the rules of the thread scheduler on the system, just like any other thread. However, sometimes you need to create threads that carry a little more or a little less weight when the scheduler algorithm is deciding which thread to execute next. You can control the priority of a managed thread via the Thread.Priority property. You can adjust this value as necessary during execution of the thread. It's actually a rare occurrence that you'll need to adjust this value. All threads start out with the priority of Normal from the ThreadPriority enumeration.

The IOU Pattern and Asynchronous Method Calls

In the section titled "Asynchronous Method Calls," where I discuss asynchronous I/O and thread pools, you'll see that the BeginProcessData/EndProcessData is a common pattern of asynchronous processing used throughout the .NET Framework. The BeginMethod/EndMethod pattern of asynchronous programming in the .NET Framework is similar to the IOU pattern described by Allan Vermeulen in his article, "An Asynchronous Design Pattern" (*Dr. Dobb's Journal*, June 1996). In that pattern, a function is called to start the asynchronous operation and in return, the caller is given an "I owe you" (IOU) object. Later, the caller can use that object to retrieve the result of the asynchronous operation. The beauty of this pattern is that it completely decouples the caller wanting to get the asynchronous work done from the mechanism used to actually do the work. This pattern is used extensively in the .NET Framework, and I suggest that you employ it for asynchronous method calls, as it will give your clients a familiar look and feel.

States of a Thread

The states of a managed thread are well defined by the runtime. Although the state transitions may seem confusing at times, they aren't much more confusing than the state transitions of an OS thread. There are other considerations to address in the managed world, so the allowable states and state transitions are naturally more complex. Figure 12-1 shows a state diagram for managed threads.

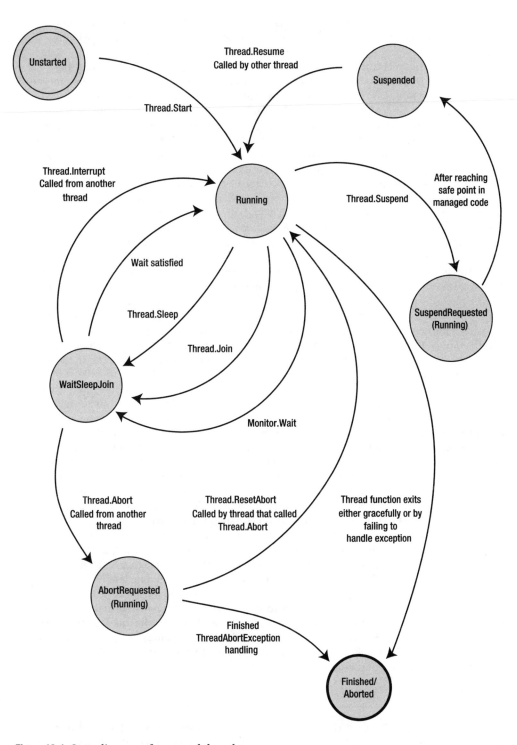

Figure 12-1. *State diagram of managed threads*

The states in the state diagram are based upon the states defined by the CLR for managed threads, as defined in the ThreadState enumeration. Every managed thread starts life in the Unstarted state. As soon as you call Start on the new thread, it enters the Running state. OS threads that enter the managed runtime start immediately in the Running state, thus bypassing the Unstarted state. Notice that there is no way to get back to the Unstarted state. The dominant state in the state diagram is the Running state. This is the state of the thread when it is executing code normally, including any exception handling and execution of any finally blocks. If the main thread method, passed in via an instance of the ThreadStart delegate during thread creation, finishes normally, then the thread enters the Finished state, as shown in Figure 12-1. Once in this state, the thread is completely dead and will never wake up again. If all of the foreground threads in your process enter the Finished state, the process will exit normally.

The three states mentioned previously cover the basics of managed thread state transition, assuming you have a thread that simply executes some code and exits. Once you start to add synchronization constructs in the execution path or wish to control the state of the thread, whether from another thread or the current thread, things become more complicated.

For example, suppose you're writing code for a new thread and you want to put it to sleep for a while. You would call Thread.Sleep and provide it a timeout, such as how many milliseconds to sleep. This is similar to how you put an OS thread to sleep. When you call Sleep, the thread enters the WaitSleepJoin state, where its execution is suspended for the duration of the timeout. Once the sleep expires, the thread reenters the running state.

Synchronization operations can also put the thread into the WaitSleepJoin state. As may be obvious by the name of the state, calling Thread.Join on another thread in order to wait for it to finish puts the calling thread into the WaitSleepJoin state. Calling Monitor.Wait also enters the WaitSleepJoin state. Now you know the three factors that went into naming the state in the first place. You can use other synchronization methods with a thread, and I'll cover those later in the chapter in the "Synchronizing Work Between Threads" section. As before, once the thread's wait requirements have been met, it reenters the Running state and continues execution normally.

It's important to note that any time the thread is sitting in the WaitSleepJoin state, it can be forcefully pushed back into the Running state when another thread calls Thread.Interrupt on the waiting thread. Win32 programmers will recognize that this behavior is similar to alertable wait states in the operating system. Beware that when a thread calls Thread.Interrupt on another thread, the interrupted thread receives a thrown ThreadInterruptedException. So, even though the interrupted thread reenters the Running state, it won't stay there for long unless an appropriate exception-handling frame is in place. Otherwise, the thread will soon enter the Finished state once the exception boils its way up to the top of the thread's stack unhandled.

Another way that the thread state can transition out of the WaitSleepJoin state is when another thread calls Thread.Abort on the current thread. Technically, a thread could call Abort on itself. However, I consider that a rare execution flow and have not shown it in Figure 12-1. Once Thread.Abort is called, the thread enters the AbortRequested state. This state is actually a form of a running state, since the thread is thrown a ThreadAbortException and must handle the exception. However, as I explain later on, the managed thread treats this exception in a special way, such that the next state will be the final Aborted state unless the thread that called Thread.Abort manages to call Thread.ResetAbort before that happens. Incidentally, there's nothing to stop the thread that is aborting from calling ResetAbort. However, you must refrain from doing such a thing since it could create some ill behavior. For example, if a foreground thread can never be aborted because it keeps resetting the abort, the process will never exit.

■**Note** Beginning in .NET 2.0, the host has the ability to forcefully kill threads during application domain shutdown by using what's called a *rude thread abort*. In such a situation, it is impossible for the thread to keep itself alive by using Thread.ResetAbort.

Finally, a running thread enters the SuspendRequested state after calling Thread.Suspend on itself, or after another thread calls Suspend on it. Very shortly after that, the thread automatically enters the Suspended state. Once a thread enters the SuspendRequested state, there is no way to keep it from eventually entering the Suspended state. Later on, in the section titled "Halting Threads and Waking Sleeping Threads," I discuss why this intermediate state is needed when a thread is suspended. But for now, it's important to realize that the SuspendRequested state is a form of a running state in the sense that it is still executing managed code.

That wraps up the big picture regarding managed-thread state transitions. Be sure to refer to Figure 12-1 throughout the rest of the chapter when reading about topics that affect the state of the thread.

Terminating Threads

When you call Thread.Abort, the thread in question eventually receives a ThreadAbortException. So, naturally, in order to handle this situation gracefully, you must process the ThreadAbortException if there is anything specific you must do when the thread is being aborted. There is also an overload of Abort that accepts an arbitrary object reference, which is then encapsulated in the subsequent ThreadAbortException. This allows the code that is aborting the thread to pass some sort of context information to the ThreadAbortException handler, such as a reason why Abort was called in the first place.

The CLR doesn't deliver a ThreadAbortException unless the thread is running within the managed context. If your thread has called out to a native function via the P/Invoke layer, and that function takes a long time to complete, then a thread abort on that thread is pended until execution returns to managed space.

Note In .NET 2.0 and later, if a finally block is executing, delivery of a ThreadAbortException is pended until execution leaves the finally block. In .NET 1.x, the abort exception is delivered anyway.

Calling Abort on a thread doesn't forcefully terminate the thread, so if you need to wait until the thread is truly finished executing, you must call Join on that thread to wait until all of the code in the ThreadAbortException exception handler is finished. During such a wait, it is wise to wait with a timeout so that you don't get stuck waiting forever for a thread to finish cleaning up after itself. Even though the code in the exception handler should follow other exception-handler coding guidelines, it's still possible for the handler to take a long time or, gasp, forever to complete its work. Let's take a look at a ThreadAbortException handler and see how this works:

```
using System;
using System.Threading;

public class EntryPoint
{
    private static void ThreadFunc() {
        ulong counter = 0;
        while( true ) {
            try {
                Console.WriteLine( "{0}", counter++ );
            }
            catch( ThreadAbortException ) {
                // Attempt to swallow the exception and continue.
                Console.WriteLine( "Abort!" );
```

```
                }
            }
        }

    static void Main() {
        Thread newThread =
            new Thread( new ThreadStart(EntryPoint.ThreadFunc) );
        newThread.Start();
        Thread.Sleep( 2000 );

        // Abort the thread.
        newThread.Abort();

        // Wait for thread to finish.
        newThread.Join();
    }
}
```

From a cursory glance at the code, it would appear that the call to Join on the newThread instance will block forever. However, that's not what happens. It would appear that since the ThreadAbortException is handled within the loop of the thread function, the exception will be swallowed and the loop will continue no matter how many times the main thread attempts to abort the thread. As it turns out, the ThreadAbortException thrown via the Thread.Abort method is special. When your thread finishes processing the abort exception, the runtime implicitly rethrows it at the end of your exception handler. It's the same as if you had rethrown the exception yourself. Therefore, any outer exception handlers or finally blocks will still execute normally. In the example, the call to Join won't be waiting forever as initially expected.

There is a way to keep the system from rethrowing the ThreadAbortException, by calling the Thread.ResetAbort static method. However, the general recommendation is that you only call ResetAbort from the thread that called Abort. This would require some sort of tricky intrathread communication technique if you wanted to cause this to happen from within the abort handler of the thread being aborted. If you find yourself trying to implement such a technique to abort a thread abort, then maybe it's time to reassess the design of the system in the first place. In other words, bad design alert!

Even though the runtime provides a much cleaner mechanism for aborting threads such that you can inform interested parties when the thread is aborting, you still have to implement a ThreadAbortException handler properly.

■**Note** The fact that ThreadAbortException instances can be thrown asynchronously into a random managed thread makes it tricky to create robust exception-safe code. Be sure to read the "Constrained Execution Regions" section in Chapter 7.

Halting Threads and Waking Sleeping Threads

Similar to native threads, there are mechanisms in place for putting a thread to sleep for a defined period of time or actually halting execution until it is explicitly released again. If a thread just wants to suspend itself for a prescribed period of time, it may call the static method Thread.Sleep. The only parameter to the Sleep method is the number of milliseconds the thread should sleep. When called, this method causes the thread to relinquish the rest of its time slice with the processor and go to sleep. After the time has expired, the thread may be considered for scheduling again. Naturally, the time duration you pass to Sleep is reasonably accurate, but not exact. That's because, at the end of the duration, the thread is not immediately given time on the processor. There could be other, higher-priority threads in the queue before it. Therefore, using Sleep to synchronize execution between two threads is strongly discouraged.

■**Caution** If you find yourself solving synchronization problems by introducing calls to Sleep within your code, you're not solving the problems at all. You're merely covering them up even more.

There is even a special value, Timeout.Infinite, that you can pass to Sleep to make the thread go to sleep forever. You can wake a sleeping thread by interrupting it via the Thread.Interrupt instance method. Interrupt is similar to Abort in that it wakes up the target thread and throws a ThreadInterruptedException. Therefore, if your thread function is not equipped to handle the exception, it will percolate all the way up the call stack until the runtime ends the thread's execution. To be safe, you should make your call to Sleep within a try block and catch the ThreadInterruptException. Unlike the ThreadAbortException, the ThreadInterruptException is not automatically rethrown by the runtime at the end of the exception handler.

■**Note** Another special parameter value for Thread.Sleep is 0. If you pass 0, Thread.Sleep will cause the thread to relinquish the rest of its time slice. The thread will then be allowed to run again once the system thread scheduler comes back around to it.

Another way to put a thread to sleep for an indefinite time is via the Thread.Suspend instance method. Calling Suspend will suspend execution of the thread until it is explicitly resumed. You can resume the thread by calling the Resume instance method or Interrupt. However, with Interrupt, the target thread needs to have a proper exception handler around the Suspend call; otherwise, the thread will exit. Technically, calling Abort on the thread will resume the thread, but only to send it a ThreadAbortException and cause the thread to exit. Keep in mind that any thread with sufficient privileges can call Suspend on a thread—even the current thread can call Suspend. If the current thread calls Suspend, it blocks at that point, waiting for the next Resume call.

It's important to note that when you call Suspend on a thread, the thread is not suspended immediately in its tracks. Instead, the thread is allowed to execute to what's called a *safe point*. Once it reaches the safe point, the thread is suspended. A safe point is a place in the managed code where it is safe to allow garbage collection. For instance, if the CLR determines it is time to perform a garbage collection, it must suspend all threads temporarily while it performs the collection. However, as you can imagine, if a thread is in the middle of a multi-instruction operation that accesses an object on the heap, and then the GC comes along and moves that object to a different place in system memory, only bad things will happen. For that reason, when the GC suspends threads for collection, it must wait until they all have reached a safe point where it is OK to move things around on the heap. For this reason, the call to Suspend allows the thread to reach a safe point before actually suspending it. I also want to stress that you should never use Suspend and Resume to orchestrate thread synchronization. Of course, the fact that the system allows the thread to continue running until it reaches a safe point is a good enough reason not to rely on this mechanism, but it's also a bad design practice.

Waiting for a Thread to Exit

In this chapter's previous examples, I've used the Join method to wait for a specific thread to exit. In fact, that is exactly what it is used for. In an unmanaged Win32 application, you may have been accustomed to waiting for the thread handle to become signaled to indicate the completion of the thread. The Join method is the same mechanism indeed. The name of the method is suggestive of the fact that you're joining the current thread's execution path to that of the thread you're calling Join on, and you cannot proceed until your joined thread arrives.

Naturally, you'll want to avoid calling Join on the current thread. The effect is similar to calling Suspend from the current thread. The thread is blocked until it is interrupted. Even when a thread is blocked from calling Join, it can be awoken via a call to Interrupt or Abort as described in the previous section.

Sometimes, you'll want to call Join to wait for another thread to complete, but you won't want to get stuck waiting forever. Join offers overloads that allow you to designate the amount of time you're willing to wait. Those overloads return a Boolean value that returns true to indicate that the thread actually terminated, or false to indicate that the timeout expired.

Foreground and Background Threads

When you create a thread in the .NET managed environment, it exists as a foreground thread by default. This means that the managed execution environment, and thus the process, will remain alive as long as the thread is alive. Consider the following code:

```
using System;
using System.Threading;

public class EntryPoint
{
    private static void ThreadFunc1() {
        Thread.Sleep( 5000 );
        Console.WriteLine( "Exiting extra thread" );
    }

    static void Main() {
        Thread thread1 =
            new Thread( new ThreadStart(EntryPoint.ThreadFunc1) );

        thread1.Start();

        Console.WriteLine( "Exiting main thread" );
    }
}
```

If you run this code, you'll see that Main exits before the extra thread finishes, as expected. (C++ developers will find that very different from the behavior they're used to, where the process normally terminates once the main routine in the application exits.)

At times, you might want the process to terminate when the main thread finishes, even when there are extra threads in the background. You can accomplish this in the runtime by turning the extra thread into a background thread by setting the Thread.IsBackground property to true. You'll want to consider doing this for threads that do stuff such as listen on a port for network connections, or some other background task such as that. Keep in mind, though, that you always want to make sure that your threads get a proper chance to clean up if they need to before they are shut down. When a background thread is shut down as the process exits, it doesn't receive an exception of any type as it does when someone calls Interrupt or Abort. So, if the thread has persistent data in some sort of half-baked state, shutting down the process will definitely not be good for that persistent data. Therefore, when creating background threads, make sure they are coded so that they can be terminated rudely at any point without any adverse effects. You can also implement some sort of mechanism to notify the thread that the process is to shut down soon. Creating such a mechanism will prove messy, since the main thread will need to wait a reasonable amount of time after firing the notification for the extra thread to do its cleanup work. At that point, it almost becomes reasonable to turn the thread back into a foreground thread.

Thread-Local Storage

You can create thread-local storage in the managed environment. Depending on your application, it may be necessary for you to have a static field of a class that is unique for each thread that the class is used in. Doing so is trivially easy in the majority of the cases in C#. If you have a static field that must be thread-relative, simply adorn it with the ThreadStaticAttribute attribute. Once you do that, the field will be initialized for each thread that accesses it. Under the covers, each thread is given its own thread-relative location to save the value or reference. However, when using references to objects, be careful with your assumptions about object creation. The following code shows a pitfall to avoid:

```
using System;
using System.Threading;

public class TLSClass
{
    public TLSClass() {
        Console.WriteLine( "Creating TLSClass" );
    }
}

public class TLSFieldClass
{
    [ThreadStatic]
    public static TLSClass tlsdata = new TLSClass();
}

public class EntryPoint
{
    private static void ThreadFunc() {
        Console.WriteLine( "Thread {0} starting...",
                            Thread.CurrentThread.GetHashCode() );
        Console.WriteLine( "tlsdata for this thread is \"{0}\"",
                            TLSFieldClass.tlsdata );
        Console.WriteLine( "Thread {0} exiting",
                            Thread.CurrentThread.GetHashCode() );
    }

    static void Main() {
        Thread thread1 =
            new Thread( new ThreadStart(EntryPoint.ThreadFunc) );
        Thread thread2 =
            new Thread( new ThreadStart(EntryPoint.ThreadFunc) );

        thread1.Start();
        thread2.Start();
    }
}
```

This code creates two threads that access a thread-relative static member of TLSFieldClass. To illustrate the trap, I've made that thread-specific slot of type TLSClass, and the code attempts to initialize that slot with an initializer in the class definition that simply calls new on the default constructor of the class. Now, look how surprising the output is:

```
Thread 3 starting...
Thread 4 starting...
Creating TLSClass
tlsdata for this thread is "TLSClass"
Thread 3 exiting
tlsdata for this thread is ""
Thread 4 exiting
```

Caution Always remember that ordering of execution in multithreaded programs is never guaranteed unless you employ specific synchronization mechanisms. This output was generated on a single-processor system. If you run the same application on a multiprocessor system, you'll likely see that the output executes in a completely different order. Nevertheless, the purpose of the example does not change.

The important thing to take note of is that the constructor for TLSClass was only called once. The constructor was called for the first thread, but not for the second thread. For the second thread, the field is initialized to null. Since tlsdata is static, its initialization is actually done at the time the static constructor for the TLSFieldClass is called. However, static constructors can only be called once per class per application domain. For this reason, you want to avoid assigning thread-relative slots at the point of declaration. That way, they will always be assigned to their default values. For reference types, that means null, and for value types, it means the equivalent of setting all of the bits in the value's underlying storage to 0. Then, upon first access to the thread-specific slot, you can test the value for null and create an instance as appropriate. Of course, the cleanest way to achieve this is always to access the thread-local slot via a static property.

As an added note, don't think that you can outsmart the compiler by adding a level of indirection, such as assigning the thread-relative slot based on the return value of a static method. You'll find that your static method will only get called once. If the CLR were to "fix" this problem for you, it would undoubtedly be less efficient because it would have to test whether the field is being accessed for the first time and call the initialization code if that is the case. If you think about it, you'll find that task is a lot harder than it sounds, since it will be impossible to do the right thing 100% of the time.

There is another way to use thread-local storage that doesn't involve decorating a static method with an attribute. You can allocate thread-specific storage dynamically by using either of the Thread.AllocateDataSlot or Thread.AllocateNamedDataSlot methods. You'll want to use these methods if you won't know how many thread-specific slots you'll need to allocate until runtime. Otherwise, it's generally much easier to use the static field method. When you call AllocateDataSlot, a new slot is allocated in all threads to hold a reference to an instance of type System.Object. The method returns a handle of sorts in the form of a LocalDataStoreSlot object instance. You can access this location using the GetData and SetData methods on the thread. Let's look at a modification of the previous example:

```
using System;
using System.Threading;

public class TLSClass
{
```

```
    static TLSClass() {
        tlsSlot = Thread.AllocateDataSlot();
    }

    public TLSClass() {
        Console.WriteLine( "Creating TLSClass" );
    }

    public static TLSClass TlsSlot {
        get {
            Object obj = Thread.GetData( tlsSlot );
            if( obj == null ) {
                obj = new TLSClass();
                Thread.SetData( tlsSlot, obj );
            }
            return (TLSClass) obj;
        }
    }

    private static LocalDataStoreSlot tlsSlot = null;
}

public class EntryPoint
{
    private static void ThreadFunc() {
        Console.WriteLine( "Thread {0} starting...",
                          Thread.CurrentThread.GetHashCode() );
        Console.WriteLine( "tlsdata for this thread is \"{0}\"",
                          TLSClass.TlsSlot );
        Console.WriteLine( "Thread {0} exiting",
                          Thread.CurrentThread.GetHashCode() );
    }

    static void Main() {
        Thread thread1 =
            new Thread( new ThreadStart(EntryPoint.ThreadFunc) );
        Thread thread2 =
            new Thread( new ThreadStart(EntryPoint.ThreadFunc) );

        thread1.Start();
        thread2.Start();
    }
}
```

As you can see, using dynamic slots is a little more involved than using the static field method. However, it does provide some extra flexibility. Notice that the slot is allocated in the type initializer, which is the static constructor you see in the example. That way, the slot is allocated for all threads at the point where the runtime initializes the type for use. Notice that I'm testing the slot for null in the property accessor of the TLSClass. When you allocate the slot using AllocateDataSlot, the slot is initialized to null for each thread.

You may find it convenient to access your thread-specific storage via a string name rather than with a reference to a LocalDataStoreSlot instance. However, you must be careful to use a reasonably unique name so that use of that same name elsewhere in the code won't cause adverse effects. You may consider naming your slot using a string representation of a GUID, so that you can reasonably assume that nobody will attempt to create one with the same name. When you need to access the slot, you can call `GetNamedDataSlot`, which will simply translate your string into a `LocalDataStoreSlot` instance. I urge you to read the MSDN documentation regarding named thread-local storage slots to get more details.

Most of this will be familiar to those developers who have used thread-local storage in Win32. There is one improvement, though: Because managed TLS slots are implemented in a different way, the limitation on the number of Win32 TLS slots doesn't apply.

How Unmanaged Threads and COM Apartments Fit In

It is possible for unmanaged threads to enter the managed environment from the outside. For example, managed objects can be exposed to native code via the COM interop layer. When the native thread calls through to the object, it enters the managed environment. When this happens, the CLR makes note of that fact, and if it is the first time the unmanaged thread has called into the CLR, it sets up the necessary bookkeeping structures allowing it to run as a managed thread within the managed runtime. As I mentioned before, threads that enter the managed environment this way initially start their managed thread existence in the `Running` state, as shown in Figure 12-1. Once this bookkeeping is set up, then each time the same unmanaged thread enters the runtime, it is associated with the same managed thread.

Just as managed objects can be exposed to the native world as COM objects, COM objects can be exposed to the managed world as managed objects. When a managed thread calls out to a COM object in this way, the runtime relinquishes control over the thread's state until it reenters the managed environment.

Suppose a COM object, written in native C++, calls the `WaitForSingleObject` Win32 API function to wait for a particular synchronization object to become signaled. Then, if a managed thread calls `Thread.Abort` or `Thread.Interrupt` to wake up the thread, the wakeup will be pended until the thread reenters the managed environment. In other words, it will have no effect while the thread is executing unmanaged code. Therefore, you want to be reasonably cognizant of what sorts of synchronization mechanisms are being used by native COM objects that your native code is calling out to.

Finally, if you've ever done an extensive amount of COM development in the past, then you're familiar with the notion of a COM apartment and the proxies and stubs that go along with them.[1] When managed code calls out into COM objects, it is important that the managed code be set up to call the unmanaged COM object through either a single-threaded apartment (STA) or a multi-threaded apartment (MTA). You can set this property on a new managed thread by setting the `Thread.ApartmentState` property. Once the thread makes a COM call, this state gets locked in. In other words, you cannot change it afterwards. You can set the property after the first COM call all you want, but it will have no effect. When you call out to COM objects from managed code, it's best to know the type of apartment the COM objects will run in. That way, you can judiciously choose which type of COM apartment you want your thread to run in. Choosing the wrong type may introduce inefficiencies by forcing calls to go through proxies and stubs. In even worse cases, COM objects may not be callable from other apartment types.

Using `Thread.ApartmentState`, you can control the COM apartment property for new managed threads that you create. But what about the main thread of an application? The fact is that once the main thread of a managed application is running, it's already too late to set the `ApartmentState` property. That's because the managed runtime initializes the main thread to the MTA state as the managed application is initialized. If you need to change the `ApartmentState` of the main thread to STA, the only way to do so is by decorating the `Main` method with the `STAThreadAttribute` attribute.

---

1. For a detailed description of COM apartments and how they work, I suggest you read Don Box's *Essential COM* (Boston, MA: Addison-Wesley Professional, 1997).

Incidentally, you could also decorate it with the MTAThreadAttribute attribute, but that would be redundant since that's the CLR's default choice. The following code shows an example of what I'm talking about:

```
public class EntryPoint
{
    [STAThread]
    static void Main() {
    }
}
```

If you've ever worked with Windows Forms applications, especially those generated by the wizards of Visual Studio, you probably have already seen this attribute and wondered what it was all about. By decorating the main UI thread of GUI applications with this attribute, you can integrate native ActiveX controls more easily in the GUI, since those normally run in an STA.

Note that the ApartmentState property of a managed thread has no effect on the execution of managed code. And more importantly, when managed objects are consumed by native applications via the COM interop layer, the ApartmentState doesn't control what apartment the object appears to live in from the perspective of the native application. From the native side of the fence, all managed objects appear as COM objects that live in the MTA and integrate the Free Threaded Marhsaller (FTM). Also, all threads created in the CLR's thread pool always live in the MTA for the process.

Synchronizing Work Between Threads

Synchronization is arguably the most difficult part of creating multithreaded applications. You can create extra threads to do work all day long without having to worry about synchronization, as long as those threads consume some data at startup that no other thread uses and do some work. Nobody needs to know when they finish or what the results of their operations are. Obviously, it's a rare case that you'll create such a thread. In most cases, you need to communicate with the running thread, wait for it to reach a defined state in the code, or possibly work on the same object or value instances that other threads are working on.

In all of those cases, and more, you must rely upon synchronization techniques to synchronize the threads to avoid race conditions and deadlocks. With race conditions, two threads may need to access the same piece of memory and only one can safely do so at a time. In these cases, you must use a synchronization mechanism that will only allow one thread at a time to access the data and lock out the other thread, making it wait until the first one is done. Multithreaded environments are stochastic in nature, and you never know when the scheduler will take away control from the thread. The classic example is where one thread gets halfway through changing a block of memory, loses control, and then the other thread is given control and starts reading the memory, assuming that it is in a valid state. An example of a deadlock is when two threads are waiting for each other to release a resource. Both threads end up waiting for each other, and since neither one of them can run until the wait is satisfied, they will end up waiting forever.

In all synchronization tasks, you should use the most lightweight sync mechanism that you can get away with and no heavier. For example, if you're trying to share a data block between two threads in the same process and you must gate access between the two, use something such as a Monitor lock rather than a Mutex. Why? Because a Mutex is meant to gate access to a shared resource between processes, and therefore, is a heavyweight OS object that slows down the process when acquiring and releasing the lock. If no interprocess locking is necessary, use the Monitor instead. Even more lightweight than the Monitor is a set of methods in the Interlocked class. These are ideal when you know that the likelihood of actually having to wait a good while when acquiring a lock is low.

■Note Any type of wait on a kernel object—such as waiting on a `Mutex`, `Semaphore`, `EventWaitHanldle`, or any other wait that boils down to waiting on a Win32 kernel object—requires a transition to kernel mode. Transitions to kernel mode are expensive, and you should avoid them if at all possible. For example, if the threads you are synchronizing live in the same process, kernel synchronization objects are probably too heavy. The lightest synchronization technique involves crafty use of the `Threading.Interlocked` class. Its methods are all implemented completely in user mode, thus allowing you to avoid the user-to-kernel mode transition.

When using synchronization objects in a multithreaded environment, you want to hold the lock for as little time as possible. For example, if you acquire a synchronization lock to read a shared structure instance, and code within the method that acquires the lock uses that instance of the structure for some purpose, it's best to make a local copy of the structure on the stack and then release the lock immediately, unless it is logically impossible. That way, you don't tie up other threads in the system that need to access the guarded variable.

When you need to synchronize thread execution, never rely upon methods such as `Thread.Suspend` or `Thread.Resume` to control thread synchronization. If you recall from a previous section in this chapter, calling `Thread.Suspend` doesn't actually suspend the thread immediately. Instead, it must get to a safe point within the managed code before it can suspend execution. And never use `Thread.Sleep` to synchronize threads. `Thread.Sleep` is appropriate when you're doing some sort of polling loop on an entity, such as device hardware that has just been reset and has no way of notifying anyone that it is back online. In that case, you don't want to check the state in a loop repeatedly. Instead, it's much nicer to sleep a little bit between polling, to allow the scheduler to let other threads run. I've said this in a previous section, but I'll say it again because it's so important: If you ever find yourself solving a synchronization bug by introducing a call to `Thread.Sleep` at some seemingly random point in the code, you're not solving the problem at all. Rather, you're hiding it even deeper. Just don't do it!

Lightweight Synchronization with the Interlocked Class

Those of you who come from the unmanaged world of programming against the Win32 API probably already know about the `Interlocked...` family of functions. Thankfully, those functions have been exposed to managed C# developers via static methods on the `Interlocked` class in the `System.Threading` namespace. Sometimes, when running multiple threads, it's necessary to maintain a simple variable—typically, a value, but possibly an object—between the multiple threads. For example, suppose you have some reason to track the number of running threads in a static integer somewhere. When a thread begins, it increments that value, and when it finishes, it decrements that value. Obviously, you must synchronize access to that value somehow, since the scheduler could take away control from one thread and give it to another when the first one is in the process of updating the value. Even worse, the same code could be executing concurrently on a multiprocessor machine. For this task, you can use `Interlocked.Increment` and `Interlocked.Decrement`. These methods are guaranteed to modify the value atomically across all processors in the system. Take a look at the following example:

```
using System;
using System.Threading;

public class EntryPoint
{
    static private int numberThreads = 0;

    static private Random rnd = new Random();
```

```csharp
        private static void RndThreadFunc() {
            // Manage thread count and wait for a
            // random amount of time between 1 and 12
            // seconds.
            Interlocked.Increment( ref numberThreads );
            try {
                int time = rnd.Next( 1000, 12000 );
                Thread.Sleep( time );
            }
            finally {
                Interlocked.Decrement( ref numberThreads );
            }
        }

        private static void RptThreadFunc() {
            while( true ) {
                int threadCount = 0;
                threadCount =
                    Interlocked.Exchange( ref numberThreads,
                                          numberThreads );
                Console.WriteLine( "{0} thread(s) alive",
                                   threadCount );
                Thread.Sleep( 1000 );
            }
        }

        static void Main() {
            // Start the reporting threads.
            Thread reporter =
                new Thread( new ThreadStart(
                                EntryPoint.RptThreadFunc) );
            reporter.IsBackground = true;
            reporter.Start();

            // Start the threads that wait random time.
            Thread[] rndthreads = new Thread[ 50 ];
            for( uint i = 0; i < 50; ++i ) {
                rndthreads[i] =
                    new Thread( new ThreadStart(
                                    EntryPoint.RndThreadFunc) );
                rndthreads[i].Start();
            }
        }
    }
}
```

This little program creates 50 foreground threads that do nothing but wait a random period of time between 1 and 12 seconds. It also creates a background thread that reports how many threads are currently alive. If you look at the RndThreadFunc method, which is the thread function that the 50 threads use, you can see it increment and decrement the integer value using the Interlocked methods. Notice that I use a finally block to ensure that the value gets decremented no matter how the thread exits. You could use the disposable trick with the using keyword by wrapping the increment and decrement in a separate class that implements IDisposable. That would get rid of the ugly finally block. But, in this case, it wouldn't help you at all, since you'd also have to create a reference type to contain the integer count variable, as you cannot store a ref to the integer as a field in the helper class.

You've already seen `Interlocked.Increment` and `Interlocked.Decrement` in action. But what about `Interlocked.Exchange`, which the reporter thread uses? Remember, since multiple threads are attempting to write to the `threadCount` variable, the reporter thread must read the value in a synchronized way as well. That's where `Interlocked.Exchange` comes in. `Interlocked.Exchange`, as its name implies, allows you to exchange the value of a variable with that of another in an atomic fashion, and it returns the value that was stored previously in that location. Since the `Interlocked` class doesn't provide a method to simply read an `Int32` value in an atomic operation, all I'm doing is swapping the `numberThreads` variable's value with its own value, and, as a side effect, the `Interlocked.Exchange` method returns to me the value that was in the slot.

INTERLOCKED METHODS ON SMP SYSTEMS

On Intel symmetric multiprocessing (SMP) platforms and most other SMP systems, simple reads and writes to memory slots that are of the native size are synchronized automatically. On an IA-32 system, reads and writes to properly aligned 32-bit values are synchronized. Therefore, in the previous example where I showed the use of `Interlocked.Exchange` merely to read an `Int32` value, it would not have been necessary if the variable were aligned properly.

By default, the CLR works hard to make sure that values are aligned properly on natural boundaries. However, you can override the placement of values within a class or structure using the `FieldOffsetAttribute` on fields, thus forcing a misaligned data field. If an `Int32` is not aligned, the guarantee mentioned in the previous paragraph is lost. In such a case, you must use `Interlocked.Exchange` to read the value reliably.

The `Interlocked...` methods are all implemented on IA-32 systems using the `lock` prefix. This prefix causes the processor LOCK# signal to be asserted. This prevents the other processors in the system from accessing the value concurrently, which is necessary for complex operations where values are incremented and so on. One handy quality of the `lock` prefix is that the misaligned data field does not adversely affect the integrity of the lock. In other words, it works perfectly fine with misaligned data. That's why `Interlocked.Exchange` is the ticket for reading misaligned data atomically.

Finally, consider the fact that the `Interlocked` class implements overloads of some of the methods so that they work with 64-bit values, floating-point numbers, and object references. In fact, `Interlocked...` even offers generic overloads for working with object references. Consider what it means to work with 64-bit values atomically on a 32-bit system. Naturally, there is no possible way to read such values atomically without resorting to the `Interlocked` class. In fact, for this very reason, the .NET 2.0 version of the `Interlocked` class introduced `Interlocked.Read` for `Int64` values. Naturally, such a beast is not necessary on 64-bit systems and should simply boil down to a regular read. However, the CLR is meant to work on multiple platforms, so you should always use `Interlocked.Read` when working with 64-bit values.

For these reasons, it would be better safe than sorry to always use `Interlocked.Exchange` for reading and writing values atomically, since it could prove troublesome to validate that the data is not misaligned and no bigger than the native size prior to reading or writing it in a raw manner. Determining the native size on the platform and basing code conditionally on such data goes against the grain of the cross-platform spirit of managed code.

The last method to cover in the `Interlocked` class is `CompareExchange`. This little method is handy indeed. It's similar to `Interlocked.Exchange`, in that it allows you to exchange the value of a location or slot in an atomic fashion. However, it only does the exchange if the original value compares equal to a provided comparand. In any event, the method always returns the original value. One extremely handy use of the `CompareExchange` method is to create a lightweight *spin lock*. A spin lock gets its name from the fact that if it cannot acquire the lock, it will spin in a tight loop until it can. Typically, when implementing a spin lock, you put your thread to sleep for a very brief slice of time with each failed attempt to acquire the lock. That way, the thread scheduler can give processor time to another thread while you wait. If you don't want the thread to sleep but only to release its time slice, you can pass a value of 0 to Thread.Sleep. Let's look at an example:

```csharp
using System;
using System.IO;
using System.Threading;

public class SpinLock
{
    public SpinLock( int spinWait ) {
        this.spinWait = spinWait;
    }

    public void Enter() {
        while( Interlocked.CompareExchange(ref theLock,
                                      1,
                                      0) == 1 ) {
            // The lock is taken, spin.
            Thread.Sleep( spinWait );
        }
    }

    public void Exit() {
        // Reset the lock.
        Interlocked.Exchange( ref theLock,
                            0 );
    }

    private int theLock = 0;
    private int spinWait;
}

public class SpinLockManager : IDisposable
{
    public SpinLockManager( SpinLock spinLock ) {
        this.spinLock = spinLock;
        spinLock.Enter();
    }

    public void Dispose() {
        spinLock.Exit();
    }

    private SpinLock spinLock;
}

public class EntryPoint
{
    static private Random rnd = new Random();
    private static SpinLock logLock = new SpinLock( 10 );
    private static StreamWriter fsLog =
        new StreamWriter( File.Open("log.txt",
                                    FileMode.Append,
                                    FileAccess.Write,
                                    FileShare.None) );
```

```
    private static void RndThreadFunc() {
        using( new SpinLockManager(logLock) ) {
            fsLog.WriteLine( "Thread Starting" );
            fsLog.Flush();
        }

        int time = rnd.Next( 10, 200 );
        Thread.Sleep( time );

        using( new SpinLockManager(logLock) ) {
            fsLog.WriteLine( "Thread Exiting" );
            fsLog.Flush();
        }
    }

    static void Main() {
        // Start the threads that wait random time.
        Thread[] rndthreads = new Thread[ 50 ];
        for( uint i = 0; i < 50; ++i ) {
            rndthreads[i] =
                new Thread( new ThreadStart(
                                EntryPoint.RndThreadFunc) );
            rndthreads[i].Start();
        }
    }
}
```

This example is similar to the previous one. It creates 50 threads that wait a random amount of time. However, instead of managing a thread count, it outputs a line to a log file. Since this writing is happening from multiple threads, and instance methods of StreamWriter are not thread-safe, you must do the writing in a safe manner within the context of a lock. That is where the SpinLock class comes in. Internally, it manages a lock variable in the form of an integer, and it uses Interlocked. CompareExchange to gate access to the lock. The call to Interlocked.CompareExchange in SpinLock.Enter is saying

1. If the lock value is equal to 0, replace the value with 1 to indicate that the lock is taken; otherwise, do nothing.

2. If the value of the slot already contains 1, it's taken, and you must sleep and spin.

Both of those items occur in an atomic fashion via the Interlocked class, so there is no possible way that more than one thread at a time can acquire the lock. When the SpinLock.Exit method is called, all it needs to do is reset the lock. However, that must be done atomically as well—hence, the call to Interlocked.Exchange.

In this example, I decided to illustrate the use of the disposable/using idiom to implement deterministic destruction, where you introduce another class—in this case, SpinLockManager—to implement the RAII idiom. This saves you from having to remember to write finally blocks all over the place. Of course, you still have to remember to use the using keyword, but if you follow the idiom more closely than this example, you would implement a finalizer that would assert in the debug build if it ran and the object had not been disposed of.[2]

---

2.   See Chapter 13 for more information on this technique.

Keep in mind that spin locks implemented in this way are not reentrant. Any function that has acquired the lock cannot be called again until it has released the lock. This doesn't mean that you cannot use spin locks with recursive programming techniques. It just means that you must release the lock before recursing, or else suffer a deadlock.

■Note If you require a reentrant wait mechanism, you can use wait objects that are more structured, such as the Monitor class, which I cover in the next section, or kernel-based wait objects.

Incidentally, if you'd like to see some fireworks, so to speak, try uncommenting the use of the spin lock in the RndThreadFunc method and run the result several times. You'll most likely notice the output in the log file gets a little ugly. The ugliness should increase if you attempt the same test on a multiprocessor machine.

Monitor Class

In the previous section, I showed you how to implement a spin lock using the methods of the Interlocked class. A spin lock is not always the most efficient synchronization mechanism, especially if you use it in an environment where a wait is almost guaranteed. The thread scheduler keeps having to wake up the thread and allow it to recheck the lock variable. As I mentioned before, a spin lock is ideal when you need a lightweight, non-reentrant synchronization mechanism and the odds are low that a thread will have to wait in the first place. When you know the likelihood of waiting is high, you should use a synchronization mechanism that allows the scheduler to avoid waking the thread until the lock is available. .NET provides the System.Threading.Monitor class to allow synchronization between threads within the same process. You can use this class to guard access to certain variables or to gate access to code that should only be run on one thread at a time.

■Note The Monitor pattern provides a way to ensure synchronization such that only one method, or a block of protected code, executes at one time. A Mutex is typically used for the same task. However, Monitor is much lighter and faster. Monitor is appropriate when you must guard access to code within a single process. Mutex is appropriate when you must guard access to a resource from multiple processes.

One potential source of confusion regarding the Monitor class is that you cannot instantiate an instance of this class. The Monitor class, much like the Interlocked class, is merely a containing namespace for a collection of static methods that do the work. If you're used to using critical sections in Win32, you know that at some point you must allocate and initialize a CRITICAL_SECTION structure. Then, to enter and exit the lock, you call the Win32 EnterCriticalSection and LeaveCriticalSection functions. You can achieve exactly the same task using the Monitor class in the managed environment. To enter and exit the critical section, you call Monitor.Enter and Monitor.Exit. Where you pass a CRITICAL_SECTION object to the Win32 critical section functions, you pass an object reference to the Monitor methods.

Internally, the CLR manages a sync block for every object instance in the process. Basically, it's a flag of sorts, similar to the integer used in the examples of the previous section describing the Interlocked class. When you obtain the lock on an object, this flag is set. When the lock is released, this flag is reset. The Monitor class is the gateway to accessing this flag. The versatility of this scheme is that every object instance in the CLR potentially contains one of these locks. I say potentially because the CLR allocates them in a lazy fashion, since not every object instance's lock will be utilized. To implement a critical section, all you have to do is create an instance of Object. Let's look at an example using the Monitor class by modifying the example from the previous section:

```csharp
using System;
using System.Threading;

public class EntryPoint
{
    static private object theLock = new Object();
    static private int numberThreads = 0;
    static private Random rnd = new Random();

    private static void RndThreadFunc() {
        // Manage thread count and wait for a
        // random amount of time between 1 and 12
        // seconds.
        try {
            Monitor.Enter( theLock );
            ++numberThreads;
        }
        finally {
            Monitor.Exit( theLock );
        }

        int time = rnd.Next( 1000, 12000 );
        Thread.Sleep( time );

        try {
            Monitor.Enter( theLock );
            --numberThreads;
        }
        finally {
            Monitor.Exit( theLock );
        }
    }

    private static void RptThreadFunc() {
        while( true ) {
            int threadCount = 0;
            try {
                Monitor.Enter( theLock );
                threadCount = numberThreads;
            }
            finally {
                Monitor.Exit( theLock );
            }

            Console.WriteLine( "{0} thread(s) alive",
                              threadCount );
            Thread.Sleep( 1000 );
        }
    }

    static void Main() {
        // Start the reporting threads.
```

```
        Thread reporter =
            new Thread( new ThreadStart(
                                EntryPoint.RptThreadFunc) );
        reporter.IsBackground = true;
        reporter.Start();

        // Start the threads that wait random time.
        Thread[] rndthreads = new Thread[ 50 ];
        for( uint i = 0; i < 50; ++i ) {
            rndthreads[i] =
                new Thread( new ThreadStart(
                                EntryPoint.RndThreadFunc) );
            rndthreads[i].Start();
        }
    }
}
```

Notice that I perform all access to the numberThreads variable within a critical section in the form of an object lock. Before each access, the accessor must obtain the lock on the theLock object instance. The type of theLock field is of type object simply because its actual type is inconsequential. The only thing that matters is that it is a reference type—that is, an instance of object rather than a value type. Since you only need the object instance to utilize its internal sync block, you can just instantiate an object of type System.Object.

One thing you've probably also noticed is that the code is uglier than the version that used the Interlocked methods. Whenever you call Monitor.Enter, you want to guarantee that the matching Monitor.Exit executes no matter what. I mitigated this problem in the examples using the Interlocked class by wrapping the usage of the Interlocked class methods within a class named SpinLockManager. Can you imagine the chaos that could ensue if a Monitor.Exit call was skipped because of an exception? Therefore, you always want to utilize a try/finally block in these situations. The creators of the C# language recognized that developers were going through a lot of effort to ensure that these finally blocks were in place when all they were doing was calling Monitor.Exit. So, they made our lives easier by introducing the lock keyword. Consider the same example again, this time using the lock keyword:

```
using System;
using System.Threading;

public class EntryPoint
{
    static private object theLock = new Object();
    static private int numberThreads = 0;
    static private Random rnd = new Random();

    private static void RndThreadFunc() {
        // Manage thread count and wait for a
        // random amount of time between 1 and 12
        // seconds.
        lock( theLock ) {
            ++numberThreads;
        }

        int time = rnd.Next( 1000, 12000 );
        Thread.Sleep( time );

        lock( theLock ) {
```

```
                    —numberThreads;
            }
        }
    }

    private static void RptThreadFunc() {
        while( true ) {
            int threadCount = 0;
            lock( theLock ) {
                threadCount = numberThreads;
            }

            Console.WriteLine( "{0} thread(s) alive",
                                    threadCount );
            Thread.Sleep( 1000 );
        }
    }

    static void Main() {
        // Start the reporting threads.
        Thread reporter =
            new Thread( new ThreadStart(
                            EntryPoint.RptThreadFunc) );
        reporter.IsBackground = true;
        reporter.Start();

        // Start the threads that wait random time.
        Thread[] rndthreads = new Thread[ 50 ];
        for( uint i = 0; i < 50; ++i ) {
            rndthreads[i] =
                new Thread( new ThreadStart(
                                EntryPoint.RndThreadFunc) );
            rndthreads[i].Start();
        }
    }
}
```

Notice that the code is much cleaner now, and in fact, there are no more explicit calls to any Monitor methods at all. Under the covers, however, the compiler is expanding the lock keyword into the familiar try/finally block with calls to Monitor.Enter and Monitor.Exit. You can verify this by examining the generated IL code using ILDASM.

In many cases, synchronization implemented internally within a class is as simple as implementing a critical section in this manner. But when only one lock object is needed across all methods within the class, you can simplify the model even more by eliminating the extra dummy instance of System.Object by using the this keyword when acquiring the lock through the Monitor class. You'll probably come across this usage pattern often in C# code. Although it saves you from having to instantiate an object of type System.Object—which is pretty lightweight, I might add—it does come with its own perils. For example, an external consumer of your object could actually attempt to utilize the sync block within your object by calling Monitor.Enter before even calling one of your methods that will try to acquire the same lock. Technically, that's just fine, since the same thread can call Monitor.Enter multiple times. In other words, Monitor locks are reentrant, unlike the spin locks of the previous section. However, when a lock is released, it must be released by calling Monitor.Exit a matching number of times. So, now you have to rely upon the consumers of your object to either use the lock keyword or a try/finally block to ensure that their call to Monitor.Enter is matched appropriately with Monitor.Exit. Any time you can avoid such uncertainty, do so. Therefore, I recommend against locking via the this keyword, and I suggest instead using a private instance of System.Object as your lock. You could achieve the same effect if there were some way to declare the sync block flag of an object private, but alas, that is not possible.

Beware of Boxing

When you're using the Monitor methods to implement locking, internally Monitor uses the sync block of object instances to manage the lock. Since every object instance can potentially have a sync block, you can use any reference to an object, even an object reference to a boxed value. Even though you can, you should never pass a value type instance to Monitor.Enter, as demonstrated in the following code example:

```
using System;
using System.Threading;

public class EntryPoint
{
    static private int counter = 0;

    // NEVER DO THIS !!!
    static private int theLock = 0;

    static private void ThreadFunc() {
        for( int i = 0; i < 50; ++i ) {
            Monitor.Enter( theLock );
            try {
                Console.WriteLine( ++counter );
            }
            finally {
                Monitor.Exit( theLock );
            }
        }
    }

    static void Main() {
        Thread thread1 =
            new Thread( new ThreadStart(EntryPoint.ThreadFunc) );
        Thread thread2 =
            new Thread( new ThreadStart(EntryPoint.ThreadFunc) );
        thread1.Start();
        thread2.Start();
    }
}
```

If you attempt to execute this code, you will immediately be presented with a SynchronizationLockException, complaining that an object synchronization method was called from an unsynchronized block of code. Why does this happen? In order to find the answer, you need to remember that implicit boxing occurs when you pass a value type to a method that accepts a reference type. And remember, passing the same value type to the same method multiple times will result in a different boxing reference type each time. Therefore, the reference object used within the body of Monitor.Exit is different from the one used inside of the body of Monitor.Enter. This is another example of how implicit boxing in the C# language can cause you grief. You may have noticed that I used the old try/finally approach in this example. That's because the designers of the C# language created the lock statement such that it doesn't accept value types. So, if you just stick to using the lock statement for handling critical sections, you'll never have to worry about inadvertently passing a boxed value type to the Monitor methods.

Pulse and Wait

I cannot overstate the utility of the Monitor methods to implement critical sections. However, the Monitor methods have capabilities beyond that of implementing simple critical sections. You can also use them to implement handshaking between threads, as well as for implementing queued access to a shared resource.

When a thread has entered a locked region successfully, it can give up the lock and enter a waiting queue by calling Monitor.Wait. The first parameter to Monitor.Wait is the object reference whose sync block represents the lock being used. The second parameter is a timeout value. Monitor.Wait returns a Boolean that indicates whether the wait succeeded or if the timeout was reached. If the wait succeeded, the result is true; otherwise, it is false. When a thread that calls Monitor.Wait completes the wait successfully, it leaves the wait state as the owner of the lock again.

If threads can give up the lock and enter into a wait state, there must be some mechanism to tell the Monitor that it can give the lock back to one of the waiting threads as soon as possible. That mechanism is the Monitor.Pulse method. Only the thread that currently holds the lock is allowed to call Monitor.Pulse. When it's called, the thread first in line in the waiting queue is moved to a ready queue. Once the thread that owns the lock releases the lock, either by calling Monitor.Exit or by calling Monitor.Wait, the first thread in the ready queue is allowed to run. The threads in the ready queue include those that are pulsed and those that have been blocked after a call to Monitor.Enter. Additionally, the thread that owns the lock can move all waiting threads into the ready queue by calling Monitor.PulseAll.

There are many fancy synchronization tasks that you can accomplish using the Monitor.Pulse and Monitor.Wait methods. For example, consider the following example that implements a handshaking mechanism between two threads. The goal is to have both threads increment a counter in an alternating manner:

```
using System;
using System.Threading;

public class EntryPoint
{
    static private int counter = 0;

    static private object theLock = new Object();

    static private void ThreadFunc1() {
        lock( theLock ) {
            for( int i = 0; i < 50; ++i ) {
                Monitor.Wait( theLock, Timeout.Infinite );
                Console.WriteLine( "{0} from Thread {1}",
                        ++counter,
                        Thread.CurrentThread.GetHashCode() );
                Monitor.Pulse( theLock );
            }
        }
    }

    static private void ThreadFunc2() {
        lock( theLock ) {
            for( int i = 0; i < 50; ++i ) {
                Monitor.Pulse( theLock );
                Monitor.Wait( theLock, Timeout.Infinite );
```

```
                Console.WriteLine( "{0} from Thread {1}",
                                ++counter,
                                Thread.CurrentThread.GetHashCode() );
            }
        }
    }

    static void Main() {
        Thread thread1 =
            new Thread( new ThreadStart(EntryPoint.ThreadFunc1) );
        Thread thread2 =
            new Thread( new ThreadStart(EntryPoint.ThreadFunc2) );
        thread1.Start();
        thread2.Start();
    }
}
```

You'll notice that the output from this example shows that the threads increment counter in an alternating fashion.

As another example, you could implement a crude thread pool using Monitor.Wait and Monitor.Pulse. It may be unnecessary to actually do such a thing, since the .NET Framework offers the ThreadPool object, which is robust and likely uses optimized I/O completion ports of the underlying OS. For the sake of example, however, I'll show how you could implement a pool of worker threads that wait for work items to be queued:

```
using System;
using System.Threading;
using System.Collections;

public class CrudeThreadPool
{
    static readonly int MAX_WORK_THREADS = 4;
    static readonly int WAIT_TIMEOUT = 2000;

    public delegate void WorkDelegate();

    public CrudeThreadPool() {
        stop = 0;
        workLock = new Object();
        workQueue = new Queue();
        threads = new Thread[ MAX_WORK_THREADS ];

        for( int i = 0; i < MAX_WORK_THREADS; ++i ) {
            threads[i] =
                new Thread( new ThreadStart(this.ThreadFunc) );
            threads[i].Start();
        }
    }

    private void ThreadFunc() {
        lock( workLock ) {
            int shouldStop = 0;
            do {
                shouldStop = Interlocked.Exchange( ref stop,
                                                    stop );
                if( shouldStop == 0 ) {
                    WorkDelegate workItem = null;
```

```
                        if( Monitor.Wait(workLock, WAIT_TIMEOUT) ) {
                            // Process the item on the front of the
                            // queue
                            lock( workQueue ) {
                                workItem =
                                    (WorkDelegate) workQueue.Dequeue();
                            }
                            workItem();
                        }
                    }
                } while( shouldStop == 0 );
            }
        }

        public void SubmitWorkItem( WorkDelegate item ) {
            lock( workLock ) {
                lock( workQueue ) {
                    workQueue.Enqueue( item );
                }

                Monitor.Pulse( workLock );
            }
        }

        public void Shutdown() {
            Interlocked.Exchange( ref stop, 1 );
        }

        private Queue     workQueue;
        private Object    workLock;
        private Thread[]  threads;
        private int       stop;
    }

    public class EntryPoint
    {
        static void WorkFunction() {
            Console.WriteLine( "WorkFunction() called on Thread {0}",
                               Thread.CurrentThread.GetHashCode() );
        }

        static void Main() {
            CrudeThreadPool pool = new CrudeThreadPool();
            for( int i = 0; i < 10; ++i ) {
                pool.SubmitWorkItem(
                    new CrudeThreadPool.WorkDelegate(
                                    EntryPoint.WorkFunction) );
            }

            pool.Shutdown();
        }
    }
```

In this case, the work item is represented by a delegate that neither accepts nor returns any values. When the CrudeThreadPool object is created, it creates a pool of threads and starts them running the main work item processing method. That method simply calls Monitor.Wait to wait for an item to be queued. When SubmitWorkItem is called, an item is pushed into the queue and it calls Monitor.Pulse to release one of the worker threads. Naturally, access to the queue must be synchronized. In this case, the reference type used to sync access is the queue itself. Additionally, the worker threads must not wait forever, because they need to wake up periodically and check a flag to see if they should shut down gracefully. Optionally, you could simply turn the worker threads into background threads by setting the IsBackground property inside the Shutdown method. However, in that case, the worker threads may be shut down before they're finished processing their work. Depending on your situation, that may or may not be favorable. Notice that I chose to use the Interlocked methods to manage the stop flag used to indicate that the worker threads should exit.

■Note Another useful technique for telling threads to shut down is to create a special type of work item that tells a thread to shut down. The trick is that you need to make sure you push as many of these special work items onto the queue as there are threads in the pool.

Locking Objects

The .NET Framework offers several high-level locking objects that you can use to synchronize access to data from multiple threads. I dedicated the previous section entirely to one type of lock: the Monitor. However, the Monitor class doesn't implement a kernel lock object; rather, it provides access to the sync lock of every .NET object instance. Previously in this chapter, I also covered the primitive Interlocked class methods that you can use to implement spin locks. One reason spin locks are considered so primitive is that they are not reentrant and thus don't allow you to acquire the same lock multiple times. Other higher-level locking objects typically do allow that, as long as you match the number of lock operations with release operations. In this section, I want to cover some useful locking objects that the .NET Framework provides.

No matter what type of locking object you use, you should always strive to write code that keeps the lock for the least time possible. For example, if you acquire a lock to access some data within a method that could take quite a bit of time to process that data, acquire the lock only long enough to make a copy of the data on the local stack, and then release the lock as soon as possible. By using this technique, you will ensure that other threads in your system don't block for inordinate amounts of time to access the same data.

ReaderWriterLock

When synchronizing access to shared data between threads, you'll often find yourself in a position where you have several threads reading, or consuming, the data, while only one thread writes, or produces, the data. Obviously, all threads must acquire a lock before they touch the data to prevent the race condition in which one thread writes to the data while another is in the middle of reading it, thus potentially producing garbage for the reader. However, it sure seems inefficient for multiple threads that are merely going to read the data rather than modify it to be locked out from each other. There is no reason why they should not be able to all read the data concurrently without having to worry about stepping on each other's toes.

The ReaderWriterLock elegantly avoids this inefficiency. In a nutshell, it allows multiple readers to access the data concurrently, but as soon as one thread needs to write the data, everyone except the writer must get their hands off. ReaderWriterLock manages this feat by using two internal queues. One queue is for waiting readers, and the other is for waiting writers. Figure 12-2 shows a high-level block diagram of what the inside of a ReaderWriterLock looks like. In this scenario, four threads are running in the system, and currently, none of the threads are attempting to access the data in the lock.

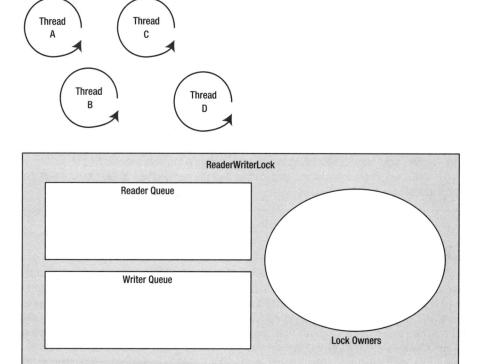

Figure 12-2. *Unutilized ReaderWriterLock*

To access the data, a reader calls AcquireReaderLock. Given the state of the lock shown in Figure 12-2, the reader will be placed immediately into the Lock Owners category. Notice the use of plural here, since multiple read lock owners can exist. Things get interesting as soon as one of the threads attempts to acquire the write lock by calling AcquireWriterLock. In this case, the writer is placed into the writer queue because readers currently own the lock, as shown in Figure 12-3.

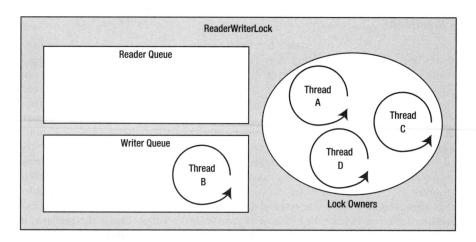

Figure 12-3. *The writer thread is waiting for ReaderWriterLock*

As soon as all of the readers release their lock via a call to ReleaseReaderLock, the writer—in this case, Thread B—is allowed to enter the Lock Owners region. But, what happens if Thread A releases its reader lock and then attempts to reacquire the reader lock before the writer has had a chance to acquire the lock? If Thread A were allowed to reacquire the lock, then any thread waiting in the writer queue could potentially be starved of any time with the lock. In order to avoid this, any thread that attempts to require the read lock while a writer is in the queue is placed into the reader queue, as shown in Figure 12-4.

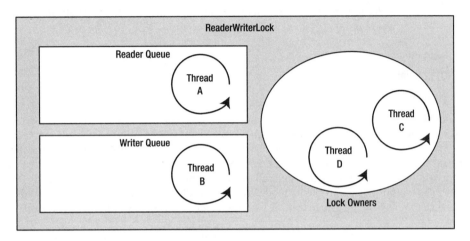

Figure 12-4. *Reader attempting to reacquire lock*

Naturally, this scheme gives preference to the writer queue. That makes sense given the fact that you'd want any readers to get the most up-to-date information. Of course, had the thread that needs the writer lock called AcquireWriterLock while the ReaderWriterLock was in the state shown in Figure 12-2, it would have been placed immediately into the Lock Owners category without having to go through the writer queue.

The ReaderWriterLock is reentrant. Therefore, a thread can call any one of the lock-acquisition methods multiple times, as long as it calls the matching release method the same number of times. Each time the lock is reacquired, an internal lock count is incremented. It should seem obvious that a single thread cannot own both the reader and the writer lock at the same time, nor can it wait in both queues in the ReaderWriterLock. It is possible, however, for a thread to upgrade or downgrade the type of lock it owns. For example, if a thread currently owns a reader lock and calls UpgradeToWriterLock, its reader lock is released no matter what the lock count is, and then it is placed into the writer queue. The UpgradeToWriterLock returns an object of type LockCookie. You should hold on to this object and pass it to DowngradeFromWriterLock when you're done with the write operation. The ReaderWriterLock uses the cookie to restore the reader lock count on the object. Even though you can increase the writer lock count once you've acquired it via UpgradeToWriterLock, your call to DowngradeFromWriterLock will release the writer lock no matter what the write lock count is. Therefore, it's best that you avoid relying on the writer lock count within an upgraded writer lock.

As with just about every other synchronization object in the .NET Framework, you can provide a timeout with almost every lock acquisition method. This timeout is given in milliseconds. However, instead of the methods returning a Boolean to indicate whether the lock was acquired successfully, these methods throw an exception of type ApplicationException if the timeout expires. So, if you pass in any timeout value other than Timeout.Infinite to one of these functions, be sure to make the call inside a try block to catch the potential exception.

ReaderWriterLockSlim

.NET 3.5 introduces a new style of reader/writer lock called ReaderWriterLockSlim. It brings a few enhancements to the table, including better deadlock protection, better efficiency, and disposability. It also does not support recursion by default, which adds to its efficiency. If you need recursion, ReaderWriterLockSlim provides an overloaded constructor that accepts a value from the LockRecursionPolicy enumeration. Microsoft recommends using ReaderWriterLockSlim rather than ReaderWriterLock for any new development.

With respect to ReaderWriterLockSlim, there are four states that the thread can be in:

- Unheld
- Read mode
- Upgradeable mode
- Write mode

Unheld means that the thread is not attempting to read or write to the resource at all. If a thread is in read mode, it has read access to the resource after successfully calling the EnterReadLock method. Likewise, if a thread is in write mode, it has write access to the thread after successfully calling EnterWriteLock. Just as with ReaderWriterLock, only one thread can be in write mode at a time and while any thread is in write mode, all threads are blocked from entering read mode. Naturally, a thread attempting to enter write mode is blocked while any threads still remain in read mode. Once they all exit, the thread waiting for write mode is released. So what is upgradeable mode?

Upgradeable mode is useful if you have a thread that needs read access to the resource but may also from time to time need write access to the resource. Without upgradeable mode, the thread would need to exit read mode and then attempt to enter write mode sequentially. During the time when it is in the unheld mode, another thread could enter read mode, thus stalling the thread attempting to gain the write lock. Only one thread at a time may be in upgradeable mode, and it enters upgradeable mode via a call to EnterUpgradeableReadLock. Upgradeable threads may enter read mode or write mode recursively, even for ReaderWriterLockSlim instances that were created with recursion turned off. In essence, upgradeable mode is a more powerful form of read mode that allows greater efficiency when entering write mode. If a thread attempts to enter upgradeable mode and another thread is in write mode or threads are in a queue to enter write mode, the thread calling EnterUpgradeableReadLock will block until the other thread has exited write mode and the queued threads have entered and exited write mode. This is identical behavior to threads attempting to enter read mode.

ReaderWriterLockSlim may throw a LockRecursionException in certain circumstances. Since ReaderWriterLockSlim instances don't support recursion by default, attempting to call EnterReadLock, EnterWriteLock, or EnterUpgradeableReadLock multiple times from the same thread will result in one of these exceptions. Additionally, whether the instance supports recursion or not, a thread that is already in upgradeable mode and attempts to call EnterReadLock or a thread that is in write mode and attempts to call EnterReadLock could deadlock the system, so a LockRecursionException is thrown in those cases too.

If you're familiar with the Monitor class, you may recognize the idiom represented in the method names of ReaderWriterLockSlim. Each time a thread enters a state, it must call one of the Enter...methods, and each time it leaves that state, it must call one of the corresponding Exit... methods. Additionally, just like Monitor, ReaderWriterLockSlim provides methods that allow you to try to enter the lock without potentially blocking forever with methods such as TryEnterReadLock, TryEnterUpgradeableReadLock, and TryEnterWriteLock. Each of the Try... methods allows you to pass in a timeout value indicating how long you are willing to wait.

The general guideline when using `Monitor` is not to use `Monitor` directly, but rather indirectly through the C# `lock` keyword. That's so that you don't have to worry about forgetting to call `Monitor.Exit` and you don't have to type out a `finally` block to ensure that `Monitor.Exit` is called under all circumstances. Unfortunately, there is no equivalent mechanism available to make it easier to enter and exit locks using `ReaderWriterLockSlim`. Always be careful to call the `Exit...` method when you are finished with a lock, and call it from within a `finally` block so that it gets called even in the face of exceptional conditions.

Mutex

The `Mutex` object is a heavier type of lock that you can use to implement mutually exclusive access to a resource. The .NET Framework supports two types of `Mutex` implementations. If it's created without a name, you get what's called a local mutex. But if you create it with a name, the `Mutex` is usable across multiple processes and implemented using a Win32 kernel object, which is one of the heaviest types of lock objects. By that, I mean that it is the slowest and carries the most overhead when used to guard a protected resource from multiple threads. Other lock types, such as the `ReaderWriterLock` and the `Monitor` class, are strictly for use within the confines of a single process. Therefore, for efficiency, you should only use a `Mutex` object when you really need to synchronize execution or access to some resource across multiple processes.

As with other high-level synchronization objects, the `Mutex` is reentrant. When your thread needs to acquire the exclusive lock, you call the `WaitOne` method. As usual, you can pass in a time-out value expressed in milliseconds when waiting for the `Mutex` object. The method returns a `Boolean` that will be `true` if the wait is successful, or `false` if the timeout expired. A thread can call the `WaitOne` method as many times as it wants, as long as it matches the calls with the same amount of `ReleaseMutex` calls.

Since you can use `Mutex` objects across multiple processes, each process needs a way to identify the `Mutex`. Therefore, you can supply an optional name when you create a `Mutex` instance. Providing a name is the easiest way for another process to identify and open the mutex. Since all `Mutex` names exist in the global namespace of the entire operating system, it is important to give the mutex a sufficiently unique name so that it won't collide with `Mutex` names created by other applications. I recommend using a name that is based on the string form of a GUID generated by `GUIDGEN.exe`.

■Note I mentioned that the names of kernel objects are global to the entire machine. That statement is not entirely true if you consider Windows fast user switching and Terminal Services. In those cases, the namespace that contains the name of these kernel objects is instanced for each logged-in user. For times when you really do want your name to exist in the global namespace, you can prefix the name with the special string "`\Global`". For more information, reference *Microsoft Windows Internals, Fourth Edition: Microsoft Windows Server 2003, Windows XP, and Windows 2000* by Mark E. Russinovich and David A. Solomon (Redmond, WA: Microsoft Press, 2004).

If everything about the `Mutex` object sounds strikingly familiar to those of you who are native Win32 developers, that's because the underlying mechanism is, in fact, the Win32 `Mutex` object. In fact, you can get your hands on the actual OS handle via the `SafeWaitHandle` property inherited from the `WaitHandle` base class. I have more to say about the `WaitHandle` class in the "Win32 Synchronization Objects and WaitHandle" section, where I discuss its pros and cons. It's important to note that since you implement the `Mutex` using a kernel mutex, you incur a transition to kernel mode any time you manipulate or wait upon the `Mutex`. Such transitions are extremely slow and should be minimized if you're running time-critical code.

■**Tip** Avoid using kernel mode objects for synchronization between threads in the same process if at all possible. Prefer more lightweight mechanisms, such as the Monitor class or the Interlocked class. When effectively synchronizing threads between multiple processes, you have no choice but to use kernel objects. On my current test machine, a simple test showed that using the Mutex took more than 44 times longer than the Interlocked class and 34 times longer than the Monitor class.

Semaphore

The .NET Framework supports semaphores via the System.Threading.Semaphore class. They are used to allow a countable number of threads to acquire a resource simultaneously. Each time a thread enters the semaphore via WaitOne or any of the other Wait...methods, the semaphore count is decremented. When an owning thread calls Release, the count is incremented. If a thread attempts to enter the semaphore when the count is zero, it will block until another thread calls Release. When a thread calls Release, the count is incremented.

Just as with Mutex, when you create a semaphore, you may or may not provide a name by which other processes may identify it. If you create it without a name, you end up with a local semaphore that is only useful within the same process. Either way, the underlying implementation uses a Win32 semaphore kernel object. Therefore, it is a very heavy synchronization object that is slow and inefficient. You should prefer local semaphores over named semaphore unless you need to synchronize access across multiple processes for security reasons.

Note that a thread can enter a semaphore recursively. However, it must call Release the appropriate number of times to restore the availability count on the semaphore. The task of matching the Wait...method calls and subsequent calls to Release is entirely up to you. There is nothing in place to keep you from calling Release too many times. If you do, then when another thread later calls Release, it could attempt to push the count above the allowable limit, at which point it will throw a SemaphoreFullException. These bugs are very difficult to find because the point of failure is disjoint from the point of error.

Events

In the .NET Framework, you can use two types to signal events: ManualResetEvent and AutoResetEvent. As with the Mutex object, these event objects map directly to Win32 event objects. If you're familiar with using Win32 events, you'll feel right at home with the .NET event objects. Similar to Mutex objects, working with event objects incurs a slow transition to kernel mode. Both event types become signaled when someone calls the Set method on an event instance. At that point, a thread waiting on the event will be released. Threads wait for an event by calling the inherited WaitHandle.WaitOne method, which is the same method you call to wait on a Mutex to become signaled.

I was careful in stating that a waiting thread is released when the event becomes signaled. It's possible that multiple threads could be released when an event becomes signaled. That, in fact, is the difference between ManualResetEvent and AutoResetEvent. When a ManualResetEvent becomes signaled, all threads waiting on it are released. It stays signaled until someone calls its Reset method. If any thread calls WaitOne while the ManualResetEvent is already signaled, then the wait is immediately completed successfully. On the other hand, AutoResetEvent objects only release one waiting thread and then immediately reset to the unsignaled set automatically. You can imagine that all threads waiting on the AutoResetEvent are waiting in a queue, where only the first thread in the queue is released when the event becomes signaled. However, even though it's useful to assume that the waiting threads are in a queue, you cannot make any assumptions about which waiting thread will be released first. AutoResetEvents are also known as *sync events* based on this behavior.

Using the AutoResetEvent type, you could implement a crude thread pool where several threads wait on an AutoResetEvent signal to be told that some piece of work is available. When a new piece of work is added to the work queue, the event is signaled to turn one of the waiting threads loose. Implementing a thread pool this way is not efficient and comes with its problems. For example, things become tricky to handle when all threads are busy and work items are pushed into the queue, especially if only one thread is allowed to complete one work item before going back to the waiting queue. If all threads are busy and, say, five work items are queued in the meantime, the event will be signaled but no threads will be waiting. The first thread back into the waiting queue will be released once it calls WaitOne, but the others will not, even though four more work items exist in the queue. One solution to this problem is not to allow work items to be queued while all of the threads are busy. That's not really a solution, because it defers some of the synchronization logic to the thread attempting to queue the work item by forcing it to do something appropriate in reaction to a failed attempt to queue a work item. In reality, creating an efficient thread pool is tricky business, to say the least. Therefore, I recommend you utilize the ThreadPool class before attempting such a feat. I cover the ThreadPool class in detail in the "Using ThreadPool" section.

Since .NET event objects are based on Win32 event objects, you can use them to synchronize execution between multiple processes. Along with the Mutex, they are also more inefficient than an alternative, such as the Monitor class, because of the kernel mode transition involved. However, the creators of ManualResetEvent and AutoResetEvent did not expose the ability to name the event objects in their constructors, as they do for the Mutex object. Therefore, if you need to create a named event, you should use the EventWaitHandle class instead.

Win32 Synchronization Objects and WaitHandle

In the previous two sections, I covered the Mutex, ManualResetEvent, and AutoResetEvent objects. Each one of these types is derived from WaitHandle, a general mechanism that you can use in the .NET Framework to manage any type of Win32 synchronization object that you can wait upon. That includes more than just events and mutexes. No matter how you obtain the Win32 object handle, you can use a WaitHandle object to manage it. I prefer to use the word *manage* rather than *encapsulate*, because the WaitHandle class doesn't do a great job of encapsulation, nor was it meant to. It's simply meant as a wrapper to help you avoid a lot of direct calls to Win32 via the P/Invoke layer when dealing with OS handles.

Note Take some time to understand when and how to use WaitHandle, because many APIs have yet to be mapped into the .NET Framework, and many of them may never be.

I've already discussed the WaitOne method used to wait for an object to become signaled. However, the WaitHandle class has two handy static methods that you can use to wait on multiple objects. The first is WaitHandle.WaitAny. You pass it an array of WaitHandle objects, and when any one of the objects becomes signaled, the WaitAny method returns an integer indexing into the array to the object that became signaled. The other method is WaitHandle.WaitAll, which, as you can imagine, won't return until all of the objects becomes signaled. Both of these methods have defined overloads that accept a timeout value. In the case of a call to WaitAny that times out, the return value will be equal to the WaitHandle.WaitTimeout constant. In the case of a call to WaitAll, a Boolean is returned, which is either true to indicate that all of the objects became signaled, or false to indicate that the wait timed out.

Prior to the existence of the EventWaitHandle class, in order to get a named event, you had to create the underlying Win2 object and then wrap it with a WaitHandle, as I've done in the following example:

```
using System;
using System.Threading;
using System.Runtime.InteropServices;
using System.ComponentModel;
using Microsoft.Win32.SafeHandles;

public class NamedEventCreator
{
    [DllImport( "KERNEL32.DLL", EntryPoint="CreateEventW",
                SetLastError=true )]
    private static extern SafeWaitHandle CreateEvent(
                                IntPtr lpEventAttributes,
                                bool   bManualReset,
                                bool   bInitialState,
                                string lpName );

    public const int INVALID_HANDLE_VALUE = -1;

    public static AutoResetEvent CreateAutoResetEvent(
                                    bool initialState,
                                    string name ) {
        // Create named event.
        SafeWaitHandle rawEvent = CreateEvent( IntPtr.Zero,
                                    false,
                                    false,
                                    name );
        if( rawEvent.IsInvalid ) {
            throw new Win32Exception(
                            Marshal.GetLastWin32Error() );
        }

        // Create a managed event type based on this handle.
        AutoResetEvent autoEvent = new AutoResetEvent( false );

        // Must clean up handle currently in autoEvent
        // before swapping it with the named one.
        autoEvent.SafeWaitHandle = rawEvent;

        return autoEvent;
    }
}
```

Here I've used the P/Invoke layer to call down into the Win32 CreateEventW function to create a named event. Several things are worth noting in this example. For instance, I've completely punted on the handle security, just as the rest of the .NET Framework standard library classes tend to do. Therefore, the first parameter to CreateEvent is IntPtr.Zero, which is the best way to pass a NULL pointer to the Win32 error. Notice that you detect the success or failure of the event creation by testing the IsInvalid property on the SafeWaitHandle. When you detect this value, you throw a Win32Exception type. You then create a new AutoResetEvent to wrap the raw handle just created. WaitHandle exposes a property named SafeWaitHandle, whereby you can modify the underlying Win32 handle of any WaitHandle derived type.

■**Note** You may have noticed the legacy Handle property in the documentation. You should avoid this property, since reassigning it with a new kernel handle won't close the previous handle, thus resulting in a resource leak unless you close it yourself. You should use SafeHandle derived types instead. The SafeHandle type also uses constrained execution regions to guard against resource leaks in the event of an asynchronous exception such as ThreadAbortException. You can read more about constrained execution regions in Chapter 7.

In the previous example, you can see that I declared the CreateEvent method to return a SafeWaitHandle. Although it's not obvious from the documentation of SafeWaitHandle, it has a private default constructor that the P/Invoke layer is capable of using to create and initialize an instance of this class.

Be sure to check out the rest of the SafeHandle derived types in the Microsoft.Win32.SafeHandles namespace. Specifically, the .NET 2.0 Framework introduced SafeHandleMinusOneIsInvalid and SafeHandleZeroOrMinusOneIsInvalid for convenience when defining your own Win32-based SafeWaitHandle derivatives.

Be aware that the WaitHandle type implements the IDisposable interface. Therefore, you want to make judicious use of the using keyword in your code whenever using WaitHandle instances or instances of any of the classes that derive from it, such as Mutex, AutoResetEvent, and ManualResetEvent.

One last thing that you need to be aware of when using WaitHandle objects and those objects that derive from the type is that you cannot abort or interrupt managed threads in a timely manner when they're blocked via a method to WaitHandle. Since the actual OS thread that is running under the managed thread is blocked inside the OS—thus outside of the managed execution environment—it can only be aborted or interrupted as soon as it reenters the managed environment. Therefore, if you call Abort or Interrupt on one of those threads, the operation will be pended until the thread completes the wait at the OS level. You want to be cognizant of this when you block using a WaitHandle object in managed threads.

Using ThreadPool

A thread pool is ideal in a system where small units of work are performed regularly in an asynchronous manner. A good example is a web server or any other kind of server listening for requests on a port. When a request comes in, a new thread is given the request and processes it. The server achieves a high level of concurrency and optimal utilization by servicing these requests in multiple threads. Typically, the slowest operation on a computer is an I/O operation. Storage devices, such as hard drives, are very slow in comparison to the processor and its ability to access memory. Therefore, to make optimal use of the system, you want to begin other work items while it's waiting on an I/O operation to complete in another thread. Creating a thread pool to manage such a system is an amazing task fraught with many details and pitfalls. However, the .NET environment exposes a pre-built, ready-to-use thread pool via the ThreadPool class.

The ThreadPool class is similar to the Monitor and Interlocked classes in the sense that you cannot actually create instances of the ThreadPool class. Instead, you use the static methods of the ThreadPool class to manage the thread pool that each process gets by default in the CLR. In fact, you don't even have to worry about creating the thread pool. It gets created when it is first used. If you have used thread pools in the Win32 world, whether it be via the system thread pool that was introduced in Windows 2000 or via I/O completion ports, you'll notice that the .NET thread pool is the same beast with a managed interface placed on top of it.

To queue an item to the thread pool, you simply call ThreadPool.QueueUserWorkItem, passing it an instance of the WaitCallback delegate. The thread pool gets created the first time your process calls this function. The callback method that is called through the WaitCallback delegate accepts a reference to System.Object and has a return type of void. The object reference is an optional context object that the caller can supply to an overload of QueueUserWorkItem. If you don't provide a context, the context reference will be null. Once the work item is queued, a thread in the thread pool will execute the callback as soon as it becomes available. Once a work item is queued, it cannot be removed from the queue except by a thread that will complete the work item. So if you need to cancel a work item, you must craft a way to let your callback know that it should do nothing once it gets called.

The thread pool is tuned to keep the machine processing work items in the most efficient way possible. It uses an algorithm based upon how many CPUs are available in the system to determine how many threads to create in the pool. However, even once it computes how many threads to create, the thread pool may, at times, contain more threads than originally calculated. For example, suppose the algorithm decides that the thread pool should contain four threads. Then, suppose the server receives four requests that access a backend database that takes some time. If a fifth request comes in during this time, no threads will be available to dispatch the work item. What's worse, the four busy threads are just sitting around waiting for the I/O to complete. In order to keep the system running at peak performance, the thread pool will actually create another thread when it knows all of the others are blocking. After the work items have all been completed and the system is in a steady state again, the thread pool will then kill off any extra threads created like this. Even though you cannot easily control how many threads are in a thread pool, you can easily control the minimum number of threads that are idle in the pool waiting for work via calls to GetMinThreads and SetMinThreads.

I urge you to read the details of the System.Threading.ThreadPool static methods in the MSDN documentation if you plan to deal directly with the thread pool. In reality, it's rare that you'll ever need to insert work items directly into the thread pool. There is another, more elegant, entry point into the thread pool via delegates and asynchronous procedure calls, which I cover in the next section.

Asynchronous Method Calls

Although you can manage the work items put into the thread pool directly via the ThreadPool class, a more popular way to employ the thread pool is via asynchronous delegate calls. When you declare a delegate, the CLR defines a class for you that derives from System.MulticastDelegate. One of the methods defined is the Invoke method, which takes exactly the same function signature as the delegate definition. The C# language, of course, offers a syntactical shortcut to calling the Invoke method. In fact, you cannot explicitly call the Invoke method in C#. But along with Invoke, the CLR also defines two methods, BeginInvoke and EndInvoke, that are at the heart of the asynchronous processing pattern used throughout the CLR. This pattern is similar to the IOU pattern introduced earlier in the chapter.

The basic idea is probably evident from the names of the methods. When you call the BeginInvoke method on the delegate, the operation is pended to be completed in another thread. When you call the EndInvoke method, the results of the operation are given back to you. If the operation has not completed at the time you call EndInvoke, the calling thread blocks until the operation is complete. Let's look at a short example that shows the general pattern in use. Suppose you have a method that computes your taxes for the year, and you want to call it asynchronously because it could take a reasonably long amount of time to do:

```
using System;
using System.Threading;

public class EntryPoint
{
    // Declare the delegate for the async call.
    private delegate Decimal ComputeTaxesDelegate( int year );
```

```csharp
// The method that computes the taxes.
private static Decimal ComputeTaxes( int year ) {
    Console.WriteLine( "Computing taxes in thread {0}",
                       Thread.CurrentThread.GetHashCode() );

    // Here's where the long calculation happens.
    Thread.Sleep( 6000 );

    // You owe the man.
    return 4356.98M;
}

static void Main() {
    // Let's make the asynchronous call by creating
    // the delegate and calling it.
    ComputeTaxesDelegate work =
        new ComputeTaxesDelegate( EntryPoint.ComputeTaxes );
    IAsyncResult pendingOp = work.BeginInvoke( 2004,
                                               null,
                                               null );

    // Do some other useful work.
    Thread.Sleep( 3000 );

    // Finish the async call.
    Console.WriteLine( "Waiting for operation to complete." );
    Decimal result = work.EndInvoke( pendingOp );

    Console.WriteLine( "Taxes owed: {0}", result );
}
}
```

The first thing you will notice with the pattern is that the BeginInvoke method's signature does not match that of the Invoke method. That's because you need some way to identify the particular work item that you just pended with the call to BeginInvoke. Therefore, BeginInvoke returns a reference to an object that implements the IAsyncResult interface. This object is like a cookie that you can hold on to so that you can identify the work item in progress. Through the methods on the IAsyncResult interface, you can check on the status of the operation, such as whether it is completed. I'll discuss this interface in more detail in a bit, along with the extra two parameters added onto the end of the BeginInvoke method declaration for which I'm passing null. When the thread that requested the operation is finally ready for the result, it calls EndInvoke on the delegate. However, since the method must have a way to identify which asynchronous operation to get the results for, you must pass in the object that you got back from the BeginInvoke method. In this example, you'll notice the call to EndInvoke blocking for some time as the operation completes.

Note If an exception is generated while the delegate's target code is running asynchronously in the thread pool, the exception is rethrown when the initiating thread makes a call to EndInvoke.

Part of the beauty of the IOU asynchronous pattern that delegates implement is that the called code doesn't even need to be aware of the fact that it's getting called asynchronously. Of course, it's rarely practical to call a method asynchronously when it was never designed to be, if it touches data in the system that other methods touch without using any synchronization mechanisms. Nonetheless, the headache of creating an asynchronous calling infrastructure around the method has been mitigated by the delegate generated by the CLR, along with the per-process thread pool. Moreover, the initiator of the asynchronous action doesn't even need to be aware of how the asynchronous behavior is implemented.

Now let's look a little closer at the IAsyncResult interface for the object returned from the BeginInvoke method. The interface declaration looks like the following:

```
public interface IAsyncResult
{
    Object AsyncState { get; }
    WaitHandle AsyncWaitHandle { get; }
    bool CompletedSynchronously { get; }
    bool IsCompleted { get; }
}
```

In the previous example, I chose to wait for the computation to finish by calling EndInvoke. I could have instead waited on the WaitHandle returned by the IAsyncResult.AsyncWaitHandle property before calling EndInvoke. The end result would have been the same in this case. However, the fact that the IAsyncResult interface exposes the WaitHandle allows you to have multiple threads in the system wait for this one action to complete if they needed to.

Two other properties allow you to query whether the operation has completed. The IsCompleted property simply returns a Boolean representing the fact. You could construct a polling loop that checks this flag repeatedly. However, that would be much more inefficient than just waiting on the WaitHandle. Nonetheless, it is there if you need it. Another Boolean property is CompletedSynchronously. The asynchronous processing pattern in the .NET Framework provides for the option that the call to BeginInvoke could actually choose to process the work synchronously rather than asynchronously. The CompletedSynchronously property allows you to determine if this happened. As it is currently implemented, the CLR will never do such a thing when delegates are called asynchronously, but this could change at any time. However, since it is recommended that you apply this same asynchronous pattern whenever you design a type that can be called asynchronously, the capability was built into the pattern. For example, suppose you have a class where a method to process generalized operations synchronously is supported. If one of those operations simply returns the version number of the class, then you know that operation can be done quickly, and you may choose to perform it synchronously.

Finally, the AsyncState property of IAsyncResult allows you to attach any type of specific context data to an asynchronous call. This is the last of the extra two parameters added at the end of the BeginInvoke signature. In my previous example, I passed in null because I didn't need to use it. Although I chose to harvest the result of the operation via a call to EndInvoke, I could have chosen to be notified via a callback. Consider the following modifications to the previous example:

```
using System;
using System.Threading;

public class EntryPoint
{
    // Declare the delegate for the async call.
    private delegate Decimal ComputeTaxesDelegate( int year );

    // The method that computes the taxes.
    private static Decimal ComputeTaxes( int year ) {
        Console.WriteLine( "Computing taxes in thread {0}",
                          Thread.CurrentThread.GetHashCode() );

        // Here's where the long calculation happens.
        Thread.Sleep( 6000 );
```

```
        // You owe the man.
        return 4356.98M;
    }

    private static void TaxesComputed( IAsyncResult ar ) {
        // Let's get the results now.
        ComputeTaxesDelegate work =
            (ComputeTaxesDelegate) ar.AsyncState;

        Decimal result = work.EndInvoke( ar );
        Console.WriteLine( "Taxes owed: {0}", result );
    }

    static void Main() {
        // Let's make the asynchronous call by creating
        // the delegate and calling it.
        ComputeTaxesDelegate work =
            new ComputeTaxesDelegate( EntryPoint.ComputeTaxes );
        work.BeginInvoke( 2004,
                          new AsyncCallback(
                                  EntryPoint.TaxesComputed),
                          work );

        // Do some other useful work.
        Thread.Sleep( 3000 );

        Console.WriteLine( "Waiting for operation to complete." );
        Thread.Sleep( 4000 );
    }
}
```

Now, instead of calling EndInvoke from the thread that called BeginInvoke, I'm requesting that the thread pool call the TaxesComputed method via an instance of the AsyncCallback delegate that I passed in as the second-to-last parameter of BeingInvoke. Using a callback to process the result completes the asynchronous processing pattern by allowing the thread that started the operation to continue to work without ever having to explicitly wait on the worker thread. Notice that the TaxesComputed callback method must still call EndInvoke to harvest the results of the asynchronous call. In order to do that, though, it must have an instance of the delegate. That's where the IAsyncResult.AsyncState context object comes in handy. In my example, I initialize it to point to the delegate by passing the delegate as the last parameter to BeginInvoke. The main thread that calls BeginInvoke has no need for the object returned by the call, since it never actively polls the state of the operation, nor does it wait explicitly for the operation to complete. The added sleep at the end of the Main method is there for the sake of the example. Remember, all threads in the thread pool run as background threads. Therefore, if you don't wait at this point, the process would exit long before the operation completes. If you need asynchronous work to occur in a foreground thread, it is best to create a new class that implements the asynchronous pattern of BeingInvoke/EndInvoke and use a foreground thread to do the work. Never change the background status of a thread in the thread pool via the IsBackground property on the current thread. Even if you try, you'll find that it has no effect.

■**Note** It's important to realize that when your asynchronous code is executing and when the callback is executing, you are running in an arbitrary thread context. You cannot make any assumptions about which thread is running your code. In many respects, this technique is similar to driver development on Windows platforms.

Using a callback to handle the completion of a work item is very handy when creating a server process that will handle incoming requests. For example, suppose you have a process that listens on a specific TCP/IP port for an incoming request. When it receives one, it replies with the requested information. To achieve high utilization, you definitely want to pend these operations asynchronously. Consider the following example that listens on port 1234 and when it receives anything at all, it simply replies with "Hello World!":

```
using System;
using System.Text;
using System.Threading;
using System.Net;
using System.Net.Sockets;

public class EntryPoint {
    private const int CONNECT_QUEUE_LENGTH = 4;
    private const int LISTEN_PORT = 1234;

    static void ListenForRequests() {
        Socket listenSock =
            new Socket( AddressFamily.InterNetwork,
                        SocketType.Stream,
                        ProtocolType.Tcp );
        listenSock.Bind( new IPEndPoint(IPAddress.Any,
                                        LISTEN_PORT) );
        listenSock.Listen( CONNECT_QUEUE_LENGTH );

        while( true ) {
            using( Socket newConnection = listenSock.Accept() ) {
                // Send the data.
                byte[] msg =
                    Encoding.UTF8.GetBytes( "Hello World!" );
                newConnection.Send( msg, SocketFlags.None );
            }
        }
    }

    static void Main() {
        // Start the listening thread.
        Thread listener = new Thread(
                        new ThreadStart(
                            EntryPoint.ListenForRequests) );
        listener.IsBackground = true;
        listener.Start();

        Console.WriteLine( "Press <enter> to quit" );
        Console.ReadLine();
    }
}
```

This example creates an extra thread that simply loops around listening for incoming connections and servicing them as soon as they come in. The problems with this approach are many. First, only one thread handles the incoming connections. If the connections are flying in at a rapid rate, it will quickly become overwhelmed. Think about a web server that could easily see thousands of requests per second. As it turns out, the Socket class implements the asynchronous calling pattern of the .NET Framework. Using the pattern, you can make the server a little bit better by servicing the incoming requests using the thread pool, as follows:

```
using System;
using System.Text;
using System.Threading;
using System.Net;
using System.Net.Sockets;

public class EntryPoint {
    private const int CONNECT_QUEUE_LENGTH = 4;
    private const int LISTEN_PORT = 1234;

    static void ListenForRequests() {
        Socket listenSock =
            new Socket( AddressFamily.InterNetwork,
                        SocketType.Stream,
                        ProtocolType.Tcp );
        listenSock.Bind( new IPEndPoint(IPAddress.Any,
                                        LISTEN_PORT) );
        listenSock.Listen( CONNECT_QUEUE_LENGTH );

        while( true ) {
            Socket newConnection = listenSock.Accept();
            byte[] msg = Encoding.UTF8.GetBytes( "Hello World!" );
            newConnection.BeginSend( msg,
                                     0, msg.Length,
                                     SocketFlags.None,
                                     null, null );
        }
    }

    static void Main() {
        // Start the listening thread.
        Thread listener = new Thread(
                            new ThreadStart(
                                EntryPoint.ListenForRequests) );
        listener.IsBackground = true;
        listener.Start();

        Console.WriteLine( "Press <enter> to quit" );
        Console.ReadLine();
    }
}
```

The server is becoming a little more efficient, since it is now sending the data to the incoming connection from a thread in the thread pool. This code also demonstrates a fire-and-forget strategy when using the asynchronous pattern. The caller is not interested in the return object that implements IAsyncResult, nor is it interested in setting a callback method to get called when the work completes. This fire-and-forget call is a valiant attempt to make the server more efficient. However, the result is less than satisfactory, since the using statement from the previous incarnation of the server is gone. The Socket is not closed in a timely manner, and the remote connections are held open until the GC gets around to finalizing the Socket objects. Therefore, the asynchronous call needs to include a callback in order to close the connection. It wouldn't make sense for the listening thread to wait on the EndSend method, as that would put you back in the same inefficiency boat you were in before.

Note When you get an object that implements `IAsyncResult` back from starting an asynchronous operation, that object must implement the `IAsyncResult.AsyncWaitHandle` property to allow users to obtain a handle they can wait on. In the case of `Socket`, an instance of `OverlappedAsyncResult` is returned. That class ultimately derives from `System.Net.LazyAsyncResult`. It doesn't actually create the event to wait on until someone accesses it via the `IAsyncResult.AsyncWaitHandle` property. This lazy creation spares the burden of creating a lock object that goes unused most of the time. Also, it is the responsibility of the `OverlappedAsyncResult` object to close the OS handle when it is finished with it.

However, before getting to the callback, consider the listening thread for a moment. All it does is spin around listening for incoming requests. Wouldn't it be more efficient if the server were to use the thread pool to handle the listening too? Of course it would! So, now, let me present the new and improved "Hello World!" server that makes full use of the process thread pool:

```csharp
using System;
using System.Text;
using System.Threading;
using System.Net;
using System.Net.Sockets;

public class EntryPoint {
    private const int CONNECT_QUEUE_LENGTH = 4;
    private const int LISTEN_PORT = 1234;
    private const int MAX_CONNECTION_HANDLERS = 4;

    private static void HandleConnection( IAsyncResult ar ) {
        Socket listener = (Socket) ar.AsyncState;

        Socket newConnection = listener.EndAccept( ar );
        byte[] msg = Encoding.UTF8.GetBytes( "Hello World!" );
        newConnection.BeginSend( msg,
                                 0, msg.Length,
                                 SocketFlags.None,
                                 new AsyncCallback(
                                     EntryPoint.CloseConnection),
                                 newConnection );

        // Now queue another accept.
        listener.BeginAccept(
            new AsyncCallback(EntryPoint.HandleConnection),
            listener );
    }

    static void CloseConnection( IAsyncResult ar ) {
        Socket theSocket = (Socket) ar.AsyncState;
        theSocket.Close();
    }

    static void Main() {
        Socket listenSock =
            new Socket( AddressFamily.InterNetwork,
                        SocketType.Stream,
                        ProtocolType.Tcp );
        listenSock.Bind( new IPEndPoint(IPAddress.Any,
                                        LISTEN_PORT) );
```

```
            listenSock.Listen( CONNECT_QUEUE_LENGTH );

            // Pend the connection handlers.
            for( int i = 0; i < MAX_CONNECTION_HANDLERS; ++i ) {
                listenSock.BeginAccept(
                    new AsyncCallback(EntryPoint.HandleConnection),
                    listenSock );
            }

            Console.WriteLine( "Press <enter> to quit" );
            Console.ReadLine();
        }
    }
```

Now, the "Hello World" server is making full use of the process thread pool and can handle incoming client requests with the best concurrency. Incidentally, testing the connection is fairly simple using the built-in Windows Telnet client. Simply run Telnet from a command prompt or from the Start ➤ Run dialog, and at the prompt enter the following command to connect to port 1234 on the local machine while the server process is running in another command window:

```
Microsoft Telnet> open 127.0.0.1 1234
```

Timers

Yet another entry point into the thread pool is via Timer objects in the System.Threading namespace. As the name implies, you can arrange for the thread pool to call a delegate at a specific time as well as at regular intervals. Let's look at an example of how to use a Timer object:

```
using System;
using System.Threading;

public class EntryPoint
{
    private static void TimerProc( object state ) {
        Console.WriteLine( "The current time is {0} on thread {1}",
                           DateTime.Now,
                           Thread.CurrentThread.GetHashCode() );
        Thread.Sleep( 3000 );
    }

    static void Main() {
        Console.WriteLine( "Press <enter> when finished\n\n" );

        Timer myTimer =
            new Timer( new TimerCallback(EntryPoint.TimerProc),
                       null,
                       0,
                       2000 );

        Console.ReadLine();
        myTimer.Dispose();
    }
}
```

When the timer is created, you must give it a delegate to call at the required time. Therefore, I've created a TimerCallback delegate that points back to the static TimerProc method. The second parameter to the Timer constructor is an arbitrary state object that you can pass in. When your timer callback is called, this state object is passed to the timer callback. In my example, I have no need for a state object, so I just pass null. The last two parameters to the constructor define when the callback gets called. The second-to-last parameter indicates when the timer should fire for the first time. In my example, I pass 0, which indicates that it should fire immediately. The last parameter is the period at which the callback should be called. In my example, I've asked for a two-second period. If you don't want the timer to be called periodically, pass Timeout.Infinite as the last parameter. Finally, to shut down the timer, simply call its Dispose method.

In my example, you may wonder why I have the Sleep call inside the TimerProc method. It's there just to illustrate a point, and that is that an arbitrary thread calls the TimerProc. Therefore, any code that executes as a result of your TimerCallback delegate must be thread-safe. In my example, the first thread in the thread pool to call TimerProc sleeps longer than the next timeout, so the thread pool calls the TimerProc method two seconds later on another thread, as you can see in the generated output. You could really cause some strain on the thread pool if you were to notch up the sleep in the TimerProc.

■**Note** If you've ever used the Timer class in the System.Windows.Forms namespace, you must realize that it's a completely different beast than the Timer class in the System.Threading namespace. For one, the Forms.Timer is based upon Win32 Windows messaging—namely, the WM_TIMER message. One handy quality of the Forms.Timer is that its timer callback is always called on the same thread. However, the only way that happens in the first place is if the UI thread that the timer is a part of has an underlying UI message pump. If the pump stalls, so do the Forms.Timer callbacks. So, naturally, the Threading.Timer is more powerful in the sense that it doesn't suffer from this dependency. However, the drawback is that you must code your Threading.Timer callbacks in a thread-safe manner.

Summary

In this chapter, I've covered the intricacies of managed threads in the .NET environment. I covered the various mechanisms in place for managing synchronization between threads, including the Interlocked, Monitor, AutoResetEvent, ManualResetEvent, WaitHandle-based objects, and so on. I then described the IOU pattern and how the .NET Framework uses it extensively to get work done asynchronously. That discussion centered around the CLR's usage of the ThreadPool based upon the Windows thread pool implementation.

Threading always adds complexity to applications. However, when used properly, it can make applications more responsive to user commands and more efficient. Although multithreading development comes with its pitfalls, the .NET Framework and the CLR mitigate many of those risks and provide a model that shields you from the intricacies of the operating system—most of the time. For example, thread pools have always been difficult to implement, even after a common implementation was added to the Windows operating system. Not only does the .NET environment provide a nice buffer between your code and the Windows thread pool intricacies, but it also allows your code to run on other platforms that implement the .NET Framework, such as the Mono runtime running on Linux. If you understand the details of the threading facilities provided by the .NET runtime and are familiar with multithreaded synchronization techniques, as covered in this chapter, then you're well on your way to producing effective multithreaded applications.

In the next chapter, I go in search of a C# canonical form for types. I investigate the checklist of questions you should ask yourself when designing any type using C# for the .NET Framework.

CHAPTER 13

■ ■ ■

In Search of C# Canonical Forms

Many object-oriented languages—C# included—don't offer anything to force developers to create well-designed software. There is no better example of this than when using C++ to implement an OO design. C# is a little more structured than C++; for example, you cannot create free static functions that exist outside the context of a defined type. Still, C# doesn't force you to create software that adheres to well-known practices of good software design.

The C++ community quickly identified some canonical forms useful for designing types to meet a specific purpose. Really and truly, these canonical forms are merely checklists, or recipes, you can use while designing new classes. Before a pilot can clear an airplane to back out of the gate, he must go through a strict checklist. The goal of this chapter is to identify such checklists for creating robust types in the C# world.

When you explore these checklists, you need to consider what sorts of behaviors are required of objects of the new type you're creating. For example, is your new type going to be cloneable? In other words, can it be copied? If instances of your new type are placed in a collection, can they be ordered? What does it mean to compare two references of this object's type for equality? In other words, do you want to know if the two references refer to the same instance? Or do you want to know if two instances referred to have exactly the same state? These are the types of questions you should ask yourself when you create a new type.

■**Note** This chapter is rather long, but it's important to keep so much useful and related information together. Overall, the chapter is sectioned into two partitions. The first partition covers reference types, and the second covers value types. I cover reference types first and at greater length, since some material applies to both reference types and value types. Finally, the chapter concludes with a pair of checklists to go through when designing new types.

Reference Type Canonical Forms

First, let's explore canonical forms for reference types in C#. In C#, objects live on the managed heap and are accessed through value types containing references to them.

Note In C++ terms, you can envision a similar system where all objects are created dynamically using new, and you only reference them through the pointer returned by new. This is essentially what is happening in the CLR, except that the CLR tracks all of these "pointers," or references, and it knows when the objects on the heap have no more references to them and thus, when they can be destroyed.

To be a little more specific, consider this: Over the years, the C++ community has utilized a vast array of idioms that rely upon the stack to help manage resources. If you create your C++ object on the stack, then the compiler will make sure that your object's constructors and destructor get called at the appropriate times, thus giving you a controlled point at which to put your resource cleanup code. The dominant idiom here is called Resource Acquisition Is Initialization (RAII), and it's used extensively in C++ and any other object-oriented language with deterministic destruction of objects. Basically, the idea behind the idiom is that any resource that requires allocation is acquired in a constructor body, and the release of the resource is in the matching destructor. This idiom is so entrenched that in order to write robust, exception-safe, and exception-neutral C++ code, you must use this idiom extensively and contain just about every usage of new and delete inside constructors and destructors. In the C# domain, this idiom is not available so easily, because C# destructors are not deterministic. Therefore, you must approach the problems solved by this idiom in a different way, as discussed throughout this section.

Default to sealed Classes

When you create a new class, I firmly believe you should automatically mark that class sealed, and only remove the sealed keyword if you can think of a bona fide reason why someone would need to derive from your class. Why not go the other way around and make the class unsealed by default and seal it when you know someone should not derive from it? Because it's impossible to predict how someone will attempt to derive from your class if you don't put in specific design measures to support inheritance. I've seen many designs over the years where someone attempted to derive from a class that was never meant to be derived from. For example, in a good design, classes that have no virtual methods are not normally intended to be derived from. The lack of virtual methods most likely indicates that the author of the class didn't consider whether anyone would even want to inherit from the type and probably should have marked the class sealed. If your class is not sealed, and you intend to allow others to inherit from it, be sure to include adequate documentation so the person deriving from your class doesn't shoot himself in the foot.

Note As hard as you may try to create self-explanatory base classes, it's nearly impossible to escape documenting them as long as you have at least one overrideable virtual method in them. Read on for more information why.

Even classes that do have virtual methods and are purposely meant to be derived from can be problematic. For example, if you derive from a class that provides a virtual method DoSomething, and you'd like to extend that method by overriding it, do you call the base class version in your override? If so, do you call it before or after you get your derived work done? Does the ordering matter? Maybe it does if protected fields are declared in the base class.[1] If you don't have really good documentation for the class you're deriving from, you may never know the answers to these questions. In

---

1. In Chapter 4, I discussed encapsulation and its importance in object-oriented design. It's important to note that protected fields break encapsulation.

fact, this is one reason why extension through containment is generally more flexible, and thus more powerful, at design time than extension through inheritance. Extension through containment is dynamic and performed at run time, whereas inheritance-based extension is more restrictive, since it is static and wired up at compile time. And better yet, you can do containment-based extension even if the class you want to extend is marked sealed.

Unless you can come up with a really good reason why your class should serve as a base class, mark your class sealed. Otherwise, be prepared to offer very detailed documentation on how to best derive from your class. I guarantee that you can produce a different design using interface inheritance together with containment rather than implementation (class) inheritance that can do the same job. Since that is the case, there's almost no reason why almost all of the classes you design should not be marked sealed. Don't misunderstand: I'm not saying that all inheritance is bad. On the contrary, it is useful when used properly. Unfortunately, it is greatly misused. A deep hierarchy tree, as opposed to a shallow, flat one, is a common sign that you should rethink the design.

■**Note** When leaf classes that derive from other classes with virtual methods are marked sealed, or when individual override methods are marked sealed, the runtime can turn calls to those methods into nonvirtual calls, since no more derived implementations of those methods can exist. Naturally, this is a performance gain.

Use the Non-Virtual Interface (NVI) Pattern

Many times, when you design a class specifically capable of acting as a base class in a hierarchy, you declare methods that are virtual so that deriving classes can modify the behavior. A first pass at such a base class may look something like the following:

```
using System;

public class Base
{
    public virtual void DoWork() {
        Console.WriteLine( "Base.DoWork()" );
    }
}

public class Derived : Base
{
    public override void DoWork() {
        Console.WriteLine( "Derived.DoWork()" );
    }
}

public class EntryPoint
{
    static void Main() {
        Base b = new Derived();
        b.DoWork();
    }
}
```

Not surprisingly, the output from the example looks like this:

```
Derived.DoWork()
```

However, the design could be subtly more robust. Imagine that you're the writer of Base, and you have deployed Base to millions of users. Many people are happily using Base all over the world when you decide, for some good reason, that you should do some pre- and postprocessing within DoWork. For example, suppose you would like to provide a debug version of Base that tracks how many times the DoWork method is called. As the code was written previously, you cannot do such a thing without forcing breaking changes onto the millions of users who have used your class Base. For example, you could introduce two more methods, named PreDoWork and PostDoWork, and ask kindly that your users reimplement their overrides so that they call these methods at the correct time. Ouch! Now, let's consider a minor modification to the original design that doesn't even change the public interface of Base:

```
using System;

public class Base
{
    public void DoWork() {
        CoreDoWork();
    }

    protected virtual void CoreDoWork() {
        Console.WriteLine( "Base.DoWork()" );
    }
}

public class Derived : Base
{
    protected override void CoreDoWork() {
        Console.WriteLine( "Derived.DoWork()" );
    }
}

public class EntryPoint
{
    static void Main() {
        Base b = new Derived();
        b.DoWork();
    }
}
```

This nifty little pattern is called the Non-Virtual Interface (NVI) pattern, and it does exactly that: It makes the public interface to the base class nonvirtual, but the overrideable behavior is moved into another, protected method, named CoreDoWork. The NVI pattern is similar to the Template Method pattern as described by Erich Gamma, Richard Helm, Ralph Johnson, and John Vlissides in *Design Patterns: Elements of Reusable Object-Oriented Software* (Boston, MA: Addison-Wesley Professional, 1995). .NET Framework libraries use the NVI pattern widely, and it's circulated in library design guidelines at Microsoft for obviously good reasons. In order to add some metering to the DoWork method, you only need to modify Base and the assembly that contains it. Any of the other classes that derive from assembly don't even have to change.

Another technique that is typically used with NVI in the C++ world is that of actually declaring the virtual method private, as in the following code that unfortunately won't compile in C# for reasons I'll explain shortly:

```
// WILL NOT COMPILE!!!!!
using System;

public class Base
```

```
{
    public void DoWork() {
        CoreDoWork();
    }

    // WILL NOT COMPILE!!!!!
    private virtual void CoreDoWork() {
        Console.WriteLine( "Base.DoWork()" );
    }
}

public class Derived : Base
{
    // WILL NOT COMPILE!!!!!
    private override void CoreDoWork() {
        Console.WriteLine( "Derived.DoWork()" );
    }
}

public class EntryPoint
{
    static void Main() {
        Base b = new Derived();
        b.DoWork();
    }
}
```

This code would actually compile in the initial .NET 1.0 release of C#, and the technique was perfectly valid in the CLR, reflecting the fact that the CLI spec at the time and C# wanted to match the C++ semantics as closely as possible. Before I explain why this won't work in C# now, let me explain why you would want to do it in the first place.

There is a fundamental difference between a method's visibility and its accessibility. If the method is in the declaration of a class or struct, no matter what its protection level, it is visible. And traditionally, in order for a derived class to override a method, it merely has to be visible, and not accessible.

■**Note** The only thing private means on a C++ private virtual method is that the derived class may not call the base class's implementation. If you don't believe me, try this example in native C++. You'll find that it works as expected.

The beauty of being able to declare private virtual methods is that you don't have to worry about derived classes misusing your Base class. For example, maybe you require that they don't call your base class implementation of the virtual method. Fine, just make it private virtual. In fact, using such a technique, you should only make your method protected virtual if you know there is a good reason why the base class would need to call it. And if you do that, you must strictly document at what point the override should call the base implementation. Many people believe that just because the method is declared private, it cannot be overridden. But in the strict sense, restricted accessibility doesn't make it invisible to overriding.

Now let me explain why this feature was turned off in the .NET 1.1 release of C#. This was a mystery to me until Brandon Bray from the Microsoft Visual C++ team explained it neatly. The fact that you can inherit across assembly boundaries turns this feature into a sort of security hole. With native C++, it was never an issue. Consider this: If a private virtual method can be overridden, then so can an internal virtual method. And therein lies the problem. It would allow you to override the behavior of an `internal virtual` method on some random class in a particular assembly, and that is the source of the security hole. So, a tradeoff was made, and every release starting with 1.1 has this feature disabled. Incidentally, this same fix was added to C++/CLI. Although native C++ classes can use the `private virtual` method feature effectively, `ref` C++ classes cannot. And that, of course, is because `ref` C++ classes represent .NET `ref` types that can be inherited across assembly boundaries. How about that!

Is the Object Cloneable?

As you know, objects in C# and in the CLR live on the heap and are accessed through references. You're not actually making a copy of the object when you assign one object variable to another, as in the following code.

```
Object obj = new Object();
Object objCopy = obj;
```

After this code executes, `objCopy` doesn't refer to a copy of `obj`; rather, you now have two references to the same `Object` instance.

However, sometimes it makes sense to be able to make a copy of an object. For that purpose, the Standard Library defines the `ICloneable` interface. When your object implements this interface, it is saying that it supports the ability to have copies of itself made. In other words, it claims that it can be used as a prototype to create new instances of objects. Objects of this type could participate in a prototype factory design pattern. Before I go any further, let's have a look at the `ICloneable` interface:

```
public interface ICloneable
{
    object Clone();
}
```

As you can see, the interface only defines one method, `Clone`, which returns an object reference. That object reference is intended to be the copy. All you have to do is return a copy of the object and you're done, right? Well, not so fast.

You see, there's a not-so-subtle problem with the definition of this interface. The documentation for the interface doesn't indicate whether the copy returned should be a deep copy or a shallow copy. In fact, the documentation leaves it open for the class designer to decide. The difference between a shallow copy and a deep copy is only relevant if the object contains references to other objects. A shallow copy of an object creates a copy whose contained object references refer to the same objects as the prototype's references. A deep copy, on the other hand, creates a copy of the prototype where all of the contained objects are copied as well. In a deep copy, the object containment tree is traversed all the way down to the bottom, and copies of each of those objects are made. Therefore, the result of a deep copy shares no underlying objects with the prototype.

This is enough to drive a good software designer insane. It seems only logical that if you really want to make a copy of an object, then a deep copy is the only true way to go. Fine! From this point onward, when I say "clone," I mean a deep copy.

In order for an object to effectively implement a clone of itself, remember that I'm saying that a clone is a deep copy, so all of its contained objects must provide a means of creating a deep copy of themselves. You can quickly see the problem that comes with that requirement. You cannot guarantee a deep copy if your object contains references to objects that themselves cannot be deep-copied. This is precisely why we suffer from the documentation for the `ICloneable` interface and its lack of specification of copy semantics. Plus, and importantly, this lack of specification forces you to clearly document the `ICloneable` implemenation on any object that implements it so that consumers will know if the object supports a shallow or deep copy.

Let's consider options for implementing the ICloneable interface on objects. If your object contains only value types, such as int, long, or values based on struct definitions where the structs contain no reference types, then you can use a shortcut to implement the Clone method by using Object.MemberwiseClone, as in the following code:

```
using System;

public sealed class Dimensions : ICloneable
{
    public Dimensions( long width, long height ) {
        this.width = width;
        this.height = height;
    }

    // ICloneable implementation
    public object Clone() {
        return this.MemberwiseClone();
    }

    private long width;
    private long height;
}
```

MemberwiseClone is a protected method implemented on System.Object that an object can use to create a *shallow* copy of itself. However, it's important to note one caveat, and that is that MemberwiseClone creates a copy of the object without calling any constructors on the new object. It's an object-creation shortcut. If your object relies upon the constructor being called during creation—for example, if you send debug traces to the console during object construction—then MemberwiseClone is not for you. If you absolutely must use MemberwiseClone, and your object requires work to be done during the constructor call, you must factor that work out into a separate method. Then you can call that method from the constructor, and, in your Clone method, you can call that worker method on the new object after calling MemberwiseClone to create the new instance. Although doable, it's a tedious approach. An alternative way to implement the clone is to make use of a private copy constructor, as in the following code:

```
using System;

public sealed class Dimensions : ICloneable
{
    public Dimensions( long width, long height ) {
        Console.WriteLine( "Dimensions( long, long) called" );

        this.width = width;
        this.height = height;
    }

    // Private copy constructor used when making a copy of this object.
    private Dimensions( Dimensions other ) {
        Console.WriteLine( "Dimensions( Dimensions ) called" );

        this.width = other.width;
        this.height = other.height;
    }
```

```
    // ICloneable implementation
    public object Clone() {
        return new Dimensions(this);
    }

    private long width;
    private long height;
}
```

This method of cloning an object is the safest way in the sense that you have full control over how the copy is made. Any changes that need to be done regarding the way the object is copied can be made in the copy constructor. You must take care to consider what happens when you declare a constructor in a class. Any time you do so, the compiler will not emit the default constructor that it normally does when you don't provide a constructor. If the private copy constructor listed here was the only constructor defined in the class, users of the class would never be able to create instances of it. That's because the default constructor is now gone, and no other publicly accessible constructor would exist. In this case, you have nothing to worry about since you also defined a public constructor that takes two parameters. Nevertheless, it's an important point to consider during class design.

Now, let's also consider objects that themselves contain references to other objects. Suppose you have an employee database, and you represent each employee with an object of type Employee. This Employee type contains vital information such as the employee's name, title, and ID number. The name and possibly the formatted ID number are represented by strings, which are themselves reference type objects. For the sake of example, let's implement the employee title as a separate class named Title. If you follow the guideline I stated previously where you always do a deep copy on a clone, then you could implement the following clone method:

```
using System;

// Title class
//
public sealed class Title : ICloneable
{
    public enum TitleNameEnum {
        GreenHorn,
        HotshotGuru
    }

    public Title( TitleNameEnum title ) {
        this.title = title;

        LookupPayScale();
    }

    private Title( Title other ) {
        this.title = other.title;

        LookupPayScale();
    }

    // ICloneable implementation
    public object Clone() {
        return new Title(this);
    }
```

```
    private void LookupPayScale() {
        // Looks up the pay scale in a database. Payscale is
        // based upon the title.
    }

    private TitleNameEnum title;
    private double minPay;
    private double maxPay;
}

// Employee class
//
public sealed class Employee : ICloneable
{
    public Employee( string name, Title title, string ssn ) {
        this.name = name;
        this.title = title;
        this.ssn = ssn;
    }

    private Employee( Employee other ) {
        this.name = String.Copy( other.name );
        this.title = (Title) other.title.Clone();
        this.ssn = String.Copy( other.ssn );
    }

    // ICloneable implementation
    public object Clone() {
        return new Employee(this);
    }

    private string name;
    private Title title;
    private string ssn;
}
```

Notice that you cannot copy the Title object with MemberwiseClone, because a side effect of the constructor is to call LookupPayScale on the new object to retrieve the pay scale for the title from the database. Let's assume it's possible that the pay scale for the position can change between the prototype's creation and the clone operation, so you always want to look that up in the database. Also, note that copies of the contained objects are made using their respective ICloneable methods. For the Title object, you merely call its implementation of Clone. It turns out that System.String implements ICloneable. However, you cannot use the Clone method to create a deep copy of Employee. If you read the fine print on the String.Clone implementation, you'll see that it just returns a reference to itself. This is a perfect example of the issues I was talking about regarding the inconsistencies of the Clone implementations out there. Instead, you have to use the static String.Copy method in order to get a real copy of the source string.

The fact that System.String returns a reference to itself when its ICloneable.Clone method is called is an optimization that its implementors introduced. Even though the implementation bars you from making a true deep clone of any object that contains string object references, the optimization is valid for two reasons. First, the documentation doesn't specify whether you need to implement a deep or shallow copy. I've already discussed the pros and cons of that omission in the contract specification. Second, System.String is an immutable object. Immutability in objects is a powerful concept that I cover in the later section "Prefer Type Safety at All Times." The general idea is that once you create a string object, you can never change it for as long as it lives. Therefore, it becomes an efficiency burden to implement String.Clone so that it always performs a deep copy. Clients of System.String work the same way, whether String.Clone performs a deep or shallow copy, because of its immutability.

In efforts to make the ICloneable implementation document itself, you can use a custom attribute to mark the Clone method. This way, consumers of your object can determine at design time or at run time whether your object supports a deep copy or a shallow copy. Consider the following custom attribute:[2]

```
using System;

namespace CloneHelpers
{

public enum CloneStyle {
    Deep,
    Shallow
}

[AttributeUsageAttribute(AttributeTargets.Method)]
public sealed class CloneStyleAttribute : Attribute
{
    public CloneStyleAttribute( CloneStyle clonestyle ) {
        this.clonestyle = clonestyle;
    }

    public CloneStyle Style {
        get {
            return clonestyle;
        }
    }

    private CloneStyle clonestyle;
}

}
```

Using this attribute, you can tag your clone implementations such that they are explicit about what type of clone operation they perform. But keep in mind that, as shown, the attribute is only a marker and doesn't enforce anything at run time. That's not to say that you cannot create some other type that enforces a policy at run time based on attached custom attributes. Let's revisit the Dimensions class and apply this attribute appropriately:

```
using System;
using CloneHelpers;

public sealed class Dimensions : ICloneable
{
    public Dimensions( long width, long height ) {
        this.width = width;
        this.height = height;
    }
```

---

2. Full coverage of custom attributes in the .NET Framework is beyond the scope of this book. For more information, consult the MSDN Library documentation or any one of the fine books covering the CLR, such as Andrew Troelsen's *Pro C# with .NET 3.0* (Berkeley, CA: Apress, 2007).

```
// ICloneable implementation
[CloneStyleAttribute(CloneStyle.Deep)]
public object Clone() {
    return this.MemberwiseClone();
}

private long width;
private long height;
}
```

There is no question as to how the Clone method is implemented, and consumers of this object will be well informed.

After this discussion, I'm sure you'll agree that implementing something so seemingly innocuous as ICloneable is not so simple after all.

■Caution Avoid implementing ICloneable. As alarming as that sounds, Microsoft is actually making this recommendation. The problem stems from the fact that the contract doesn't specify whether the copy should be deep or shallow. In fact, as noted in Krzysztof Cwalina and Brad Abrams' *Framework Design Guidelines: Conventions, Idioms, and Patterns for Reusable .NET Libraries* (Boston, MA: Addison-Wesley Professional, 2005), Cwalina searched the entire code base of the .NET Framework and couldn't find any code that uses ICloneable. Had the Framework designers and developers been using this interface, they probably would have stumbled across the omission in the ICloneable specification and fixed it.

However, this recommendation is not to say that you shouldn't implement a Clone method if you need one. If your class needs a clone method, you can still implement one on the public contract of the class without actually implementing ICloneable.

Is the Object Disposable?

I've already covered the ins and outs of disposable objects, but let's cover more of the effects they can have on your design. First, you need to determine if your object should be disposable in the first place. Generally, if it manages some sort of unmanaged resource, such as a chunk of virtual memory (or any other native resource), then the object needs to be disposable. If your object contains other objects that are themselves disposable, then your object should be disposable as well. For example, an object that holds a reference to a file opened with exclusive read/write privileges should be disposable so that the client of the object can control when the underlying resource is closed or cleaned up.

An object is declared to be disposable if it implements the IDisposable interface. The IDisposable interface is another one of those simplistic-looking interfaces, similar to ICloneable, that has a lot of issues lurking under the covers. Let's have a look at the interface itself:

```
public interface IDisposable
{
    void Dispose();
}
```

It looks simple enough. Just implement the Dispose method so that it cleans up the resource, and you're done, right? Well, maybe.

If you create a disposable object that contains other objects that are disposable, then in your Dispose implementation, you should call the Dispose method on the contained objects. Also, it's perfectly valid for clients to call Dispose multiple times. So, instead of throwing an exception on subsequent calls, which is invalid based upon the documentation for IDisposable, you should simply do nothing. Therefore, you'll need to maintain some sort of internal flag so that your code doesn't explode if Dispose gets called multiple times. This internal flag can be used for another purpose, too. It is normally invalid to call a method on a disposed object, so in those cases, you can check the flag and if it indicates that the object has been disposed previously, you can throw an ObjectDisposedException. You can already see that the requirements for implementing IDisposable are mounting, and what appeared to be a simple interface is becoming more and more difficult to implement properly. Let's look at an example of implementing IDisposable. The following code consists of a custom heap object that uses Win32 functions to manage a local heap:

```
using System;
using System.Runtime.InteropServices;

public sealed class Win32Heap : IDisposable
{
    [DllImport("kernel32.dll")]
    static extern IntPtr HeapCreate(uint flOptions, UIntPtr dwInitialSize,
                                    UIntPtr dwMaximumSize);

    [DllImport("kernel32.dll")]
    static extern bool HeapDestroy(IntPtr hHeap);

    public Win32Heap() {
        theHeap = HeapCreate( 0, (UIntPtr) 4096, UIntPtr.Zero );
    }

    // IDisposable implementation
    public void Dispose() {
        if( !disposed ) {
            HeapDestroy( theHeap );
            theHeap = IntPtr.Zero;
            disposed = true;
        }
    }

    private IntPtr theHeap;
    private bool disposed = false;
}
```

This object doesn't contain any objects that implement IDisposable, so you don't need to iterate through the containment tree calling Dispose.

It's important to note that in the Disposable pattern, the implementation of the contained objects shapes the container object by forcing it to implement IDisposable if the contained objects implement IDisposable. It's an inside-out relationship.

Since the IDisposable pattern requires the user to call the Dispose method explicitly, the onus is thrown on the user to make sure that it is called, even in the face of exceptions. This makes the client code tedious to produce. For example, consider the following code, which opens a file for writing:

```
using System;
using System.IO;

public sealed class WriteStuff
{
    static void Main(){
        StreamWriter sw = new StreamWriter("Output.txt");
        try {
            sw.WriteLine( "This is a test of the emergency dispose mechanism" );
```

```
        }
        finally {
            if( sw != null ) {
                ((IDisposable)sw).Dispose();
            }
        }
    }
}
```

The C# designers recognized how writing code like this can be a royal pain, so at the same time the .NET Framework introduced the IDisposable interface, the designers overloaded the using keyword to provide a using statement to help us out. In a using statement, you declare the disposable variables within a pair of parentheses and then, when the scope leaves the following code block, the objects are disposed of. Internally, the using statement does essentially the same thing as the try/finally construct. You can look at the generated IL code to prove this. The using statement definitely does help; however, the client of the object is still required to remember to use it in the first place. Let's modify the previous example with a using statement:

```
using System;
using System.IO;

public sealed class WriteStuff
{
    static void Main(){
        using( StreamWriter sw = new StreamWriter("Output.txt") ) {
            sw.WriteLine( "This is a test of the emergency dispose mechanism" );
        }
    }
}
```

Now, can you think of what happens if the client of your object forgets to call Dispose or doesn't use a using statement? Clearly, there is the chance that you will leak the resource. And that's why you need to also implement a finalizer, as I describe in the next section.

■**Note** In the previous examples, I have not considered what would happen if multiple threads were to call Dispose concurrently. Although the situation seems diabolical, you must plan for the worst if you're a developer of library code that unknown clients will consume.

Does the Object Need a Finalizer?

A finalizer is a method that you can implement on your class and that is called prior to the GC cleaning up your unused object from the heap. Let's get one important concept clear up front: Finalizers are not destructors, nor should you view them as destructors.

Destructors are associated with deterministic destruction of objects. Finalizers are associated with nondeterministic destruction of objects. Unfortunately, much of the confusion between finalizers and destructors comes from the fact that the C# language designers chose to map finalizers into the C# destructor syntax, which is identical to the C++ destructor syntax. In fact, you'll find that it's impossible to overload Object.Finalize explicitly in C#. You overload it implicitly by using the destructor syntax that you're used to if you come from the C++ world. The only good thing that comes from C# implementing finalizers this way is that you never have to worry about calling the base class finalizer. The compiler does that for you.

Most of the time when your object needs some sort of cleanup code—for example, an object that abstracts a file in the file system—it needs to happen deterministically; for example, when manipulating unmanaged resources. In other words, it needs to happen explicitly when the user is finished with the object and not when the GC finally gets around to disposing of the object. In these cases, you need to implement this functionality using the Disposable pattern by implementing the IDisposable interface. Don't be fooled into thinking that the destructor you wrote for the class using the familiar destructor syntax will get called when the object goes out of scope as it does in C++. In fact, if you think about it, you'll see that it is extremely rare that you'll need to implement a finalizer. It's difficult to think of a cleanup task that you cannot do using IDisposable.

■**Note** In reality, it's rare that you'll ever need to write a finalizer. Most of the time, you should implement the Disposable pattern to do any resource cleanup code in your object. However, finalizers can be useful for cleaning up unmanaged resources in a guaranteed way—that is, when the user has forgotten to call IDisposable. Dispose.

In a perfect world, you could simply implement all of your typical destructor code in the IDisposable.Dispose method. However, there is one serious side effect of the C# language's not supporting deterministic destruction. The C# compiler doesn't call IDisposable.Dispose on your object automatically when it goes out of scope. C#, as I have mentioned previously, throws the onus on the user of the object to call IDisposable.Dispose. The C# language does make it easier to guarantee this behavior in the face of exceptions by overloading the using keyword, but it still requires the client of your object not to forget the using keyword in the first place. This is important to keep in mind, and it's what can ruin your "perfect world" dream.

We don't live in a perfect world, so in order to clean up directly held resources reliably, it's wise for any objects that implement the IDisposable interface to also implement a finalizer that merely defers to the Dispose method.[3] This way, you can catch those errant mistakes where users forget to use the Disposable pattern and don't dispose of the object properly. Of course, the cleanup of undisposed objects will now happen at the discretion of the GC, but at least it will happen. Beware; the GC finalizer calls the finalizer for the objects being cleaned up from a separate thread. Now, all of a sudden, you may have to worry about threading issues in your disposable objects. It's unlikely that threading issues will bite you during finalization, since, in theory, the object being finalized is not being referenced anywhere. However, it could become a factor depending on what you do in your Dispose method. For example, if your Dispose method uses an external, possibly unmanaged, object to get work done that another entity may hold a reference to, then that object needs to be *thread-hot*—that is, it must work reliably in multithreaded environments. It's better to be safe than sorry and consider threading issues when you implement a finalizer.

There is one more important thing to consider that I touched on in a previous chapter. When you call your Dispose method via the finalizer, you should not use reference objects contained in fields within this object. It may not sound intuitive at first, but you must realize that there is no guaranteed ordering of how objects are finalized. The objects in the fields of your object could have been finalized before your finalizer runs. Therefore, it would elicit the dreaded undefined behavior if you were to use them and they just happened to be destroyed already. I think you'll agree that could be a tough bug to find. Now, it's becoming clear that finalizers can drag you into a land of many pitfalls.

---

3. It's important to note that objects that implement IDisposable only because they contain types that implement IDisposable should not have a finalizer. They don't manage resources directly, and the finalizer will impose undue stress on the finalizer thread of the GC.

■**Caution** Be wary of any object used during finalization, even if it's not a field of your object being finalized, because it, too, may already be marked for finalization and may or may not have been finalized already. Using object references within a finalizer is a slippery slope indeed. In fact, many schools of thought recommend against using any external objects within a finalizer. But the fact is that any time an object that supports a finalizer is moved to the finalization queue in the GC, all objects in the object graph are moved, whether they are finalizable or not. So if your finalizable object contains a private, nonfinalizable object, then you can touch the private contained object in the finalizer because you know it's still alive, since it got promoted to the finalization queue with your object, and it cannot have been finalized before your object since it has no finalizer. However, see the next Note in the text!

Let's revisit the Win32Heap example from the previous section and modify it with a finalizer. Follow the recommended Disposable pattern, and see how it changes:

```
using System;
using System.Runtime.InteropServices;

public class Win32Heap : IDisposable
{
    [DllImport("kernel32.dll")]
    static extern IntPtr HeapCreate(uint flOptions, UIntPtr dwInitialSize,
                                    UIntPtr dwMaximumSize);

    [DllImport("kernel32.dll")]
    static extern bool HeapDestroy(IntPtr hHeap);

    public Win32Heap() {
        theHeap = HeapCreate( 0, (UIntPtr) 4096, UIntPtr.Zero );
    }

    // IDisposable implementation
    protected virtual void Dispose( bool disposing ) {
        if( !disposed ) {
            if( disposing ) {
                // It's ok to use any internal objects here. This class happens
                //   not to have any, though.
            }

            // If using objects that you know do still exist, such as objects
            // that implement the Singleton pattern, it is important to make
            // sure those objects are thread-safe.

            HeapDestroy( theHeap );
            theHeap = IntPtr.Zero;
            disposed = true;
        }
    }

    public void Dispose() {
        Dispose( true );
        GC.SuppressFinalize( this );
    }

    ~Win32Heap() {
        Dispose( false );
```

```
    }

    private IntPtr theHeap;
    private bool disposed = false;
}
```

Let's analyze the changes made to support a finalizer. First, notice that I've added the finalizer using the familiar destructor syntax.[4] Also, notice that I've added a second level of indirection in the Dispose implementation. This is so you know whether your private Dispose method was called from a call to Dispose or through the finalizer. Also, in this example, Dispose(bool) is implemented virtually, so that any deriving type merely has to override this method to modify the dispose behavior. If the Win32Heap class was marked sealed, you could change that method from protected to private and remove the virtual keyword. As I mentioned before, you cannot reliably use subobjects if your Dispose method was called from the finalizer.

Note Some people take the approach that all object references are off limits inside the Dispose method that is called by the finalizer. There's no reason you cannot use objects that you know to be alive and well. However, beware if the finalizer is called as a result of the application domain shutting down; objects that you assume to be alive may not actually be alive. In reality, it's almost impossible to determine if an object reference is still valid in 100% of the cases. So, it's best just to not reference any reference types within the finalization stage if you can avoid it.

The Dispose method features a performance boost; notice the call to GC.SuppressFinalize. The finalizer of this object merely calls the private Dispose method, and you know that if your public Dispose method gets called, the finalizer doesn't need to do that any longer. So you can tell the GC not to put the object instance on the finalization queue when the IDisposable.Dispose method is called. This optimization is more than trivial once you consider the fact that objects that implement a finalizer live longer than those that don't. When the GC goes through the heap looking for dead objects to collect, it normally just compacts the heap and reclaims their memory. However, if an object has a finalizer, instead of reclaiming the memory immediately, the GC moves the object over to a finalization list that gets handled by the separate finalization thread. Once the finalization thread has completed its job on the object, the object is remarked for deletion, and the GC reclaims the space during a subsequent pass. That's why objects that implement a finalizer live longer than those that don't. If your objects eat up lots of heap memory, or your system creates lots of those objects, finalization starts to become a huge factor. Not only does it make the GC inefficient, but it also chews up processor time in the finalization thread. This is why you suppress finalization inside Dispose if possible.

Note When an object has a finalizer, it is placed on an internal CLR queue to keep track of this fact, and, clearly, GC.SuppressFinalize affects that status. During normal execution, as previously mentioned, you cannot guarantee that other object references are reachable. However, during application shutdown, the finalizer thread actually finalizes the objects right off of this internal finalizable queue, and therefore, those objects are reachable and can be referenced in finalizers. You can determine if this is the case by using Environment. HasShutdownStarted or AppDomain.IsFinalizingForUnload. However, just because you can do it does not mean that you should do so without careful consideration. Don't be surprised if this behavior changes in future versions of the CLR.

---

4. But keep telling yourself that it's not a destructor!

Let's consider the performance impact of finalizers on the GC a little more closely. The CLR GC is implemented as a generational GC. This means that allocated objects that live in higher generations are assumed to live longer than those that live in lower generations and are collected less frequently than the generation below them. The fine details of the GC's collection algorithm are beyond the scope of this book. However, it's beneficial to touch upon them at a high level. For example, the GC normally attempts to allocate any new objects in generation 0. Moreover, the GC assumes that objects in generation 0 will live a relatively short lifespan. So, when the GC attempts to allocate space for an object, and it sees that the heap must be compacted, it releases space held by dead generation 0 objects, and objects that are not dead get promoted to generation 1 during the compaction. Upon completion of this stage, if the GC is able to find enough space for the allocation, it stops compacting the heap. It won't attempt to compact generation 1 unless it needs even more space or it sees that the generation 1 heap is full and likely needs to be compacted. It will iterate through all the generations as necessary. However, during the entire pass of the garbage collector, an object can only be promoted one level. So, if an object is promoted from generation 0 to generation 1 during a collection and the GC must subsequently continue compacting generation 1 in the same collection pass, the object just promoted stays in generation 1. Currently, the CLR heap consists of only three generations. So, naturally, if an object lives in generation 2, it cannot be promoted to a higher generation. The CLR also contains a special heap for large object allocation, which in the current release contains objects greater than 80 KB in size. That number may change in future releases, though, so don't rely on it staying static.

Now, consider what happens when a generation 0 object gets promoted to generation 1 during a compaction. Even if all root references to an object in generation 1 are out of scope, the space may not be reclaimed for a while, since the GC will not compact generation 1 very often.

Objects that implement finalizers get put on the finalization queue. That reference on the queue counts as a root reference. Therefore, the object will be promoted to generation 1 if it currently lives in generation 0. But you already know that the object is dying. In fact, once the finalization queue is drained, the object most likely will be dead, unless it is resurrected during the finalization process. So, there's the rub. This object with the finalizer is dying, but since it was put on the finalization queue and thus promoted to a higher generation, its shell will likely lie around rotting in the GC until a higher-generation compaction occurs.

For this reason, it's important that you not implement a finalizer unless you have to. And as previously mentioned, that should only be necessary when your object directly maintains resources that must be freed or cleaned up deterministically.

■**Note** Resources that must be cleaned up deterministically can be both managed and unmanaged resources. An example of an unmanaged resource is something like an instance of `System.IO.FileStream`, where `IDisposable.Dispose` calls through to `FileStream.Close`, which releases the underlying unmanaged resources. It is likely undesirable for you to wait until the GC feels like calling the finalizer on the `FileStream` before the file is unlocked.

I want to focus a little more on the fact that `Dispose` is never called automatically, and how your finalizer can help point out potential efficiency problems to your client. Let's suppose you create an object that allocates a nontrivial chunk of unmanaged system resources. And suppose that the client of your object has created a web site that takes many hits per minute and, with each hit, the client creates a new instance of your object. The client's system's performance will degrade significantly if the client forgets to dispose of these objects in a timely manner before all references to the object are gone. Of course, if you implement a finalizer as shown previously, the object will eventually be disposed of. However, disposal only happens when the GC feels it necessary, so resources will probably run dry and cripple the system. Moreover, failing to call `Dispose` will likely result in more finalization, which will cripple the GC even more. Client code can force GC collection through

the GC.Collect method. However, it is strongly recommended that you never call it, since it inter-
feres with the GC's algorithms. The GC knows how to manage its memory better than you do 99.9%
of the time.

It would be nice if you could inform the clients of your object when they forget to call Dispose
in their debug builds. Well, in fact, you can log an error whenever the finalizer for your object runs
and it notices that the object has not been disposed of properly. You can even point clients to the
exact location of the object creation by storing off a stack trace at the point of creation. That way,
they know which line of code created the offending instance. Let's modify the Win32Heap example
with this approach:

```
using System;
using System.Runtime.InteropServices;
using System.Diagnostics;

public sealed class Win32Heap : IDisposable
{
    [DllImport("kernel32.dll")]
    static extern IntPtr HeapCreate(uint flOptions,
                                    UIntPtr dwInitialSize,
                                    UIntPtr dwMaximumSize);

    [DllImport("kernel32.dll")]
    static extern bool HeapDestroy(IntPtr hHeap);

    public Win32Heap() {
        creationStackTrace = new StackTrace(1, true);

        theHeap = HeapCreate( 0, (UIntPtr) 4096, UIntPtr.Zero );
    }

    // IDisposable implementation
    private void Dispose( bool disposing ) {
      if( !disposed ) {
        if( disposing ) {
          // It's ok to use any internal objects here.  This
          // class happens not to have any, though.
        } else {
          // OOPS!  We're finalizing this object and it has not
          // been disposed.  Let's let the user know about it if
          // the app domain is not shutting down.
          AppDomain currentDomain = AppDomain.CurrentDomain;
          if( !currentDomain.IsFinalizingForUnload() &&
              !Environment.HasShutdownStarted ) {
            Console.WriteLine(
                        "Failed to dispose of object!!!" );
            Console.WriteLine( "Object allocated at:" );
            for( int i = 0;
                 i < creationStackTrace.FrameCount;
                 ++i ) {
              StackFrame frame =
                  creationStackTrace.GetFrame(i);
              Console.WriteLine( "    {0}",
                                  frame.ToString() );
            }
          }
        }
```

```
        // If using objects that you know do still exist, such
        // as objects that implement the Singleton pattern, it
        // is important to make sure those objects are thread-
        // safe.

        HeapDestroy( theHeap );
        theHeap = IntPtr.Zero;
        disposed = true;
      }
    }

    public void Dispose() {
        Dispose( true );
        GC.SuppressFinalize( this );
    }

    ~Win32Heap() {
        Dispose( false );
    }

    private IntPtr theHeap;
    private bool disposed = false;
    private StackTrace creationStackTrace;
}

public sealed class EntryPoint
{
    static void Main()
    {
        Win32Heap heap = new Win32Heap();
        heap = null;
        GC.Collect();
        GC.WaitForPendingFinalizers();
    }
}
```

In the Main method, notice that I allocate a new Win32Heap object, and then I immediately force it to be finalized. Since the object was not disposed, this triggers the stack dumping code inside the private Dispose method. Since you probably don't care about objects being finalized as a result of the app domain getting unloaded, I wrapped the stack-dumping code inside a block conditional on the result of AppDomain.IsFinalizingForUnload && Environment.HasShutdownStarted. Had I called Dispose prior to setting the reference to null in Main, then the stack trace would not be sent to the console. Clients of your library may thank you for pointing out undisposed objects. I know I would.

■Note When you compile the previous example, you'll get much more meaningful and readable output if you compile with the /debug+ compiler switch. You may even want to consider turning on such reporting only in debug and testing builds.

I hope, after this discussion, you can see the perils of implementing finalizers. They are potential tremendous resource sinks, since they make objects live longer, and yet they are hidden behind the innocuous syntax of destructors. The one redeeming quality of finalizers is the ability to point out when objects are not disposed of properly, but I advise using that technique only in debug builds. Be aware of the efficiency implications you impose on your system when you implement a finalizer on an object. I recommend that you avoid writing a finalizer if at all possible.

Developers familiar with finalizers are also familiar with the cost incurred by the finalization thread that walks through the finalization queue calling the objects' finalizers. However, many more hidden costs are easy to miss. For example, the creation of finalizable objects takes a little bit longer due to the bookkeeping that the CLR must maintain to denote the object as finalizable. Of course, for a single object instance, this cost is extremely minimal, but if you're creating tens of thousands of small, finalizable objects very quickly, the cost will add up. Also, some incarnations of the CLR create only one finalization thread, so if you're running code on a multiprocessor system and several processors are allocating finalizable objects quicker than the finalization thread can clean them up, you'll have a resource problem. What's worse is if you can imagine what would happen if one of your finalizers blocked the thread for a long period of time or indefinitely. Additionally, even though you can introduce dependencies between finalizable objects using some crafty techniques, be aware that the CLR team is actively considering moving finalization to the process thread pool rather than using a single finalization thread. That would mean that those crafty finalization techniques would need to be thread-safe. Be careful out there, and avoid finalizers if at all possible.

What Does Equality Mean for This Object?

`Object.Equals` is the virtual method that you call to determine, in the most general way, if two objects are equivalent. On the surface, overriding the `Object.Equals` method may seem trivial. However, beware that it is yet another one of those simplistic-looking things that can turn into a semantic hair ball. The key to understanding `Object.Equals` is to understand that there are generally two semantic meanings of equivalence in the CLR. The default meaning of equivalence for reference types—a.k.a. objects—is identity equivalence. This means that two separate references are considered equal if they both reference the same object instance on the heap. So, with identity equality, even if you have two references each referencing different objects that just happen to have completely identical internal states, `Object.Equals` will return `false` for those.

The other form of equivalence in the CLR is that of value equality. Value equality is the default equivalence for value types, or structs, in C#. The default version of `Equals`, which is provided by the override of `Equals` inside the `ValueType` class that all value types derive from, uses reflection to iterate over the internal fields of two values, comparing them for value equality. With two semantic meanings of `Equals` in the CLR possible, some confusion can come from the fact that both value types and reference types have different default semantic meanings for `Equals`. In this section, I'll concentrate on implementing `Object.Equals` for reference types. I'll save value types for a later section.

Reference Types and Identity Equality

What does it mean to say that a type is a reference type? Basically, it means that every variable of that type that you manipulate is actually a pointer to the actual object on the heap. When you make a copy of this reference, you get another reference that points to the same object. Consider the following code:

```
public class EntryPoint
{
    static void Main()
    {
        object referenceA = new System.Object();
        object referenceB = referenceA;
    }
}
```

In Main, I create a new instance of type System.Object, and then I immediately make a copy of the reference. What I end up with is something that resembles the diagram in Figure 13-1.

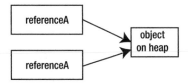

Figure 13-1. *Reference variables*

In the CLR, the variables that represent the references are actually value types that embody a storage location (for the pointer to the object they represent) and an associated type. However, note that once a reference is copied, the actual object pointed to is not copied. Instead, you have two references that refer to the same object. Operations on the object performed through one reference will be visible to the client using the other reference.

Now, let's consider what it means to compare these references. What does equality mean between two reference variables? The answer is, it depends on what your needs are and how you define equality. By default, equality of reference variables is meant to be an identity comparison. What that means is that two reference variables are equal if they refer to the same object, as in Figure 13-1. Again, this referential equality, or identity, is the default behavior of equality between two references to a heap-based object.

From the client code standpoint, you have to be careful about how you compare two object references for equality. Consider the following code:

```
public class EntryPoint
{
    static bool TestForEquality( object obj1, object obj2 )
    {
        return obj1.Equals( obj2 );
    }

    static void Main()
    {
        object obj1 = new System.Object();
        object obj2 = null;

        System.Console.WriteLine( "obj1 == obj2 is {0}",
                                  TestForEquality(obj1, obj2) );
    }
}
```

Here I create an instance of System.Object, and I want to find out if the variables obj1 and obj2 are equal. Since I'm comparing references, the equality test determines if they are pointing to the same object instance. From looking at the code, you can see that the obvious result is that obj1 != obj2 because obj2 is null. This is expected. However, consider what would happen if you swapped the order of the parameters in the call to TestForEquality. You would quickly find that your program crashes with an unhandled exception where TestForInequality tries to call Equals on a null reference. Therefore, you should modify the code to account for this:

```
public class EntryPoint
{
    static bool TestForEquality( object obj1, object obj2 )
    {
        if( obj1 == null && obj2 == null ) {
```

```
            return true;
        }

        if( obj1 == null )
        {
            return false;
        }

        return obj1.Equals( obj2 );
    }

    static void Main()
    {
        object obj1 = new System.Object();
        object obj2 = null;

        System.Console.WriteLine( "obj1 == obj2 is {0}",
                              TestForEquality(obj2, obj1) );
        System.Console.WriteLine( "null == null is {0}",
                              TestForEquality(null, null) );
    }
}
```

Now, the code can swap the order of the arguments in the call to TestForEquality, and you get the expected result. Notice that I also put a check in there to return the proper result if both arguments are null. Now, TestForEquality is complete. It sure seems like a lot of work to test two references for equality. Well, the designers of the .NET Framework Standard Library recognized this problem and introduced the static version of Object.Equals that does this exact comparison. Thankfully, as long as you call the static version of Object.Equals, you don't have to worry about creating the code in TestForEquality in this example.

You've seen how equality tests on references to objects test identity by default. However, there may be times when this type of equivalence test makes no sense. Consider an immutable object that represents a complex number:

```
public class ComplexNumber
{
    public ComplexNumber( int real, int imaginary )
    {
        this.real = real;
        this.imaginary = imaginary;
    }

    private int real;
    private int imaginary;
}

public class EntryPoint
{
    static void Main()
    {
        ComplexNumber referenceA = new ComplexNumber( 1, 2 );
        ComplexNumber referenceB = new ComplexNumber( 1, 2 );

        System.Console.WriteLine( "Result of Equality is {0}",
                              referenceA == referenceB );
    }
}
```

The output from that code looks like this:

```
Result of Equality is False
```

Figure 13-2 shows the diagram representing the in-memory layout of the references.

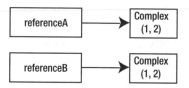

Figure 13-2. *References to* ComplexNumber

This is the expected result based upon the default meaning of equality between references. However, this is hardly intuitive to the user of these ComplexNumber objects. It would make better sense for the comparison of the two references in the diagram to return true, since the values of the two objects are the same. To achieve such a result, you need to provide a custom implementation of equality for these objects. I'll show how to do that shortly, but first, let's quickly discuss what value equality means.

Value Equality

From the preceding section, it should be obvious what value equality means. Equality of two values is true when the actual values of the fields representing the state of the object or value are equivalent. In the ComplexNumber example from the previous section, value equality is true when the values for the real and imaginary fields are equivalent between two instances of the class.

In the CLR, and thus in C#, this is exactly what equality means for value types defined as structs. Value types derive from System.ValueType, and System.ValueType overrides the Object.Equals method. ValueType.Equals uses reflection to iterate through the fields of the value type while comparing the fields. This generic implementation will work for all value types. However, it is much more efficient if you override the Equals method in your struct types and compare the fields directly. Although using reflection to accomplish this task is a generally applicable approach, it's very inefficient.

■**Note** Before the implementation of ValueType.Equals resorts to using reflection, it makes a couple of quick checks. If the two types being compared are different, it fails the equality. If they are the same type, it first checks to see if the types in the contained fields are simple data types that can be bitwise-compared. If so, the entire type may be bitwise-compared. Failing both of these conditions, the implementation then resorts to using reflection. As the default implementation of ValueType.Equals iterates over the value's contained fields using reflection, it determines the equality of those individual fields by deferring to the implementation of Object.Equals on those objects. Therefore, if your value type contains a reference type field, you may be in for a surprise, depending on the semantics of the Equals method implemented on that reference type. Generally, containing reference types within a value type is not recommended.

Overriding Object.Equals for Reference Types

Many times, you may need to override the meaning of equivalence for an object. You may want equivalence for your reference type to be value equality as opposed to referential equality, or identity. Or, as you'll see in a later section, you may have a custom value type where you want to override the default Equals method provided by System.ValueType in order to make the operation more efficient. No matter what your reason for overriding Equals, you must follow several rules:

- x.Equals(x) == true. This is the reflexive property of equality.
- x.Equals(y) == y.Equals(x). This is the symmetric property of equality.
- x.Equals(y) && y.Equals(z) implies x.Equals(z) == true. This is the transitive property of equality.
- x.Equals(y) must return the same result as long as the internal state of x and y has not changed.
- x.Equals(null) == false for all x that are not null.
- Equals must not throw exceptions.

An Equals implementation should adhere to these hard-and-fast rules. You should follow other suggested guidelines in order to make the Equals implementations on your classes more robust.

As already discussed, the default version of Object.Equals inherited by classes tests for referential equality, otherwise known as identity. However, in cases like the example using ComplexNumber, such a test is not intuitive. It would be natural and expected that instances of such a type are compared on a field-by-field basis. It is for this very reason that you should override Object.Equals for these types of classes that behave with value semantics.

Let's revisit the ComplexNumber example once again to see how you can do this:

```
public class ComplexNumber
{
    public ComplexNumber( int real, int imaginary )
    {
        this.real = real;
        this.imaginary = imaginary;
    }

    public override bool Equals( object obj )
    {
        ComplexNumber other = obj as ComplexNumber;

        if( other == null )
        {
            return false;
        }

        return (this.real == other.real) &&
               (this.imaginary == other.imaginary);
    }

    public override int GetHashCode()
    {
        return (int) real ^ (int) imaginary;
    }

    public static bool operator==( ComplexNumber me, ComplexNumber other )
    {
        return Equals( me, other );
    }

    public static bool operator!=( ComplexNumber me, ComplexNumber other )
    {
```

```
        return Equals( me, other );
    }

    private double real;
    private double imaginary;
}

public class EntryPoint
{
    static void Main()
    {
        ComplexNumber referenceA = new ComplexNumber( 1, 2 );
        ComplexNumber referenceB = new ComplexNumber( 1, 2 );

        System.Console.WriteLine( "Result of Equality is {0}",
                                  referenceA == referenceB );

        // If we really want referential equality.
        System.Console.WriteLine( "Identity of references is {0}",
                                  (object) referenceA == (object) referenceB );
        System.Console.WriteLine( "Identity of references is {0}",
                                  ReferenceEquals(referenceA, referenceB) );
    }
}
```

In this example, you can see that the implementation of Equals is pretty straightforward, except that I do have to test some conditions. I must make sure that the object reference I'm comparing to is both not null and does, in fact, reference an instance of ComplexNumber. Once I get that far, I can simply test the fields of the two references to make sure they are equal. You could introduce an optimization and compare this with other in Equals. If they're referencing the same object, you could return true without comparing the fields. However, comparing the two fields is a trivial amount of work in this case, so I'll skip the identity test.

In the majority of cases, you won't need to override Object.Equals for your reference type objects. It is recommended that your objects treat equivalence using identity comparisons, which is what you get for free from Object.Equals. However, there are times when it makes sense to override Equals for an object. For example, if your object represents something that naturally feels like a value and is immutable, such as a complex number or the System.String class, then it could very well make sense to override Equals in order to give that object's implementation of Equals() value equality semantics.

In many cases, when overriding virtual methods in derived classes, such as Object.Equals, it makes sense to call the base class implementation at some point. However, if your object derives directly from System.Object, it makes no sense to do this. This is because Object.Equals likely carries a different semantic meaning from the semantics of your override. Remember, the only reason to override Equals for objects is to change the semantic meaning from identity to value equality. Also, you don't want to mix the two semantics together. But there's an ugly twist to this story. You *do* need to call the base class version of Equals if your class derives from a class other than System.Object and that other class does override Equals. This is because the most likely reason a base class overrode Object.Equals is to switch to value semantics. This means that you must have intimate knowledge of your base class if you plan on overriding Object.Equals, so that you will know whether to call the base version. That's the ugly truth about overriding Object.Equals for reference types.

Sometimes, even when you're dealing with reference types, you really do want to test for referential equality no matter what. You cannot always rely on the Equals method for the object to determine the referential equality, so you must use other means, because the method can be overridden as in the ComplexNumber example.

Thankfully, you have two ways to handle this job, and you can see them both at the end of the Main method in the previous code sample. The C# compiler guarantees that if you apply the == operator to two references of type Object, you will always get back referential equality. Also, System. Object supplies a static method named ReferenceEquals that takes two reference parameters and returns true if the identity test holds true. Either way you choose to go, the result is the same.

If you do change the semantic meaning of Equals for an object, it is best to document this fact clearly for the clients of your object. If you override Equals for a class, I would strongly recommend that you tag its semantic meaning with a custom attribute, similar to the technique introduced for iCloneable implementations previously. This way, people who derive from your class and want to change the semantic meaning of Equals can quickly determine if they should call your implementation in the process. For maximum efficiency, the custom attribute should serve a documentation purpose. Although it's possible to look for such an attribute at run time, it would be very inefficient.

Note You should never throw exceptions from an implementation of Object.Equals. Instead of throwing an exception, return false as the result instead.

Throughout this entire discussion, I have purposely avoided talking about the equality operators because it is beneficial to consider them as an extra layer in addition to Object.Equals. Support of operator overloading is not a requirement for languages to be CLS-compliant. Therefore, not all languages that target the CLR support them thoroughly. Visual Basic is one language that has taken a while to support operator overloading, and it only started supporting it fully in Visual Basic 2005. Visual Basic .NET 2003 supports calling overloaded operators on objects defined in languages that support overloaded operators, but they must be called through the special function name generated for the operator. For example, operator== is implemented with the name op_Equality in the generated IL code. The best approach is to implement Object.Equals as appropriate and base any operator== or operator!= implementations on Equals while only providing them as a convenience for languages that support them.

Note Consider implementing IEquatable<T> on your type to get a type-safe version of Equals. This is especially important for value types, since type-specific versions of methods avoid unnecessary boxing.

If You Override Equals, Override GetHashCode Too

GetHashCode is called when objects are used as keys of a hash table. When a hash table searches for an entry after given a key to look for, it asks the key for its hash code and then uses that to identify which hash bucket the key lives in. Once it finds the bucket, it can then see if that key is in the bucket. Theoretically, the search for the bucket should be quick, since the buckets should have very few keys in them. This occurs if your GetHashCode method returns a reasonably unique value for instances of your object that support value equivalence semantics.

Given the previous discussion, you can see that it would be very bad if your hash code algorithm could return a different value between two instances that contain values that are equivalent. In such a case, the hash table may fail to find the bucket your key is in. For this reason, it is imperative that you override GetHashCode if you override Equals for an object. In fact, if you override Equals and not GetHashCode, the C# compiler will let you know about it with a friendly warning. And since we're all diligent with regard to building our release code with zero warnings, we should take the compiler's word seriously.

Note The previous discussion should be plenty of evidence that any type used as a hash table key should be immutable. After all, the GetHashCode value is normally computed based upon the state of the object itself. If that state changes, then the GetHashCode result will likely change with it.

GetHashCode implementations should adhere to the following rules:

- If, for two instances, x.Equals(y) is true, then x.GetHashCode() == y.GetHashCode().
- Hash codes generated by GetHashCode need not be unique.
- GetHashCode is not permitted to throw exceptions.

If two instances return the same hash code value, they must be further compared with Equals to determine if they're equivalent. Incidentally, if your GetHashCode method is very efficient, you can base the inequality code path of your operator!= and operator== implementations on it, since different hash codes for objects of the same type imply inequality. Implementing the operators this way can be more efficient in some cases, but it all depends on the efficiency of your GetHashCode implementation and the complexity of your Equals method. In some cases, when using this technique, the calls to the operators could be less efficient than just calling Equals, but in other cases, they can be remarkably more efficient. For example, consider an object that models a multidimensional point in space. Suppose the number of dimensions (rank) of this point could easily approach into the hundreds. Internally, you could represent the dimensions of the point by using an array of integers. Say you want to implement the GetHashCode method by computing a CRC32 on the dimension points in the array. This also implies that this Point type is immutable. This GetHashCode call could potentially be expensive if you compute the CRC32 each time it is called. Therefore, it may be wise to precompute the hash and store it in the object. In such a case, you could write the equality operators as shown in the following code:

```
sealed public class Point
{
    // Other methods removed for clarity

    public override bool Equals( object other ) {
        bool result = false;
        Point that = other as Point;
        if( that != null ) {
            result = (this.coordinates == that.coordinates);
        }

        return result;
    }

    public override int GetHashCode() {
        return precomputedHash;
    }

    public static bool operator ==( Point pt1, Point pt2 ) {
        if( pt1.GetHashCode() != pt2.GetHashCode() ) {
            return false;
        } else {
            return Object.Equals( pt1, pt2 );
        }
    }

    public static bool operator !=( Point pt1, Point pt2 ) {
```

```
            if( pt1.GetHashCode() != pt2.GetHashCode() ) {
                return true;
            } else {
                return !Object.Equals( pt1, pt2 );
            }
        }
    }

    private float[] coordinates;
    private int precomputedHash;
}
```

In this example, as long as the precomputed hash is sufficiently unique, the overloaded operators will execute quickly in some cases. In the worst case, one more comparison between two integers—the hash values—is executed along with the function calls to acquire them. If the call to Equals is expensive, then this optimization will return some gains on a lot of the comparisons. If the call to Equals is not expensive, then this technique could add overhead and make the code less efficient. It's best to apply the old adage that premature optimization is poor optimization. You should only apply such an optimization after a profiler has pointed you in this direction and if you're sure it will help.

Object.GetHashCode exists because the developers of the Standard Library felt it would be convenient to be able to use any object as a key to a hash table. The fact is, not all objects are good candidates for hash keys. Usually, it's best to use immutable types as hash keys. A good example of an immutable type in the Standard Library is System.String. Once such an object is created, you can never change it. Therefore, calling GetHashCode on a string instance is guaranteed to always return the same value for the same string instance. It becomes more difficult to generate hash codes for objects that are mutable. In those cases, it's best to base your GetHashCode implementation on calculations performed on immutable fields inside the mutable object.

Detailing algorithms for generating hash codes is outside the scope of this book. I recommend that you reference Donald E. Knuth's *The Art of Computer Programming, Volume 3: Sorting and Searching, Second Edition* (Boston, MA: Addison-Wesley Professional, 1998). For the sake of example, suppose you want to implement GetHashCode for a ComplexNumber type. One solution is to compute the hash based on the magnitude of the complex number, as in the following example:

```
using System;

public sealed class ComplexNumber
{
    public ComplexNumber( double real, double imaginary ) {
        this.real = real;
        this.imaginary = imaginary;
    }

    public override bool Equals( object other ) {
        bool result = false;
        ComplexNumber that = other as ComplexNumber;
        if( that != null ) {
            result = (this.real == that.real) &&
                        (this.imaginary == that.imaginary);
        }

        return result;
    }

    public override int GetHashCode() {
        return (int) Math.Sqrt( Math.Pow(this.real, 2) *
                            Math.Pow(this.imaginary, 2) );
```

```
    }

    public static bool operator ==( ComplexNumber num1, ComplexNumber num2 ) {
        return Object.Equals(num1, num2);
    }

    public static bool operator !=( ComplexNumber num1, ComplexNumber num2 ) {
        return !Object.Equals(num1, num2);
    }

    // Other methods removed for clarity

    private readonly double real;
    private readonly double imaginary;
}
```

The GetHashCode algorithm is not meant as a highly efficient example. In fact, it's not efficient at all, since it is based on nontrivial floating-point mathematical routines. Also, the rounding could potentially cause many complex numbers to fall within the same bucket. In that case, the efficiency of the hash table would degrade. I'll leave a more efficient algorithm as an exercise to the reader. Notice that I don't use the GetHashCode method to implement operator!= because of the efficiency concerns. But more importantly, I rely on the static Object.Equals method to compare them for equality. This handy method checks the references for null before calling the instance Equals method, saving you from having to do that. Had I used GetHashCode to implement operator!=, I would have had to check the references for null values before calling GetHashCode on them. Also, note that both fields used to calculate the hash code are immutable. Thus, this instance of this object will always return the same hash code value as long as it lives. In fact, you may consider caching the hash code value once you compute it the first time to gain greater efficiency.

Does the Object Support Ordering?

Sometimes you'll design a class for objects that are meant to be stored within a collection. When the objects in that collection need to be sorted, such as by calling Sort on an ArrayList, you need a well-defined mechanism for comparing two objects. The pattern that the Base Class Library designers provided hinges on implementing the following IComparable interface:[5]

```
public interface IComparable
{
    int CompareTo( object obj );
}
```

Again, another one of these interfaces merely contains one method. Thankfully, IComparable doesn't contain the same depth of pitfalls as ICloneable and IDisposable. The CompareTo method is fairly straightforward. It can return a value that is either positive, negative, or zero. Table 13-1 lists the return value meanings.

Table 13-1. *Meaning of Return Values of* IComparable.CompareTo

CompareTo Return Value	Meaning
Positive	this > obj
Zero	this == obj
Negative	this < obj

---

5. For value types, you should consider using the generic IComparable<T> interface as shown in Chapter 10.

You should be aware of a few points when implementing IComparable.CompareTo. First, notice that the return value specification says nothing about the actual value of the returned integer. It only defines the sign of the return values. So, to indicate a situation where this is less than obj, you can simply return -1. When your object represents a value that carries an integer meaning, an efficient way to compute the comparison value is by subtracting one from the other. It can be tempting to treat the return value as an indication of the degree of inequality. Although this is possible, I don't recommend it, since relying on such an implementation is outside the bounds of the IComparable specification, and not all objects can be expected to do that.

Second, keep in mind that CompareTo provides no return value definition for when two objects cannot be compared. Since the parameter type to CompareTo is System.Object, you could easily attempt to compare an Apple instance to an Orange instance. In such a case, there is no comparison, and you're forced to indicate such by throwing an ArgumentException object.

Finally, semantically, the IComparable interface is a superset of Object.Equals. If you derive from an object that overrides Equals and implements IComparable, then you're wise to both override Equals and reimplement IComparable in your derived class, or do neither. You want to make certain that your implementation of Equals and CompareTo are aligned with each other.

Based upon all of this information, a compliant IComparable interface should adhere to the following rules:

- x.CompareTo(x) must return 0. This is the reflexive property.

- If x.CompareTo(y) == 0, then y.CompareTo(x) must equal 0. This is the symmetric property.

- If x.CompareTo(y) == 0, and y.CompareTo(z) == 0, then x.CompareTo(z) must equal 0. This is the transitive property.

- If x.CompareTo(y) returns a value other than 0, then y.CompareTo(x) must return a non-0 value of the opposite sign. In other terms, this statement says that if x < y, then y > x, or if x > y, then y < x.

- If x.CompareTo(y) returns a value other than 0, and y.CompareTo(z) returns a value other than 0 with the same sign as the first, then x.CompareTo(y) is required to return a non-0 value of the same sign as the previous two. In other terms, this statement says that if x < y and y < z, then x < z, or if x > y and y > z, then x > z.

The following code shows a modified form of the ComplexNumber class that implements IComparable and consolidates some code at the same time in private helper methods:

```
using System;

public sealed class ComplexNumber : IComparable
{
    public ComplexNumber( double real, double imaginary ) {
        this.real = real;
        this.imaginary = imaginary;
    }

    public override bool Equals( object other ) {
        bool result = false;
        ComplexNumber that = other as ComplexNumber;
        if( that != null ) {
            result = InternalEquals( that );
        }

        return result;
    }
```

```csharp
public override int GetHashCode() {
    return (int) this.Magnitude;
}

public static bool operator ==( ComplexNumber num1, ComplexNumber num2 ) {
    return Object.Equals(num1, num2);
}

public static bool operator !=( ComplexNumber num1, ComplexNumber num2 ) {
    return !Object.Equals(num1, num2);
}

public int CompareTo( object other ) {
    ComplexNumber that = other as ComplexNumber;
    if( that == null ) {
        throw new ArgumentException( "Bad Comparison!" );
    }

    int result;
    if( InternalEquals(that) ) {
        result = 0;
    } else if( this.Magnitude > that.Magnitude ) {
        result = 1;
    } else {
        result = -1;
    }

    return result;
}

private bool InternalEquals( ComplexNumber that ) {
    return (this.real == that.real) &&
            (this.imaginary == that.imaginary);
}

public double Magnitude {
    get {
        return Math.Sqrt( Math.Pow(this.real, 2) +
                            Math.Pow(this.imaginary, 2) );
    }
}

// Other methods removed for clarity

private readonly double real;
private readonly double imaginary;
}
```

Is the Object Formattable?

When you create a new object, or an instance of a value type for that matter, it inherits a method from System.Object called ToString. This method accepts no parameters and simply returns a string representation of the object. In all cases, if it makes sense to call ToString on your object, you'll need to override this method. The default implementation provided by System.Object merely returns a string representation of the object's type name, which of course is not useful for an object requiring a string representation based upon its internal state. You should always consider overriding Object.ToString for all of your types, even if only for the convenience of logging the object state to a debug output log.

Object.ToString is useful for getting a quick string representation of an object; however, it's sometimes not useful enough. For example, consider the previous ComplexNumber example. Suppose you want to provide a ToString override for that class. An obvious implementation would output the complex number as an ordered pair within a pair of parentheses, such as "(1, 2)" for example. However, the real and imaginary components of ComplexNumber are of type double. Also, floating-point numbers don't always appear the same across all cultures. Americans use a period to separate the fractional element of a floating-point number, whereas most Europeans use a comma. This problem is solved easily if you utilize the default culture information attached to the thread. By accessing the System.Threading.Thread.CurrentThread.CurrentCulture property, you can get references to the default cultural information detailing how to represent numerical values, including monetary amounts, as well as information on how to represent time and date values.

Note I cover globalization and cultural information in greater detail in Chapter 8.

By default, the CurrentCulture property gives you access to System.Globalization.DateTimeFormatInfo and System.Globalization.NumberFormatInfo. Using the information provided by these objects, you can output the ComplexNumber in a form that is appropriate for the default culture of the machine the application is running on. Check out Chapter 8 for an example of how this works.

That solution seems easy enough. However, you must realize that there are times where using the default culture is not sufficient, and a user of your objects may need to specify which culture to use. Not only that, the user may want to specify the exact formatting of the output. For example, a user may prefer to say that the real and imaginary portions of a ComplexNumber instance should be displayed with only five significant digits while using the German cultural information. If you develop software for servers, you know that you need this capability. A company that runs a financial services server in the United States and services requests from Japan will want to display Japanese currency in the format customary for the Japanese culture. You need to specify how to format an object when it is converted to a string via ToString without having to change the CurrentCulture on the thread beforehand.

In fact, the Standard Library provides an interface for doing just that. When a class or struct needs the capability to respond to such requests, it implements the IFormattable interface. The following code shows the simple-looking IFormattable interface. However, don't be fooled by its simplistic looks, because depending on the complexity of your object, it may be tricky to implement:

```
public interface IFormattable
{
   string ToString( string format, IFormatProvider formatProvider );
}
```

Let's consider the second parameter first. If the client passes null for formatProvider, you should default to using the culture information attached to the current thread as previously described. However, if formatProvider is not null, you'll need to acquire the formatting information from the provider via the IFormatProvider.GetFormat method. IFormatProvider looks like this:

```
public interface IFormatProvider
{
   object GetFormat( Type formatType );
}
```

In an effort to be as generic as possible, the designers of the Standard Library designed GetFormat to accept an object of type System.Type. Thus, it is extensible as to what types the object that implements IFormatProvider may support. This flexibility is handy if you intend to develop custom format providers that need to return as-of-yet-undefined formatting information.

The Standard Library provides a System.Globalization.CultureInfo type that will most likely suffice for all of your needs. The CultureInfo object implements the IFormatProvider interface, and you can pass instances of it as the second parameter to IFormattable.ToString. Soon, I'll show an example of its usage when I make modifications to the ComplexNumber example, but first, let's look at the first parameter to ToString.

The format parameter of ToString allows you to specify how to format a specific number. The format provider can describe how to display a date or how to display currency based upon cultural preferences, but you still need to know how to format the object in the first place. All of the types within the Standard Library, such as Int32, support the standard format specifiers as described under "Standard Numeric Format Strings" in the MSDN library. In a nutshell, the format string consists of a single letter specifying the format, and then an optional number between 0 and 99 that declares the precision. For example, you can specify that a double be output as a five-significant-digit floating-point number with F5. Not all types are required to support all formats except for one—the G format, which stands for "general." In fact, the G format is what you get when you call the parameterless Object.ToString on most objects in the Standard Library. Some types will ignore the format specification in special circumstances. For example, a System.Double can contain special values that represent NaN (Not a Number), PositiveInfinity, or NegativeInfinity. In such cases, System.Double ignores the format specification and displays a symbol appropriate for the culture as provided by NumberFormatInfo.

The format specifier may also consist of a custom format string. Custom format strings allow the user to specify the exact layout of numbers as well as mixed-in string literals and so on by using the syntax described under "Custom Numeric Format String" in the MSDN library. The client can specify one format for negative numbers, another for positive numbers, and a third for zero values. I won't spend any time detailing these various formatting capabilities. Instead, I encourage you to reference the MSDN material for detailed information regarding them.

As you can see, implementing IFormattable.ToString can be quite a tedious experience, especially since your format string could be highly customized. However, in many cases—and the ComplexNumber example is one of those cases—you can rely upon the IFormattable implementations of standard types. Since ComplexNumber uses System.Double to represent its real and imaginary parts, you can defer most of your work to the implementation of IFormattable on System.Double. Let's look at modifications to the ComplexNumber example to support IFormattable. Assume that the ComplexNumber type will accept a format string exactly the same way that System.Double does and that each component of the complex number will be output using this same format. Of course, a better implementation may provide more capabilities such as allowing you to specify whether the output should be in Cartesian or polar format, but I'll leave that to you as an exercise:

```
using System;
using System.Globalization;

public sealed class ComplexNumber : IFormattable
{
    public ComplexNumber( double real, double imaginary ) {
        this.real = real;
        this.imaginary = imaginary;
    }
```

```
    public override string ToString() {
        return ToString( "G", null );
    }

    // IFormattable implementation
    public string ToString( string format,
                            IFormatProvider formatProvider ) {
        string result = "(" +
            real.ToString(format, formatProvider) +
            " " +
            real.ToString(format, formatProvider) +
            ")";
        return result;
    }

    // Other methods removed for clarity

    private readonly double real;
    private readonly double imaginary;
}

public sealed class EntryPoint
{
    static void Main() {
        ComplexNumber num1 = new ComplexNumber( 1.12345678,
                                                2.12345678 );

        Console.WriteLine( "US format: {0}",
                           num1.ToString( "F5",
                                new CultureInfo("en-US") ) );
        Console.WriteLine( "DE format: {0}",
                           num1.ToString( "F5",
                                new CultureInfo("de-DE") ) );
        Console.WriteLine( "Object.ToString(): {0}",
                           num1.ToString() );
    }
}
```

Here's the output from running this example:

```
US format: (1.12346 2.12346)
DE format: (1,12346 2,12346)
Object.ToString(): (1.12345678 2.12345678)
```

In Main, notice the creation and use of two different CultureInfo instances. First, the ComplexNumber is output using American cultural formatting, and second, using German cultural formatting. In both cases, I specify to output the string using only five significant digits. You will see that System.Double's implementation of IFormattable.ToString even rounds the result as expected. Finally, you can see that the Object.ToString override is implemented to defer to the IFormattable.ToString method using the G (general) format.

IFormattable provides the clients of your objects with powerful capabilities when they have specific formatting needs for your objects. However, that power comes at an implementation cost. Implementing IFormattable.ToString can be a very detail-oriented task that takes a lot of time and attentiveness.

Is the Object Convertible?

The C# compiler provides support for converting instances of simple built-in value types, such as int and long, from one type to another via casting by generating IL code that uses the conv IL instruction. The conv instruction works well for the simple built-in types, but what do you do when you want to convert a string to an integer or vice versa? The compiler cannot do this for you automatically, because such conversions are potentially complex and even require parameters, such as cultural information.

The .NET Framework provides several ways to get the job done. For nontrivial conversions that you cannot do with casting, you should rely upon the System.Convert class. I won't list the functions that Convert implements here, as the list is extremely long. I encourage you to look it up in the MSDN library. The Convert class contains methods to convert from just about any built-in type to another as long as it makes sense. So, if you want to convert a double to a String, you would simply call the ToString static method, passing it the double as follows:

```
static void Main()
{
    double d = 12.1;
    string str = Convert.ToString( d );
}
```

In similar form to IFormattable.ToString, Convert.ToString has various overloads that also allow you to pass a CultureInfo object or any other object that supports IFormatProvider, in order to specify cultural information when doing the conversion. You can use other methods as well, such as ToBoolean and ToUint32. The general pattern of the method names is obviously ToXXX, where XXX is the type you're converting to. System.Convert even has methods to convert byte arrays to and from base64-encoded strings. If you store any binary data in XML text or any other text-based medium, you'll find these methods very handy.

Convert will generally serve most of your conversion needs between built-in types. It's a one-stop shop for converting an object of one type to another. You can see this just by looking at the wealth of methods that it supports. However, what happens when your conversion involves a custom type that Convert doesn't know about? The answer lies in the Convert.ChangeType method.

ChangeType is System.Convert's extensibility mechanism. It has several overloads, including some that take a format provider for cultural information. However, the general idea is that it takes an object reference and converts it to the type represented by the passed-in System.Type object. Consider the following code, which uses the ComplexNumber from previous examples and tries to convert it into a string using System.Convert.ChangeType:

```
using System;

public sealed class ComplexNumber
{
    public ComplexNumber( double real, double imaginary ) {
        this.real = real;
        this.imaginary = imaginary;
    }

    // Other methods removed for clarity

    private readonly double real;
    private readonly double imaginary;
}

public sealed class EntryPoint
{
```

```
static void Main() {
    ComplexNumber num1 = new ComplexNumber( 1.12345678, 2.12345678 );

    string str =
        (string) Convert.ChangeType( num1, typeof(string) );
    }
}
```

You'll find that the code compiles just fine. However, you'll get a surprise at run time when you find that it throws an InvalidCastException with the message, "Object must implement IConvertible." Even though ChangeType is System.Convert's extensibility mechanism, extensibility doesn't come for free. You must do some work to make ChangeType work with ComplexNumber. And, as you probably guessed, the work required is to implement the IConvertible interface.

The IConvertible interface is the last defense when it comes to converting objects. If you want your custom objects to play nice with System.Convert and the types of conversions the user may desire to perform, then you had better implement IConvertible. As with System.Convert, I won't list the IConvertible methods here, since there are quite a few of them. I encourage you to look them up in the MSDN documentation. You'll see one method for converting to each of the built-in types. In addition, Convert uses a catch-all method, IConvertible.ToType, to convert one custom type to another custom type. Also, the IConvertible methods accept a format provider so that you can provide cultural information to the conversion method.

Remember, when you implement an interface, you're required to provide implementations for all of the interface's methods. However, if a particular conversion makes no sense for your object, then you can throw an InvalidCastException. Naturally, your implementation will most definitely throw an exception inside IConvertible.ToType for any generic type that it doesn't support conversion to.

To sum up, it may appear that there are many ways to convert one type to another in C#, and in fact, there are. However, the general rule of thumb is to rely on System.Convert when casting won't do the trick. Moreover, your custom objects, such as the ComplexNumber class, should implement IConvertible so they can work in concert with the System.Convert class.

■Note C# offers conversion operators that allow you to do essentially the same thing you can do by implementing IConvertible. However, C# implicit and explicit conversion operators aren't CLS-compliant. Therefore, not every language that consumes your C# code may call them to do the conversion. It is recommended that you not rely on them exclusively to handle conversion. Of course, if your project is coded using .NET languages that do support conversion operators, then you can use them exclusively, but it's recommended that you also support IConvertible.

The .NET Framework offers yet another type of conversion mechanism, which works via the System.ComponentModel.TypeConverter. It is another converter that is external to the class of the object instance that needs to be converted, such as System.Convert. The advantage of using TypeConverter is that you can use it at design time within the IDE as well as at run time. You create your own special type converter for your class that derives from TypeConverter, and then you associate your new type converter to your class via the TypeConverterAttribute. At design time, the IDE can examine the metadata for your type and, from the information gleaned from the metadata, create an instance of your type's converter. That way, it can convert your type to and from representations that it sees fit to use. I won't go into the details of creating a TypeConverter derivative, but if you'd like more information, look up the "Generalized Type Conversion" topic in the MSDN documentation.

CHAPTER 13 ■ IN SEARCH OF C# CANONICAL FORMS   **399**

Prefer Type Safety at All Times

You already know that C# is a strongly typed language. A strongly typed language and its compiler form a dynamic duo capable of sniffing out bugs before they strike. Even though every object in the managed world derives from System.Object, it's a bad idea to treat every object generically via a System.Object reference. One reason is efficiency; for example, if you were to maintain a collection of Employee objects via references to System.Object, you would always have to cast instances of them to type Employee before you can call the Evaluate method on them. Although this inefficiency problem is slight when reference types are used and the cast succeeds, it is amplified by magnitudes with value types, since unnecessary boxing operations are generated in the IL code. I'll cover the boxing inefficiencies in the following sections dealing with value types. The biggest problem with all of this casting when using reference types is when the cast fails and an exception is thrown. By using strong types, you can catch these problems and deal with them at compile time.

Another prominent reason to prefer strong type usage is associated with catching errors. Consider the case when implementing interfaces such as ICloneable. Notice that the Clone method returns an instance as type Object. Clearly, this is done so that the interface will work generically across all types. However, it can come at a price.

C++ and C# are both strongly typed languages. Every variable is declared with a type. Along with this comes type safety, which the compiler supplies to help you avoid errors. For example, it keeps you from assigning an instance of class Apple from an instance of class MonkeyWrench. However, C# (and C++) allows you to work in a less type-safe way. You can reference every object through the type Object; however, doing so throws away the type safety, and the compiler will allow you to assign an instance of type Apple from an instance of type MonkeyWrench as long as both references are of type Object. Unfortunately, even though the code will compile, you run the risk of generating a runtime error once the CLR executes code that realizes what sort of craziness you're attempting to do. So, the more you utilize the type safety of the compiler, the more error detection it can do at compile time, and catching errors at compile time is *always* more desirable than catching errors at run time.

Let's have a closer look at the efficiency facet of the problem. Treating objects generically can impose a runtime inefficiency when you need to downcast to the actual type. In reality, this efficiency hit is very minor with managed reference types in C#, unless you're doing it many times within a loop.

In some situations, the C# compiler will generate much more efficient code if you provide a type-safe implementation of a well-defined method. Consider this typical foreach statement in C#:

```
foreach( Employee emp in collection ) {
    // Do Something
}
```

Quite simply, the code loops over all the items in collection. Within the body of the foreach statement, a variable emp of type Employee references the current item in the collection during iteration. One of the rules enforced by the C# compiler for the collection is that it must implement a public method named GetEnumerator, which returns a type used to enumerate the items in the collection. This method is implemented as a result of the collection type implementing the IEnumerable interface and typically returns a forward iterator on the collection of contained objects.[6] One of the rules for the enumerator type is that it must implement a public property named Current, which allows access to the current element. This property is part of the IEnumerator interface; however, notice that IEnumerator.Current is typed as System.Object. This leads to another rule with regard to the foreach statement. It states that the object type of IEnumerator.Current, the real

---

6. I use the word *typically* here, since the iterators could be reverse iterators. In Chapter 9, I show how you can easily create reverse and bidirectional iterators that implement IEnumerator.

object type, must be explicitly castable to the type of the iterator in the foreach statement, which in this example is type Employee. If your collection's enumerator types its Current property as System. Object, the compiler must always perform the cast to type Employee. However, you can see that the compiler can generate much more efficient code if your Current property on your enumerator is typed as Employee.

So, what can you do to remedy this situation in the C# world? Basically, whenever you implement an interface that contains methods with essentially nontyped return values, consider using explicit interface implementation to hide the method from the public interface of the class, while implementing a more type-safe version as part of the public interface of the class. Let's look at an example using the IEnumerator interface:

```
using System;
using System.Collections;

public class Employee
{
    public void Evaluate() {
        Console.WriteLine( "Evaluating Employee..." );
    }
}

public class WorkForceEnumerator : IEnumerator
{
    public WorkForceEnumerator( ArrayList employees ) {
        this.enumerator = employees.GetEnumerator();
    }

    public Employee Current {
        get {
            return (Employee) enumerator.Current;
        }
    }

    object IEnumerator.Current {
        get {
            return enumerator.Current;
        }
    }

    public bool MoveNext() {
        return enumerator.MoveNext();
    }

    public void Reset() {
        enumerator.Reset();
    }

    private IEnumerator enumerator;
}

public class WorkForce : IEnumerable
{
    public WorkForce() {
        employees = new ArrayList();
```

```
        // Let's put an employee in here for demo purposes.
        employees.Add( new Employee() );
    }

    public WorkForceEnumerator GetEnumerator() {
        return new WorkForceEnumerator( employees );
    }

    IEnumerator IEnumerable.GetEnumerator() {
        return new WorkForceEnumerator( employees );
    }

    private ArrayList employees;
}

public class EntryPoint
{
    static void Main() {
        WorkForce staff = new WorkForce();
        foreach( Employee emp in staff ) {
            emp.Evaluate();
        }
    }
}
```

Look carefully at the example and notice how the typeless versions of the interface methods are implemented explicitly. Remember that in order to access those methods, you must first cast the instance to the interface type. However, the compiler doesn't do that when it generates the foreach loop. Instead, it simply looks for methods that match the rules already mentioned.[7] So, it will find the strongly typed versions and use them. I encourage you to step through the code using a debugger to see it in action. In fact, these types aren't even required to implement the interfaces that they implement—namely, IEnumerable and IEnumerator. You can comment the interface names out and simply implement the methods that match the signatures of the ones in the interfaces. Also, you can make this code considerably more efficient by using generics, which I covered in Chapter 11.

Let's take a closer look at the foreach loop generated by the compiler to get a better idea of what sorts of efficiency gains you get. In the following code, I've removed the strongly typed versions of the interface methods, and as expected, the example runs pretty much the same as before from an outside perspective:

```
using System;
using System.Collections;

public class Employee
{
    public void Evaluate() {
        Console.WriteLine( "Evaluating Employee..." );
    }
}
```

---

7. This technique is commonly referred to as *duck typing*. Duck typing is a programming style whereby a type implements a contract or an interface simply by implementing the methods defined in the contract rather than inheriting from a specific type or interface. For more information, reference http://en.wikipedia. org/wiki/Duck_typing.

```csharp
public class WorkForceEnumerator : IEnumerator
{
    public WorkForceEnumerator( ArrayList employees ) {
        this.enumerator = employees.GetEnumerator();
    }

    public object Current {
        get {
            return enumerator.Current;
        }
    }

    public bool MoveNext() {
        return enumerator.MoveNext();
    }

    public void Reset() {
        enumerator.Reset();
    }

    private IEnumerator enumerator;
}

public class WorkForce : IEnumerable
{
    public WorkForce() {
        employees = new ArrayList();

        // Let's put an employee in here for demo purposes.
        employees.Add( new Employee() );
    }

    public IEnumerator GetEnumerator() {
        return new WorkForceEnumerator( employees );
    }

    private ArrayList employees;
}

public class EntryPoint
{
    static void Main() {
        WorkForce staff = new WorkForce();
        foreach( Employee emp in staff ) {
            emp.Evaluate();
        }
    }
}
```

Of course, the generated IL is not as efficient. To see the efficiency gains within the foreach loop, you must load the compiled versions of each example into ILDASM and open up the IL code for the Main method. You'll see that the weakly typed example has extra castclass instructions that are not present in the strongly typed example. On my development machine, I ran the foreach loop 20,000,000 times in a tight loop to create a crude benchmark. The typed version of the enumerator was 15% faster than the untyped version. That's a considerable gain if you're working on the game loop in the next best-selling Managed DirectX game.

Using Immutable Reference Types

When creating a well-designed contract or interface, you should always consider the mutability or immutability of types declared in the contract. For example, if you have a method that accepts a parameter, you should consider whether it is valid for the method to modify the parameter. Suppose you want to ensure that the method body cannot modify a parameter. If the parameter is a value type that is passed without the ref keyword, then the method receives a copy of the parameter, and you're guaranteed that the source value is not modified. However, for reference types, it's much more complicated, since only the reference is copied rather than the object the reference points to.

■**Note** If you come from a C++ background, you'll recognize that immutability is implemented via the const keyword. To follow this technique is to be const-correct. Even though C++ may seem superior to those who are upset that C# doesn't support const, keep in mind that in C++, you can cast away the const-ness using const_cast. Therefore, an immutable implementation is actually superior to the C++ const keyword, since you can't simply cast it away.

A great example of an immutable class within the Standard Library is System.String. Once you create a String object, you can't ever change it. There's no way around it; that's the way the class is designed. You can create copies, and those copies can be modified forms of the original, but you simply cannot change the original instance for as long as it lives, without resorting to unsafe code. If you understand that, you're probably starting to get the gist of where I'm going here: For a reference-based object to be passed into a method, such that the client can be guaranteed that it won't change during the method call, it must itself be immutable.

In a world such as the CLR where objects are held by reference by default, this notion of immutability becomes very important. Let's suppose that System.String was mutable, and let's suppose you could write a method such as the following fictitious method:

```
public void PrintString( string theString )
{
    // Assuming following line does not create a new
    // instance of String but modifies theString
    theString += ": there, I printed it!";
    Console.WriteLine( theString );
}
```

Imagine the callers' dismay when they get further along in the code that called this method and now their string has this extra stuff appended onto the end of it. That's what could happen if System.String were mutable. You can see that String's immutability exists for a reason, and maybe you should consider adding the same capability to your design.

There are many ways to solve the C# const parameter problem for objects that must be mutable. One general solution is to create two classes for each mutable class you create if you'll ever want your clients to be able to pass a const version of the object to a parameter. As an example, let's revisit the previous ComplexNumber class. If implemented as an object rather than a value type, ComplexNumber is a perfect candidate to be an immutable type, similar to String. In such cases, an operation such as ComplexNumber.Add would need to produce a new instance of ComplexNumber rather than modify the object referenced by this. But for the sake of argument, let's consider what you would want to do if ComplexNumber were allowed to be mutable. You could allow access to the real and imaginary fields via read-write properties. But how would you be able to pass the object to a method and be guaranteed that the method won't change it by accessing the setter of the one of the properties? One answer, as in many other object-oriented designs, is the technique of introducing another class. Consider the following code:

```
using System;

public sealed class ComplexNumber
{
    public ComplexNumber( double real, double imaginary ) {
        this.real = real;
        this.imaginary = imaginary;
    }

    public double Real {
        get {
            return real;
        }

        set {
            real = value;
        }
    }

    public double Imaginary {
        get {
            return imaginary;
        }

        set {
            imaginary = value;
        }
    }

    // Other methods removed for clarity

    private double real;
    private double imaginary;
}

public sealed class ConstComplexNumber
{
    public ConstComplexNumber( ComplexNumber pimpl ) {
        this.pimpl = pimpl;
    }

    public double Real {
        get {
            return pimpl.Real;
        }
    }

    public double Imaginary {
        get {
```

```
            return pimpl.Imaginary;
        }
    }

    private readonly ComplexNumber pimpl⁸;
}

public sealed class EntryPoint
{
    static void Main() {
        ComplexNumber someNumber = new ComplexNumber( 1, 2 );
        SomeMethod( new ConstComplexNumber(someNumber) );

        // We are guaranteed by the contract of ConstComplexNumber that
        // someNumber has not been changed at this point.
    }

    static void SomeMethod( ConstComplexNumber number ) {
        Console.WriteLine( "( {0}, {1} )",
                           number.Real,
                           number.Imaginary );
    }
}
```

Notice that I've introduced a shim class named ConstComplexNumber. When a method wants to accept a ComplexNumber object but guarantee that it won't change that parameter, then it accepts a ConstComplexNumber rather than a ComplexNumber. Of course, for the case of ComplexNumber, the best solution would have been to implement it as an immutable type in the first place.[9] But, you can easily imagine a class much more complex than ComplexNumber (no pun intended . . . really!) that may require a technique similar to this to guarantee that a method won't modify an instance of it.

As with many problems in software design, you can achieve the same goal in many ways. This shim technique isn't the only way to solve this problem. You could also achieve the same goal with interfaces. You could define one interface that declares all of the methods that modify the object—say, IModifiableComplexNumber—and another interface that declares methods that don't modify the object—say, IConstantComplexNumber. Then, you could create a third interface, IComplexNumber, which derives from both of these, and, finally, ComplexNumber would then implement the IComplexNumber interface. For methods that must take the parameter as immutable, you can simply pass the instance as the IConstantComplexNumber type.

Before you write these techniques off as academic exercises, please take time to consider and understand the power of immutability in robust software designs. So many articles on const-correctness exist in the C++ community for good reason. And there is no good reason that you shouldn't apply these same techniques to your C# designs.

Value Type Canonical Forms

While investigating the notions of canonical forms for value types, you'll find that some of the concepts that apply to reference types may be applied here as well. However, there are many notable

---

8. For those of you curious about the curious name of this field, read about the Pimpl Idiom in Herb Sutter's *Exceptional C++: 47 Engineering Puzzles, Programming Problems, and Solutions* (Boston, MA: Addison-Wesley Professional, 2000).

9. To avoid this complex ball of yarn, many of the value types defined by the .NET Framework are, in fact, immutable.

differences. For example, it makes no sense to implement ICloneable on a value type. Technically, you could, but since ICloneable returns an instance of type Object, your value type's implementation of ICloneable.Clone would most likely just be returning a boxed copy of itself. You can get exactly the same behavior by simply casting a value type instance into a reference to System.Object, as long as your value type doesn't contain any reference types. In fact, you could argue that value types that contain mutable reference types are bordering on poor design. Value types are best used for immutable, lightweight data chunks. So, as long as the reference types your value type does contain are immutable—similar to System.String, for example—you don't have to worry about implementing ICloneable on your value type. If you find yourself being forced to implement ICloneable on your value type, take a closer look at the design. It's possible that your value type should be a reference type.

Value types don't need a finalizer, and, in fact, C# won't let you create a finalizer via the destructor syntax on a struct. Similarly, value types have no need to implement the IDisposable interface, unless they contain objects by reference, which implement IDisposable, or if they hold onto scarce system resources. In those cases, it's important that value types implement IDisposable. In fact, you can use the using statement with value types that implement IDisposable.

■ **Tip** Since value types cannot implement finalizers, they cannot guarantee that the cleanup code in Dispose executes even if the user forgets to call it explicitly. Therefore, declaring fields of reference type within value types should be discouraged. If the field is a value type that requires disposal, you cannot guarantee that disposal happens.

Value types and reference types do share many implementation idioms. For example, it makes sense for both to consider implementing IComparable, IFormattable, and possibly IConvertible.

In the rest of this section, I'll cover the different canonical concepts that you should apply while designing value types. Specifically, you'll want to override Equals for greater runtime efficiency, and you'll want to be cognizant of what it means for a value type to implement an interface. Let's get started.

Override Equals for Better Performance

You've already seen the main differences between the two types of equivalence in the CLR and in C#. For example, you now know that reference types (class instances) define equality as an identity test by default, and value types (struct instances) use value equality as an equivalence test. Reference types get their default implementation from Object.Equals, whereas value types get their default implementation from System.ValueType's override of Equals. All struct types implicitly derive from System.ValueType.

You should implement your own override of Equals for each struct that you define. You can compare the fields of your object more efficiently, since you know their types and what they are at compile time. Let's update the ComplexNumber example from previous sections, converting it to a struct and implementing a custom Equals override:

```
using System;

public struct ComplexNumber : IComparable
{
    public ComplexNumber( double real, double imaginary ) {
        this.real = real;
        this.imaginary = imaginary;
    }
```

```csharp
public override bool Equals( object other ) {
    bool result = false;
    if( other is ComplexNumber ) {
        ComplexNumber that = (ComplexNumber) other ;

        result = InternalEquals( that );
    }

    return result;
}

public override int GetHashCode() {
    return (int) this.Magnitude;
}

public static bool operator ==( ComplexNumber num1,
                                ComplexNumber num2 ) {
    return num1.Equals(num2);
}

public static bool operator !=( ComplexNumber num1,
                                ComplexNumber num2 ) {
    return !num1.Equals(num2);
}

public int CompareTo( object other ) {
    if( !(other is ComplexNumber) ) {
        throw new ArgumentException( "Bad Comparison!" );
    }

    ComplexNumber that = (ComplexNumber) other;

    int result;
    if( InternalEquals(that) ) {
        result = 0;
    } else if( this.Magnitude > that.Magnitude ) {
        result = 1;
    } else {
        result = -1;
    }

    return result;
}

private bool InternalEquals( ComplexNumber that ) {
    return (this.real == that.real) &&
            (this.imaginary == that.imaginary);
}

public double Magnitude {
    get {
        return Math.Sqrt( Math.Pow(this.real, 2) +
                          Math.Pow(this.imaginary, 2) );
    }
}
```

```
        // Other methods removed for clarity

        private readonly double real;
        private readonly double imaginary;
    }

    public sealed class EntryPoint
    {
        static void Main()
        {
            ComplexNumber num1 = new ComplexNumber( 1, 2 );
            ComplexNumber num2 = new ComplexNumber( 1, 2 );

            bool result = num1.Equals( num2 );
        }
    }
```

Looking at the example code, you can see that it has only minimal changes compared to the reference type version. The type is now declared as a struct rather than a class, and notice that it also still supports IComparable. I'll have more to say about structs implementing interfaces later, in the section titled "Do Values of This Type Support Any Interfaces?" The keen reader may notice that the efficiency still stands to improve by a fair amount. The trick lies in the concept of boxing and unboxing. Remember, any time a value type instance is passed as an object in a method parameter list, it must be implicitly boxed if it is not boxed already. That means that when the Main method calls the Equals method, it must first box the num2 value. What's worse is that the method will typically unbox the value in order to use it. Thus, in the process of comparing two values for equality, you've made two more copies of one of them.

To solve this problem, you can define two overloads of Equals. You want a type-safe version that takes a ComplexNumber as its parameter type, and you still need to override the Object.Equals method as before.

Note The .NET 2.0 Framework formalized this concept with the generic interface IEquatable<T>, which declares one method that is the type-safe version of Equals.

Let's take a look at how the code changes:

```
using System;

public struct ComplexNumber : IComparable,
                              IComparable<ComplexNumber>,
                              IEquatable<ComplexNumber>
{
    public ComplexNumber( double real, double imaginary ) {
        this.real = real;
        this.imaginary = imaginary;
    }

    public bool Equals( ComplexNumber other ) {
        return (this.real == other.real) &&
               (this.imaginary == other.imaginary);
    }
```

```csharp
public override bool Equals( object other ) {
    bool result = false;
    if( other is ComplexNumber ) {
        ComplexNumber that = (ComplexNumber) other ;

        result = Equals( that );
    }

    return result;
}

public override int GetHashCode() {
    return (int) this.Magnitude;
}

public static bool operator ==( ComplexNumber num1,
                                ComplexNumber num2 ) {
    return num1.Equals(num2);
}

public static bool operator !=( ComplexNumber num1,
                                ComplexNumber num2 ) {
    return !num1.Equals(num2);
}

public int CompareTo( object other ) {
    if( !(other is ComplexNumber) ) {
        throw new ArgumentException( "Bad Comparison!" );
    }

    return CompareTo( (ComplexNumber) other );
}

public int CompareTo( ComplexNumber that ) {
    int result;
    if( Equals(that) ) {
        result = 0;
    } else if( this.Magnitude > that.Magnitude ) {
        result = 1;
    } else {
        result = -1;
    }

    return result;
}

public double Magnitude {
    get {
        return Math.Sqrt( Math.Pow(this.real, 2) +
                          Math.Pow(this.imaginary, 2) );
    }
}

// Other methods removed for clarity
```

```
        private readonly double real;
        private readonly double imaginary;
}

public sealed class EntryPoint
{
    static void Main()
    {
        ComplexNumber num1 = new ComplexNumber( 1, 2 );
        ComplexNumber num2 = new ComplexNumber( 1, 2 );

        bool result = num1.Equals( num2 );
    }
}
```

Now, the comparison inside Main is much more efficient, since the value doesn't need to be boxed. The compiler chooses the closest match of the two overloads, which, of course, is the strongly typed overload of Equals that accepts a ComplexNumber rather than a generic object type. Internally, the Object.Equals override delegates to the type-safe version of Equals after it checks the type of the object and unboxes it. It's important to note that the Object.Equals override first checks the type to see if it is a ComplexNumber, or more specifically a boxed ComplexNumber, before it unboxes it so as to avoid throwing an exception. The Standard Library documentation for Object.Equals clearly states that overrides of Object.Equals must not throw exceptions. Finally, notice that the same rule of thumb for GetHashCode exists for structs as well as classes. If you override Object.Equals, you must also override Object.GetHashCode, or vice versa.

Note that I also implemented IComparable<ComplexNumber>, which uses the same technique as IEquatable<ComplexNumber> to provide a type-safe version of IComparable. You should always consider implementing these generic interfaces so the compiler has greater latitude when enforcing type safety.

Do Values of This Type Support Any Interfaces?

The difference in behavior between value types and reference types within the CLR can sometimes cause headaches and confusion, especially to those who are new to the CLR and C#. Those headaches usually derive from the tricky nature of bridging the two worlds between reference types and value types. Consider the fact that all value types (structs) implicitly derive from System.ValueType. Also, consider the fact that System.ValueType derives from System.Object. You might be inclined to think that you could simply cast a value type, such as an instance of ComplexNumber, into Object and thus bridge the gap between the value-type world and the reference-type world. This is what happens, but probably not as you may expect.

What actually happens is that the CLR creates a new object for you, and that new object contains a copy of your value type. You have already seen this concept defined as boxing. Under the covers, when the CLR encounters a definition for a struct, or value type, it also internally defines a reference type, which is the box I'm talking about when I talk about a boxing operation. You can't create an instance of that type explicitly, but that's what you're doing when you incur a boxing operation on a value instance.

When the CLR creates this internal boxing type at run time, it uses reflection to implement all of the methods that your value type implements, and the method implementations simply forward the calls to the contained copy of your value type. By the same token, the dynamically generated boxing type also implements any interfaces that the value type implements. Thus, references to instances of the dynamic box type, which is a reference type, can be cast to references of the implemented interface types, as is natural for reference types. But what do you think happens when you cast a value type instance into an interface type? The answer is that the value must be boxed first. It makes sense when you consider that an interface reference always references a reference type.

You've already seen how boxing can be a nuisance in C#. This is because boxing happens automatically, as if to help you out. But unless you know what's going on under the covers, it can cause more confusion than not, since you can inadvertently modify a value within a box and then throw it away without propagating those changes back into the original value from the boxed value. Dizzying, isn't it?

Can you think of a way whereby you can modify a value that lives inside a box? If you cast the box instance back to its value type, you get a new copy of the value in the box. So, that cannot do the trick. What you need is a way to touch the internal boxed value. Interfaces are the answer. As I said before, the internally created boxing reference type that you never see implements all of the interfaces that the struct implements. Since interface references refer to objects, they can modify the state of the value inside the box, if you make calls through the interface. You cannot modify the contents of a value within a box except through an interface.

In closing, it's important to note that value types that implement interfaces will incur implicit boxing if you cast one of those types to an interface type that it implements. At the same time, interfaces are the only mechanism through which you can change the value inside a box. For an example of how to do this, check out the "Boxing and Unboxing" section in Chapter 4.

Implement Type-Safe Forms of Interface Members and Derived Methods

I already covered this topic with respect to reference types in the "Prefer Type Safety at All Times" section. Most of the same points are applicable to value types, along with some added efficiency considerations. These efficiency problems stem from explicit conversion operations from value types to reference types, and vice versa. As you know, these conversions produce hidden boxing and unboxing operations in the generated IL code. Boxing operations can easily kill your efficiency in many situations. The points made previously about how type-safe versions of the enumeration methods help the C# compiler create much more efficient code in a foreach loop apply tenfold to value types. That is because boxing operations from conversions to and from value types take much more processor time when compared to a typecast of a reference type, which is relatively quick.

You've already seen how the ComplexNumber value type implements an interface—in this case, IComparable. That is because you still want value types to be sortable if they're stored within a container. You'll notice that core types within the CLR, such as System.Int32, also support interfaces such as IComparable. However, from an efficiency standpoint, you don't want to box a value type each time you want to compare it to another. In fact, as it is currently written, the following code boxes both values:

```
public void Main()
{
    ComplexNumber num1 = new ComplexNumber( 1, 3 );
    ComplexNumber num2 = new ComplexNumber( 1, 2 );

    int result = ((IComparable)num1).CompareTo( num2 );
}
```

Can you see both of the boxing operations? As was shown in the previous section, the num1 instance must be boxed in order to acquire a reference to the IComparable interface on it. Secondly, since CompareTo accepts a reference of type System.Object, the num2 instance must be boxed. This is terrible for efficiency. Technically, I didn't have to box num1 in order to call through IComparable. However, if the previous ComplexNumber example had implemented the IComparable interface explicitly, I would have had no choice.

To solve this problem, you want to implement a type-safe version of the CompareTo method, while at the same time implementing the IComparable.CompareTo method. Using this technique, the comparison call in the previous code will incur absolutely no boxing operations. Let's look at how to modify the ComplexNumber struct to do this:

```csharp
using System;

public struct ComplexNumber : IComparable,
                              IComparable<ComplexNumber>,
                              IEquatable<ComplexNumber>
{
    public ComplexNumber( double real, double imaginary ) {
        this.real = real;
        this.imaginary = imaginary;
    }

    public bool Equals( ComplexNumber other ) {
        return (this.real == other.real) &&
               (this.imaginary == other.imaginary);
    }

    public override bool Equals( object other ) {
        bool result = false;
        if( other is ComplexNumber ) {
            ComplexNumber that = (ComplexNumber) other ;

            result = Equals( that );
        }

        return result;
    }

    public override int GetHashCode() {
        return (int) this.Magnitude;
    }

    public static bool operator ==( ComplexNumber num1,
                                    ComplexNumber num2 ) {
        return num1.Equals(num2);
    }

    public static bool operator !=( ComplexNumber num1,
                                    ComplexNumber num2 ) {
        return !num1.Equals(num2);
    }

    public int CompareTo( ComplexNumber that ) {
        int result;
        if( Equals(that) ) {
            result = 0;
        } else if( this.Magnitude > that.Magnitude ) {
            result = 1;
        } else {
            result = -1;
        }
```

```
            return result;
        }

        int IComparable.CompareTo( object other ) {
            if( !(other is ComplexNumber) ) {
                throw new ArgumentException( "Bad Comparison!" );
            }

            return CompareTo( (ComplexNumber) other );
        }

        public double Magnitude {
            get {
                return Math.Sqrt( Math.Pow(this.real, 2) +
                                  Math.Pow(this.imaginary, 2) );
            }
        }

        // Other methods removed for clarity

        private readonly double real;
        private readonly double imaginary;
    }

    public sealed class EntryPoint
    {
        static void Main()
        {
            ComplexNumber num1 = new ComplexNumber( 1, 3 );
            ComplexNumber num2 = new ComplexNumber( 1, 2 );

            int result = num1.CompareTo( num2 );

            // Now, try the type-generic version
            result = ((IComparable)num1).CompareTo( num2 );
        }
    }
```

After the modifications, the first call to CompareTo in Main will incur no boxing operations. You'll also notice that I went one step further and implemented the IComparable.CompareTo method explicitly; this makes it harder to call the typeless version of CompareTo inadvertently without first explicitly casting the value instance to a reference of type IComparable. For good measure, the Main method demonstrates how to call the typeless version of CompareTo. Now, the idea is that clients who use the ComplexNumber value can write code in a natural-looking way and get the benefits of better performance. Clients who require going through the interface, such as some container types, can use the IComparable interface, albeit with some boxing. If you're curious, go ahead and open up the compiled executable with the previous example code inside ILDASM and examine the Main method. You'll see that the first call to CompareTo results in no superfluous boxing, whereas the second call to CompareTo does, in fact, result in two boxing operations as expected.

As a general rule of thumb, you can apply this idiom to just about any value type's methods that accept or return a boxed instance of the value type. So far, you've seen two such examples of the idiom in use. The first was while implementing Equals for the ComplexNumber type, and the second was while implementing IComparable.CompareTo.

Summary

This entire chapter can be summarized into a pair of handy checklists that you can use whenever you design a new type in C#. When you design a new class or struct, it's good design practice to go through the checklist for each type, just as a pilot does before the plane leaves the gate. If you take this approach, you can always feel confident about your designs.

These checklists have been a work in progress for some time. They are, by no means, meant to be complete. You may find the need to augment them or create new entries for new scenarios where you may use classes or structs. These checklists are meant to address the most common scenarios that you're likely to encounter in a C# design process.

Checklist for Reference Types

- *Should this class be unsealed?* Classes should be declared sealed by default unless they're clearly intended to be used as a base class. Even then, you should well document how to use them as a base class. Choose sealed classes over unsealed classes.

- *Is an object cloneable?*

    - *Implement* ICloneable *while defaulting to a deep copy*: If an object is mutable, default to a deep copy. Otherwise, if it's immutable, consider a shallow copy as an optimization.

    - *Avoid use of* MemberwiseClone: Calling MemberwiseClone creates a new object without calling any constructors. This practice can be dangerous.

- *Is an object disposable?*

    - *Implement* IDisposable: If you find the need to implement a conventional destructor, use the IDispose pattern instead.

    - *Implement a finalizer*: Disposable objects should implement a finalizer to either catch objects that clients forgot to dispose of or to warn clients that they forgot to do so. Don't do deterministic destruction work in the C# destructor, which is the finalizer. Only do that kind of work in the Dispose method.

    - *Suppress finalization during a call to* Dispose: This will make the GC perform much more efficiently. Otherwise, objects live on the heap longer than they need to.

- *Should object equivalence checks carry value semantics?*

    - *Override* Object.Equals: Before changing the semantic meaning of Equals, be sure you have a solid argument to do so; otherwise, leave the default identity equivalence in place for objects. It is an error to throw exceptions from within your Equals override.

    - *Know when to call the base class* Equals *implementation*: If your object derives from a type whose version of Equals differs in semantic meaning from your implementation, don't call the base class version in the override. Otherwise, be sure to do so and include its result with yours.

    - *Override* GetHashCode *too*: This is a required step to ensure that you can use objects of this type as a hash code key. If you override Equals, always override GetHashCode too.

- *Are objects of this type comparable?*

    - *Implement* IComparable *and override* Equals *and* GetHashCode: You'll want to override these as a group, since they have intertwined implementations.

- *Is the object convertible to* System.String *or vice versa?*

  - *Override* Object.ToString: The implementation inherited from Object.ToString merely returns a string name of the object's type.

  - *Implement* IFormattable *if users need finer control over string formatting.* Implement the Object.ToString override by calling IFormattable.ToString with a format string of G and a null format provider.

- *Is an object convertible?*

  - *Override* IConvertible *so the class will work with* System.Convert: In C#, you must implement all methods of the interface. However, for conversion methods that don't make sense for your class, simply throw an InvalidCastException object.

- *Should this object be immutable?*

  - *Consider making fields read-only and provide only read-only properties*: Objects that fundamentally represent a simple value, such as a string or a complex number, are excellent candidates to be immutable objects.

- *Do you need to pass this object as a constant immutable method parameter?*

  - *Consider implementing an immutable shim class that contains a reference to a mutable object, which can be passed a method parameter*: First, see if it makes sense for your class to be immutable. If so, then there's no need for this action. If you do need to be able to pass your mutable objects to methods as immutable objects, you can achieve the same effect by using interfaces.

Checklist for Value Types

- *Do you desire greater efficiency for your value types?*

  - *Override* Equals *and* GetHashCode: The generic version of ValueType.Equals is not efficient, because it relies upon reflection to do the job. Generally, it's best to provide a type-safe version of Equals by implementing IEquatable<T> and then have the typeless version call it. Don't forget to override GetHashCode too.

  - *Provide type-safe overloads of inherited typeless methods and interface methods*: For any method that accepts or returns a parameter of type System.Object, provide an overload that uses the concrete value type in its place. That way, clients of the value type can avoid unnecessary boxing. For interfaces, consider hiding the typeless implementation behind an explicit interface implementation, if desired.

- *Need to modify boxed instances of value?*

  - *Implement an interface to do so*: Calling through an interface member implemented by a value type is the only way to change a value type within a boxed instance.

- *Are values of this type comparable?*

  - *Implement* IComparable, *and override* Equals *and* GetHashCode: You'll want to override these as a triplet, since they have intertwined implementations. If you override Equals, take the previous advice and create a type-safe version as well.

- *Is the value convertible to* System.String *or vice versa?*

  - *Override* ValueType.ToString: The implementation inherited from ValueType merely returns a string name of the value's type.

- *Implement* IFormattable *if users need finer control over string formatting*: Implement a ValueType.ToString override that calls IFormattable.ToString with a format string of G and a null format provider.

- *Is the value convertible?*

  - *Override* IConvertible *so struct will work with* System.Convert: In C#, all methods of the interface must be implemented. However, for conversion methods that don't make sense for your struct, simply throw an InvalidCastException object.

- *Should this struct be immutable?*

  - *Consider making fields read-only, and provide only read-only properties*: Values are excellent candidates to be immutable types.

CHAPTER 14

■■■

Extension Methods

Using extension methods, you can declare methods that appear to augment the public interface, or contract, of a type. At first glance, they may appear to provide a way to extend classes that are not meant to be extended. However, it's very important to note that extension methods can only access public members of the type they are extending. That's because they're not really instance methods at all and thus cannot crack the shell of encapsulation on the type they are extending.

Introduction to Extension Methods

As previously mentioned, extension methods make it appear that you can modify the public interface of any type. Let's take a quick look at a small example showing extension methods in action.

```
using System;

namespace ExtensionMethodDemo
{

public static class ExtensionMethods
{
    public static void SendToLog( this String str ) {
        Console.WriteLine( str );
    }
}

public class ExtensionMethodIntro
{
    static void Main() {
        String str = "Some useful information to log";

        // Call the extension method.
        str.SendToLog();

        // Call the same method the old way.
        ExtensionMethods.SendToLog( str );
    }
}

}
```

Take a look at the Main method first. Notice that I declared a System.String first and then called the method SendToLog on the str instance. But wait! There is no method named SendToLog in the System.String type definition. That's because SendToLog is an extension method declared in the previous class, named ExtensionMethods.

At first glance, it appears that ExtensionMethods.SendToLog is just like any other plain static method. But notice two things. It is declared inside a static class, namely ExtensionMethods, and the first parameter to the static method SendToLog has its type prefixed with the keyword this. Using the this keyword in this way is how you tell the compiler that the method is an extension method.

Notice that in the end of the Main method, I demonstrate that you can still call the SendToLog method just like any other normal static method. In fact, functionally, extension methods do not give you any more functionality over regular static methods. Extension methods add a certain amount of syntactic sugar to the language to allow you to call them as if they were an instance method of the type instance you are operating on. But just like any other feature of the language, they can be abused. Therefore, later, in the "Recommendations for Use" section, I present some best practices and guidelines when using extension methods.

How Does the Compiler Find Extension Methods?

When you call an instance method on a type instance, the compiler must derive which method you are actually calling by considering things such as the instance's type, its base type (if there is one), and any interfaces it and its base type may implement, etc. As shown in Chapter 5, the steps the compiler goes through to determine which method to call can be quite complex. So how does the compiler handle the added complexity of finding an extension method to call?

Extension methods are typically imported into the current compilation unit via namespaces with the using keyword. When you use the using keyword to import the types from a particular namespace into the current scope, you also make all of the extension methods implemented in static classes in that namespace available for call via the new syntax. If you don't import the namespace with the static classes implementing the extension methods you need, then you can only call them as static methods using their fully qualified names. Remember that it is not required that you import a namespace in order to use the types within it. For example, you can use the System.Console type in your application without actually importing the types of the System namespace. But you typically do it for convenience. Similarly, in order to call extension methods using the instance method call syntax, you must import the namespace.

■**Note** In C# 3.0, importing a namespace as a more convenient way to address the types within it has a side effect if that namespace also contains extension methods. I discuss this more fully in the "Recommendations for Use" section later on.

When you invoke an instance method, the compiler searches the type for the matching instance method. If the search yields no matching methods, the compiler proceeds to look for matching extension methods. It starts by searching all of the extension methods declared in the containing namespace, and if it does not find a match, searches the next outer enclosing namespace recursively up to the default namespace as it looks for a match. If it fails to find a match, the compiler will stop with a compilation error. Conversely, if the current namespace has more than one extension method imported that matches, the compiler will issue an error complaining about the ambiguity. In such cases, you must fall back to calling the method as a static method while specifying the fully qualified method name.

Consider the following example, which illustrates all of these points:

```
using System;

public static class ExtensionMethods
{
    static public void WriteLine( this String str ) {
        Console.WriteLine( "Default Namespace: " + str );
    }
}

namespace A
{
    public static class ExtensionMethods
    {
        static public void WriteLine( this String str ) {
            Console.WriteLine( "Namespace A: " + str );
        }
    }
}

namespace B
{
    public static class ExtensionMethods
    {
        static public void WriteLine( this String str ) {
            Console.WriteLine( "Namespace B: " + str );
        }
    }
}

namespace C
{
    using A;

    public class Employee
    {
        public Employee( String name ) {
            this.name = name;
        }

        public void PrintName() {
            name.WriteLine();
        }

        private String name;
    }
}

namespace D
{
    using B;
```

```
    public class Dog
    {
        public Dog( String name ) {
            this.name = name;
        }

        public void PrintName() {
            name.WriteLine();
        }

        private String name;
    }
}

namespace E
{
    public class Cat
    {
        public Cat( String name ) {
            this.name = name;
        }

        public void PrintName() {
            name.WriteLine();
        }

        private String name;
    }
}

namespace Demo
{
    using A;
    using B;

    public class EntryPoint
    {
        static void Main() {
            C.Employee fred = new C.Employee( "Fred" );
            D.Dog thor = new D.Dog( "Thor" );
            E.Cat sylvester = new E.Cat( "Sylvester" );

            fred.PrintName();
            thor.PrintName();
            sylvester.PrintName();

            // String str = "Etouffe";
            // str.WriteLine();
        }
    }
}
```

In this example, the same extension method is declared in three different namespaces, specifically, namespace A, namespace B, and the default namespace. Additionally, three types are defined, each in its own namespace; they are Employee, Dog, and Cat. In the Main method, an instance of each is created, and then the PrintName method is called on each instance. The body of each type's PrintName method then calls the WriteLine extension method on the field of type String, and this is where things get interesting. If you compile and execute the code, you will see the following output on the console:

```
Namespace A: Fred
Namespace B: Thor
Default Namespace: Sylvester
```

Notice that, in this case, the exact implementation of the extension method that gets called is governed by which namespace is imported into the namespace where the type (either Employee, Dog, or Cat) is defined. Because namespace C imports namespace A, it follows that Employee will end up calling the WriteLine defined in namespace A. Similarly, since namespace D imports namespace B, the WriteLine extension method in namespace B will get called. Because namespace E imports neither namespaces A nor B, the search proceeds out to the default namespace, which also includes an implementation of the WriteLine extension method. And finally, notice the commented code at the end of the Main method. If you uncomment these lines and attempt to compile, you will see the compiler complain that it cannot figure out which WriteLine to call since the Demo namespace imports both namespaces A and B. This example highlights the dangers of improperly using this new syntax.

Under the Covers

How does the compiler implement extension methods? Since extension methods are just a syntactic shortcut, no modifications were needed to the runtime to support extension methods. Instead, the compiler implements extension methods completely with metadata. Following is the IL code for the ExtensionMethods.WriteLine method from the default namespace generated by compiling the previous example:

```
.method public hidebysig static void  WriteLine(string str) cil managed
{
  .custom instance void [System.Core]System.Runtime.CompilerServices. ➥
ExtensionAttribute::.ctor() = ( 01 00 00 00 )
  // Code size       19 (0x13)
  .maxstack  8
  IL_0000:  nop
  IL_0001:  ldstr      "Default Namespace: "
  IL_0006:  ldarg.0
  IL_0007:  call       string [mscorlib]System.String::Concat(string,
                                                                string)
  IL_000c:  call       void [mscorlib]System.Console::WriteLine(string)
  IL_0011:  nop
  IL_0012:  ret
} // end of method ExtensionMethods::WriteLine
```

The bold text is wrapped to fit the page width, but what it shows you is that the method has a new attribute applied to it. That attribute is ExtensionAttribute and it is defined in the System.Runtime.CompilerServices namespace. The compiler also applies the attribute to the containing class, which in this case, is ExtensionMethods. At compile time, it references this information when searching for potential extension methods to call. This is a perfect example of the power of metadata and the kinds of things you can achieve with custom attributes in metadata.

If you look at the generated IL at the call site of an extension method, you will see that the extension method is called as a normal static method.

Code Readability vs. Code Understandability

Let's face it. There are too many companies out there that provide very little documentation of their applications' code. Many companies may have high-level design documents that essentially show the big components of the application and some vague lines joining them together to express the relationships between them. But all too often, companies are in such a hurry to get to market that once they start coding the app and the design makes a few turns here and there, they never bother to update the original design documents. Give the product a few versions for the code and documentation to diverge further, and then you may as well just send the documents to the recycle bin. At the other end of the spectrum, you very occasionally see organizations that document everything, even up to the point of designing every piece of the application with a UML modeling tool, and so on, before coding.

Most successful projects fall somewhere in between. You typically have just enough documentation so that if the lead developer who conjured up the guts of a rendering engine meets an unfortunate fate, then the next developer can come in behind him and couple the information in the documentation with the information in the code and move forward. One key to this puzzle is easily readable code, but it should also be easy-to-understand code.

What's the difference? Code that's easily readable makes the programmer's intentions at the place you are reading easy to absorb. For example, imagine you are reading someone's code and they have a need to send some string to some log file. You could come across something like the following:

```
String s = "tasty information";
Logger.LogOutput( s );
```

For the most part, it's easy to see what is going on. Or is it? What does LogOutput do? Does it write the string to a file? Does it send it to the console? Does it send it to the debug output stream? It's impossible to tell from looking at this code. Instead, we have to look at the Logger.LogOutput method's code to understand what's going on. So one may argue that the key to understandable code is code that is easy to navigate, thus making it easy to follow.

Consider what that code might look like with extension methods in play:

```
String info = "tasty information";
info.WriteTo( logFile );
```

Instantly, the code is much easier to read. It almost reads like a written sentence. This is a technique you see used all throughout the .NET Framework. In the second line, it starts with a subject, in the middle there is a verb, and at the end is an indirect object. You could read it as if it were an imperative command given to the info object.

But what if WriteTo is implemented as an extension method? Is the code just as easy to understand as it is to read? It actually may depend on your tools. Intellisense in Visual Studio definitely can help here because it can help you find which static class implements the WriteTo extension method. But if your favorite editor is Emacs or Vim, you are stuck having to determine which namespaces have been imported into the current scope, and then you must start searching those namespaces for a class that implements the extension method. Depending on the complexity of the application code and how many namespaces the current compilation unit imports, that could be a nightmare!

So the moral of the story is this. Just as with any other language feature, be sure to use extension methods correctly, sparingly, and only when needed. Just because you can implement something with an extension method doesn't mean that you always should. The entire engineering discipline is built around making *engineering decisions* whereby we gather information and make the best decision based upon the data even though none of the options may be perfect.[1]

Recommendations for Use

The following sections detail some best-use practices and guidelines for using extension methods. Of course, as extension method use evolves in the language, this set will grow.

Consider Extension Methods Over Inheritance

When one first encounters extension methods, it's natural to view the feature as a way to extend the public contract of a single type or a group of types. That's an obvious conclusion given the fact that extension methods can be invoked through the instance method call syntax. However, I think it's much more effective to view extension methods as a way to provide operations that you can apply to a given type, or multiple types, in a more attractive syntactic way—because again, they do not actually extend a type's contract at all.

Previously, I showed trivial examples of using extension methods to be able to call WriteLine on instances of type String. Alternatively, one could have attempted to inherit from String in order to provide the same behavior. In this case, you'll find that such a technique is impossible, because String is sealed. In Chapter 13, I explain why I believe it is best to prefer sealing the types you create by default. You should only unseal them after you put in the extra thought and design (and documentation) required to make them suitable as base classes. The designers of System.String clearly had good reason to keep us from using it as a base type.

Additionally, gratuitous use of inheritance for this purpose unnecessarily complicates your design. Chapter 4 describes how you should use inheritance sparingly and how using containment is generally more flexible than inheritance. Inheritance is one of the strongest forms of binding two types together statically. Overuse of that glue creates a monolith that's extremely difficult to work with.

For example, you may have the need to apply your WriteLine operation, or some other useful extension method, on a type instance that you do not create. Consider an instance of a type that's returned from some factory method, as in the following code:

```
public class MyFactory
{
    public Widget CreateWidget() {
        ...
    }
}
```

Here CreateWidget is the method that is creating the instance of the returned Widget. It's what is called a factory method. Typically, you'll have a hierarchy of type specializations derived from Widget, and CreateWidget may take some parameters telling it exactly what type of Widget to create. Regardless of that, we don't have control over how or when the object is created. Therefore, it's impossible for us to use inheritance to extend the Widget type's contract unless we also control the CreateWidget method. And even if we do, maybe that method is already published in some other assembly that's been certified and cannot be easily changed. Clearly inheritance is not the correct approach to add the WriteLine functionality to types of Widget in this situation.

---

1. The jaded might call this choosing between the lesser of two evils.

Extension methods also allow you to provide an operation that one can apply to an entire hierarchy of types' instances. For example, consider an extension method whose first parameter is of type System.Object. That extension method can be called on any type. You can't achieve that with inheritance. To do so would require that you have some ability to create a derived type from System.Object, say MyObject, and then somehow get every type in the CLR to derive from MyObject rather than System.Object. Clearly, there's no reason to think too much about the impossible. But just because you can create an extension method that is callable on all objects does not mean you should. Unless the extension method operates only on the public interface of System.Object, you'll most likely have some code in the extension method to determine type at run time so that you can perform some type-specific operation. Such a coding style defeats the strongly typed nature of C# and its compiler.

■**Note** You can also use generics to apply extension methods to multiple types. You can declare generic extension methods just as easily as declaring generic instance methods or generic delegates. In the section titled "The Visitor Pattern" I show an example of using a generic extension method.

Isolate Extension Methods in Separate Namespace

One of the fundamental disciplines in writing methods is that you should avoid side effects. What that means is that, if you create a method such as LogToFile and within its implementation you decide to modify some global state that is used by other components in the application, you have just introduced a potentially dangerous side effect. Side effects such as these are usually the cause of many hard-to-find bugs because, in this case, the modification of the global state may not be intuitive based on the method name.

In the same regard, try to avoid introducing side effects to your clients when they import namespaces. Specifically, it's best if you declare any extension methods in their own namespace separate from the namespace of the types they extend. Typically, the extension methods are in a nested namespace. Not giving your clients this granularity can cause confusion when the compiler attempts to look up a method for an instance method call.

Imagine, for a moment, the confusion that could come from defining your extension methods in the System namespace. There's no mechanism that keeps you from doing so. Just about everyone imports the System namespace into their code. Thus, if you define your extensions that way, most everyone will import them and the only way to keep it from happening is for them to live with the inconvenience of not importing the System namespace at all!

If you think this is no big deal, then allow me to paint a scenario. Imagine you have an application that uses a library from Acme Widgets. The developers of Acme Widgets thought that it would be handy to introduce an extension method named WriteToLog so that you can have another debugging tool in your toolbox when using their library. Being good designers, they defined the extension method in a namespace called AcmeWidgetExtensions. Now, two versions later, you come across a library from Ace Objects that you just must have. Before making any changes to your code, you reference their assembly in your project and now all of a sudden your code won't build; the compiler is complaining with error CS0121 that calls to WriteToLog are ambiguous! Further investigation reveals that Ace Objects also thought it would be handy to provide an extension method called WriteToLog. Unfortunately, they defined it in the System namespace, which all of your code files import. Ouch!

Thus, the moral of the story is to always define your extension methods in a separate namespace in order to allow your clients the granularity they need when importing them into their scope.

Moreover, if you are offering a large set of extension methods, consider whether it would be appropriate to further partition them into multiple namespaces to offer greater granularity to your clients.

Changing a Type's Contract Can Break Extension Methods

When the compiler looks for a name that matches an instance method call, extension methods are the last place it looks. This makes sense because if you have a class that already implements an instance method named WriteToLog, then you don't want an extension method to replace that functionality. However, consider the following scenario.

You have an application that uses a library from Acme Widgets. To further help debug your system and to produce a rich logging mechanism, you created an extension method named WriteToLog that you can use to send information about a particular widget to a log file. Time passes and now you have decided to upgrade to version 2 of the Acme Widgets library. But in the meantime, the creators of the Acme Widgets library decided to extend the public contract of some of their types and add a WriteToLog method because, before you implemented your own WriteToLog extension method, you sent them a feature request expressing how valuable such a thing would be. Without knowing that they added this method to their types, you recompile your code. There are no errors, because the new instance method's signature just happens to match your extension method's signature exactly. But then the next time you run your application, you see some different behavior and all of a sudden, the formatting in your log file is completely different! This happens because now the compiler prefers the instance method over the extension method. It turns out that similar bad things can happen if the type definition includes a new property with the same name as your extension method. But in that case, you get a compiler error as it complains that you are attempting to call a property as if it was a method.

The only real solution to this problem, if you ever come across it, is to switch to calling the extension method through the classic static method call syntax rather than the extension method instance call syntax. But if you're unlucky enough to have the switch happen silently, as in our scenario, it may be a little while before you realize that you need to start calling the extension method differently.

Transforms

Even though extension methods are merely syntactic shortcuts for calling static methods using the standard method call syntax, sometimes even such seemingly insignificant features can trigger a different thought process, thus opening up a plethora of new ideas. For example, imagine that you have a collection of data. Let's say that collection implements IEnumerable<T>. Now, let's say that we want to apply an operation to each item in the list and produce a new list. For the sake of example, let's assume that we have a list of integers and that we want to transform them into a list of doubles that are 1/3 of the original value. You could approach the problem as shown in this example:

```
using System;
using System.Collections.Generic;

public class TransformExample
{
    static void Main() {
        var intList = new List<int>() { 1, 2, 3, 4, 5 };

        var doubleList = new List<double>();

        // Compute the new list.
        foreach( var item in intList ) {
```

```
            doubleList.Add( (double) item / 3 );
            Console.WriteLine( item );
        }
        Console.WriteLine();

        // Display the new list.
        foreach( var item in doubleList ) {
            Console.WriteLine( item );
        }
        Console.WriteLine();
    }
}
```

The technique here is a typical imperative programming style and a valid solution to the problem. Unfortunately, it's not very scalable or reusable. For example, imagine if you wanted to apply some other operation to the result of the first one, or maybe three operations chained together. Or maybe you want to make as much of this code reusable as possible.

There are really at least two fundamental operations taking place in this example. The first is that of iterating over the input collection and producing a new collection. Another operation, which is fundamentally orthogonal to the first, is that of dividing each item by 3. Wouldn't it be nice to decouple these two? Then, if coded correctly, the transformation code can be reused with a variety of operations. So, first, let's break out the operation from the transformation and see what the code may look like:

```
using System;
using System.Collections.Generic;

public class TransformExample
{
    delegate double Operation( int item );

    static List<double> Transform( List<int> input, Operation op ) {
        List<double> result = new List<double>();
        foreach( var item in input ) {
            result.Add( op(item) );
        }

        return result;
    }

    static double DivideByThree( int n ) {
        return (double)n / 3;
    }

    static void Main() {
        var intList = new List<int>() { 1, 2, 3, 4, 5 };

        // Compute the new list.
        var doubleList = Transform( intList, DivideByThree );

        foreach( var item in intList ) {
            Console.WriteLine( item );
        }
        Console.WriteLine();

        // Display the new list.
        foreach( var item in doubleList ) {
```

```
            Console.WriteLine( item );
        }
        Console.WriteLine();
    }
}
```

The new code is better. Now, the operation has been factored out and is passed via a delegate to the Transform static method. As you can imagine, we can convert the Transform method to an extension method. But that's not all! We can also use generics to make the code even more reusable. But wait, there's even more! We can use iterators to make the Transform method calculate its items in a lazy fashion. Check out the next example for a more reusable version of Transform:

```
using System;
using System.Linq;
using System.Collections.Generic;

public static class MyExtensions
{
    public static IEnumerable<R> Transform<T, R>(
                        this IEnumerable<T> input,
                        Func<T, R> op ) {
        foreach( var item in input ) {
            yield return op( item );
        }
    }
}

public class TransformExample
{
    static double DivideByThree( int n ) {
        return (double)n / 3;
    }

    static void Main() {
        var intList = new List<int>() { 1, 2, 3, 4, 5 };

        // Compute the new list.
        var doubleList =
            intList.Transform( new Func<int, double>(DivideByThree) );

        foreach( var item in intList ) {
            Console.WriteLine( item );
        }
        Console.WriteLine();

        // Display the new list.
        foreach( var item in doubleList ) {
            Console.WriteLine( item );
        }
    }
}
```

Now we're getting there! First notice that Transform<T> is now a generic extension method. Moreover, it takes and returns IEnumerable<T> types. Now Transform<T> can be used on any generic collection and accepts a delegate describing how to transform each item. The Func<TArg0,TResult> type is defined in the System namespace and is new to .NET 3.0. Since an iterator is used to return items from Transform<T>, each item is only processed each time the returned IEnumerable<T> type's cursor is advanced. In this example, the computational savings are trivial. However, you can easily imagine a situation where the passed-in operation can take quite a bit of time to process each item in the input collection. The input collection could contain long strings and the operation could be an encryption operation, for example. Another reason lazy evaluation is so handy is that the input collection could even be an infinite series. How? Check out the next example, which also shows a teaser for lambda expressions, covered in Chapter 15:

```
using System;
using System.Linq;
using System.Collections.Generic;

public static class MyExtensions
{
    public static IEnumerable<R> Transform<T, R>(
                    this IEnumerable<T> input,
                    Func<T, R> op ) {
        foreach( var item in input ) {
            yield return op( item );
        }
    }
}

public class TransformExample
{
    static IEnumerable<int> CreateInfiniteSeries() {
        int n = 0;
        while( true ) {
            yield return n++;
        }
    }

    static void Main() {
        var infiniteSeries1 = CreateInfiniteSeries();

        var infiniteSeries2 =
            infiniteSeries1.Transform( x => (double)x / 3 );

        IEnumerator<double> iter =
            infiniteSeries2.GetEnumerator();

        for( int i = 0; i < 25; ++i ) {
            iter.MoveNext();
            Console.WriteLine( iter.Current );
        }
    }
}
```

How cool is that? Of course, in my loop I could not use `foreach` otherwise the program would never finish and you would have to terminate it forcefully. The funny syntax within the `Transform<T>` method call is a lambda expression. A lambda expression used this way defines a function which in this case is passed as a delegate. You can envision lambda expressions as a terse syntax for defining anonymous methods. If you just can't wait to see what lambda expressions are all about, jump to Chapter 15.

Used this way, extension methods allow us to implement more of a functional programming style.[2] After all, the Transform<T> method just shown fits into that category. In fact, you will find that most of the new additions offered by C# 3.0 facilitate the functional programming paradigm. Those features include extension methods, lambda expressions, and LINQ. Each of these features places the emphasis on the computational operation rather than the structure of the computation itself. The benefits of functional programming are numerous, and one could fill the pages of an entire book describing them. For example, functional programming facilitates parallelism, since variables are typically never changed after initial assignment; thus, fewer locks and sync blocks are necessary.

■**Note** C++ developers familiar with template metaprogramming as described in the excellent book *C++ Template Metaprogramming: Concepts, Tools, and Techniques from Boost and Beyond* by David Abrahams and Aleksey Gurtovoy (Boston, MA: Addison-Wesley Professional, 2004) will be right at home with this style of functional programming. In fact, template metaprogramming provides a more purely functional programming environment because once a variable (or *symbol*, in functional programming lingo) is assigned, it can never be changed. C#, on the other hand, offers a hybrid environment where you are free to implement functional programming if you choose. Also, those familiar with the Standard Template Library (STL) will get a familiar feeling from this style of programming. STL swept through the C++ programming community back in the early 1990s and encouraged a more functional programming thought process.

Operation Chaining

Using extension methods, operation chaining becomes a more natural process. Again, it's nothing that you could not have done in C# 2.0 using plain static methods and anonymous methods. However, with the streamlined syntax, chaining actually removes the clutter and can trigger some innovative thinking. Let's start with the example from the previous section where we took a list of integers and transformed them into a list of doubles. This time, we'll look at how we can actually chain operations in a fluid way. Let's suppose that after dividing the integers by three, we want to then compute the square of the result. The code below shows how we could do that.

```
using System;
using System.Linq;
using System.Collections.Generic;

public static class MyExtensions
{
    public static IEnumerable<R> Transform<T, R>(
                    this IEnumerable<T> input,
                    Func<T, R> op ) {
        foreach( var item in input ) {
            yield return op( item );
        }
    }
}

public class TransformExample
{
```

---

2. For more on functional programming, search "functional programming" on www.wikipedia.org.

```
static IEnumerable<int> CreateInfiniteList() {
    int n = 0;
    while( true ) yield return n++;
}

static double DivideByThree( int n ) {
    return (double)n / 3;
}

static double Square( double r ) {
    return r * r;
}

static void Main() {
    var divideByThree =
        new Func<int, double>( DivideByThree );
    var squareNumber =
        new Func<double, double>( Square );

    var result = CreateInfiniteList().
                    Transform( divideByThree ).
                    Transform( squareNumber );

    var iter = result.GetEnumerator();
    for( int i = 0; i < 25; ++i ) {
        iter.MoveNext();
        Console.WriteLine( iter.Current );
    }
}
}
```

Isn't that cool? In one statement of code, I took an infinite list of integers and applied a divisor followed by a squaring operation, and the end result is a lazy-evaluated IEnumerable<double> type that computes each element as needed. Functional programming is actually pretty useful when you look at it this way. Of course, you could chain as many operations as necessary. For example, you may want to append a rounding operation at the end. Or maybe you want to append a filtering operation such that only the results that match a certain criteria are considered. To do that, you could create a generic Filter<T> extension method, similar to Transform<T>, that takes a predicate delegate as a parameter and uses it to filter the items in the collection.

At this point, I'm sure that you're thinking of all of the really useful extension methods you could create to manipulate data. You may be wondering if a host of these extension methods already exists. Check out the System.Linq.Queryable class. This class provides a whole host of extension methods that are typically used with LINQ, which I cover in Chapter 16. The main difference is that all of these extension methods operate on types of IQueryable<T>, which derives from IEnumerable<T>. Also, the System.Linq.Enumerable class provides the same functionality for types that implement IEnumerable<T>.

Custom Iterators

In Chapter 9 I covered iterators, which were added to the language in C# 2.0. I also described some ways you could create custom iterators. Extension methods offer even more flexibility to create custom iterators for collections in a very expressive way. By default, every collection that implements IEnumerable or IEnumerable<T> has a forward iterator, so a custom iterator would be necessary to walk through a collection in a different way than its default iterator. Also, you will need to create a custom iterator for types that don't support IEnumerable<T> as I'll show in the next section, titled "Borrowing from Functional Programming." Let's look at how you can use extension methods to implement custom iterators on types implementing IEnumerable<T>.

For example, imagine a two-dimensional matrix implemented as a List<List<int>> type. When performing some operations on such matrices, it's common to require an iterator that walks through the matrix in row-major fashion. What that means is that the iterator walks all of the items of the first row, and then the second row, etc., until it reaches the end of the last row.

You could iterate through the matrix in row-major form as shown here:

```
using System;
using System.Collections.Generic;

public class IteratorExample
{
    static void Main() {
        var matrix = new List<List<int>> {
            new List<int> { 1, 2, 3 },
            new List<int> { 4, 5, 6 },
            new List<int> { 7, 8, 9 }
        };

        // One way of iterating the matrix.
        foreach( var list in matrix ) {
            foreach( var item in list ) {
                Console.Write( "{0}, ", item );
            }
        }

        Console.WriteLine();
    }
}
```

Yes, this code gets the job done, but it is not very reusable. Let's see one way this can be redone using an extension method:

```
using System;
using System.Collections.Generic;

public static class CustomIterators
{
    public static IEnumerable<T> GetRowMajorIterator<T>(
                                 this List<List<T>> matrix ) {
        foreach( var row in matrix ) {
            foreach( var item in row ) {
                yield return item;
            }
        }
    }
}

public class IteratorExample
{
    static void Main() {
        var matrix = new List<List<int>> {
            new List<int> { 1, 2, 3 },
            new List<int> { 4, 5, 6 },
            new List<int> { 7, 8, 9 }
```

```
        };

        // A more elegant way to enumerate the items.
        foreach( var item in matrix.GetRowMajorIterator() ) {
            Console.Write( "{0}, ", item );
        }

        Console.WriteLine();
    }
}
```

In this version, I have externalized the iteration into the `GetRowMajorIterator<T>` extension method. At the same time, I made the extension method generic so it will accept two-dimensional nested lists that contain any type, thus making it a bit more reusable.

Borrowing from Functional Programming

You might have already noticed that many of the new features of C# 3.0 facilitate a functional programming model. You've always been able to implement functional programming models in C#, but the new language features make it easier syntactically by making the language more expressive. Sometimes, the functional model facilitates easier solutions to various problems. Various languages are categorized as functional languages, and Lisp is one of them.

If you've ever programmed using Lisp, you know that the list is one of the core constructs in that language. In C#, we can model such a list using the following interface definition at the core:

```
public interface IList<T>
{
    T Head { get; }
    IList<T> Tail { get; }
}
```

The structure of this list is a bit different than the average linked list implementation. Notice that instead of one node containing a value and a pointer to the next node, it instead contains the value at the node and then the rest of the list. In fact, it's rather recursive in nature. That's no surprise, since recursive techniques are part of the functional programming model. For example, if you were to represent a list on paper by writing values within parentheses, a traditional list might look like the following:

(1 2 3 4 5 6)

whereas a list defined using the `IList<T>` interface above could look like this:

(1 (2 (3 (4 (5 (6 (null null)))))))

Each set of parentheses contain two items: the value of the node and then the remainder of the list within a nested set of parentheses. So, to represent a list with just one item in it, such as just the number one, we could represent it this way:

(1 (null null))

And of course, the empty list could be represented this way:

(null null)

In the following example code, I create a custom list called `MyList<T>` that implements `IList<T>`. The way it is built here is not very efficient, and I'll have more to say about that shortly.

```
using System;
using System.Collections.Generic;
```

```
public interface IList<T>
{
    T Head { get; }
    IList<T> Tail { get; }
}

public class MyList<T> : IList<T>
{
    public static IList<T> CreateList( IEnumerable<T> items ) {
        IEnumerator<T> iter = items.GetEnumerator();
        return CreateList( iter );
    }

    public static IList<T> CreateList( IEnumerator<T> iter ) {
        if( !iter.MoveNext() ) {
            return new MyList<T>( default(T), null );
        }

        return new MyList<T>( iter.Current, CreateList(iter) );
    }

    private MyList( T head, IList<T> tail ) {
        this.head = head;
        this.tail = tail;
    }

    public T Head {
        get {
            return head;
        }
    }

    public IList<T> Tail {
        get {
            return tail;
        }
    }

    private T         head;
    private IList<T> tail;
}

public static class CustomIterators
{
    public static IEnumerable<T>
        LinkListIterator<T>( this IList<T> theList ) {

        for( var list = theList;
            list.Tail != null;
            list = list.Tail ) {
            yield return list.Head;
        }
    }
}

public class IteratorExample
{
```

```
static void Main() {
    var listInts = new List<int> { 1, 2, 3, 4 };
    var linkList =
        MyList<int>.CreateList( listInts );

    foreach( var item in linkList.LinkListIterator() ) {
        Console.Write( "{0}, ", item );
    }

    Console.WriteLine();
}
}
```

First, notice in Main that I am initializing an instance of MyList<int> using a List<int>. The CreateList static method recursively populates MyList<int> using these values. Once CreateList is finished, we have an instance of MyList<int> that can be visualized as below:

(1 (2 (3 (4 (null null)))))

You're probably wondering why the list is not represented using the following:

(1 (2 (3 (4 null))))

You could do that; however, you will find that it is not as easy to use either when composing the list or consuming it. Speaking of consuming the list, you can imagine that there are times when you need to iterate over one of these lists. In that case, you need a custom iterator, which I have highlighted in the example. The code in Main uses this iterator to send all of the list items to the console. The output is as follows:

1, 2, 3, 4,

In the example, notice that the LinkListIterator<T> method creates a forward iterator by making some assumptions about how to determine if it has reached the end of the list and how to increment the cursor during iteration. What if we externalized this information? How could we do that? If the idea of delegates pops into your mind, then you're right on track. Check out the following revised version of the iterator extension method and the Main method:

```
public static class CustomIterators
{
    public static IEnumerable<T>
        GeneralIterator<T>( this IList<T> theList,
                            Func<IList<T>, bool> finalState,
                            Func<IList<T>, IList<T>> incrementer ) {
        while( !finalState(theList) ) {
            yield return theList.Head;
            theList = incrementer( theList );
        }
    }
}

public class IteratorExample
{
```

```
static void Main() {
    var listInts = new List<int> { 1, 2, 3, 4 };
    var linkList =
        MyList<int>.CreateList( listInts );

    var iterator = linkList.GeneralIterator( delegate( IList<int> list ) {
                                                 return list.Tail == null;
                                             },
                                             delegate( IList<int> list ) {
                                                 return list.Tail;
                                             } );

    foreach( var item in iterator ) {
        Console.Write( "{0}, ", item );
    }

    Console.WriteLine();
}
}
```

Notice how the GeneralIterator<T> method accepts two more delegates, one of which is then called upon to check if the cursor is at the end of the list, and the other to increment the cursor. In the Main method, I am passing two delegates in the form of anonymous methods. Now, the GeneralIterator<T> method can be used to iterate over every other item in the list simply by modifying the delegate passed in through the incrementer parameter.

■**Note** Some of you may already be familiar with lambda expressions, which are new in C# 3.0. Indeed, using lambda expressions you can clean up this code considerably by using the lambda expression syntax to replace the anonymous delegates above. I cover lambda expressions in Chapter 15.

As a final extension method example for operations on the IList<T> type, consider how we could create an extension method to reverse the list and return a new IList<T>. There are several ways one could consider doing this, and some are much more efficient than others. However, I want to show you an example that uses a form of recursion. Consider the following Reverse<T> custom method implementation:

```
public static class CustomIterators
{
    public static IList<T> Reverse<T>( this IList<T> theList ) {
        var reverseList = new List<T>();
        Func<IList<T>, List<T>> reverseFunc = null;

        reverseFunc = delegate(IList<T> list) {
            if( list != null ) {
                reverseFunc( list.Tail );
                if( list.Tail != null ) {
                    reverseList.Add( list.Head );
                }
            }
            return reverseList;
        };

        return MyList<T>.CreateList( reverseFunc(theList) );
    }
}
```

If you've never encountered this style of coding, it can surely make your mind twist inside your head. The key to the work lies in the fact that there is a delegate defined that calls itself and captures variables along the way.[3] In the code above, the anonymous method is assigned to the reverseFunc variable. And as you can see, the anonymous method body calls reverseFunc, or more accurately, itself! In a way, the anonymous method captures itself! The trigger to get all of the work done is in the last line of the Reverse<> method. It initiates the chain of recursive calls to the anonymous method and then passes the resulting List<T> to the CreateList method, thus creating the reversed list.

Those who pay close attention to efficiency are likely pointing out the inefficiency of creating a temporary List<T> instance that is then passed to CreateList. For example, if the constructor to MyList<T> is made public, you can eliminate the temporary List<T> entirely and build the new MyList<T> using a captured variable as shown below:

```
public static class CustomIterators
{
    public static IList<T> Reverse<T>( this IList<T> theList ) {
        var reverseList = new MyList<T>(default(T), null);
        Func<IList<T>, MyList<T>> reverseFunc = null;

        reverseFunc = delegate(IList<T> list) {
            if( list.Tail != null ) {
                reverseList = new MyList<T>( list.Head, reverseList );
                reverseFunc( list.Tail );
            }

            return reverseList;
        };

        return reverseFunc(theList);
    }
}
```

Those of you who are more familiar with functional programming are probably saying that the Reverse<T> extension method above can be cleaned up by eliminating the captured variable and using the stack instead. Therefore, my final example of the Reverse<T> method uses only the stack as a temporary storage location while building the new reversed list:

```
public static class CustomIterators
{
    public static IList<T> Reverse<T>( this IList<T> theList ) {
        Func<IList<T>, IList<T>, IList<T>> reverseFunc = null;

        reverseFunc = delegate(IList<T> list, IList<T> result) {
            if( list.Tail != null ) {
                return reverseFunc( list.Tail, new MyList<T>(list.Head, result) );
            }

            return result;
        };

        return reverseFunc(theList, new MyList<T>(default(T), null));
    }
}
```

---

3. Computer Science wonks like to call a delegate that captures variables a *closure,* which is a construct where a function is packaged with an environment (such as variables).

■**Note** This code uses the Func<> definition, which is a generic delegate that is defined in the System name-space. Using Func<> is a shortcut you can employ to avoid having to declare delegate types all over the place. You use the Func<> type parameter list to declare what the parameter types (if any) and return type of the dele-gate are.

The MyList<T> class used in the previous examples builds the linked list from the IEnumerable<T> type entirely before the MyList<T> object can be used. I used a List<T> as the seed data but I could have used anything that implements IEnumerable<T> to fill the contents of MyList<T>. But what if IEnumerable<T> were an infinite iterator similar to the one created by CreateInfiniteList in the "Operation Chaining" section of this chapter? If you fed the result of CreateInfiniteList to MyList<T>.CreateList, you would have to kill the program forcefully or wait until your memory runs out as it tries to build the MyList<T>. If you are creating a library for general use that contains a type like MyList<T>, which builds itself given some IEnumerable<T> type, then you should do your best to accommodate all scenarios that could be thrown at you. The IEnumerable<T> given to you could take a very long time to calculate each item of the enumeration. For example, it could be enumerating over a database of live data where database access is very costly. For an example of how to create the list in a lazy fashion where each node is created only when needed, check out Wes Dyer's excellent blog, specifically the entry titled "Why all the love for lists?"[4] The technique of lazy evaluation while iterating is a fundamental feature of LINQ, which I cover in Chapter 16.

The Visitor Pattern

The Visitor pattern, as described in the seminal pattern book *Design Patterns: Elements of Reusable Object-Oriented Software* by the Gang of Four,[5] allows you to define a new operation on a group of classes without changing the classes themselves. Extension methods present a handy option for implementing the Visitor pattern.

For example, consider a collection of types that may or may not be related by inheritance, and imagine that you want to add functionality to validate instances of them at some point in your application. One option, although very unattractive, is to modify the public contract of all of the types, introducing a Validate method on each of them. One may even jump to the conclusion that the easiest way to do it is to introduce a new base type that derives from System.Object, implements Validate as an abstract method, and then makes all of the other types derive from the new type instead of System.Object. That would be nothing more than a maintenance nightmare in the end.

By now you should agree that an extension method or a collection of extension methods will do the trick nicely. Given a collection of unrelated types, you will probably implement a host of extension methods. But the beauty is that you don't have to change the already defined types. In fact, if they're not your types to begin with, you cannot change them anyway. Consider the following code:

```
using System;
using ValidatorExtensions;

namespace ValidatorExtensions
{
```

---

4. You can find Wes Dyer's blog titled "Yet Another Language Geek" at blogs.msdn.com/wesdyer/.

5. *Design Patterns: Elements of Reusable Object-Oriented Software* by Erich Gamma, Richard Helm, Ralph John-son, and John Vlissides (Boston, MA: Addison-Wesley Professional, 1995) is cited in the references at the end of this book.

```csharp
    public static class Validators
    {
        public static void Validate( this String str ) {
            // Do something to validate the String instance.

            Console.WriteLine( "String with \"" +
                                    str +
                                    "\" Validated." );
        }

        public static void Validate( this SupplyCabinet cab ) {
            // Do something to validate the SupplyCabinet instance.

            Console.WriteLine( "Supply Cabinet Validated." );
        }

        public static void Validate( this Employee emp ) {
            // Do something to validate the Employee instance.

            Console.WriteLine( "** Employee Failed Validation! **" );
        }
    }
}

public class SupplyCabinet
{
}

public class Employee
{
}

public class MyApplication
{
    static void Main() {
        String data = "some important data";

        SupplyCabinet supplies = new SupplyCabinet();

        Employee hrLady = new Employee();

        data.Validate();
        supplies.Validate();
        hrLady.Validate();
    }
}
```

Notice that for each type of object we want to validate (in this example there are three), I have defined a separate Validate extension method. The output from the application shows that the proper Validate method is being called for each instance and is as follows:

```
String with "some important data" Validated.
Supply Cabinet Validated.
** Employee Failed Validation! **
```

In this example, it's important to note that the visitors, in this case the extension methods named Validate, must treat the instance that they are validating as black boxes. By that I mean that they do not have the validation capabilities of a true instance method, since only true instance methods have access to the internal state of the objects. Nevertheless, in this example, it may make sense to validate the instances from a client's perspective.

Using generics and constraints, you can slightly extend the previous example and provide a generic form of the Validate extension method that can be used if the instance supports a well-known interface. In this case, the well known interface is named IValidator. Therefore, it would be nice to create a special Validate method that will be called if the type implements the IValidator interface. Consider the following code, which shows the changes marked in bold:

```csharp
using System;
using ValidatorExtensions;

namespace ValidatorExtensions
{
    public static class Validators
    {
        public static void Validate( this String str ) {
            // Do something to validate the String instance.

            Console.WriteLine( "String with \"" +
                               str +
                               "\" Validated." );
        }

        public static void Validate( this Employee emp ) {
            // Do something to validate the Employee instance.

            Console.WriteLine( "** Employee Failed Validation! **" );
        }

        public static void Validate<T>( this T obj )
                           where T: IValidator {
            obj.DoValidation();
            Console.WriteLine( "Instance of following type" +
                               " validated: " +
                               obj.GetType() );
        }
    }
}

public interface IValidator
{
    void DoValidation();
}

public class SupplyCabinet : IValidator
{
    public void DoValidation() {
        Console.WriteLine( "\tValidating SupplyCabinet" );
    }
}

public class Employee
{
```

```
}

public class MyApplication
{
    static void Main() {
        String data = "some important data";

        SupplyCabinet supplies = new SupplyCabinet();

        Employee hrLady = new Employee();

        data.Validate();
        supplies.Validate();
        hrLady.Validate();
    }
}
```

Now, if the instance that we're calling Validate on happens to implement IValidator and there is not a version of Validate that specifically takes the type as its first parameter, then the generic form of Validate will be called, which then passes through to the DoValidation method on the instance.

Notice that I removed the extension method whose first parameter was of type SupplyCabinet, so that the compiler would choose the generic version. If I had left it in, the code as written in Main above would call the version that I removed. However, even if I had not removed the nongeneric extension method, I could have forced the compiler to call the generic one by changing the syntax at the point of call as shown here:

```
public class MyApplication
{
    static void Main() {
        String data = "some important data";

        SupplyCabinet supplies = new SupplyCabinet();

        Employee hrLady = new Employee();

        data.Validate();

        // Force generic version
        supplies.Validate<SupplyCabinet>();

        hrLady.Validate();
    }
}
```

In the Main method, I have given the compiler more information to limit its search of the Validate method to generic forms of the extension method that accept one generic type parameter.

Summary

In this chapter, I have introduced you to extension methods, including how to declare them, how to call them, and also how the compiler implements them under the covers. Additionally, we saw how they really are just syntactic sugar and don't require any changes to the underlying runtime in order to work. Extension methods can cause confusion when defined inappropriately, so we looked at some caveats to avoid. I showed you how they can be used to create such useful things such as iterators (IEnumerable<T> types) on containers that are not enumerable by default. Even for types that do have enumerators, you can define enumerators that iterate in a custom way. As you'll see in Chapter 15, when they are combined with lambda expressions, extension methods provide a certain degree of expressiveness that is extremely useful. While showing how to create custom iterators, I took a slight detour (using anonymous functions rather than lambda expressions) to show you the world of functional programming that the new C# 3.0 features unlock. The code for those examples will become much cleaner when you use lambda expressions instead of anonymous methods.

In the next chapter, I'll introduce you to lambda expressions, which really make functional programming in C# syntactically succinct. Additionally, they allow you to convert a functional expression into either code or data in the form of IL code or an expression tree, respectively.

## CHAPTER 15

Lambda Expressions

Most of the new features of C# 3.0 open up a world of expressive functional programming to the C# programmer. Functional programming, in its pure form, is a programming methodology built on top of immutable variables (sometimes called symbols), functions that can produce other functions, and recursion, just to name a few of its foundations. Some prominent functional programming languages include Lisp, Haskell, F#,[1] and Scheme.[2] However, functional programming does not require a pure functional language and one can use and implement functional programming disciplines in traditionally imperative languages like the C-based languages (including C#). The new C# 3.0 features transform the language into a more expressive hybrid language where both imperative and functional programming techniques can be utilized in harmony. Lambda expressions are arguably the biggest piece of this functional programming pie.

Introduction to Lambda Expressions

Using lambda expressions, you can succinctly define function objects for use at any time. C# has always supported this capability via delegates, whereby you create a function object (in the form of a delegate) and wire it up to the backing code at the time of creation. Lambda expressions join these two actions—creation and connection—into one expressive statement in the code. Additionally, you can easily associate an environment with function objects. A *functional* is a function that takes functions in its parameter list and operates on those functions, possibly even returning another function as the result. For example, a functional could accept two functions, where one performs one mathematical operation and the other performs a different mathematical operation, and return a third function that is a composite function built from the two. Lambda expressions provide a more natural way to create and invoke functionals.

In simple syntactic terms, lambda expressions are a syntax whereby you can declare anonymous functions (delegates) in a more fluid and expressive way. At the same time, they are very much more than that, as you will see. Just about every use of an anonymous method can be replaced with a lambda expression. That said, there's no reason you can't utilize functional programming techniques in C# 2.0.[3] At first, the syntax of lambda expressions may take some time to

---

1. F# is an exciting new functional programming language for the .NET Framework. For more information, I invite you to read Robert Pickering's *Foundations of F#* (Berkeley, CA: Apress, 2007).

2. One of the languages that I use often is C++. Those of you who are familiar with metaprogramming in C++ are definitely familiar with functional programming techniques. If you use C++ and you're curious about metaprogramming, I invite you to check out David Abrahams' and Aleksey Gurtovoy's excellent book *C++ Template Metaprogramming: Concepts, Tools, and Techniques from Boost and Beyond* (Boston, MA: Addison-Wesley Professional, 2005).

3. I covered some examples of functional programming with anonymous methods in Chapter 14.

get used to. Overall, the syntax is very straightforward when you are looking at a lambda expression all by itself. However, when embedded in code, they can be a little tricky to decipher and it may take some time to get used to their syntax.

Lambda expressions really take two forms. The form that most directly replaces anonymous methods in syntax includes a statement block within braces. I like to refer to these as lambda statements. These lambda statements are a direct replacement for anonymous methods. Lambda expressions, on the other hand, provide an even more abbreviated way to declare an anonymous method and do not require code within braces nor a return statement. Both types of lambda expressions can be converted to delegates. However, lambda expressions without statement blocks offer something truly impressive. You can convert them into expression trees based on the types in the `System.Linq.Expressions` namespace. In other words, the function described in code is turned into data. I cover the topic of creating expression trees from lambda expressions in the section titled "Expression Trees" later in this chapter.

Lambda Expressions

First let's look at the simpler form of lambda expressions; that is, the ones without a statement block. As mentioned in the previous section, a lambda expression is a shorthand way of declaring a simple anonymous method. The following lambda expression can be used as a delegate that accepts one parameter and returns the result of performing the operation on that parameter:

```
x => x / 2
```

What this says is "take x as a parameter and return the result of following operation on x." Notice that the lambda expression is devoid of any type information. It does not mean that the expression is typeless. Rather, the compiler will deduce the type of the argument x and the type of the result depending on the context where it is used, and by that, it means that if you are assigning a lambda expression to a delegate, the types of the delegate definition are used to determine the types within the lambda expression. The following code shows what happens when a lambda expression is assigned to a delegate type:

```
using System;
using System.Linq;

public class LambdaTest
{
    static void Main() {
        Func<int, double> expr = x => x / 2;

        int someNumber = 9;
        Console.WriteLine( "Result: {0}", expr(someNumber) );
    }
}
```

I have marked the lambda expression in bold so that it stands out. The `Func<>` type is a new helper type provided by the `System` namespace that you can use to declare simple delegates that take up to four arguments and return a result. In this case, I am declaring a variable expr that is a delegate that accepts an `int` and returns a `double`. When the compiler assigns the lambda expression to the expr variable, it uses the type information of the delegate to determine that the type of x must be `int` and the type of the return value must be `double`.

Now, if you execute that code, you'll notice that the result is not entirely accurate. That is, the result has been rounded. This is expected since the result of x/2 is represented as an `int` which is then cast to a double. You can fix this by specifying different types in the delegate declaration, as shown here:

```
using System;
using System.Linq;

public class LambdaTest
{
    static void Main() {
        Func<double, double> expr = (double x) => x / 2;

        int someNumber = 9;
        Console.WriteLine( "Result: {0}", expr(someNumber) );
    }
}
```

This lambda expression has what's called an explicitly typed parameter list, and in this case, x is declared as type double. Also notice that the type of expr is now Func<double, double> rather than Func<int, double>. The compiler requires that any time you use a typed parameter list in a lambda expression and assign it to a delegate, the delegate's argument types must match exactly. However, since an int is explicitly convertible to a double, you can pass someNumber to expr at call time as shown.

■**Note** When using typed parameter lists, notice that the parameter list must be enclosed in parentheses. Parentheses are also required when declaring a delegate that accepts either more than one parameter or no parameters, as I'll show later on. In fact, you can use parentheses at any time; they are optional in lambda expressions of only one implicitly typed parameter.

When the lambda expression is assigned to a delegate, the return type of the expression is generally derived from the argument types. So, in the following code statement, the return type of the expression is double since the inferred type of the parameter x is double:

```
Func<double, int> expr = (x) => x / 2;    // Compiler Error!!!!
```

However, since double is not implicitly convertible to int, the compiler will complain:

```
error CS1662: Cannot convert 'lambda expression' to
        delegate type 'System.Func<double,int>' because some of the return
        types in the block are not implicitly convertible to the delegate return
        type
```

You can "fix" this by casting the result of the lambda expression body to int:

```
Func<double, int> expr = (x) => (int) x / 2;
```

■**Note** Explicit types in lambda expression parameter lists are required if the delegate you are assigning them to has out or ref parameters. One could argue that fixing the parameter types explicitly within a lambda expression defeats some of the elegance of their expressive power. It definitely can make the code harder to read.

Now I would like to show you a simple lambda expression that accepts no parameters:

```
using System;
using System.Linq;

public class LambdaTest
{
    static void Main() {
        int counter = 0;

        WriteStream( () => counter++ );

        Console.WriteLine( "Final value of counter: {0}",
                            counter );
    }

    static void WriteStream( Func<int> counter ) {
        for( int i = 0; i < 10; ++i ) {
            Console.Write( "{0}, ", counter() );
        }
        Console.WriteLine();
    }
}
```

Notice how simple it was, using this lambda expression, to pass a function as a parameter into the WriteStream method. Moreover, the function passed in captures an environment within which to run, namely, the counter value in Main. Back in the "good old days" of C# 1.0, this was a painful process indeed and one needed to do something like the following:

```
using System;

unsafe public class MyClosure
{
    public MyClosure( int* counter )
    {
        this.counter = counter;
    }

    public delegate int IncDelegate();
    public IncDelegate GetDelegate() {
        return new IncDelegate( IncrementFunction );
    }

    private int IncrementFunction() {
        return (*counter)++;
    }

    private int* counter;
}

public class LambdaTest
{
    unsafe static void Main() {
        int counter = 0;

        MyClosure closure = new MyClosure( &counter );

        WriteStream( closure.GetDelegate() );
```

```
            Console.WriteLine( "Final value of counter: {0}",
                                counter );
        }

        static void WriteStream( MyClosure.IncDelegate incrementor ) {
            for( int i = 0; i < 10; ++i ) {
                Console.Write( "{0}, ", incrementor() );
            }
            Console.WriteLine();
        }
    }
}
```

Look at all of the work involved without lambda expressions. I have bolded the extra work and other changes in the code. The first order of business is to create an object to represent the delegate and its environment. In this case, the environment is a pointer to the counter variable in the Main method. I decided to use a class to encapsulate the function and its environment. Notice the use of unsafe code in the MyClosure class to accomplish this. Then, in the Main method, I created an instance of MyClosure and passed a delegate created by calling GetDelegate to WriteStream.

What a lot of work! And on top of that, it sure makes for some hard-to-follow code.

In C# 2.0, anonymous methods were introduced to reduce the burden I just described. However, they are not as functionally expressive as lambda expressions since they still carry the old imperative programming style with them and require parameter types in the parameter list. Additionally, the anonymous method syntax is rather bulky. For good measure, the following shows how the previous example would be implemented using anonymous methods, so you can see the difference in syntax from lambda expressions.

```
using System;

public class LambdaTest
{
    static void Main() {
        int counter = 0;

        WriteStream( delegate () {
                        return counter++;
                     } );

        Console.WriteLine( "Final value of counter: {0}",
                            counter );
    }

    static void WriteStream( Func<int> counter ) {
        for( int i = 0; i < 10; ++i ) {
            Console.Write( "{0}, ", counter() );
        }
        Console.WriteLine();
    }
}
```

I have bolded the differences between this example and the original lambda expression example. It's definitely much cleaner than the way you would have implemented it in the C# 1.0 days. However, it's still not as expressive and succinct as the lambda expression version. Finally, in C# 3.0, we have an elegant means of defining potentially very complex functions using lambda expressions that can even be built by assembling together other functions.

█Note In the previous code example, you likely noticed the implications of referencing the `counter` variable within the lambda expression. After all, `counter` is actually a local variable within the scope of `Main`, yet within the scope of `WriteStream` it is referenced while invoking the delegate. In the Chapter 10 section "Beware the Captured Variable Surprise," I describe how you can do the same thing with anonymous methods. In functional programming lingo, this is called a *closure*. In essence, any time a lambda expression incorporates the environment around it, a closure is the result. As I'll show in a following section, "Closures (Variable Capture) and Memoization," closures can be very useful. However, when used inappropriately, they can create some nasty surprises.

Finally, I want to show you an example of a lambda expression that accepts more than one parameter:

```
using System;
using System.Linq;
using System.Collections.Generic;

public class LambdaTest
{
    static void Main() {
        var teamMembers = new List<string> {
            "Lou Loomis",
            "Smoke Porterhouse",
            "Danny Noonan",
            "Ty Webb"
        };

        FindByFirstName( teamMembers,
                    "Danny",
                    (x, y) => x.Contains(y) );
    }

    static void FindByFirstName(
                    List<string> members,
                    string firstName,
                    Func<string, string, bool> predicate ) {
        foreach( var member in members ) {
            if( predicate(member, firstName) ) {
                Console.WriteLine( member );
            }
        }
    }
}
```

In this case, the lambda expression is used to create a delegate that accepts two parameters of type string and returns a bool. As you can see, lambda expressions provide a nice, succinct way of creating predicates. In the later section "Iterators Revisited," I'll build upon an example from Chapter 14 showing how to use lambda expressions as predicates to create flexible iterators.

Lambda Statements

All of the lambda expressions I have shown so far have been purely of the expression type. Another type of lambda expression is one I like to call a lambda statement. It is similar in form to the lambda expressions of the previous section except that it is composed of a compound statement block within curly braces. Because of that, a lambda with statement blocks must have a return statement. In general, all lambda expressions shown in the previous section can be converted to a lambda with a statement block simply by surrounding the expression with curly braces after prefixing the right side with a return statement. For example, the following lambda expression:

```
(x, y) => x * y
```

can be rewritten as the following lambda with a statement block:

```
(x, y) => { return x * y; }
```

In form, lambdas with statement blocks are almost identical to anonymous methods. And there is one major difference between lambdas with statement blocks and lambda expressions. Lambdas with statement blocks can only be converted to delegate types, whereas lambda expressions can be converted both to delegates and to expression trees typed by the family of types centered around System.Linq.Expressions.Expression<T>. I'll discuss expression trees in the next section.

■**Note** The big difference between lambdas with statement blocks and anonymous methods is that anonymous methods must explicitly type their parameters, whereas the compiler can infer the types of the lambda based on context in almost all cases. The abbreviated syntax offered by lambda expressions fosters a more functional programming thought process and approach.

Expression Trees

So far, I have shown you lambda expressions that replace the functionality of delegates. If I stopped there, I would be doing you a great disservice. That's because the C# 3.0 compiler also has the ability to convert lambda expressions into expression trees based on the types in the System.Linq. Expressions namespace. I'll explain why this is such a great thing in a later section, "Functions as Data." For example, you've already seen how you can convert a lambda expression into a delegate as shown here:

```
Func<int, int> func1 = n => n+1;
```

In this line of code, the expression is converted into a delegate that accepts a single int parameter and returns an int. However, check out the following modification:

```
Expression<Func<int, int>> expr = n => n+1;
```

This is really cool! The lambda expression, instead of being converted into a callable delegate, is converted into a data structure that represents the operation. The type of the expr variable is Expression<T>, where T is replaced with the type of delegate the lambda can be converted to. The compiler notices that you are trying to convert the lambda expression into an Expression<Func<int,int>> instance and generates all of the code internally to make it happen. At some point later in time, you can then compile the expression into a usable delegate as shown in the next example:

```
using System;
using System.Linq;
using System.Linq.Expressions;

public class EntryPoint
{
    static void Main() {
        Expression<Func<int, int>> expr = n => n+1;
```

```
        Func<int, int> func = expr.Compile();

        for( int i = 0; i < 10; ++i ) {
            Console.WriteLine( func(i) );
        }

    }
}
```

The line in bold shows the step at which the expression is compiled into a delegate. If you think about it a little bit, you may quickly start imagining how you could modify this expression tree or even combine multiple expression trees to create more complex expression trees prior to compiling them. One could even define a new expression language or implement a parser for an already existing expression language. In fact, the compiler acts as an expression parser when you assign a lambda expression into an Expression<T> type instance. Under the covers, it generates the code to build the expression tree and if you use ILDASM to look at the generated code, you can see it in action. The previous example could be rewritten without using the lambda expression as follows:

```
using System;
using System.Linq;
using System.Linq.Expressions;

public class EntryPoint
{
    static void Main() {
        var n = Expression.Parameter( typeof(int), "n" );
        var expr = Expression<Func<int,int>>.Lambda<Func<int,int>>(
                        Expression.Add(n, Expression.Constant(1)),
                        n );

        Func<int, int> func = expr.Compile();

        for( int i = 0; i < 10; ++i ) {
            Console.WriteLine( func(i) );
        }

    }
}
```

The bolded lines here replace the single line in the prior example in which the expr variable is assigned the lambda expression n => n+1. I think you'll agree that the first example is much easier to read. However, this longhand example helps express the true flexibility of expression trees. Let's break down the steps of building the expression. First, you need to represent the parameters in the parameter list of the lambda expression. In this case, there is only one, the variable n. Thus we start with:

```
var n = Expression.Parameter( typeof(int), "n" );
```

■Note In these examples, I am using implicitly typed variables to save myself a lot of typing and to reduce clutter for readability. Remember, the variables are still strongly typed. The compiler simply infers their type at compile time rather than requiring you to provide the type.

This line of code says that we need a variable named n that is of type int. Remember that in a plain lambda expression, this type can be inferred based upon the delegate type provided. Now, we need to construct a BinaryExpression instance that represents the addition operation, as shown next:

```
Expression.Add(n, Expression.Constant(1))
```

Here, I've said that my BinaryExpression should consist of adding a constant, the number one, to the parameter n. You may have already started to notice a pattern. The framework implements a form of the Abstract Factory design pattern for creating instances of expression elements. That is, you cannot create a new instance of BinaryExpression, or any other building block of expression trees, using the new operator along with the constructor of the type. The constructor is not accessible, and therefore, you must use the static methods on the Expression class to create those instances. They give us as consumers the flexibility to express what we want and allow the Expression implementation to decide which type we really need.

Now that we have the BinaryExpression, we need to use the Expression.Lambda<> method to bind the expression (in this case n+1) with the parameters in the parameter list (in this case n). Notice that in the example I use the generic Lambda<> method so that I can create the type Expression<Func<int,int>>. Using the generic form gives the compiler more type information to catch any errors I may have introduced at compile time rather than let those errors bite me at run time.

■Note If I had used the nongeneric version of the Expression.Lambda method, the result would have been an instance of LambdaExpression. LambdaExpression also implements the Compile method; however, instead of a strongly typed delegate, it returns an instance of type Delegate. Before you can invoke the Delegate instance, you must cast it to the specific delegate type, in this case Func<int, int> or another delegate with the same signature, or you must call DynamicInvoke on the delegate. Either one of those could throw an exception at run time if you have a mismatch between your expression and the type of delegate you think it should generate.

Operating on Expressions

Now, I would like to show you an example of how you can take an expression tree generated from a lambda expression and modify it to create a new expression tree. In this case, I will take the expression (n+1) and turn it into 2*(n+1):

```
using System;
using System.Linq;
using System.Linq.Expressions;

public class EntryPoint
{
    static void Main() {
        Expression<Func<int,int>> expr = n => n+1;

        // Now, reassign the expr by multiplying the original
        // expression by 2.
        expr = Expression<Func<int,int>>.Lambda<Func<int,int>>(
                Expression.Multiply( expr.Body,
                                        Expression.Constant(2) ),
                expr.Parameters );

        Func<int, int> func = expr.Compile();
```

```
    for( int i = 0; i < 10; ++i ) {
        Console.WriteLine( func(i) );
    }


  }
}
```

The bolded lines show the stage at which I multiply the original lambda expression by two. It's very important to notice that the parameters passed into the Lambda<> method need to be exactly the same instances of the parameters that come from the original expression; that is, expr.Parameters. This is required. You cannot pass a new instance of ParameterExpression to the Lambda<> method above; otherwise, at run time you will receive an exception similar to the following since the new ParameterExpression instance, even though it may have the same name, is actually a different parameter instance.

```
System.InvalidOperationException: Lambda Parameter not in scope
```

There are many classes derived from the Expression class and many static methods for creating instances of them and combining other expressions. It would be a waste for me to describe them all here. Therefore, I recommend that you refer to the MSDN Library documentation regarding the System.Linq.Expressions namespace for all of the fantastic details.

Functions As Data

If you have ever studied functional languages such as Lisp, you may notice the similarities between expression trees and how Lisp and similar languages represent functions as data structures. Most people encounter Lisp in an academic environment and many times concepts that one learns in academia are not directly applicable to the real world. But before you eschew expression trees as merely an academic exercise, I want to point out how they are actually very useful.

As you may already guess, within the scope of C# 3.0, expression trees are extremely useful when applied to LINQ. I will give a full introduction to LINQ in Chapter 16, but for our discussion here, the most important fact is that LINQ provides a language-native, expressive syntax for describing operations on data that are not naturally modeled in an object-oriented way. For example, you can create a LINQ expression to search a large in-memory array (or any other IEnumerable type) for items that match a certain pattern. LINQ is extensible and can provide a means of operating on other types of stores, such as XML and relational databases. In fact, out of the box, C# 3.0 provides implementations for LINQ on relational databases (including LINQ to SQL, LINQ to Dataset, LINQ to Entities, LINQ to XML, and LINQ to Objects), which collectively allow you to perform LINQ operations on any type that supports IEnumerable.

So how do expression trees come into play here? Imagine you are implementing LINQ to SQL to query relational databases. The user's database could be a half a world away and it may be very expensive to perform a simple query. On top of that, you have no way of judging how complex the user's LINQ expression may be. Naturally, you want to do everything you can to provide the most efficient experience possible.

If the LINQ expression is represented in data (as an expression tree) rather than in IL (as a delegate), then you can operate on it. Maybe you have an algorithm that can spot places where an optimization may be utilized, thus simplifying the expression. Or maybe when your implementation analyzes the expression, you determine that the entire expression can be packaged up, sent across the wire, and executed in its entirety on the server.

Expression trees give you this important capability. Then, when you are finished operating on the data, you can translate the expression tree into the final executable operation via a mechanism like the LambdaExpression.Compile method and go. Had the expression only been available as IL code from the beginning, your flexibility would have been severely limited. I hope now you can appreciate the true power of expression trees in C# 3.0.

Useful Applications of Lambda Expressions

Now that I have shown you what lambda expressions look like, let's consider some of the things you can do with them. You can actually implement most of the following examples in C# 2.0 using anonymous methods or delegates. However, it's amazing how a simple syntactic addition to the language can clear the fog and open up the possibilities of expressiveness.

Iterators and Generators Revisited

I've described how you can create custom iterators with C# in a couple of places in this book already.[4] Now I would like to demonstrate how one can use lambda expressions to create custom iterators. The point I would like to stress is how the code implementing the algorithm, in this case the iteration algorithm, is then factored out into a reusable method that can be applied in almost any scenario.

■**Note** Those of you who are also C++ programmers and familiar with using the Standard Template Library (STL) will find this notion a familiar one. Most of the algorithms defined in the std namespace in the <algorithm> header require you to provide predicates to get their work done. When the STL arrived on the scene back in the early 1990s, it swept the C++ programming community like a refreshing functional programming breeze.

I want to show how you can iterate over a generic type that may or may not be a collection in the strict sense of the word. Additionally, you can externalize the behavior of the iteration cursor as well as how to access the current value of the collection. With a little thought, one can factor out just about everything from the custom iterator creation method, including the type of the item stored, the type of the cursor, the start state of the cursor, the end state of the cursor, and how to advance the cursor. All of these are demonstrated in the following example:

```
using System;
using System.Linq;
using System.Collections.Generic;

public static class IteratorExtensions
{
    public static IEnumerable<TItem>
        MakeCustomIterator<TCollection, TCursor, TItem>(
                this TCollection collection,
                TCursor cursor,
                Func<TCollection, TCursor, TItem> getCurrent,
                Func<TCursor, bool> isFinished,
                Func<TCursor, TCursor> advanceCursor) {
        while( !isFinished(cursor) ) {
            yield return getCurrent( collection, cursor );
```

---

4. Chapter 9 introduces iterators via the `yield` statement, and Chapter 14 expands on custom iterators in the section titled "Borrowing from Functional Programming."

```
                cursor = advanceCursor( cursor );
            }
        }
    }
}

public class IteratorExample
{
    static void Main() {
        var matrix = new List<List<double>> {
            new List<double> { 1.0, 1.1, 1.2 },
            new List<double> { 2.0, 2.1, 2.2 },
            new List<double> { 3.0, 3.1, 3.2 }
        };

        var iter = matrix.MakeCustomIterator(
                    new int[] { 0, 0 },
                    (coll, cur) => coll[cur[0]][cur[1]],
                    (cur) => cur[0] > 2 || cur[1] > 2,
                    (cur) => new int[] { cur[0] + 1,
                                         cur[1] + 1 } );

        foreach( var item in iter ) {
            Console.WriteLine( item );
        }
    }
}
```

Look how reusable MakeCustomIterator<> is! Admittedly, it takes some time to get used to the lambda syntax and those used to reading imperative coding styles may find it hard to follow. Notice that it takes three generic type arguments. TCollection is the type of the collection, which in this example is specified as List<List<double>> at the point of use. TCursor is the type of the cursor, which in this case is a simple array of integers which can be considered coordinates of the matrix variable. And TItem is the type that the code returns via the yield statement. The rest of the parameters to MakeCustomIterator<> are delegate types that it uses to determine how to iterate over the collection. First, it needs a way to access the current item in the collection, which is expressed in the following lambda expression:

```
(coll, cur) => coll[cur[0]][cur[1]]
```

Then it needs a way to determine if we have reached the end of the collection, for which I supply the following lambda expression:

```
(cur) => cur[0] > 2 || cur[1] > 2
```

And finally, it needs to know how to advance the cursor, which I have supplied in the following lambda expression:

```
(cur) => new int[] { cur[0] + 1, cur[1] + 1 }
```

Other implementations of MakeCustomIterator<> could accept a first parameter of type IEnumerable<T>, which in this example would be IEnumerable<double>. However, when you impose that restriction, whatever you pass to MakeCustomIterator<> must implement IEnumerable<>. The matrix variable does implement IEnumerable<>, but not in the form that is easily usable, since it is IEnumerable<List<double>>. Additionally, you could assume that the collection implements an indexer as described in the Chapter 4 section "Indexers," but then again, to do so would be restricting the reusability of MakeCustomIterator<> and which objects you could use it on. In the example above, the indexer is actually used to access the current item, but its use is externalized and wrapped up in the lambda expression given to access the current item.

Moreover, since the operation of accessing the current item of the collection is externalized, you could even transform the data in the original matrix variable as you iterate over it. For example, I could have multiplied each value by two in the lambda expression that accesses the current item in the collection, as shown here:

```
(coll, cur) => coll[cur[0]][cur[1]] * 2;
```

Can you imagine how painful it would have been to implement MakeCustomIterator<> using delegates in the C# 1.0 days? This is exactly what I mean when I say that even just the addition of the lambda expression syntax to C# 3.0 opens one's eyes to the incredible possibilities. If you execute the previous example, you'll see that I walked the diagonal of the matrix as shown in the following output:

```
1
2.1
3.2
```

As a final example, consider the case where your custom iterator does not even iterate over a collection of items at all and is used as a number generator instead, as shown here:

```
using System;
using System.Linq;
using System.Collections.Generic;

public class IteratorExample
{
    static IEnumerable<T> MakeGenerator<T>( T initialValue,
                                            Func<T, T> advance ) {
        T currentValue = initialValue;
        while( true ) {
            yield return currentValue;
            currentValue = advance( currentValue );
        }
    }

    static void Main() {
        var iter = MakeGenerator<double>( 1,
                                          x => x * 1.2 );

        var enumerator = iter.GetEnumerator();
        for( int i = 0; i < 10; ++i ) {
            enumerator.MoveNext();
            Console.WriteLine( enumerator.Current );
        }
    }
}
```

After executing this code, you will see the following results:

```
1
1.2
1.44
1.728
2.0736
2.48832
2.985984
3.5831808
4.29981696
5.159780352
```

You could allow this method to run infinitely, and it would only stop if you experienced an overflow exception or you stopped execution. But the point is, the items you are iterating over don't exist as a collection; rather, they are generated on an as-needed basis each time you advance the iterator. You can apply this concept in many ways, even creating a random number generator implemented using C# iterators.

Closures (Variable Capture) and Memoization

In the Chapter 10 section titled "Beware the Captured Variable Surprise," I described how anonymous methods can capture the contexts of their lexical surroundings. Many refer to this phenomenon as variable capture. In functional programming parlance, it's also known as a closure.[5] Here is a simple closure in action:

```
using System;
using System.Linq;

public class Closures
{
    static void Main() {
        int delta = 1;
        Func<int, int> func = (x) => x + delta;

        int currentVal = 0;
        for( int i = 0; i < 10; ++i ) {
            currentVal = func( currentVal );
            Console.WriteLine( currentVal );
        }
    }
}
```

The variable delta and the delegate func embody the closure. The expression body references delta, and therefore must have access to it when it is executed at a later time. To do this, the compiler "captures" the variable for the delegate. Under the covers, what this means is that the delegate body contains a reference to the actual variable delta. Moreover, since the captured variable is accessible to both the delegate and the context containing the lambda expression, it means that the captured variable can be changed outside the scope and out of band of the delegate. This behavior can be used to your advantage, but when unexpected, it can cause serious confusion.

---

5. For a more general discussion of closures, visit http://en.wikipedia.org/wiki/Closure_%28computer_science%29.

Note In reality, when a closure is formed, the C# 3.0 compiler takes all of those variables and wraps them up in a generated class. It also implements the delegate as a method of the class. In very rare cases, you may need to be concerned about this, especially if it is found to be an efficiency burden during profiling.

Now I would like to show you a great application of closures. One of the foundations of functional programming is that the function itself is treated as a first class object that can be manipulated and operated upon as well as invoked. You've already seen how lambda expressions can be converted into expression trees so you can operate on them, producing more or less complex expressions. But one thing I have not discussed yet is the topic of using functions themselves as building blocks for creating new functions. As a quick example of what I mean, consider two lambda expressions:

```
x => x * 3
x => x + 3.1415
```

You could create a method to combine such lambda expressions to create a compound lambda expression as I've shown here:

```
using System;
using System.Linq;

public class Compound
{
    static Func<T, S> Chain<T, R, S>( Func<T, R> func1,
                                      Func<R, S> func2 ) {
        return x => func2( func1(x) );
    }

    static void Main() {
        Func<int, double> func = Chain( (int x) => x * 3,
                                        (int x) => x + 3.1415 );

        Console.WriteLine( func(2) );
    }
}
```

The Chain<> method accepts two delegates and produces a third delegate by combining the two. In the Main method, you can see how I used it to produce the compound expression. The delegate that you get after calling Chain<> is equivalent to the delegate you get when you convert the following lambda expression into a delegate:

```
x => (x * 3) + 3.1415
```

Having a method to chain arbitrary expressions like this is useful indeed, but let's look at other ways you can produce a derivative function. Imagine an operation that takes a really long time to compute. Examples are the factorial operation or the operation to compute the nth Fibonacci number. An example that I would ultimately like to show demonstrates the Reciprocal Fibonacci constant, which is:

$$\sum_{k=1}^{\infty} \frac{1}{F_k} = 3.35988566\ldots$$

where F_k is a Fibonacci number.[6]

---

6. Weisstein, Eric W. "Reciprocal Fibonacci Constant." From MathWorld—A Wolfram Web Resource. http://mathworld.wolfram.com/ReciprocalFibonacciConstant.html.

To begin to demonstrate that this constant exists computationally, we need to first come up with an operation to compute the nth Fibonacci number:

```
using System;
using System.Linq;

public class Proof
{
    static void Main() {
        Func<int, int> fib = null;
        fib = (x) => x > 1 ? fib(x-1) + fib(x-2) : x;

        for( int i = 30; i < 40; ++i ) {
            Console.WriteLine( fib(i) );
        }
    }
}
```

When you look at this code, the first thing that jumps up and grabs you is the formation of the Fibonacci routine, that is, the `fib` delegate. It forms a closure on itself! This is definitely a form of recursion and behavior that I desire. However, if you execute the example, unless you have a quad-core powerhouse of a machine, you will notice how slow it is, even though all I did was output the 30th to 39th Fibonacci numbers! If that is the case, then we don't even have a prayer at demonstrating the Fibonacci constant. The slowness comes from the fact that for each Fibonacci number that we compute, we have to do a little more work than we did to compute the two prior Fibonacci numbers, and you can see how this work quickly mushrooms.

We can solve this problem by trading a little bit of space for time by caching the Fibonacci numbers in memory. But instead of modifying the original expression, let's look at how we can create a method that accepts the original delegate as a parameter and returns a new delegate to replace the original. The ultimate goal is to be able to replace the first delegate with the derivative delegate without affecting the code that consumes it. One such technique is called memoization.[7] This is the technique whereby you cache function return values and each return value's associated input parameters. This only works if the function has no entropy, meaning that for the same input parameters, it always returns the same result. Then, prior to calling the actual function, you first check to see if the result for the given parameter set has already been computed and return it rather than calling the function. Given a very complex function, this technique trades a little bit of memory space for significant speed gain. Let's look at an example.

```
using System;
using System.Linq;
using System.Collections.Generic;

public static class Memoizers
{
    public static Func<T,R> Memoize<T,R>( this Func<T,R> func ) {
        var cache = new Dictionary<T,R>();
        return (x) => {
            R result = default(R);
            if( cache.TryGetValue(x, out result) ) {
                return result;
            }
```

---

7. You can read more about memoization at http://en.wikipedia.org/wiki/Memoization. Also, Wes Dyer has an excellent entry regarding memoization on his blog at http://blogs.msdn.com/wesdyer/archive/2007/01/26/function-memoization.aspx.

```
            result = func(x);
            cache[x] = result;
            return result;
        };
    }
}

public class Proof
{
    static void Main() {
        Func<int, int> fib = null;
        fib = (x) => x > 1 ? fib(x-1) + fib(x-2) : x;
        fib = fib.Memoize();

        for( int i = 30; i < 40; ++i ) {
            Console.WriteLine( fib(i) );
        }
    }
}
```

First of all, notice how in Main, I have added only one more statement where I apply the Memoize<> method to the delegate to produce a new delegate. Everything else stays the same, so the transparent replaceability goal is achieved. The Memoize<> method wraps the original delegate that's passed in via the func argument with another closure that includes a Dictionary<> instance to store the cached values of the given delegate func. In the process of Memoize<> taking one delegate and returning another, it has introduced a cache that greatly improves the efficiency. Each time the derivative delegate is called, it first checks the cache to see if the value has already been computed.

■**Caution** Of course, memoization only works for functions that are deterministically repeatable in the sense that you are guaranteed to get the same result for the same parameters. For example, a true random number generator cannot be memoized.

Run the two previous examples on your own machine to see the amazing difference. Now we can move on to the business of computing the Reciprocal Fibonacci constant by modifying the Main method as follows:

```
static void Main() {
    Func<ulong, ulong> fib = null;
    fib = (x) => x > 1 ? fib(x-1) + fib(x-2) : x;
    fib = fib.Memoize();

    Func<ulong, decimal> fibConstant = null;
    fibConstant = (x) => {
        if( x == 1 ) {
            return 1 / ((decimal)fib(x));
        } else {
            return 1 / ((decimal)fib(x)) + fibConstant(x-1);
        }
    };
    fibConstant = fibConstant.Memoize();

    Console.WriteLine( "\n{0}\t{1}\t{2}\t{3}\n",
                       "Count",
                       "Fibonacci".PadRight(24),
```

```
                            "1/Fibonacci".PadRight(24),
                            "Fibonacci Constant".PadRight(24) );

        for( ulong i = 1; i <= 93; ++i ) {
            Console.WriteLine( "{0:D5}\t{1:D24}\t{2:F24}\t{3:F24}",
                                i,
                                fib(i),
                                (1/(decimal)fib(i)),
                                fibConstant(i) );
        }
    }
```

The bold text shows the delegate I created to compute the nth Reciprocal Fibonacci constant. As you call this delegate with higher and higher values for x, you should see the result get closer and closer to the Reciprocal Fibonacci constant. Notice that I memoized the fibConstant delegate as well. If you don't do this, you may suffer a stack overflow due to the recursion as you call fibConstant with higher and higher values for x. So you can see that memoization also trades stack space for heap space. On each line of output, the code outputs the intermediate values for informational purposes, but the interesting value is in the far right column. Notice that I stopped calculation with iteration number 93. That's because the ulong will overflow with the 94th Fibonacci number. I could solve the overflow problem by using BigInteger in the System.Numeric namespace. However, that's not necessary since the 93rd iteration of the Reciprocal Fibonacci constant shown here is close enough to prove the point of this example.

3.**35988566**62431777553039387

I have bolded the digits that are significant.[8] I think you will agree that memoization is extremely useful. For that matter, many more useful things can be done with methods that accept functions and produce other functions as I'll show in the next section.

Currying

In the previous section on closures I demonstrated how to create a method that accepts a function, given as a delegate, and produces a new function. This concept is a very powerful one and memoization, as shown in the previous section, is a powerful application of it. In this section, I would like to show you the technique of currying,[9] which essentially means creating an operation (usually a method) that accepts a function of multiple parameters (usually a delegate) and produces a function of only a single parameter.

■**Note** If you are a C++ programmer familiar with the STL, you have undoubtedly used the currying operation if you've ever utilized any of the parameter binders such as Bind1st and Bind2nd.

Suppose you have a lambda expression that looks like the following:

```
(x, y) => x + y
```

---

8. You can see many more decimal locations of the Reciprocal Fibonacci constant at http://www.research.att.com/~njas/sequences/A079586.

9. For a lot more information about currying, go to http://en.wikipedia.org/wiki/Currying.

Now, suppose you have a list of doubles and you want to use this lambda expression to add a constant value to each item on the list, producing a new list. What would be nice is to create a new delegate based on the original lambda expression where one of the variables is forced to a static value. This notion is called *parameter binding*, and those who have used STL in C++ are likely very familiar with it. Check out the next example, where I show parameter binding in action:

```
using System;
using System.Linq;
using System.Collections.Generic;

public static class CurryExtensions
{
    public static Func<TArg1, TResult>
        Bind2nd<TArg1, TArg2, TResult>(
            this Func<TArg1, TArg2, TResult> func,
            TArg2 constant ) {
        return (x) => func( x, constant );
    }
}

public class BinderExample
{
    static void Main() {
        var mylist = new List<double> { 1.0, 3.4, 5.4, 6.54 };
        var newlist = new List<double>();

        // Here is the original expression.
        Func<double, double, double> func = (x, y) => x + y;

        // Here is the curried function.
        var funcBound = func.Bind2nd( 3.2 );

        foreach( var item in mylist ) {
            Console.Write( "{0}, ", item );
            newlist.Add( funcBound(item) );
        }

        Console.WriteLine();
        foreach( var item in newlist ) {
            Console.Write( "{0}, ", item );
        }
    }
}
```

The meat of this example is in the Bind2nd<> extension method, which I have bolded. You can see that it creates a closure and returns a new delegate that accepts only one parameter. Then, when that new delegate is called, it passes its only parameter as the first parameter to the original delegate and passes the provided constant as the second parameter. For the sake of example, I iterate through the mylist list, building a second list held in the newlist variable while using the curried version of the original method to add 3.2 to each item.

Just for good measure, I want to show you another way you can perform the currying, slightly different from that shown in the previous example.

```
using System;
using System.Linq;
using System.Collections.Generic;
```

```
public static class CurryExtensions
{
    public static Func<TArg2, Func<TArg1, TResult>>
        Bind2nd<TArg1, TArg2, TResult>(
            this Func<TArg1, TArg2, TResult> func ) {
        return (y) => (x) => func( x, y );
    }
}

public class BinderExample
{
    static void Main() {
        var mylist = new List<double> { 1.0, 3.4, 5.4, 6.54 };
        var newlist = new List<double>();

        // Here is the original expression.
        Func<double, double, double> func = (x, y) => x + y;

        // Here is the curried function.
        var funcBound = func.Bind2nd()(3.2);

        foreach( var item in mylist ) {
            Console.Write( "{0}, ", item );
            newlist.Add( funcBound(item) );
        }

        Console.WriteLine();
        foreach( var item in newlist ) {
            Console.Write( "{0}, ", item );
        }
    }
}
```

I have bolded the parts that are different from the previous example. In the first example, Bind2nd<> returned a delegate that accepted a single integer and returned an integer. In this example, I changed Bind2nd<> to return a delegate that accepts a single parameter (the value to bind the second parameter of the original function to) and returns another delegate that is the curried function. Both forms are perfectly valid. But the purists may prefer the second form over the former.

Anonymous Recursion

In the earlier section titled "Closures (Variable Capture) and Memoization," I showed a form of recursion using closures while calculating the Fibonacci numbers. For the sake of discussion, let's look at a similar closure that one can use to calculate the factorial of a number.

```
Func<int, int> fact = null;
fact = (x) => x > 1 ? x * fact(x-1) : 1;
```

This code works because fact forms a closure on itself and also calls itself. That is, the second line, where fact is assigned the lambda expression for the factorial calculation, captures the fact delegate itself. Even though this recursion works, it is extremely fragile and you must be very careful when using it as written.

Remember that even though a closure captures a variable for use inside the anonymous method, which is implemented here as a lambda expression, the captured variable is still accessible and mutable from outside the context of the capturing anonymous method or lambda expression. For example, consider what happens if you perform the following:

```
Func<int, int> fact = null;
fact = (x) => x > 1 ? x * fact(x-1) : 1;
Func<int, int> newRefToFact = fact;
```

Since objects in the CLR are reference types, newRefToFact and fact now reference the same delegate. Now, imagine that you then do something similar to this:

```
Func<int, int> fact = null;
fact = (x) => x > 1 ? x * fact(x-1) : 1;
Func<int, int> newRefToFact = fact;
fact = (x) => x + 1;
```

Now the recursion is broken! Can you see why? The reason is that we modified the captured variable fact. We reassigned fact to reference a new delegate based on the lambda expression (x) => x+1. But newRefToFact still references the lambda expression (x) => x > 1 ? x * fact(x-1) : 1. However, when the delegate referenced by newRefToFact calls fact, it ends up getting the new expression (x) => x+1 which is different behavior than the recursion we had before.

There are several ways to fix this problem, but the typical method is to use anonymous recursion.[10] What ends up happening is that you modify the factorial lambda expression above to accept another parameter which is the delegate to call when it's time to recurse. Essentially, this removes the closure and converts the captured variable into a parameter to the delegate. What you end up with is something similar to the following:

```
delegate TResult AnonRec<TArg,TResult>( AnonRec<TArg,TResult> f, TArg arg );
AnonRec<int, int> fact = (f, x) => x > 1 ? x * f(f, x-1) : 1;
```

The key here is that instead of recursing by relying on a captured variable that is a delegate, you instead pass the delegate to recurse on as a parameter. In this example, the recursion delegate is represented by the parameter f. Therefore, notice that fact not only accepts f as a parameter, but calls it in order to recurse and then passes f along to the next iteration of the delegate. In essence, the captured variable now lives on the stack as it is passed to each recursion of the expression. However, since it is on the stack, the danger of it being modified out from underneath the recursion mechanism is now gone.

For more details on this technique I strongly suggest that you read Wes Dyer's blog entry titled "Anonymous Recursion in C#" at http://blogs.msdn.com/wesdyer. Wes is one of the members of the C# team and a functional programming aficionado extraordinaire. In his blog entry he demonstrates how to implement a Y fixed-point combinator that generalizes the notion of anonymous recursion shown earlier.[11]

---

10. For more theoretical details on anonymous recursion, reference the article at http://en.wikipedia.org/wiki/Anonymous_recursion.

11. Read more about Y fixed-point combinators at http://en.wikipedia.org/wiki/Fixed_point_combinator.

Summary

In this chapter I introduced you to the syntax of lambda expressions, which are, for the most part, replacements for anonymous methods. In fact, it's a shame lambda expressions did not come along with C# 2.0, because then there would have been no need for anonymous methods. I showed how you can convert lambda expressions, with and without statement bodies, into delegates. Additionally, you saw how lambda expressions without statement bodies are convertible to expression trees based on the Expression<T> type as defined in the System.Linq.Expression namespace. Using expression trees, you can apply transformations to the expression tree before actually compiling it into a delegate and calling it. I finished the chapter by showing you useful applications of lambda expressions. These included creating generalized iterators, memoization by using closures, delegate parameter binding using currying, and an introduction to the concept of anonymous recursion. Just about all of these concepts are foundations of functional programming. Even though one could implement all of these techniques in C# 2.0 using anonymous methods, the introduction of lambda syntax to the language makes using such techniques more natural and less cumbersome.

The following chapter introduces LINQ, the culmination of all of the new C# 3.0 features. I will also continue to focus on the functional programming aspects that it brings to the table.

CHAPTER 16

■ ■ ■

LINQ: Language Integrated Query

C-style languages (including C#) are imperative in nature, meaning that the emphasis is placed on the state of the system, and changes are made to that state over time. Data-acquisition languages such as SQL are functional in nature, meaning that the emphasis is placed on the operation and there is little or no immutable data used during the process. LINQ bridges the gap between the imperative programming style and the functional programming style. LINQ is a huge topic that deserves entire books devoted to it and what you can do with it.[1] There are several implementations of LINQ readily available and they are LINQ to Objects, LINQ to SQL, LINQ to Dataset, and LINQ to XML. I will be focusing on LINQ to Objects since I'll be able to get the LINQ message across without having to incorporate extra layers and technologies.

■**Note** Development for LINQ started some time ago at Microsoft and was born out of the efforts of Anders Hejlsberg and Peter Golde. The idea was to create a more natural and language-integrated way to access data from within a language such as C#. However, at the same time, it was undesirable to implement it in such a way that it would destabilize the implementation of the C# compiler and become too cumbersome for the language. As it turns out, it made sense to implement some building blocks in the language in order to provide the functionality and expressiveness of LINQ. Thus we have features like lambda expressions, anonymous types, extension methods, and implicitly typed variables. All of them are excellent features in themselves but arguably were precipitated by LINQ.

LINQ does a very good job of allowing the programmer to focus on the business logic while spending less time coding up the mundane plumbing that is normally associated with data access code. If you have experience building data-aware applications, think about how many times you have found yourself coding up the same type of boilerplate code over and over again. LINQ removes some of that burden.

A Bridge to Data

Throughout this book, I have stressed how just about all of the new features introduced in C# 3.0 foster a functional programming model. There's a good reason for that, in the sense that data query is typically a functional process. For example, a SQL statement tells the server exactly what you want and what to do. It does not really describe objects and structures and how they are related both statically and dynamically, which is typically what you do when you design a new application in an object-oriented language. Therefore, functional programming is the key here and any techniques that you may be familiar with from other functional programming languages such as Lisp, Scheme, or F# are applicable.

---

1. For more extensive coverage of LINQ, I suggest you check out *Pro LINQ: Language Integrated Query in C# 2008* by Joseph C. Rattz, Jr. (Berkeley, CA: Apress, 2007).

Query Expressions

At first glance, LINQ query expressions look a lot like SQL expressions. But make no mistake. LINQ is not SQL. For starters, LINQ is strongly typed. After all, C# is a strongly typed language, and therefore, so is LINQ. The language adds eight new keywords for building query expressions. However, their implementation from the compiler standpoint is pretty simple. LINQ query expressions get translated into a chain of extension method calls on a sequence or collection. That set of extension methods is clearly defined, and they are called *standard query operators*.

■**Note** This LINQ model is quite extensible. If the compiler merely translates query expressions into a series of extension method calls, it follows that you can provide your own implementations of those extension methods. In fact, that is the case. For example, the class System.Linq.Enumerable provides implementations of those methods for LINQ to Objects, whereas System.Linq.Queryable provides implementations of those methods for LINQ to SQL.

Let's jump right in and have a look at what queries look like. Consider the following example where I create a collection of Employee objects and then perform a simple query:

```
using System;
using System.Linq;
using System.Collections.Generic;

public class Employee
{
    public string FirstName { get; set; }
    public string LastName { get; set; }
    public Decimal Salary { get; set; }
    public DateTime StartDate { get; set; }
}

public class SimpleQuery
{
    static void Main() {
        // Create our database of employees.
        var employees = new List<Employee> {
            new Employee {
                FirstName = "Joe",
                LastName = "Bob",
                Salary = 94000,
                StartDate = DateTime.Parse("1/4/1992") },
            new Employee {
                FirstName = "Jane",
                LastName = "Doe",
                Salary = 123000,
                StartDate = DateTime.Parse("4/12/1998") },
            new Employee {
                FirstName = "Milton",
                LastName = "Waddams",
                Salary = 1000000,
                StartDate = DateTime.Parse("12/3/1969") }
        };
```

```
var query = from employee in employees
            where employee.Salary > 100000
            orderby employee.LastName, employee.FirstName
            select new { LastName = employee.LastName,
                         FirstName = employee.FirstName };

Console.WriteLine( "Highly paid employees:" );
foreach( var item in query ) {
    Console.WriteLine( "{0}, {1}",
                          item.LastName,
                          item.FirstName );
    }

    }
}
```

First of all, 99% of the time, you will need to import the System.Linq namespace, as I show in the following section titled "Standard Query Operators." In this example, I marked the query expression in bold to make it stand out. It's quite shocking if it's the first time you have seen a LINQ expression! After all, C# is a language that syntactically evolved from C++ and Java, and the LINQ syntax looks nothing like those languages.

■ Note For those of you familiar with SQL, the first thing you probably noticed is that the query is backwards from what you are used to. In SQL, the select clause is normally the beginning of the expression. There are several reasons why the reversal makes sense in C#. One reason is so that Intellisense will work. In the example, if the select clause appeared first, Intellisense would have a hard time knowing which properties employee provides, since it would not even know the type of employee yet.

Prior to the query expression, I created a simple list of Employee instances just to have some data to work with. Each query expression starts off with a from clause, which declares what's called a *range variable*. The from clause in our example is very similar to a foreach statement in that it iterates over the employees collection and stores each item in the collection in the variable employee during each iteration. After the from clause, the query consists of a series of clauses where we can use various query operators to filter the data represented by the range variable. In my example I applied a where clause and an orderby clause, as you can see. Finally, the expression closes with a *projection* operator. When you perform a projection in the query expression, you are typically creating another collection of information, or a single piece of information, that is a transformed version of the collection iterated by the range variable. In the previous example, I wanted just the first and last names of the employees in my results.

The end result of building the query expression culminates in what's called a *query variable*, which is query in this example. Notice that I reference it using an implicitly typed variable. After all, can you imagine what the type of query is? If you are so inclined, you can send query.GetType to the console and you'll see that the type is as shown here:

```
System.Linq.Enumerable+<SelectIterator>d__b`2[Employee, ➥
<>f__AnonymousType0`2[System.String,System.String]]
```

Another thing to note is my use of anonymous types in the select clause. I wanted the query to create a transformation of the original data into a collection of structures, where each instance contains a FirstName property, a LastName property, and nothing more. Sure, I could have defined such a structure prior to my query and made my select clause instantiate instances of that type, however, doing so defeats some of the convenience and expressiveness of the LINQ query.

And most importantly, as I'll detail a little later in the section "The Virtues of Being Lazy," the query expression does not execute at the point the query variable is assigned. Instead, the query variable in this example implements the generic form of IEnumerable, and the subsequent use of foreach on the query variable produces the end result of the example.

Extension Methods and Lambda Expressions Revisited

Before I break down the elements of a LINQ expression in more detail, I would like to show you an alternate way of getting the work done. In fact, it's more or less what the compiler is doing under the covers.

The LINQ syntax is very foreign looking in a predominantly imperative language like C#. It's easy to jump to the conclusion that the C# language underwent massive modifications in order to implement LINQ. Actually, the compiler simply transforms the LINQ expression into a series of extension method calls that accept lambda expressions.

If you look at the System.Linq namespace, you'll see that there are two interesting static classes full of extension methods: Enumerable and Queryable. Enumerable defines a collection of generic extension methods useable on IEnumerable types whereas Queryable defines the same collection of generic extension methods usable on IQueryable types. If you look at the names of those extension methods, you'll see they have names just like the clauses in query expressions. That's no accident, since the extension methods implement the standard query operators I mentioned in the previous section. In fact, the query expression in the previous example can be replaced with the following code:

```
var query = employees
    .Where( emp => emp.Salary > 100000 )
    .OrderBy( emp => emp.LastName )
    .OrderBy( emp => emp.FirstName )
    .Select( emp => new {LastName = emp.LastName,
                         FirstName = emp.FirstName} );
```

Notice that it is simply a chain of extension method calls on IEnumerable, which is implemented by employees. In fact, you could go a step further and flip the statement inside out by removing the extension method syntax and simply call them as static methods, as shown here:

```
var query =
    Enumerable.Select(
      Enumerable.OrderBy(
       Enumerable.OrderBy(
        Enumerable.Where(
          employees, emp => emp.Salary > 100000),
        emp => emp.LastName ),
       emp => emp.FirstName ),
      emp => new {LastName = emp.LastName,
                  FirstName = emp.FirstName} );
```

But why would you want to do such a thing? I merely show it here for illustration purposes so you know what is actually going on under the covers. Those who are really attached to C# 2.0 anonymous methods could even go one step further and replace the lambda expressions with anonymous methods. Needless to say, the Enumerable and Queryable extension methods are very useful even outside the context of LINQ.

Standard Query Operators

LINQ is built upon the use of standard query operators, which are methods that operate on sequences such as collections that implement IEnumerable or IQueryable. As discussed previously, when the C# compiler encounters a query expression, it converts the expression into a series or chain of calls to those extension methods that implement the behavior.

There are two benefits to this approach. One is that you can generally perform the same actions as a LINQ query expression by calling the extension methods directly. The resulting code is not as easy to read as code with query expressions. However, there may be times when you need functionality from the extension methods and a complete query expression may be overkill.

The greatest benefit of this approach is that LINQ is extensible. That is, you can define your own set of extension methods and the compiler will generate calls to them while compiling a LINQ query expression. For example, suppose you did not import the System.Linq namespace and instead wanted to provide your own implementation of Where and Select. You could do that as shown here:

```
using System;
using System.Collections.Generic;

public static class MySqoSet
{
    public static IEnumerable<T> Where<T> (
            this IEnumerable<T> source,
            System.Func<T,bool> predicate ) {
        Console.WriteLine( "My Where implementation called." );
        return System.Linq.Enumerable.Where( source,
                                             predicate );
    }

    public static IEnumerable<R> Select<T,R> (
            this IEnumerable<T> source,
            System.Func<T,R> selector ) {
        Console.WriteLine( "My Select implementation called." );
        return System.Linq.Enumerable.Select( source,
                                              selector );
    }
}

public class CustomSqo
{
    static void Main() {
        int[] numbers = { 1, 2, 3, 4 };

        var query = from x in numbers
                    where x % 2 == 0
                    select x * 2;

        foreach( var item in query ) {
            Console.WriteLine( item );
        }
    }
}
```

Notice that I did not have to import the System.Linq namespace. Aside from the added convenience, this helps prove my point as not importing the System.Linq namespace prevents the compiler from automatically finding the extension methods in System.Linq.Enumerable. In the MySqoSet static class, I provide my own implementations of the standard query operators Where and Select that simply log a message and then forward to the ones in Enumerable. If you run this example, the output will look as follows:

```
My Where implementation called.
My Select implementation called.
4
8
```

You could take this exercise a little further and imagine that you want to use LINQ against a collection that does not support IEnumerable. Although you would normally make your collection support IEnumerable, for the sake of argument, let's say it supports the custom interface IMyEnumerable instead. In that case, you can supply your own set of standard query operators that operate on IMyEnumerable rather than IEnumerable. There is one drawback, though. If your type does not derive from IEnumerable, then you cannot use a LINQ query expression because the from clause requires a data source that implements IEnumerable. However, you can call the standard query operators on your IMyEnumerable type to achieve the same effect. I will show an example of this in the later section titled "Techniques from Functional Programming," where I build upon an example from Chapter 14.

C# Query Keywords

C# 2008 introduces a small set of new keywords for creating LINQ query expressions. They are from, join, where, group, into, let, orderby, and select. In the following sections, I cover the main points regarding their use.

The from Clause and Range Variables

Each query begins with a from clause. The from clause is a generator that also defines the range variable, which is a local variable of sorts used to represent each item of the input collection as the query expression is applied to it. The from clause is just like a foreach construct in the imperative programming style and the range variable is identical in purpose to the iteration variable in the foreach statement.

A query expression may contain more than one from clause. In that case, you have more than one range variable, and it's analogous to having nested foreach clauses. The next example uses multiple from clauses to generate the multiplication table you may remember from grade school, albeit not in tabular format and with a slight bit of repetition:

```
using System;
using System.Linq;

public class MultTable
{
    static void Main() {
        var query = from x in Enumerable.Range(0,10)
                    from y in Enumerable.Range(0,10)
                    select new {
                        X = x,
                        Y = y,
                        Product = x * y
                    };
```

```
    foreach( var item in query ) {
        Console.WriteLine( "{0} * {1} = {2}",
                            item.X,
                            item.Y,
                            item.Product );
    }
  }
}
```

Remember that LINQ expressions are compiled into strongly typed code. So in this example, what is the type of x and what is the type of y? The compiler infers the types of those two range variables based upon the type argument of the IEnumerable<T> interface returned by Range. Since Range returns a type of IEnumerable<int>, the type of x and y is int. Now, you may be wondering what happens if you want to apply a query expression to a collection that only supports the nongeneric IEnumerable interface. In those cases, you must explicitly specify the type of the range variable, as shown here:

```
using System;
using System.Linq;
using System.Collections;

public class NonGenericLinq
{
    static void Main() {
        ArrayList numbers = new ArrayList();
        numbers.Add( 1 );
        numbers.Add( 2 );

        var query = from int n in numbers
                    select n * 2;

        foreach( var item in query ) {
            Console.WriteLine( item );
        }
    }
}
```

You can see where I am explicitly typing the range variable n to type int. At run time, a cast is performed, which could fail with an InvalidCastException. Therefore, it's best to strive to use the generic, strongly typed IEnumerable<T> rather than IEnumerable so these sorts of errors are caught at compile time rather than run time.

■Note As I've emphasized throughout this book, the compiler is your best friend. Use as many of its facilities as possible to catch coding errors at compile time rather than run time. Strongly typed languages such as C# rely upon the compiler to verify the integrity of the operations we perform on the types defined within the code. If you cast away the type and deal with general types such as System.Object rather than the true concrete types of the objects, you are throwing away one of the most powerful capabilities of the compiler. Then, if there is a type-based mistake in your code and quality assurance does not catch it before it goes out the door, you can bet your customer will let you know about it, in the most abrupt way possible!

The join Clause

Following the from clause, you may have a join clause used to correlate data from two separate sources. Join operations are not typically needed in environments where objects are linked via hierarchies and other associative relationships. However, in the relational database world, there typically are no hard links between items in two separate collections, or tables, other than the equality between items within each record. That equality operation is defined by you when you create a join clause. Consider the following example:

```
using System;
using System.Linq;
using System.Collections.Generic;

public class EmployeeId
{
    public string Id { get; set; }
    public string Name { get; set; }
}

public class EmployeeNationality
{
    public string Id { get; set; }
    public string Nationality { get; set; }
}

public class JoinExample
{
    static void Main() {
        // Build employee collection
        var employees = new List<EmployeeId>() {
            new EmployeeId{ Id = "111-11-1111",
                            Name = "Ed Glasser" },
            new EmployeeId{ Id = "222-22-2222",
                            Name = "Spaulding Smails" },
            new EmployeeId{ Id = "333-33-3333",
                            Name = "Ivan Ivanov" },
            new EmployeeId{ Id = "444-44-4444",
                            Name = "Vasya Pupkin" }
        };

        // Build nationality collection.
        var empNationalities = new List<EmployeeNationality>() {
            new EmployeeNationality{ Id = "111-11-1111",
                                     Nationality = "American" },
            new EmployeeNationality{ Id = "333-33-3333",
                                     Nationality = "Russian" },
            new EmployeeNationality{ Id = "222-22-2222",
                                     Nationality = "Irish" },
            new EmployeeNationality{ Id = "444-44-4444",
                                     Nationality = "Russian" }
        };

        // Build query.
        var query = from emp in employees
                    join n in empNationalities
```

```
                on emp.Id equals n.Id
            orderby n.Nationality descending
            select new {
                Id = emp.Id,
                Name = emp.Name,
                Nationality = n.Nationality
            };

    foreach( var person in query ) {
        Console.WriteLine( "{0}, {1}, \t{2}",
                            person.Id,
                            person.Name,
                            person.Nationality );
    }
  }
}
```

In this example, I have two collections. The first one contains just a database of employees and their employee identification numbers. The second contains a database of employee nationalities where each employee is only identified by employee ID. To keep the example simple, every piece of data is a string. Now, I would like a list of all employee names and their nationalities and I would like to sort the list by their nationality but in descending order. A join clause comes in handy here because there is no single data source that contains this information. But join lets us meld the information from the two data sources, and LINQ makes this a snap! In the query expression I have highlighted the join clause. For each item that the range variable emp references, it finds the item in the collection empNationalities where the Id is equivalent to the Id referenced by emp. Then, my projector clause, the select clause, takes data from both collections when building the result and projects that data into an anonymous type. Thus, the result of the query is a single collection where each item from both employees and empNationalities is melded into one. If you execute this example, the results are as shown here:

```
333-33-3333, Ivan Ivanov,        Russian
444-44-4444, Vasya Pupkin,       Russian
222-22-2222, Spaulding Smails,   Irish
111-11-1111, Ed Glasser,         American
```

When your query contains a join operation, the compiler converts it to a Join extension method call under the covers unless it is followed by an into clause. If the into clause is present, the compiler uses the GroupJoin extension method which also groups the results. For more information on the more esoteric things you can do with join and into clauses, reference the MSDN documentation on LINQ or see *Pro LINQ: Language Integrated Query in C# 2008* by Joseph C. Rattz, Jr. (Apress, 2007).

■**Note** There's no reason you cannot have multiple join clauses within the query to meld data from three different collections all at once. In the previous example you may have a collection that represents languages spoken by each nation, and you could join each item from the empNationalities collection with the items in that language's spoken collection. To do that, you would simply have one join clause following another.

The where Clause and Filters

Following one or more from clause generators or the join clauses if there are any, you typically place one or more filter clauses. Filters consist of the where keyword followed by a predicate expression. The where clause is translated into a call to the Where extension method, and the predicate is passed to the Where method as a lambda expression. Calls to Enumerable.Where, which are used if you are performing a query on an IEnumerable type, convert the lambda expression into a delegate. Conversely, calls to Queryable.Where, which are used if you perform a query on a collection via an IQueryable interface, convert the lambda expression into an expression tree.[2] I'll have more to say about expression trees in LINQ later, in the section titled "Expression Trees Revisited."

The orderby Clause

The orderby clause is used to sort the sequence of results in a query. Following the orderby keyword is the item you want to sort by, which is commonly some property of the range variable. You can sort in either ascending or descending order and if you don't specify that with either the ascending or descending keyword, ascending is the default order. Following the orderby clause, you can have an unlimited set of sub-sorts simply by separating each sort item with a comma, as demonstrated here:

```
using System;
using System.Linq;
using System.Collections.Generic;

public class Employee
{
    public string LastName { get; set; }
    public string FirstName { get; set; }
    public string Nationality { get; set; }
}

public class OrderByExample
{
    static void Main() {
        var employees = new List<Employee>() {
            new Employee {
                LastName = "Glasser", FirstName = "Ed",
                Nationality = "American"
            },
            new Employee {
                LastName = "Pupkin", FirstName = "Vasya",
                Nationality = "Russian"
            },
            new Employee {
                LastName = "Smails", FirstName = "Spaulding",
                Nationality = "Irish"
            },
            new Employee {
                LastName = "Ivanov", FirstName = "Ivan",
                Nationality = "Russian"
            }
        };
```

---

2. In Chapter 15, I show how lambda expressions that are assigned to delegate instance variables are converted into executable IL code, whereas lambda expressions that are assigned to Expression<T> are converted into expression trees, thus describing the expression with data rather than executable code.

```
    var query = from emp in employees
                orderby emp.Nationality,
                        emp.LastName descending,
                        emp.FirstName descending
                select emp;

    foreach( var item in query ) {
        Console.WriteLine( "{0},\t{1},\t{2}",
                        item.LastName,
                        item.FirstName,
                        item.Nationality );
    }
}
}
```

Notice that since the `select` clause simply returns the range variable, this whole query expression is nothing more than a sort operation. But it sure is a convenient way to sort things in C#. In this example, I sort first by `Nationality` in ascending order, then the second expression in the `orderby` clause sorts the results of each nationality group by `LastName` in descending order, and finally, each of those groups is sorted by `FirstName` in descending order.

At compile time, the compiler translates the first expression in the `orderby` clause into a call to the `OrderBy` standard query operator extension method. Any subsequent secondary sort expressions are translated into chained `ThenBy` extension method calls.

The select Clause and Projection

In a LINQ query, the `select` clause is used to produce the end result of the query. It is called a *projector* because it projects, or translates, the data within the query into a form desired for consumption. If there are any filtering `where` clauses in the query expression, they must precede the `select` clause. The compiler converts the `select` clause into a call to the `Select` extension method. The body of the `select` clause is converted into a lambda expression that is passed into the `Select` method, which uses it to produce each item of the result set.

Anonymous types are extremely handy here and you would be correct in guessing that the anonymous types feature was born from the `select` operation during the development of LINQ. To see why anonymous types are so handy in this case, consider the following example:

```
using System;
using System.Linq;

public class Result
{
    public Result( int input, int output ) {
        Input = input;
        Output = output;
    }
    public int Input { get; set; }
    public int Output { get; set; }
}

public class Projector
{
    static void Main() {
        int[] numbers = { 1, 2, 3, 4 };
```

```
        var query = from x in numbers
                    select new Result( x, x*2 );

        foreach( var item in query ) {
            Console.WriteLine( "Input = {0}, Output = {1}",
                               item.Input,
                               item.Output );
        }
    }
}
```

This works. However, notice how I had to declare a new type Result just to hold the results of the query. Now, what if I wanted to change the result to include x, x*2, and x*3 in the future? I would have to first go modify the definition of the Result class to accommodate that. Ouch! It's so much easier just to use anonymous types as follows:

```
using System;
using System.Linq;

public class Projector
{
    static void Main() {
        int[] numbers = { 1, 2, 3, 4 };

        var query = from x in numbers
                    select new {
                        Input = x,
                        Output = x*2 };

        foreach( var item in query ) {
            Console.WriteLine( "Input = {0}, Output = {1}",
                               item.Input,
                               item.Output );
        }
    }
}
```

Now that's much better! I can go and add a new property to the result type and call it Output2, for example, and it would not force any changes on anything other than the anonymous type instantiation inside query expression. Existing code will continue to work, and anyone who wants to use the new Output2 property can use it.

Of course, there are some circumstances where you do want to use predefined types in the select clause. However, the more you can get away with using anonymous types, the more flexibility you will have later on.

The let Clause

The let clause introduces a new local identifier that can subsequently be referenced in the remainder of the query. Think of it as a local variable that is visible only within the query expression, just as a local variable inside a normal code block is visible only within that block. Consider the following example:

```
using System;
using System.Linq;
using System.Collections.Generic;
```

```
public class Employee
{
    public string LastName { get; set; }
    public string FirstName { get; set; }
}

public class OrderByExample
{
    static void Main() {
        var employees = new List<Employee>() {
            new Employee {
                LastName = "Glasser", FirstName = "Ed"
            },
            new Employee {
                LastName = "Pupkin", FirstName = "Vasya"
            },
            new Employee {
                LastName = "Smails", FirstName = "Spaulding"
            },
            new Employee {
                LastName = "Ivanov", FirstName = "Ivan"
            }
        };

        var query = from emp in employees
                    let fullName = emp.FirstName +
                                     " " + emp.LastName
                    orderby fullName
                    select fullName;

        foreach( var item in query ) {
            Console.WriteLine( item );
        }
    }
}
```

In this example, I wanted to sort the names in ascending order, but by sorting on the full name created by putting the FirstName and LastName together. I introduce this construct by using the let clause to define the fullName variable.

One other nice quality of local identifiers introduced by let clauses is that if they reference collections, then you can use the variable as input to another from clause to create a new, derived range variable. In the previous section titled "The from Clause and Range Variables," I gave an example using multiple from clauses to generate a multiplication table. Following is a slight variation of that example using a let clause:

```
using System;
using System.Linq;

public class MultTable
{
    static void Main() {
        var query = from x in Enumerable.Range(0,10)
                    let innerRange = Enumerable.Range(0, 10)
                    from y in innerRange
```

```
                        select new {
                            X = x,
                            Y = y,
                            Product = x * y
                        };

            foreach( var item in query ) {
                Console.WriteLine( "{0} * {1} = {2}",
                                        item.X,
                                        item.Y,
                                        item.Product );
            }
        }
    }
```

I have bolded the changes in this query from the earlier example. Notice how I added a new intermediate identifier named innerRange and I then iterate over that collection with the from clause following it.

The group Clause

The query expression can have an optional group clause, which is very powerful at partitioning the input of the query. The group clause is a projector as it projects the data into a collection of IGrouping interfaces. Because of that, the group clause can be the final clause in the query, just like the select clause. The IGrouping interface is defined in the System.Linq namespace and it also derives from the IEnumerable interface. Therefore, you can use an IGrouping interface anywhere you can use an IEnumerable interface. IGrouping comes with a property named Key, which is the object that delineates the subset. Each result set is formed by applying an equivalence operator between Key and a piece of input data or data derived from input data. Let's take a look at an example that takes a series of integers and partitions them into the set of odd and even numbers.[3]

```
using System;
using System.Linq;

public class GroupExample
{
    static void Main() {
        int[] numbers = {
            0, 1, 2, 3, 4, 5, 6, 7, 8, 9
        };

        // partition numbers into odd and
        // even numbers.
        var query = from x in numbers
                        group x by x % 2;

        foreach( var group in query ) {
            Console.WriteLine( "mod2 == {0}", group.Key );
            foreach( var number in group ) {
                Console.Write( "{0}, ", number );
            }
```

---

3. In the discussion of the group clause, I am using the word *partition* in the set theory context. That is, a set partition of a space S is a set of disjoint subsets whose union produces S.

```
            Console.WriteLine( "\n" );
        }
    }
}
```

First of all, notice that there is no select clause in this query. The end result of the query is a sequence of two instances of IGrouping. The first instance in the result sequence contains the even numbers and the second one contains the odd numbers, as shown in the following output:

```
mod2 == 0
0, 2, 4, 6, 8,

mod2 == 1
1, 3, 5, 7, 9,
```

The first foreach iterates over the two groups, or rather, the two instances of IGrouping. And since each IGrouping implements IEnumerable, there is a nested foreach loop that iterates over all of the items in the group. As you can see, this simple query iterated over all of the items from the source data collection, numbers, and produced two resultant groups. Internally, the compiler translates each group clause into a call to the GroupBy standard query operator.

The group clause can also partition the input collection using multiple keys, also known as compound keys. I prefer to think of it as sorting on one key that consists of multiple pieces of data. In order to perform such a grouping, you can use an anonymous type to introduce the multiple keys into the query, as demonstrated in the following example:

```
using System;
using System.Linq;
using System.Collections.Generic;

public class Employee
{
    public string LastName { get; set; }
    public string FirstName { get; set; }
    public string Nationality { get; set; }
}

public class OrderByExample
{
    static void Main() {
        var employees = new List<Employee>() {
            new Employee {
                LastName = "Jones", FirstName = "Ed",
                Nationality = "American"
            },
            new Employee {
                LastName = "Ivanov", FirstName = "Vasya",
                Nationality = "Russian"
            },
            new Employee {
                LastName = "Jones", FirstName = "Tom",
                Nationality = "Welsh"
            },
            new Employee {
```

```
                        LastName = "Smails", FirstName = "Spaulding",
                        Nationality = "Irish"
                    },
                    new Employee {
                        LastName = "Ivanov", FirstName = "Ivan",
                        Nationality = "Russian"
                    }
                };

            var query = from emp in employees
                        group emp by new {
                            Nationality = emp.Nationality,
                            LastName = emp.LastName
                        };

        foreach( var group in query ) {
            Console.WriteLine( group.Key );
            foreach( var employee in group ) {
                Console.WriteLine( employee.FirstName );
            }
            Console.WriteLine();
        }
    }
}
```

Notice the anonymous type within the group clause. What this says is that I want to partition the input collection into groups where both the Nationality and LastName are the same. In this example, every group ends up having one entity except one, and it's the one where Nationality is Russian and LastName is Ivanov. Essentially how it works is that for each item, it builds an instance of the anonymous type and checks to see if that key instance is equal to the key of an existing group. If so, the item goes in that group. If not, a new group is created with that instance of the anonymous type as the key.

The grouping by itself is useful indeed. However, what if you want to operate further on each of the groups within the query, thus treating the resulting partition as an intermediate step? That's when you use the into keyword, described in the next section.

The into Clause and Continuations

The into keyword is similar to the let keyword in that it defines an identifier local to the scope of the query. Using an into clause you tell the query that you want to assign the results of a group or a join operation to an identifier that can then be used later on in the query. In query lingo, this is called a *continuation* since the group clause is not the final projector in the query. However, the into clause acts as a generator, much as from clauses do, and the identifier introduced by the into clause is similar to a range variable in a from clause. Let's look at some examples:

```
using System;
using System.Linq;

public class GroupExample
{
    static void Main() {
        int[] numbers = {
```

```
            0, 1, 2, 3, 4, 5, 6, 7, 8, 9
        };

        // Partition numbers into odd and
        // even numbers.
        var query = from x in numbers
                        group x by x % 2 into partition
                        where partition.Key == 0
                        select new {
                            Key = partition.Key,
                            Count = partition.Count(),
                            Group = partition
                        };

        foreach( var item in query ) {
            Console.WriteLine( "mod2 == {0}", item.Key );
            Console.WriteLine( "Count == {0}", item.Count );
            foreach( var number in item.Group ) {
                Console.Write( "{0}, ", number );
            }
            Console.WriteLine( "\n" );
        }
    }
}
```

In this query, the continuation, that is the part of the query after the into clause, filters the series of groups where Key is 0 by using a where clause. This filters out the group of even numbers. I then project that group out into an anonymous type, producing a count of items in the group to go along with the Key property and the items in the group. Thus the output to the console only includes one group.

But what if I wanted to add a count to each group in the partition? As I said before, the into clause is a generator. So I can produce the desired result by changing the query to this:

```
        var query = from x in numbers
                        group x by x % 2 into partition
                        select new {
                            Key = partition.Key,
                            Count = partition.Count(),
                            Group = partition
                        };
```

When executed with this version of the query, the example produces the following desired output:

```
mod2 == 0
Count == 5
0, 2, 4, 6, 8,

mod2 == 1
Count == 5
1, 3, 5, 7, 9,
```

The Virtues of Being Lazy

When you build a LINQ query expression and assign it to a query variable, very little code is executed in that statement. The data only becomes available when you iterate over that query variable, which executes the query once for each result in the result set. So, for example, if the result set consists of 100 items and you only iterate over the first ten, then you don't pay the price for computing the remaining 90 items in the result set.

■**Note** You can use the `Take` extension method to reduce the number of items in the result set; however, it still produces an enumerator that uses deferred execution. Similarly useful methods are `TakeWhile`, `Skip`, and `SkipWhile`.

The benefits to this deferred execution approach are many. First of all, the operations described in the query expression could be quite expensive. Since those operations are provided by the user, and the designers of LINQ have no way of predicting the complexity of those operations, it's best to harvest each item only when necessary. Also, the data could be in a database halfway around the world. You definitely want lazy evaluation on your side in that case. And finally, the range variable could actually iterate over an infinite sequence. I'll show an example of that in the next section.

C# Iterators Foster Laziness

Internally, the query variable is implemented using C# iterators by using the `yield` keyword. I explained in Chapter 9 that code containing `yield` statements actually compiles into an iterator object. Therefore, when you assign the LINQ expression to the query variable, just about the only code that is executed is the constructor for the iterator object. The iterator may depend on other nested objects and they are initialized as well. You get the results of the LINQ expression once you start iterating over the query variable using a `foreach` statement, or by using the `IEnumerator` interface.

As an example, let's have a look at a query slightly modified from the code in the earlier section "LINQ Query Expressions." For convenience, here is the relevant code:

```
var query = from employee in employees
            where employee.Salary > 100000
            select new { LastName = employee.LastName,
                         FirstName = employee.FirstName };

Console.WriteLine( "Highly paid employees:" );
foreach( var item in query ) {
   Console.WriteLine( "{0}, {1}",
                      item.LastName,
                      item.FirstName );
```

Notice that the only difference is that I removed the `orderby` clause from the original LINQ expression; I'll explain why in the next section. Remember that this query is translated into a series of chained extension method calls on the `employees` variable. Each of those methods returns an object that implements `IEnumerable<T>`. In reality, those objects are iterators created from a `yield` statement.

Let's consider what happens when you start to iterate through the results in the `foreach` block. To obtain the next result, first, the `from` clause grabs the next item from the `employees` collection and makes the range variable employee reference it. Then, under the covers, the where clause passes the next item referenced by the range variable to the Where extension method. If it gets trapped by the filter, execution backtracks to the from clause to obtain the next item in the collection. It keeps executing that loop until either employees is completely empty or an element of employees passes the where clause predicate. Then, the select clause projects the item into the format we want by creating an anonymous type and returning it. Once it returns the item from the select clause, its work is done until the query variable cursor is advanced by the next iteration.

■**Note** LINQ query expressions can be reused. For example, suppose you have started iterating over the results of a query expression. Now, imagine that the range variable has iterated over just a few of the items in the input collection, and the variable referencing the collection is changed to reference a different collection. You can continue to iterate over the same query and it will pick up the changes in the new input collection without requiring you to redefine the query. How is that possible? Hint: think about closures and variable capture and what happens if the captured variable is modified outside the context of the closure.

Subverting Laziness

In the previous section, I removed the orderby clause from the query expression, and you may have been wondering why. That's because there are certain query operations that foil lazy evaluation. After all, how can orderby do its work unless it has a look at all of the results from the previous clauses? Of course it can't, and therefore orderby forces the clauses prior to it to iterate to completion.

■**Note** orderby is not the only clause that subverts lazy evaluation, or deferred execution, of query expressions. group . . . by and join do as well. Additionally, anytime you make an extension method call on the query variable that produces a singleton value, such as Count, you force the entire query to iterate to completion.

The original query expression used in the earlier section "LINQ Query Expressions" looked like the following:

```
var query = from employee in employees
            where employee.Salary > 100000
            orderby employee.LastName, employee.FirstName
            select new { LastName = employee.LastName,
                         FirstName = employee.FirstName };

Console.WriteLine( "Highly paid employees:" );
foreach( var item in query ) {
    Console.WriteLine( "{0}, {1}",
                       item.LastName,
                       item.FirstName );
}
```

I have bolded the orderby clause to make it stand out. When you ask for the next item in the result set, the from clause sends the next item in employees to the where clause filter. If it passes, that is sent on to the orderby clause. However, now the orderby clause needs to see the rest of the input that passes the filter, so it forces execution back up to the from clause to get the next item that passes the filter. It continues in this loop until there are no more items left in the employees collection. Then, after ordering the items based on the criteria, it passes the first item in the ordered set to the select projector. When foreach asks for the next item in the result set, evaluation starts with the orderby clause since it has cached all of the results from every clause prior. It takes the next item in its internal cache and passes it on to the select projector. This continues until the consumer of the query variable iterates over all of the results, thus draining the cache formed by orderby.

Now, earlier I mentioned the case where the range variable in the expression iterates over an infinite loop. Consider the following example:

```
using System;
using System.Linq;
using System.Collections.Generic;

public class InfiniteList
{
    static IEnumerable<int> AllIntegers() {
        int count = 0;
        while( true ) {
            yield return count++;
        }
    }

    static void Main() {
        var query = from number in AllIntegers()
                    select number * 2 + 1;

        foreach( var item in query.Take(10) ) {
            Console.WriteLine( item );
        }
    }
}
```

Notice in the bolded query expression, it makes a call to AllIntegers, which is simply an iterator that iterates over all integers starting from zero. The select clause projects those integers into all of the odd numbers. I then use Take and a foreach loop to display the first ten odd numbers. Notice that if I did not use Take, the program would run forever unless you compile it with the /checked+ compiler option to catch overflows.

■**Note** Methods that create iterators over infinite sets like the AllIntegers method in the previous example are sometimes called streams. The Queryable and Enumerable classes also contain useful methods that generate finite collections. Those methods are Empty, which returns an empty set of elements, Range, which returns a sequence of numbers, and Repeat, which generates a repeated stream of constant objects given the object to return and the number of times to return it. I wish Repeat would iterate forever if a negative count is passed to it.

Consider what would happen if I modified the query expression ever so slightly as shown here:

```
var query = from number in AllIntegers()
            orderby number descending
            select number * 2 + 1;
```

If you attempt to iterate even once over the query variable to get the first result, then you had better be ready to terminate the application. That's because the orderby clause forces the clauses before it to iterate to completion. In this case, that will never happen.

Even if your range variable does not iterate over an infinite set, the clauses prior to the orderby clause could be very expensive to execute. So the moral of the story is, be careful of the performance penalty associated with using orderby, group . . . by, and join in your query expressions.

Executing Queries Immediately

Sometimes you need to execute the entire query immediately. Maybe you want to cache the results of your query locally in memory or maybe you need to minimize the lock length to a SQL database. You can do this in a couple of ways. You could immediately follow your query with a foreach loop that iterates over the query variable, stuffing each result into a List<T>. But that's so imperative! Wouldn't you rather be functional? Instead, you could call the ToList extension method on the query variable, which does the same thing in one simple method call. As with the orderby example in the previous section, be careful when calling ToList on a query that returns an infinite result set. There is also a ToArray extension method for converting the results into an array. I show an interesting usage of ToArray in the later section titled "Replacing foreach Statements."

Along with ToList, there are other extension methods, known as aggregate operators, that force immediate execution of the entire query. They include such methods as Count, Sum, Max, Min, Average, Last, Reverse and any other method that must execute the entire query in order to produce its result.

Expression Trees Revisited

In Chapter 15 I described how lambda expressions can be converted into expression trees. I also made a brief mention of how this is very useful for LINQ to SQL.

When you use LINQ to SQL, the bodies of the LINQ clauses that boil down to lambda expressions are represented by expression trees. These expression trees are then used to convert the entire expression into a SQL statement for use against the server. When you perform LINQ to Objects as I have done throughout this chapter, the lambda expressions are converted to delegates in the form of IL code instead. Clearly that's not acceptable for LINQ to SQL. Can you imagine how difficult it would be to convert IL into SQL?

As you know by now, LINQ clauses boil down to extension method calls implemented in either System.Linq.Enumerable or System.Linq.Queryable. But which set of extension methods are used and when? If you look at the documentation for the methods in Enumerable, you can see that the predicates are converted to delegates, since the methods all accept a type based on the Func<> generic delegate type. However, the extension methods in Queryable, which have the same names as those in Enumerable, all convert the lambda expressions into an expression tree since they take a parameter of type Expression<T>. Clearly, LINQ to SQL uses the extension methods in Queryable.

■Note Incidentally, when you use the extension methods in Enumerable, you can pass either lambda expressions or anonymous functions to them since they accept a delegate in their parameter lists. However, the extension methods in Queryable can only accept lambda expressions, since anonymous functions cannot be converted into expression trees.

Techniques from Functional Programming

In the following sections, I would like to explore some more of the functional programming concepts that are prevalent throughout the new features in C# 3.0. As you'll soon see, some problems are solved with clever use of delegates created from lambda expressions to add the proverbial extra level of indirection. I'll also show how you can replace many uses of the imperative programming style constructs such as for loops and foreach loops using a more functional style.

Custom Standard Query Operators and Lazy Evaluation

In this section, I will revisit an example introduced in Chapter 14, where I showed how to implement a Lisp-style forward-linked list along with some extension methods to perform on that list. The primary interface for the list is shown here:

```
public interface IList<T>
{
    T Head { get; }
    IList<T> Tail { get; }
}
```

and a possible implementation of a collection based on this type was shown in Chapter 14; I repeat it here for convenience:

```
public class MyList<T> : IList<T>
{
    public static IList<T> CreateList( IEnumerable<T> items ) {
        IEnumerator<T> iter = items.GetEnumerator();
        return CreateList( iter );
    }

    public static IList<T> CreateList( IEnumerator<T> iter ) {
        if( !iter.MoveNext() ) {
            return new MyList<T>( default(T), null );
        }

        return new MyList<T>( iter.Current, CreateList(iter) );
    }

    public MyList( T head, IList<T> tail ) {
        this.head = head;
        this.tail = tail;
    }

    public T Head {
        get {
            return head;
        }
    }

    public IList<T> Tail {
        get {
            return tail;
        }
    }

    private T        head;
    private IList<T> tail;
}
```

Notice how I have provided two CreateList methods so that one can create an instance of
MyList using an IEnumerable or an IEnumerator type. Now, let's say that we want to implement the
Where and Select standard query operators. Based on this implementation of MyList, those opera-
tors could be implemented as shown here:

```
public static class MyListExtensions
{
    public static IEnumerable<T>
        GeneralIterator<T>( this IList<T> theList,
                            Func<IList<T>, bool> finalState,
                            Func<IList<T>, IList<T>> incrementer ) {
        while( !finalState(theList) ) {
            yield return theList.Head;
            theList = incrementer( theList );
        }
    }

    public static IList<T> Where<T>( this IList<T> theList,
                                     Func<T, bool> predicate ) {
        Func<IList<T>, IList<T>> whereFunc = null;

        whereFunc = list => {
            IList<T> result = new MyList<T>(default(T), null);

            if( list.Tail != null ) {
                if( predicate(list.Head) ) {
                    result = new MyList<T>( list.Head, whereFunc(list.Tail) );
                } else {
                    result = whereFunc( list.Tail );
                }
            }

            return result;
        };

        return whereFunc( theList );
    }

    public static IList<R> Select<T,R>( this IList<T> theList,
                                        Func<T,R> selector ) {
        Func<IList<T>, IList<R>> selectorFunc = null;

        selectorFunc = list => {
            IList<R> result = new MyList<R>(default(R), null);

            if( list.Tail != null ) {
                result = new MyList<R>( selector(list.Head),
                                        selectorFunc(list.Tail) );
            }

            return result;
        };

        return selectorFunc( theList );
    }
}
```

Each of the two methods, Where and Select, uses an embedded lambda expression that is converted to a delegate in order to get the work done.

Note Chapter 14 demonstrated a similar technique, but since lambda expressions had not been introduced yet, it used anonymous methods instead. Of course, lambda expressions clean up the syntax quite a bit.

In both methods, the embedded lambda expression is used to perform a simple recursive computation to compute the desired results. The final result of the recursion produces the product we want from each of the methods.

The GeneralIterator method in the previous example is used to create an iterator that implements IEnumerable on the MyList object instances. It is virtually the same as that shown in the example in Chapter 14.

Finally, you can put all of this together and execute the following code to see it in action:

```
public class SqoExample
{
    static void Main() {
        var listInts = new List<int> { 5, 2, 9, 4, 3, 1 };
        var linkList =
            MyList<int>.CreateList( listInts );

        // Now sort.
        var linkList2 = linkList.Where( x => x > 3 ).Select( x => x * 2 );
        var iterator2 = linkList2.GeneralIterator( list => list.Tail == null,
                                                   list => list.Tail );
        foreach( var item in iterator2 ) {
            Console.Write( "{0}, ", item );
        }

        Console.WriteLine();
    }
}
```

Of course, you will have to import the appropriate namespaces in order for the code to compile. Those namespaces are System, System.Linq, and System.Collections.Generic. If you execute this code, you will see the following results:

10, 18, 8,

There are some very important points and problems to address in this example, though. First of all, notice that my query was not written using a LINQ query expression even though I do make use of the standard query operators Where and Select. This is because the from clause requires that the given collection must implement IEnumerable. Since our IList interface does not implement IEnumerable, it is impossible to use foreach or a from clause. One could use the GeneralIterator extension method to get an IEnumerable interface on the IList and then use that in the from clause of a LINQ query expression. In that case, there would be no need to implement custom Where and Select methods. However, your results of the query would be in the form of an IEnumerable and not an IList, so you would then have to reconvert the results of the query back to an IList. Although these conversions are all possible, for the sake of example, let's assume that the requirement is that the standard query operators must accept an IList type and return an IList type. Under such a requirement, it is impossible to use LINQ query expressions and we must invoke the standard query operators directly.

Note You can see the power of the LINQ layered design and implementation. Even when your custom collection type does not implement IEnumerable, you can still perform operations using custom standard query operators even though you cannot use LINQ query expressions.

There is one major problem with the implementation of MyList and the extension methods in the MyListExtensions class as shown so far. They are grossly inefficient! One of the functional programming techniques employed throughout the LINQ implementation is that of lazy evaluation. In the section titled "The Virtues of Being Lazy" I showed how when you create a LINQ query expression, very little code is executed at that point and operations are performed only as needed while you iterate the results of the query. The implementations of Where and Select for IList as shown so far don't follow this methodology. For example, when you call Where, the entire input list is processed before any results are returned to the caller. That's bad, because what if the input IList was an infinite list? The call to Where would never return.

Note When developing implementations of the standard query operators or any other method where lazy evaluation is desirable, I like to use an infinite list for input as the litmus test of whether my lazy evaluation code is working as expected. Of course, as shown in the section "Subverting Laziness," there are certain operations that just cannot be coded using lazy evaluation.

Let's turn our attention to reimplementing the custom standard query operators in the previous example using lazy evaluation. Let's start by considering the Where operation. How could we reimplement it to use lazy evaluation? It accepts an IList and returns a new IList, so how is it possible that Where could only return one item at a time? The solution actually lies in the implementation of the MyList class. Let's consider the typical IEnumerator implementation for a moment. It has an internal cursor that points to the item that the IEnumerable.Current property returns, and it has a MoveNext method to go to the next item. The IEnumerable.MoveNext method is the key to retrieving each value only when needed. When you call MoveNext, you are invoking the operation to produce the next result but only when needed, thus using lazy evaluation.

I've mentioned Andrew Koenig's "Fundamental Theorem of Software Engineering," where all problems can be solved by introducing an extra level of indirection.[4] Although it's not really a theorem, it is true and very useful. In the C language, that form of indirection is typically in the form of a pointer. In C++ and other object-oriented languages, that extra level of indirection is typically in the form of a class, or sometimes called a wrapper class. In functional programming, that extra level of indirection is typically a function in the form of a delegate.

So how can we fix this problem in MyList by adding the proverbial extra level of indirection? It's actually fundamentally quite simple. Don't compute the IList that is the IList.Tail until it is asked for. Consider the changes in the MyList implementation as shown here:

```
public class MyList<T> : IList<T>
{
    public static IList<T> CreateList( IEnumerable<T> items ) {
        IEnumerator<T> iter = items.GetEnumerator();
        return CreateList( iter );
    }
}
```

---

4. I first encountered Koenig's so-called fundamental theorem of software engineering in his excellent book co-authored with Barbary Moo titled *Ruminations on C++* (Boston, MA: Addison-Wesley Professional, 1996).

```
public static IList<T> CreateList( IEnumerator<T> iter ) {
    Func<IList<T>> tailGenerator = null;
    tailGenerator = () => {
        if( !iter.MoveNext() ) {
            return new MyList<T>( default(T), null );
        }

        return new MyList<T>( iter.Current, tailGenerator );
    };

    return tailGenerator();
}

public MyList( T head, Func<IList<T>> tailGenerator ) {
    this.head = head;
    this.tailGenerator = tailGenerator;
}

public T Head {
    get {
        return head;
    }
}

public IList<T> Tail {
    get {
        if( tailGenerator == null ) {
            return null;
        } else if( tail == null ) {
            tail = tailGenerator();
        }
        return tail;
    }
}

private T              head;
private Func<IList<T>> tailGenerator;
private IList<T>       tail = null;
}
```

I have bolded the portions of the code that are interesting. Notice that the constructor still accepts the item that is assigned to head, but instead of taking an IList tail as the second argument it accepts a delegate that knows how to compute tail instead. There's our extra level of indirection! Also, notice how the get accessor of the Tail property then uses that delegate on an as-needed basis to compute tail when asked for it. And finally, the CreateList static method that builds an IList from an IEnumerator must pass in a delegate that simply grabs the next item out of the IEnumerator. So, even if you initialize a MyList with an IEnumerable, the IEnumerable type is not fully consumed at creation time as it was in the example from Chapter 14. That's a definite plus because even the IEnumerable passed in can reference an infinite stream of objects.

Now, let's turn our attention to the modifications necessary for the standard query operators so they can work on this new implementation of MyList. Consider the modifications shown here:

```
public static class MyListExtensions
{
    public static IEnumerable<T>
        GeneralIterator<T>( this IList<T> theList,
                            Func<IList<T>,bool> finalState,
```

```
                        Func<IList<T>,IList<T>> incrementer ) {
    while( !finalState(theList) ) {
        yield return theList.Head;
        theList = incrementer( theList );
    }
}

public static IList<T> Where<T>( this IList<T> theList,
                                 Func<T, bool> predicate ) {
    Func<IList<T>> whereTailFunc = null;

    whereTailFunc = () => {
        IList<T> result = null;

        if( theList.Tail == null ) {
            result = new MyList<T>( default(T), null );
        }

        if( predicate(theList.Head) ) {
            result = new MyList<T>( theList.Head,
                                    whereTailFunc );
        }

        theList = theList.Tail;
        if( result == null ) {
            result = whereTailFunc();
        }

        return result;
    };

    return whereTailFunc();
}

public static IList<R> Select<T,R>( this IList<T> theList,
                                    Func<T,R> selector ) {
    Func<IList<R>> selectorTailFunc = null;

    selectorTailFunc = () => {
        IList<R> result = null;

        if( theList.Tail == null ) {
            result = new MyList<R>( default(R), null );
        } else {
            result = new MyList<R>( selector(theList.Head),
                                    selectorTailFunc );
        }

        theList = theList.Tail;
        return result;
    };

    return selectorTailFunc();
}
}
```

Now, the implementations for Where and Select build a delegate that knows how to compute the next item in the result set and pass that delegate to the new instance of MyList that they return. Thus, we have achieved lazy evaluation. Notice that each lambda expression in each method forms a closure that uses the passed-in information to form the recursive code that generates the next element in the list. Now, let's test the lazy evaluation by introducing an infinite linked list of values.

Before you can prove the lazy evaluation with an infinite list, you need to either iterate through the results using a for loop (since a foreach loop will attempt to iterate to the nonexistent end) or, instead of using a for loop, implement the standard query operator Take, which returns a given number of elements from the list. Following is a possible implementation of Take using our new lazy MyList implementation.

```
public static class MyListExtensions
{
    public static IList<T> Take<T>( this IList<T> theList,
                                    int count ) {
        Func<IList<T>> takeTailFunc = null;

        takeTailFunc = () => {
            IList<T> result = null;

            if( theList.Tail == null || count-- == 0 ) {
                result = new MyList<T>( default(T), null );
            } else {
                result = new MyList<T>( theList.Head,
                                        takeTailFunc );
            }

            theList = theList.Tail;
            return result;
        };

        return takeTailFunc();
    }
}
```

This implementation of Take is very similar to that of Select except that the closure formed by the lambda expression assigned to takeTailFunc also captures the count parameter.

■**Note** Using Take is a more functional programming approach rather than using a for loop to count through the first few items in a collection.

Armed with the Take method, we can prove that lazy evaluation works with the following code:

```
public class SqoExample
{
    static IList<T> CreateInfiniteList<T>( T item ) {
        Func<IList<T>> tailGenerator = null;

        tailGenerator = () => {
            return new MyList<T>( item, tailGenerator );
        };

        return tailGenerator();
    }
```

```
    static void Main() {
        var infiniteList = CreateInfiniteList<int>( 21 );

        var linkList = infiniteList.Where( x => x > 3 )
                                   .Select( x => x * 2 )
                                   .Take( 10 );
        var iterator = linkList.GeneralIterator(
                                    list => list.Tail == null,
                                    list => list.Tail );
        foreach( var item in iterator ) {
            Console.Write( "{0}, ", item );
        }

        Console.WriteLine();
    }
}
```

The `Main` method uses the `CreateInfiniteList` method to create an infinite `IList` stream that returns the constant 21. Following the creation of `infiniteList` are chained calls to our custom standard query operators. Notice that the final method in the chain is the `Take` method, where I am only asking for the first 10 items in the result set. Without that call, the `foreach` loop later on would loop indefinitely. Since the `Main` method actually runs to completion, it proves that the lazy evaluation coded into the new `MyList` and the new implementations of `Where`, `Select`, and `Take` are working as expected. If any of them were broken, execution would get stuck in an infinite loop.

Replacing foreach Statements

As with most of the new features of C# 3.0, LINQ imparts a taste of functional programming on the language that, when used appropriately, can leave a sweet after-taste on the palate. Since functional programming has, over the years, been considered less efficient in its consumption of memory and CPU resources, it's possible that inappropriate use of LINQ could actually lead to inefficiencies. As with just about anything in software development, moderation is often the key to success. With enough use and given enough functional programming examples, you may be surprised at how many problems can be solved in a different, and sometimes clearer way using LINQ and functional programming practices rather than the typical imperative programming style of C-style languages such as C#, C++, and Java.

In many of the examples in this book, I send a list of items to the console to illustrate the results of the example. Typically I have used a `Console.WriteLine` method call within a `foreach` statement to iterate over the results when the result set is a collection. Now, I would like to show you how this can be done differently using LINQ, as in the following example:

```
using System;
using System.Linq;
using System.Collections.Generic;

public static class Extensions
{
    public static string Join( this string str,
                               IEnumerable<string> list ) {
        return string.Join( str, list.ToArray() );
    }
}

public class Test
{
    static void Main() {
```

```
        var numbers = new int[] { 5, 8, 3, 4 };

        Console.WriteLine(
            string.Join(", ",
                        (from x in numbers
                         orderby x
                         select x.ToString()).ToArray()) );
    }
}
```

I have bolded the interesting part of the code. In one statement, I sent all of the items in the numbers collection to the console separated by commas and sorted in ascending order. Isn't that cool? The way it works is that my query expression is evaluated immediately, since I call the ToArray extension method on it to convert the results of the query into an array. That's where the typical foreach clause disappears to. The static method String.Join should not be confused with the LINQ join clause or the Join extension method you get when using the System.Linq namespace. What it does is intersperse the first string, in this case a comma, among each string in the given array of strings, building one big string in the process. I then simply pass the results of String.Join to Console.WriteLine.

■**Note** In my opinion, LINQ is to C# what the Standard Template Library (STL) is to C++. When STL first came out in the early 1990s, it really jolted C++ programmers into thinking more functionally. It was definitely a breath of fresh air. LINQ has this same effect on C#, and I believe that as time goes on, you will see more and more crafty usage of functional programming techniques using LINQ. For example, if a C++ programmer used the STL effectively, there was little need to write a for loop, since the STL provides algorithms where one passes a function into the algorithm along with the collection to operate on and it invokes that function on each item in the collection. One may wonder why this technique is so effective. One reason is that for loops are a common place to inadvertently introduce an off-by-one bug. Of course, the C# foreach keyword also helps alleviate that problem.

With enough thought, you could probably replace just about every foreach block in your program with a LINQ query expression.

Summary

LINQ is clearly the culmination of most of the new C# 3.0 features. Or put another way, most of the new features of C# 3.0 were born from LINQ. In this chapter, I showed the basic syntax of a LINQ query including how LINQ query expressions ultimately compile down to a chain of extension methods known as the standard query operators. I then described all of the new C# keywords introduced for LINQ expressions. Although you are not required to use LINQ query expressions and you can choose to call the extension methods directly, it sure makes for easily readable code. However, I also described how when you implement standard query operators on collection types that don't implement IEnumerable, you may not be able to use LINQ query expressions.

I then explored the usefulness of lazy evaluation, or deferred execution, which is used extensively throughout the library provided LINQ standard operators on IEnumerable and IQueryable types. And finally, I closed the chapter by exploring how to apply the concept of lazy evaluation when defining your own custom implementations of the standard query operators.

LINQ is such a huge topic that there is no way I could possibly cover every nuance in one chapter. For example, you'll notice that I only covered LINQ to Objects and not LINQ to SQL, XML, or DataSet. Entire books are devoted to LINQ. I highly suggest that you frequently reference the MSDN documentation on LINQ. Additionally, you may consider *LINQ for Visual C# 2005* by Fabio Claudio Ferracchiati or *Pro LINQ: Language Integrated Query in C# 2008* by Joseph C. Rattz, Jr., both published by Apress.

APPENDIX

∎∎∎

References

The following list of publications are listed as references and/or recommended reading:

Abrams, Brad. *.NET Framework Standard Library Annotated Reference, Volumes 1 and 2*. Boston, MA: Addison-Wesley Professional, 2004, 2005.

Alexandrescu, Andrei. *Modern C++ Design: Generic Programming and Design Patterns Applied*. Boston, MA: Addison-Wesley Professional, 2001.

Archer, Tom, and Andrew Whitechapel. *Inside C#, Second Edition*. Redmond, WA: Microsoft Press, 2002.

Box, Don. *Essential COM*. Boston, MA: Addison-Wesley Professional, 1997.

Box, Don, with Chris Sells. *Essential .NET, Volume 1: The Common Language Runtime*. Boston, MA: Addison-Wesley Professional, 2003.

Box, Don with Anders Hejlsberg. "The LINQ Project." http://msdn2.microsoft.com/en-us/library/aa479865.aspx, September 2005.

Brown, Keith. *The .NET Developer's Guide to Windows Security*. Boston, MA: Addison-Wesley Professional, 2004.

Coplien, James O. *Advanced C++ Programming Styles and Idioms*. Boston, MA: Addison-Wesley Professional, 1991.

Cwalina, Krzysztof, and Brad Abrams. *Framework Design Guidelines: Conventions, Idioms, and Patterns for Reusable .NET Libraries*. Boston, MA: Addison-Wesley Professional, 2005.

Ecma International. *Standard ECMA-334: C# Language Specification, Third Edition*. June 2005.

Ecma International. *Standard ECMA-335: Common Language Infrastructure (CLI), Third Edition*. June 2005.

Ecma International. *Standard ECMA-372: C++/CLI Language Specification*. December 2005.

Gamma, Erich, Richard Helm, Ralph Johnson, and John Vlissides. *Design Patterns: Elements of Reusable Object-Oriented Software*. Boston, MA: Addison-Wesley Professional, 1995.

Hejlsberg, Anders, Scott Wiltamuth, and Peter Golde. *The C# Programming Language*. Boston, MA: Addison-Wesley Professional, 2003.

Horton, Anson. "The Evolution of LINQ and It's Impact On the Design of C#," *MSDN Magazine*, June 2007.

Kaplan, Michael, and Cathy Wissink. "Custom Cultures: Extend Your Code's Global Reach with New Features in the .NET Framework 2.0," *MSDN Magazine*, October 2005.

LaMacchia, Brian A., Sebastian Lange, Matthew Lyons, Rudi Martin, and Kevin T. Price. *.NET Framework Security*. Upper Saddle River, NJ: Pearson Education, 2002.

Meyers, Scott. *Effective C++, Second Edition: 50 Specific Ways to Improve Your Programs and Designs.* Boston, MA: Addison-Wesley Professional, 1997.

Meyers, Scott. *More Effective C++: 35 New Ways to Improve Your Programs and Designs.* Boston, MA: Addison-Wesley Professional, 1995.

Microsoft Corporation. "C# Language Specification Version 3.0." September 2007.

Miller, Jim, and Susann Ragsdale. *The Common Language Infrastructure Annotated Standard.* Boston, MA: Addison-Wesley Professional, 2003.

Nathan, Adam. *.NET and COM: The Complete Interoperability Guide.* Indianapolis, IN: Sams, 2002.

Richter, Jeffrey. *Applied Microsoft .NET Framework Programming.* Redmond, WA: Microsoft Press, 2002.

Robbins, John. "Unhandled Exceptions and Tracing in the .NET Framework 2.0," *MSDN Magazine,* July 2005.

Russinovich, Mark E., and David A. Solomon. *Microsoft Windows Internals, Fourth Edition: Microsoft Windows Server 2003, Windows XP, and Windows 2000.* Redmond, WA: Microsoft Press, 2004.

Schmidt, Douglas C. "Monitor Object: An Object Behavioral Pattern for Concurrent Programming," Department of Computer Science and Engineering, Washington University, St. Louis, MO, April 2005.

Stroustrup, Bjarne. *The Design and Evolution of C++.* Boston, MA: Addison-Wesley Professional, 1994.

Sutter, Herb. *Exceptional C++: 47 Engineering Puzzles, Programming Problems, and Exception-Safety Solutions.* Boston, MA: Addison-Wesley Professional, 1999.

Sutter, Herb. *Exception C++ Style: 40 New Engineering Puzzles, Programming Problems, and Solutions.* Boston, MA: Addison-Wesley Professional, 2004.

Sutter, Herb. *More Exceptional C++: 40 New Engineering Puzzles, Programming Problems, and Solutions.* Boston, MA: Addison-Wesley Professional, 2001.

Toub, Stephen. "High Availability: Keep Your Code Running with the Reliability Features of the .NET Framework," *MSDN Magazine,* October 2005.

Troelsen, Andrew. *Pro C# 2005 and the .NET 2.0 Platform.* Berkeley, CA: Apress, 2005.

Vermeulen, Allan. "An Asynchronous Design Pattern," *Dr. Dobb's Journal,* June 1996.

Blogs

http://blogs.msdn.com/brada/

http://blogs.msdn.com/cbrumme/

http://blogs.msdn.com/kcwalina/

http://blogs.msdn.com/maoni/

http://blogs.msdn.com/ricom/

http://pluralsight.com/blogs/dbox/

http://pluralsight.com/blogs/hsutter/

http://www.sellsbrothers.com/news/

http://blogs.msdn.com/wesdyer/

http://blogs.msdn.com/charlie/default.aspx

Index

Symbols

@ character, preceding verbatim strings, 196
{ } (curly braces), 268, 284
+ (addition) operator, 151, 209
++ (postfix) operators, 151
+= operator, 264
-= operator, 264
— (prefix) operators, 151
; (semicolon), 19
?: (ternary) operator, 153, 158

A

Abort method, 322–324
AbortRequested state, thread, 322
Abrahams, David, 429
Abrams, Brad, 27, 64, 75, 247
abstract classes, 65
Abstract Factory pattern, 451
abstract keyword, 65, 115
abstract methods, 115
access modifiers, 41, 55, 56, 125
accessibility, 41, 55, 56, 57, 125
accessor properties, 47–48
AcquireReaderLock method, 346
AcquireWriterLock method, 346
Active Template Library (ATL), 296
Add method, 273, 287, 289, 304
Adder property, 270
addition (+) operator, 151, 209
aggregate operators, 485
A.InitZ method, 42
Alexandrescu, Andrei, 296
allocated resources, working with, 186–190
AllocateDataSlot method, 328
AllocateNamedDataSlot method, 328
anonymous methods
    advantages, 270
    captured variables, 270–272
    declaration, 3
    delegates, 266–271, 272–274, 276
    described, 5, 45
    function members, compared, 56
    generic, 286
    hiding, 126, 134, 137
    lambda expressions, 444, 447, 449
    matching rules, 135–139
    naming conventions, 124
    overriding, 115
    parameters, 268
    scoping, 268, 270
    uses, 267–268
    virtual, 115–118
anonymous recursion, 462–463
anonymous types, 6, 81–82, 84, 475–476, 480
AOP (aspect-oriented programming), 23
AOSD (aspect-oriented software development), 23
ApartmentState property, 330
AppDomain.UnhandledException, 164
AppDomain.UnloadException, 165
Append method, 210
AppendFormat method, 204, 210
ApplicationException, 186
applications
    managed, 1, 10
    native, 2
ApplyRaiseOf method, 261
ArgumentException, 232
ArgumentOutOfRangeException, 164, 166, 171, 175, 210
Array class, 280
array covariance rules, compared to constructed generic types, 224, 280
Array.GetLength method, 228, 229
Array.Length property, 228
ArrayList, 281
Array.Rank property, 229
arrays
    covariance and, 224, 280
    creating, 221
    declaring, 221
    implicit typing, 222–224
    jagged, 229–231
    multidimensional, 228–231
    rank, 225, 229
    rectangular, 228
    sortability, 225
    vectors, 226
The Art of Computer Programming Volume 3: Sorting and Searching Second Edition (Knuth), 390
as operator, 29–30
aspect-oriented programming (AOP), 23
aspect-oriented software development (AOSD), 23
assemblies, 11–14
asynchronous code, 320, 354–361
"An Asynchronous Design Pattern" (Vermeulen), 320
asynchronous method calls, 320

Find it faster at http://superindex.apress.com/